Minor Lives

A Collection of Biographies by John Nichols

John Nichols, Esq., F.S.A.

Minor Lives

A Collection of Biographies by John Nichols

Annotated and with an Introduction on John Nichols and the Antiquarian and Anecdotal Movements of the late Eighteenth Century

Edward L. Hart, Editor

Harvard University Press   Cambridge, Massachusetts   1971

© Copyright 1971 by the President and Fellows of Harvard College
All rights reserved
Distributed in Great Britain by Oxford University Press, London
Library of Congress Catalog Card Number 73-131470
SBN 674-57630-6
Printed in the United States of America

for **ELEANOR**

Contents

	Page
PREFACE	ix
INTRODUCTION	xiii
SHORTENED TITLES OF NICHOLS' WORKS	xxxi
PART I ANTIQUARIANS	1
Isaac Reed	3
Richard Farmer	17
George Steevens	41
William Cole	63
Richard Gough	82
Browne Willis	100
Samuel Pegge the Elder	127
Joseph Warton and Thomas Warton the Younger	148
John Nichols	167
PART II BOOKSELLERS AND PRINTERS	195
John Dunton	197
Bernard Lintot	221
David Henry	232
Thomas Davies	237
James Dodsley	250
Thomas Longman	254
Thomas Payne	256
Peter Elmsly	259
Thomas Cadell	265
Andrew Millar	271
William Strahan	275
Joseph Johnson	282
PART III ILLUSTRATORS AND DESIGNERS	287
Isaac Basire and the three James Basires	289
John Baskerville	291
William Caslon (with accompanying brief memoirs of Thomas Cottrell, Joseph Jackson, and Vincent Figgins)	306

PART IV CURATE, SCHOLAR, GRUB, POET 315
    John Jones 317
    Thomas Tyrwhitt 329
    Samuel Boyse 341
    John Hughes 351

INDEX 353

Illustrations

Frontispiece

John Nichols, Esq., F.S.A. Engraved by A. Cardon from an original drawing by H. Eldridge

Following page 110

Isaac Reed. Published in London on May 1, 1791, by E. Harding of 132 Fleet Street

The Reverend Richard Farmer, D.D. Engraved by T. Hodgetts from an original in Emmanuel College, Cambridge, 1816

George Steevens, Esq., F.R.S. Painted by Zoffany. Engraved by T. Hodgetts. Published for John Murray, March 1816

The Reverend William Cole, A.M., of Cambridge and F.A.S., 1768. Engraved from an original drawing. From *Literary Anecdotes*, I, 657

Following page 206

Browne Willis, Esq., died February 5, 1760, aged 78. From *Literary Anecdotes*, VIII, 219

The Reverend Samuel Pegge the Elder, LL.D., F.S.A. 1704-1796. Engraved by Philip Audinet from an original painting, 1788. From *Illustrations*, IV, 721

The Reverend Thomas Warton, B.D., F.S.A., 1728-1790. From *Illustrations*, IV, 738

James Basire, 1730-1802. Published by J. Nichols, & Co., August 1, 1815. From *Literary Anecdotes*, IX, frontispiece

Preface

A number of conditions justify the production of this volume. The first is that although the works of John Nichols are basic tools for scholars of the latter half of the eighteenth century, these works have now become rare enough that even many libraries, especially newer ones with beginning collections, are unable to obtain copies of original impressions. A recent reprint edition offers a set of the *Literary Anecdotes* and *Illustrations of the Literary History of the Eighteenth Century* in seventeen volumes for five hundred dollars. Reprint issues of other works of Nichols are available at comparable prices. Clearly, there is a demand for the writings of Nichols; clearly, also, these writings will remain off the shelves of many individual scholars.

The second condition justifying this volume is Nichols' own biographical method. He frequently introduced a sketch of a person's life into the *Gentleman's Magazine*, later transferred it to some other collection, and still later put additions and corrections to the original sketch in half-a-dozen or more subsequent publications. An advantage of this one-volume collection of lives, then, is that the reader will find here something that he does not find in Nichols himself—all the relevant materials regarding a selected number of biographical subjects brought together, annotated, and related to each other. This, I hope, will prove useful to the young scholar in showing him the effective use of Nichols as a source, and pleasurable to the mature scholar in presenting him with an array of familiar faces in a new setting.

A third consideration that prompted the production of this book is that the biographical work of Nichols needed to be related to surviving manuscript materials and to efforts expended on his subjects since he wrote. It has been my aim, therefore, to supply the reader not only with the biographies of Nichols but also with references to work that has been done since (including some of the use made of Nichols by succeeding writers) and to the locations of some of the more important manuscript resources. Over fifty hitherto unpublished letters are reproduced in this volume by way of introducing the reader to new and significant biographical material.

Perhaps the most important reason of all for such a volume as this is that through it Nichols may be related to the men and movements of his time, especially to the antiquarians and the anecdotists. The writers involved in antiquarian and anecdotal pursuits in the late eighteenth century were an unusually gregarious group and developed to a high degree the arts of corresponding and cooperating with each other. One cluster of lives in this collection is designed to reveal the interrelationships among some of these writers, and in one central scene, the Sturbridge Fair at Cambridge in September of 1782, six members of the group, including Nichols, are brought together at one time and place.

Several criteria have governed the selection of lives included in this volume. Among the most important of these are the intrinsic interest of the biographical subject, his relation to literature or to literary figures, and his relation to others whose lives are also here. Although I have placed some emphasis on the antiquarians, the anecdotists, and other special groups to which Nichols belonged, I have recognized that his multifarious writings are broad in scope; I have, therefore, tried to include in the list of lives some that will illustrate the complete range of Nichols' interests, resources, and modes of procedure. That Nichols may be fully appreciated as a biographer, I have placed him, in the Introduction that follows, in the setting out of which his works grew.

The text of Nichols' writings has been reproduced, to the extent possible, just as he presented it. No changes have been made in punctuation or spelling (even when a word may be spelled in two different ways on the same page). Nichols' text is sufficiently modern that I felt nothing could be gained and a great deal could be lost by Americanizing or normalizing it. All interpolations and changes have been indicated by square brackets, and Nichols' own square brackets have been changed to parentheses except where he used them to indicate his own interpolation in another author's text (in which instance a footnote will indicate that they are his). All omissions from Nichols' text are indicated by ellipsis dots. No attempt has been made to preserve the ligatures employed in the printing of the original work.

A few minor liberties with Nichols' text were inevitable: obvious typographical errors, such as inverted letters, have been corrected silently. I must add, however, that this kind of error is relatively rare. A punctuation mark with which I have taken some liberties is the dash. Nichols used it not only as we use it today, but also in long footnotes, to designate paragraph separations (presumably for saving space). For the sake of a more readable text, I have omitted the dash when used to indicate a paragraph break and in its place have ended the old paragraph and begun the new in the regular way. I have not indicated in the text when I have done this, and I have used my own judgment to determine when a dash is a dash and when a paragraph indicator.

Because Nichols has very many and very long footnotes, sometimes occupying almost an entire page—and because often these footnotes contain matter of great interest, easily overlooked because of their location, I have frequently raised notes to the status of text and introduced them at the appropriate point. Wherever I have done this, I have indicated with an editor's note or a footnote of my own that the material was originally in a note. I have tried to make use of Nichols' own corrections and additions (often given in later volumes); these changes are always indicated by distinctive brackets. I have introduced material relevant to a particular life from whatever place I have been able to find it in the writings of Nichols, attempting to bring together all his materials on a particular biographical subject, indicating the source as each separate piece of information is introduced.

For introducing me to John Nichols, whose affable good sense and industry have long recommended their possessor, I am lastingly grateful to Miss Mary M. Lascelles. I wish to thank Professor Bertrand H. Bronson for first suggesting to me that I undertake this book. I am likewise under obligation to Professors William K. Wimsatt, Jr., and Frederick W. Hilles for encouraging me to complete it, and to Professor James L. Clifford for drawing my attention to the existence of some important manuscript materials. I deeply appreciate the painstaking care of my copyeditor, Miss M. Kathleen Ahern.

I am grateful to many persons and to many libraries for permission to use printed and manuscript materials; and in particular I am indebted to the following for permission to reproduce manuscripts or portions of manuscripts in their possession, as indicated at the place each is introduced: to the Bodleian Library for one letter; to Mr. John G. Murray of John Murray Publishers, London, for twelve letters in the Warton Collection in the British Museum (all those taken from Add. Mss. 42,560 or 42,561); to the British Museum for three additional letters and a page of William Cole's journal; to the Columbia University Special Collections Library for fourteen letters; to the Folger Shakespeare Library for all or part of sixteen letters; to the Osborn Collection at Yale for four letters; and to the Beinecke Rare Book and Manuscript Library at Yale for three letters.

For providing me with a grant to travel to England during the summer of 1964 I wish to express appreciation to the American Philosophical Society. I am also grateful for material assistance given me by Brigham Young University.

E. L. H.

Introduction

The Antiquarian Movement

An antiquarian, in the late eighteenth-century application of the term, was basically a writer of local histories of towns, counties, parishes, abbeys, or even of individual churches, houses, or monuments; he was an antiquarian because he was dedicated to the preservation of antiquities. Thomas Warton the Younger expressed this attraction for the ancient in the last two lines of his sonnet "Written in a Blank Leaf of Dugdale's Monasticon":

> Nor rough nor barren are the winding ways
> Of hoar Antiquity, but strown with flowers.

The Augustan Age produced a society of refined tastes, elegance, and sophistication. The nostalgic appeal of a more simple past had existed from the beginning of the period. Dryden and Pope had been attracted by Chaucer (who, although not simple was certainly medieval), and Addison had discovered the elemental charm of the ballad. During the latter half of the eighteenth century, interest in antiquities developed into the common pursuit of the educated man: Percy was collecting his *Reliques;* Warton was collecting materials for histories of Winchester and of Kidlington, exposing Rowley, and writing a history of English poetry; Horace Walpole was collecting a catalogue of the works of royal and noble authors and writing a Gothic novel; Nichols was preparing his monumental history of Leicestershire; and all of these men, along with almost everyone who was doing any writing at all, were looking up information for each other, copying inscriptions, collecting anecdotes, and writing innumerable letters.

The antiquarians were, then, a group with wide and diverse interests: a cross section of the educated class. They were historians, novelists, medievalists, and letter writers. They were bishops and parish priests, nobles and commoners of any business or profession. The uniting force, the effort to preserve the past, threw them into communication with each other, and their joint product made it possible for the succeeding generation to revel almost effortlessly in a past spread open before them.

Ana and Anecdotes

An activity of the late eighteenth century that was as pervasive as antiquarianism was the collecting of ana and anecdotes. The two activities are, of course, related: one preserves the past and the other preserves one's contemporaries. It was of Edmund Curll, the publisher of Pope's letters, that Professor Walter Raleigh wrote (in an essay on "Early Lives of the Poets," *Six Essays on Johnson* [Oxford, 1910, 1927]) that he was the genius who hit upon the epoch-making idea of entertaining men handsomely upon one another's remains. Such entertainment has an obvious relation to biography and therefore deserves observation here.

Rich backgrounds existed, of course, for the appearance of the anecdotists of the late eighteenth century, as will be readily acknowledged by anyone calling to mind such names as Thomas Fuller, John Aubrey, or Anthony à Wood. To begin with the century, however, we see first the flighty publisher, John Dunton, a contemporary of Curll. Dunton's *Life and Errors* of 1705 contains an account of himself and of a great many others.

After Dunton, one of the earliest and most influential collectors of anecdotes of the eighteenth century was Joseph Spence. His *Essay on Pope's Odyssey* (1726) had brought him into Pope's favor, and thereafter he was permitted frequently to be in Pope's company. Spence, surely a forerunner of Boswell, kept records of Pope's conversations and wrote down anecdotes that he heard concerning Pope's friends and enemies and others. During Spence's lifetime, his manuscripts were loaned to Warburton and Warton. Owen Ruffhead used them for his *Life of Pope* (1769), and later a copy supplied to Johnson provided important materials for his lives of Pope and Addison. A transcription of Spence's papers was also used by Edmond Malone for his life of Dryden. The story is well known of how two rival editions of Spence's anecdotes were published the same day in 1820 by John Murray and Samuel Weller Singer. Singer's edition, being more complete and more accurate, was the standard reference until the appearance of James M. Osborn's edition, *Joseph Spence: Observations, Anecdotes and Characters of Books and Men,* 2 vols. (Oxford, 1966).

The copy of Spence's anecdotes published by Murray was the one transcribed for Malone, and it came to Murray by way of William Beloe, who intended to edit it, but who died before doing so. Beloe himself made a desultory collection of anecdotes about men and books of all ages, published in six volumes as *Anecdotes of Literature and Scarce Books* (1807-1812). For the most part, these materials were collected while Beloe was keeper of printed books at the British Museum. While he was holding that position, some manuscripts were stolen by a man to whom they had been loaned, and Beloe was dismissed. Feeling that his dismissal was unjust, he poured his bitterness into his last work, *The Sexagenarian* (2 vols., 1817). He died just after this had gone through the press, and it was published immediately after his death. Some of the offensive passages were omitted in the edition of 1818. A key to the 1817 edition, made by the Rev. Mark Noble (1773-1826), is attached to a copy in the Bodleian Library (shelfmark Hope 8º 893).

Another eminent compiler of anecdotes was Horace Walpole, who published his two-volume *Royal and Noble Authors* in 1758 and the first three volumes of his *Anecdotes of Painting* in 1762. The *Royal and Noble Authors* contains much information not now obtainable elsewhere. In addition to these works which Walpole himself published are, of course, his voluminous letters, ranging in subject matter all the way from local historical antiquities to character vignettes, biographical data, and all the rest of his varied interests. Once considered a mere dilettante, he is every year rising in the estimation of scholars as volumes of his letters continue to appear.

A few other anecdotists need to be mentioned to fill out the picture. William Seward published in three volumes his *Anecdotes of Some Distinguished Persons* in 1795; and in 1799 he brought out in two volumes his *Biographiana*. Thomas Frognall Dibdin made his great contribution with *Bibliomania* in 1809. Isaac D'Israeli produced three works of interest to us here, his *Curiosities of Literature* (2 vols., 1791-1793), his *Calamities of Authors* (2 vols., 1812), and his *Quarrels of Authors* (3 vols., 1814).

Less important anecdotists are numerous—numerous enough to justify the use of the word *movement* in referring to them. All but a few shall remain nameless. Those to be named will be the elder Samuel Pegge, who contributed many articles to the *Bibliotheca Topographica Britannica*, some of which are of biographical significance. His *Anonymiana; or, Ten Centuries of Observations on Various Authors and Subjects,* was published in 1809, after Pegge's death. The younger Samuel Pegge produced *Anecdotes of the English Language* (1803) and *Curialia*, of which the fourth and fifth parts were published posthumously by Nichols in 1806.

Descending still lower in the scale of importance, we come to two works known as *Almon's Anecdotes* and the *Percy Anecdotes*. John Almon issued his work with the title: *Biographical, Literary, and Political Anecdotes* (3 vols., 1797). *The Percy Anecdotes. Original and Select. By Sholto and Reuben Percy, Brothers of the Benedictine Monastery, Mont Benger.,* was published in twenty volumes, 1821-1823. The authors' names were fictitious; Sholto Percy in reality was Joseph Clinton Robertson, and Reuben Percy was Thomas Byerley. Their anecdotes are divided into departments by subject. Two other works, these by anonymous writers, should also be mentioned. The first, called simply *Anecdotes of Polite Literature,* came out in five volumes in 1764. To this day there is no clue to the authorship, but Walpole supposed it to be no more than a bookseller's collection (see a letter from John C. Bryce in the *Times Literary Supplement* for 18 April 1936, p. 340). Another collection, the authorship of which is also still unknown, appeared from 1796 to 1797 in sixteen volumes entitled *Interesting Anecdotes, Memoirs, Allegories, Essays, and Poetical Fragments. . . . By Mr. Addison.* The name *Addison* was used to attract attention and was a pseudonym.

No list of eighteenth-century anecdotists would be complete without Mrs. Thrale. Her *Anecdotes of the Late Samuel Johnson* (1786) is hardly the equal of Boswell's *Life*, but her *Thraliana* (1942) has an important place in the history of anecdotal literature. It contains anecdotes of a great number of literary people; and, more important, it shows a side of Johnson which Boswell was never permitted to see. In a sense, Boswell himself may be viewed as the proper culmination of the whole movement. The multifarious collecting of literary conversations, anecdotes, and biographical information going on through the whole century had set a pattern which Boswell could organize into a method and focus upon one man.

At the Center: John Nichols

In the center of the antiquarian and anecdotal movement is John Nichols. He is more central than any other figure, very often the hub from whom radiate spokes of people and projects. Some connection can be found between him and almost every significant antiquarian or biographical activity of his day—and his day was a long one. He had, for example, some direct connection with all those mentioned in the preceding section, with the exception of Dunton and Spence and certain others who either died before his time or still remain anonymous (and possibly with these latter also). With Dunton he had an indirect connection since Nichols was involved with the republication of Dunton's book. It should follow, then, that by pursuing Nichols we shall find ourselves at the heart of the Antiquarian Movement and of the anecdote and literary biography collecting of the late eighteenth century.

Nichols produced more biographical data regarding the writers of his time than did all his contemporaries combined—including Boswell and Johnson. He is a standard reference with whom all scholars of the period are acquainted. But until recent times there has been a striking contrast between the wide use made of Nichols and the amount of work devoted to him as a subject. After his death in November 1826, Alexander Chalmers wrote a memoir, drawn largely from personal acquaintance, for the December issue of the *Gentleman's Magazine,* and at the end he incorporated a list of works compiled by Nichols for his own life in the sixth volume of *Literary Anecdotes.* In succeeding years, two further accounts of Nichols appeared. G. A. Aitken wrote an excellent short life for the *Dictionary of National Biography,* and Austin Dobson wrote a discursive paper entitled "A Literary Printer," published first in the *National Review,* 61:1086-1104 (1913), and later in his *Rosalba's Journal* (1915). A short bibliographical note by William Bates, "Nichols' 'Biographical Anecdotes of William Hogarth,'" appeared in *Notes and Queries,* 4th ser., 1:97 (February 1868).

Since the publication of the works mentioned in the preceding paragraph, John Nichols has been receiving an increasing amount of attention. The printing firm that he took over from William Bowyer was passed on to his son John Bowyer Nichols and his grandson John Gough Nichols. In 1939 the firm of "J. B. Nichols & Son, Printers, Westminster" closed for business. A ten-page pamphlet commemorating its history has on its title page, under an emblem of the head of Cicero: "At the Sign of Cicero's Head. A Short

History of the House of Nichols, Printers during the Reign of Twelve Sovereigns, 1699 to 1939." This pamphlet, described in some detail because it is rare, was made available to me through the kindness of Mr. S. J. Osborne, Assistant Clerk of Stationers' Hall, who further informed me that the letter transmitting a copy of the pamphlet to Stationers' Hall was written by Mr. G. E. Dunstone, who says in the letter that he prepared the pamphlet and that he had been manager of the Nichols printing firm for thirty years. Near the end of the *House of Nichols,* Mr. Dunstone wrote (p. 9): "At the end of 1939 the history of this firm will cease. It occupied for 240 years a prominent place in the sphere of printing." The pamphlet concludes with a list of the names of the principals of the firm from 1699 to 1939. The closing of the Nichols printing office was further memorialized in an unsigned note, "Printers and Scholars: John Nichols and his Descendants," in the *Times Literary Supplement* (9 December 1939), p. 724.

Additional important work on Nichols' trade relations has been done by Mr. Albert H. Smith in his article, "John Nichols, Printer and Publisher," *The Library,* 5th ser., 18:169-190 (September 1963). Two other works by Mr. Smith have bibliographical interest: "John Nichols and Hutchins's *History and Antiquities of Dorset,*" *The Library,* 5th ser., 15:81-95 (June 1960), and "Nichols' Anecdotes of Hogarth," *Notes and Queries,* new ser., 4:352-353 (August 1957), in the latter of which the author discusses passages modified by Nichols to avoid offending Horace Walpole. Two other articles on Nichols should be mentioned here. The first, an unsigned note called "Old Papers," is in the *Times Literary Supplement* (2 November 1951), p. 693; it discusses the Nichols tradition and mentions a sale of "the second portion of the Nichols papers" at Sotheby's, 6 November 1951. The second, by G. B. Schick, " 'Kind Hints' to John Nichols, by Joseph Warton and others," is in *Notes and Queries,* new ser., 3:76-78 (1956); it deals with Nichols' selection of materials for the *Select Collection.*

My own work on Nichols began with a doctoral thesis at Oxford: "A Study of the Biographical Works of John Nichols" (1950), and extended from this to the publication of a number of articles which analyzed Nichols' biographical methods, traced some of his contributions to other authors, and revealed him as the foremost collector of biographical information during the latter half of the eighteenth century. The earliest of these articles was "Some New Sources of Johnson's *Lives,*" *PMLA,* 65:1088-1111 (December 1950); the second was "The Contributions of John Nichols to Boswell's *Life of Johnson,*" *PMLA,* 67:391-410 (June 1952); the third was "An Ingenious Editor: John Nichols and the *Gentleman's Magazine,*" *Bucknell Review,* 10:232-242 (March 1962); and the most recent was "Portrait of a Grub: Samuel Boyse," *Studies in English Literature,* 7:415-425 (Summer 1967).

I should like to think it true that my work has been partially responsible for stimulating the efforts of another scholar whose concern for Nichols is indeed welcome. Mr. James M. Kuist wrote his doctoral dissertation at Duke University (1965) on "The *Gentleman's Magazine,* 1754-1800: A Study of its

Development as a Vehicle for the Discussion of Literature," and I understand that he plans a study of the entire history of that periodical. He has also, in the meantime, become the editor of the Kraus reprint edition of *The Works of John Nichols,* to which he has written an excellent and useful introduction (1968).

One final illustration of a growing contemporary interest in Nichols is the publication of an assortment of lives from *Literary Anecdotes* by Southern Illinois University Press at Carbondale (1967). The lives in this one-volume collection were chosen by Mr. Colin Clair, who also wrote a brief introduction to them. This volume has almost no usefulness to scholars, however, because of the total absence of scholarly apparatus—even of marks to show omissions.

Although one can draw satisfaction from the increasing amount of effort being devoted to Nichols, a great deal more remains to be done. And because no single and thorough standard biography yet exists, it is necessary to review his life here.

Nichols was born on 2 February 1745. Before he was quite thirteen, he was apprenticed to William Bowyer the Younger, who was, wrote Nichols, "confessedly the most learned Printer of the Eighteenth Century." Later, Nichols became Bowyer's partner, and on Bowyer's death he became sole master of the printing house. In 1804 he became master of the Stationers' Company. In achieving the summit of his calling as a printer, Nichols is the archetype of the successful industrious apprentice. Concerning John Nichols as a printer, Edward Gibbon wrote that he was "the last, or one of the last, of the learned Printers in Europe" *(Lit. Anec.,* VIII, 557).

Nichols inherited many literary friendships from Bowyer, and he greatly added to these, with the result that (in partnership with Bowyer and alone) he printed some of the most important books of his age, including, since we are particularly interested in literature here, the first collected edition of the poems of Mark Akenside (1772) and of Lord Lyttelton (1774), the *Works of the English Poets* (1779-1781), and Johnson's collected prefaces to these works as the *Lives of the English Poets* (1781). He also printed the first editions of George Crabbe's *The Library* (1781) and *The Village* (1783) and Thomas Sheridan's *Life of Swift* (1784). In addition to printing these and many other literary works, Nichols also printed, for some time, the proceedings of the Society of Antiquaries, of which he became a fellow, and the votes of the House of Commons.

He held a political appointment under John Wilkes, as his deputy for the ward of Farringdon Without, and later he was elected into the common council for that ward, on 21 December 1784, after which he continued to serve as a member (except for his failure to be elected in 1786) until he resigned in 1811. A large correspondence between Nichols and Wilkes is in *Literary Anecdotes.* Wilkes had his speeches printed by Nichols, and he employed Nichols also in printing a number of editions of classical authors, including the flawless printing of the poems of Catullus (1778). In 1779

Wilkes discontinued a collection of newspapers he had been making since 1768 and gave to Nichols the entire set, consisting of "35 large volumes in folio, illustrated with many MS remarks by himself, detached printed papers on various subjects, and some curious caricatures." These papers were saved from the fire that destroyed Nichols' printing office on 8 February 1808 only to be "stolen by a faithless servant, to whom the care of my warehouse had been considerably confided; and never afterwards could be traced, having probably been consigned, as waste paper, to the shop of some distant cheesemonger" (*Lit. Anec.,* IX, 464n). Thus these papers are not part of the great collection made by Nichols himself and acquired by the Bodleian Library in 1865. Through these and similar resources, Nichols possessed privately great stores of information, and his acquaintance with living men was equal to his resources among the dead.

Though Nichols' prestige as a printer was great, he was probably even better known by his contemporaries as *Sylvanus Urban,* third editor of the *Gentleman's Magazine.* The founder and first editor had been Edward Cave, the friend, benefactor, and one of the earliest employers of Samuel Johnson. It was Cave, Johnson said, "who never looked out of his window but with a view to the *Gentleman's Magazine*" (Hill-Powell, *Boswell,* IV, 409). Although the diligence of Cave was of first importance in establishing the *Gentleman's Magazine* as one of the leading periodicals of the day, Johnson assisted in this achievement. His contributions—poems, translations, reviews, and especially the parliamentary debates—helped the magazine attain and hold its leading position.

Edward Cave was succeeded in the editorship by his brother-in-law, David Henry. Nichols first became associated with Henry in 1778 by buying what he called "a considerable share of the Proprietorship" of the magazine. I deduce from statements made by Nichols, however, that the "considerable share" was less than half, and that the principal part remained in the hands of the Henry family. (See the "Preface" to the *General Index to the Gentleman's Magazine* [1821], III, lvii-lviii.)

The first result of Nichols' connection with the magazine was that he became its printer, partially after 1778 and entirely after 1781. After having some hand in the management from 1778 to 1792, he became sole manager and editor on the death of Henry in 1792. For the next thirty-four years— that is, until his death in 1826—Nichols continued to run the magazine. The period of his influence extended over forty-eight years, and during this time the *Gentleman's Magazine* remained at the height of its influence. After Nichols' death it declined rapidly.

Nichols' *Gentleman's Magazine* was not a *magazine* in the original sense of the term. It was not just a collection (or storehouse) of materials gathered from other sources, nor had it been from the beginning. The *Gentleman's Magazine* was not really much different from the modern magazine. Actually, it can be said that except for the use of materials not then in existence, such as short stories and photographs, there is nothing in modern magazines that did not have a counterpart in the magazines of the late eighteenth century. The *Gentleman's Magazine* had engraved illustrations, letters to the editor, obituaries, summaries of foreign and domestic news, biographical accounts of leading persons, and accounts of industrial progress (such as a description of Franklin's American stove). It contained book reviews, original poems and essays, and historical accounts of people and places having some claim to attention. One could have found in the *Gentleman's Magazine* everything that now would have to be sought in a dozen periodicals: *The Atlantic, Harpers, Time,* the various digests, the *National Geographic,* and the daily newspaper.

Though Nichols was not just an editor, the amount of work he expended on his magazine was more than many another editor has made a life's work of. As soon as he became editor in 1782, he set about building up two departments: obituaries and correspondence with the editor. By 1794 he began to receive so much correspondence that he had to advise contributors concerning the type of material that would be acceptable:

> In one department of our Miscellany it is not arrogant to assert, that we stand unrivalled. The Obituary forms a Body of Biography, which posterity will look back to with a satisfaction which any one may conceive who for a moment considers the defects of similar annals in preceding periods. In this branch of our labours, we have to acknowledge the assistance of many friends. At the same time we request those who in future may be inclined to favour us with intelligence of this kind to confine themselves in general to dates and facts, and to avoid expatiating on that which, arising from circumstances of private knowledge, or a local nature, may serve equally for thousands, as the favourite individual to whom it is promiscuously applied (*General Index to the Gent. Mag.* [1821], III, lxxi).

We may scoff at anyone who places such emphasis on "dates and facts." And one of Nichols' contemporaries did scoff. John Wolcot, alias Peter Pindar, disliked Nichols for political reasons and made fun of the obituaries thus:

> Behold, amidst their short'ning, panting breath,
> Poor souls! the dying dread thee more than death:
> "Oh! save us from JOHN NICHOLS!" is the cry,
> "Let not that death-hunter know where we lie;
> What in *delirium* from our lips may fall,
> Oh! hide—our letters, burn them, burn them all!
> Oh! let not from the tomb our ghosts complain!

> O Jesu! we shall soon be up again;
> Condemn'd, alas! to grin with grisly mien,
> 'Midst the pale horrors of his Magazine."
>
> ("A Benevolent Epistle to Sylvanus Urban, Alias Master John Nichols, Printer, Common-councilman of Farringdon Ward, and Censor-general of Literature. . . ," *The Works of Peter Pindar* [London, 1794], II, 382)

Perhaps all that needs to be said with reference to these facetious lines is that today the bound volumes of the *Gentleman's Magazine* on the open shelves of the British Museum are among the most frequently consulted books in the library. Apparently Nichols' obituaries are no duller than, say, the *Stationers' Register*. And this should remind us that Nichols was interested primarily in facts and not in their literary presentation. Judging Nichols on any other basis is unfair to him, though I do not mean to disparage his style, which is often surprisingly good.

It is easy to see how the stores of information provided in the obituaries and in correspondence would be useful to biographers of the century. But Nichols was not content to take merely what happened to turn up. His manipulation of the magazine correspondence reveals a deft and sometimes a wily hand—or perhaps one should say *hands,* because occasionally he can be detected in a game of writing letters from one hand to the other, and of passing elegant compliments from his left hand to his right. These discoveries are the result of a pursuit of his various pseudonyms: *Alphonso, Eugenio, M. Green, A London Antiquary, J. N.,* and so on (see *Lit. Anec.,* VI, 628). Under the name of *Eugenio,* Nichols wrote:

> Nov. 6.
>
> Mr. Urban,
> The following authentic dates will essentially clear up a circumstance in which the ingenious editor of the "Select Collection of Miscellany Poems" has been misled by an unusual similarity of names. . . (*Gent. Mag.,* 51:515 [November 1781]).

Nichols was editor of this *Select Collection,* which, incidentally, contains biographical notes that will be used in this volume. For a man to call himself an "ingenious editor" in his own magazine while correcting his own mistake, and above all to get away with it, is almost proof of his right to the title he gave himself.

Nichols' frequent manipulation of the correspondence of the magazine was mostly for the purpose of obtaining information on projects that he was currently working on. From 1775 to 1779, for instance, he was engaged in bringing out three supplements to the works of Swift, which will be discussed in detail later. In November of 1778 Nichols wrote a letter, signed *J. N.*, asking readers to supply specific, detailed information about Swift (*Gent. Mag.*, 48:521-523 [November 1778]). In 1782, while working on the first two volumes of his *Atterbury Correspondence*, he wrote asking for such information as Mrs. Atterbury's maiden name (52:335-336 [July 1782]). As *M. Green*, in a letter to Mr. Urban in July 1783, Nichols ended with a request: "I should also be much pleased to see some memorials of Mr. Ellis, the schoolmaster of Sir R. Steele" (53:552). In 1786 Nichols brought out an edition of the *Tatler*, and in 1788 he published Steele's correspondence.

Because of his reputation for judgment and reliability, Nichols came into possession of a great deal of material that might not have been entrusted to another publisher. Among these materials were some important manuscripts. The family of Richard Steele sold him Steele's letters, and Richard Farmer passed on to him freely all the materials he had gathered for a history of Leicester. Other manuscripts he received were from people not so well known. One of these was John Jones, who had received a curacy from Edward Young, author of *Night Thoughts*. Jones left, at his death, a bundle of papers directed to Nichols (*Lit. Anec.*, I, 633-634). A great deal of information from Jones's papers is scattered across the pages of the *Gentleman's Magazine* (see, for example, 53:101-103 [February 1783]; 227-229 [March 1783]; 62:463-464 [June 1792]). When Samuel Johnson applied to Nichols for information about Gilbert West for *Lives of the Poets*, Nichols found material among the contributions of John Jones. This information now constitutes part of Johnson's life of West.*

There is no end to the examples that could be cited to illustrate Nichols' use of the magazine for secondary purposes; others will appear in relation to lives presented later in this volume.

As indicated previously, the other department of the magazine upon which Nichols lavished his attention was that of the obituary. In the statement of 1794, cited earlier, Nichols had made a prediction: "The Obituary forms a Body of Biography, which posterity will look back to with a satisfaction which any one may conceive who for a moment considers the defects of similar annals in preceding periods." No one can question that the hopes he held for the magazine have been fulfilled, but at an expense to himself of endless personal interviews, letters, and searches through records. Facts published monthly in the magazine could be verified, as they would still be fresh in the memories of those who knew the deceased person. If mistakes were made they would be pointed out by correspondents.

To the end of his life Nichols was occupied with making corrections and

---

* See my article, "Some New Sources of Johnson's *Lives*," *PMLA*, 65:1099-1101 (December 1950).

additions to his huge accumulations of data. And to the end he prized the *Gentleman's Magazine* beyond all other receivers of his effort. He was an ingenious editor. He handled the magazine with loving care. If he possessed anything worthy of being printed, it went to the *Gentleman's Magazine* first and was later farmed out to one of his book collections. Thus we find, for example, that the publication of Johnson's letters begins immediately after his death in the magazine he had helped to build. We find spread over the same period and in the same place Nichols' many anecdotes of Johnson, later gathered for Boswell and the enrichment of his *Life of Johnson*.*

Still later biographers made use of Nichols. He is, of course, the primary source of information for the lives of most who appear in this collection. We can, without exaggeration, sum up Nichols' contribution to biography by saying that there is no life of a literary figure of the eighteenth century included in the *Dictionary of National Biography* that is not indebted to some extent to John Nichols. And this, in turn, implies an indebtedness to the *Gentleman's Magazine*. I find some lives in the DNB continuing Nichols' original phraseology; in a few instances whole sentences are transplanted unaltered. (See examples in "An Ingenious Editor: John Nichols and the *Gentleman's Magazine*," pp. 241-242.) In this way the hundreds of anonymous authors writing letters to Mr. Urban have become collaborators with Nichols as authors of the largest part of the biography of their age.

It has been so easy to borrow from Nichols' inexhaustible store of facts that the process of doing so without acknowledging the source began even during Nichols' lifetime. He wrote the following in an introduction to a life he had published previously: "The former Edition of these 'Anecdotes' having served as the ground-work of Dr. Kippis's Memoir of this 'learned Divine and Antiquary' in the *Biographia Britannica;* I have no hesitation in reclaiming, with *legal interest,* the scattered materials. Thus books are constantly made; but not always thus honestly acknowledged" (introduction to life of William Clarke, *Lit. Anec.,* IV, 363). The process of borrowing from Nichols has been going on ever since. Facts attributable to him appear in countless books written on eighteenth-century subjects. There are footnote references and guides to them in the indexes. That which had been contributed by Nichols has become the property of new writers, and most people who read the books will pay little attention to either notes or indexes. Such is the fame of Nichols and his host of silent partners; but to them we owe an inestimable debt of gratitude for their contribution to our knowledge of eighteenth-century writers.

Nichols' activities do not end, however, with his being a printer and the editor of the *Gentleman's Magazine*. He was also an author in his own right. During his lifetime he wrote more than forty volumes. This is not to mention, of course, writing that he contributed to the *Gentleman's Magazine*

---

* See my account of this in "The Contributions of John Nichols to Boswell's *Life of Johnson*," *PMLA,* 67:391-410 (June 1952).

over a period of nearly fifty years; he became, in fact, its historian by writing "A Prefatory Introduction Descriptive of the Rise and Progress of the Magazine" for the *General Index* (1821).

The most important biographical writings of John Nichols, and consequently the most useful to students of the period, are the seventeen volumes of the *Literary Anecdotes of the Eighteenth Century* and *Illustrations of the Literary History of the Eighteenth Century*. These works began as a pamphlet of fifty-two pages (1778) of which only twenty copies were printed, with the title: "Anecdotes, biographical and literary, of the late Mr. William Bowyer, Printer. Compiled for private use. [Phoenix design.] London: printed in the year MDCCLXXVIII." (Three copies are in the British Museum, shelfmarks 619.f.7; 1415.d.52; and G.16621.) At the end of 1778, an abridged version appeared in installments of the *Gentleman's Magazine* (48:409-412 [September]; 449-456 [October]; 513-516 [November]; 569-572 [December]). Still later it formed the core of a large quarto volume of 666 pages entitled *Biographical and Literary Anecdotes of William Bowyer* (1782), referred to at times by Nichols as the "first edition" of *Literary Anecdotes*. The growth of a pamphlet in such a manner, reaching such proportions, can be explained only in relation to the *Gentleman's Magazine* and the use Nichols made of it in gathering information.

The original intention was for *Literary Anecdotes* to be six volumes. These were duly issued in 1812, to be followed by the first part of Volume 7, an index to the first six volumes (1813). In time, two supplementary volumes came out, Volume 8 in 1814 and Volume 9, in 1815, with the second half of Volume 7, an index to the last two volumes, appearing in 1816. Then the series of *Illustrations* was begun, the first two volumes issued by John Nichols in 1817 and the last, Volume 8, by his son, John Bowyer Nichols, in 1858, eighty years after the first start had been made upon the "Life of Bowyer."

Literary Anecdotes was, to begin with, set up as a chronological listing of books printed at the Bowyer (later Nichols) press. But the books had authors, and notes containing memoirs, anecdotes, and letters crowd beneath the text of the annals of the press until sometimes the text disappears altogether and nothing is left but notes. In later volumes there are memoirs of the writers of letters to the original author, and sometimes there are memoirs of everyone mentioned in the letters. Fortunately, there are good indexes in which one can find something about nearly everyone of any importance in the century.

In a class by itself among Nichols' biographical writings is his work on Hogarth. His first publication on this subject was his *Anecdotes of Mr. Hogarth* (1780?). In 1781 Nichols published the first edition, in one octavo volume, of his *Biographical Anecdotes of William Hogarth*. It was reprinted in increasingly large volumes in 1782 and 1785. Between 1810 and 1817 it became three volumes. In 1780 Horace Walpole issued the long-awaited fourth volume of his *Anecdotes of Painting in England*. This volume, containing an account of Hogarth, had done much to create interest in the artist. Edmond Malone, writing to Lord Charlemont on 18 June 1781, mentioned the current excitement regarding Hogarth, an excitement that must go a long way toward explaining the phenomenal growth of Nichols' work. "People here," wrote Malone, "are seized at present with an Hogarthomania ... Mr. Walpole's book first gave rise to it, and a new life of Hogarth that is just published [by Nichols] will probably greatly add to the disorder" (*Hist. MSS. Commission Reports,* Charlemont, I, 382-383). George Steevens, whose life by Nichols is included in this volume, assisted Nichols with the work on Hogarth. Earlier the two had collaborated on editing *Six Old Plays* (2 vols., 1779), sources of six of Shakespeare's plays, and in 1799 Nichols published an edition of Shakespeare from Steevens' text. For the work on Hogarth, Steevens wrote critiques on the plates and Nichols wrote the biography. Their work is still the primary source for any latter-day biographer of Hogarth. Walpole completed his list of Hogarth's works from Nichols' and acknowledged that Nichols' work on the subject of Hogarth was more accurate and satisfactory than his own (see *Lit. Anec.,* VI, 632n).

Nichols' biographical writings are likely to be found in many places and works other than those that appear on the surface to be biographical. His *Select Collection of Poems* (8 vols., 1780-1782), for example, contains biographical notes on over one hundred and fifty people, including Samuel Boyse, whose life is included in this volume. Nichols' note on William Broome in the *Select Collection* provided Johnson with a good deal of the material that went into his life of Broome in the *Lives of the Poets* ("Some New Sources of Johnson's *Lives,*" pp. 1094-1095).

Many biographical sketches are also to be found in Nichols' historical works, especially in his magnum opus as an antiquarian, the monumental *History of Leicester* (7 vols. folio, 1795-1811). People with Leicester associations should be especially sought for in this work. One indication of the value Nichols placed upon preserving antiquities is the fact that he suffered a tremendous financial loss—at least £5,000, to bring out his *History of Leicester* (*Illustr.,* VI, 589-590). Two other works of Nichols are certainly of great importance as histories: the first, *The Progresses of Queen Elizabeth* (3 vols. folio, 1778-1804), and the second, *The Progresses of King James I* (gathered by Nichols but published in 1828, two years after his death). These two works are of special historical value now because many of the manuscripts and scarce pamphlets reprinted in them are printed nowhere else or are lost.

Other biographical notes of Nichols are scattered throughout his various contributions to the *Bibliotheca Topographica Britannica,* edited by him and Richard Gough (9 vols., 1812-1815). He supplied, in addition, biographies to works of others, including "several hundred new lives" to the second edition of *The General Biographical Dictionary* (1784), a feat which he dismisses with utmost brevity (*Lit. Anec.*, VI, 633). One can, in short, expect to find biographical notes in almost any of the numerous works which Nichols wrote or edited or to which he contributed.

Although we have considered Nichols briefly as a printer, as a magazine editor, and as an author, we are not done with him yet. He also edited over one hundred and fifty volumes of the writings of other men, and some of this editing was of great literary importance. He edited, for example, the first collection of the letters of Richard Steele (2 vols., 1788). He reprinted the letters in 1809, and that was the last collecting and editing of Steele's letters until the definitive edition of Rae Blanchard in 1941. Nichols had purchased the letters from the Steele family, and after finishing his editing he deposited them in the British Museum (MSS. 5145 ABC). Earlier, Nichols had brought out an edition of *The Tatler* (1786), the first to be adequately annotated. Nichols was assisted by many persons still living who had known Steele, and Nichols' notes to this edition included those collected by Thomas Percy. Percy's notes to the 1786 edition of *The Tatler* came to Nichols by way of John Calder (*Lit. Anec.*, IX, 805). Without this edition, much of the information in the notes would have been irrecoverably lost. Nichols also brought out annotated editions of some of Steele's lesser known works: *The Lover and Reader* (1789), *The Town Talk, Fish Pool, Plebian, Old Whig, Spinster, &c.* (1790), and *The Theatre and Anti-theatre, &c.* (1791).

In addition to his work on Steele, Nichols also edited the *Works of William King* (3 vols., 1776). The twenty-page memoir prefixed to the first volume provided Johnson with the materials for his life of King ("Some New Sources of Johnson's *Lives*," pp. 1101-1111). The *Works of Leonard Welsted* (1787), with a memoir of the author, was also edited by Nichols, as was Francis Atterbury's *Epistolary Correspondence* (4 vols., 1783-1787; 5 vols., 1799) and a new edition of Fuller's *Worthies* (2 vols., 1811).

Nichols' greatest literary contribution as an editor, however, was the effort he gave to Swift over a period of many years. He first became interested in Swift while assisting his partner, William Bowyer, in adding a thirteenth and a fourteenth volume in 1762 to Hawkesworth's twelve-volume edition of 1755. Nichols continued to interest himself in the editing of Swift from the time of this introduction by Bowyer until 1808, a period of forty-six years.

By the time Nichols began his independent work on Swift, a fifteenth and a sixteenth volume of the London booksellers' edition of Swift's works had been added by Deane Swift in 1765 to the fourteen volumes already mentioned. In addition, six volumes of correspondence had been published. The first three were edited by John Hawkesworth in 1766 and contained letters I and XLI-LXV of the *Journal to Stella*; the other three were edited by Deane Swift in 1768 and contained letters I-XL of the *Journal* (see edition of Harold Williams [Oxford, 1948], I, xlviii-l).

Nichols edited his first supplementary volume to the works of Swift in 1775, and it became Vol. XVII of the trade edition. It contained an index to all previous volumes, including the six volumes of correspondence. The second supplementary volume (Vol. XXIV of the trade edition) was issued by Nichols in 1776. By the time it appeared, Nichols had become deeply interested in the editorial problems involved and he had gone a long way toward solving some of them. He had, first of all, brought order to a good deal of Swift by a close and intelligent reading of the *Journal to Stella* and by making notes of what Swift himself had said of his writing. In the supplement of 1776 Nichols printed many of the pieces by Swift that he had discovered, and in the preface listed the titles of those he had been unable to find (*Illustr.*, V, 392-393).

The attention given by Nichols to the *Journal to Stella* led him to another important discovery. He noticed a difference in style between the twelve volumes edited by Hawkesworth and the two volumes edited by Deane Swift and went to the originals to find the explanation (Williams, I, l-li). Along the way he began his long and important work of making corrections, supplying excisions and obliterations, and filling in the little language.

Nichols secured the interest in his projects of Edmond Malone, a man imbued with the same methodical habit of accuracy that characterized Nichols; Malone was impressed by the pains Nichols was taking with Swift, and as is shown in the following extract from a letter from Malone to Lord Charlemont, the search for the missing pieces of Swift was carried to Ireland. The letter is undated, but the list of works at the end is the same as the one in the preface to the 1776 *Supplement*. The letter was probably sent in 1776, or at the latest the following year.

> He [Nichols] has taken infinite pains about Swift. He has examined all the original letters (of which so many collections have been printed within these few years) which are now deposited in the British Museum, and on collating them with the printed copies, he found that Dr. Hawkesworth and the other editors had taken most unwarrantable liberties with them, mutilating and suppressing passages ad libitum. When he applied to me on the subject, which I shall just now mention to you, he shewed me several sheets of paper which he had covered with these omitted passages, and which he had been at the pains of transcribing from the originals. By an attentive perusal of Swift's "Journal to Stella," he has discovered him to be the author of many little pieces in the time of Queen Anne, which have not yet been inserted in his works; and he has procured almost all the original editions of Swift's political pieces, as they were published in threepenny and sixpenny pamphlets, by which he has been enabled to correct many errors. But there are a few papers which, after all his researches, he has not been able to meet with; and he requested me to write to Ireland in order to get some intelligence about them. A complete edition of Swift is so national a work that I am sure you will be ready to contribute to it, yet I fear it will be difficult, if not impossible, to procure the pieces

he wants. The titles of them are as follows: ... (*Hist. MSS. Commission Reports,* Charlemont, II, 402.)

Malone, writing again to Charlemont in a letter dated 29 April 1779, says that Nichols has discovered some of the works on the previous list and has some new ones to add to it. Malone also reports that Nichols has been again at work on the *Journal to Stella* (Charlemont, I, 346-347). The third supplement printed by Nichols to the *Works of Swift* was Vol. XXV of the trade edition.

"In his *Supplement to Dr. Swift's Works,* 1779," wrote Harold Williams, "he [Nichols] printed a list of 'Omissions and principal Corrections' in which he noted the deliberate excisions of the 1766 edition, and he also supplied much of the little language" (Williams, *Journal to Stella,* I, li). The list of missing works printed in the 1779 supplement makes it of great importance in the bibliography of Swift, and it is useful even today. All three supplements were reprinted in 1779 (in 1 vol. 4to, 3 vols. 8vo, and 3 vols. 18mo).

Nichols' collection of Swift materials had been made from the first with the intention of using them eventually in a complete edition of Swift's works (see *Illustr.,* V, 391); but before he could gain possession of all the scattered copyrights (*ibid.,* 394), Thomas Sheridan had, in 1784, brought out his edition of Swift's works. In Sheridan's edition the two parts of the letters to Stella (those edited earlier by Hawkesworth and Deane Swift) were brought together for the first time, with the title *Dr. Swift's Journal to Stella,* though Nichols had used the *Journal to Stella* title in his 1779 supplement and so must be considered its originator (Williams, I, 1, n. 1).

It was not until 1801 that Nichols was enabled to bring out his complete edition of Swift (issued in 19 vols. 8vo; reprinted in 1804 in 24 vols. 18mo; again reprinted in 1808 in 19 vols. 8vo). The importance of Nichols' editions of Swift's works to the text of the *Journal to Stella* is summarized by Harold Williams:

> It would be difficult to conceive more indolent editorial method than that exhibited by Sheridan's presentation of *The Journal to Stella.*
>
> Nichols's edition of Swift's *Works,* published in 1801, showed a real advance. He embodied in the *Journal* the corrections and additions which he had printed in 1779, and since that time he had evidently turned once again to decipher the original letters. On the other hand, the reproduction of his earlier notes was neither verbally accurate nor faithful to the original. But, for the first time, the letters appeared in a form which made some approximation to the manuscript, although there were serious omissions, and spelling and punctuation were normalized. He also added a large number of footnotes, especially to the part of the *Journal* printed by Deane Swift, and he altered many others.

[Sir Walter] Scott, in 1814, very considerably amplified and added to the annotations of the *Journal,* but he was content to take his text directly from Nichols.

Not for nearly one hundred years after John Nichols had studied the original letters to Stella was a serious attempt again made to decipher the obliterated passages, correct mistakes of reading, note omissions, and interpret the little language. (Williams, I, lii.)

Nichols had had great difficulty in gathering his materials and in obtaining copyrights for Swift's *Works.* Scott's ungracious lifting of the text of the *Journal* without even spelling Nichols' name correctly in his inadequate acknowledgment drew from Nichols one of the few passages in which he wrote with asperity of a fellow author.

Here ends my own Literary History as Editor of the Works of the far-famed Dean of St. Patrick's; for, about that period, the great Magician of the North, (not then Unknown,) having made a solid breakfast on John Dryden, conceived the idea of a pleasant dinner and supper on Jonathan Swift; which, from the entertainment I had prepared, he found a task of no great difficulty. Laying his potent wand on my humble labours, he very soon, by a neat shuffling of the cards, and by abridging my tedious annotations, (turning lead to gold,*) he presented to the Booksellers of Edinburgh an Edition somewhat similar to mine, and consisting of the same number of volumes; condescending, however, to honour me with this brief compliment:

"The Valuable and laborious Edition of Mr. *Nicol* (the misnomer is of no consequence) was the first which presented to the publick any thing resembling a complete collection of Swift's Works; and unquestionably those who peruse it, must admire the labour and accuracy of the Editor."

---

* The Pecuniary remuneration to Sir Walter Scott was precisely *thirty* times as much as I had received, or expected, for my Three Editions. NICHOLS. (*Illustr.,* V, 396-397.)

Malone rendered great assistance to Nichols. Through him Nichols got possession of the essay of Dr. Barrett on the early life of Swift (Williams, *The Poems of Jonathan Swift* [Oxford, 3 vols., 1958], I, xli). Malone also procured for Nichols "a drawing of the very excellent likeness of the Dean, taken after his death, which appears in the Edition of 1808; and an original Letter to Dr. [Henry] Jenny" [dated 8 June 1732, *Illustr.,* V, 396; for dating of letter see Nichols' 1808 *Swift,* XII, 352-357]. A hitherto unpublished letter from Nichols to Malone, in the Bodleian Library (MS Malone 39, fol. 148), refers to the engraving of Swift and expresses a sense of the importance attached by Nichols to the help of Malone.

> Dear Sir,   June 20, 1808
>
> I send you a Proof of the Engraving of Swift; to which the Writing will be added as directed in your last.—I am now winding up the Fragments at the End of the several Volumes; but will keep a Niche open till the last moment in hopes of further Contributions.
> I am Sir
>   Very gratefully yours,
>   J Nichols

Malone's assistance to Nichols went beyond Swift and included help with the two-volume edition of Fuller's *Worthies* published by Nichols in 1811 (*Illustr.*, V, 466-467); and Nichols reciprocated with help given to Malone. Of particular significance is Nichols' supplying letters of Dryden's famous master, Richard Busby, to Malone for his edition of *Critical and Miscellaneous Prose Works of John Dryden* (3 vols., 1800), acknowledged thus by Malone: "The Letters of Dr. Busby have been already made publick; but are here printed from the originals, which have been obligingly communicated by Mr. John Nichols, author of the History of Leicestershire" (I, pt. 2, 18). Additional illustrations of assistance given by Nichols to Malone—this time to his editing of Boswell's *Life of Johnson*—have been given by me elsewhere.*

In moving as we have, however, from the subject of the works written or edited by Nichols to the subject of assistance given and received by him, we have left a lagoon and entered the great ocean of eighteenth-century literary life. Here, Nichols' collaborators were not only Malone, but also Johnson, Boswell, Walpole, Steevens, the Wartons, and almost every other literate man, known or unknown, in the England of that day. At the lower end of the scale of the known are such figures as E. E. Raspe, the peripatetic embezzler, better known as the author of the *Adventures of Baron Munchausen*. Raspe made extracts from the Domesday Book for Nichols' *History of Leicester*, and Nichols printed a number of works written by Raspe himself (*Lit. Anec.*, III, 216-218). Among the unknown are the forever anonymous contributors to the *Gentleman's Magazine*, supplying Nichols with information he sought to fill up his never-ending collections. At this point, however, we must abandon the impossible task of presenting here all of Nichols' relationships with all of his literary associates and turn to our main object, the observation of the lives of an interesting group of men as these lives came from the pen of John Nichols.

---

* "The Contributions of John Nichols to Boswell's *Life of Johnson*," *PMLA*, 67:406-410 (June 1952).

Shortened Titles of Nichols' Works

In addition to using such universally recognized abbreviations as *DNB* and *PMLA*, I have shortened the titles of a number of works. Hill-Powell, *Boswell*, is used consistently to refer to *Boswell's Life of Johnson*, ed. G. B. Hill and rev. L. F. Powell, 6 vols. (Oxford: Clarendon Press, 1934-1950). The *Gentleman's Magazine*, edited by John Nichols from 1792 to 1826, is shortened in notes to *Gent. Mag.* I have, in addition, shortened the titles of some other works by John Nichols. Following are three titles of works cited frequently in text and notes. Given first (except for the last item) is the shortened version of the title used only in notes; second is the short title used commonly in other places; finally, the full title and dates are given.

Illustr.—Illustrations: Illustrations of the Literary History of the Eighteenth Century. Consisting of Authentic Memoirs and Original Letters of Eminent Persons; and intended as a Sequel to The Literary Anecdotes (8 vols., 1817-1858; Vols. I-VI name John Nichols as author; Vols. VII-VIII name his son John Bowyer Nichols as author).

Lit. Anec.—Literary Anecdotes: Literary Anecdotes of the Eighteenth Century; comprizing Biographical Memoirs of William Bowyer, Printer, F.S.A. and many of his Learned Friends; an Incidental View of the Progress and Advancement of Literature in this Kingdom during the Last Century; and Biographical Anecdotes of a Considerable Number of Eminent Writers and Ingenious Artists; with a very Copious Index (9 vols., all by John Nichols, 1812-1816).

Select Collection: A Select Collection of Poems: with Notes, Biographical and Historical (8 vols., all edited by John Nichols, 1780-1782).

Part I Antiquarians

Isaac Reed

[Isaac Reed died 5 January 1807, and the *Gentleman's Magazine* for January 1807 contains "Biographical Memoirs of the late Isaac Reed, Esq.," signed *J.N.* At the conclusion of the memoir Nichols wrote: "On the bed of pain and anguish, another of his oldest friends (though unable to hold a pen) feels a soothing satisfaction in dictating this last tribute of respect to so exemplary a character." Nichols' "bed of pain and anguish" was the result of a fall and fracture of "one of his thighs" on 8 January, and at the age of sixty-two.[1]

Another memoir of Reed appeared in February in the *European Magazine*. In this memoir, the author states that Reed had been formerly "both Editor and a Proprietor" of that magazine, though during his lifetime Reed had denied being editor. Henry Meen wrote in a letter to Thomas Percy, *Illustr.*, VII, 48, "He is not the editor, he asserts; nor does he wish to be so considered." He was without question, however, a part owner. The memoir in the *European Magazine* is signed *J.B.* and was written by James Bindley, a friend of both Reed and Nichols. Some facts from Nichols' life of Reed are repeated by Bindley, though there is no evidence of direct assistance. Since, however, the information in the following comparison came from a letter from Reed to Nichols, we may assume that Nichols' memoir, especially as it appeared a month earlier than Bindley's, was the source.

Nichols	Bindley
So extremely averse indeed was he to appearing before the publick, that, when he was asked, as a matter of course, to add only his initials at the end of the prefatory advertisement to the volume of Dr. Young,[2] his answer was nearly in these words: "I solemnly declare, that I have such a thorough dread of putting my name to any publication whatever, that, if I were placed in the alternative either of so doing or of standing in the pillory, I believe I should prefer the latter."[3]	It is remarkable, that when he was requested to suffer his name, or his initials, to appear in the title-page, or advertisement, he made answer, (so great was his dread on that occasion,) "he believed he should prefer the pillory itself, if it were proposed as an alternative."[4]

1. *Lit. Anec.*, VI, 629.
2. Reed edited the sixth volume of the works of Edward Young, 1778.
3. *Gent. Mag.*, 77:80 (January 1807).
4. *Europ. Mag.*, 51:83 (February 1807).

When Nichols reprinted the memoir of Reed in *Lit. Anec.*, II, 664-672, he added a note to the material used in the comparison above: "This was written from memory. But the following Letter, which I have since found, confirms the fact." The exact words of Reed, taken from his letter to Nichols, are: "I declare I have such a horror of seeing my name as Author or Editor, that if I had the option of standing in the pillory, or in standing formally before the publick in either of those lights, I should find it difficult to determine which to choose." (II, 666 n)

Bindley's memoir, however, contributed new information to a life of Reed as well as using some already provided by Nichols; and when Nichols transferred his memoir of Reed from the *Gentleman's Magazine* to *Literary Anecdotes*, he made some corrections to his own material from Bindley's account. In *Literary Anecdotes* Nichols also added a number of letters from Reed to himself, and it seems that there is now no other source for these letters, which are reprinted by Claude E. Jones in the notes to his edition of the *Isaac Reed Diaries, 1762-1804* (University of California Publications in English, vol. 10, 1946). Aside from the memoir proper, many other matters concerning Reed appear in various volumes of *Literary Anecdotes* and *Illustrations*. Of special interest is some correspondence between Reed and Thomas Percy in *Illustr.*, VIII, 296-298.

Reed was well informed and was very free with his assistance. He had the reputation of being willing to give literary help to all who asked it. Nichols benefited greatly from his association with Reed; nor, to tell the complete story, was the matter of assistance a one-way street. Nichols contributed notes to Reed's edition of Dodsley's *Old Plays*, 1780 (*Lit. Anec.*, VI, 630 n), assistance that was acknowledged by Reed in his preface: "and those [notes] which have the letter N annexed to them, are such observations as occurred to the printer of the first six volumes, in reading the proof sheets." In addition, Nichols solicited help for Reed, in connection with this same work, from other authors, including Samuel Pegge (*Lit. Anec.*, III, 267 n).

Nichols' success as a biographer depended to some extent, surely, on his personal association with many of those people about whom he wrote. It appears that Nichols called upon Reed for legal assistance upon at least one occasion, according to a letter in the Columbia University collection of Nichols papers. The letter, which is transcribed below, is about Thomas Bowyer, only surviving son of Nichols' former employer and partner William Bowyer. Thomas Bowyer was intended by his father to succeed him in the printing business, but the son disliked the employment and became in turn a cleric of the Church of England, a military man, and a Quaker, being known at times simply as Mr. Thomas: a fact which caused him some difficulty over his inheritance when his father died and resulted in his having to prove his legitimacy. Nichols assisted him in gaining possession of his estate. When Thomas Bowyer died, he left most of his property to a distant relative, an apothecary named Francis Mewburn (*Lit. Anec.*, III, 273-277). It is with respect to the latter fact that Reed wrote the following letter. Mewburn also corresponded with Nichols (see *ibid.*), and the validity of Thomas Bowyer's will was eventually established by the verdict of a jury.

Dear Sir,   Staple Inn/Feb. 2. 1784
    I am about to take a liberty which I think your good nature will pardon and as I am unacquainted with any person in Durham you will oblige me much if you will furnish me with the information I now apply for.
    A Person is lately dead in Durham of the name of Thomas Bowyer [b. 5 September 1730; d. 27 December 1783] or as he was sometimes called Mr Thomas only. He has left a Will by which Mr Mewburn an Apothecary where he lodged is bequeathed almost the whole of his property. A Report is gone abroad & from circumstances it is not improbable that he was not in a sufficiently sound mind to make a Will at all. This how ever must depend upon Evidence and a good deal upon the character of the persons who attested it as Witnesses. Their names I find are Francis Smorles an Attorney of Patrick and William Henderson both Shopkeepers & I think Grocers. Sho^d the Testator not have been sufficiently sane to execute a Will Mr Nichols the Printer will become intitled to a considerable sum of money but as he is not desirous of a groundless litigation it is probable he will give up his claim or rather not assert it if the witnesses are persons of good and respectable characters.
    If you will be so obliging as to let me know whe^r they are credible persons or not by the return of post [you] will do me and Mr Nichols a singular favo[ur]. I beg an answer early as Mewburn & his . . . are both in Town & nothing can be done [until the] fact is ascertained.
                                             I am as . . .
                                             [Isaac Reed]

    One of the great attractions of the life of Reed by Nichols is that in it we find Nichols present in person at the Sturbridge (or Stirbitch) Fair in company with five of his biographical subjects: Isaac Reed, George Steevens, Richard Farmer, Richard Gough, and William Cole.
    Since the publication of *Literary Anecdotes,* Reed has been written about from time to time. Alexander Chalmers included a life of him in his *General Biographical Dictionary* (London, 1816). Chalmers, later to be Nichols' own biographer, made two acknowledgments: "Life in Europ. Mag. 1807.—Nichols's Bowyer." By *Bowyer,* Chalmers meant *Literary Anecdotes;* he added nothing in his account to the details provided by his two sources. Edward Dowden wrote a discursive account of Reed (see n. 31). Sidney Lee's life of Reed in *DNB* uses Nichols as a main source.
    Scholars interested in pursuing Reed further will find the greatest abundance of manuscript materials at the Folger Shakespeare Library, which holds not only diaries and other papers but a great collection of autograph letters as well, both to and from Reed. The most important Reed collection at the Folger (C.b.2) is especially rich in his correspondence with George

Steevens, Elizabeth Steevens, Richard Farmer, Edmond Malone, and William Hayley. Many other libraries also have important holdings. In the Osborn collection at Yale, for instance, are thirteen letters and three other manuscripts, including more Reed correspondence with Steevens and others and a "Poetical Obituary; lists, in dated order, of Poets dying from 1638-1797." At Yale's Beinecke Library are several other letters and memoranda. The Bodleian Library has at least ten letters to or from Reed, including one each from Farmer, Percy, and Thomas Warton.]

[I trust that I shall be excused in presenting this memoir of a worthy Friend in the words *dictated from the heart* at a period when, from an unfortunate accident, I was unable to *read a line, or to hold a pen*.—I am aware that some Memoirs of Mr. Reed, drawn up by a gentleman who knew him well, were printed in the European Magazine for February 1808; from which a few corrections shall be taken in the way of Notes.[5]]

This very eminent Collector of Books and able Commentator [Reed] was born in the parish of St. Dunstan in the West,* where his father passed unambitiously through life, in the useful occupation of a baker, and had the satisfaction of witnessing the son's literary attainments† with that enthusiasm which frequently prevails in a strong uncultivated mind.

He commenced his public life very reputably, as a solicitor and conveyancer; but for several years before his death had confined the practical part of his business to the last-mentioned branch of his profession. [He was articled as a Clerk to Messrs. Perrott and Hodgson, eminent Attorneys; and was afterwards an assistant to Mr. Hoskins, a respectable Barrister and Conveyancer; with whom he continued about a year, and then commenced practice in chambers in Gray's Inn, as a Conveyancer.—He had been heard to say, "The practice of the Law was intolerable."][6] Placed in a situation which, above all others, is frequently the road to riches and honour, Mr. Reed's principal ambition was, to acquire a fundamental knowledge of the jurisprudence of his Country; and thus far he was eminently successful. But the Law, however alluring its prospects, had not charms sufficient to engage his whole attention; he loved, he venerated, that admirable system,

---

* I understood, from himself, that his father resided there; but Isaac was born in Stewart-street, Old Artillery Ground. NICHOLS.

† Being of a delicate constitution, his earliest years were passed at home with his parents; and he was afterwards placed at a school in Streatham. NICHOLS.

5. This paragraph appears as a note in *Lit. Anec.* Alexander Chalmers wrote (*Illustr.*, VIII, xix): "In the case of the fracture, the present writer had an opportunity to witness an instance of patient endurance and of placid temper which he can never forget. Only three days after the accident, he found Mr. Nichols, supported by the surgical apparatus usual on such occasions, calmly reading the proof of a long article which he had that morning dictated to one of his daughters, respecting the life and death of his old friend Isaac Reed, which went to press as he left it, and indeed wanted no correction. This accident left some portion of lameness, and abridged his usual exercise, but his general health was little impaired."

6. The parenthetical material appears as a note in *Lit. Anec.*

which, from the days of Alfred and Canute, from the bold usurping Norman to the present amiable Father of his People, has been regularly ameliorating; but he detested the chicanery of which he was almost daily a witness in many of its professors. If ever there was a mind devoid of guile, it was Isaac Reed's; and an attempt to make "the worse appear the better cause"[7] would have been with him a breach of moral obligation. Hence an extensive line of business was necessarily precluded; but he had the satisfaction of numbering among his clients many highly-valued friends; and other avenues to Fame, if not to Fortune, were open to his capacious mind. His intimate knowledge of antient English Literature was unbounded. His own publications, though not very numerous, were all valuable; and he was more satisfied with being a faithful editor, than ambitious of being an original composer.

In the year 1768, he collected into one volume, 12mo, "The Poetical Works of the Hon. Lady M(ar)y W(ortle)y M(ontagu)e." His other publications were, [Thomas] Middleton's "Witch, a Tragi-Coomodie," a few copies only for his Friends, 1778; the Sixth Volume of Dr. Young's Works, 1778, 12mo;[8] "Biographia Dramatica," 2 volumes, 8vo, 1782, founded upon "[David Erskine] Baker's Companion to the Playhouse:" the biographical department of this work is the result of diligent enquiry, and his strictures on the productions of the English Drama display sound judgment and correct taste;‡ an improved edition of Dodsley's Old Plays, with Notes, 12 vols. 8vo, 1780; Dodsley's Collection of Poems, with Biographical Notes, 6 vols. 8vo, 1782; "The Repository: a select Collection of Fugitive Pieces of Wit and Humour, in Prose and Verse, by the most eminent Writers," 4 vols. 8vo, 1777-1783; Pearch's Collection of Poems, with Biographical Notes, 4 volumes, 8vo, 1783 (which some have ascribed to the late George Keate, esq.);[9] "A complete Collection of the Cambridge Prize Poems, from their first Institution, in 1750, to the present Time," 8vo, 1773; an edition of Johnson and Steevens's Shakspeare, 10 vols. 8vo, 1785, which he undertook at the request of Dr. Farmer and Mr. Steevens, the latter of whom resigning, for this time, the office of Editor; some short Lives of those English Poets who were added to Dr. Johnson's Collection, in 1790;[10] the last and splendid Edition of

---

‡ Mr. Reed had occasionally interested himself in arranging and collecting materials for an improved edition; but, finding himself unequal to continue his exertions, the property of this work, before he had actually much enlarged it, was transferred to the London Booksellers; and on Mr. Reed's strongest recommendation, the completion of it was undertaken by Mr. Stephen Jones, in whose hands it will not fail to appear before the publick with every advantage. NICHOLS.

7. A paraphrase of Milton, whose Belial, in *Paradise Lost* II. 113-114, "could make the worse appear / The better reason. . ."

8. See headnote and n.2.

9. George Pearch's collection of poems was intended as a supplement to that of Robert Dodsley, referred to just before the Pearch collection in the text. Nichols' *Select Collection* contained no poems in either Dodsley's or Pearch's collections and was intended as a supplement to both.

10. Johnson, in a letter to Nichols, conjecturally dated May 1780 and numbered 670 in

Shakspeare, in 21 vols. 8vo, 1803, with his name prefixed; an effort which he with some difficulty was persuaded to make. So extremely averse indeed was he to appearing before the publick, that, when he was asked, as a matter of course, to add only his initials at the end of the prefatory advertisement to the volume of Dr. Young,[11] his answer was nearly in these words: "I solemnly declare, that I have such a thorough dread of putting my name to any publication whatever, that, if I were placed in the alternative either of so doing or of standing in the pillory, I believe I should prefer the latter." [This was written from memory. But the following Letter, which I have since found, confirms the fact.][12]

DEAR SIR,   *Staple-inn*, (1778.)
Your note yesterday surprized me much, as I never had the least idea that it would be expected that my name should be to Young; and I was the more astonished, as you speak of the matter as one of perfect indifference. I declare I have such a horror of seeing my name as Author or Editor, that if I had the option of standing in the pillory, or in standing formally before the publick in either of those lights, I should find it difficult to determine which to choose. It is what I never did in my life, and what I neither can or will, let the consequence turn out as it may. As the agreement with the Bookseller was as to him under that idea, I think he ought not to be bound by it. I will readily refund the money, the first I ever received for any literary undertaking, at Christmas, and expect it will never be taken any notice of. The Work which I have taken the most pains about, I mean Dodsley's Plays, where I might expect some credit on the score of my industry, will not have my name to them; nor shall any thing else, if I ever undertake any thing more (which I think doubtful); for I heartily detest all the squabbles and paltry tricks which are used by authors against one another, and which no one who gives his name to the publick has a right to suppose himself insignificant enough to be exempt from. Writing is very painful to me, and I do not know that I am perfectly intelligible.

I thank you very heartily for Dryden;§ it came very seasonably to fill up the taedium of a solitary evening. There are two or three errors in points of fact, which must be rectified. My illness is more stubborn than can be imagined.

ISAAC REED.

The two following Letters are of a somewhat similar nature:

DEAR SIR,   *Staple-inn, Thursday*, (1781.)
I have made some alteration in the note you desired me to look at, and wish my recollection would enable me to be more positive about the fact.

Chapman, *Letters of Johnson*, II, 360, objected to the *Works* of the English poets (for which he wrote the *Lives* as prefaces) being called *his*. Johnson referred to the *Works* as "*your* Edition, which is very impudently called mine. . . ." By *your* he meant the London booksellers.

§ See the "Select Collection of Miscellany Poems, 1780-1782," I, 56, 181; II, 88, 90. NICHOLS. (The references are to poems by John Dryden and his son Charles.)

11. See headnote and n. 2.

12. The parenthetical sentences and the letters to Nichols which follow appear as notes in *Lit. Anec.*

I am certain you are safe in ascribing the poem to Croxall.|| The permission you offered me of drawing upon you for the money I wanted I yesterday accepted. Should Mr. ——— refuse to repay you, pray let me know; I will then write into the country to get some money raised upon some property I have at Chesterfield, that you may be put to no inconvenience. It is, I confess, what I would willingly avoid; but as it will be the least of two evils, I shall not hesitate about it. The illiberality of Mr. ———'s behaviour to me, I believe and hope, is without a parallel in the present times. Curll himself, whatever liberties he took with the miserable wretches who were dependant upon him, never assumed the right of affronting a person who had either character or respectability in the world: and I protest, upon a review of my life, I know of no circumstance in it by which I have forfeited my claim to be treated with decency. I may, I am sure, appeal to you, whether the note I sent warranted an answer written by a servant, and not transmitted immediately to me, containing at the same time nothing from which I could collect a decisive reply to the request which I had made, though from the nature of it a positive answer might be expected. The rudeness and incivility of this conduct will, however, be attended with some good to me. What neither the hints of some, nor the remonstrances of other of my friends, could effect, this transaction will bring about. I will renounce the beggarly employment by which I have been too long disgracing myself, and return to my own profession, which I am ashamed to have so much neglected. I confess, I am the more mortified at this business, as I cannot but reflect on the very different treatment I met with from Mr. Dodsley on a similar occasion. At a time when from illness I could not proceed on his work, and when, from appearances, it seemed probable that I never might be able to finish it, he without scruple, or any pitiful hesitation, advanced me the loan I asked of him; and I do not believe has ever repented that he behaved to me like a gentleman. What I requested as a favour, I now will expect as a stipulation. I therefore will not look at the work again till you have satisfaction for the draft I have drawn. I am neither poor enough, nor sufficiently abject for such a humiliating situation as Mr. ——— seems to wish me in; and therefore he may take the alternative. There were other names mentioned for the honourable task besides mine. Let him employ any of them. From the review I have taken of it, I see, I can get as much money in the time I must employ about it, even though I hire myself out to write for a stationer; and if I do I cannot be more disgraced than I have been. I ought to apologize for plaguing you with this scrawl; but I want to forget the subject of it.

I.R.

DEAR SIR *Staple-inn, Monday,* (1787.)

I this morning in the City met Mr. Kearsley,[13] when, to my utter astonishment, he told me he had been informed that I was the writer of the unfavourable criticisms on his publication in the Gentleman's Magazine. How such a report can have originated I cannot conjecture. The falsehood of it you know; and I trust will do me the justice to refute it.‡

After every recollection on the subject, I cannot recall to my mind that I ever wrote a Review of any kind, except [Sir William] Jones's Isaeus, about ten years ago, in the Gentleman's Magazine (see vol. XLIX. p. 257.) If you

---

|| Ibid. vol. VII. p. 345. NICHOLS.
‡ Mr. Kearsley was assured by me, that this was fact. NICHOLS.
13. For another reference to George Kearsley see the life of George Steevens.

remember any, pray let me know; and if it is not too much trouble I will thank you to tell Kearsley every circumstance you know of my writing in the Magazine. I am sure there is not a syllable either there or any where else that I would not avow; and when I say that, I should be sorry there was any thing that could be injurious (as he tells me this has been) to a man of business, who has always been represented to me as one struggling hard for the support of a large family. If you will either write to him, or see him, I shall hold myself much obliged. Yours very truly,

ISAAC REED.

He was a valuable contributor to the Westminster Magazine from 1773-4 to about the year 1780. The biographical articles in that Miscellany are from his pen. He became also very early one of the proprietors of the European Magazine, and was a constant contributor to it for many years, particularly in the biographical and critical departments. He was also an occasional volunteer in the pages of Sylvanus Urban. So ample indeed was his collection of literary curiosities, so ready was he in turning to them, and so thoroughly able to communicate information, that no man of character ever applied to him in vain. Even the labours of Dr. Johnson were benefited by his accuracy; and, for the last 30 years, there has scarcely appeared any literary work in this country, of the least consequence, that required minute and extensive research, which had not the advantage of his liberal assistance, as the grateful prefaces of a variety of writers have abundantly testified. Among the earliest of these was the Edition of Dr. King's Works, 1776,[14] and the Supplement to Swift, in the same year.[15] In both these works Mr. Nichols was most materially indebted to the judicious remarks of Mr. Reed, whose friendly assistance also in many instances contributed to render his "Anecdotes of Mr. Bowyer," in 1782,[16] completer than they otherwise could possibly have been. He contributed also many useful Notes to the later Editions of Dr. Johnson's Lives of the Poets. To enumerate the thanks of the Authors whom he had assisted by his advice would be endless; but in a Preface which

---

14. *The Original Works, in Prose and Verse, of William King* was edited and published by Nichols in 3 volumes. A twenty-page memoir of King by Nichols was prefixed to this work; it furnished Johnson his material for his own life of King in the *Lives of the Poets*. See my essay "Some New Sources of Johnson's *Lives*," *PMLA*, 65:1101-1110 (December 1950).

15. Nichols edited three supplementary volumes of Swift's writings for the edition of the London booksellers. His first supplement, 1775, became Vol. 17 of the trade edition; his second supplement, 1776, became Vol. 24; and his third supplement, 1779, became Vol. 25. In the last supplement, Nichols supplied many excisions made deliberately by earlier editors of Swift's letters to Stella and he went a long way also toward supplying much of the little language. Nichols used the title *Journal to Stella* in the 1779 *Supplement*, the first time the letters had been so designated; thus Nichols must be considered the originator of the title. In 1801 Nichols brought out his own complete edition of Swift, reprinted in 1804 and again in 1808.

16. Nichols' *Biographical and Literary Anecdotes of William Bowyer*, 1782, is a quarto volume of 666 pages. It grew out of a slim pamphlet of 52 pages, 1778, and in its turn became the basis of the 17 volumes of *Anecdotes* and *Illustrations*.

I have seen, those thanks are so happily expressed that I feel a great pleasure in referring to it.*

With the late Dr. Farmer, the worthy master of Emanuel College, Cambridge, he was long and intimately acquainted, and regularly for many years spent an autumnal month with him at that pleasant seat of learning. At that period the Theatricals of Stirbitch Fair had powerful patronage in the Combination-room of Emanuel, where the routine of performance was regularly settled, and where the charms of the bottle were early deserted for the pleasures of the sock and buskin. In the boxes of this little theatre Dr. Farmer was the *Arbiter Elegantiarum,* and presided with as much dignity and unaffected ease as within the walls of his own College. [This I state from my own knowledge, having been present with him at the Stirbitch Theatre.][17]

[Editor's Note: In September 1782 Reed and Steevens were guests of Farmer at Cambridge. Both had come to see the Fair. Reed's diary indicates that he had never been to the Fair before,[18] nor had Steevens, according to the following note from Richard Gough to Nichols:

Enfield, Sept. 11, 1782.

I am just returned . . . from a most pleasant excursion. I spent two agreeable days in Cambridge with Messrs. Cole,[19] Steevens, and Farmer . . . . The second is in high spirits in the prospect of the *Nundinae Sturbrigienses,* which he never saw; and the third enjoys his friends. Mr. Reed should have been added to the party, but he seemed fatigued with the journey. . .

Yours faithfully,   R. GOUGH.[20]

The two days spent in Cambridge by Gough were 9 and 10 September. Reed mentions Gough in his diary for those two days. In his entry for the ninth, Reed wrote, "On my arrival at Emmanuel College, Dr. Farmer and Mr. Steevens were gone to Sir. John Cotton's. They arrived at 8 o'clock and

---

* By Mr. [William] Beloe. See Gent. Mag. vol. LXXVII. p. 18. NICHOLS. (Beloe, a contributor to *Lit. Anec.,* published in 6 vols. *Anecdotes of Literature and Scarce Books,* 1807-1812. Beloe was later dismissed as keeper of printed books at the Britism Museum after some manuscripts were stolen by someone to whom he had entrusted them. Feeling he had been unjustly treated, he poured his bitterness into his last work, *The Sexagenarian,* 1817.)

17. This sentence appears as a note in *Lit. Anec.*
18. See Claude E. Jones, *Isaac Reed Diaries, 1762-1804* (Berkeley and Los Angeles, University of California Publications in English, vol. 10, 1946), for entries prior to 1782. This work lists in the index some references belonging to John Nichols under the entry "Nichols, Nathaniel."
19. See n. 3 to the life of Farmer.
20. *Lit. Anec.,* I, 667n.

I spent the Evening with them, Mr. Gough, (and others). . . ." On the tenth, Reed "Breakfasted at Jude's with Mr. Steevens, Gough and Kirby."[21]

On 18 September Farmer and Reed had gone to the Fair, and Steevens, remaining at Emmanuel, wrote to Nichols:

> DEAR NICHOLS,   *Emmanuel College, Sept.* 18, 1782.
> . . . Stirbitch Fair has so thoroughly dissipated us all, that we have no taste for critical investigations. Reed is gone to dinner with the Vice-Can. &c. at the Fair; but will possibly add his scrawl to mine when he returns . . . as the bell rings for dinner, I cannot wait to express myself with studied civility; though with much sincerity,
> When I assure you I am entirely yours, &c.
> As Reed, it seems, will not be back till the post is gone out, he must take the consequences of his idleness, and provide a frank for himself if he has any thing to send . . . . The Master and Cole desire their compliments.
>   G. STEEVENS.[22]

On 28 September 1782 Nichols was at the Fair himself, according to the entry in Reed's diary for that day: "In the afternoon Mr. Nichols came from London and he, Dr. Farmer, Dr. Pennington and myself played at Cards until 10 o'clock, when we went home and supped in the Parlour."[23] On 1 October Nichols is again mentioned by Reed in his diary:

> Tuesday 1st Octr. Breakfasted at Jude's and then went to the Fair with Wilcox, Homer and Steevens. We were met by the Master and Mr. Nichols there and adjourned to a Booth to eat Pork. Dined at the College Hall and in the afternoon went with the Master and Mr. Nichols to the Theatre. Saw *As you like it* and *Tom Thumb.* Supped in the Parlour. This day has been a more than ordinary pleasant one.[24]

Two days later, on 3 October, Nichols and Reed left Cambridge for London, traveling together by coach.[25] Ten days after that Reed was back

---

21. Jones, *Reed Diaries*, pp. 117-118.
22. *Lit. Anec.*, VIII, 388-389. Steevens had been in Cambridge to see Farmer before, but he had not gone to the fair. Edmond Malone, in a letter dated 15 July 1780 to James, First Earl of Charlemont, said that he and Steevens had been at Cambridge "last summer." See *Hist. MSS. Comm.*, 12th Report, App. X, p. 373.
23. Jones, *Reed Diaries*, p. 121.
24. *Ibid.*, p. 122. This was printed earlier by Edward Dowden in the chapter "Some Old Shakespearians" in *Essays Modern and Elizabethan* (London, 1910), pp. 223-224.
25. Jones, *Reed Diaries*, p. 122 (entry for 3 October 1782).

at Staple Inn, Gough was at Enfield, Cole was at Milton, Steevens and Farmer were still at Cambridge, and Nichols was on a tour of Leicestershire. It is impossible that these people were ever all together again.

Steevens, remaining at the fair till it ended, wrote to Reed on 10 October. The letter, which follows, is from the Folger Shakespeare Library (ART Vol. a9).

Dear Sir. Emmanuel Octr 10th 1782

I am much obliged by your punctuality in delivering my letters. All the articles wanted, arrived in proper time.

On Tuesday Evening our players finished their campaign, and (to use Melisander's words with a slight alteration)

—I never heard
a sound so dismal as their parting thanks.

We have agreed, however, to dance away another fortnight, and make up, as well as we can, for the loss of the Theatre, which is almost taken down already. The last house was a very full one. From an enclosed document you will learn that I carried three & twenty out of this college. I have engaged a party to go to Bury Fair & attend the Benefit of M^r & Mrs Murray, who signalized themselves greatly after you left us.

I send you Playbills to complete your series, together with a book you left behind you.

If you have a quarter of an hour's leisure, I shall be glad to hear how Mrs Siddons was received, or, rather, what reception she really deserved. I cannot be expected to place any confidence in Newspaper accounts.

I shall thank you much if you will leave the enclosed packet at White's. A few days ago Mr Cole assured me he expected Nichols here. If he does not come, please to tell him that the Locke who lies buried in Trinity Chapel, was not the person whose portrait was painted by Hogarth. Cole intends to offer Nichols some other curious MSS. for publication; but it will be necessary that he should come here, if he can, for a day or two, that they may understand each other; for my old friend will by no means submit to the interpolations of Mr G.—— [Gough].

Your friends, the Master [Farmer], Messieurs Wilcox, Homer, &c, desire to be remembered to you. Let me trouble you to put the letter in the Parcel into the Penny Post, & believe me,

Your very faithful
& obed^t
GS.

Reed received the above letter from Steevens on the twelfth and wrote to Nichols the same day, primarily to inform Nichols about Cole's manuscripts:

DEAR SIR, *Staple-inn,* 12 *Oct.* 1782.

Understanding that a frank will be sent to you this night, I just inclose a few lines, to inform you that I received a letter from Mr. Steevens this morning, in which he says you were expected at Cambridge, and that Mr. Cole had some curious MSS. to offer you, which he wished to confer with you about in person.† If your arrangements are not finally made, perhaps you may contrive to return that way.‡ If you do not, suppose you write to Mr. Cole upon the subject. His health is so precarious that it will be hazardous to lose any time; and therefore I thought it worth while to send you the hint. I wish you all possible enjoyment of the country. I.R.[26]

Cole decided that he was too ill to publish the "curious MSS." mentioned in the letter, and he had Steevens carry a letter to Nichols telling him not to visit Milton.[27] Before any arrangements could be made for Nichols to receive these papers, Cole died (16 December 1782) and the manuscripts went to the British Museum.[28]]

He [Farmer] was regularly surrounded by a large party of congenial friends and able Criticks; among whom Mr. Reed and Mr. Steevens were constantly to be found. The last-mentioned gentleman, it may not here improperly be noticed, had so inviolable an attachment to Mr. Reed, that, notwithstanding a capriciousness of temper which often led him to differ from his dearest friends, and occasionally to lampoon them, there were three persons with whom through life he scarcely seemed to have a shade of difference of opinion; but those three were gentlemen with whom it was not possible for the most captious person to have differed—Dr. Farmer, Mr. [Thomas] Tyrwhitt, and Isaac Reed.

To follow Mr. Reed into the more retired scenes of private and domestic life: he was an early riser; and, whenever the avocations of business permitted leisure, applied, in general, several hours in the morning either in study or in the arrangement of his numerous scarce tracts. His collection of Books, which were chiefly English, was perhaps one of the most extensive

---

† On the subject of Browne Willis's Buckinghamshire MSS.—See [*Lit. Anec.,*] vol. VI. pp. 199-202. NICHOLS.
‡ I was then on an excursion in Leicestershire. NICHOLS.
26. *Lit. Anec.,* II. 671n.
27. See Horace Walpole's *Correspondence with the Rev. William Cole,* ed. W. S. Lewis and A. Dayle Wallace (New Haven, 1937), II, 338 (letter dated 7 November 1782).
28. *Lit. Anec.,* VI, 200-202.

in that kind that any private individual ever possessed; and he had a short time before his death made arrangements for disposing of a great part of it. The whole was afterwards sold by auction.[29]

He was naturally companionable; and frequently enjoyed the conversation of the table at the houses of a select circle of friends, to whom his great knowledge of men and books, and his firm but modest mode of communicating that knowledge, always rendered him highly acceptable.

Exercise was to him a great source both of health and pleasure. Frequently has the compiler of this article enjoyed a twelve miles walk to partake with him in the hospitalities of Mr. Gough at Enfield, and the luxury of examining with perfect ease the rarer parts of an uncommonly rich topographical library. But the most intimate of his friends was the friend of human kind at large, the mild, benevolent Daniel Braithwaite, esq. late comptroller of the Foreign Post-office, who has frequently beguiled him into an agreeable saunter of near 20 miles to his delightful retreat in the pleasant village of Amwell, where he was always as happy and as much at home as Dr. Johnson was at Mr. Thrale's at Streatham.

With Mr. [James] Bindley, senior Commissioner of the Stamp-office, whose skill and taste in collecting rare and valuable articles of Literature were so congenial to his own, Mr. Reed had many interchanges of reciprocal obligation. But his more immediate associates were, James Sayer, esq. of Great Ormond-street; Mr. [George] Romney and Mr. [William] Hayley, the eminent Painter and Poet; William Long, esq. the celebrated Surgeon; Edmund [sic] Malone, esq. the great rival Commentator on Shakspeare; J. P. Kemble, esq. not only an excellent Critick and Collector of dramatic curiosities, but himself (perhaps with the exception of his Sister [Sarah Siddons] only) the best living exemplar of Shakspeare's text; the Rev. H. J. Todd, the illustrator of Milton and Spenser, to whom he left a legacy for his trouble in superintending the sale of his library; Francis Newbery, esq. of Heathfield, co. Sussex; Richard Sharp, esq. M.P. for Castle Rising; and George Nicol, esq. the judicious perveyor of literary curiosities for the King. Some of these gentlemen were members of a select dining-club [the Unincreasable], of which he [Reed] had from its origin been the President.

On the bed of pain and anguish, another of his oldest friends (though unable to hold a pen) feels a soothing satisfaction in dictating this last tribute of respect to so exemplary a character. He died Jan. 5, 1807, at his chambers in Staple-inn, of which honourable Society he had long been one of the antients, worn out by natural debility, which for the last two or three years had rendered his hands unable to do their office, though his mind retained its original firmness. [His remains were interred at Amwell, agreeably to his own request, on Tuesday the 13th of January, attended by

---

29. In a note at this point Nichols quotes from Dibdin, *Bibliomania*, p. 690, concerning Reed's library and the auction.

Mr. Braithwaite, Thomas Green, esq. and George Nicol, esq.; and his relations, Mr. Aubrey Joseph Lum and Mr. Robert Lum.[30]]

Mr. Reed left considerable property to some relations, and small pecuniary remembrances to most of his friends.

[See a copy of Mr. Reed's will, with Twelve Codicils, in the Monthly Mirror, 1807, p. 130.—The first of these Codicils contains only, "I give to Mr. John Nichols, Printer, two guineas." The third, "I revoke the legacy given to John Nichols. I. R. See additional codicil, dated 7th August 1799. I. R." No codicil, however, of *such date* appears; nor am I conscious of ever having given him the slightest offence. I have, therefore, every reason to believe that he intended to have *augmented* the legacy.[31]]

[In *Illustr.*, VII, 66-68, is a letter from Henry Meen to Thomas Percy describing the illness and death of Reed. The letter, dated 20 January 1807, is reproduced in part below.]

In the mean time, I once more venture to trespass upon your Lordship's patience and time, by giving you the earliest information of the loss we have sustained, by the death of our excellent and justly-valued friend, Mr. Isaac Reed. His paralytic affections have for some years been gradually increasing. To persons thus afflicted all exertion is painful. It has long been an effort of no common sort to move from his room, in which he constantly sat, surrounded by his books, and occasionally relieved by the calls of his friends. Importuned by them, he sometimes, though but seldom, consented to dine out. He dined with Mr. Braithwaite on New-year's day. His appetite continued to the last, as did that of his friend Mr. Steevens; for their complaints were similar. On Sunday evening, Jan. 4th, I called, as usual, to drink tea with him; when, to my surprise and sorrow, I found him confined to his bed. On the morning of the following day it was the misfortune of his surrounding friends to see him dying and dead. The talents and virtues of this excellent man are too well known to your Lordship to need any recital from me. His books will be sold by auction, according to the directions given in his will; which was drawn up by himself with perspicuity and precision, and bore the evident marks of a benevolent mind.

30. This sentence appears as a note in *Lit. Anec.*
31. This paragraph appears as a note in *Lit. Anec.*

Richard Farmer

[At the time of Farmer's death, a short account of his life was printed in the *Gentleman's Magazine* in three installments: September, October, and December 1797. In 1799 William Seward included him in his *Biographiana;* but the largest part of Seward's material is a contribution from Isaac Reed and is more a laudatory sketch of Farmer's character than an attempt at biography. The first extended life was written by George Dyer, signed G.D., in *The Annual Necrology, for 1797-8; including also, various articles of neglected Biography* (1800). Dyer's work, although it contains several inaccuracies and a strong political bias, is important for a considerable amount of factual information. The second account of Farmer appeared in 1801 in the "supplement to the third edition of the *Encyclopaedia Britannica* . . . by George Gleig, LL.D. F.R.S. Edin." This life added a few details but is much indebted to Dyer.

Nichols' account of Farmer was published for the first time in his monumental *History of Leicester,* IV, pt. 2, 943-949, which appeared in 1811. The account was reproduced with only very minor changes the following year in *Lit. Anec.,* II, 618-649, from which the account that follows is primarily drawn. Although *Literary Anecdotes* is listed as a source of Farmer's life by both the DNB (in the life by Thompson Cooper) and the CBEL, neither mentions Nichols' earlier account in the *History of Leicester.*

A few other minor published sources exist. E. S. Schuckburgh filled in some of the background of Farmer's Cambridge in *Laurence Chaderton, D.D. (first Master of Emmanuel) translated from a Latin memoir of Dr. Dillingham with notes and Illustrations. Richard Farmer, D.D. (Master of Emmanuel, 1775-1797)*, Cambridge, 1884. Farmer is also mentioned in J. A. Venn, *Alumni Cantabrigienses* (Cambridge, 1944), II (pt. 2), 460. A pamphlet by Sydney C. Roberts, *Richard Farmer* (London, 1961), is a copy of the Arundell Esdaile Memorial Lecture delivered by Roberts before the Library Association in 1960.

By far the most impressive recent scholarship on Farmer is that of Mr. Cleanth Brooks in *The Correspondence of Thomas Percy and Richard Farmer,* which is Volume II of the Percy Letters series (Louisiana State University Press, 1946). It is to this collection that a scholar should turn first if he wishes to begin a further pursuit of Farmer; afterwards, if his interests carry him to manuscripts, he will do well to begin with the Folger Shakespeare Library, which has letters of Gray, Percy, and others to Farmer and letters of Farmer to Malone, Steevens, and others. The Folger also has an interleaved copy of Farmer's *Essay on the Learning of Shakespeare* (S.a. 138) and Farmer's notes on Shakespeare (S.b. 114-117). The Bodleian has more of Farmer's notes and a few letters, including one from Cole. The Osborn collection at Yale contains two Farmer items, one of which is a letter from Farmer to Malone dated 29 August 1787.]

This learned Critick and distinguished Scholar (who is justly celebrated in the "Encyclopaedia Britannica" as "a man of pleasing, though singular manners") was the descendant of a family long seated at Ratcliffe Culey,* a hamlet within the parish of Shepey, in the county of Leicester.[1] His grandfather (who died in 1727, aet. 63) is described on his tomb, in St. Mary's church at Leicester as "John Farmer, of Nuneaton, gent."[2] His father, who was largely engaged in Leicester in the profession of a maltster, married in 1732-3 Hannah Knibb, by whom he had five sons and four daughters. He died in 1778, at the age of 80. His widow survived him more than thirty[3] years, dying Dec. 14, 1808, at the advanced age of nearly 97. Their first-born son, John, died an infant.

Richard, the second son, was born, Aug. 28, 1735, in the antient Borough of Leicester; and received the early part of his education, under the Rev. Gerrard Andrewes (father of the present truly respectable Dean of Canterbury,) in the Free Grammar-school of his native Town; a seminary in which many eminent persons were his contemporaries.

About the year 1753, he left the school, with the character of being estimable for temper and talents; and was entered a pensioner at Emanuel College, Cambridge, when Dr. Richardson was master, and Mr. Bickham and Mr. Hubbard tutors.[4]

Mr. Farmer, when an under-graduate, applied himself chiefly to classical learning and the belles lettres; was known to be a man of reading, distin-

---

* See an ample Pedigree of Dr. Farmer's ancestors under *Ratcliffe Culey*, in the History of Leicestershire, vol. IV. p. 950. NICHOLS.

1. So closely has Nichols' wording been followed by later biographers that Thompson Cooper begins his life of Farmer in DNB by saying that he was "the descendant of a family long seated at Ratcliffe Culey, a hamlet in the parish of Sheepy, Leicestershire."

2. In addition to having previous biographies of Farmer at his disposal, Nichols had another resource not previously available. The Rev. William Cole left a manuscript collection to the British Museum with orders that it was to be kept locked up for twenty years after his death, which took place in 1782. The manuscripts, thus, must have become public by 1802. Nichols made extensive use of Cole's papers, and at this point in the text quotes Cole with reference to Farmer's coat of arms: "Dr. Farmer gives arms on his seal, Argent, a chevron Sable, between three Roman lamps, burning proper. Motto, *non extinguentur*. Dr. Farmer shewed Mr. Cole his arms and pedigree in Guillim." Cole had introduced himself to Nichols by letter in 1781 (*Lit. Anec.*, I, 661), and thereafter Cole made many contributions to Nichols' works in progress (ibid.). It appears that at one time Cole intended leaving his papers with the library of Emmanuel College until he detected in Farmer what he interpreted to be an indifference to the proposal (ibid., VIII, 387). Nichols probably knew of the existence of the manuscripts before they became public; when they were finally opened to inspection he ransacked them thoroughly for information regarding Farmer and others, finding enough material to fill over five columns of index references in *Literary Anecdotes*. New interest in Cole has been created by the editing of two volumes of his diaries by Francis Griffin Stokes: *A Journal of my Journey to Paris* and *The Blecheley Diary* (both in London, 1931).

3. Originally *twenty*, corrected to *thirty* in *Lit. Anec.*, VIII, 421.

4. According to Venn's *Alumni Cantabrigienses*, Farmer was admitted at Emmanuel on 12 April 1753. (See headnote.) William Richardson, who had never been a Fellow of Emmanuel, was chosen Master in 1736. He was one of the innumerable contributors to the works of Nichols (*Lit. Anec.*, III, 300, n.), and Nichols wrote a short sketch of his life (ibid., V, 157-159). The two tutors were James Bickham and Henry Hubbard.

guished rather for sprightly parts than profound speculations; and much esteemed in the circle of his friends.

He took his degree of B.A. in 1757; ranked as a Senior Optime; and was of the same year with Dr. Waring and Dr. Jebb. The degree, though not of the first class, procured him notice in College; and he successfully contested the silver cup given at Emanuel to the best graduate of that year with Mr. Wanley Sawbridge, brother to the Alderman. This cup is preserved with great care in Dr. Farmer's family.

His Cambridge Verses were, a Poem on laying the first Stone of the Public Library, 1755; and a Sonnet on the late King's death, 1760.

In 1760 he proceeded M.A.; and succeeded as classical tutor to Mr. Bickham, who went off to the valuable rectory of Loughborough in Leicestershire, in the gift of Emanuel College. In discharge of the part of his office more immediately classical, Mr. Farmer was entitled to considerable respect. He was a good scholar; but Theology and Mathematics were not his favourite studies. He did not give lectures in Euclid many years; but in Grotius and the Greek Testament he continued to lecture till he resigned the tuition. By his pupils, as formerly by his fellow students, he was generally esteemed; though an occasional want of punctuality sometimes exposed him to censure from their parents.

For many years, while tutor, he served the curacy of Swavesey, a village about eight miles from Cambridge, not far from the road to Huntingdon, which had been formerly served by the celebrated Dr. [John] Jortin. In this situation he gained the respect of his congregation, rather by his affability and social manners, than by the solemnity of his carriage, or the rigour of his doctrines. At this time also he formed an intimacy with Sir Thomas Hatton, bart. a good-humoured country gentleman of Long-Stanton in Cambridgeshire.

He was elected a Fellow of the Society of Antiquaries, May 19, 1763.

In 1765 he was junior proctor of the University of Cambridge.

On the 15th of May 1766, he published, from the University Press "Proposals for printing, by Subscription, The History and Antiquities of the Town of Leicester; originally collected by *William* Staveley, Esq. [a mistake —for *Thomas* Staveley—who is called *William* in the *Imprimatur* which Mr. Farmer obtained for it in 1767] Barrister at Law, and formerly of Peterhouse in that University. Now first offered to the Publick from the Author's Manuscript; with very large Additions and Improvements; and an Appendix of Papers relative to the Subject. By Richard Farmer, M.A. Fellow of Emanuel College in Cambridge, and of the Society of Antiquaries, London."

That he set about this Work with the full intention of pursuing it with diligence, is evident from the tenor of many of the Letters which he addressed at that period to his Antiquarian Friends.† But, in a very few months,

---

† Several of these may be seen in an Advertisement prefixed to the Third Volume of the History of Leicestershire, p. vi—viii. NICHOLS.

he began to perceive that the task he had undertaken was much more laborious than he had at first imagined; and in his "Essay on the Learning of Shakspeare, 1766," addressed to his worthy Friend and Schoolfellow Joseph Cradock, Esq. of Gumley (a Work by which, as Dr. Warton very justly and emphatically expresses it, "an end is put for ever to the dispute concerning the Learning of Shakspeare, by the masterly and convincing and unanswerable Essay‡ of Dr. Farmer on this subject") he laments that *"he had been persuaded into that employment.* Though I have as much," he says, "of the *Natale Solum* about me as any man whatsoever, yet, I own, the *Primrose Path* is still more pleasing than the *Fosse* of the *Watling-street:*

> Age cannot wither it, nor custom stale
> Its infinite variety.—

And when I am fairly rid of the dust of Topographical Antiquity, which hath continued much longer about me than I expected, you may very probably be troubled again with the ever-fruitful subject of Shakspeare and his Commentators."

To an Advertisement of his "Essay," which appeared Jan. 22, 1767, is added, "Mr. Farmer takes this opportunity of informing the Subscribers to the History and Antiquities of the Town of Leicester, that many of the Plates are already finished; and that the whole Work is prosecuted with all Expedition consistent with the Nature of the undertaking. But the important Communications he has been favoured with, which greatly enlarge his Book, must necessarily defer its Publication somewhat longer than he expected. Subscriptions will be received till Lady-day next, at Half a Guinea the small, and 15s. the large Paper." And in a letter to a venerable Antiquary, on the 16th of April following, he says, "I am much obliged by your attention to my attempt on Antiquities; which is a sacrifice of time to my native Town, with little or no view to profit or reputation."—Certainly not to profit; for the price of the quarto volume was to have been only half a guinea!

In 1767, he took the degree of B.D.; and in 1769, July 8, was appointed by Dr. Terrick, then Bishop of London, one of the Preachers at the Chapel Royal at Whitehall; an engagement that required him to be in London a certain number of months in the year, a situation favourable to one now becoming a collector of books. His place of residence was usually the house of Dr. Anthony Askew, the very eminent physician, in Queen-square, Bloomsbury; who died in 1774.

‡ A second edition of this valuable performance was called for in 1767, in which are only a few corrections of style, but no additional information. A third was printed in 1789, without any additions except a note at the end, accounting for his finally abandoning his intended publication of the Antiquities of Leicester. The Essay is also given at large in Mr. Steevens's edition of Shakespeare, printed in fifteen volumes, 1793; and in Mr. Reed's edition, twenty-one volumes, 1803. NICHOLS. (The main thesis of Farmer's *Essay* is that Shakespeare's knowledge of the classics was obtained through English translations.)

Feb. 13, 1770, Mr. Farmer appears the profound Antiquary, in thus addressing Mr. Thomas Warton;

DEAR SIR,
I should have been particularly happy to have seen you at Askew's, as perhaps he has more matters worth your notice, than he himself in the multitude of his business might have time to exhibit; but I am sure he would at least be willing, for I know not a more communicative man in the world. I wish I could give you a satisfactory account of Leland . . . . Have you no job in the *History of Poetry* for your very obliged and affectionate servant,

R. FARMER?[5]

On the subject of the "History of Leicester," he thus addressed Mr. H. Baldwin, Nov. 12, 1772:

SIR:
A Correspondent of yours, in the Chronicle of Saturday, informs you that he is a Subscriber to some Book, which he has long wished to receive; and complains, with seeming justice, of the delay of publication. He must, however, be candid enough to own, that there may be causes which do not originate in the Author, and those unforseen ones; such at least, he will soon find, in the preface to the *History of Leicester,* has been the case with that Work. The matter is too long for a Newspaper disquisition; but it will appear, that Mr. Farmer has been the person most deceived in his reasonable expectations; and that not his Time only, but his Money, has been sacrificed to the Honour of his Town, and the Interest of his Subscribers. When the delay proved inevitable, it was repeatedly advertized in the Country Journals, that the Subscription-money would be returned by the Booksellers to all those who should please to accept it; and the same notice was given to Mr. Beecroft, in London, from whom almost all the Town Receipts were taken. This is again offered; and Mr. Farmer flatters himself that no room is left for complaint.

Some time ago Mr. Farmer, on the authority of some persons whom he supposed to be better acquainted than himself with the business of Plates and Printing, was induced to tell his friends in the country, that the Work would be finished in the course of the Winter. He is very sorry to find himself unavoidably deceived, and must necessarily beg a little further indulgence; he hopes only *to* the Summer; certainly not *beyond* it.

The further prosecution of his "History of Leicester," a task which he had in many respects found unpleasant, he soon after thought it prudent to abandon; a circumstance thus noticed by himself:

This Work was just begun at the press, when the Writer was called to the

---

5. For a full treatment of Farmer's relations with another historian of antiquities see *The Correspondence of Thomas Percy and Richard Farmer,* ed. Cleanth Brooks (Baton Rouge, Louisiana, 1946). In the introduction, p. vii, Brooks agrees with Nichols that Farmer's correspondence proves that he was not the indolent man some have taken him to be and that his giving up the *History of Leicester* was due to the fact "that Farmer's college and university duties gradually came to absorb more and more of his time."

superintendance of a large College, and was obliged to decline the undertaking. The Plates, however, and some of the Materials, have been long ago put into the hands of a Gentleman who is every way qualified to make a proper use of them.§

The handsome present was thus acknowledged:

The Collections of Thomas Staveley, esq. and the Rev. Samuel Carte, with several original MSS. and some engraved Plates, were the gift of a learned Dignitary of the Church, from whom the Publick long expected a History of his native Town of Leicester; and the handsome manner in which this has been publicly noticed, is an inducement for wishing to deserve the compliment which Dr. Farmer has bestowed.||

[At the distance of more than twenty years, Dr. Farmer was publicly called upon, in a manner which the following letter (written wholly unknown to him, and whilst he was labouring under a severe indisposition) will fully explain:

MR. URBAN,   July 3, 1797.
In a periodical publication of December last, it is asked, whether Dr. Farmer received subscriptions for the Antiquities of Leicester, and whether the book has been published. Without entering into the motives for such a question, I will answer, that Dr. Farmer did receive such subscriptions, and that the book is not yet published. But let me add, that the very respectable Dignitary here called in question, more than twenty years ago, advertized in the St. James's Chronicle that he had declined the undertaking, and that the subscription-money was ready to be returned. Should any one doubt this assertion, I am ready to give the best proof of it, by repeating the same offer in the Doctor's name. You may, therefore, Sir, assure your Readers, that, if by chance there should be still any one or more subscriptions outstanding, the money will, on demand, be returned by
                                                                              J. NICHOLS.

I did not expect that many would apply for the return of such small sums as *five shillings* and *seven shillings and six pence*. I paid, however, those sums to *five Subscribers;* and two of them came from the Executors of my rich Friend Mr. James Dodsley!—my generosity, however, (though two of the receipts were for *large paper*) cost me only thirty shillings![6]]

§ Essay on the Learning of Shakespeare, ed. 1789, p. 95. NICHOLS. (It was, of course, Nichols to whom Farmer gave all his Leicester materials, and these helped to make Nichols' *History of Leicester* "the best history of this county," as it is called by Charles Gross in *A Bibliography of British Municipal History* [New York, 1897], p. 99, item 624. "Nichols was a most careful and accurate compiler, and in genealogy and heraldry there are few county historians to compare to him.... His work will always stand high among the best of the English county histories," said William Page, editor of *The Victoria History of the Counties of England: A History of Leicestershire* [London, 1907], I, xvii.)
|| Preface to the History of Leicestershire; and Gent. Mag. vol. IXV, p. 185. NICHOLS.
6. This paragraph, the letter preceding it, and the sentence introducing the letter appear as a note to the text in *Lit. Anec.* Nichols may well have exclaimed over such a

In 1775, on the death of Dr. Richardson, he [Farmer] was chosen Master of Emanuel College; Mr. Hubbard, the senior Fellow, declining it on account of age and infirmities.

On the death of Dr. Richardson, the College assembled March 21, 1775, when they unanimously elected Mr. Henry Hubbard to succeed him, who was so long an ornament in that respectable Society; but who, having, with his wonted moderation and disinteredness, declined that honour, gave his full suffrage to his friend Mr. Farmer.[7]

He now took the degree of D.D.; and was very soon succeeded in the tutorship by Dr. William Bennet, an elegant and profound scholar, who was afterwards most deservedly honoured with a mitre, and is now Bishop of Cloyne.

In 1775-6 Dr. Farmer served, in his turn, the office of Vice-chancellor of the University; and in that elevated office acquired a considerable degree of reputation, and was afterwards frequently the *Pro-vicecancellarius*.

The disturbances in America having by this time become serious, the University of Cambridge, with numberless other loyal Bodies, voted an Address to the King, approving of the measures adopted by Government to reduce the factious Colonists to their duty; the Address, however, was not carried unanimously. It was, of course, opposed by the Rev. John Jebb, so well known for his free opinions in politics and religion, and by some others; of whom one man, a member of the *Caput,* carried his opposition so far, as actually to refuse the key of the place which contained the seal necessary on such occasions. In this emergency, Dr. Farmer, who was then Vice-chancellor, is said to have forced open the door with a sledge-hammer; an exploit which his democratical biographers affect to ridicule, by calling it *his* courtly zeal, and the occasion of all his subsequent preferments.‡ If it be indeed true that he broke the door in pieces with his own hands, his conduct must be acknowledged to have been not very decorous; but, if the office which he filled be taken into consideration, we apprehend it would be as difficult to prove that conduct essentially wrong, as to vindicate the obstinate arrogance of him who occasioned it. The seal was the property of the University, of which this outrageous supporter of the Bill of Rights was but an individual member. The University had resolved that it should be employed

---

minor loss as thirty shillings since he lost at least £5,000 on publishing the *History of Leicester.* Even though he suffered a loss by fire of his printing presses and warehouses, he wrote to Thomas Percy that he was in honor bound to complete the *Leicester.* See *Illustr.,* VI, 589-590.

7. This interpolated paragraph, a footnote in *Lit. Anec.,* II, 629, is quoted by Nichols from the Cole manuscripts.

‡ The Author of Dr. Farmer's Life in the "Annual Necrology," [George Dyer] evidently impressed with great personal esteem for his *quondam* Tutor, but differing *toto coelo* from him in political opinions, observes, "that the two parties of Whig and Tory, at Cambridge, had for some time carried their contentions rather high; till, on the 17th of March 1769, an Address was presented to the King by the Tories, containing nothing short of a reprobation of the principles and conduct of the popular party.—A few years after happened the American War. An Address was again presented by the Tories, justifying the cruel measures then pursued, and the men who adopted them." *Annual Necrology.* NICHOLS.

for a certain purpose, which it was the duty of the Vice-chancellor to carry into effect; and, since the seal was refused to him, he had no alternative but to get possession of it by force. We hope, however, that he employed a servant to break the door; and, indeed, as Vice-chancellor, he must have had so many servants at his command, that it is not conceivable he would wield the sledge-hammer himself.*

On the death of Dr. Barnadiston, Master of Bene't College, he was (June 27, 1778,) unanimously elected *Proto-Bibliothecarius,* or Principal Librarian, of the University;† to which (as well as to the Headship of his College) he was well entitled from his literary character.

In a very few days after he was admitted to the office, he thus addressed his friend Mr. [Richard] Gough:

DEAR SIR, *Emanuel, July 27, 1778.*
You have repeatedly called me a very *idle and ungrateful fellow;* but I think you will pardon me when you hear my situation. When I received your Letter, I was confined by the rheumatism; and, as soon as possible, carried into the country to get rid of it. The death of your Master‡ brought me back, when I was very little able to canvass for his place; and had, besides, a Sermon to make for our Infirmary business; at which instant, I had an account of the death of my Father: the consequences of which have totally engaged me till last night. When I returned, I found myself obliged to go into Suffolk this morning; whence I mean to return about the middle of the week; and if I live, and any thing appears worth transcription, you shall hear by the end of it from
Yours very affectionately,

R. FARMER.
I must go the Libraries, as I have little or nothing of my own.

Dr. Farmer, when a young man, wrote some very excellent "Directions for studying the English History;" which, with his permission, were printed in the European Magazine for 1791; and are also copied in Mr. Seward's "Biographiana."[8]

In April 1780 Dr. Farmer was collated by Bp. Hurd, then Bishop of Lichfield and Coventry, to the Prebend of Aldrewas, and the Chancellorship annexed, founded in the Cathedral Church of Lichfield, vacant by the death of Dr. Greene, Dean of Salisbury.

About this period, he lent Mr. Cole[9] "The Negotiations of Cardinal Thomas Woolsey," in MS. which Mr. Cole transcribed (vol. LIX. of his MSS.) It was a MS. of about 400 leaves, apparently written about the reign

---

* Encyclopaedia Britannica. NICHOLS. (This quotation is from the account of Farmer written by George Gleig.)
† *Cole MSS.* NICHOLS.
‡ Mr. [Richard] Gough had been educated, at Bene't College, under Dr. [John] Barnadiston. NICHOLS.
8. See the headnote to this life.
9. See n. 3.

of Charles the First. Mr. Gray[10] (to whom the MS. was lent about 1770) returned it with this note, written on a blank leaf of the book itself:

Mr. Gray returns Mr. Farmer's Books, with many thanks. The MS Letters would be of some value, if the Transcriber had better understood what he was about; but there are so many words mistaken, so many omitted, that the sense can often only be made out by conjecture. Does not recollect, that they have been printed in any of the Collections; but thinks, he has seen several of them (the originals) in the Harleian Library. Lord Herbert plainly had seen them, and (as far as they go) has made them the foundation of his History. They serve to shew, as he says, that the Cardinal, in his Dispatches, was more copious than eloquent. The Instructions to Tunstall and Wingfield, after the Battle of Pavia, and the King's Directions after he had signed the Peace with France, are most remarkable.
Pemb. Hall, 12 *April.*§

It was about 1770, that Mr. Farmer and Mr. Gray became acquainted.

Before, they had been shy of each other, and, though Dr. Farmer was then esteemed one of the most ingenious of men in the University, yet Mr. Gray's singular niceness in the choice of his acquaintance, made him appear fastidious to a great degree to all who were not acquainted with his manner. Indeed, there did not seem to be any probability of any great intimacy, from the style and manner of each of them; the one a cheerful, companionable, hearty, open, downright man, of no great regard to dress, or common forms of behaviour; the other of a most fastidious and recluse distance of carriage, rather averse to all sociability, but of the graver turn, nice and elegant in his person, dress, and behaviour, even to a degree of finicalness and effeminacy: so that nothing but their extensive learning and abilities could ever have coalesced two such different men; and both of great value in their own line and walk. They were ever after great friends; and Dr. Farmer and all his acquaintance had soon after too much reason to lament his loss, and the shortness of their acquaintance.||

Some time after this, he was made Prebendary of Canterbury; we believe, through the recommendation of Lord North, then Premier: and it was at Canterbury that the Writer of this sketch [George Gleig] had the happiness of being introduced to him, and witnessing his hospitality.‡

He was appointed Prebendary, on the death of Dr. William Tatton, in February 1782; and was installed in March. When he returned thanks* at Court for this last preferment, the King very politely asked him, "Whether

---

§ This article was purchased at Dr. Farmer's sale by Mr. [James] Bindley, in whose possession it now remains. NICHOLS.
|| Cole, MSS. vol LIX, pp, 57, 58. NICHOLS.
‡ Encyclopaedia Britannica. NICHOLS. (This paragraph is quoted by Nichols.)
* "Feb. 12, 1782, he came to London, to kiss hands for the prebend of Canterbury, vacant by the death of Dr. Tatton." *W. Cole, MS.* NICHOLS.
10. Thomas Gray the poet.

the University was flourishing, and what Noblemen were resident; and told him, that he could wish every one of that rank had as good principles instilled into them as the Earl of Westmoreland." Dr. Farmer had before told Mr. Cole, that Charles Fox, the vehement haranguer in Parliament against the Court, had publicly reflected on him, as breeding up the Earl, his pupil, in Emanuel and Tory principles: the mention, therefore, of this Earl to Dr. Farmer was as polite as *àpropos*. The Queen, who came to him, in her broken English, accosted him thus—"Doctour! in what part of the Kingdom do you reside?"—"Always at Cambridge, Madam,"—"Oh, College!" replied her Majesty, and gave him joy of his preferment.†

After enjoying his Prebend for several years, he resigned it on being preferred by the late Mr. Pitt, then Premier, to a Residentiaryship of St. Paul's;‡ and we have reason to believe that he declined a Bishoprick, which was offered to him as a reward for the constitutional principles which he was at pains to propagate, not only in college, but, as far as his influence went, through the whole University.§

Dr. Farmer had not yet arrived at the zenith of his prosperity; and, indeed, declined being raised to that dignity, to which the Minister was inclined to advance him. The offer of a Bishoprick was twice made him by Mr. Pitt. The promise, at least influence, made personally, as well as by letter, may be, as it always is, considered as the sure forerunner of advancement. But the truth is, the solemnity and formality of the Episcopal character would have sat but awkwardly on Farmer. He chose to move without restraint; and to enjoy himself without responsibility. To use his own language to a friend, "One that enjoyed the Theatre, and the Queen's Head in the evening, would have made but an indifferent Bishop." A piece of preferment, however, was soon conferred on him by Mr. Pitt, no less agreeable to his taste, in point of situation, than valuable in point of income, a Residentiaryship of St. Paul's. This was given him in exchange for the Prebend of Canterbury. It was agreeable to his taste, as requiring three months residence in the capital, and only three in the year; enabling him to enjoy in succession his literary clubs in London, and his literary retreat at Cambridge. It was valuable, for its clear income is twelve or fourteen hundred a year, besides perquisites, which, though not easily ascertained, are considerable. The ingenious, good-humoured Doctor now expressed himself in terms of perfect satisfaction. He looked for nothing higher. He enjoyed a plentiful income himself, and possessing with it a considerable share of patronage, had the means (an important consideration to a kind-hearted man) of rendering essential services to his friends. Independently, therefore, of the political principles originally imbibed by Dr. Farmer, it was natural enough for him to express,

† *Cole's MSS*. NICHOLS.

‡ In an hour or two after he had received the official information of this appointment, I met him near Amen Corner; and he pleasantly observed to me, "I could now, if I thought proper, cheat the Minister; for I have in my pocket an appointment to the Residentiaryship of St. Paul's, without having resigned the Prebend of Canterbury." NICHOLS.

§ Encyclopaedia Britannica. NICHOLS. (This paragraph is quoted by Nichols.)

and, in his conduct through life, to exhibit, a warm attachment to Mr. Pitt, and to support with great cordiality the measures of his administration.[11]

On the vacancy of the small vicarage of St. Nicholas at Leicester, then worth only 45*l.* a year, the Rev. William Bickerstaffe, an old schoolfellow with Dr. Farmer, applied for it by petition to Lord Chancellor Thurlow; and, at the same time, in the hope of forwarding his suit, wrote also to Dr. Farmer . . . .
It has been said, that the delights of the pipe and the bottle, in Emanuel parlour, outweighed, in his estimation, the dazzling splendour of the mitre: but he had other and better reasons for preferring a private to a public station. In early life, at least before he was advanced in years, he had felt the power of love, and had suffered such a disappointment as sunk deep in his mind, and for a time threatened his understanding.[12]

[[Nichols' note:] This attachment, formed whilst curate of Swavesey, when his situation in life was inadequate to the union, continued for many years unimpaired: and, when his fame and fortune rendered his situation in life at least adequate to the rank of the object of his affections, he began to think seriously of Matrimony; but, on mature reflexion, found that his habits of life were then too deeply rooted to be changed into those of domestic arrangements with any probable chance of perfect happiness to either party.—Mr. Cole, however, says, "Dr. Colman told me, May 3, 1782, that he had it from sufficient authority, that Sir Thomas Hatton had refused his eldest daughter to Dr. Farmer, but on what foundation he knew not. The lady is 27 or 28, and Dr. Farmer about 47 or 48. It will probably be a great mortification to both, as to every one it seemed that their regard for each other was reciprocal. Dr. Farmer's preferment is equal to 800*l. per annum;* and I guess the lady's fortune, there being six daughters and two sons, not very great."]

From that period, though he retained his faculties entire, he acquired some peculiarities of manner; of which he was so far conscious, as to be sensible that they would hardly become the character of a Bishop: being likewise strongly attached to dramatic entertainments (which, if we mistake not, the English Bishops never witness), and delighting in clubs, where he could have rational conversation without state or ceremony of any kind—he very wisely preferred his Residentiaryship to the highest dignity in the Church.
His voice was strong and his manner of speaking rapid and quick. So, that

---

11. This quotation from Dyer's memoir of Farmer in the *Annual Necrology* is given as a note by Nichols in *Lit. Anec.*
12. This paragraph, including the part following the interpolated note of Nichols, is quoted in the text of Farmer's life and attributed to Gleig's account in the *Encyclopaedia Britannica.*

one day a lady hearing him preach at St. Mary's and end his Sermon abruptly, turned to an officer of dragoons who was with her, and said that Dr. Farmer knew how to stop short in a full gallop as well as any of the men in his company.||

The latter years of Dr. Farmer's life were pretty equally divided between Emanuel College and the Residentiary house in Amen-Corner.

His residence in London was favourable, as already hinted, to his love of literary society; and for many years he was a member of different clubs, composed of men of letters, by whom he was much esteemed.

Of this class was the Eumélean club, at Blenheim tavern, Bond-street, of which Dr. [John] Ash was President; and of which Sir Joshua Reynolds, Mr. Boswell, Mr. [William] Windham, . . . Mr. [William] Seward, Doctor Charles Burney, &c. &c. were members.

He was also a member of the Unincreasable Club, Queen's head, Holborn, of which Mr. Isaac Reed was the President; Mr. George Romney the Painter, . . . &c. &c. were members.#

Dr. Farmer was elected a member of the Literary Club (founded by Dr. Johnson and sir Joshua Reynolds) Feb. 3, 1795.

He died, after a long and painful illness, at the Lodge of Emanuel College, September 8, 1797; and was buried in the Chapel.

[Just a year before his death, Farmer wrote a letter to Steevens from Bath. The letter, reproduced below, is preserved in the Folger Shakespeare Library (C.b.10):

Dear *Sir*   *Bath.* Sep^t 11. 1796. (Sunday)
I intend to leave this Place for Leicester before the End of this Week —I believe, it has been of *some service* to me, & I must *pay* for it. Perhaps you know some one here, who may facilitate a Draft upon you. I hope to be at *Cambridge* on the 24th & shall be glad if you can come to see us at *Michaelmas*. If any thing be settled about *leases* &c, you will inform me; and you may let me have the half year's Account as early as may be. My Brother & Nephew are here.
                    Comp^{ts} to all Friends, yours sincerely
                                                            R. Farmer.

|| Cole's MSS. Nichols. (This paragraph is quoted by Nichols.)
Annual Necrology; where the Club in Essex-street, founded by Dr. Johnson and his friends, is also mentioned. But of that Club Dr. Farmer was not a member, though in the later period of it he once or twice was a visitor. See Gent. Mag. vol. LV. pp. 8. 99. Nichols. (Nichols was in a position to know this, since he himself was a member of the Essex Head Club. This and the preceding two paragraphs are quoted from the *Annual Necrology*.)

Farmer's belief that Bath had been of "some service" to him appears to have been groundless, for only a little over a month later Steevens added a P.S. to a letter to Thomas Percy (*Illustr.*, VII, 5-6):

> On the 24th of last month, when our excellent friend Dr. Farmer returned from Bath to college, he was the mere shadow of what he had been. He assured me, he had neither the benefit of appetite, sleep, or spirits. In the course of the next three weeks, however, he eat as much as he ought, slept with few interruptions, and enlivened his companions as much as ever. But in these circumstances, I must confess, I have little confidence. He still wants flesh and the genuine colour of health. His disorder, I am afraid, is referable to the state of his liver. I should add, that this supposition is merely my own, and has not been authorised by our London or Cambridge physicians. I sincerely wish I could, consistently with truth, have transmitted you more welcome intelligence.

As time went on, reports of the ill health of Farmer continued to circulate among his friends. On 23 January 1797, Henry Meen wrote as follows to Thomas Percy (*Illustr.*, VII, 42-43):

> The state of Dr. Farmer's health will not permit him to return to town in February, which is his month of residence; I therefore took the first opportunity that offered to pay my respects to him in college, and spend a few days with my college-friends. It will, I am certain, be satisfactory to your Lordship, to know how Dr. Farmer does. I wish it were in my power to give you, my Lord, a more favourable account of our worthy friend's health. But he is very far from well. There is a visible change in his person and appearance. He looks enfeebled and emaciated. Occasionally his spirits revive, and he recovers for a time his usual cheerfulness. He complains much of the cramp, which frequently disturbs his rest; and he is apprehensive that it will finally seize some vital part, and prove fatal. No arguments will prevail upon him to alter his habits. He takes but little exercise, and sees but little company, except that of his own society, with whom he spends his most comfortable hours. But I am happy to hear him say that he intends to be with us in June. I sincerely wish that he would exert himself a little; and not sink under his infirmities with a langour bordering upon a despondency. Much, it is thought, might yet be done by a change of air, diet, and exercise: and nothing surely should be omitted, that can prolong a life valuable as *his*.

Meen again reported to Percy on the state of health of Farmer in a letter dated 30 August 1797, nine days before his death (*Illustr.*, VII, 46).

I wish I could give your Lordship a more favourable account of Dr. Farmer's health, than that which I have very lately received from his nephew Mr. Farmer, who is constantly with his uncle at college. He writes thus: "The Master seems to be no worse now than when you last saw him, some months ago; though in the interim he has been very bad indeed. Professor Harwood thinks Dr. Farmer might in some measure reinstate his health, if he would get into the air. But he has not been down stairs these two months and upwards."

The nephew in attendance would have been Tom, the son of Thomas, one of the two surviving brothers of Richard Farmer. His other brother, Joseph, was an officer of the Leicester Volunteers and died unmarried. Richard Farmer's nephew had been presented to the vicarage of St. Luke, Middlesex, by his uncle in 1796 (*Lit. Anec.*, II, 640, n.). On the day of Richard Farmer's death, Tom Farmer wrote to George Steevens. The letter is in the Folger Shakespeare Library (C.b.10).

My Dear Sir,   Eman. Coll: Sep. 8th [1797]
    I was sorry I had not the Pleasure of seeing you during my short Stay in London. When I left Cambridge we were in Hopes the Master was getting much better; He however on Wednesday last was surprised by the continual throwing up of Bile, under the severe Exertions of which He died this Morning at seven o Clock—Melancholy Event for all his Friends; but scarcely supportable by me who have attended him very strictly for some Time. He fell as if a Sleep & left this World without the least Struggle. He has said He has left a Will & given every thing to Captn F. With the utmost Wishes for your Health &c I am yours very truly,

                                                                                T Farmer

The information in the letter above was passed on by Steevens to Percy in a letter dated 14 September 1797 (*Illustr.*, VII, 32-33).

    I foretold, that the first effort of nature to relieve poor Farmer would be the last moment of his existence. He was striving to throw up some bile, and died in his exertion. He sunk back on his bed, as if asleep, and left the world without the slightest struggle. His nephew Tom was with him; and Captain Farmer [Joseph] (who, I believe, is his executor) was immediately sent for from Leicester. Dr. Farmer will be buried in the chapel at Emmanuel, near the remains of his friend and predecessor, Harry Hubbard. About the contents of his will, and the destination of his library, I have nothing to say at present; nor can I learn that his successor in Amen-corner is announced. I am equally doubtful respecting the Mastership of the College.]

The following epitaph in the Cloisters of the College, written by Dr. [Samuel] Parr, accurately exhibits his more amiable and respectable qualities; and reflects honour on the candour of the learned writer; between whom and Dr. Farmer there subsisted great differences of opinion on political subjects.

> Ricardus Farmer, S.T.P.
> Magister hujus Collegii,
> vir facetus et dulcis festivique sermonis,
> Graecè et Latinè doctus,
> in explicandâ veterum Anglorum Poesi
> subtilis atque elegans,
> Academiae Cantabrigiensis stabiliendae
> et amplificandae studiosus,
> Regis et Patriae amantissimus
> vixit ann. LXII. mens. III. dies XIIII;
> decessit sexto id. Septemb.
> anno Domini
> M DCC LXXXX VII;
> et conditus est juxta aram vicini sacelli
> in sepulcro quod sibi vivus nuncupaverat.

[In a few days after the Doctor's death, the following *jeu d'esprit* (not improbably by his friend Mr. George Steevens) appeared in one of the daily papers:[13]]

This eminent Critick and enlightened Scholar has left few of equal celebrity behind him at Cambridge: he has turned his mind more to the Belles Lettres than men do in general who are educated in the trammels of that Monkish Establishment. The Doctor composed some of his pleasantest Works in an arbour on the verge of a pond where he resided, where a pipe was his principal companion; and, when he relaxed from his labours, he amused himself with a variety of water-fowls, which covered his pond; and which, with others not of an aquatic nature, were much admired by all those who visited his hospitable mansion. These birds, a Cambridge friend informs me, he has disposed of in the following manner:

My Geese I give and bequeath—to the Heads of the University.
My ducks and Drakes—to Sir Henry Vane Tempest.
My Peacock—to the Duchess of Gordon.
My Guinea Fowl—to Colonel Cawthorne.
My Pigeons—to Lady Buckinghamshire, &c. &c.

13. This introductory statement and the quotation that follows it are a note in *Lit. Anec.*

My Doves—to the Princesses.
My Screech-owl—to Mrs. Mattocks.
My Humming-bird—to Mr. Courtney.
My Bantams—to Tommy Onslow.
My Chicken—to M. A. Taylor
My King-fisher—to the French Directors.
My Cock Sparrow—to the Duke of Queensbury.
My Old Grey Parrot—To Mrs. Cowley.
My Pullets—to Lord William Gordon
My Cuckoo—to Mr. Esten.
My Cormorant—to the Duke of Marlborough.
My Goldfinches—to Sir William Pultney.
My Vulture—to Lord Lonsdale.
My Eagle—to Mr. Pitt.
My Jack-daws—to the Bond-street Beaux.
My Magpie—to Mr. George Colman.
And my Rooks—to the Club at Brookes's.
Oracle, Sept. 21 ONE OF THE COCK AND HEN CLUB.

His will, dated about 1792, was written on a blank leaf torn out of an old book, and was nearly as under: "I give to my brother, Joseph Farmer, all my property, not doubting of his using it for the benefit of our Family." [Dr. Farmer left two surviving brothers, Thomas and Joseph, both of whom are living in great respectability at Leicester . . .[14]]

Though a good classical scholar, Dr. Farmer has been celebrated only for that kind of literature which is connected with the English Drama; and, having a strong predilection for old English writers, he ranked high among the Commentators upon Shakespeare. His 'Essay upon the Learning of Shakespeare' was, in fact, the first foundation of his fame, which an unconquerable indolence prevented him from carrying to that height to which the exercise of his literary talents could not have failed to raise it:[15] so great, indeed, was his love of ease, that, after having announced for subscriptions a History of Leicestershire, and actually begun to print it, rather than submit to the fatigue of carrying it through the press, he returned the subscriptions. Indolence and the love of ease were, indeed, the Doctor's chief characteristicks; and to them, with the disappointment already mentioned, may be attributed a want of attention to his external appearance, and to the usual forms of behaviour belonging to his station. In the company of strangers, the eccentricity of his appearance and of his manners made him sometimes be taken for a person half crazed. The Writer of this sketch [George Gleig] saw him one morning at Canterbury, dressed in stockings of unbleached thread, brown breeches, and a wig not worth a shilling; and when a Brother Prebendary of his, remarkable for elegance of manners and

14. This sentence is a note in *Lit. Anec.* The omitted part names Farmer's surviving brothers and sisters and their families.
15. See n. 8 for a refutation of the idea that Farmer was indolent, as Gleig here said he was. In his DNB life of Farmer, Thompson Cooper kept alive the myth of Farmer's indolence.

propriety of dress, put him in mind that they were to attend on the Archbishop, Dr. Farmer replied, that it had totally escaped him; but he went home, and dressed himself like a Clergyman. That he sat late reading, and occasionally drinking brandy and water, cannot be denied; and it is literally true, that he could not easily be prevailed upon to settle his accompts. His accompts with some of his pupils, when Tutor of his College, were never settled to the day of his death; and the young gentlemen not unfrequently took advantage of this unconquerable indolence to borrow of him considerable sums, well knowing that there was little chance of a demand being ever made upon their parents. One gentleman, in particular, told a friend of ours, who was himself a pensioner of Emanuel, that, when he left that College, he was near 50*l*. in debt to Dr. Farmer; 'a debt,' said he, 'which I would have scrupulously paid, but, after repeated solicitations, I could get no bill from him.'

Having been a warm partizan of Government during the American war, it will readily be believed that Dr. Farmer was the determined enemy of Levellers and Anarchists. He was such a Whig as those who placed King William on the throne; and of course deemed a violent Tory by our present Republicans, of whom, to say the truth, he could hardly speak with temper. By his enemies he is admitted to have been a man of generosity. As he obtained money easily, so he parted with it easily. Whilst he was always ready to relieve distress, his bounty was frequently bestowed on the patronage of learned men, and learned publications: he was, accordingly, a favourite with all good men who knew him. In his own College he was adored. In the University he had, for many years, more influence than any other individual; and, with all his eccentricities, his death was a loss to that learned Body, which, in the opinion of some of its members, will not soon be made up.*

My friend Isaac Reed (than whom no man was better acquainted with the honest, undisguised sentiments of the benevolent Master of Emanuel) has thus delineated his character. [Nichols quotes the following four paragraphs.]

Dr. Farmer was the architect of his own fortune, and, without the air of friends of powerful connections, elevated himself to an honourable and lucrative situation, in the enjoyment of which he bounded his ambition at a time when he might have obtained higher preferment. From his entrance into the University, he seemed to have fixed on Cambridge as the place destined for his future residence; and uniformly rejected every offer, the acceptance of which would occasion his entire removal from that place. His attention to the interests of the Town and University never was suspended; and by his exertions every improvement and convenience introduced for the last thirty years were either originally proposed, or ultimately forwarded and carried into execution. The plan for paving, watching, and lighting the Town, after many ineffectual attempts, was accomplished in his

---

* Encyclopaedia Britannica. NICHOLS. (Three paragraphs are quoted.)

second vice-chancellorship, greatly to the satisfaction of all parties; whose petty objections and jealousies, and discordant and jarring interests, he exerted himself with success to obviate, to moderate, and to reconcile. As a Magistrate, he was active and diligent; and, on more than one occasion of riots, displayed great firmness of mind in dangerous conjunctures. As the Master of his College, he was easy and accessible, cultivating the friendship of the Fellows and inferior members by every mark of kindness and attention; and this conduct was rewarded in the manner he most wished, by the harmony which prevailed in the society, and by an entire exemption from those feuds and animosities which too often tore to pieces and disgraced other Colleges.

In his office of Residentiary of St. Paul's, if he was not the first mover, he was certainly the most strenuous advocate for promoting the art of Sculpture, by the introduction of Statuary into the Metropolitan Cathedral: and many of the regulations on the subject were suggested by him and adopted in consequence of his recommendation.†

His literary character rests on one small Work—"The Essay on the Learning of Shakespeare," composed in the early period of his life, and which completely settled a much litigated and controverted question, contrary to the opinions of many eminent writers, in a manner that carried conviction to the mind of every one who had either carelessly or carefully reflected on the subject. It may, in truth, be pointed out as a master-piece, whether considered with a view to the sprightliness and vivacity with which it is written, the clearness of the arrangement, the force and variety of the evidence, or the compression of scattered materials into a narrow compass; materials which inferior Writers would have expanded into a large volume. He had no taste for the prevailing pursuit in the University, the Mathematicks, nor ever paid any regard to it, after he had obtained his first two degrees; but he cultivated the Belles Lettres with great assiduity, though with little appearance of regular study. His knowledge of books in all languages, and in every science, was very comprehensive. He was fond of reading; and continued the habit until the last stage of his existence. His good humour, liberality, pleasantry, and hospitality, might afford subjects for unmixed panegyric, to which every one who knew him would readily assent. These will live in the memory of his surviving friends; who, whenever his name occurs, cannot but sigh at the reflection that those qualities, which have so often soothed and gladdened life, were suffered to exist no longer in the possessor than until he had attained the age of sixty-two years.

The illiberal practice of the present times may expect a drawback of the foibles of a man of genius and virtue. That Dr. Farmer had some, it would

† Dr. Farmer, as a member of the Chapter, very zealously lent his powerful aid on this occasion, but, having been myself, in conjunction with my friends Dr. Warner and Dr. Lettsom, an active agent in obtaining admission for Mr. Howard's monument, I can speak with certainty also of the readiness with which the Right Reverend the Dean and the rest of the Dignitaries of the Cathedral... acceded to the proposal. NICHOLS.

be ridiculous to deny, and useless to conceal. They were, however, such as superseded no duty, encouraged no vice, and might pass in review, before the most rigid Moralist, without calling for more than a very slight censure: in reality, they were lost in the recollection of his many amiable qualities. Some of them, however, are delicately glanced at in the following masterly character, drawn by the Reverend Dr. Parr,[16] and published a short time before Dr. Farmer's death:

Of any undue partiality towards the Master of Emanuel College I shall not be suspected, by those persons who know how little his sentiments accord with my own upon some ecclesiastical and many political matters. From rooted principle and antient habit, he is a Tory—I am a Whig; and we have both of us too much confidence in each other, and too much respect for ourselves, to dissemble what we think upon any grounds, or to any extent: let me, then, do him the justice, which, amidst all our differences in opinion, I am sure that he will ever be ready to do to me. His knowledge is various, extensive, and recondite. With much seeming negligence, and perhaps in later years some real relaxation, he understands more, and remembers more, about common and uncommon subjects of Literature, than many of those who would be thought to read all the day, and meditate half the night. In quickness of apprehension, and acuteness of discrimination, I have not often seen his equal. Through many a convivial hour have I been charmed by his vivacity; and upon his genius I have reflected in many a serious moment with pleasure, with admiration; but not without regret, that he has never concentrated and exerted all the great powers of his mind, in some great Work, upon some great subject. Of his liberality in patronizing learned men, I could point out numerous instances. Without the smallest propensities to avarice, he possesses a large income; and, without the mean submissions of dependance, he is risen to high station. His ambition, if he has any, is without insolence; his munificence is without ostentation; his wit is without acrimony; and his learning without pedantry.‡

Two letters of Dr. Johnson to Dr. Farmer are preserved in Boswell's Life; the one, in 1770, requesting (for Mr. Steevens and himself) such information concerning Shakspeare as Dr. Farmer was "more able to give than any other man;"[17] the other, in 1780, soliciting information concerning "Ambrose Philips, Broome, and Gray, who were all of Cambridge; and of whose lives he was to give such accounts as he could gather."[18]

---

‡ Seward's Biographiana, vol. II. p. 579. NICHOLS.
16. Samuel Parr, who composed the epitaph on Samuel Johnson's monument in St. Paul's, was another of that army of contributors to Nichols' works. See *Lit. Anec.*, IX, v.
17. This letter, dated 21 March 1770, is number 227 in *The Letters of Samuel Johnson*, ed. R. W. Chapman (Oxford, 1952), I, 233-234.
18. This letter, dated 23 May 1780, is number 673 in ibid., II, 363. Farmer, it seems, did not respond to Johnson's appeal for information. As a result, Johnson wrote to Nichols on 16 June 1780 (letter 683) thanking him for material on Broome and asking for "dates for A. Philips." Johnson concludes the letter: "I wrote to Cambridge about them, but have had no answer." For information regarding the assistance given by Nichols to Johnson on the life of William Broome and others see my article, "Some New Sources of Johnson's *Lives*," *PMLA*, 65:1088-1111 (December 1950). In addition to the two letters from

In the European Magazine, vol. XXV. 1794, p. 410, is an excellent Letter from Dr. Farmer to Isaac Reed, esq. Jan. 28, 1794, occasioned by a question which Mr. Reed had proposed to him on the subject of [John] Dennis the Critic having been expelled from the University of Cambridge; a fact asserted in the "Biographia Dramatica," but denied by Dr. Kippis in the "Biographia Britannica," under the article *Dennis*.§

Mr. Hawkins, in an advertisement prefixed to his edition of "Ignoramus, 1787," very handsomely observes, that "it would have been an injury to his reputation to conceal that the Editor was indebted to the Rev. Dr. Farmer for the knowledge of many facts which no one but himself could have furnished."[19]

His Library, which was particularly rich in scarce Tracts and old English Literature, was sold, under the title of "*Bibliotheca Farmeriana;* a Catalogue of the curious, valuable, and extensive Library, in Print and Manuscript, of the late Rev. Richard Farmer, D.D. Canon Residentiary of St. Paul's, Master of Emanuel College, and Fellow of the Royal and Antiquary Societies, deceased; comprehending many rare Editions of the Greek and Roman Classicks, and of the most eminent Philogers; a fine Collection of English History, Antiquities, and Topography; including all the old Chronicles; the most rare and copious Assemblage of old English Poetry that, perhaps, was ever exhibited at one View; together with a great Variety of old Plays, and early printed Books, English and Foreign, in the Black Letter, many of which are extremely scarce," &c. &c. The sale to commence Monday, May 7, 1798, and continue 35 days, by Mr. King, King Street, Covent-garden.||

The Catalogue extends to 379 pages, and the articles of books amount to 8155.

The Library is supposed to have cost him less than 500*l*. It sold for 2210*l*. independent of his Pictures.

Dr. Farmer once proposed himself to have had a Catalogue taken of his

---

Johnson to Farmer mentioned by Nichols, Chapman has two others: number 244 dated 18 February 1771 and number 530 dated 22 July 1777.

§ After some pleasant arguments and remarks, Dr. Farmer concludes, "Yet we have not proved that Dennis was expelled from *Caius*, his original College; but this matter is soon settled; though the *tradition* more fully expresses the cause of it. On turning to their *Gesta* Book, under the head 'Sir Dennis sent away,' appears this entry: 'March 4, 1680. At a meeting of the master and fellows, sir Dennis mulcted 3*l*.; his scholarship taken away, and he *sent out of College*, for assaulting and wounding sir Glenham with a sword.'" NICHOLS.

19. John Sidney Hawkins, eldest son of Sir John Hawkins, spent nearly ten years on this edition of George Ruggle's comedy, published by Nichols upon the recommendation of Johnson, who sent proposals for its publication along with his letter. See *Lit. Anec.,* IX, 35n. Johnson's letter, dated 12 April 1784, is number 950 in Chapman, *Letters of Johnson,* III, 151.

|| "Dr. Farmer's copies were, in general, in sorry condition: the possessor caring little for large margins and splendid bindings. His own name, generally accompanied with a bibliographical remark, and both written in a sprawling character, usually preceded the title-page. . . ." Dibdin's Bibliomania, *ubi supra.* NICHOLS. (Thomas F. Dibdin's *Bibliomania* was first published in London in 1809.)

Library, to which he intended to have prefixed the following Advertisement: "This Collection of Books is by no means to be considered as an essay towards a perfect library: the circumstances and the situation of the Collector made such an attempt both unnecessary and impracticable. Here are few publications of great price which were already to be found in the excellent Library of Emanuel College; but, it is believed, that not many private collections contain a greater number of really curious and scarce books; and, perhaps, no one is so rich in the antient philogical English literature. R. FARMER."

[The material that follows is in "Additions to the Second Volume," *Lit. Anec.*, VIII, 420-421, and is signed "T. M." These initials belong to a contributor listed by Nichols in the "Advertisement" to the volume in which the addition occurs as "Rev. Thomas Martyn, Professor of Botany at Cambridge." A number of notes with this same signature occur in *Literary Anecdotes,* and one of them, only three pages away from the one reproduced below, is acknowledged to be Martyn's by Nichols in his *Illustr.*, IV, 243, n. Nichols has a short biographical sketch of Martyn in *Lit. Anec.*, III, 156-158n]

I observe that you have been very large in your account of my intimate friend Dr. Farmer. He was admitted of Emanuel College, not in 1753, but in October 1752, and came into residence at the same time. Though he arrived within a few days after me, yet he was a year my junior, because he had not been admitted before the Commencement. We were near neighbors in Bungay-court, and almost always together. I could have wished a fairer account of our most respectable tutor and Dr. Farmer's firm friend Mr. Hubbard. He was a Tory, but not the least of a Jacobite; nor was Dr. Richardson. They were both Disciplinarians; and considered *minutiae*, perhaps with some reason, as the outworks of discipline. We see now the consequence of their having been given up. The citadel has been stormed. Bickham, the junior tutor, was a bold man, and had been a bruiser when young. I do not think he was of any party. It is inaccurate to call him the Classical Tutor, for he gave us lectures in Euclid. He did not want parts, but he was idle.

Dr. Farmer's degree should not have been called *inconsiderable;* it was even reputable.[20] Considering how idle he was, and how little inclination he had for mathematicks, it shewed the goodness of his parts. There was no contest between him and Sawbridge for the cup; Farmer had it of course, as senior in the Proctor's list. I was much oftener Curate of Swavesey than Dr. Farmer. Mr. Allenson, the Vicar, went every other year to see his relations in Yorkshire, and was absent 12 months. At these times Dr. Farmer or I were his substitutes. I never recollect there being any Methodists in the

---

20. Nichols had not said that Farmer's degree was "inconsiderable"; he had said simply that it was "not of the first class" but that it had "procured him notice in College."

parish.[21] Dr. Farmer was not famous as a Preacher. His Sermons were florid, and composed in haste; his enunciation was loud and hurried; his setting-off was so violent as to make nervous people start. As a proof of his hurrying, I heard him relate, that, having been to preach at Huntingdon, and on his return riding over the bridge, he heard a man say to his companion, 'Ay, there he goes; if he rides as fast as he preaches, he will soon be at Cambridge.' He was occasionally writing Remarks on Shakspeare from the very first of his residing at Cambridge. I perfectly recollect his little *porte-feuille*, filled with scraps of paper of all sizes, in no order, which I occasionally attempted to arrange; and sometimes he would bring me some of his own writing to decypher, when he could not make it out himself.

Farmer's engagement at Whitehall did not require him to be in London a certain number of *months* in the year, but only two Sundays, or at most two and a half. It was his Canonry of St. Paul's, which Mr. Pitt gave him many years after, that required three months residence.

He very justly writes *raptim,* or *calamo rapidissimo,* at the end of his letters, for he was always in a hurry. He suffered a disappointment in love very early in life. From his first coming to College he always gave Miss Benskin as a toast, and never could mention her name without evident feelings of the most ardent affection. We were then so intimate that his joys and sorrows were poured into my bosom. After a lapse of almost 60 years, it is no wonder if I do not correctly remember how the connexion terminated; but I have some notion that at length she married another person, there being little prospect of the connexion with Dr. Farmer speedily taking place. But as she was a Leicester girl, Mr. Nichols may perhaps know this circumstance better than I do. This I am certain of, that the disappointment affected his mind very deeply, and was the source of his peculiarities. Of his latter connexion with Miss Hatton I cannot speak with the same certainty, because at that time I did not reside in the University, and our intimacy had ceased, though we continued very good friends to Dr. Farmer's death; as indeed who could be otherwise than friendly with so kind and good-humoured a man as he was? Dr. Colman was likely to know the truth of the affair with Miss Hatton.[22] To the Character given of him I make no objection. The *Encyclopaedia,* Mr. Isaac Reed, Mr. Dibdin, and Dr. Parr,

---

21. Nichols, in a note, *Lit. Anec.,* II, 621, had quoted from Dyer's *Annual Necrology:* "Swavesey was at that time frequented by Methodists. . . . Between these gentlemen and Farmer there existed no great cordiality; for Farmer was no friend to their doctrines, which appeared to him irrational and gloomy. He classed them with Presbyterians; and both Presbyterians and Methodists he considered as Puritans and Roundheads. Farmer was a greater adept in cracking a joke, than in unhinging a Calvinist's creed, or in quieting a gloomy conscience. He, however, possessed a spirit of benevolence; and knew how to perform a generous action to a distressed family. There are men who can read over a person's grave 'He was a kind man,' with greater satisfaction than 'He was a great Preacher.'"

22. On 21 May 1788 Michael Lort wrote the following in a letter to Thomas Percy, *Illustr.,* VII, 495: ". . . I think I mentioned . . . Dr. Farmer's succeeding Dr. Douglas in a residentiaryship of St. Paul's, supposed now to be worth 1,000*l.* a year, on the strength of which he renewed his proposals of marriage to Miss Hatton, whose father, the late Sir T. Hatton, had resisted the former proposals; but now the young lady and her mother very readily acceded to them, and the former was ushered to Amen Corner to give directions about the house, and to a painter to sit for her picture. But so it happens, that the lover's cold fit is come on, and he has absolutely declined all further proceedings. No good reason has yet been publicly assigned, so that all his friends, as well as the lady's, are much hurt, none more than G. Steevens, the common friend of both, under whose guidance and direction the whole business has proceeded, and was to have been completed."

have done him justice. There is nought set down in malice; nor is the truth concealed or even varnished.—I still look back to him with great affection. T.M.

[In December 1818, the *New Monthly Magazine*, p. 388, published a letter of the Rev. Baptist Noel Turner of Emmanuel College describing a visit of Dr. Johnson at Cambridge. Dr. L. F. Powell refers to this letter as "a rambling account of Johnson's visit which is not to be trusted in some details." (Hill-Powell, *Boswell*, I, 518, Appendix C.) It seems, however, that it is mainly Turner's dating of the visit that has been called in question; perhaps the error is understandable as Turner, writing in 1818, was describing a visit that took place in 1765. Dr. Powell is able to place the date of the visit precisely as taking place between Saturday 16 and Tuesday 19 February. The dating was made possible by a letter from Farmer to Thomas Percy. (See Hill-Powell, *ibid.*, p. 555, Appendix G. Farmer's letter is reproduced there, as it is also in *The Correspondence of Percy and Farmer*, ed. Brooks, pp. 84-86.) Turner's letter, along with some others about Johnson, was reprinted by Nichols (or perhaps by his son John Bowyer Nichols) in the posthumous Volume VI of *Illustrations*, 1831 (Nichols had died in 1826). Only the parts of the letter which refer to Farmer are reproduced below, and they are placed in chronological order. The text comes from pp. 146-159 of *Illustrations*. With reference to this Cambridge trip, Turner tells us that Johnson went to see Farmer, "on whose account principally the journey was undertaken."]

... At another time he [Johnson] said, "That Mr. Farmer, of your College, is a very clever man indeed, Sir." And on my asking him whether he knew the fact with respect to the learning of Shakspeare, before that gentleman's publication? Johnson. "Why, yes, Sir, I knew in general that the fact was as he represents it; but I did not know it, as Mr. Farmer has now taught it me, by *detail*, Sir." I was several times the bearer of messages between them; and my suggesting and expressing a hope that we should some time or other have the pleasure of seeing him at Cambridge, when I should be most happy to introduce them to each other, might somewhat conduce to his taking the journey I am about to describe. . . .

When I mentioned a wish to introduce him to our common friend Farmer, the Doctor did not seem disinclined to the proposal; and it was on Saturday in the beginning of March 1765,[23] that having accepted the offer of Topham Beauclerk, Esq. to drive him down in his phaeton, they arrived at the Rose Inn, Cambridge. . . .

The long-wished for interview of these unknown friends was uncommonly joyous on both sides. After the salutations, said Johnson, "Mr. Farmer, I understand you have a large collection of very rare and curious books." Farmer. "Why yes, Sir, to be sure I have plenty of all such reading as was

---

23. Johnson arrived on a Saturday, but the actual date, as indicated in the headnote to these excerpts from Turner's letter, was 16 February 1765. Boswell mentions Johnson's visit to Cambridge and quotes part of a letter describing it, a letter written by John Sharp, another Cambridge man. Sharp's letter first appeared in the *Gent. Mag.* (March 1785). See Hill-Powell, *Boswell*, I, 487. The text of Sharp's letter is reproduced in full in *ibid.*, p. 517.

never read." Johnson. "Will you favour me with a specimen, Sir?" Farmer, considering for a moment, reached down "Markham's Booke of Armorie,"[24] and turning to a particular page, presented it to the Doctor, who, with rolling head, attentively perused it. The passage having been previously pointed out to myself, I am luckily enabled to lay it before the reader, because I find it quoted, *totidem verbis*, as a great curiosity, which it certainly is, at line 101 of the first part of "The Pursuits of Literature."[25] The words in question are said to be the conclusion of the first chapter of "Markham's Booke," intituled, "The difference between Charles and Gentleman," and is as follows: "From the offspring of gentlemanly Japhet came Abraham, Moses, Aaron, and the Prophets, &c. &c.—and also the king of the right line of Mary, of whom that only absolute gentleman, Jesus, gentleman by his mother Mary, Princess of Coat Armorie," &c. Towards the conclusion of which unaccountable and almost incredible folly, . . . if you can conceive a cast of countenance expressive at once of both pleasantry and horror, that was the one which our sage assumed when he exclaimed, "Now I am shocked, Sir—now I am shocked!" which was only answered by Farmer with his usual ha! ha! ha! for even blasphemy, where it is unintentional, may be so thoroughly ridiculous as merely to excite the laugh of pity! . . .

In the height of our convivial hilarity, our great man exclaimed: "Come, now, I'll give you a test; now I'll try who is a true antiquary amongst you. Has any one of this company ever met with the History of Glorianus and Gloriana?" Farmer, drawing the pipe out of his mouth, followed by a cloud of smoke, instantly said, "I've got the book." "Gi' me your hand, gi' me your hand," said Johnson, "you are the man after my own heart." And the shaking of two such hands, with two such happy faces attached to them, could hardly, I think, be matched in the whole annals of literature! . . .

Though he must have been well known to many of the Heads and Doctors at this seat of learning, yet he seemed studious to preserve a strict incognito; his only aim being an introduction to his favourite scholar, his brother patriot and antiquary, who was then Mr. but afterwards Dr. Farmer, and master of his college, and who finally declined episcopacy. Merit like Johnson's seeks not publicity . . . .

---

24. "The Book of Armorie" is the third and last part of Gervase Markham's *The Gentlemans Academie. Or, the booke of S. Albans*, 1595, an edition of Juliana Barnes' *Book of St. Albans*. See DNB life of Gervase Markham by Clements Robert Markham.

25. Published anonymously by T. J. Mathias in 1794 and reprinted many times.

George Steevens

[Upon the death of George Steevens on 22 January 1800, small obituary notices appeared in various periodicals. Among these was the following from the *Gent. Mag.*, 70:92 (January 1800): "22nd. At his house at Hampstead, George Steevens, esq. F. R. and A. SS. the celebrated Commentator on Shakespeare; of whom our next shall give some particulars." In the *European Magazine*, 37:87, for the same month was a similar notice, followed by the following parenthetical statement: "A further account will be given of this gentleman." The *Gentleman's Magazine* kept its promise and produced in February (70:178-180), "Biographical Anecdotes of George Steevens, Esq." Steevens' epitaph was printed in the *Gent. Mag.*, 72:62 (January 1802), two years later.

John Nichols had been editor of the *Gentleman's Magazine* since 1792; we may also believe him to be the author of the account of Steevens (except for the inclusion of a letter signed ETONIENSIS since he, a man careful about such things, reproduced it as his own in *Lit. Anec.*, II, 650-663.

The *European Magazine* fulfilled its promise to produce a "further account," but only after twelve years had passed. When it finally appeared, 61:46-47 (January 1812), it was an abbreviated version of the *Gentleman's Magazine* account with the exception of a few minor details presumably supplied by Daniel Lysons, to whom the memoir is attributed.[1] Lysons may not have taken his account directly from Nichols, however; he might have taken it from an intermediate source: the *Monthly Mirror*, for instance, which reprinted verbatim, 12:307-311 (November 1801), Nichols' memoir of Steevens without so much as a word of acknowledgment.

Several other lives of Steevens were written in the years that immediately followed his death, and all were based on Nichols' account. In the life in the *Thespian Dictionary* (London 1802 and 1805), some of the sentences from the *Gentleman's Magazine* have been omitted and others rearranged, but the wording within the sentences remains unaltered. T. F. Dibdin gives details of the life of Steevens in his *Bibliomania* (London 1811), p. 570, but he attributes many of them to the "respectable compiler of the *Gentleman's Magazine*." After the publication of Nichols' life of Steevens in *Literary Anecdotes* in 1812, two other authors wrote accounts interesting enough to be mentioned. Both acknowledged Nichols as a source. The first of these is in John James Park, *The Topography and Natural History of Hampstead* (London 1814), p. 354; and the second is in Alexander Chalmers, *The General Biographical Dictionary* (London 1816), XXVIII, 366n. Exactly how far Nichols' memoir of Steevens may have gone is impossible for me to say. But the diction and sentence structure of Nichols are apparent in at least one translation, that in the *Biographie universelle, ancienne et moderne ... redige par une societe de gens de lettres et de savants* (Paris 1825), XLIII, 494-495.

---

1. See Daniel Lysons, *Environs of London* (London, 1810), II, 699.

In his *Illustr.*, V, 427-443, Nichols published an extension of the memoir of Steevens in *Literary Anecdotes*. Although the volume in which this work appeared was issued posthumously, Nichols had, at the time of his death, worked nearly two hundred pages beyond the Steevens addition. (See the statement of Nichols' son, John Bowyer Nichols, in *Illustr.*, V, iii.) In addition to the memoir proper, there are numerous references to Steevens throughout the *Anecdotes* and *Illustrations*. Especially important among these printed sources are Steevens' many letters to Percy, Nichols, and others, most of which will not be reproduced here. An excellent biography of Steevens by Sidney Lee is in the DNB. Adequate acknowledgment is made to Nichols, who must always be considered a primary source by any biographer of Steevens.

A great many manuscript materials are available to the scholar who wishes to seek Steevens beyond Nichols' writings. The Folger Shakespeare Library, in its C.b.10 holding, has seventy letters from correspondents to Steevens (1736-1800) and four letters written by him (1763-1799) among the 191 items on Steevens in the collection. His correspondents here include Farmer, Malone, Percy, Reed, Fuseli, Joseph Ritson, and Sir Joseph Banks. A number of additional letters to and from Steevens are scattered through other Folger holdings. The British Museum is also rich in Steevens material. Eleven letters from Steevens to Thomas Warton the Younger are in the volume bound as Add. Mss. 42,561. In other places in the Museum's manuscript collections are five items (1781-1782) of Steevens correspondence with Cole, Steevens correspondence with others, and his will (Add. Mss. 20,082. f. 126). The Osborn collection at Yale holds twenty-nine letters and three other Steevens manuscripts; among the correspondents in this group are Farmer, Reed, Nichols, Garrick, Percy, and Banks. The Bodleian Library possesses at least eight items written by Steevens, to him, or about him. A few, and of course only a few, of these manuscript letters will be introduced below as they have a particular relevance to Nichols' life of Steevens.

Portraits of Steevens are in *Illustr.*, V, facing 427, and VII, facing 1.]

THIS eminent Scholar and profoundly learned Commentator was the only son of George Steevens, esq. of Stepney, many years an East-India Captain, and afterwards a Director of the East India Company, who died in 1768.

[Editor's note: In its list of deaths for January of 1768, the *Gentleman's Magazine* for February of the same year (38:93) has the following obituary, apparently assigning the wrong given name to the father of George Steevens: "Thomas Stevens, Esq; formerly an East-India captain."

In the *Gent. Mag.*, 60:865 (September 1790), under the date of the 16th, is this obituary: "At her house at Poplar, in her 79th year, Mrs. Anna Steevens, relict of Wm. S. esq. a commander in the Honourable East India

Company's service, and mother of George S. esq. editor of Shakspeare."
With reference to this obituary, George Steevens wrote to Isaac Reed in a
letter of 5 October 1790 (Folger C.b.2): "Though I took the pains to leave
a transcript of the article inserted in your obituary, with Mr Nichols, he
has thought proper, in the Gent. Mag. to convert my *Aunt* (whose death
happen'd on the 16th of last month,) into my Mother, who died at least
28 years ago. By these means also my father & mother have been new-
christened; and the former, who never was in the East, has been made a Captain in the India Company's service.—I have sent Mr Urban a Perstringer,
& can easily suppose that, next month, he will supersede his old blunders
by a set of new ones.—Pray contradict this circumstance that it may not
be imagined I could desert an aged Parent confin'd to her bed, that I might
indulge myself in the pleasures of Stirbich Fair."

The *Gentleman's Magazine* for October 1790 (60:953) contains this cor-
rection: "At the end of the article announcing the death of Mrs. *Anna
Steevens,* omit the words 'and mother of Geo. Steevens, esq. Editor of
Shakspeare.' " No correction is made, however, of the statement that George
Steevens' father had been "a commander in the honourable East India
Company's service." He remains in its service in Nichols' life of Steevens
in *Lit. Anec.,* II, 650, as he does also in Sidney Lee's DNB life and in Venn's
Alumni Cantabrigienses; but in *Lit. Anec.,* IX, 784 (as a correction to II,
650) is this note by Richard Gough: "The Father of George Steevens, Esq.
was an Elder Brother of the Trinity-house, and Captain of a Ship, but not
to the East Indies. R. G."]

He [George Steevens] was born at Stepney, May 10, 1736,* and admitted of
King's College, Cambridge, about 1751 or 1752 [actually 29 March 1753; see
Venn, *Alumni Cantabrigienses*]. But he is best known as editor of Shak-
speare's Plays, Twenty of which he published 1766, in four volumes, 8vo.[2]

A year before the appearance of this edition, Dr. Johnson had published
an edition, with notes, in eight volumes, 8vo. A coalition between these
two editors having been negotiated, another edition, known by the name of
"Johnson and Steevens's Edition," made its appearance in 10 vols. 8vo, 1773.

It was reprinted by these gentlemen, in the same number of volumes, five
years after; and again, in 1785, under the care of Isaac Reed, esq. of Staple-
inn, who, at the request of his friends Mr. Steevens and Dr. Farmer, undertook the office of editor.

A fourth edition of this work, with great additions and improvements,
was published by Mr. Steevens in fifteen volumes, 8vo, 1793, which at the
time was certainly the most complete edition extant of Shakspeare's Plays.

---

* "George, son of George Steevens, of Poplar, mariner, and Mary his wife, baptized
May 19, 1736, nine days old." NICHOLS.

2. At this point Nichols introduces in a note the letter signed *Etonensis*. This letter,
which I have placed at the end of Nichols' own memoir, was published first in the *Gent.
Mag.,* 70:180 (February 1800).

This work, which, through the indefatigable exertions of the editor, was carried through the press in the space of eighteen months, is enriched with much novelty of remark, and contains the accumulated result of his acute and critical observations, made during a long course of reading, chiefly devoted to the illustration of his favourite Bard. The diligent editor has taken all possible pains to render his work full, clear, and convenient; and whoever considers the prolegomena and notes, joined to the elegance of the typographical execution, will be of opinion that our immortal Bard was edited in a manner worthy his fame.†

But this talent at explaining and illustrating the difficulties and beauties of Shakspeare was disgraced by the worst of foils, a severity of satire,‡ which too strongly marked a malevolence of heart, from which his best friends cannot vindicate the editor.[3] The severity of his satire has, in some instances, recoiled on himself; and perhaps the retort courteous was never better played off against him than by our friend, honest and generous Tom Davies,[4] in his vigorous character of *Master Stephen*.§ It would be happy for him could as much be said for him as for that unfortunate and worthy man on a similar occasion. But "Peace be to his soul, if God's good pleasure be!"

---

† A subsequent edition of this valuable Work was edited by Mr. Reed in 1803. . . . NICHOLS.

‡ Of this Sir John Hawkins felt the keenest force. NICHOLS.

3. In his *Curiosities of Literature* (London, 1859), III, 297, Isaac D'Israeli says that "it is to be regretted that Mr. Nichols, who might have furnished much secret history of this extraordinary literary forger, has, from delicacy, mutilated his collective vigour." One can but guess how many examples of Steevens' bad conduct Nichols might have collected, but in the one or two instances in which D'Israeli charges Nichols with being too delicate, it can be demonstrated that Nichols' treatment was adequate. That there were in Steevens' private life faults more terrible than any revealed is doubted by Sidney Lee in his DNB life of Steevens: "The proofs that Steevens was guilty of publishing anonymous libels on his boon companions are happily incomplete. . . . But many of his contributions have been identified, and, although biting enough, do not transgress the bounds of social decency." New evidence, however, indicates questions not yet answered. In the *Private Papers of James Boswell from Malahide Castle*, ed. Goeffrey Scott and F. A. Pottle (privately printed, New York, 1928-34), XIV, 178, Boswell wrote of Steevens: "He has the character of being very Malignant. He will, it is said, write in the Newspapers against people with whom he is living intimately. Said Dr. Johnson: 'No, Sir, he is not malignant. He is mischievous. He only means to vex them.' But surely there is evil in this, though the distinction by the Doctor be well put. I said he was a man of good principles but bad practice; for he defends religion, yet he carried off a man's wife. The Doctor said I was right." Boswell omitted the name and the part about carrying off a man's wife when he introduced this material into his *Life of Johnson;* see Hill-Powell, *Boswell*, IV, 274. In the *Life*, Boswell said Johnson had defended Steevens "from the spirit of contradiction as I thought." In the Malahide *Boswell Papers*, VI, 51, Steevens is identified as the man who "would rather have the character of Sodomite than Infidel. I, not; Johnson, yes. 'An infidel would be it if he inclined.' " Steevens was a member of Johnson's Literary Club and of his Essex Head Club.

4. Davies assumed that Steevens had written a review in the *Gent. Mag.* severely critical of Davies' *Dramatic Miscellanies*, which had originally appeared in Dublin in 3 volumes, 1783-84, and which had just been issued in 1785. Nichols informs us, however, in *Lit. Anec.*, VI, 443n, that Steevens had not written the review; it had in fact been written by John Duncombe. "Nor had I myself at that time," said Nichols, "any power over the *Review*."

§ Mr. [Arthur] Murphy also has strongly pourtrayed him in his Address to the *Malevoli*. NICHOLS.

Mr. Steevens was a good classical scholar, and was remarkable for the brilliancy of his wit, and for his satirical talents. The latter he occasionally indulged in some excellent *jeux d'esprit,* which made their appearance in various periodical publications.

"The Frantic Lover,["] mentioned in p. 651,[5] appeared in Almon's "New Foundling Hospital for Wit, 1771," vol. IV. p. 189. And see the St. James's Chronicle, Jan. 11, 1774, for a Song written by him in the character of a Stationer; and two or three other poems, one called "The Insensible Lover," just before or after, in the same Chronicle, which were all written as coming from a very worthy man who carried on that trade under the Exchange.

See also Gent. Mag. vol. LII. page 276, for a portrait, invented by him, of Chedder, a poet older than Rowley; and, for his sketch of Dean Milles's wig, see the same volume, p. 288 [June 1782].

[Editor's note: In a letter from Steevens to Thomas Warton the Younger dated 27 April 1782 (British Museum Add. Mss. 42,561. f. 114), Steevens wrote: "I think I find somewhat of the Revd T. Warton in the last St James's Chronicle. The immense white wig seems to be of his make . . . . I wish you would throw away a few minutes now & then by assisting to keep up a fire in the aforesaid paper. I am going into Essex for about a fortnight and must neglect my Post."]

He died January 22, 1800, at his house at Hampstead, where he had lived several years in the most recluse and unsocial retirement; and was buried in the chapel at Poplar, where, in the North aile, there is a monument to his memory by [John] Flaxman, of which an engraving, in an elegant outline, is given by the Rev. Daniel Lysons in the Supplementary Volume of his "Environs of London."[6]

Underneath is the following inscription; the verses in which are from the pen of Mr. [William] Hayley:

> In the middle aile of this chapel
> lie the remains of George Steevens, esq.
> who, after having cheerfully employed
> a considerable portion of his life and fortune
> in the illustration of Shakspeare,
> expired at Hampstead the 22d day of January 1800,
> in his 64th year.

> Peace to these reliques, once the bright attire
> Of spirits sparkling with no common fire;
> How oft has pleasure in the social hour

---

5. Of *Lit. Anec.,* vol. II. This refers to a reference in the letter signed *Etonensis;* see above p. 41.
6. See n. 1; an engraving of Flaxman's monument is in *Illustr.,* V, facing 427.

Smil'd at his wit's exhilarating power;
And truth attested with delight intense
The serious charms of his colloquial sense;
His talents, varying as the diamond's ray,
Could strike the grave, or fascinate the gay.
His critic labours of unwearied force
Collected light from every distant source;
Want with such true beneficence he cheer'd,
All that his bounty gave, his zeal endear'd;
Learning as vast as mental power could seize,
In sport displaying, and with graceful ease;
Lightly the stage of checquer'd life he trod,
Careless of chance, confiding in his God.
                                            W. H.

A capital portrait of Mr. Steevens was accidentally discovered, a few years since, which he had looked all London through to find, but to no purpose. It was the intention of the Original to serve this inimitable likeness as he had before done a miniature of himself by [Christopher] Myers,[7] and a whole-length, in the character of Barbarossa, which Mr. Steevens played on a private theatre with great eclat. Fortunately the third and last picture of this extraordinary man escaped the ravage of the self-destroyer. It was painted by [Johan] Zoffanii before he went to India, and sold, with many others, to a Mr. Clark, in Princes-street, having been left in the Painter's hands, who got rid of all his portraits when he set out on his Eastern expedition. From this picture an excellent print was engraved for sale, at the expence of Mr. Sylvester Harding, in whose family the plate now remains.[8]

Mr. Steevens was rich in books and prints. He bought largely at Mr. Baker's auction of sir Clement Dormer's library, 1764, collected by General Dormer, where he got the French translation of Xenophon's Works by Pyramus de Candale, Cologn, 1613, bound in Morocco and gilt leaves, worth 40*l.* and upwards, for 12*l.* 12*s.*

He had the Second Folio of Shakspeare, with notes, and alterations of the scenes, by King Charles the First; together with that Monarch's name and motto, *Dum spiro spero,* in his own hand-writing. This curious volume Mr. Steevens bought at Dr. Askew's sale of books; and at his own sale it was purchased for the Royal Library, where it now remains.

Mr. Steevens had also illustrated a copy of his own edition of Shakspeare, 1793, with 1500 portraits of all the persons and places mentioned in the notes and text, of which he could make drawings, or procure engravings.

His set of Hogarth's prints may be considered as the completest that ever was collected;[9] and his commentary on the productions of that inimitable

---

7. Nichols has a brief memoir of Myers in *Lit. Anec.,* IX, 508, where it appears as an addition to II, 658.

8. See the engraving of Steevens by George Dance in *Illustr.,* VII, facing 1.

9. Nichols and Steevens collaborated on the *Biographical Anecdotes of William Hogarth,* issued first in 1781 and reissued in 1782, 1785, and 1810-1817. For this work Nichols wrote the biographical part and Steevens wrote the critiques on the plates of Hogarth.

Painter, which accompanies Mr. Nichols's "Biographical Anecdotes," would alone have stamped a lasting fame on his critical acumen.||

His illustrated copy of Shakspeare he bequeathed to Earl Spencer; his Hogarth (perfect, with the exception of one or two pieces) to that eminent statesman the late Mr. Windham, of Fellbrig in Norfolk; and his corrected copy of Shakspeare to Mr. Reed, with a bequest of 200 guineas.

[Editor's note: At the beginning of his diary for 1800, Reed wrote: "W. Jan. 22. My friend George Steevens Esq. died this day. T.30. I attended his funeral at Poplar Chapel. He was buried close to the reading desk. Besides myself there were Mr. Wheeler, the Clergyman of the place, the Revd. Mr. Grant, the Clergyman of Hampstead, the Revd. Mr. Meen, Mr. Nettleship, and Mr. Bliss, Apothecary. Requiscat [sic] in pace." In May of the same year, Reed wrote: "T. 13th. The Sale of Mr. Steevens's Library commenced. S 24. Mr. Steevens' Sale finished." In June, this entry occurs: "T. 12th. Went to Poplar chapel with Mr. Flaxman the Statuary, Mr. Long, and Mr. Braithwaite to fix on a place for Mr. Steevens's monument." See Jones, *Reed Diaries*, pp. 223-224.]

To his niece, Miss [Elizabeth] Steevens, who was the residuary legatee, he left the bulk of his fortune, including his well-stored Library.[10]

[Editor's note: Elizabeth Steevens was the cousin of George Steevens. A letter from her to her cousin is in the Osborn collection at Yale; and six letters from her to Isaac Reed are in the Folger Shakespeare Library (C.b.2). Two letters from George Steevens to Reed from the same collection as the six from Elizabeth Steevens were written during the same period, as was one other letter, this one from Isaac Reed to George Steevens (Folger C.b.10). Brief excerpts of all these letters in the Folger C.b.2 collection are in the notes for 1799 and 1800 of the *Reed Diaries*, pp. 294-295; but in that place no reference is made, under the date of 25 December 1799, to the letter from Reed to Steevens in the Folger C.b.10 collection. The full text of all ten of these letters, in chronological order, follows.]

1. Elizabeth Steevens to George Steevens (Osborn Collection).

Dear Sir.

Your swift footed messenger has afforded me an opportunity to gratify two senses—my sight by the print which we esteem excellent and the likeness strong—my taste by the hare whose goodness I shall

---

|| See the Preface to the Quarto Edition of Hogarth's Works, published by the Editor of these "Anecdotes," 1810. NICHOLS.

10. See below, n. 24.

prove tomorrow—you have thanks for each from its proper channel—if Turk Mudge deprives me of the picture by no other means than that which you warn me against I doubt not to remain in quiet possession of it—my mother & cousin join me in Respects

Your much obliged Cousin
Elisa Steevens.

Poplar Monday evening
Feb:ʸ yᵉ 19th 1781.

2. Elizabeth Steevens to Isaac Reed (Folger C.b.2).

Miss Steevens, presents her respectful Compliments to Mʳ Reed, & earnestly begs to know if he has seen or heard of Mʳ Steevens since last Wednesday.
Tyndale Place   Tuesday afternoon [3 December 1799].

3. Elizabeth Steevens to Isaac Reed (Folger C.b.2).

Miss Steevens, presents her respectful Compliments to Mʳ Reed, & returns him many thanks for the comfortable intelligence his Note conveyed.
Tyndale Place   Saturday Mornᵍ [7 December 1799].

4. Elizabeth Steevens to Isaac Reed (Folger C.b.2).

Sir /   Tyndale Place   Sunday Noon [15 December 1799].
Your friendly zeal in my unfortunate Cause, demands my most grateful thanks, your favour which I received this morning, has prepared me, to expect the last sad tale of my greatly valued Cousin.—Mʳ Nicholls wrote me on Monday, that he had long, & serious, discourse, with Mʳ Steevens, but could prevail nothing in my behalf, on the contrary he obliged Mʳ N. to promise that I should not be sent to him, this law, I am determined never to infringe, for the consequence might be instantly fatal in his now weak state.—I shall be highly obliged to you for such information as may reach you in the course of this week.—
I remain Sir with respect

Your very humble Servant
Elizabeth Steevens.

[Editor's note: Jones, in the *Reed Diaries,* p. 294, dates the above letter 16 December. The postmark is 12 o'clock noon of 16 December 1799, but the "Sunday Noon" written by Elizabeth Steevens on her letter would be the day before, 15 December.]

5. George Steevens to Isaac Reed (Folger C.b.2).

My Dear Sir   Hampstead Heath Dec^{ber} 20 [1799]

With the utmost Sincerity I thank you for the very Eminent Services you have done me, and am very sorry that such an Accident shou'd have hapen^d on my Account.

When your present Indisposition permits, I shall be obliged to the Banker to send me a Hundred Pound in small Bills and Money.

So far from being better, I think myself worse, and to Correspond with any Person is Painful if not Impossible.

I have heard nothing of the Servant you wrote me about. I would not have this Money sent, till I am sure of my Draughts having reach^d your hand.

God Bless you! I am sorry to say I am not at present able to express one fiftieth part of my obligation to you.

Farewell, Dear Sir, and once more believe me to be your Faithfull Servant   George Steevens

PS The Conveyance of the Money will be time enough a Week hence.

6. Isaac Reed to George Steevens (Folger C.b.10).

My Dear Sir   Staple Inn / Decr 25th [1799]

I am very anxious to hear how your health is but very averse to your taking upon yourself the trouble of writing. May I beg you will direct one of your servants to give me the requested information? If it is only in two words it will be satisfactory—especially if they pronounce you to be better.

My intercourse with Mr Long whose skill I have great confidence in has led me to state your case for his opinion and he has no doubt but yours is a Bath case and that if you remove thither and use the proper remedies a short time you would be perfectly restored. A person he knows twelve years older than you are has lately received a perfect cure. With the strength of your sound constitution every thing is to be hoped for. Pray let me recommend you to take further advice.

I expected to have received your directions about the Money at the Bankers. Though I am unable to go into the City myself, I can get the business done without the least trouble.

As to myself every thing I am told goes on well but that I must be patient.

I am D^{er sr} / your obliged faithful / Servt / Isaac Reed.
                                                              Thursday 26th Dec^r

I wrote the above last night. The account your Servant gives affords me great satisfaction. I still however wish you would have more advice. It will tend to a more speedy recovery.

I waited for your directions about the money. To day or at farthest tomorrow you will receive some.

My arm goes on well I believe. There is no great sacrifice in being confined this weather.

I am D^e S^r / Your faithful hble Servt / Isaac Reed.

7. George Steevens to Isaac Reed (Folger C.b.2).

My Dear Sir   Hampstead Heath Dec. 26 [1799]

Let me beg you to let me know the State of the Accident into which your kindness to me has ledd you. I hope by this time you can make a good Report of it.

I have heard nothing from the Banker yet, and shall be once more more oblig^d to you for your Interposition with him.

I will be at any Expences whatever of the Subject in question, I mean the Money, which I begin to be much in want of.

I cannot boast of any Amendment in my Health.

But as long as I live, must confess the number and quality of my Obligations to you. Once again

Dear Sir, I remain with perfect Gratitude, your most Faithfull and obedient Ser^{vt} George Steevens

8. Elizabeth Steevens to Isaac Reed (Folger C.b.2).

Sir/   [Postmark date 22 January 1800, the date of
          George Steevens' death]

I should certainly have answered your favour of Friday—but that I waited in hopes of better news from Hampstead. Mr Nettleshipp, saw Mr Steevens, on Sunday, he was up & dressed—but I fear in a State trully lamentable both of body & mind. If you have the opportunity of again seeing Mr Boydell—I shall be greatly obliged if you would present my most respectful thanks, to him, for his very polite offer—but of that situation or any other in that neighbourhood I will never avail myself while M^r S lives—for to him, it could be no benefit—& to myself a great breach of decorum.

I sincerely congratulate you Sir on the recovery from your late accident—but I fear your Surgeons will not think this weather fit for a first attempt to go abroad.

I have the Honour to remain Sir your obliged & obd^t Sert.

                 E Steevens.

9. Elizabeth Steevens to Isaac Reed (Folger C.b.2).

Sir /   Hampstead Heath May ye 29th 1800.

Permit me to offer you my most thankful acknowledgment for the great trouble & attention you have given to the disposal of my late

Cousins Library—I hear its success far exceeds your expectation.— Another curcumstance which I heard from Mr Nettleshipp, more highly gratifying, that there is an Inscription written for the Tablet proposed to be put up to the memory of Mr Steevens, I should be very much obliged for a copy of it.

I have the Honour to be Sir your very obedient Sert.

E Steevens.

10. Elizabeth Steevens to Isaac Reed (Folger C.b.2).

Sir /   Hampstead Heath June ye 1st 1800.

I am delighted, in the highest degree—with the Zeal, that has been shewn by the public, in purchasing almost at any rate, the Books that were once the property of my late friend.—it strongly proves the universal high opinion of his Judgment & Taste.

It is utterly impossible that *I* who am under such infinite obligations to Mr Steevens, should wish to limit within narrow bounds, any memorial thought proper to perpetuate his character. I should esteem it a very great favor, if you would undertake to give such orders, for a Tablet, to the Sculptor you have named, as you think will be consistant with the fortune & rank in life which he bore.

I admire exceedingly the Epitaph, & request when you have opportunity, that you will offer my most respectful thanks to Mr Hayley for it.—I am Sir, quite of your opinion, that it in no point exagerates his worth.—I have often heard Mr Steevens speak of Mr Hayley, & he has given me some of his Poetical works.

In answer to your obliging enquiry concerning my health, I can only say, that it is not improved, I have been under medical care many months, but with no sensible benefit.

I have the honor to remain Sir your very Obed^t Servant

E Steevens.

[Editor's note: This concludes the interpolated correspondence. The text of Nichols' life of Steevens is resumed.]

There were only two or three other small legacies in money.

Mr. Steevens was a most valuable member of the literary world, and a bright star in the constellation of editors of that century in which the names of Pope, Theobald, Rowe, Warburton, Garrick, Johnson, Capel, and Malone, are conspicuous. Adorned with a versatility of talents, he was eminent both by his pen and his pencil; with the one there was nothing he could not compose, and with the other nothing he could not imitate so closely, as to leave a doubt which was the original and which the copy. But his chief excellence lay in his critical knowledge of an author's text, and the best pattern of his great abilities is his edition of Shakspeare, in which he has left every competitor far behind him; and even Johnson, with his giant strides, could not walk by his side.

Mr. Steevens had a happy memory, richly stored, was a very pleasant tête-à-tête companion, communicative of his knowledge, but jealous of other men's.

He was a man of the greatest perseverance in every thing he undertook; often constant, but not always consistent, as he would sometimes break off his longest habits without any ostensible reason. He discontinued his daily visits at Mr. White's, the bookseller, after many years regular attendance, for no real cause; and left Mr. Stockdale, whom he took up on quitting Mr. White, all at once in the same eccentric and unaccountable manner. He never took a pinch of snuff after he lost his box in St. Paul's Church-yard, though it had been the custom of his life, and he was much addicted to the practice, and in the habit of making his memorandums by bits of paper in his box.

His Library (which contained a valuable collection of Classics, and was particularly rich in dramatic and other poetry, and in the miscellaneous productions of the English press during the reigns of Queen Elizabeth and James I.[)] was sold by auction (with the exception of the three curious articles before mentioned as bequeathed to Lord Spencer, Mr. Windham, and Mr. Reed,) in the month of May 1800, and produced the sum of 2700*l*.

Six Plays sold for 158*l*. 4*s*.—Fuller's Worthies,[11] full of MS notes by the late Mr. [William] Oldys, Mr. [Ralph] Thoresby, and Mr. Steevens, 43*l*.—Rapin, 51 guineas.—Purchas' Pilgrims, 22 guineas.—Beaver's Military Punishments, 13*l*. 5*s*.—Tracts relative to Mary Toft, 14*l*. 10*s*.—Dodsley's Old Plays, 12 vols. L.P. 12 guineas.—Nichols's Hogarth, with MS notes by Mr. S. 13*l*.—Ireland's Pamphlets, with Imitations of the old Deeds, &c. sold originally from [Samuel] Ireland, jun. to F. G. Waldron, for 18*s*. and purchased of him by Mr. S. for 2*l*. 2*s*. 17 guineas.—Plot of two Plays prior to the time of Shakspeare on two pasteboards, 11*l*.—Paradise of Dainty Devices, 21*l*. 10*s*. 6*d*.—The second folio of Shakspeare, 18 guineas, and a copy of "Dido," [in which Steevens had written, "This copy was given me by Mr. Reed. Such liberality in a Collector of old Plays is at least as rare as the rarest of our dramatic pieces. G.S."], 17 guineas.

[This ends the account from Vol. II of *Literary Anecdotes*. The continuation in Vol. V of *Illustrations* follows.]

---

11. Nichols and Steevens collaborated on *Six Old Plays, On Which Shakspeare Grounded a like Number of His*, 1799; Nichols edited and published an edition of Thomas Fuller's *History of the Worthies of England* in 1811.

Of this unrivaled Commentator on Shakspeare a brief Memoir has been given in the "Literary Anecdotes," vol. II. p. 680; and frequent mention is made of him in other parts of these volumes. Of his true character it is difficult to form a just estimate.

Possessing naturally an extremely robust bodily frame, and endowed with intellectual power of equal strength, there was scarcely any thing within the range of human possibility which he could not have achieved.[12] His retentive memory had in early life been abundantly stored with classical literature; and to the end of his life he could quote from the strains of the Greek and Roman Poets as readily as he could from Shakspeare, Dryden, or Pope. He wrote rapidly; but his hand-writing was perfect, and his style correct. But woe to the hopeless wight who chanced to give him the slightest offence; as nothing could exceed the severity of his satire. Yet, in his general habits, he was polite in the extreme; and his attachment to some of his friends was most exemplary; to Dr. Farmer particularly, to Isaac Reed, and Mr. [Thomas] Tyrwhitt.

Frugal, and even abstemious in his own solitary meal, he was liberal to the distressed; and in his literary communications he was unremittingly attentive and obliging.

He was always an early riser; and, unless prevented by extraordinary bad weather, rarely failed walking to London and back again. His usual custom was to call on Isaac Reed in Staple-Inn at or before seven o'clock in the morning; and then, after a short conference with his intelligent Friend, he paraded to John Nichols,‡ in Red Lion-passage; then hastened to the shop of Mudge and Dutton, the celebrated watch-makers, to regulate his watch; and to his steady and judicious friend Thomas Longman, in search of new publications, and literary news. This was in general his *ultima Thule*.

In returning, he constantly visited his much respected Friend Henry Baldwin; and then generally passed some time in converse with the Paragon of Literature, Dr. Samuel Johnson; rarely omitting to call at the well-stored shop of Ben White; the political storehouse of George Kearsley,* or the literary conversational lounge at Archibald Hamilton's. Thence occasionally at one, two, or more of the following noted Bibliopoles: Cadell, Peter Elms-

---

‡ Who acknowledges much obligation to him for various literary communications, particularly when publishing the Biographical Anecdotes of Hogarth; yet who more than once experienced his unaccountable caprices. NICHOLS. (See n. 13 below.)

* Where he indulged his satirical vein by hints to Peter Pindar. NICHOLS. (*Peter Pindar* was the pseudonym of John Wolcot, who occasionally satirized Nichols. See above pp. xx-xxi.)

12. In *Lit. Anec.* IX, 803 (an addition to VI, 209), Nichols introduced a description of Steevens given by William Cole. "It was at a late period of Mr. Cole's life, that he became acquainted with Mr. Steevens, whom he thus describes: 'I met him at dinner, with Dr. Farmer, &c. at Dr. Lort's chambers in Trinity College, Aug. 9, 1780. He is much of a gentleman, well bred, civil, and obliging; Editor of Shakspeare. He told me, he was admitted in King's College, 1754, the year after I quitted it. He is an Essex Gentleman; in the Militia; well-made, black, and tall."

ly, Tom Davies, Tom Payne, Debrett, or Stockdale. Regularly finishing in Bond-street either with Robson or Faulder, he hastened to an early dinner at his pleasant residence on Hampstead Heath.

His fertile pen was frequently employed in the "Critical Review," sometimes in the "Morning," and occasionally in the "General Evening Post;" but the "St. James's Chronicle," of which he was one of the early Proprietors, was the principal *arena* of his various literary squibs. Of these it may suffice to mention his cruel and unwarrantable attacks on Sir John Hawkins's "History of Music:" which for a long time injured the sale of that valuable publication, to the very serious injury of "honest Tom Payne," one of the worthiest Booksellers that this country could ever boast.

The "Gentleman's Magazine" too was occasionally the deposit of his satirical effusions; in which the benevolent Dean [Jeremiah] Milles was severely handled for his credulity in Rowley's Poems.

[Editor's note: In the British Museum Warton collection are eight letters from Steevens to Thomas Warton the Younger on the subject of the Rowley controversy. The following letter (Add. Mss. 42,561. f. 110) is the earliest and is typical of the others. After its interpolation, Nichols' text is resumed. More material on the Rowley controversy will be found in the life of Tyrwhitt.]

Dear Sir: Hampstead Heath Feb[y] 23[d] 1782

Farmer, who is come up from Cambridge to be prebendized, tells me that the old Library at Bristol, during the life of Chatterton, was open to every body, and that he believes our hero obtained an introduction to it by means of Catcott's brother who wrote on the Deluge—Farmer likewise says, he has the greatest reason to suppose Chatterton had recourse to Fuller's Church History respecting Battle Abbey Roll, &c. I do not apologize for sending you these hints, as I happen to have a frank by me.—[Jacob] Bryant[13] has not made a single convert, even at Cambridge. D[r] [Robert] Glynn is very angry with him for not having introduced more of what the Doctor calls his proofs; and Bryant is heartily sorry he ever meddled with the business.

I am D[r] Sir / Most faithfully Yours /   G Steevens

His malevolent attack on Arthur Murphy is well known; and that he received from that spirited writer a "Rowland for his Oliver," is equally well remembered.

With the accomplished and artful Samuel Ireland, Mr. Steevens was at open variance. The pretended MSS. of Shakspeare were sufficient to call forth the indignation of one who could so well appreciate the matchless style of "the sweet Swan of Avon." But to this were superadded numerous sketches *ascribed* to the inimitable Hogarth, several of which were stifled in their birth by the penetrating glance of Steevens, among whose various endowments the greatest skill as a Draughtsman, and punctuality as a Copyist, were of the most conspicuous. In him therefore, Ireland found a formidable opponent; and every new print produced by Ireland as Hogarth's, was critically analysed by Steevens. But what most especially galled that very ingenious artist [Ireland], was the severe inscription furnished by his [Steevens'] satire, under an uncommonly fine Portrait among the inimitable Caricatures of [James] Gil[l]ray.†

After all, the *chef-d'oeuvre* of Steevens's malevolence was the very ingenious fabrication of the supposed monumental memorial of Hardyknute; a deep-laid trap into which that excellent artist Jacob Schnebbelie was instantly ensnared, as appears by his beautiful *fac-simile* of the supposed relick. But the shaft was levelled at higher game—as it more than glanced at the whole Society of Antiquaries, and more especially their worthy Director, Mr. [Richard] Gough. It is needless to notice that the Hero—

Rode in the Tempest and enjoyed the Storm.[14]

This deeply-planned and well executed imposition was publicly avowed by Mr. Steevens, who gloried in having entrapped the worthy Director of the Society of Antiquaries.[15] The imposition, however, was detected in time to prevent the appearance of a learned comment on the supposed Saxon inscription, which was actually written by Dr. [Samuel] Pegge, who had no opportunity of seeing the stone on which it was placed, but to whom Mr. [Jacob] Schnebbelie's accurate drawing of it had been submitted.

[Here the whole might have ended;[16] but so little was the intended venom felt, that Schnebbelie's neat drawing, well copied by [James] Basire, was given to the publick in the Gentleman's Magazine for 1790, p. 217, with the following brief notice: "The inscription is copied from a piece of stone

---

† Four Forgers born in one prolific age,
  Much critical acumen did engage;
  The first [Lauder] was soon by doughty Douglas scar'd,
  Though Johnson would have screen'd him had he dar'd;
  The next [Macpherson] had all the cunning of a Scot;
  The third [Chatterton] invention, genius, nay, what not?
  Fraud, now exhausted, only could dispense
  To his fourth son their threefold impudence.

14. This line is, of course, a paraphrase of Addison's famous line about the angel in *The Campaign* who "Rides in the whirlwind and directs the storm."

15. With reference to this fabrication of Steevens, see D'Israeli, *Curiosities of Literature*, III, 304, n.

16. This and the following three paragraphs appear as a note to the text in Nichols.

exhibited above a twelve-month at the window of a cutler's shop beyond Blackfriar's-bridge, and pretended to have been found in Kennington-lane. From internal evidence, from the letters being eaten in by aquafortis, and above all, from the studied reserve affected as to all circumstances respecting the discovery, there was from the first every reason to suppose (what is now avowedly the case) that it was a *forgery*. The most guarded manner in which it was communicated to a learned Society could not, however, secure them from the waggery of a newspaper correspondent, who laid the trap, and then ridiculed those whom he supposed to have fallen into it.—Beware of counterfeit copies of the Inscription, for such are abroad!"

This produced from Mr. Steevens, in p. 292, of the same volume, a most intemperate and abusive letter not worth transcribing; and in the Morning Herald, of April 7, 1790, the following brief notice: "Mr. Steevens has been teazing the Antiquarians by a fabricated piece of antiquity. A stone, bearing the name of Hardyknute, and a Saxon inscription, all cut in by aquafortis, was artfully thrown in the way of Director Gough; but it is not to the impeachment of sagacity a thing with the marks of *genuinity* is admitted to be such." The transaction was thus facetiously stated by Mr. Steevens in the General Evening Post of October 25, 1790:

". . . . A well known ingenious gentleman, whose knowledge and researches into antiquity enabled him to carry on such a scheme, had a coarse marble stone inscribed with *Saxon letters,* importing it to be part of the *sarcophagus* of *Hardyknute,* and describing the manner of his death, which was that of dropping suddenly dead, after drinking a gallon flaggon of wine at the marriage of a Danish Lord.

"This stone was carried to a founder's in Southwark, who was in the secret, and a private buz whispered about, that such a curiosity was found. The antiquarians instantly surrounded the house, to purchase it at any price; no, the owner loved antiquity too well himself to part with it. They might take drawings of it with pleasure, but the piece was invaluable. This, however, was some comfort; to work they went, and a very accurate drawing was taken of it, and sent down to one of the greatest antiquarians in Derbyshire for his approbation; he returned for answer, 'That it was a great discovery, and perfectly answerable to the spelling and cut of the Saxon characters in the eleventh century.' The joke having thus travelled far enough, an ample discovery was made, which occasioned a good deal of innocent merriment on all sides; and the original marble was shewn on Saturday night last at Sir Joseph Banks's *Converzatione,* for the *inspection of the curious."*

I shall conclude these desultory anecdotes with one which in a slight degree affects myself.

In a very fair copy of Bale's "Illustrium Majoris Britanniae Scriptorum," &c. printed at Ipswich in 1548, is the following memorandum in the neat hand-writing of Mr. Steevens:

"The opposite vacancy was once filled by a beautiful impression of a very elegant and elaborate wooden cut of John Bale presenting his book to King Edward the Sixth, in all probability the work of Holbein. I have removed it:

> Abi, Successor! et plora.‡
>
> See also the bottom of the page before the Preface, from which I have taken two neat wooden cuts, the one representing John Wicliff, the other John Bale and King Edward differently grouped, and in a smaller size. The second block was printed off on the back of the first   G. STEEVENS."]

[The following excerpt of a letter, dated 14 February 1800, from Henry Meen to Thomas Percy, *Illustr.*, VII, 49-50, tells of Steevens' death.]

The unwelcome news of the death of your old friend George Steevens, Esq. has, I presume, long since reached your Lordship's ear. His decline was rapid. Repeated strokes of the palsy, quick in their succession, and more violent in their return, shook, impaired, and at last destroyed an understanding the most vigorous, and a body apparently strong enough to combat with ordinary diseases for many years to come. But the palsy was, I understand, a family complaint; and he seems to have had a presentiment that such would be his end. He left by will, to Dr. Farmer an 100*l.*, and an 100*l.* to Mr. Reed, with benefit of survivorship. The valuable copy of his own edition of Shakspeare, enriched and ornamented with more than 450 heads, he bequeathed to Lord Spencer. To Mr. Windham, the member, he left his complete and curious collection of Hogarth's works. Not a single book, besides these now mentioned, has he reserved, as a token of regard, for any of his friends: neither has he consigned them to any public body or museum. They are become the property of his relation Miss [Elizabeth] Steevens,[17] to whom he left the bulk of his fortune, and whom he has appointed his sole executrix. His collection of books, though not large, is more curious and valuable than was generally suspected. They will be disposed of, most probably before May, at a public auction, and their destination will be announced, as usual, by the fall of the hammer. This inglorious end, which Mr. Steevens's sagacity must have foreseen, his vanity, one might have thought, would have determined him to prevent. On the 30th of January his remains were interred in the chapel of Poplar. This was his native place, and here his family was buried. He was followed to his grave by the clergymen of Poplar and Hampstead in one coach; and by Mr. [Isaac] Reed. . . and myself in another. . . . Every token of regard which friendship could shew, or merit claim, was liberally manifested on this mournful occasion.

[Editor's note: A letter signed ETONIENSIS, included with Nichols' first account of Steevens in the *Gentleman's Magazine*, was reprinted as a footnote in *Lit. Anec.*, II, 650-653. It is reproduced in full below.]

If, as Dr. Johnson has observed, the chief glory of every people arises from its authors; from those who have extended the boundaries of learning, and advanced the interests of science; it may be considered as an act of

---

‡ That Successor (alas!) was JOHN NICHOLS. NICHOLS.
17. In another letter from Meen to Percy, dated 8 April 1801, we read: "Miss Steevens, who succeeded to our late friend's property, and lived in his house, died there lately, after having enjoyed this considerable accession to her fortune only one year. Her complaint was a dropsy for which she had been tapped. Her age was about 52." A note to the letter adds that she died 26 January 1801.

public duty, as well as of private friendship to attend, with the regret of the patriot as well as the sensibility of the friend, the closing scene of those men, whose superior genius has improved, extended, or adorned, the literature of their country. Mr. George Steevens may be said to have possessed a pre-eminent claim to this character; and, though he is known rather as a commentator than as an original writer, yet, when we consider the works which he illustrated, the learning, sagacity, taste, and general knowledge, which he brought to the task, and the success which crowned his labours, it would not only be an act of injustice, but a most glaring proof of obstinacy and ignorance, to refuse him a place among the first literary characters of the age in which we live. The early editors of Shakspeare looked to little more than verbal accuracy; and even Warburton consigned the sagacity of his mighty mind to the restoring certain readings, and explaining dubious passages. Johnson, who possessed more of the knowledge necessary to an editor of Shakspeare than those who had preceded him in that character, was found wanting; and his first edition of Shakspeare's Plays, which had been expected with much impatience, brought disappointment along with it. In a subsequent edition, he accepted the assistance of Mr. Steevens; and consented that the name of that gentleman should be in editorial conjunction with his own. Mr. Steevens possessed that knowledge which qualified him in a superior degree for the illustration of our divine Poet, and without which the utmost critical acumen would prove abortive. He had, in short, studied the age of Shakspeare, and had employed his persevering industry in becoming acquainted with the writings, manners, and laws, of that period, as well as the provincial peculiarities, whether of language or custom, which prevailed in different parts of the kingdom, but more particularly in those where Shakspeare passed the early years of his life. This store of knowledge he was continually increasing by the acquisition of the rare and obsolete publications of a former age, which he spared no expence to obtain; while his critical sagacity and acute observation were employed incessantly in calling forth the hidden meanings of our great dramatic Bard from their covert, and, consequently, enlarging the display of his beauties. This advantage is evident from his last edition of Shakspeare, which contains so large a portion of new, interesting, and accumulated illustration.

It is to his own indefatigable industry, and the exertions of his printer, that we are indebted for the most perfect edition of our immortal Bard that ever came from the English press. In the preparation of it for the printer, he gave an instance of editorial activity and perseverance which is without example. To this work he devoted solely and exclusively of all other attentions a period of 18 months; and, during that time, he left his house every morning at one o'clock with the Hampstead patrole, and, proceeding without any consideration of the weather or the season, called up the compositor and woke all his devils:[18]

> Him late from Hampstead journeying to his book
> Aurora oft for Cephalus mistook;
> What time he brush'd the dews with hasty pace,
> To meet the printer's dev'let face to face.

18. Compare this with the account in the *Biographie Universelle*, referred to in the headnote: "Pendant dix-huit mois, tous les jours, et quelque temps qu'il fît, Steevens se levait régulièrement à une heure du matin, au signal que lui donnait la patrouille, pour aller à l'imprimerie s'emparer d'une feuille humide, qu'il ne quittait qu'après en avoir fait disparaître toutes les incorrections."

At the chambers of Mr. Reed, where he was allowed to admit himself, with a sheet of the Shakspeare letter-press ready for correction, and found a room prepared to receive him: there was every book which he might wish to consult; and on Mr. Reed's pillow he could apply, on any doubt or sudden suggestion, to a knowledge of English literature perhaps equal to his own. The nocturnal toil greatly accelerated the printing of the work; as, while the printers slept, the editor was awake: and thus, in less than 20 months, he completed his last splendid edition of Shakspeare, in 15 large 8vo volumes; an almost incredible labour, which proved the astonishing energy and persevering powers of his mind. That he contented himself with being a commentator, arose probably from the habits of his life, and his devotion to the name with which his own will descend to the latest posterity. It is probable that many of his *jeux-d'esprit* might be collected; but I am not acquainted with any single production of his pen but a poem of a few stanzas in Dodsley's Annual Register, under the title of "The Frantic Lover;" which is superior to any similar production in the English language. Mr. Steevens was a classical scholar of the first order. He was equally acquainted with the *Belles Lettres* of Europe. He had studied History, antient and modern, but particularly that of his own country. How far his knowledge of the sciences extended, I cannot tell, whether it was merely elementary or profound; but when any application was made to them in conversation, he always spoke of, and drew his comparisons from, them with the easy familiarity of intimate acquaintance. He possessed a strong original genius and an abundant wit; his imagination was of every colour, and his sentiments were enlivened with the most brilliant expressions. With these qualities, I need not add that his colloquial powers surpassed those of other men. In argument he was uncommonly eloquent; and his eloquence was equally logical and animated. His descriptions were so true to nature, his figures were so finely sketched, of such curious selection, and so happily grouped, that I have sometimes considered him as a speaking Hogarth. He would frequently, in his sportive and almost boyish humours, condescend to a degree of ribaldry but little above [John] O'Keeffe: with him, however, it lost all its coarseness, and assumed the air of classical vivacity. He was indeed too apt to catch the ridiculous, both in character and things, and to indulge rather an indiscreet animation wherever he found it. It must be acknowledged, that he scattered his wit and his humour, his gibes and his jeers, too freely around him: and they were not lost for want of gathering. This disposition made him many enemies, and attached an opinion of malignity to his character which it did not in reality possess.[19] But there are many who would rather receive a serious injury than be the object of a joke, or at least of such jokes as were uttered by Steevens, which were remembered by all who heard them, and repeated by all who remembered them. A characteristic *bon mot* is a kind of oral caricature, copies of which are multiplied by every tongue which utters it; and it is much less injurious or mortifying to be the object of a satirical work, which is seldom read but once, and is often thought of no more, than to be hitched into a sarcastic couplet, or condensed into a stinging epithet, which will be equally treasured up by good-humour or ill-nature, for the different purposes of mirth or resentment. Mr. Steevens loved what is called fun; a disposition which has, I fear, a tendency to mischief. It is a hobby horse, which, while it curvets and prances merely to frighten a timorous rider, will sometimes unintentionally throw him in the

---

19. See above, n. 6.

dirt. Some open charges of a malignant disposition have been made against him; and, in the Preface to the works of a distinguished literary character, he is accused, while in the habits of intimate friendship and daily intercourse with that gentleman, of writing calumniating paragraphs in the newspapers against him.[20] But these paragraphs Mr. Steevens did not write; and the late Mr. [William] Seward assured me, that Mr. [John] Bicknell, the author of a poem, called "The Dying Negro," acknowledged to him, that he was the author of them.[21] It is impossible to pass by, even in such a cursory account of Mr. Steevens as this, the very severe note, in the "Pursuits of Literature,"[22] which was written to be applied to him. I am a sanguine admirer of that work; at the same time I have ever regretted, that the partialities and resentments of its author should have occasionally led him into a wantonness of praise and of censure. I think the censure of Mr. Steevens, as well as the praise of Mr. Samuel Lysons[23] (and I am not singular in my opinion), are equally ridiculous, and without foundation.[24] Mr. Steevens possessed a very handsome fortune, which he managed with discretion, and was enabled by it to gratify his wishes, which he did without any regard to expence, in forming his distinguished collections of Classical Learning, Literary Antiquity, and the Arts connected with it. His generosity also was equal to his fortune; and, though he was not seen to give eleemosynary sixpences to sturdy beggars or sweepers of the crossings, few persons distributed Bank-notes with more liberality; and some of his acts of pecuniary kindness might be named, and probably among many others that are not known, which could only proceed from a mind adorned with the noblest sentiments of humanity. He possessed all the grace of exterior accomplishment, acquired in a period when civility and politeness were the characteristicks of a gentleman; a mortifying contrast to the manners of our present young men of fashion, which would have disgraced the servants' halls of their grandfathers. Mr. Steevens received the first part of his education at Kingston upon Thames; he went thence to Eton, and was afterwards a fellow-commoner of King's college, Cambridge. He also accepted a commission in the Essex militia on its first establishment. The latter years of his life he chiefly passed at Hampstead in unvisitable retirement, and seldom mixed with society but in bookseller's shops, or the Shakspeare Gallery, or the morning *converzazione* of sir Joseph Banks. I have heard of his caprices, of the fickleness of his friendships, and the sudden transition of his regards. These, however, I cannot censure; for I know not his motives: nor shall I attempt to analyse his sensibilities. But, whatever may have been his failings, I do not fear contradiction when I assert, that George Steevens, was a man of extraordinary talents, erudition, and attainments; and that he was an honour to the literature of his country. When Death, by one stroke, and in one moment, makes

20. Ibid.
21. Bicknell is mentioned in the *Life of Johnson*. See Hill-Powell, *Boswell*, I, 315.
22. See n. 48 to the life of Richard Farmer.
23. Samuel Lysons, author of *An Account of Roman Antiquities Discovered at Woodchester* (London, 1797), for which he was praised by Mathias in his *Pursuits of Literature*, was the brother of Daniel Lysons, author of the *Environs of London* referred to in n. 1 above.
24. *Etoniensis* later modified his opinion of Lysons' work: "I appeal to any Antiquary, whether the "Roman Antiquities of Woodchester," and the "Environs of London," are not among the first productions of the present day, notwithstanding what the author of the "Pursuits of Literature" has thought proper to observe with regard to the latter in that narrow-minded scale upon which the whole book is conducted." See *Lit. Anec.*, II, 654n.

such a dispersion of knowledge and intellect—when such a man is carried to his grave—the mind can feel but one emotion: we consider the vanity of every thing beneath the sun—we perceive what shadows we are—and what shadows we pursue. ETONIENSIS.

[In a note concerning Steevens' library, Nichols quotes from T. F. Dibdin's *Bibliomania,* and after a time the subject becomes Steevens rather than his books. Nichols thus introduces Dibdin's transition from the library to the man: "After filling nearly twelve pages with the prices of the *rarer articles,* Mr. Dibdin proceeds. . . ." The text comes from *Lit. Anec.,* II, 659-662n.]

It remains to say a few words of the celebrated Collector of this very curious library. The wit, taste, and classical acquirements of George Steevens, are every where recorded and acknowledged. As an editor of his beloved Shakspeare, he stands unrivalled; for he combined, with much recondite learning and indefatigable research, a polish of style, and vigour of expression, which are rarely found united in the same person. . . .

We will now say somewhat of the man himself. Mr Steevens lived in a retired and eligibly situated house, just on the rise of Hampstead Heath. It was paled in, and had, immediately before it, a verdant lawn skirted with a variety of picturesque trees. Formerly, this house had been a tavern, which was known by the name of *The Upper Flask;* and which my fair readers (if a single female can have the courage to peruse these bibliomaniacal pages) will recollect to have been the same to which Richardson sends Clarissa in one of her escapes from Lovelace. Here Steevens lived embosomed in books, shrubs, and trees: being either too coy, or too unsociable, to mingle with his neighbours. His habits were indeed peculiar; not much to be envied or imitated; as they sometimes betrayed the flights of a madman, and sometimes the asperities of a cynic. His attachments were warm, but fickle both in choice and duration. He would frequently part from one, with whom he had lived on terms of close intimacy, without any assignable cause; and his enmities, once fixed, were immovable. There was, indeed, a kind of venom in his antipathies; nor would he suffer his ears to be assailed, or his heart to relent, in favour of those against whom he entertained animosities, however capricious and unfounded. In *one* pursuit only was he consistent: *one* object only did he woo with an inflexible attachment; and that object was *Dame Drama.* I have sat behind him, within a few years of his death, and watched his sedulous attention to the performances of strolling players, who used to hire a public room in Hampstead; and towards whom his gallantry was something more substantial than mere admiration and applause: for he would make liberal presents of gloves, shoes, and stockings—especially to the female part of the company. His attention, and even delight, during some of the most wretched exhibitions of the dramatic art, was truly surprising; but he was then drooping under the pressure of age, and what passed before him might serve to remind him of former days, when his discernment was quick, and his judgment matured. . . .

It is now time to bid farewell to the subject of this tremendous note: and most sincerely do I wish I could "draw the curtain" upon it, and say "good night" with as much cheerfulness and satisfaction as [Francis] Atterbury did upon the close of his professional labours.—But the latter moments of Steevens were moments of mental anguish. He grew not only irritable, but outrageous; and, in full possession of his faculties, he raved in a manner which could have been expected only from a creature bred up without notions of morality or religion. Neither complacency nor "joyful hope" soothed his bed of death. His language was, too frequently, the language of imprecation; and his wishes and apprehensions such, as no rational Christian can think upon without agony of heart. Although I am not disposed to admit the whole of the testimony of the good woman who watched by his bed-side, and paid him, when dead, the last melancholy attentions of her office—although my prejudices (as they may be called) will not allow me to believe that the windows shook, and that strange noises and deep groans were heard at midnight in his room—yet no creature of common sense (and this woman possessed the quality in an eminent degree) could mistake oaths for prayers, or boisterous treatment for calm and gentle usage. If it be said—why

> draw his frailties from their drear abode?[25]

the answer is obvious, and, I should hope, irrefragable. A duty, and a sacred one too, is due To The Living. Past examples operate upon future ones: and posterity ought to know, in the instance of this accomplished scholar and literary antiquary, that neither the sharpest wit, nor the most delicate intellectual refinement, can, alone, afford a man "Peace at the Last." The vessel of human existence must be secured by other anchors than these, when the storm of Death approaches.

25. The word *drear* rather than *dread* is used by both Dibdin and Nichols, perhaps on purpose, in this line from "The Epitaph" at the end of Gray's *Elegy*.

William Cole

[The source of Nichols' life of William Cole is *Lit. Anec.*, I, 657-701, with an addition to this account in VIII, 382-388. Besides the memoir proper, Nichols makes references to Cole innumerable times throughout *Anecdotes* and *Illustrations,* such references in the former alone amounting to over five columns in the indexes. In *Illustr.*, VIII, 572-587, are excerpts from Cole's great work, left in manuscript to the British Museum, the "Athenae Cantabrigienses." These excerpts, numerous references, and many letters of Cole are not reproduced in the following account because a great deal of his correspondence was directed to the correcting and improving of the antiquarian works of others, often consisting entirely of transcripts of old documents or of inscriptions from monuments. Only such correspondence as illustrates his own life has been included.

The British Museum is the richest manuscript source of Cole materials: notes, diaries, and papers of various kinds, including those that at one time he contemplated giving to John Nichols, who describes the collection as "100 volumes in folio" in the life that follows. Cole's letters have a wider distribution. The Bodleian Library possesses (MS. Top. Gen. c. 9) a collection of letters from Cole to Browne Willis, Zachary Grey, A. C. Ducarel, Michael Lort, Farmer, Gough, and Nichols; and additional correspondence of Cole can be found in many other places. He had, for example, an extensive correspondence with Horace Walpole. Fifty-five pages of his correspondence with James Granger appear in a book printed by Nichols, Granger's *Letters* (London, 1805), pp. 320-375. In the Beinecke Library at Yale is a ten-page work in Cole's hand: "Index to Mr. Gray's Life—MS written by Wm Cole in a fit of the Gout. 16 May 1775." Several books written by others but with manuscript notes by Cole are in the British Museum, referred to under his name in the catalogue of printed books. An *Index to the Contents of the Cole Manuscripts in the British Museum* by George J. Gray was published in 1912. References to other sources for his life and correspondence are at the end of the account of Cole by Thompson Cooper in the DNB, where Nichols is listed as a source immediately following Cole's own manuscripts.

Cooper was, as a matter of fact, greatly indebted to Nichols and to Alexander Chalmers, whose life of Cole in the *General Biographical Dictionary* (1812-1817) was partially reproduced by Nichols in his addition to the original memoir. Nichols and Chalmers were, actually, good friends and assisted each other with many works. Chalmers made use of Nichols' original account of Cole, and Nichols in turn made use of Chalmers' work. Chalmers, eventually, was to become Nichols' own biographer, *Gent. Mag.*, 96:489-504 (December 1826) and *Illustr.*, VIII, v-xxv. The importance of Nichols as a biographer is again attested by the following comparison of the text of Nichols and Chalmers with that of Cooper.

Nichols

On examination of dates, and Pedigrees of the *Coles*, . . . it appears that their ancestors, who were yeomen of respectability, lived for several generations in that part of Cambridgeshire which borders on Essex.

William Cole, the father of our Antiquary, had a little farm at Baberham in Cambridgeshire; and had four wives: . . .

3. Catharine, daughter of Theophilus Tuer, of Cambridge, merchant, widow of Charles Apthorp . . . .

Cooper

COLE, WILLIAM (1714-1782), The Cambridge antiquary, was descended from a family of respectable yeomen, who lived for several generations in that part of Cambridgeshire which borders on Essex. The antiquary's father, William Cole of Baberham, Cambridgeshire, married four times, his third wife, the mother of the antiquary, being Elizabeth, daughter of Theophilus Tuer, merchant, of Cambridge, and widow of Charles Apthorp.

Chalmers

but in 1735, on the death of his father, from whom he inherited a handsome estate, he entered himself a fellow-commoner of Clare Hall, and next year removed to King's College, where he had a younger brother, then a Fellow. . . . In April 1736 he travelled for a short time in French Flanders with his half-brother, the late Dr. Stephen Apthorp. In 1737, in consequence of bad health, he went to Lisbon, where he remained six months, and returned to College in May 1738. The following year he was put into the commission of the peace for the county of Cambridge, in which capacity he acted for many years.

Cooper

but in 1735, on the death of his father, from whom he inherited a handsome estate, he entered himself as a fellow-commoner of Clare Hall, and the next year migrated to King's College, where he had a younger brother, then a fellow. . . . In April 1736 he travelled for a short time in French Flanders with his half-brother, Dr. Stephen Apthorp, . . . In 1737, in consequence of bad health, he went to Lisbon for six months, returning to college in May 1738. The following year he was put into the commission of the peace for Cambridgeshire, in which capacity he acted for many years.

This kind of comparison could be continued at length, but perhaps that given is sufficient to demonstrate that quite often Nichols' (or Chalmers') own phraseology will be read by the modern student who turns to a life of one of Nichols' subjects.]

On examination of dates, and of the Pedigrees of the *Coles,* in the Manuscript Volumes in the British Museum,* it appears that their ancestors, who were yeomen of respectability, lived for several generations in that part of Cambridgeshire which borders on Essex. [All his father's family were seated about Shepereth, and the borders of Essex adjoining to Cambridgeshire.—A William Cole lived at Shepereth 18 Richard II.—The Earliest ancestor from whom he could trace descent in a direct line was John Cole, of Ashden in Essex, who occurs in a will in the Ely Register, 1521.[1]]

William Cole, the father of our Antiquary, had a little farm at Baberham† in Cambridgeshire; and had four wives:

1. Anne, daughter of . . . . . Mole, of Elmdon, in Essex, who died 1697.

2. Elizabeth, daughter of . . . . Babbes, of Ongar, in Essex, widow of Mr. Meyer, who died 1712.

3. Catharine, daughter of Theophilus Tuer,‡ of Cambridge, merchant, widow of Charles Apthorp, who died April 25, 1725.

4. Margaret, daughter of Berkeley Green, of Cotteridge in Worcestershire.

Our Antiquary, who was a son of the third wife, was born at Little Abbindon, a village adjoining to Baberham, Aug. 3, 1714. His mother died April 25, 1725; and his step-mother, whilst he was a boy at Eton school, in 1729, or 1730. His father died Jan. 14, 1735.

Mr. Cole received the early part of his education under the Rev. Mr. Butts at Saffron Walden. He learned French of a Mons. Henebert, who was then teacher of the modern languages at Cambridge, whom he describes as an ingenious man, and above the common run of that sort of people.

After going to these several schools, a Dame's school at Cambridge, Linton, Saffron Walden, and Eton, where he was five years on the foundation, he was entered a Pensioner of Clare Hall (where he was a Fellow in 1735); and after three or four years' stay removed to King's, where he had a younger brother§ then a Fellow, and was accommodated with better apartments, which was the occasion of his removal. He took the degree of B.A. in 1736; proceeded M.A. in 1740; and was ordained in the Collegiate Church of Westminster, by Dr. Wilcocks, Bishop of Rochester, Dec. 25, 1744, by

---

* Cole's MSS. vol. XI. pp. 164. NICHOLS.

† "The first arms I ever tricked out from painted glass in windows of churches were in Baberham church in Cambridgeshire, where my father lived, and in Moulton church in Lincolnshire; so early a taste had I for Antiquities, even when at school at Eton. I have the notes still by me, this 24 July, 1772." Cole's MSS. vol. XLIII. 339. NICHOLS.

‡ Whose mother Catharine Tuer was the third and youngest daughter of Owen Vaughan of Llwydiart; which Owen Vaughan married Margaret, second sister of Mr. George Herbert the Poet, fifth son of Richard Herbert, of Montgomery, by Magdalen his wife, daughter of Sir Richard Newport by Margaret his wife, daughter and sole heir of Sir Thomas Bromley, of the Privy Council to Henry VIII. NICHOLS.

§ "Cole, John, *mon cher frere,* buried in Moulton church," MSS. vol. XXII. 43. 339, 373, 374. NICHOLS.

1. The three sentences beginning "All his father's family" are in a note in *Lit. Anec*

letters dismissory from Dr. Gooch, Bishop of Norwich, on the Curacy of Wethersfield in Suffolk.

In 1749, he was resident at Haddenham in the Isle of Ely; and in that year was collated by Bishop Sherlock to the Rectory of Hornsey in Middlesex (at his institution Father Courayer was present); but resigned it Jan. 9, 1751, in favour of Mr. Territ, who had just been appointed by Bishop Sherlock to instruct the young Prince of Anamaboe on the Coast of Guinea, and then in England, in the principles of the Christian Religion.

In 1753, he was presented by his early Friend and Patron Browne Willis, esq. to the Rectory of Bletchley in Buckinghamshire; which he resigned, March 20, 1768, in favour of his Patron's Grandson.

In 1755 he was confined by a broken leg.[2]

Mr. Cole was an early and intimate acquaintance of the Honourable Horace Walpole, afterwards Earl of Orford. They went to France together in 1765; Mr. Walpole to enjoy the world of gaiety, but Cole to seek a residence in a cheap part of the country, to which he might retire altogether. The *Droit d'Aubaine* had not at that time been revoked;

On this subject he received the following letter from Mr. Walpole, dated *March 9, 1765*:

You know I am not cordially disposed to your French journey, which is now more serious, as it is to be much more lasting. However, though I may suffer by your absence, I would not dissuade what may suit your inclination and circumstances. One thing, however, has struck me, which I must mention, though it would depend on a circumstance that would give me the most concern. It was suggested to me by that great fondness I have for your MSS. for your kindness about which I feel the utmost gratitude. You would not, I think, leave them behind you; and are you aware of the danger they would run, if you settled entirely in France? Do you know that the King of France is heir to all strangers who die in his dominions, by what they call the *Droit d'Aubaine?* Sometimes, by great interest and favour, persons have obtained a remission of this right in their life-time; and yet even that has not secured their effects from being embezzled. Old Lady Sandwich had obtained this remission; and yet, though she left every thing to the present Lord her grandson, a man for whose rank one should have thought they would have had regard, the King's officers forced themselves into the house, after her death, and plundered. You see, if you go, I shall expect to have your MSS. deposited with me. Seriously, you must leave them in safe custody behind you.[3]

---

2. In *Lit. Anec.*, IX, 391, is a letter from Cole to Joseph Bentham in which he refers to his broken leg: "It may be proper to tell you, that you may not be surprized when you see me, that although I am very well, and my leg is well joined together, yet it is very crooked: but the fault is my own; for the Surgeon would have remedied it, had I been consenting, after it had been set a fortnight; but I considered that it was very little significant, whether a person who generally wears pettycoats, and is no dancer at assemblies, had a strait or crooked leg, so it served the purpose of conveying him from place to place; so as it would have put me to some pain, to which I was always a great enemy, I rather chose to have it as it is."

3. This excerpt from Walpole's letter and the statement that introduces it are in a note in *Lit. Anec.*

but Mr. Cole thought it no obstacle to his fixing on Normandy for his retreat. The visit, however, impressed his mind so strongly (even at that time) with the certainty of an impending Revolution, that he preferred remaining in England.

He wrote the Account of Pythagoras's School at Cambridge in "Grose's Antiquities;" and was a great contributor to the Rev. James Bentham's "History of Ely, 1771," writing the Lives of the Bishops and Deans, and the Description of the Ely Tablet. [Among Mr. Cole's alphabetical volumes, B. part 1. f. 113. b. is a long account of Mr. Bentham, and the share Mr. Cole had in the History of Ely. "The History, proposed to be sold to the subscribers for 18s. was increased (though with about 50 copper-plates) only to a guinea; got up, even Aug. 1, 1778, to three guineas. The fund Mr. Bentham set out with, were his Father's Collections, which were very large. He was assisted in the overlooking and correction by his brother Dr. Bentham; and it was in a great measure managed by Mr. Cole"[4]]

In 1767, he went into a hired house at Waterbeche, and continued there two years, while a house was fitting for him at Milton, a small village, on the Ely road near Cambridge, where he passed the remainder of his days.

In 1772, Bishop Keene, unasked, sent Mr. Cole an offer of the Vicarage of Maddingley, about seven miles from Milton; which, for reasons of convenience, he civilly declined; and in 1773 had the first regular fit of the gout. He was instituted by Dr. John Green, the Bishop of Lincoln, to the Vicarage of Burnham, in Buckinghamshire, on the presentation of Eton College, June 10, 1774, void by the cession of his uterine brother, Stephen Apthorp, D.D.

His industry as a Topographical Collector was very great. He had a curious Library of printed books, and was very liberal with his communications.

To Dr. Ducarel, in 1754, he communicated a complete list of the Chancellors of Ely; and afterwards several useful hints respecting his Tour in Normandy.

To Mr. Gough's "Anecdotes of British Topography," he contributed in 1772 some valuable Remarks; as he afterwards did in 1774, respecting the "Sepulchral Monuments;" and when the "Memoirs of the Gentlemen's Society at Spalding" were printing, in 1780, he supplied several anecdotes of the early members.||

In 1779, in compliance with a public request, he communicated to Mr. Urban an account of St. Nicholas;‡ and gave, in the same volume of the Gentleman's Magazine, some Remarks on Sir John Hawkins's "History of Music."*

In 1781, I was for the first time favoured with his correspondence;

|| These were communicated through the medium of Mr. [Richard] Gough. . . . NICHOLS.
‡ Gent. Mag. vol. XLIX. pp. 119. 131. 157. 208. NICHOLS.
* Ibid. p. 219. NICHOLS.
4. The four sentences beginning "Among Mr. Cole's alphabetical volumes" appear as a note to the text in Lit. Anec.

SIR,   *Milton, near Cambridge, April* 4, 1781.
    Though unknown to you, I take the liberty to address a letter to you as the Printer of the Gentleman's Magazine....[5]

and was afterwards indebted to him for several biographical hints and corrections relative to four volumes of "A Select Collection of Miscellaneous Poems," then lately published; all which were adopted in the four succeeding Volumes.

SIR,   *Saturday, April* 14, 1781, *Milton.*
    Since I wrote my first Letter to you, near a fortnight ago, your *Select Collection of Poems* was put into my hands by the *Master of Emanuel* [Richard Farmer], the bearer of this: and I am sorry I did not meet with the Collection sooner, when I might, perhaps, have been more diffuse than I can be at present, running over the work in an hasty manner, and putting down a few hasty observations, which you, as a correct man, no doubt, will be glad to have. I am at present so ill, that I can barely hold my pen, and therefore you will excuse my mistakes also.[6]

A similar good office he performed towards improving the "Anecdotes of Hogarth."

DEAR SIR,   *Milton, near Cambridge, Sunday, May* 6,1781.
    .... I can send you no farther particulars about Mr. Hogarth than what you know. I have a sister, who was much acquainted with his wife, and was often at Chiswick with them. You are aware, no doubt, of his life in the last volume of the Anecdotes on Painting in England. The picture you mention I have never seen since it was finished and sent home; Chancellor Hoadly and Mr. Harry Taylor were frequently at Rivenhall, when I was used to be there in my early age; but I do not remember their pictures being in the Family Conversation piece: they might be added afterwards. I sat for my picture, with Mr. Western, his mother, a daughter of Sir Anthony Shirley, with Archdeacon Charles Plumptre, to Mr. Hogarth at his house, in a square at the West end of the town, about the year 1736: at which time Mr. Western sat to him for a full length picture, for me, and which I have now in my gallery, and is one of the most resembling portraits I ever met with: he is drawn sitting in his Fellow Commoner's habit, and square cap with a gold tassell, in his chamber at Clare Hall, over the arch, towards the river; and Mr. Hogarth, as the chimney could not be expressed, has drawn a cat sitting near it, to express the situation, agreeably to his humour. But I am tired, and hope you will excuse, Dear Sir, the scrawl of Yours, &c. WM. COLE.
    P.S. Mr. Taylor was then curate of Rivenhall, and a great favourite in the family.[7]

In the latter end of 1781, and the beginning of 1782, I had frequent

---

    5. This letter, in which Cole introduces himself to Nichols, is given in full as a note in *Lit. Anec.*
    6. This letter appears as part of a note in *Lit. Anec.* When men, so ill that they can barely hold their pens, will send Nichols corrections and additions to his works, Nichols' completeness and accuracy can be better understood.
    7. The letter of which this is a part appears in a note in *Lit. Anec.*

occasion of consulting Mr. Cole, whilst I was compiling the "History of Hinckley;" and the enquiries were in general both expeditiously and very satisfactorily answered.[8]

In the Autumn of 1782, Mr. Cole would have presented to me his friend Mr. Browne Willis's "History of the Hundreds of Newport and Cotslow in Buckinghamshire;" which Mr. Cole had transcribed and methodized in ten folio volumes, from the originals in four volumes, which Mr. Willis had delivered to him a few weeks before his death, with an earnest request that he would prepare them for publication. Unluckily I had not at the time sufficient leisure to pay him a visit at Milton. [From Mr. Cole I afterwards received the following Letter:]

DEAR SIR, *Milton, Tuesday, Sept.* 24, 1782.
Your two last Books of Mr. Bowyer, and the proof-sheets of Hinckley, greatly please me: Dr. Farmer sent me the last.[9] Your anecdotes in both will render your works valuable to every Antiquary; and to none more than to, Dear Sir, your most obedient servant, W. COLE.[10]

Mr. Cole did not long survive the date of this kind offer [of the Buckinghamshire papers]. His death is thus noticed by Mr. [Richard] Gough:

At Milton, a small village on the Ely road, was the retirement of the eminent Antiquary, the Rev. Mr. William Cole, vicar of Burnham, in the county of Bucks, and the intimate friend of Browne Willis. Here, Dec. 16, 1782, in his 68th year, he closed a life spent in learned research into the history and antiquities of this County in particular, which nothing but his declining state of health prevented this work from sharing the benefit of. He left to the British Museum, to be locked up for twenty years, his valuable collection in 100 volumes in folio, fairly written in his own hand, which was not unlike that of Mr. Thomas Baker, to whose memory he has bequeathed a monument in St. John's College Chapel. Mr. Cole was buried under the belfry of St. Clement's church in Cambridge.†

My own Epitaph, in due time, when it pleases God, after taking me out of this world, to make it proper for me.

Underneath
lyeth the body of
W.C. A.M. and F.A.S.
the son of W.C. of Baberham, in the County
of Cambridge, gent.
lord of the manor of Halls, in this parish,
by Catherine his wife,

---

† Camden's Britannia, Cambridgeshire, vol. II. p. 143. NICHOLS. (This paragraph and the following, including the epitaph, are quoted from Gough.)

8. Nichols published his *History and Antiquities of Hinckley* in 1782.

9. This sentence seems misleading in its construction. There were not two books of Mr. Bowyer, only one. The *two* refers to the *Bowyer* and the *Hinckley*. The preface to the *Biographical and Literary Anecdotes of William Bowyer* is dated 11 June 1782. Nichols and his friends sometimes refer to *Literary Anecdotes* as the "second edition" of *Bowyer*.

10. This letter and the sentence which introduces it are a note in *Lit. Anec.*

daughter of Theophilus Tuer,
of Cambridge, Merchant.
He was educated in the College of Eton,
and from thence removed to Clare Hall
in the University of Cambridge.
In the former part of his life, and while he
resided in the University
(which he did for 20 years)
he was in the Commission of the Peace for the
County of Cambridge,
and acted for many years in that capacity;
and one of his Majesty's Deputy-lieutenants
for the said County;
and was afterwards Justice of the Peace for the
Borough of Cambridge.
On his going into holy orders, he was
first collated by Thomas Sherlock, Bp. of London,
to the Rectory of Hornsey in Middlesex;
then by that industrious Antiquary, Browne Willis,
Esq. to the Rectory of Blecheley in Buckinghamshire;
and lastly presented by Eton College to the
Vicarage of Burnham near Windsor.
He departed this life
. . . . in the . . . . . . year of his age.
Memento, homo, quia pulvis es,
et in pulverem reverteris.
Miserere mei, Deus, secundùm multitudinem
misericordiarum tuarum.
O Christe, Soter & Judex,
mihi Gulielmo Cole, peccatorum maximo
misericors & propitius esto.

[It is singular that, in an epitaph prepared *by* himself *on* himself, he should make no mention of his migration to, and residence at, King's College. An instance scarcely ever occurs of a person's changing his College, except for a Fellowship or Mastership; neither of which was his lot at King's. He probably resided there as a Fellow Commoner Master. On the arms engraved for his Book Plate he is styled of King's College. I suppose he liked living well with his old Eton Friends, the Fellows of that Society.[11]]

A half sheet print of Mr. Cole, from Mr. Kerrich's drawing, was engraved by Facius a short time since.—A portrait of him was also published in Mr. Malcolm's Collection of "Letters to Mr. Granger, 1806;"[12] and, by the favour of Mr. [William] Richardson, is here inserted.

Mr. Cole had a great predilection for *Alma Mater Cantabrigiensis*. In one of his alphabetical volumes he says, Oxford is *ill served with water, and unwholesomely seated*. He was a Churchman of the highest class; and considered our Ecclesiastical Establishment to be under more obligation to

---

11. This paragraph is a note in *Lit. Anec.*
12. James Granger's *Letters*, ed. J. P. Malcolm, were printed by Nichols. The engraving of Cole referred to here appears in *Lit. Anec.*, I, facing p. 657.

Archbishop Laud than to any Prelate that had filled the Metropolitan Chair since St. Austin.‡

He numbered among his friends and correspondents some of the most learned and ingenious men of his time. Among the principal of these were, the Honourable Horace Walpole; the Poet Gray; the Rev. Dr. Michael Lort;[13] George Steevens, esq. the eminent Commentator on Shakspeare;[14] the Rev. Dr. Farmer, the learned and worthy Master of Emanuel; Jacob Bryant, esq. the eminent Mythologist; Dr. William Bennet, the present excellent and benevolent Bishop of Cloyne, the late profoundly learned Antiquary Richard Gough, esq.,[15] and very many others of the highest eminence.

Of the Manuscript Collections in his own hand, which he ordered to be locked up for twenty years, a satisfactory account is given in the Synopsis of the British Museum. The largest and most valuable portion is taken up by his Collections for Cambridgeshire, and his "Athenae Cantabrigienses." Many of the volumes exhibit striking traits of Mr. Cole's own character; and a man of sufficient leisure might pick out from them abundance of curious matter. His Diary, however, is truly laughable. It is worse than honest Humphrey Wanley's;[16] *e.g.*

Jan. 25, 1766. Foggy, My beautiful parrot died at ten at night, without knowing the cause of his illness, he being very well last night.

Feb. 1. Saturday. Fine day and cold, Will Wood junior carried three or four loads of dung into the Clay-pit close. Baptized William the son of William Grace, blacksmith, who I married about six months before.

March 3, Monday. I baptized Sarah, the bastard daughter of the Widow Smallwood of Eton, aged near 50, whose husband died above a year ago.

6, Thursday. Very fine weather. My man was blooded. I sent a loin of pork and a spare-rib to Mr. Cartwright in London.[17]

8, Saturday. Very fine weather. Mr. Cartwright brought me a quarter of house lamb from London.

9, Sunday. Very fine time. At matins and vespers. Mr. Armsteed the apothecary of Fenny Stratford (who came to see my man Tom, who was very ill with a distemper called the shingles) dined with me, as did John Perrot and William Travel. I catechized the children as usual, buried the son of Francis Perrot; and drank coffee with Mrs. Willis, who was very ill of an asthma.

‡ MSS. vol. I. p. 536. NICHOLS.
13. Two letters of Cole to Lort are reproduced by Nichols in a note.
14. See note 12 to the life of Steevens.
15. In an addition concerning Gough in *Lit. Anec.*, I, 712, Nichols wrote: "Mr. George Steevens, who delighted in mischievous wit, having, by an early purchase, after the death of Mr. Cole, obtained his copy of the 'Anecdotes of British Topography,' in which were two or three severe remarks on the learned Author; transcribed them in a hand resembling that of Mr. Cole, and transmitted them to Enfield [Gough's residence], with the following direction: 'To Richard Gough, esq. F.S.A. William Cole doth, in all good humour, dedicate, present, and consecrate, these his labours, to live with the Eternity of his Fame.' "
16. Librarian of the Harleian collection, excerpts from whose diary Nichols also reproduces in *Lit. Anec.*, I, 85-105.
17. The text of the diary here is as Nichols has it. See *The Blecheley Diary of the Rev. William Cole, M.A. F.S.A., 1765-67*, ed. Francis Griffin Stokes (London, 1931).

27, Thursday. I sent my two French wigs to my London barber to alter them, they being made so miserably I could not wear them.

May 3, Cold and rainy. My knee, where it was strained, uneasy. I had it pumped upon at the pump in the yard.

June 17, Tuesday. Windy, cold and rainy. I went to our new Archdeacon's Visitation at Newport Pagnel. I took young H. Travel with me on my dun horse, as his father had formerly desired me, in order that he might hear the organ at Newport, he being a great Psalm-singer. Mr. Tanquerary, rector of Bow-Brick-hill, preached the sermon before the Archdeacon, who gave a Charge. The most numerous appearance of Clergy that I remember: Forty-four dined with the Archdeacon, and what is extraordinary not one smoked tobacco. My new coach-horse very *ungain*.

Aug. 16, Saturday. Cool day. Tom reaped for Joe Holdom. I cudgelled Jem for staying so long on an errand at Newton Longueville.

In one of Horace Walpole's letters to him, May 4, 1781, he says, "My poor dear Madame du Deffand's little dog is arrived. She made me promise to take care of it, the last time I saw her, should I survive her. That I will most religiously, and make it as happy as it is possible."

Mr. Cole's answer is amusing.

May 7, 1781. I congratulate the little Parisian dog that he has fallen into the hands of so humane a master. I have a little diminutive dog, *Busy,* full as great a favourite, and *never out of my lap:* I have already, in case of an accident, ensured it a refuge from starvation and ill-usage. It is the least we can do, for poor harmless, shiftless, pampered animals, that have amused us, and we have spoilt.—

How could he ever have got through the transcript of a Bishop's Register, or a Chartulary, with Busy in his lap!

So minute was Mr. Cole in penning almost every action of his life, that in one of his volumes he has preserved the very weight of his body at different aeras of his life.

1759. Weighing myself at my Lord Montfort's, as I often used to do, with others, there being scales for that purpose in the collonade under the house, I then weighed only 13 stone 9 pounds: but on Oct. 28, 1763, I had gained greatly, weighing now 14 stone 4 pounds. Nov. 12, 1749, 11 stone 8 pounds. Nov. 14, 1758, 13 stone 3 pounds. Aug. 23, 1768, 14 stone 2 pounds. Christmass 1769, I had lost 4 pounds, weighing 13 stone 12 pounds. Aug. 1, 1774, 14 stone 8 pounds. Jan. 25, 1775, 15 stone.

In the XXXIXth volume of Mr. Cole's MSS. toward the end, are some additional particulars in regard to Rowley and Chatterton§ as related by Dr. Fry;|| and in the Gentleman's Magazine for 1784,‡ are two specimens of his Remarks on Books—the one panegyrical, the other satirical. In the

---

§ See MS Athenae Cantabrigienses, vol. E. p. 138. NICHOLS.
|| Fellow of St. John's College, Oxford, and an assistant in the Bodleian Library. NICHOLS.
‡ Vol. LIV. p. 333. NICHOLS.

Magazine for 1806, p. 693, is a long extract from a remarkable Letter of his to Dr. Lort.*

My intelligent young friend Mr. Philip Bliss, of St. John's College, Oxford, who has undertaken to re-publish Wood's "Athenae Oxonienses," possesses a copy of that useful work, the margins of which are filled with the notes of Mr. Cole,† superadded to those of Mr. Thomas Baker.‡

I shall close this account of a very worthy though eccentric writer, by four other specimens of his epistolary correspondence; the first of which is to his very early Friend and Patron Browne Willis, esq; the second to Dr. Zachary Grey; the third to Dr. Farmer, when he was about to publish the "History of Leicester;"[18] the last to Mr. William Herbert, re-publisher of Ame's "Typographical Antiquities."[19]

[An addition to the above account appears in "Additions to the first Volume," *Lit. Anec.*, VIII, 382-388. The greater part of this is quoted by Nichols from Alexander Chalmers' *Biographical Dictionary* and from D'Israeli's *Calamities of Authors*.]

Mr. Cole, speaking of Baberham, says, "I call this my native parish, though I was born in Little Abington just by, as my father and mother constantly and uniformly went to church to Baberham, he holding the great farm there. It is remarkable for its honey, which to this day I always have from thence. W.C." The Father of this eminent Benefactor to the History and Antiquities of England was a gentleman, it appears, of some considerable landed property. . . .

Whilst the present sheet was preparing for the press, I had the opportunity of perusing the well-digested Memoirs of Mr. Cole in the Tenth Volume of the "Biographical Dictionary," gathered by my accurate friend Mr.

---

* The letter is chiefly on the subject of Rowley's Poems. . . . NICHOLS.

† Transcribed by Mr. Cole from a copy in the Public Library at Cambridge, in which is written, "The Rev. Mr. Thomas Baker, of St. John's College, in Cambridge, having made a vast quantity of notes upon Mr. Wood's Athenae Oxonienses, and inserted them in his edition of that work in 1691, all under their proper heads; which book he left to the Library of our University of Cambridge, I shall exactly copy the same into this edition 1721; and to prevent any injury to Mr. Baker's memory, by being mixed with some of my own, I shall add at the end of each note or observation of Mr. Baker the initial letters of his name, T.B. to distinguish them from any that are there at present, or may hereafter be inserted by W.C.

"Finished these Notes at Haddenham, in the Isle of Ely, Sunday, 29 Oct. an. 1749. W.C." NICHOLS.

‡ "This book I leave in trust with my worthy friend Dr. Middleton, for the Public Library. And I desire of my executor, that it may be delivered accordingly, though not mentioned in my will, and was otherwise disposed of when my will was made, now void as to that particular. THOMAS BAKER." NICHOLS.

18. See the life of Farmer.

19. Specimens of the correspondence of Cole with all four men mentioned in this paragraph are given by Nichols in his notes.

Chalmers from a diligent perusal of the several MS Volumes in Mr. Cole's Collection; and shall here supply, from that article some particulars which I had not before the opportunity of obtaining.—

His stepmother (his father's *fourth* wife) was a relation of Lord Montfort. "By her," says the son, "he had no issue, and very little quiet. After four or five years' jarring, they agreed to a separation."

At Eton young Cole was placed under Dr. Cooke, afterwards Provost, but to whom he seems to have contracted an implacable aversion. After remaining five years on the foundation at this seminary, he was admitted a pensioner of Clare Hall, Cambridge, Jan. 25, 1733; and in April 1734 was admitted to one of Freeman's scholarships, although not exactly qualified according to that benefactor's intention: but in 1735, on the death of his father, from whom he inherited a handsome estate, he entered himself a fellow-commoner of Clare Hall, and next year removed to King's College, where he had a younger Brother, then a Fellow, and was accommodated with better apartments. This last circumstance, and the society of his old companions of Eton, appear to have been his principal motives for changing his College. In April 1736 he travelled for a short time in French Flanders with his half-brother, the late Dr. Stephen Apthorp. In 1737, in consequence of bad health, he went to Lisbon, where he remained six months, and returned to College in May 1738. The following year he was put into the commission of the peace for the county of Cambridge, in which capacity he acted for many years. In 1740 Ld. Montfort, then lord lieutenant of the county, appointed him one of his deputy lieutenants. In 1743, his health being again impaired, he took another trip through Flanders for five or six weeks, visiting St. Omer's, Lisle, Tournay, &c. and other principal places, of which he has given an account in his MS. Collections.

In December 1744 he was ordained Deacon; and was for some time curate to Dr. Abraham Oakes, rector of Wethersfield in Suffolk. In 1745, after being admitted to priest's orders, he was made chaplain to Thomas Earl of Kinnoul; in which office he was continued by the succeeding Earl, George. He was elected a Fellow of the Society of Antiquaries in November 1747; and appears to have resided at Haddenham, in the Isle of Ely, in 1749, when he was collated by Bp. Sherlock to the rectory of Hornsey in Middlesex, which he retained only a very short time. Speaking of that Prelate, he says, "He gave me the rectory of Hornsey; yet his manner was such that I soon resigned it to him again. I have not been educated in episcopal trammels, and liked a more liberal behaviour; yet he was a great man, and I believe an honest man." The fact, however, was, as Mr. Cole elsewhere informs us, that he was inducted Nov. 25; but, finding the house in so ruinous a condition as to require rebuilding, and in a situation so near the Metropolis, which was always his aversion, and understanding that the Bishop insisted on his residing, he resigned within a month. This the Bishop refused to accept, because Mr. Cole had made himself liable to dilapidations and other expences by accepting of it. Cole continued, therefore, as rector until January 9, 1751, when he resigned it into the hands of the Bishop in favour of Mr. Territt. During this time he had never resided, but employed a curate, the Rev. Matthew Mapletoft.

In 1753 he quitted the University, on being presented, by his early friend and patron Browne Willis, esq. to the rectory of Bletchley in Buckinghamshire, which he resigned March 20, 1767, in favour of his patron's grandson, the Rev. Thomas Willis; and this very honourably, and merely because he knew it was his patron's intention to have bestowed it on his grandson had he lived to effect an exchange.

I have already noticed Mr. Cole's journey to France with Mr. Walpole in 1765; on which Mr. Chalmers remarks, that,

from the whole tenour of Mr. Cole's sentiments, and a partiality, which in his MSS. he takes little pains to disguise, in favour of the Roman Catholic religion and ceremonies, we may suspect that cheapness was not the only motive for this intended removal. He had at this time his personal estate, which he tells us was a "handsome one;" and he held the living of Bletchley, both together surely adequate to the wants of a retired scholar, a man of little personal expence, and who had determined never to marry. He was, however, diverted from residing in France by the laws of that country, particularly the *Droit d'Aubaine,* by which the property of a stranger dying in France becomes the King's, and which had not at that time been revoked. Mr. Cole at first supposed this could be no obstacle to his settling in Normandy; but his friend Mr. Walpole represented to him that his MSS. on which he set a high value, would infallibly become the property of the King of France, and probably be destroyed. This had a persuasive effect; and, in addition to it, we have his own authority that this visit impressed his mind so strongly with the certainty of an impending revolution, that upon that account he preferred remaining in England. His expressions on this subject are remarkable, but not uncharacteristic: "I did not like the plan of settling in France at that time, *when the Jesuits were expelled,* and the philosophic Deists were so powerful as to threaten the destruction, not only of all the religious orders, but of Christianity itself." There is a Journal of this Tour in vol. XXXIV. of his Collections.[20]

In May 1771, by Lord Montfort's favour, he was put into the commission of the peace for the Town of Cambridge; and in 1772 Bp. Keene, without any solicitation, sent him an offer of the vicarage of Maddingley, about seven miles from Milton, which, for reasons of convenience, he civilly declined; but has not spoken so civilly of that Prelate in his "Athenae." He was, however, instituted to the vicarage of Burnham in Buckinghamshire in 1774; but still continued to reside at Milton, where he died Dec. 16, 1782, in his 68th year, his constitution having been shattered and worn down by repeated attacks of the gout.

Mr. Chalmers thus justly characterises "Cole of Milton" (for so this intelligent Collector was familiarly styled):

He was an Antiquary almost from the cradle, and had in his boyish days made himself acquainted with those necessary sciences, Heraldry and Architecture. He says, the first "essay of his Antiquarianism was taking a copy both of the inscription and tomb of Ray the Naturalist, in 1734;" but it appears that, when he was at Eton School, he used during the vacations to copy, in trick, arms from the painted windows of churches, particularly Baberham in Cambridgeshire, and Moulton in Lincolnshire. Yet, although he devoted his whole life to Topography and Biography, he did not aspire

---

20. See *A Journal of my Journey to Paris in the Year 1765 By the Rev. William Cole,* ed. Francis Griffin Stokes (London, 1931).

to any higher honour than that of a collector of information for the use of others; and certainly was liberal and communicative to his contemporaries, and so partial to every attempt to illustrate our English Antiquities, that he frequently offered his services, where delicacy and want of personal knowledge would have perhaps prevented his being consulted. What he contributed was in general, in itself, original and accurate, and would have done credit to a separate publication, if he had thought proper. Among the works which he assisted, either by entire dissertations, or by minute communications and corrections, we may enumerate. . . Mr. Nichols's "Collection of Poems," "Anecdotes of Hogarth," "History of Hinckley," and "Life of Bowyer." . . .

Mr. Cole himself was a collector of portraits at a time when this *trade* was in few hands, and had a very valuable series, in the disposal of which he was somewhat unfortunate, and somewhat capricious, putting a different value on them at different times. When in the hope that Lord Mountstuart would purchase them, he valued them at a shilling each, one with another, which he said would have amounted to 160*l*. His collection must therefore have amounted to 3200 prints; but among these were many topographical articles: 130*l*. was offered on this occasion, which Mr. Cole declined accepting. This was in 1774; but previous to this, in 1772, he met with a curious accident, which had thinned his collection of portraits. This was a visit from an eminent Collector. "He had," says Mr. Cole, "heard of my collection of prints, and a proposal to see them was the consequence. Accordingly, he breakfasted here next morning; and, on a slight offer of accommodating him with such heads as he had not, he absolutely has taken one hundred and eighty-seven of my most valuable and favourite heads, such as he had not, and most of which had never seen; and all this with as much ease and familiarity as if we had known each other ever so long. However, I must do him the justice to say, that I really did offer him, at Mr. Pemberton's that he might take such in exchange as he had not; but this I thought would not have exceeded above a dozen, or thereabouts, &c." In answer to this account of the devastation of his collection, his correspondent Horace Walpole writes to him in the following style, which is not an unfair specimen of the manner in which these correspondents treated their contemporaries:

> I have had a relapse (of the gout), and have not been able to use my hand, or I should have lamented with you on the plunder of your prints by that *Algerine hog*. I pity you, dear Sir, and feel for your awkwardness, that was struck dumb at his repaciousness. The *beast* has no sort of taste neither, and in a twelvemonth will sell them again. This *Muley Moloch* used to buy books, and now sells them. He has hurt his fortune, and ruined himself to have a collection, without any choice of what it should be composed. It is the most *under-bred swine* I ever saw, but I did not know *it* was so *ravenous*. I wish you may get paid any how.

Mr. Cole, however, after all this epistolary scurrility, acknowledges that he was 'honourably paid' at the rate of two shillings and six pence each head; and one, on which he and Walpole set an uncommon value, and demanded back, was accordingly returned.

Mr. Cole's MS Collections had two principal objects; first, the compilation of a work in imitation of Anthony Wood's "Athenae," containing the Lives of the Cambridge Scholars, and, secondly, a County History of Cambridge; and he appears to have done something to each as early as 1742. They now amount to an hundred volumes, small folio, into which he appears to have transcribed some document or other almost every day of his life, with very little intermission. He began with fifteen of these volumes, while at College, which he used to keep in a lock-up case in the University Library, until he had examined every book in that collection from which he could derive any information suitable to his purpose, and transcribed many MS lists, records, &c. The grand interval from this labour was from 1752 to 1767, while he resided at Bletchley; but even there, from his own collection of books, and such as he could borrow, he went on with his undertaking, and, during frequent journeys, was adding to his topographical drawings and descriptions, He had some turn for drawing, as his works every where demonstrate, just enough to give an accurate but coarse outline. But it was at Cambridge and Milton where his biographical researches were pursued with most effect, and where he carefully registered every anecdote he could pick up in conversation; and, in characterising his contemporaries, may literally be said to have spared neither friend nor foe. He continued to fill his volumes in this way almost to the end of his life, the last letter he transcribed being dated Nov. 25, 1782. Besides his topography and biography, he has transcribed the whole of his literary correspondence. Among his correspondents, Horace Walpole must be distinguished as apparently enjoying his utmost confidence; but their letters add very little to the character of either, as men of sincerity or candour. Both were capable of writing polite and even flattering letters to gentlemen, whom in their mutual correspondence, perhaps by the same post, they treated with the utmost contempt and derision.

Throughout the whole of Mr. Cole's MSS. his attachment to the Roman Catholic Religion is clearly to be deduced, and is often almost avowed. He never can conceal his hatred to the eminent Prelates and Martyrs who were the promoters of the Reformation. In this respect at least he resembled Anthony Wood, whose friends had some difficulty in proving that he died in communion with the Church of England; and Cole yet more closely resembled him in his hatred of the Puritans and Dissenters. When, in 1767, an order was issued from the Bishops for a Return of all Papists or reputed Papists in their Dioceses, Cole laments that in some places *none* were returned, and in other places *few;* and assigns as a reason for this regret, that "their principles are much more conducive to a peaceful and quiet subordination in government, and they might be a proper balance, in time of need, not only to the tottering state of Christianity in general, but to this Church of England in particular, *pecked* against by every fanatic Sect, whose good allies the Infidels are well known to be; but hardly safe from its own lukewarm members; and whose safety depends solely on a political balance." The "lukewarm members" he elsewhere characterises as Latitudinarians, including Clarke, Hoadly, and their successors, who held preferments in a Church whose doctrines they oppose.[21]

As late as 1778 we find Mr. Cole perplexed as to the disposal of his MSS. "I have long wavered how to dispose of all my MS volumes; to give them to *King's College,* would be to throw them into a *horse-pond;* and I had as lieve do one as the other; they are generally so *conceited of their Latin and Greek, that all other studies are barbarism.*" He once thought of Eton College; but, the MSS. relating principally to Cambridge University and County, he inclined to deposit them in one of the libraries there; not in the Public Library, because too public, but in Emanuel, with the then Master of which, Dr. Farmer, he was very intimate. Dr. Farmer, however, happening to suggest that he might find a better place for them, Mr. Cole, who was become

---

21. Dr. Samuel Clarke and Dr. Benjamin Hoadly, Bishop of Winchester.

peevish, and wanted to be courted, thought proper to consider this "coolness and indifference" as a refusal. In this dilemma he at length resolved to bequeath them to the British Museum, with this condition, that they should not be opened for twenty years after his death. For such a condition, some have assigned as a reason that the characters of many living persons being drawn in them, and that in no very favourable colours, it might be his wish to spare their delicacy; but, perhaps with equal reason, it has been objected that such persons would thereby be deprived of all opportunity of refuting his assertions, or defending themselves. Upon a careful inspection, however, of the whole of these volumes, we are not of opinion that the quantum of injury inflicted is very great, most of Cole's unfavourable anecdotes being of that gossiping kind on which a judicious Biographer will not rely, unless corroborated by other authority. Knowing that he wore his pen at his ear, there were probably many who amused themselves with his prejudices. His Collections, however, upon the whole are truly valuable; and his biographical references, in particular, while they display extensive reading and industry, cannot fail to assist the future labours of Writers interested in the History of the Cambridge Scholars.

—Thus far from Mr. Chalmers.
The character of Mr. Cole is thus also well delineated by Mr. D'Israeli:

He had a gossip's ear, and a tatler's pen—and, among better things, wrote down every grain of literary scandal his insatiable and minute curiosity could lick up; as patient and voracious as an ant-eater, he stretched out his tongue, till it was covered by the tiny creatures, and drew them all in at one digestion. All these tales were registered with the utmost simplicity, as the reporter received them; but, being only tales, the exactness of his truth made them still more dangerous lies, by being perpetuated; in his reflections he spared neither friend nor foe; yet, still anxious after truth, and usually telling lies, it is very amusing to observe, that, as he proceeds, he very laudably contradicts or explains away in subsequent memoranda what he had before written. Walpole, in a correspondence of forty years, he was perpetually flattering, though he must imperfectly have relished his fine taste, while he abhorred the more liberal feelings to which sometimes he addressed a submissive remonstrance. He has at times written a letter coolly, and, at the same moment, chronicled his suppressed feelings in his diary, with all the flame and sputter of his strong prejudices. He was expressively nick-named *Cardinal Cole*. These scandalous chronicles, which only shew the violence of his prejudices, without the force of genius, or the acuteness of penetration, were ordered not to be opened till twenty years after his decease; he wished to do as little mischief as he could, but loved to do some. When the lid was removed from this Pandora's box, it happened that some of his intimate friends lived to perceive in what strange figures they were exhibited by their quondam admirer!

Cole, however, bequeathed to the Nation, among his unpublished works, a vast mass of antiquities, historical collections, and one valuable legacy; he was a literary Antiquary, and the *Cardinal* disappeared, when I witnessed the labours, and heard the cries, of a *literary Martyr*.

Cole had passed a long life in the pertinacious labour of forming an *Athenae Cantabrigienses,* and other literary collections—designed as a companion to the work of Anthony Wood. These mighty labours exist in more than fifty folio volumes in his own writing. He began these Collections about the year 1745; and in a fly-leaf of 1777 I found the following melancholy state of his feelings, and a literary confession, as forcibly expressed as it is painful to read, when we consider that they are the wailings of a most zealous votary:

> In good truth, whoever undertakes this drudgery of an *Athenae Cantabrigienses* must be contented with no prospect of credit and reputation to himself, and with the mortifying reflection that, after all his pains and study through life, he must be looked upon in a humble light, and only as a journeyman to Anthony Wood, whose excellent book of the same sort will ever preclude any other, who shall follow him in the same track, from all hopes of fame; and will only represent him as an imitator of so original a pattern. For, at this time of day, all great characters, both Cantabrigians and Oxonians, are already published to the world, either in his book, or various others; so that the Collection, unless the same characters are reprinted here, must be made up of second-rate persons, and the refuse of Authorship.—However, as I have begun, and made so large a progress in this undertaking, *it is death to think of leaving it off,* though, from the former considerations, so little credit is to be expected from it.

Such were the fruits, and such the agonies, of nearly half a century of assiduous and zealous literary labour! *Calamities of Authors,* vol. I. p. 237. [1812]

[Editor's note: In illustration of the kinds of comments made by Cole about his friends in his manuscripts, referred to above by Chalmers and D'Israeli, I insert the following attack on Richard Gough and others, British Museum Add. Mss. 5843. p. 242 (verso of f. 117), occurring immediately under the title "Foundress's Cup at Pembroke Hall in Cambridge."]

I can't help at this Time, shewing or expressing a little Resentment both against Mr Gough & his Fauters & Abetters, whose real & private Pique against Mr Horace Walpole, I am as well satisfied of, as if they had told me so in plain words. Pride, as well as Jealousy, & Envy at so eminent a Writer as Mr Walpole, are the Movers of all this outward & inward Spleen & Grumbling against him. Mr Walpole some 2 Years ago, when I was with him at Strawberry Hill, gave me a few, not many, Notes & Additions to Mr Gough's Topography: when that Gentleman, with Messrs [Michael] Tyson & [Edward] Haistwell dined with me at Milton sometime this Summer past (1772) I gave them to Mr Gough: but whether Mr W.^{s} Mode of Expression in them displeased him, or, as I rather think, because not sent to him from himself immediately, or both possibly, he seemed to set light by them: full as much as the Rest of the Company did to his Historic Doubts: the same Cause or Causes, I have sufficient Reason & Evidence to know, is the Foundation of the

Pique, tho' more latent, from another of these Gentlemen, Mr Tyson. That [Robert] Masters's was so, I have also full & clear conviction: for when First the Anecdotes on Painting were published, this Bungler in Antiquities, sent, in his usual forward Manner, a Letter to the Author, no Doubt in Hopes of a better, (for Interest he never yet lost Sight of) offering him an old Picture (assuredly a most vile one, but of a Piece with all his Rest) of Frances Duchess of Richmond: for which Favour, tho' Mr Walpole told me, he sent him a polite & civil Refusal; yet the distant Manner, (to keep off so forward & impertinent an Intruder) it was done in, was never forgiven by that sour & malevolent Person; who never afterwards could speak of him with Candour; so that this Rebuff, which he looked on as a Reproach to his Authorship, lying broiling & rankling for years in his Stomach, he watched an Opportunity when some of Mr Walpole's Enviers were playing off their Squibs at him, at the Meetings of Society of Antiquaries, to add his Excrements to their Dunghill; & taking a further opportunity of getting his crude Performance, red at their Meetings, published just before Christmass, when he usually lodges at Caius College to feast in such Colleges as will admit him during the Holydays, Mr Gough & he knowing that Mr Walpole had been in a dying Condition for above 2 Months, with the Gout in every Part of him, the public Papers announcing his Death, & even giving his Place of 2000£ per an. to Mr Jenkinson, they contrived that this dull, heavy Nonsense should come down to Cambridge at such a Conjuncture: accordingly in the last Week of December 1772, a Packet of 30 of this Nastiness was sent by Mr Gough to Mr Masters in order to distribute among such as he calls his Friends: who these were I know not: except that dining 24. Dec: 1772 at the Master of Pembroke's Lodge, who thought it came to him as his Neighbour at Stretham, where the Master is Rector, one came as a Present while I was there; & calling that Evening at Mr Tyson's at Benet College, there laid 2 on his Table, one for him & another for Mr Nasmith, who was then at Norwich: so I borrowed Mr Tyson's, after reading as dull & dronish a Performance as ever was written. I am sorry to see our Society lending their Assistance to so poor an Animal, who will be totally forgotten, when Mr Walpole's Name will add a Lustre to their List of Members, (of which however he has lately thought proper to deprive them of) so long as polite Litterature will have its Admirers. My Zeal for Mr Walpole, whose *Doubts* however may be justly remarked on, tho' this Blunderer has overlooked the Passages, & Resentment against such Detractors, have led me astray from my Subject. . . .

[Editor's note: Here Cole returns to a description of the Foundress's Cup. A note from George Steevens to Nichols dated the 24th, n.y., concludes this account. It is from the Osborn Collection at Yale.]

Dʳ Nichols.

You may send or show the enclosed, if you please, to Mʳ Gough. You cannot conceive the acrimony with which poor Cole has written about many of his friends. His abuse of Mʳ Walpole is quite unpardonable. But say nothing of this to Mʳ Gough.

                Yours &c GS.

Richard Gough

[Nichols' first biographical account of Richard Gough (in part extracted from Stebbing Shaw's *History of Staffordshire,* 1798-1801) appeared in the *Gentleman's Magazine* in two installments in March and April of 1809; subsequently this account was prefixed to the catalogue of Gough's library, 1810. These early versions were the basis for Nichols' life of Gough in *Lit. Anec.,* VI, 262-343, 613-626, from which the account that follows is taken. Gough was one of Nichols' closest friends and was godfather to his grandson, John Gough Nichols. Letters and other materials relating to Gough occur with such frequency throughout Nichols' works that it has been impossible to reproduce or even allude to all of them; and the life itself is so long that it has had to be trimmed.

As indicated in the text of the life that follows, Gough left his topographical library to the Bodleian Library at Oxford. These volumes include many that contain manuscript notes by Gough. The Bodleian also has a manuscript letter from Thomas Warton to Gough, dated 30 June 1777 (MS. Montagu d. 2. f. 39). The Osborn collection at Yale contains fourteen Gough items, including letters to him from George Allen and Thomas Warton and letters from him to several correspondents. The Beinecke Library at Yale has letters to Gough from Daniel Prince. Two letters from Gough to Thomas Warton are in the British Museum (Add. Mss. 42,561. ff. 106, 133). A letter from the antiquarian John Milner to Gough is in the Folger Shakespeare Library (ART vol. a12). Among the Nichols materials in the Special Collections of Columbia University Library are four letters from Nichols to Gough, one from Gough to Nichols, one from Gough to John Pridden (husband of Anne, eldest daughter of John Nichols), and one from Gough to John Bowyer Nichols at the time his father fell and fractured his leg, January 1807. A life of Gough by Thompson Cooper is in the DNB, and at the end is a useful list of references to works about Gough written by others besides Nichols and to other manuscripts of Gough in the British Museum. Nichols is, of course, the primary source of information about Richard Gough.]

It was my fond wish to have inscribed an improved Edition of these Anecdotes to almost the last Survivor of the many Friends to whom (nearly thirty years ago) I was materially indebted for assistance in the original publication; who, when the present work was announced to him, exclaimed *Gaudeo, cupioque videre;* and afterwards demonstrated his zeal for the subject, by bequeathing to me his interleaved copy of the former edition,[1] replete with

---

1. Nichols considered *Literary Anecdotes* to be the second edition of *Biographical and*

notes and letters illustrative of these Anecdotes. It becomes, therefore, an indispensable duty to enroll his name in this *Mausoleum of departed Worthies.*

In a Work indeed devoted to the commemoration of Literary Ornaments of the Eighteenth Century, and more particularly of those who were the intimate associates of Mr. BOWYER; it would be unpardonable to neglect the name of Mr. GOUGH; a name endeared also to my own feelings by every social and every grateful recollection. I shall here, therefore, enlarge the Memoirs which appeared in the Gentleman's Magazine, and were prefixed to the "Catalogue of his Library," originally formed on the basis of long and unreserved habits of intimacy, and from materials furnished by himself.

RICHARD GOUGH was born Oct. 21, 1735, in a large house in Winchester-street, London, on the site of the Monastery of the Austin Friars, founded by Humfry de Bohun, Earl of Hereford and Essex, in the year 1253.*

He was the only son of Harry Gough, Esq. by Elizabeth his wife,† daughter of Morgan Hynde,‡ esq. of London; who, with two brothers, raised a fortune by the breweries in Long Acre and Portpool-land; originating from some village in Dorsetshire, which themselves forgot; and, being Dissenters, were not registered.§

Of his father Mr. Gough was proud, and justly proud; but I shall copy his own words:

Harry Gough, esq. of Perry hall, was born April 2, 1681, whom the Editor of the new edition of Camden's Britannia[2] justly "glories in calling father," was highly distinguished for his abilities by some excellent judges of their merit. He went, when only eleven years old, with Sir Richard Gough, his uncle, to China, kept all his accompts, and was called by the Chinese *Ami Whangi,* or the *white-haired* boy. In 1707 he commanded the ship Streatham; his younger brother Richard purser, 1709. He continued to command this ship till 1715; and with equal ability and integrity he acquired a decent competency, the result of many hardships and voyages in the service of the East-India Company, to which his whole life was devoted while he presided among their Directors, being elected one of them in 1731, if not sooner.

Literary Anecdotes of William Bowyer, Printer, F.S.A. and of many of his Learned Friends, 1782. This 666-page precursor of *Literary Anecdotes* grew out of a 52-page pamphlet called *Anecdotes, Biographical and Literary, of the late Mr. William Bowyer, Printer,* 1778.

* See Mr. Gough's edition of Camden, vol. II. p. 383. NICHOLS.

† "She was married in 1719; and, dying May 27, 1774, was buried (where the remains of her husband had been deposited in 1751) in the Rector's vault in St. Andrew's Holborn." R.G.—See Gent. Mag. vol. XLIV. pp. 287, 446. NICHOLS.

‡ Morgan Hynde, esq. was nominated sheriff of London and Middlesex in 1708; and paid the accustomed fine. He died in October 1714. By the undertaker's bills, which I have seen, it appears that both Morgan and one of his brothers were buried with very great funeral pomp. NICHOLS.

§ They were originally from one of the *Ockfords* in Dorsetshire. . . . NICHOLS. (This and the succeeding passages shown as quotations are quoted by Nichols from Gough's own account of himself.)

2. Gough is here, of course, referring to himself as the new editor of Camden's *Britannia.* Gough's edition was issued in three volumes, 1789.

Possessed of great application and great activity, one of his friends used to say, "if he would take the whole East-India Company on him, he must answer for it; for nobody would assist him, though they would contradict him." Nor was his duty in Parliament less attended to, while he represented the borough of Bramber, from 1734 to his death, and refused several offices from the then Chancellor of the Exchequer, Sir Robert Walpole, afterwards Earl of Orford, whose confidence he possessed. The long and late debates during the opposition to that Minister hurt his health; for he would often go to the House with a fit of the gout coming on. He purchased, 1717, of the wife of Sir Richard Shelley, one moiety of the Middlemore estate in Warwickshire (the other moiety of which he before possessed); which afterwards descended to his son Richard, together with the property at Enfield, which he purchased in 1723, and from which, in compliment to him, an East-India ship took her name, in 1730.

Mr. [Richard] Gough received the first rudiments of Latin under the tuition of——Barnewitz. . . . On his death, he was committed to the care of the Rev. Roger Pickering, one of the most learned, most independent, and most ill-treated, of the Dissenting Ministers of his time. . . . On his death, May 18, 1755, Mr. Gough finished his Greek studies under Mr. Samuel Dyer, the friend of Johnson and contemporary Literati.||

At the very early age of eleven, he commenced a task that would have reflected credit on any period of life; which, by the indulgence of his Mother, appeared in print, under the title of "The History of the Bible, translated from the French,‡ by R. G. Junior, 1746. London, printed [by James Waugh] in the year 1747." Of this curious Volume, consisting of 160 sheets in folio, no more than 25 copies were printed, as presents to a few particular Friends;* and when completed at the press, it is marked, by way of colophon, "*Done at twelve years and a half old.*"

Another juvenile work was, "The Customs of the Israelites; translated from the French of the Abbot Fleury, by R. G. 1750," 8vo. [This was also printed by Mr. Waugh; but not for sale.†]

He had also fully prepared for the press, even to the title-page and preface, a work of infinite labour and research, under the title of "*Atlas Renovatus; or, Geography modernized, being a particular description of the World as far as known to the Antients. . . . Drawn upon the Plans of Hornius' and Cellarius' Maps, 1751.*" This is a folio volume, fairly written, which I retain as a memorial of his consummate industry.

|| "Of Mr. Dyer, under whom Mr. Gough completed his Greek studies, see Sir John Hawkins's Life of Johnson; and also Mr. Malone's Life of Dryden in the excellent edition of his Prose Works. At the suggestion of Dr. Johnson, Mr. Dyer was induced to sink his fortune in annuities on Lord Verney's estates, which brought to an untimely end a man much to be regretted for his moral and intellectual talents." R. G.

‡ Printed at Amsterdam, in 2 vols. folio, with plates, 1700. NICHOLS.

* By the generosity of his worthy Relict, I have a copy of this Work with Mr. Gough's corrections in maturer age. NICHOLS.

† Translated from the "Moeurs des Israelites" of the Abbé Fleury; printed at the Hague, 1682. NICHOLS. (Square brackets in this and preceding paragraph supplied by Nichols.)

On the death of his father (which happened July 13, 1751), Mr. Gough was admitted, in July 1752, fellow-commoner of Bene't college, Cambridge, where his relations Sir Henry Gough and his brother John had before studied under Dr. Mawson, afterwards successively Master of his College, and Bishop of Landaff, Chichester, and Ely. The College tutor, 1752, was Dr. John Barnardiston, afterwards Master.

His private tutor was the Rev. John Cott, fellow of the College, son of the Town-clerk of Lynne, and afterwards rector of Braxted in Essex, where he died in 1781, having married a niece of the late Dr. Keene, Bishop of Chester.

Under the immediate tuition of the three excellent Scholars before mentioned, Mr. Gough early imbibed a taste for Classical Literature and Antiquities; and it is not to be wondered at that his connexion with a College eminent for producing a succession of British Antiquaries inspired him with a strong propensity to the study of our National Antiquities. Here was first planned the BRITISH TOPOGRAPHY.

His associates at College were not numerous, but they were judiciously selected; and the friendships then commenced remained unbroken but by Death. Among these, particularly, were, the Rev. Benjamin Forster, the Rev. George Griffiths, the Rev. Michael Tyson, and Edward Haistwell, esq. (who all died before him); and the Rev. Edward Fisher, whom (with the daughters of Mr. Haistwell) he has remembered in his will.

From Cambridge, July 13-16, 1756, he visited Peterborough, Croyland, and Stamford; and, in the History long after published of Croyland, thus adopted the words of Dr. [William] Stukeley: "When I was a youth, and began to have an inclination to the study of Antiquities, I visited Crowland [sic] Abbey; and now, once at least in the year, my affairs calling me that way, I visit it with as much pleasure as *Petrus Blesensis* formerly looked upon it. . . ."‡

He continued these visits every year to various parts of the kingdom, taking notes, which, on his return, were digested into a form which furnished materials for the new edition of CAMDEN's BRITANNIA, the result of twenty years excursions.

With two of his most intimate Friends Mr. Gough made an excursion, in 1759 and 1760, through the greater part of Essex; of which he kept a regular Itinerary, which I now possess; and which he thus inscribed to the Companions of his Tour:

To the Rev. Mr. B. F[orster], Curate of Bromfield and Chignel Smeely, in this County; and to E. H[aistwell], Esq.[3]

To you of right, I, *more Stukeliano*, inscribe this Journey, to which your company and my inclination to see somewhat of the world allured me. I

‡ Palaeographia Britannica, No. II. p. 34. NICHOLS.
3. Square brackets and punctuation are Nichols'.

willingly take this opportunity of recognizing how I ought to esteem it a happiness that you chanced to be seated in place so near that of my residence. Having lived from time *to myself* immemorial on the edges of the marshy level of Essex, I might ascribe my passion for antiquarian studies to a melancholic disposition thence contracted; but your great knowledge of antiquity and all polite learning was a spur to me, and to you in great measure do I owe what may not be discommendable in amusements of the following kind; therefore to you I offer the earliest fruits of our friendship, this small account of the most pleasurable journey I can reckon to myself. CIƆIƆCCLX.[4]

His first regular publication was anonymous: "The History of Carausius; or, an Examination of what has been advanced on that Subject by Genebrier and Dr. Stukeley, 1762." 4to.§

Mr. Gough was much respected and esteemed by the great Philanthropist JOHN HOWARD; who frequently pressed him to become his travelling companion. In 1767, particularly, he strongly endeavoured to persuade him to take a trip to Holland; assuring his mother that "he would take great care of the young voyager;" and in 1769, invited him as earnestly "to pass over to Calais, spend the winter at Geneva, and visit Italy in the Spring."||

Feb. 26, 1767, he was elected Fellow of the Society of Antiquaries of London; and, by the partiality of the late worthy President, Dr. Milles, Dean of Exeter, (his own words are here used) was, on the death of Dr. Gregory Sharpe, Master of the Temple, nominated Director of the same Society, 1771;‡ which office he held till Dec. 12, 1797, when he quitted the Society altogether.

He was chosen Fellow of the Royal Society of London 1775; but quitted that Society also in 1795.

He opened a correspondence with Mr. URBAN in 1767, with an account of the village of Aldfriston in Sussex, under the signature of D. H.; which signature he retained to the last, but not altogether uniformly; nor is another signature in some later volumes* with the same letters to be mistaken for his. And on the death of his fellow-collegian Mr. [John] Duncombe,† in 1786, the department of the Review in that valuable Miscellany was, for the most part, committed to him. If he criticised with warmth and severity certain innovations attempted in Church and State, he wrote his sentiments with sincerity and impartiality—in the fullness of a heart deeply impressed with a sense of the excellence and happiness of the English Constitution both in Church and State.

§ See *Gent. Mag.* vol. XXXII. p. 298.—This "elaborate disquisition" was noticed by the Monthly Reviewers; who add, that "the work appears to be learnedly and critically conducted." NICHOLS.

|| This appears from Mr. Howard's unpublished Letters. NICHOLS.

‡ How ably Mr. Gough fulfilled the duties of this office for 26 years, the publications of the Society will best testify. NICHOLS.

* This correspondence was continued to 1808. NICHOLS. (*Sylvanus Urban* was, of course, the title of the editor of the *Gentleman's Magazine*.)

† By whom the critique on Mr. Gough's Topography in Gent. Mag. (vol. XLII. p. 273) was written; as well as that on the second edition in vol. L. pp. 377, 530. "All that has been done, is doing, and is still wanting for illustration of our Antiquities," Mr. Duncombe justly observes, "is discussed with great accuracy in Mr. Gough's Preface." NICHOLS.

4. 1760.

In 1768 he published, in one quarto volume, his "Anecdotes of British Topography;"[5] re-printed in two of the same size in 1780;‡ and left ready for a *third edition,* with many considerable additions.

To have re-published this useful work would have been to Mr. Gough an event of the highest gratification. A THIRD Edition, begun at the press in 1806, was rapidly advancing when the destructive fire of Feb. 8, 1808,[6] and the then declining state of Mr. Gough's health, which for more than two years had been gradually impaired by repeated fits of epilepsy, interrupted an undertaking, which neither the Author nor his Printer had sufficient spirits to resume. This work had been consigned to the Bodleian Library by Mr. Gough's Will; but he subsequently gave the corrected copy, with the Plates, to Mr. Nichols; who will readily relinquish his right, if the respectable Curators of the Oxford Press think proper to undertake a new Edition.[7]

In 1773 he formed the design of a new edition of CAMDEN's BRITANNIA, which he was seven years translating, and nine printing, and which was published in three volumes, folio, 1789.[8]

This National Work was thus properly inscribed: "To the Patron of Arts and Sciences, the Father of his people, GEORGE III. who has condescended to encourage Researches into Antiquity, this Work, the earliest general Account of his Kingdom, is humbly dedicated by his most dutiful Subject,
RICHARD GOUGH."

* * *

Of this valuable work it may not be superfluous to observe, that Mr. Gough translated it from the original, and supplied his additions, with so little interruption of the ordinary intercourse of life, that none of his family were aware that he was at any time engaged in so laborious an undertaking. The copy-right he gave (without any other consideration than a few copies for presents) to his old and worthy friend Mr. Thomas Payne; who defrayed the expence of engraving the copper-plates; and afterwards disposed of the whole of his interest in the work to Messrs. Robinsons.

Mr. Gough superintended the *first* volume of a new edition; but, March

---

‡ "Mr. Nichols the Printer sent in, as a present from our worthy and learned Member Mr. Director Gough, a new edition (being the second) of his British Topography, in two volumes, quarto. The Society expressed their obligation and thanks to their worthy member for his valuable and kind present." *Minutes of the Society of Antiquaries, May 4, 1780.* NICHOLS.

5. Nichols inserts in a note here several letters of Gough sent with presentation copies of his book.

6. Nichols suffered a loss of nearly £10,000 beyond his insurance in this fire which destroyed not only his press and warehouse, but, in addition to the work mentioned here, a number of other significant books, including Percy's edition of Surrey's poems. See Nichols' letter to Percy, *Illustr.,* VI, 587-588.

7. This paragraph appears as a note in Nichols.

8. Nichols introduces in a note a considerable correspondence concerning the publication of this work.

14, 1806, thus publicly disclaimed any connexion with the succeeding volumes: "The Copy-right of the BRITANNIA having devolved, by purchase, from Messrs. Robinsons to Mr. Stockdale, when the first volume of a second Edition was far advanced in the press; Mr. Gough, finding it of importance to his health that he should suspend such pursuits, considers himself at full liberty to decline proceeding any further than to complete the Volume which Messrs. Robinsons had begun to print."

[Editor's note: Here Nichols resumes Gough's life of himself.] Being on a visit to the late Rev. Mr. Howel, then Dissenting Minister at Pool, and hearing of the difficulties under which Mr. Hutchins laboured respecting his History of Dorsetshire, he set on foot a subscription; and was the means of bringing into light a most valuable County History, which he superintended through the press, whence it issued in 2 vols. folio, 1774. Its Author did not live to see it completed; but his daughter having been enabled to proceed to Bombay, and form a happy connexion with a gentleman to whom she had long been engaged: Major Bellasis (afterwards advanced to the rank of General of Artillery, and since deceased), in grateful return to the memory of his father-in-law, at his own expence set on foot a new edition of the History of Dorsetshire;§ and Mr. Gough contributed his assistance to this second edition twenty years after the first. Except Dr. Thomas's revision and continuation of Dugdale's Warwickshire, and the paltry re-publication of Burton's Leicestershire and Philpot's Kent by Whittingham of Lynne, and Thoroton's Nottinghamshire by Throsby, not much superior, this is the first instance of a County History attaining a second edition.

Having purchased the Collections of Mr. Thomas Martin, he put out an improved "History of Thetford, 1779," 4to; with plates from views taken by the then Captain Grose, who accompanied him in the snowy season of 1778.‖

Having also purchased the plates of the Medals, Coins, and Great Seals,# executed by the celebrated Simon, and first published by Vertue in 1753, he gave a new and enlarged edition of them in 1780.

He assisted Mr. Nichols in the "Collection of Royal and Noble Wills, 1780;"* to which he wrote the Preface, and compiled the Glossary.

He superintended the printing of Dr. [Treadway] Nash's "Collections for a History of Worcestershire," in 2 vols. folio, 1781; a short Supplement to which was printed in 1799.

§ At three different periods was Dorsetshire traversed by Mr. Gough and Mr. Nichols, assisted by Mr. Basire and other able Draftsmen, for the improvement of a second edition; the result of which, to the extent of two volumes, is already before the Publick. The *Third*, with the exception of a single copy, was unfortunately burnt; but, if proper encouragement be given, may yet possibly see the light. NICHOLS. (See above, n. 6.)

‖ To this work, Mr. Gough prefixed a biographical Preface, inserted in these "Anecdotes," vol. V. p. 384. NICHOLS.

All these plates, with several others on Antiquarian subjects (most of which were the joint property of Mr. Gough and Mr. Nichols) are now deposited in the Bodleian Library. NICHOLS.

* The first projector of this curious work was Dr. [Andrew Coltée] Ducarel; and by the joint assistance of that eminent Civilian and Mr. Gough it was conducted through the press, not without a very considerable inconvenience to the Printer [Nichols], who paid the whole expence occasioned by the various notes added by his learned Friends. . . . NICHOLS.

In 1781 he was chosen an honorary member of the Society of Antiquaries at Edinburgh; and in 1785, of a similar Society at Perth.

In 1786, he published the first volume of the SEPULCHRAL MONUMENTS OF GREAT BRITAIN, applied to illustrate the History of Families, Manners, Habits, and Arts, at the different Periods from the Norman Conquest to the Seventeenth Century. With Introductory Observations. Vol. I. Containing the First Four Centuries.

This splendid Volume was published without the Author's name; about which, however, there was no secrecy, as the Plate of his Family Arms appears in the Title-page.

[At this point Nichols introduces, in a note, two letters of thanks to Gough for presentation copies of the first volume of the *Sepulchral Monuments,* the latter of which is from Horace Walpole. A part of Walpole's letter is interesting here because of a reference to William Cole: "Your partiality, I doubt, Sir, has induced you to insert a paper not so worthy of the public regard as the rest of your splendid performance. My letter to Mr. Cole, which I am sure I had utterly forgotten to have ever written, was a hasty indigested sketch, like the rest of my scribblings, and never calculated to lead such well-meditated and accurate works as yours. Having lived familiarly with Mr. Cole from our boyhood, I used to write to him carelessly on the occasions that occurred. As it was always on subjects of no importance, I never thought of enjoining secrecy. I could not forsee that such idle communications would find a place in a great national work, or I should have been more attentive to what I said. Your taste, Sir, I fear, has for once been misled, and I shall be sorry for having innocently blemished a single page."

Interesting also is the note Nichols appended to this letter: "It is remarkable that Mr. Walpole should treat Mr. Gough with such profound respect in his answers to him; whereas, in his correspondence with his friend Cole (in the Museum) he is often very unceremonious in his notices of our learned Antiquary. The modern *Horace,* like his namesake of old, was, there is reason to think, an egregious flatterer."

Walpole had been cordial in his correspondence with Nichols. In his letters to others, however, Walpole was contemptuous. He wrote, for example, to William Mason on 5 May 1783 (*Horace Walpole's Correspondence with William Mason,* II [Vol. 29 of the Yale Edition of *Horace Walpole's Correspondence,* New Haven, 1955], pp. 292-296), concerning Nichols' publication that year of the first two volumes of his *Atterbury Correspondence:* ". . . . That silly fellow Nichols the printer, who, between a furor of scribbling and a furor of getting money, vomits out volumes upon volumes filled with as insignificant rubbish as a scavanger gathers in his cart, has just published two octavos of Atterburyana in humble imitation of his prototype Curl, who gravely says in his preface *has been transmitted* (he should have said, through the pillory) *to posterity with an obloquy he ill deserved*—can one help laughing at this apostle's sympathy for the martyr his master?—*whatever were his demerits,* adds this yet unpelted disciple, *they were amply atoned for by his indefatigable industry in preserving our national remains*—so does a scavanger—*nor did he publish a single volume, but what amidst a profusion of baser metal contained some precious ore*—a gold finder again! .... In this new repository of obsolete squabbles, Nichols ... makes everything relate to everything, if they do but begin with the same letter...."]

The Second Volume, published in 1796, and an Introduction to it in 1799, contained the Fifteenth Century; with which Mr. Gough thought proper to conclude his labours, instead of continuing the Work to the end of the Sixteenth Century, as was originally intended.

This truly magnificent work would alone have been sufficient to perpetuate his fame, and the credit of the Arts in England; where few works of superior splendour have before or since appeared. The independent master of an ample fortune, he was in all respects pre-eminently qualified for the labours of an Antiquary; the pain of whose researches can but rarely meet an adequate remuneration. This magnificent work must long ago have convinced the world, that he possessed not only the most indefatigable perseverance, but an ardour which no expence could possibly deter.

One great object of his wishes was, to prepare the "Sepulchral Monuments" for a new Edition. With this constantly in view, he spared neither trouble nor expence in obtaining an ample store of new and accurate drawings by the FIRST artists; all which, with the numerous and beautiful plates already engraved, principally by the BASIRES, form part of his noble bequest to the UNIVERSITY OF OXFORD; and the Curators of the Press will doubtless have great pleasure in fulfilling the wishes of so generous a Benefactor, by an improved Edition.

In 1794, Mr. Gough published an Account of the beautiful Missal presented to Henry VI. by the Duchess of Bedford, which Mr. Edwards (then an eminent bookseller in Pall Mall), purchased at the Duchess of Portland's sale, and still possesses. ... He drew up the History of the Society of Antiquaries of London, prefixed to the first volume of their Archaeologia, 1770.... :

In Mr. Nichols' "Bibliotheca Topographica Britannica," the design of which he both suggested and forwarded, several Essays bear his name....†

He assisted in the copious, well-digested, and accurate "History of Leicestershire;" undertaken and conducted with a perseverance which would baffle common County Historians, by the same Friend; to whose benevolence, impartiality, and integrity, he is proud to bear this public testimony.

† Particularly the Memoirs of Edward Rowe-Mores, No. I.; of the Gales, and of the Gentlemen's Society at Spalding, No. II. and XX.; Preface to Antiquities of Aberdeen, No. III.; of Sir John Hawkwood, No. IV. and XIX.; History of Croyland (to which he afterwards added, a "Second Appendix," in addition to one previously communicated by Mr. Essex), No. XI.; Genealogical View of the Family of Cromwell, No. XXXI. And Dr. Pegge's Sylloge of Inscriptions, No. XLI. is inscribed to him. NICHOLS.

[Nichols' note to this praise from Gough:] ["I may be accused of vanity for publishing this very honourable testimonial; but the suppressing of it would be an unpardonable weakness and affectation."]

Pleshy in Essex, the seat of the High Constables of England, and particularly of Thomas of Woodstock, the unfortunate uncle of Richard the Second, having been an early attachment of Mr. Gough, he was at no small pains and expence to draw up a full account of it, from the Records of the Duchy of Lancaster; in which he was most kindly assisted by Mr. Harper, the keeper of them. This he illustrated with a variety of plates of views, seals, &c.; and published it in 4to, 1803....

In the same year [1803] he was called upon by the express desire of his friend Mr. Manning, to assist in the publication of his "History of Surrey," in which William Bray, esq. of Shere, was a principal coadjutor, of which the first volume appeared in 1804; a second in 1810; and the third and last is now [1809] in the press.

He counted some of the first Antiquaries of the Three Kingdoms among his Correspondents; [Nichols' note:] [Among these he particularly specified, in alphabetical order: George Allan, esq. of Darlington; Hon. Daines Barrington; Right Rev. Dr. William Bennet, Bishop of Cloyne; William Bray, esq. Treasurer of the Society of Antiquaries; J. C. Brooke, Esq. Somerset Herald; Rev. Dr. Campbell, of Ireland; Rev. John Carter, Master of Lincoln School; Rev. Ralph Churton, Middleton Cheney; Rev. William Cole, of Milton; Rev. Sir John Cullum, Bart.; Mr. Henry Ellis, British Museum; Mr. James Essex, of Cambridge; Rev. Thomas Falconer, Editor of Strabo; Rev. Richard Farmer, D.D. Master of Emanuel College; Sir John Fenn, Editor of the Paston Letters, &c.; Rev. John Gutch, M.A. Registrar of Oxford; Rev. Edward Ledwich, B.D. of Ireland; Rev. Michael Lort, D.D.; Rev. Jeremiah Milles, D.D. Dean of Exeter, Pres. A. S. (Antiquarian Society); Craven Ord, Esq.; Rev. Samuel Pegge, LL.D. and his son Samuel Pegge, Esq.; Rev. John Price, of the Bodleian Library; Robert Riddell, Esq. of Friar's Carse; Rev. Rogers Ruding, B.D. Vicar of Maldon, Surrey; J. C. Walker, Esq. of Dublin.][9] but, having once incorporated their observations in his various publications, he guarded their correspondence from the impertinence of modern Editors.

Of his own Notes, written in Printed Books, he had made the BRITISH MUSEUM the depository; [Nichols' note:] [This depository he altered, by his last will, to the BODLEIAN LIBRARY. The next sentence, with the subsequent paragraph, may, in some degree, account for the change.] though, like others of his friends, *he never attained to the honour of being one of the Trustees;* which, he has heard it observed, should be the *blue ribband of literary men,*‡ and is now become an object of successful canvass.

So unambitious was he of public honours, that, as he took no degree at Cambridge, and that University confers no honorary ones, he resisted the solicitations of many members of the Sister University, and of his old and valuable friend Dr. Pegge, to share his honours with him in 1791; though he felt real satisfaction in assisting at them, and retained to the last a grateful sense of the good wishes of that learned Seminary.

In Politicks, he was, as his Father had been before him, a firm friend to the House of Brunswick, and a stranger to the mutability of his contemporaries. That independence which he gloried in possessing as his inheri-

‡ This was first said by Dr. [John] Taylor, Editor of Demosthenes. NICHOLS.
9. Nichols' note, with the list of Gough's antiquarian friends, is included here because the names are indispensable to anyone wishing to pursue Gough further.

tance, and which he maintained by a due attention to his income, discovered itself in his opinions and his attachments. As he could not hastily form connexions, he may seem to have indulged strong aversions. But he could not accommodate himself to modern manners and opinions; and he had resources within himself, to make it less needful to seek them from without. And perhaps the greatest inconvenience arising from this disposition was the want of opportunities to serve his friends. But he saw enough of the general temper of mankind, to convince him that favours should not be too often asked; and that as to be too much under obligation is the worst of Bondage, so to confer obligations is the truest Liberty.

[Nichols' note to above paragraph] [The following sketch of an advertisement, written in 1775, will shew his ideas of what a Candidate for a Seat in Parliament should say to his Constituents:] "I offer myself a Candidate to represent the County (or Borough) of ———, with a determined resolution neither to solicit, or influence, the votes of the free electors. Superior to such influence myself, I cannot condescend to bribe or intimidate my countrymen. I stand forth, therefore, on no other ground than public virtue. If there is so much left in this place as to direct your choice to me, I shall be happy in calling it forth, whether I succeed in the election or not. I shall neither make nor authorize any other application than this. As I have no ends of my own to serve, I profess myself of no party; and resolve to follow the dictates of my own conscience, with respect to my duty to my Country, my Sovereign, and my Constituents."

The account thus far given of Mr. GOUGH, the greatest part of which is literally from his own pen, it may now be allowable to enlarge.

One of the most prominent features in his character was an insatiable thirst for Literature; and particularly that branch of it in which he so eminently excelled, the study of our National Antiquities. Young as he was at the time of his Father's death, in 1751; not having then attained his 16th year; an only son, with the certainty of inheriting a plentiful fortune; his attention was principally turned to the improvement of his mind, and the foundation of a noble Library. Hence the pleasurable diversions of the age to him had little charms. The well-stored shop of *honest Tom Payne* at the Mews Gate, or the auction-rooms of the *two Sams*, Baker and Paterson, had beauties far transcending the alluring scenes of fashionable dissipation.

[Nichols' note to above paragraph:] [Mr. Dibdin, in his Memoirs of Mr. Gough, in "Typographical Antiquities," observes:] "While the greater number of his associates might have been emulous of distinguishing themselves in the gaities of the table or the chace, it was the peculiar feeling and master passion of young Gough's mind, to be constantly looking upon every artificial object without, as food for mediation and record. The mouldering turret and the crumbling arch, the moss-covered stone and the obliterated inscription, served to excite, in his mind, the most ardent sensations, and to kindle that fire of antiquarian research, which afterwards never knew decay: which burnt with undiminished lustre at the close of his existence, and which prompted him, when in the full enjoyment of his bodily faculties, to explore long-deserted castles and mansions, to tread long-neglected byeways, and to snatch from impending oblivion many a precious relick, and many a venerable ancestry! He is the CAMDEN of modern times. He spared no labour, no toil, no expence, to obtain the best information; and to give it publicity, when obtained, in a manner the most liberal and effective."

At Cambridge his studies were regular and severe; diverted only by occasional visits to the Metropolis; or by excursions to various parts of the kingdom.

During this period he prepared for the press. . . . [six works listed]

All these remain in MS.; as do also the following proofs of his industry and abilities. . . . [thirteen works listed]

Mr. Gough had a natural turn for Poetry; and in some of his smaller essays was not unfrequently happy. A few specimens shall be given at the end of this article (*Lit. Anec.*, VI, 332-343).

His attentions, meanwhile, were not so entirely devoted to Literature, as to exclude him from social duties and the rational pleasures of life.

Aug. 18, 1774, soon after the death of his Mother, an event by which he came into possession of an excellent family residence at Enfield, with the large estate bequeathed to him in reversion by his Father, he added considerably to his other comforts, by marrying Anne, fourth daughter of Thomas Hall, esq. of Goldings, Herts; a lady of distinguished merit; whose family was equally respectable with his own; and who, after a long and happy union, has to lament the loss of him whose object through life was to increase her happiness.

[Nichols' note to preceding paragraph:] [To the property at Enfield (where he afterwards constantly resided) he made considerable additions by purchase, particularly of a large additional garden, and of a field nearly adjoining, adorned with a long row of beautiful chestnut-trees, which, as he has often observed, "were planted by his father, and were coaeval with himself"—and which he bought as full-grown timber.]

Those only who have had the satisfaction of seeing Mr. Gough in his domestic and familiar circle can properly appreciate his merits. Though highly and deservedly distinguished as a scholar, the pleasantry and the easy condescension of his convivial hours still more endeared him, not only to his intimates, but even to those with whom the forms and customs of the world rendered it necessary that he should associate.

There was, however, another class of society to which, if possible, he was still more dear—the poor and the afflicted, to whom he was at all times a father, a protector, and a benefactor.

[Nichols' note to preceding paragraph:] "I wish," says an ingenious writer, "it were in my power to add any thing to this well-merited eulogium. I had the happiness to enjoy his friendship and good opinion many years; and had numerous opportunities of observing the benevolence and humanity of his disposition towards *the sick poor*: my appeals to him on their account were always received with a kindness and cheerfulness which encouraged the repetition: it may, indeed, be truly said, that his *Cellar* was as open to the necessities of afflicted industry, as his *noble Library* to the wants and wishes of literary men. Such was his liberality in this respect, that many a time, when I have expressed a wish to look into a scarce book for the purpose of enabling me to establish an opinion respecting the antiquity of Rowley's Poems[10] hostile to his own, he hath so far anticipated my wishes and my labour, that, far from suffering me to send for it, I have found the book at my own house long before the fatigues of the day would permit me to open it." Dr. [John] SHERWEN, *Gent. Mag.* 1810, *vol. LXXX, p.* 9.

The faithful domestick, when unable to continue his services, continued to receive his pay, in the shape of an annuity, with additional comforts.

Nor was his benevolence confined to the human species. The generous steed exempt by age from labour, the cow no longer useful to the dairy, were permitted to close their useful lives in a luxuriant meadow reserved for that express purpose; and domestic animals experienced great indulgence.

Greatly as the blessing of a long life is to be esteemed, the circumstances which attend it are often of the most afflicting nature; and amongst these, the loss of our earliest and most valuable friends is not the least distressing. This observation is not new; but it forcibly recurs, on recollecting the valuable Friend who is the subject of this memoir.[11]

During the period of more than thirty years, in which the present Editor of the Gentleman's Magazine has had the melancholy satisfaction of recording the departure of numberless Worthies with whom it has been his happiness and his pride to have formed an intimacy, he never felt himself so inadequate to the task. The loss of Mr. Gough was the loss of more than a Brother—it was losing a part of himself.

For a long series of years he had experienced in Mr. Gough the kind, disinterested friend; the prudent, judicious adviser; the firm, unshaken patron. To him every material event in life was confidentially imparted. In those that were prosperous, no man more heartily rejoiced; in such as were less propitious, no man more sincerely condoled, or more readily endeavoured to alleviate. This was more particularly the case in two calamities of the most trying nature![12]

The deep concern, indeed, which Mr. Gough felt at the dreadful event which terminated his labours at the press was shewn in a series of the kindest consolatory letters.

Of these, the last may sufficiently serve as examples:

"*Enfield, Feb.* 10, 1808. My dear Nichols, God preserve and comfort you and yours under your severe calamity, of which we were first apprised by our friend Mr. [Daniel] Moore, but in a less perfect manner. I send ——— to make all possible enquiries, and to convey to you *all my assurances of assistance,* which I hope you will call upon me for. When I shall be able to

10. By Thomas Chatterton.
11. Cf. Johnson's animadversions on old age in *The Vanity of Human Wishes.*
12. Nichols fractured one of his thighs in an accidental fall on 8 January 1807; and on 8 February 1808 he lost his printing works and warehouse in a fire.

come myself I am uncertain; but shall embrace and wish for every opportunity of hearing from you, and of you.

"We are much obliged for the tender manner of communicating the event; and are all as well as circumstances will allow.

"Yours most sincerely, R. GOUGH."

In the last of these affectionate letters, near the end of September 1808, he requests Mr. Nichols to execute a confidential commission; "which," he emphatically adds, *"may be the last office* you will have to do for your sincere Friend." This was nearly prophetic; for there was little now to be done, that could contribute to his comforts.

The bright gem of intellect, though frequently clouded, had intervals of its former splendour; and the frequent emanations of benevolence displayed through a long and painful illness, whilst they comforted and delighted those around him, added poignance to the regret they experienced for those bitter sufferings, which threatened to overwhelm a noble mind with total imbecility; from which he was mercifully relieved, without any apparent struggle at the last, on the 20th of February 1809; and was buried on the 28th, in the church-yard of Wormley, Herts, in a vault built for that purpose, on the South side of the chancel, not far from the altar which for several years he had devoutly frequented.

The funeral, in conformity to his own directions, was as little ceremonious as propriety would permit....

The solemn procession was followed from Enfield to Wormley by crowds, whose lamentations and regrets were unequivocally shewn....

Mr. Gough's publications, not already noticed, are, [twelve works listed].

His assistance to any of his friends who were engaged in literary pursuits were more extensive than will probably be ever known.

He gave considerable help to Dr. [Andrew] Kippis, in the five volumes which have been published of the second edition of the "Biographia Britannica;" and prepared the Life of Sir John Fastolf, and the Farrars of Little Gedding, for the sixth volume, which perished in the fire of February 1808....[13]

In 1785 the Compiler of these Anecdotes, "in acknowledgment of many literary favours conferred on his Predecessor [William Bowyer the Younger] and himself," inscribed to Mr. Gough a volume of the "Miscellaneous Tracts of Mr. Bowyer; whom he valued as a Friend, and respected as a Scholar." Mr. Gough materially assisted him also in collecting the "Progresses of Queen Elizabeth,"[14] published in 1788; and wrote the Preface to the First

---

13. Some animosity developed between Kippis and Gough, introduced in a note by Nichols thus: "I scarcely know whether to place the following Anecdotes among the "Quarrels," or the "Calamities" of Authors" (*Lit. Anec.,* IX, 184-185). Gough had written in a review of one of the early volumes that he hoped Kippis would stick to it so "that his labours and his life may not end the one before the other." In Vol. IV Kippis replied that "Of Mr. Gough I have no reason to speak with personal respect." Their differences continued to be kept alive in succeeding volumes.

14. "Two volumes of The Progresses of Queen Elizabeth were published in 1788; and

Volume; and in 1798 he superintended the second edition of Dr. White Kennett's famous Sermon, preached at the Funeral of William Duke of Devonshire, 1707; to which he added several Notes, and an Appendix....

In 1808, "An Account of the Church and Remains of the Manor-house of Stanton Harcourt, in the County of Oxford," was published by the then noble Owner of that mansion, with the following brief, but emphatic, inscription:

> To RICHARD GOUGH, esq.
> GEORGE SIMON EARL HARCOURT
> (although personally unknown
> to that distinguished Antiquary)
> inscribes the following pages.
> Nuneham-Courtney, Nov. 1, 1808.

[Nichols' note to the above inscription:] [Peers formerly were the great Patrons of Literature, and the Rewarders of it. But the instances in any time are rare, when a Nobleman high in rank, and eminent himself in merits of every description, has condescended to inscribe his labours to a Scholar. Both the one and the other have since paid the great debt of Nature, and nearly at the same age. But the compliment paid to the Father of "British Topography," we know, was a ray of comfort to him in the severest part of his last illness; and he recollected himself sufficiently to dictate a short but expressive tribute of thanks for the present of the book, and for the noble Lord's "remembrance of him at the close of life, and in declining health."]

The prefaces to numerous other works acknowledge the extensive patronage which, during the whole of his literary career, he was not only so able, but so ready to bestow.

His Library (with the exception of the valuable Department of British Topography bequeathed to the Bodleian Library), was sold, agreeably to his own direction, by Messrs. Leigh and Sotheby, in 20 days, beginning April 5, and ending April 28, 1810; and produced 3552*l*. 3*s*.

His Prints, Drawings, Coins, Medals, Seals, Painted Glass, Paintings, Pottery, Brass Monuments, Marble Fragments, Chinese and other Bronzes, Miniatures, and Miscellaneous Antiquities, were sold July 19, 1810, and the two following days; and produced 517*l*. 6*s*. 6*d*.

By his last will, Mr. Gough gave to the UNIVERSITY OF OXFORD all his printed Books and Manuscripts on Saxon and Northern Literature, "for the use of the Saxon Professor:"—all his "Manuscripts, printed Books and Pamphlets, Prints and Drawings, Maps, and Copper Plates, relating to

---

a third volume was added to the Collection in 1800. In consequence of the fire at Mr. Nichols's premises in 1808, the work had become so scarce, and brought such high prices when it occurred in book sales, that Mr. Nichols was induced to remodel the work, and republish it in 3 vols. 4to. in 1823. To which he afterwards added The Progresses of King James I. in 4 vols. 1826." JOHN BOWYER NICHOLS, *Illustr.*, VII, 17n.

British Topography (of which, in 1808, he had nearly printed a complete Catalogue); his interleaved Copies of the "British Topography," "Camden's Britannia," and the "Sepulchral Monuments of Great Britain," with all the Drawings relative to the latter Work; and all the Copper Plates of the "Monuments" and the "Topography."—And XIV Volumes of Drawings of "Sepulchral and other Monuments in France."—All these he wills and desires may "be placed in the BODLEIAN LIBRARY, in a building adjoining to the picture Gallery, known by the name of *The Antiquaries Closet,* erected for keeping Manuscripts, printed Books, and other Articles relating to British Topography; so that all together they may form one uniform Body of English Antiquities."—And he particularly desires that Mr. John Nichols (or his son John-Bowyer Nichols) will assist his Executors in selecting the said articles, and transmitting them to Oxford.

He gives to Mr. Nichols his Set of the "Gentleman's Magazine," and of the "Anecdotes of Mr. Bowyer." And then directs that the other parts of his very valuable Library and Curiosities shall be sold by Messieurs Leigh and Sotheby.

To Mrs. Gough he has very properly secured a life-interest in nearly the whole of his property (with the exception of annuities to some particular friends, and faithful domesticks; and a few legacies to be paid within twelve months). . . .

[The following is taken from an "Addition to Mr. Gough" in the same volume as the foregoing account, *Lit. Anec.,* VI, 613-626. The introductory paragraphs deal with Gough's early schooling and are presented with these words: "In a fragment of his own Memoirs, fairly transcribed, June 14, 1779, Mr. Gough says. . . ." All that follows is in quotation marks, indicating that it is all Gough's writing concerning himself. The part below begins with a description of Gough's antiquarian experiences at Cambridge.]

The study of our National Antiquities was a favourite pursuit; and was it to be wondered at, that it should be fostered within those venerable walls, which owed their support and splendour to Archbishop Parker, and had nursed a succession of British Antiquaries to the present time? or that, without any view to a degree or a profession, I should exceed the time usually spent in College? or that, as I was to return home again to books and study, without any prospect of being able to gratify my wish of visiting foreign countries, that desire should, by recoil, impel me powerfully to ramble over my own?

I had little opportunity to gratify this desire while at College; but, when I quitted College, I by little and little every year made excursions over the greatest part of England and Scotland, with only a servant. Such were and are the difficulties and embarrassments that attend forming parties for such purposes; and my attention was too much fixed on buildings and scenery, to apply myself to the more obvious help for obtaining information in travelling by applying to living informants.

The year 1774, by the death of my Mother, made me completely master of myself. An agreeable marriage, which had been for some years before in contemplation, fixed me in a happy train of domestic life, at the same time enlarging my connexions and scene of action: and if my life for the last eleven years has not been distinguished by any considerable events, but passed on in the uniform succession of literary unambitious retirement, blest with that decent competency which suffices for bounded wishes; it has not in return been checquered by dishonourable or reproachful traits of conduct to myself or others. Be it my constant endeavour that it never shall.

If I have relieved the wants and distresses of the unhappy without ostentation, have done justice without interest, have served the common cause of Literature without vanity, maintained my own independence without pride or insolence, have moderated my attachment to external objects, and placed my affections on the virtuous and honest character, and may trust to have so passed through things temporal as finally not to lose things eternal—I shall have *lived enough.*

After a period of more than seven years, Mr. Gough thus resumed his narrative:

June 1, 1786. When a man has laid in a fund of knowledge, in any branch, from Books, or other means of attainment, it is not to be wondered that the itch for scribbling seizes him. My Authorship was fixed to the line of Antiquity. While at College, I had begun to make additions to the list of Writers on the Topography of Great Britain and Ireland, prefixed to Gibson's Camden. I inserted these in Rawlinson's "English Topographer," till I fancied I might commence Topographer myself. I formed a Quarto Volume; and it was printed, 1768, at Mr. Richardson's§ press—*on credit:* my allowance not permitting any advance of money before publication. Mr. Richardson refused interest on his labour. The sale was rapid beyond expectation; and I was, on the balance between me and *honest Tom Payne,* gainer of seven pounds.||

I had been elected F.A.S. the year before (1767)....

Having now leisure, reputation, and an unincumbered income, I was induced, by the assistance of friends, to publish a new Edition of the "British Topography," augmented to two volumes, 4to, in 1780; which I have reason to think has not injured the reputation I had already acquired.

On Christmas-day 1770, I began a translation of "Camden's Britannia," from the original, and last Edition of 1607. Essex was the first County whose translation I attempted. I went on till the whole "Britannia" was completed; and then I set about the additions on the opposite pages....

About 1772 or 1773, I formed another design, of illustrating our National Antiquities, by selecting from my notes all the Sepulchral Monuments and Inscriptions which I had collected in my excursions. When I had written these out fair in chronological arrangement, I had the vanity to think of publishing them in the manner of Montfaucon's "Monumens de la Monarchie Françoise." This was likely to prove a more costly work than any I had yet undertaken. I undertook it, however, by degrees. Mr. [James] Basire's

---

§ It was printed by Mr. William Richardson (nephew to the celebrated Writer, [*Lit. Anec.*] IV. p. 580.) who at that time was in partnership with Mr. S. Clarke, a Quaker, who died about 1768. NICHOLS.

|| The names of T. Payne and W. Brown occur in the title-page; and Mr. Gough, with the anxious solicitude of a young Author, thus minuted the result.... NICHOLS. (Nichols' biographical note on the printer and bookseller Thomas Payne is in this volume.)

specimens of drawing and engraving gave me so much satisfaction, that it was impossible to resist the impulse of carrying such a design into execution. ... The First Part of the Work is now completed, and before the Publick; who must crown my labours, and reimburse my cost—if they approve what I have done for them. [[Let it be recollected that this was written in 1786. NICHOLS.]] Lesser or anonymous publications, the things of the present moment, I shall not here stop to enumerate; nor what I have done towards the [Antiquarian] Society's publications.

I will boast, however, of my Library and Literary Collections, which are my delight and pride. Those who know the value of such articles will pardon my vanity, and, it may be, not think them a small accession to the National Fund in the British Museum when I am tired of them, or to bequeath them when I can make no further use of them. [[I must repeat, that this also was written in 1786. NICHOLS.]. . . .]

Every year now materially affects my enjoyments, I see my friends decaying with age, or broken down by malady. A course of eleven years has deprived me of many whom I lived in habits of intimacy with from my childhood, of others whom a congenial turn of mind endeared to me..., at a time too when their conversation and correspondence was become most essential to me, and when I find myself neither in a situation nor humour to replace them by new acquaintance—if indeed in the general mortality of persons of their turn and disposition it were easy to replace them at all. [(*Here the MS. ends.*)]

Browne Willis

[Nichols' account of Browne Willis comes principally from *Lit. Anec.*, VI, 186-211, and an addition to it in VIII, 217-223. Numerous references to him are scattered throughout *Literary Anecdotes* and *Illustrations;* and since Nichols possessed a large collection of his letters, he put them in wherever he could find an appropriate place. Nichols acknowledged that a good deal of his material was taken from a memoir of Willis read by Andrew Coltée Ducarel before the Society of Antiquaries in 1760; but, as is his usual procedure, Nichols augmented his borrowed material with a great many details supplied by himself, much of it in the notes he appended to Ducarel's text. To the extent that such notes are interesting or of some significance, they will be supplied.

Willis, a man of considerable means, had associations with a number of other men whose lives are in this volume, principally with William Cole, who received the gift of his living at Bletchley from Willis. As will be seen, Nichols came near to obtaining some of Willis's Buckinghamshire manuscripts by means of Cole. Willis used his fortune in pursuit of antiquities and in gifts to charities and to his ten children; in his early twenties he was a Member of Parliament and a man of means, but in his later years he was reduced to penurious living and was often taken to be a beggar.

Letters and manuscripts of Willis are now located in a number of libraries on both sides of the Atlantic. Many of his notes and manuscripts are in the British Museum, including his letters to William Cole and others. Cole's letters to Willis are in the Bodleian Library. The Osborn Collection at Yale has in it the manuscript of Ducarel's memoir of Willis, and inserted in it are a number of letters and other manuscripts.

A brief life of Willis by William Prideaux Courtney, listing *Literary Anecdotes* as a primary source, is in the DNB; the author, however, does not mention the earlier appearance of Nichols' life of Willis in the *Biographical and Literary Anecdotes of William Bowyer* of 1782. The most recent work on Willis is that of John G. Jenkins in a book entitled *The Dragon of Whaddon* (1953).]

BROWNE WILLIS, esq. LL.D. was born Sept. 14, 1682, at St. Mary Blandford, in the county of Dorset. He was grandson of Dr. Thomas Willis, the most celebrated physician of his time, and the eldest son of Thomas Willis, esq. of Bletchley, in the county of Bucks. His mother was daughter of Robert Browne, esq. of Frampton, in Dorsetshire.

[Nichols' note to the above, *Lit. Anec.*, VI, 186-187:] [Mr. Willis's father and mother, Thomas and Alice, were buried in the chancel at Bletchley, both in one year, 1699, as their inscriptions on separate slabs set forth. His father died 1699, aged 41. His mother died a few weeks after her husband, of a broken heart for her loss, aged 35; and on her death her son left Westminster school. Out of regard to their memory, he contributed largely between 1704 and 1707 to the repairing Bletchley church, of which he was a patron; and of which a view is inserted in the Gentleman's Magazine, vol. LXIV. p. 304. An account, fairly written, of the repairs and expenditures thereon by Browne Willis, amounting to 800*l*. (a faculty for which was obtained in the Commons, signed Thomas Ayloffe, LL.D.) is preserved in the church chest. Mr. Willis gave eight musical bells, cast by Rudhall of Gloucester, 1712; and exceeding handsome communion plate, with his own and wife's arms engraved on each piece, and inscriptions commemorating her as the donor, instead of himself. Jane, sister of Mr. Willis, was married to Germanicus Sheppard; and had issue Thomas Sheppard, who died without issue.

The following lines are also placed in Fenny Stratford Chapel,

>to the Memory of THOMAS WILLIS, M.D.
>
>In honour to thy mem'ry, blessed Shade!
>Was the foundation of this Chapel laid.
>Purchas'd by thee, thy son, and present heir,
>Owes these three manors to thy sacred care.
>For this, may all thy race thanks ever pay,
>And yearly celebrate St. Martin's day!   B.W.]]

He had the first part of his education under Mr. Abraham Freestone at Bechampton; whence he was sent to Westminster school;* and at the age of seventeen was admitted a gentleman commoner of Christ Church college, Oxon, under the tuition of Edward Wells, D.D. the famous Geographer.

[Nichols' note:] Amongst Mr. Browne Willis's publications is a little tract, intituled, "Reflecting Sermons considered; occasioned by several Discourses delivered in the Parish Church of Bletchley, in the County of Bucks (of which Dr. Willis was Patron), by Dr. E. Wells, rector, and Dr. E. Wells (his nephew), Curate," on some dispute with Mr. Edward Wells, who had been his tutor at Christ Church, and whom he presented to this living on the death of Matthew Disney, 1715.... He addressed to his patron a dialogue on "the great and indispensable duty to contribute liberally to the re-building, building, repairing, beautifying, and adorning churches, perused and approved of by the late most pious Robert Nelson, esq." Yet it appears he took the opportunity of the pulpit to "mark out by slander his benefactor, the very man who by mistake in an uncommon manner gave him the stand and opportunity of his misbehaviour." Dr. Wells was succeeded at Bletchley, in 1727, by Dr. Martin Benson, afterwards Bishop of Gloucester; and he, in

---

* The neighbouring Abbey drew his admiration: here he loved to walk and contemplate. The solemnity of the building, the antique appearance, the monuments, filled his whole mind. He delighted himself in reading old inscriptions. Here he first imbibed the love of antiquities, and the impression grew indelible. NICHOLS.

1740, by John, second son of Browne Willis; he by Thomas Willis, son of Henry, Browne Willis's third son, for whom the living was held by the Rev. W[illiam]. Cole of Milton, the well-known antiquary.... In a letter from Mr. Cole to Dr. Ducarel, 1760, he says Mr. Willis was no otherwise acquainted with Dr. Wells than by his works, when he gave him the living. It is believed that Mr. Adams, whose picture was at Whaddon hall, was his tutor.

When he left Oxford, he lived for three years under the tuition of Dr. William Wotton.

[Nichols' note:] "Mr. Willis always used to mention this friend of his by the style of William Wotton *Bachelor of Divinity,* that he might testify his protest against degrees given at Lambeth; for W. Wotton was in reality a Lambeth Doctor, and was consequently a titular Doctor at least." BOWYER, MS.—"A Doctor in all respects." *T.F.* [Editor's note: T.F. stands for "Taylor's Friend," the Rev. George Ashby. Another example of Willis's attitude toward Lambeth doctors is given by Nichols in a note to his life of Thomas Herring, Archbishop of Canterbury, in which he reports a visit paid by Willis to Dr. Herring, *Illustr.,* III, 455.] [Another free speaker, Browne Willis, being on a visit to him, and a certain Doctor being named by his Grace, "Doctor T.!" quoth the Antiquary, "and pray how came he to be a Doctor?" "I gave him the degree." "Oh! a Lambeth Doctor!" exclaimed Willis: "Yet (said the Archbishop when he related it) he came to ask a favour of me, nor did he fare the worse for the freedom."]

In 1702 he proved a considerable benefactor to Fenny Stratford, by reviving the market of that town; and between the years 1704 and 1707 he contributed very largely towards the repairing and beautifying Bletchley church.

[Nichols' note to the above:] "An estate called Burlton, in the parish of Burghill, near Hereford, at the beginning of this (the eighteenth) century belonged to Browne Willis, the celebrated Antiquary, who together with Mr. Brown and Mr. Mostyn, were the contemporaries and intimate friends of Philips the poet." *Price's Hereford,* p. 161.

In 1705 he was chosen member of parliament for the town of Buckingham, in the room of Sir Richard Temple, bart. who had made his election for the county of Bucks; and, during the short time he was in parliament, he was a constant attendant, and generally upon committees.

In 1707 he married Catharine, daughter of Daniel Elliot, esq. of a very antient family in Cornwall, with whom he had a fortune of 8000*l.* and by whom he had a numerous issue. She died October 2, 1724, aged 34, and was buried at Bletchley.

[Nichols' note to the above:] "Mr. Browne Willis's *wife* wrote a book intituled, 'The Established Church of England, the true Catholic Church, free from Innovations, or diminishing the Apostolick Doctrines, the Sacraments and Doctrines whereof are herein set forth.' Lond. printed for R.

Gosling, 1718, small 8vo, pp. 140.—Browne Willis had a copy in which is the following MS note, among others of the ludicrous kind. 'N.B. All the connexion in this book, is owing to the book-binder.' Browne Willis used to make a great joke of this book." *Mr. Cole, MS.*

In 1717-18, the Society of Antiquaries being revived, Mr. Willis became an active member of it.

Aug. 23, 1720, the degree of M.A. was conferred on him, by diploma, by the University of Oxford.

Mr. Willis, in a letter to the Rev. Mr. Williams, 1723, speaks as if he had an employment in the Tower; and says, "Mr. [William] Sliford, who has been with Mr. [John] Brydges, and was my amanuensis seven years (being at that time at Lincoln, picking up what he can out of the registers there), shall, if you will give me your orders, endeavour to furnish you a better Catalogue (of the Inhabitants of Wickdive).

Again, to another friend, "If I can serve you in the Tower, or any where else in my trade, I shall heartily rejoice to be employed." Feb. 1723-4.

To the extracts from Wanley's Diary, vol. I. p. 87, add, "Mr. Browne Willis came, wanting to peruse one of Holmes's MSS. marked L, and did so; and also L_2, L_3, and L_4, without finding what he expected. He would have explained to me his design in his intended book about Cathedrals; but I said I was about my Lord's necessary business, and had not leisure to spend upon any matter foreign to that. He wanted the liberty to look over Holmes's MSS. and indeed over all this library, that he might collect materials for amending his former books, and putting forth new ones. I signified to him that it would be too great a work; and that I, having business appointed me by my Lord, which required much dispatch, could not in such a case attend upon him. He would have teazed me here this whole afternoon, but I would not suffer him. At length he departed in great anger, and I hope to be rid of him." December 13, 1725.

At his solicitation, and in concurrence with his cousin, Dr. Martin Benson, afterwards Bishop of Gloucester, rector of Fenny-Stratford, a subscription was raised for building the beautiful chapel of St. Martin's† in that parish; which was begun in 1724, and consecrated by Dr. Richard Reynolds, bishop of Lincoln, May 27, 1730.

A dreadful fire having destroyed above 50 houses, and the church, at Stoney-Stratford, May 19, 1746, Mr. Willis, besides collecting money among his friends for the benefit of the unhappy sufferers, repaired, at his own expence, the tower of the church; and afterwards gave a lottery-ticket towards the rebuilding of that church, which came up a prize.

In 1741 he presented the University of Oxford with his fine cabinet of English coins, at that time looked upon as the most complete collection in England, and which he had been upwards of forty years in collecting;

---

† A remarkable circular letter on this occasion (most probably written by Mr. Willis) is printed in the Political Register, 1725, vol. XXX. p. 596. NICHOLS.

but the University thinking it too much for him, who had then a large family, to give the gold ones, purchased them for 150 guineas, which were paid to Mr. Willis for 167 English gold coins, at the rate of four guineas per ounce weight; and even in this way the gold coins were a considerable benefaction. This cabinet Mr. Willis annually visited upon the 19th of October, being St. Frideswide's day, and never failed making some addition to it.‡ He also gave some MSS. to the Bodleian Library, together with a picture of his grandfather, Dr. Thomas Willis.—In 1749 he was honoured by the University with the degree of LL.D. by diploma.

In 1752 he laid out 200*l.* towards the repairs of the fine tower at Buckingham church; and was, upon every occasion, a great friend to that town.

[Nichols' notes to the above:] (1) This tower fell down in the year 177., just as Mr. Pennant was gone out, and so completely ruined the church, that it was necessary to take it down; and being rebuilt on the Castle Hill, it exhibits a fine view from Lord Temple's gardens at Stowe.—This instance, however it may shew Browne Willis's church-munificence, should yet make us cautious how we raise ponderous additions to old and decayed buildings. Who can say that the original builders here, and in many other places, might not stop short in despair of completing their designs with safety? It should seem, from the tradition of the inhabitants, that the fall of this tower was not altogether unexpected.—Counsellor Charles Cole visiting the church, and seeing a decent looking person, asked him if they had any *presentiment?* He said, "I always told my family to shut the pew-door softly after them!" *T.F.* (George Ashby)

(2) "Browne Willis had a most passionate regard for the town of Buckingham, which he represented in parliament one session, or part of a session. This he shewed on every occasion, and particularly in endeavouring to get a new charter for them, and to get the bailiff changed into a mayor; by unwearied application in getting the assizes held once a year there, and procuring the archdeacon to hold his visitations, and also the bishop there, as often as possible; by promoting the building of a jail in the town; and, above all, by procuring subscriptions, and himself liberally contributing, to the raising the tower of the church 24 feet higher. As he cultivated an interest opposite to the Temple family, they were never upon good terms; and made verses on each other on their several foibles." *Mr. Cole, MS.*

In 1756, Bow Brickhill church, which had been disused near 150 years, was restored and repaired by the generosity of Dr. Willis.

In 1757, he erected, in Christ Church, Oxford, a handsome monument for Dr. Iles, canon of that cathedral, to whom his grandfather was an exhibitioner;§ and in 1759 he prevailed upon University College to do the same in Bechampton church for their great benefactor Sir Simon Benet, bart.|| above 100 years after his death; he also, at his own expence, placed

‡ "And, as is said, subtractions." *T.F.* NICHOLS. (*T. F.* is "Taylor's Friend," George Ashby.)

§ One who contributes towards the expences of a person at the University. NICHOLS.

|| "As Sir Simon Benet's monument was set up by University College without the date of his death, I have, at my own expence, laid a small neat marble over his grave, and

a square marble stone over him, on account of his benefactions at Bechampton, Buckingham, Stoney-Stratford, &c.

Dr. Willis died at Whaddon hall, Feb. 5, 1760; and was buried in Fenny-Stratford chapel,‡ Feb. 11, with this inscription (drawn up by himself), on a white marble tablet set in a black frame:

> Hic situs est
> BROWNE WILLIS, Antiquarius,
> cujus avi cl^{mi}. aeternae memoriae,
> Thomae Willis,
> Archiatri totius Europae celeberrimi,
> defuncti die Sancti Martini, A.D. 1675,
> haec capella exiguum monumentum est.
> Obiit 5º die Feb. A.D. 1760,
> aetatis suae 78.
> O Christe, soter et judex,
> huic peccatorum primo
> misericors et propitius esto.

He had been in a declining state for several months before. His last letter to Dr. Ducarel, dated Jan. 6, 1760, is scarcely legible; expressing how exceeding ill he was, and little capable of writing; yet, wishing for "interest with his Grace of Canterbury, to do something for a most valuable minister here, who had served this parish (Whaddon) with the utmost duty for about nine years, and he could vouch for his worth." This must be Mr. Gibberd,[1] who, in a letter to the Doctor, Feb. 5, tells him Mr. Willis died that morning, with great ease, and without the usual agonies of death.

[Nichols' note:] [The following is the character drawn of him by Mr. Gibberd:] "He was strictly religious, without any mixture of superstition or enthusiasm. The honour of God was his prime view in almost every action of his life. He was a constant frequenter of the church, and never absented himself from the holy communion; and, as to the reverence he had for places more immediately set apart for religious duties, it is needless to mention what his many public works, in building, repairing, and beautifying churches, are standing evidences of. In the time of health he called his family together every evening, and, besides his private devotions in the

---

supplied that defect. My service and thanks ever to University College for their generous regard to their benefactor. What they have done looks very handsome, and all the country commend it much." *Browne Willis, MS.* NICHOLS.

‡ "This chapel was founded by him, through he assumed no merit to himself on that account, but attributed all to the munificence of others, who were in reality only contributors. He left particular directions as to his funeral, and desired that no people might be invited to it, except the mayor and aldermen of Buckingham; to each of whom he left his first volume of 'Notitia Parliamentaria,' and a small legacy besides." *Mr. [John] Gibberd to Dr. Ducarel.* NICHOLS.

1. John Gibberd performed the service at Willis's funeral. Nichols, in a note, quotes from a letter written by Gibberd: "I have on this occasion sustained an immense loss, Dr. Willis having always shewn the greatest kindness and regard to me from my first coming into this parish. . . . 'Ah! Mr. Gibberd, God bless you for ever, Mr. Gibberd!' were almost the last words of my dying friend."

morning, he always retired into his closet in the afternoon at about 4 or 5 o'clock. In his intercourse with men he was in every respect, as far as I could judge, very upright. He was a good landlord, and scarce ever raised his rents; and that his servants likewise have no reason to complain of their master is evident from the long time they generally lived with him. He had many valuable and good friends, whose kindness he always acknowledged. And though perhaps he might have some disputes with a few people, the reason of which it would be disagreeable to enter into, yet it is with great satisfaction that I can affirm that he was perfectly reconciled with every one. He was, with regard to himself, peculiarly sober and temperate; and he has often told me, that he denied himself many things, that he might bestow them better. Indeed, he appeared to me to have no greater regard to money than as it furnished him with an opportunity of doing good. He supplied yearly three charity schools at Whaddon, Bletchley, and Fenny Stratford; and, besides what he constantly gave at Christmas, he was never backward in relieving his poor neighbours with both wine and money when they were sick, or in any kind of distress. He was a faithful friend where he professed it, and always ready to contribute any thing to their advantage."

Mr. Cole, then rector of Bletchley, Mr. John Gibberd, A.M. of Magdalen hall, curate of Whaddon, and Mr. Francis, minister of Fenny Stratford, attended his funeral in a mourning coach, and near 60 of his neighbours and tenants on horseback; the last offices being, by particular desire, performed by Mr. Gibberd.

Of ten children which Mr. Willis had, he left surviving only two twin daughters, Gertrude and Catharine, who both died the same year, 1772.[2] His son Thomas died before him, of the gout, 1756, leaving, by his second wife, two sons, Thomas and John, and a daughter Anne, married to —— Smith, esq. who left no issue. His youngest son, born 1743, being 17 years old, Aug. 1, 1760, now of Stoneham, Hants, took the name of Fleming. On his mother, who died of an asthmatic complaint, June 1767, aged 51, Dr. Willis settled his estate at Whaddon for life, and after her decease to her eldest son, Thomas (11 years old, 1760, who died before her, 1767, under age), &c. subject to the payment of an annuity of 20*l.* to her third son Henry's son Thomas for life, for whom Mr. Cole held the living of Bletchley, and then to his daughters Gertrude and Catharine.

[Nichols' note:] His grandson was third in the entail of Whaddon, and the two before him not very good lives. The living of Bletchley in 1768 was in the trustees of Thomas Willis, esq. His daughter-in-law sold the estate at Whaddon, in 1760, to Thomas James Selby, esq. who pulled down the principal part of the house, and re-built it in a good style. Part of the old brick building remains behind, with some wreathed brick chimnies. And, by will dated August 19, 1768, he left it, with the estate (in case no heir at law should be found within 12 months after his decease) to William Lowndes, esq. of Winslow, who, on a decision of the Court of King's Bench in his favour, Dec. 5, 1776, took possession of the estate, and has taken the

---

2. In a long note taken from Gough's mss. Nichols gives the names and vital statistics of Willis's children, their spouses, and their children.

name of Selby, and given the house at Whaddon, with part of his estate, to his son William Lowndes, esq. When Mr. Willis first came to the possession of this estate it was worth 2000*l*. a year. The manor of Whaddon was purchased in 1698 by James Selby and Thomas Willis, father of Browne Willis, who retired for a few years to Shrub lodge, in Whittlesey forest, and the manor-house, and that part of the manor called Whaddon Hall, being separated on the partition of lands, came to Browne Willis as heir to his father. This part, being one-third, he by his last will invested in trustees for the payment of younger children's fortunes. In this affair he had very hard usage; his part being sold for not more hundred than it was worth thousand pounds. He built Water hall, in Bletchley, at an expence of more than 5000*l*. which has been lately pulled down by Lord Spencer's Steward, who bought it; and, after building this house, Mr. Willis purchased Whaddon hall, which is about 100*l*. a year. His lady's family was descended from Walter Gifford, earl of Bucks, in the reign of the Conqueror, lord of the manor of Bletchley. Her fortune was 8000*l*. The family estate, of about 2000*l*. a year, was given by her father to Edward Gifford, esq. a relation, whom she refused on account of his relationship. Upon the decease of the Rev. Thomas Willis, grandson of Browne Willis, esq. (who left the presentation of Bletchley rectory by will to the said Thomas Willis, whose widow, a son, and five daughters, are now living at Bath), John Willis Fleming, esq. of Stoneham, Hants, grandson of the said Browne Willis, presented to the living of Bletchley the Rev. Edward Orlebar Smith, of Holcot, by Aspley, who married Miss Charlotte Hervey, daughter of the Rev. Edward Hervey, by Mary, daughter of the said Browne Willis. The said John Willis Fleming is now living at North Stoneham; he married Miss Knightley of Northamptonshire, and has no issue, and on failure of issue this estate goes to his cousin of the name of Willis.—I George III. 1761, an act passed for selling a messuage and lands in Whaddon, in the county of Bucks, settled by the late Browne Willis, esq. on the marriage of his son; and for purchasing another estate in lieu thereof to be settled to the same uses. *Mr. Gough MS.*

He gave to his eldest grandson and heir (whom he appointed sole executor) all his books, pictures, &c. except "Rymer's Foedera," in 17 folio volumes, which he bequeathed to Trinity College, Oxford, and the choice of one book to the Rev. Mr. Francis Wise; and ordered his manuscripts to be sent within a quarter of a year to the University of Oxford.

In 1710, when Mr. Gale published his "History and Antiquities of Winchester Cathedral," Mr. Willis supplied him with the History of Hyde Abbey, and Lists of the Abbots of Newminster and Hyde, therein published. In 1712, he published "Queries for the History and Survey of the County of Buckingham," in one sheet folio. In 1715 and 1716 his "Notitia Parliamentaria, or an History of the Counties, Cities, and Boroughs in England and Wales," 2 vols. 8vo; to which he added a third in 1750. The first volume was reprinted in 1730, with additions; and a single sheet, so far as relates to the borough of Windsor, in folio, 1733. In 1717 he published "The Whole Duty of Man, considered under its Three principal and general Divisions; namely, the Duties we owe to God, ourselves, and Neighbours, faitfully extracted from that excellent Book so intituled, and published for the Benefit of the poorer Sort. By a Gentleman." In the "Antiquities of the

Cathedral Church of Worcester," written by Thomas Abingdon, esq. and published by Dr. Rawlinson, in 8vo, London, 1717, at page 116 is a list of the Priors of Worcester, by Browne Willis, esq. In 1717 he published "A Survey of the Cathedral Church of St. David's, and the Edifices belonging to it, as they stood in the Year 1715," 8vo; in 1718 and 1719, "An History of the Mitred Parliamentary Abbies and Conventual Cathedral Churches,* 2 vols. 8vo; in 1719, 1720, 1721, "Surveys of the Cathedral Churches of Landaff, St. Asaph, and Bangor, and the Edifices belonging to each," 8vo, with cuts. In Peck's Stanford, the South-west prospect of Mr. Browne's Hospital is inscribed, "To that curious and communicative Antiquary Browne Willis, esq." In 1720 he assisted Mr. Strype in an edition of Stowe's Survey of London; in 1729, he published "A Prayer, &c." 8vo; "Survey of the Cathedrals of England, with *Parochiale Anglicanum*, illustrated with Draughts of the Cathedrals," 3 vols. 4to, in 1727, 1730, 1733.

[Nichols' note:] The title-page, dated 1742, is a bookseller's trick, to give a new title to an old book, in order to get rid of unsold copies. The Surveys were printed for R. Gosling, at the Middle Temple Gate in Fleet-street, in 1727.—My bookseller, Mr. Francis Gosling (now, *anno* 1757, a banker), having left off that trade, he sold the copies of my Cathedrals to Mr. Osborne, who, to dispose of them very knavishly advertised, that I had given the histories of all the 26 Cathedrals. On which account, in my own vindication, I printed the underwritten Advertisement, in the London Evening Post, March 5—8, 1743: "Whereas it hath been lately advertised in several public papers, and particularly at the end of the Proposals for printing by subscription the two first volumes of Bibliotheca Harleiana, that there is now republished, in three volumes, 4to, 'A Survey of the Cathedrals of Durham, &c. By Browne Willis, esq.:' this is to inform the publick, that the said Browne Willis has not published any account of the Members, or given any description, history, or draughts whatsoever of these following Cathedrals; viz. Canterbury, Norwich, Salisbury, Wells, and Exeter; and that what he has published in relation to the History of the Four Welsh Cathedrals; viz. St. David's, Landaff, Bangor, and St. Asaph, is in four separate 8vo volumes, printed about 20 years ago." *From Browne Willis's MS. in his own Copy.*

"A Table of the Gold Coins of the Kings of England, by B.W.† Esq. a Member of the Society of Antiquaries, London, 1733," in one sheet folio, making Plate XL. of their "Vetusta Monumenta," was of his compiling; as were the series of Principals of Religious Houses, at the end of Bishop Tanner's "Notitia Monastica" in folio, 1744, sent by him 1743 to Mr. John Tanner, editor of that work.—In 1748, in answer to Mr. Morant, who had asked permission to dedicate to him a plate of the "History of Colchester," he said, "he had just married his children; and, in acting the part of a Father, had reduced himself so low that he knew not how to be Patron."— In 1749 he published "Proposals for printing a Journal of the House of

---

* A recommendatory letter by Dr. Wotton is prefixed to the second volume of this work. NICHOLS.

† In some copies it is printed "W.B. esq." NICHOLS.

Commons." Before the year 1752 he printed, in 8 pages of 4to, an address, "to the Patrons of Ecclesiastical Livings," with the good view to prevent plurality and non-residence; and in 1754, an improved edition of "Ecton's Thesaurus Rerum Ecclesiasticarum," 4to. His last publication was the "History and Antiquities of the Town, Hundred, and Deanry, of Buckingham, London, 1755," 4to. His large collections for the whole county are now among his MSS. in the Bodleian Library.

His old friend Mr. Cole transcribed and methodized, in two volumes folio, his "History of the Hundreds of Newport and Cotslow," from the originals, in four volumes, which Mr. Willis delivered to him a few days before his death,‡ with an earnest request that he would prepare them for publication; for which they were ready in 1782, when Mr. Cole would have given them to the Compiler of these Anecdotes, if leisure had then permitted him to visit Milton. They are now, however, with Mr. Cole's valuable MSS. in the British Museum, and it is much to be lamented that this part of the labours of a most industrious Antiquary, from 1712 to his death 1760, should be lost to the publick, who derive so much advantage from such of them as are published.

[Nichols' note to the statement that Cole would have given the papers to him if he had visited Milton:] [This will appear by the following correspondence.

1. Mr. GOUGH to Mr. COLE.]
DEAR SIR, *Enfield, Sept.* 25, 1782.

Mr. Nichols most readily accepts your offer of *Mr. Willis's Bucks MSS;* and will print them out of hand, without any trouble or expence to you. If you have no objection to his using your transcript, it may be forwarded to me, or to Mr. Nichols, as soon as you please. It will be printed in a form and type to suit the History of Buckingham; to which I suppose it would make a good second volume. I will gladly correct the press, and hope it will make its appearance early in the winter. . . . Hoping no ill effects followed from our soliciting you into the company of your friends; and with the sincerest wishes for the re-establishment and long continuance of your health; I am dear Sir, yours, &c. R. GOUGH.

[2. Mr. COLE to Mr. GOUGH.]
DEAR SIR, *Milton, Friday morning, Oct.* 4, 1782.

I love to put things on a right footing. It was not I that made the offer to Mr. Nichols to print Mr. Willis's Hundreds of Newport and Cotslow, but you. They would never have been thought of, had not you proposed it. I had no objections, especially as I like well Mr. Nichols's writings, and don't observe any party reflections in them. Yet I should shudder at the thoughts of the trouble (which all along deterred my indolence from printing them, when well), did not your kind and obliging offer of correcting the press (without any trouble or expence to me) encourage me to put them into Mr. Nichols's hands, to whom I have wrote to-day on the subject, and

---

‡ Mr. Cole received the MS. Jan. 30, 1760; and had transcribed 503 pages on the 13th of February. NICHOLS.

proposed to him to look at the volumes; for, without seeing him, I can resolve on nothing; there being many other volumes which relate to the same subject, which must necessarily be sent to him.

[3. Mr. COLE to Mr. NICHOLS.]

DEAR SIR, *Milton, Frid. morn. Oct.* 4, 1782.

I wanted to answer your obliging letter before, but have been so ill all the week that I had no powers to write, though Mr. Steevens told me on Sunday, that Mr. [Isaac] Reed would take any books or letters with him to town about Wednesday. I have seen neither since; and am obliged to make you pay postage again. In Mr. Gough's inclosed letter he tells me, that you readily accept *my offer* of Mr. Willis's Buckinghamshire MSS. I love to put things in their proper order: it was no offer of mine; nor would the books have been mentioned, had not Mr. Gough first proposed it. I told him, that I had no exception to your printing them, but under certain preliminaries, which it is impossible to fix without shewing you the books; for I must send you more than the two folio volumes; as I have in my other volumes many things pertaining to the several parishes and the two hundreds, which I have methodized and arranged pretty exactly. It has been fear of trouble that has prevented me from publishing them, according to Mr. Willis's request; and now I am less able to do it; except you and Mr. Gough, as he has been so kind as to offer, will correct the press: I dare not undertake it. I will insist upon no interpolations; and that Mr. Willis's book may not have two or three different complexions. Both he and I would not be ashamed of our Tory principles, let them be ever so unfashionable. With Mr. Steevens's§ leave, I will give the etching of Mr. Willis, to be put before the first volume; for I am satisfied there is enough for two, equal to his Buckingham Hundred, which must be the pattern, rough as it is, to what will follow. I hope it will be no unreasonable request, to expect a few copies to give to such friends as have presented me with their publications. I don't mean more than a dozen, or ten. And shall expect to have the proof-sheet of every parish sent to me before concluded. I will endeavour to get franks for you and me, on the occasion; and if a few slight etchings of a few tombs and antient arms were here and there spread, it would enliven a work that, I am afraid, will want such embellishments. I believe Mr. Steevens will stay all next week: possibly longer. Could not you contrive, without great inconvenience, to take a trip hither for a day or two? And, though I am in no condition for company, being the greatest part of the day on the bed, and much talking oppressive to me; yet I don't see it possible for you to go on without first looking at my books, and my telling you what I would have omitted, if you approve of it, in order to lessen the bulk of it. After a good night, I am tolerable to-day; and am, dear Sir,

Your much obliged servant, WM. COLE.

[4. Mr. COLE to Mr. GOUGH.]

DEAR SIR, *Milton, Tuesday, Oct.* 29, 1782.

Yours of Oct. 21 I did not receive till Sunday noon, Oct. 27. . . . Mr. Steevens, who leaves Cambridge on Saturday, has been so kind to offer to carry my volume of Croyland, and any thing else, to Mr. Nichols's. . . . If Mr. Nichols comes, I shall be heartily glad to see him, and keep to my

§ The late George Steevens, esq. of Hampstead Heath, editor of Shakspeare. NICHOLS.

Isaac Reed

Reverend Richard Farmer, D.D.

George Steevens, Esq., F.R.S.

Reverend William Cole, A.M.

promise; but I was rather glad that he seemed indifferent; and will now, by no means, as I told you by word of mouth, have the obligation to lie on my side; especially as I mean to receive no emolument from it. Yet I make no doubt but Mr. Archdeacon would print them for me, with advantage, at the University press, was I to shew them to him. But I never shewed them to him, or any other person in the world, but to you, on your asking after them; and to Mr. Steevens, since I saw you. He dined here yesterday, *téte à téte.*

I am, yours faithfully,   WM. COLE.

[5. Mr. COLE to Mr. NICHOLS.]
DEAR SIR,   *Milton, Tuesd. Oct.* 29, 1782.

I did not receive your packet, and letter of 22, till Sunday noon. I am much obliged to you for the care of Mr. [Thomas] Pennant's packet; and shall be sincerely glad to see you at Milton, whenever it suits your best convenience; but it would have been much to my satisfaction, if it could have been while Mr. Steevens was in the neighbourhood; who is so kind to interest himself in my matters, now I am so unable to do it, to any purpose, myself. After a stay of six or seven weeks, he proposes to leave Cambridge on Saturday, and undertakes to deliver *this,* and a *parcel* for *Mr. Gough,* to your care. In good truth, the alarms and fears I had of a great increase of trouble, at a time I am so ill disposed to undergo it, made me receive your letter with pleasure, as it seemed to defer, and put off at a distance, what so embarrassed me. Besides your saying, that you had rather I would print it myself, or some bookseller: if those are your present sentiments, I had much rather let the undertaking cool longer. But if, upon your inspection (and without it, it is impossible for me to conclude any thing on the subject), you will think it worth your while to undertake it, I will not be worse than my word. Mr. Steevens, when you see him, will probably tell you my difficulties. If you mean for Cambridgeshire, be so good to give me a day or two's notice; and I will send my carriage for you to Cambridge, if you come by the fly, or the coach, or diligence, where you will meet with a well-aired bed. And in the mean time, I am, dear Sir,

Your much obliged and faithful servant,   WM. COLE.

I am indebted for great part of this memoir to the "Account of Mr. Willis," which was read before the Society of Antiquaries in 1760, by Dr. Ducarel, who thus sums up the character of his friend: "This learned Society, of which he was one of the first revivers, and one of the most industrious members, can bear me witness, that he was indefatigable in his researches; for his works were the most laborious kind. But what enabled him, besides his unwaried diligence, to bring them to perfection, was, his being blessed with a most excellent memory. He had laid so good a foundation of learning, that though he had chiefly conversed with records, and other matters of antiquity, which are not apt to form a polite style, yet he expressed himself, in all his compositions, in an easy and genteel manner. He was, indeed, one of the first who placed our ecclesiastical history and antiquities upon a firm basis, by grounding them upon records and registers; which, in the main, are unexceptionable authorities. During the course of his long life, he had visited every Cathedral in England and Wales, except Carlisle; which journeys he used to call his *pilgrimages.*

[Nichols' note:] Among the innumerable stories that are told of him, and the difficulties and rebuffs he met with in his favourite pursuits, the following may suffice as a specimen. One day he desired his neighbour, Mr. [Richard] Lowndes, to go with him to one of his tenants, whose old habitation he wanted to view. A coach driving into the farm-yard, sufficiently alarmed the family, who betook themselves to close-quarters; when Browne Willis, spying a woman at a window, thrust his head out of the coach, and cried out, "Woman, I ask you if you have got no *arms* in your house." As the transaction happened to be in the Rebellion of 1745, when searches for arms were talked of, the woman was still less pleased with her visitor, and began to talk accordingly. When Mr. Lowndes had enjoyed enough of this absurdity, he said, "Neighbour, it is rather cold sitting here; if you will let me put my head out, I dare say we shall do our business much better." So the late Dr. [John] Newcome, going in his coach through one of the villages near Cambridge, and seeing an old mansion, called out to an old woman, "Woman, is this a *religious house*?" "I don't know what you mean by a religious house," retorted the woman; "but I believe the house is as honest an house as any of yours at Cambridge." *Dr. Taylor's Friend* [George Ashby]. —Riding over Mendip or Chedder, he came to a church under the hill, the steeple just rising above them, and near 20 acres of water belonging to Mr. Cox. He asked a countryman the church's name—"Emburrough." "When was it dedicated?" "Talk English, or don't talk at all." "When is the revel, or wake?" The fellow thought, as there was a match at quarter-staff for a hat in the neighbourhood, he intended to make one; and, struck with his mean appearance besides, challenged him in a rude way, and so they parted. He used, when taxed with this adventure, to put it off with—"people will have their jokes." He told Mr. S. Bush he was going to Bristol on St. Austin's-day to see the cathedral, it being the dedication day. He would lodge in no house at Bath but the Abbey-house. He said, when he was told that Wells cathedral was 800 years old, there was not a stone of it left 500 years ago. *Mr. Gough, MS.*

In his friendships, none more sincere and hearty; always communicative, and ever ready to assist every studious and inquisitive person. This occasioned an acquaintance and connexion between him and all his learned contemporaries. For his mother, the University of Oxford, he always expressed the most awful respect and the warmest esteem. As to his piety and moral qualifications, he was strictly religious, without any mixture of superstition or enthusiasm, and quite exemplary in this respect: and of this, his many public works, in building, repairing, and beautifying of churches, are so many standing evidences. He was charitable to the poor and needy; just and upright towards all men.

[Nichols' note:] [He was, however, a striking instance of the contrariety of feelings which sometimes operate in the same person in different extremes. Thus Mr. Cole remarks:] "I had occasion to see this year, 1760, the fever and violence of passion (for money), when a gentleman in the very agonies of death, on seeing a person come into his chamber, whom he expected to bring him a small sum of money, could not help crying out, though hardly to be understood, 'Where is the money?' This gentleman was Browne Willis; when Mr. Cook of Water-Eaton, a kind of steward to him, came into the room at Whaddon, when he was dying. I was by. This I write Dec. 7, 1766. Mr. Cooke paid the money to his grandson, Mr. Thomas Willis. It was only four or five pounds." *Mr. Cole, MS.*

In a word, no one ever deserved better of the Society of Antiquaries; if industry and an incessant application, throughout a long life, to the investigating the antiquities of this national church and state, is deserving of their countenance."

To this well-drawn character I shall take the liberty to annex a sportive sally of a female pen, the late Miss [Catharine, daughter of Archdeacon Edward] Talbot, who, in an unprinted letter to a lady of first-rate quality (dated from the rectory-house of St. James's parish, Jan. 2, 1738-9) very humorously characterizes Mr. Willis and his daughters.

[Nichols' note:] "You know Browne Willis, or at least it is not my fault that you do not; for when at any time some of his oddities have peculiarly struck my fancy, I have writ you whole volumes about him. However, that you may not be forced to recollect how I have formerly tired you, I will repeat, that, with one of the honestest hearts in the world, he has one of the oddest heads that ever dropped out of the moon. Extremely well versed in coins, he knows hardly any thing of mankind; and you may judge what kind of education such an one is likely to give to four girls, who have had no female directress to polish their behaviour, or any habitation than a great rambling mansion-house in a country village. As, by his little knowledge of the world, he has ruined a fine estate, that was, when he first had it, 2000*l. per annum;* his present circumstances oblige him to an odd-headed kind of frugality, that shews itself in the slovenliness of his dress, and makes him think London much too extravagant an abode for his daughters; at the same time that his zeal for Antiquities makes him think an old copper farthing very cheaply bought for a guinea, and any journey properly undertaken that will bring him to some old Cathedral on the Saint's day to which it was dedicated. As, if you confine the natural growth of a tree, it will shoot out in a wrong place—in spite of his expensiveness, he appears saving in almost every article of life that people would expect him otherwise in; and, in spite of his frugality, his fortune, I believe, grows worse and worse every day. I have told you before, that he is the dirtiest creature in the world; so much so, that it is quite disagreeable to sit by him at table: yet he makes one suit of clothes serve him at least two years; and then his great coat has been transmitted down, I believe, from generation to generation, ever since Noah. One Sunday he was quite a beau. The bishop of Gloucester is his idol; and if Mr. Willis were Pope, St. Martin, as he calls him, would not wait a minute for canonization. To honour last Sunday as it deserved, after having run about all the morning to all the St. George's churches whose difference of hours permitted him, he came to dine with us in a tie-wig, that exceeds indeed all description. 'Tis a tie-wig (the very colour of it is inexpressible) that he has had, he says, these nine years; and of late it has lain by at his barber's, never to be put on but once a year, in honour of the Bishop of Gloucester's (Martin Benson) birth-day.—But, you will say, what is all this to my engagement this morning? Why, you must know, Browne distinguishes his four daughters into the *Lions* and the *Lambs*. The Lambs are very good and very insipid; they were in town about ten days, that ended the beginning of last week; and now the Lions have succeeded them, who have a little spirit of rebellion, that makes them infinitely more agreeable than their sober sisters. The Lambs went to every church Browne pleased every day; the Lions came to St. James's church on St. George's-day. The Lambs thought of no higher entertainment than going to see some collections of shells; the Lions would see every thing, and go every where. The Lambs dined here one day, were thought good awkward girls, and then were laid out of our thoughts for ever. The Lions dined with us on Sunday, and were so extremely diverting, that we spent all yesterday morning, and are engaged to spend all this, in entertaining them, and going to a Comedy, that, I think, has no ill-nature in it; for the simplicity of these girls has nothing blameable in it, and the contemplation of such unassisted nature is infinitely amusing. They follow Miss Jenny's rule, *of never being strange in a strange place*; yet in them this is not boldness. I could send you a thousand traits of them, if I were sure they would not lose by being writ down; but there is no imitating that inimitable *naïveté* which is the grace of their character. They were placed in your seat on Sunday. (Alas! I was used to seeing it filled with people that were quite indifferent to me, till seeing you in it once has thrown a fresh melancholy upon it!) I wondered to have heard no remarks on the Prince and Princess; their remarks on every thing else are admirable. As they sat in the drawing-room before dinner, one of them called to Mr. Secker [brother of the Bishop of Oxford], *I wish you would give me a glass of sack!* The Bishop of Oxford [Thomas Secker, later Archbishop of Canterbury] came in; and one of them broke out very abruptly, *But we heard every word of the Sermon where we sat; and a very good Sermon it was,* added she, with a decisive nod. The Bishop of Gloucester gave them tickets to go to a play; and one of them took great pains to repeat to him, till he heard it, *I would not rob you; but I know you are very rich, and can afford it; for I ben't covetous, indeed I an't covetous.* Poor girls, their father will make them go out of town to-morrow; and they begged very hard that we would all join in entreating him to let them stay a fortnight, as their younger sisters have done; but all our entreaties were in vain, and to-morrow the poor Lions return to their den in the stage-coach. Indeed in his birth-day tie-wig he looked so like the Father in the Farce Mrs. Secker was so diverted with, that I wished a thousand times for the invention of Scapin, and I would have made no scruple of assuming the character, and inspiring my friends with the laudable spirit of rebellion. I have picked out some of the dullest of their traits to tell you. They pressed us extremely to come and breakfast with them at their lodgings four inches square, in Chapel-street, at eight o'clock in the morning, and bring a stay-maker and the Bishop of Gloucester with us. We put off the engagement till eleven, sent the stay-maker to measure them at nine, and Mrs. Secker and I went and found the ladies quite undressed; so that, instead of taking them to Kensington Gardens, as we promised, we were forced, for want of time, to content ourselves with carrying them round Grosvenor Square into the Ring, where, for want of better amusement, they were fain to fall upon the basket of dirty sweet-meats and cakes that an old woman is always teizing you with there, which they had nearly dispatched in a couple of rounds. It were endless to tell you all that has inexpressibly diverted me in their behaviour and conversation. I have yet told you nothing; and yet I have, in telling you nothing, wasted all the time that my heart ought to have employed in saying a thousand things to you, that it is more deeply interested in. I wanted to express a thousand sentiments; but I hope you know them already, and at present my time is all spent. If you have a mind to a second part (which I assure you will far exceed the first) of the Memoirs

of the Lions, tell me so, and you shall have it when you please; for there is no fear of my forgetting what is fixed on my memory by such scenes of mirth.
Yours most faithfully,   C. TALBOT."

[Miss Talbot's letter is a very pleasant one; but would be thought highly satirical in any body else. Dr. [John] Taylor could tell a thousand such stories of Browne Willis and his family.]

"In the summer of 1740, after Mr. Baker's death,[3] his executor came to take possession of the effects, and lived for some time in his chambers at College [St. John's, Cambridge]. Here Browne Willis waited upon him to see some of the MSS. or books; and, after a long visit, to find and examine what he wanted, the old bed-maker of the rooms came in; when the gentleman said, 'What noise was that I heard just as you opened the door?' (he had heard the rustling of silk)—'Oh!' says Browne Willis, 'it is only one of my daughters that I left on the stair case.' This we may suppose was a *Lamb*, by her patient waiting; else a *Lion* would have been better able to resist any petty rudenesses.

"Once, after long teizing, the young ladies prevailed on him to give them a London Jaunt; unluckily the lodgings were (unknown to them) at an undertaker's, the irregular and late hours of whose business was not very agreeable to the young ladies; but they comforted themselves with the thoughts of the pleasure they should have during their stay in town; when, to their great surprize and grief, as soon as they had got their breakfast, the old family coach rumbled to the door, and the father bid them get in, as he had done the business about which he came to town." T. F. [George Ashby]

[I cannot resist the temptation to increase the immoderate length of this note by an extract of a letter from an accomplished and valuable friend (the late Rev. John Kynaston, M.A. fellow of Brasen Nose College [Oxford]), who had seen the preceding paragraphs:]

"*Hot Wells, Bristol, Feb.* 7, 1781.

"Your Anecdotes of the Lions and the Lambs have entertained me prodigiously, as I so well knew the griesly Sire of both. Browne Willis was indeed an original. I met with him at Mr. Cartwright's, at Aynhoe, in Northhamptonshire, in 1753, where I was at that time chaplain to the family, and curate of the parish. Browne came here on a visit of a week that summer. He looked for all the world like an old portrait of the aera of Queen Elizabeth, that had walked down out of its frame. He was, too truly, the very dirty figure Miss Talbot describes him to be; which, with the antiquity of his dress, rendered him infinitely formidable to all the children in the parish. He often called upon me at the parsonage house, when I happened not to dine in the family; having great, and, as it seemed, a very favourite point to carry, which was no less than to persuade me to follow his example, and to turn all my thoughts and studies to *venerable Antiquity;* he deemed *that* the *summum bonum,* the height of all human felicity. I used to entertain Mr. and Mrs. Cartwright highly, by detailing to them Browne's arguments to debauch me from the pursuit of polite literature, and such studies as were most agreeable to my turn and taste; and by parceling out

---

3. This is the Rev. Thomas Baker, who gave a present of a fine common prayer book to Willis's new chapel of St. Martin at Fenny Stratford. Nichols has a memoir of Baker in *Lit. Anec.,* V, 106-117; 662-663.

every morning after prayers... the progress Browne had made the day before in the arts of seduction. I amused him with such answers as I thought best suited to his hobby-horse, till I found he was going to leave us; and then, by a stroke or two of spirited raillery, lost his warm heart and his advice for ever. My egging him on served us, however, for a week's excellent entertainment, amid the dullness and sameness of a country situation. He represented me, at parting, to Mr. Cartwright, as one incorrigible, and lost beyond all hopes of recovery to every thing truly valuable in learning, by having unfortunately let slip that I preferred, and feared I ever should prefer, one page of Livy or Tacitus, Sallust or Caesar, to all the Monkish writers (with Bede at the head of them)...." J.K.

At the rectory house at Bletchley were pictures of his father and mother, and his grandfathers Willis and Browne; all supposed to be still remaining there, with others of the family, and of Archbishop Laud. In the parlour there were also portraits of Bishop [Martin] Benson, and two ladies, and a little girl.

A portrait of Browne Willis was etched in 1781, at the particular request of Mr. Cole, from a drawing made by the Rev. Michael Tyson, from an original painting by [Michael] Dahl.

[Nichols' note:] [Of this portrait of his venerable friend, which is alluded to in the correspondence printed in p. 200 [of *Lit. Anec.*], Mr. Cole speaks thus:] "The copy pleases me infinitely; nothing can be more exact and like the copy I sent, and which, as well as I can recollect, is equally so to the original. To a person who only remembers Mr. Willis's figure in his latter age, it will convey no resemblance of him; and few people are living who remember him young. When I knew him first, about 35 years ago, he had more the appearance of a mumping beggar than of a gentleman; and the most like resemblance of his figure that I can recollect among old prints, is that of Old Hobson the Cambridge carrier. He then, as always, was dressed in an old slouched hat, more brown than black, a weather-beaten large wig, three or four old-fashioned coats, all tied round by a leathern belt, and over all an old blue cloak, lined with black fustian, which he told me he had new made when he was elected member for the town of Buckingham, about 1707. I have still by me, as relicks, this cloak and belt, which I purchased of his servant. No wonder will it be, when the print is given to any one who remembers this figure of Mr. Willis, that they immediately pronounce it unlike; and so it is in good truth; and if I had two pictures of myself, one taken when I was in Blooming youth, and the other in decrepid old age, and was to give the world a print of one of them, would it be judicious to exhibit myself in deformity, when it was in my power to shew away with equal truth as a young man? Notwithstanding the distance of time when Dahl drew this portrait, and that in which I knew him, and the strange metamorphose that age and caprice had made in his figure, yet I could easily trace some lines and traits of what Mr. Dahl had given of him."

[The preceding note formed part of a letter from Mr. Cole to Mr. Steevens; by whom it was communicated, in my former edition,[4] with the

---

4. Nichols habitually refers to his *Biographical and Literary Anecdotes of William Bowyer* of 1782 as the "first edition" of *Literary Anecdotes*. A large part of the life of

consent of Mr. Cole; who, in a letter dated Feb. 6, 1781, says, "You are at liberty to use my letter to Mr. Steevens, on a presumption that there is nothing disrespectful to the memory of Mr. Willis; for what I said I don't recollect. . . ." The *disrespect* was certainly leveled at the mere external foibles of the respectable Antiquary; whose goodness of heart and general spirit of philanthropy were amply sufficient to bear him out in those whimsical peculiarities of dress which were irresistible sources of ridicule.]

Browne Willis was humorously satirized in some doggrel lines written by Dr. Darrell, of Lillington Darrell; and first printed in the Oxford Sausage, 1774.[5]

[The text of the poem that follows appears as a note in Nichols.]

An Excellent BALLAD
To the Tune of *Chevy-Chace.*

Whilome there dwelt near Buckingham,
   That famous county town,
At a known place, hight Whaddon Chace,
   A Squire of odd renown.—

A Druid's sacred form he bore,
   His robes a girdle bound:
Deep vers'd he was in antient lore,
   In customs old, profound.

A stick torn from that hallow'd tree,
   Where Chaucer us'd to sit,
And tell his tales with leering glee,
   Supports his tott'ring feet.

High on a hill his mansion stood,
   But gloomy dark within;
Here mangled books, as bones and blood
   Lie in a giant's den.

Crude, undigested, half-devour'd,
   On groaning shelves they're thrown;
Such manuscripts no eye could read,
   Nor hand write—but his own.

No prophet he, like Sydrophel,

Browne Willis is in the earlier work, pp. 244-250; Cole's letter concerning the portrait is in a note on pp. 581-582. The portrait itself is usually in *Literary Anecdotes,* somewhere in the addition to the life of Willis, VIII, 217-223.

5. In *Lit. Anec.,* VI, 176, is an entry in the life of Thomas Warton: "His next publication was 'The Oxford Sausage,' 1764; of which a second edition appeared in 1777, and a third in 1806." In IX, 803, in "Additions to the Fifth Volume," is a note to the preceding: "It is said the *Oxford Sausage* was published in 1764; but a second Edition in 1777; and a third in 1786.—In the same Volume, p. 210, it is observed, that Browne Willis was satirized in some lines first printed in the *Oxford Sausage* 1774; and my copy of that publication was printed in 1772. The former account cannot, therefore, be correct." JAMES DOWLAND.

    Could future times explore;
But what had happen'd, he could tell,
    Five hundred years and more.

A walking Alm'nack he appears,
    Stept from some mouldy wall,
Worn out of use thro' dust and years,
    Like scutcheons in his hall.

His boots were made of that cow's hide,
    By Guy of Warwick slain;
Time's choicest gifts, aye to abide
    Among the chosen train.

Who first receiv'd the precious boon,
    We're at a loss to learn,
By Spelman, Camden, Dugdale, worn,
    And then they came to Hearne.

Hearne strutted in them for awhile;
    And then, as lawful heir,
Browne claim'd and seiz'd the precious spoil.
    The spoil of many a year.

His car himself he did provide,
    To stand in double stead;
That it should carry him alive,
    And bury him when dead.

By rusty coins old kings he'd trace,
    And know their air and mien:
King Alfred he knew well by face,
    Tho' George he ne'er had seen.

This wight th' outside of churches lov'd,
    Almost unto a sin;
Spires Gothic of more use he prov'd
    Than pulpits are within.

Of use, no doubt, when high in air,
    A wand'ring bird they'll rest,
Or with a Bramin's holy care,
    Make lodgments for its nest.

Ye Jackdaws, that are us'd to talk,
    Like us of human race,
When nigh you see Browne Willis walk,
    Loud chatter forth his praise.

Whene'er the fatal day shall come,
    For come, alas! it must,
When this good 'squire must stay at home,
    And turn to antique dust;

The solemn dirge, ye Owls, prepare,
    Ye Bats, more hoarsly screak;
Croak, all ye Ravens, round the bier,
    And all ye Church-mice, squeak!

[Nichols' note:] [Mr. Cole gives the following anecdotes of Browne Willis, as notes to the above poem.] "Mr. Willis never mentioned the adored town of Buckingham without the addition of *county-town*. His person and dress were so singular, that, though a gentleman of 1000*l. per annum,* he has often been taken for a beggar. An old leathern girdle or belt always surrounded the two or three coats he wore, and over them an old blue cloak.—He wrote the worst hand of any man in England—such as he could with difficulty read himself; and what no one, except his old correspondents, could decypher.— His boots, which he almost always appeared in, were not the least singular part of his dress. I suppose it will not be falsity to say they were forty years old; patched and vamped up at various times. They are all in wrinkles, and don't come up above half way of his legs. He was often called in the neighbourhood, *Old Wrinkle Boots*. They are humorously historized in the above poem.—The chariot of Mr. Willis was so singular that from it he was called himself, *The old Chariot*. It was his wedding chariot, and had his arms on brass plates about it, not unlike a coffin, and painted black.—He was as remarkable probably for his love to the walls and structures of churches, as for his variance with the clergy in his neighbourhood. He built, by subscription, the chapel at Fenny-Stratford; repaired Bletchley church very elegantly, at a great expence; repaired Bow Brickill church, desecrated and not used for a century; and added greatly to the height of Buckingham church tower.—He was not well pleased with any one who in talking of, or with him, did not call him *Squire*.—I wrote these notes when I was out of humour with him for some of his tricks. God rest his soul, and forgive us all. Amen!"

[Some farther particulars of Mr. Willis may be found in Ballard's Letters,[6] vol. II. pp. 41. 55. 107. 158. 163. His great attempts in his old age, ib. 179. ill used by Mr. Cole, ibid. V. 13. VII. 15. 21. XV. 53. XVIII. 42. Curious peculiarities of him, ibid. 109, 110, 111. Letters from Katharine Willis to Dr. Charlett, XIX. 6, 7, 20, 23, 34, 36. 41. 43. 46. 48, 51, 52, 65. 85. Rachel Willis 67.—Offered to give Mr. Thomas Hearne the rich rectory of Bletchley (if he would have taken the oaths), which he afterwards gave to Mr. Cole, LIX. 43.]

I could easily have extended this single article to a volume; from a very large collection which I possess of the MS Letters of Mr. Willis for a long series of years—*Sed manuum de tabulâ.*

[This ends the account of Browne Willis from Vol. VI of *Lit. Anec.* The material that follows is from the continuation of his life in Vol. VIII, 217-223.]

---

6. George Ballard, a maker of women's clothing turned Saxon scholar, is memorialized by Nichols, *Lit. Anec.*, II, 466-470, who says that Ballard "completed a transcript of a Saxon Dictionary, which he borrowed of Mr. Browne Willis" (p. 466). Ballard published only one work, *Memoirs of several Ladies of Great Britain, who have been celebrated for their Writings or Skill in the learned Languages, Arts, and Sciences* (Oxford, 1752); but Nichols ends his memoir of Ballard with this statement: "A very large Collection of his Epistolary Correspondence is preserved in the Bodleian Library." Nichols quotes from this collection of letters from time to time in *Literary Anecdotes*.

Since the Memoirs of this distinguished Antiquary were printed, in vol. VI. pp. 186-211; a farther examination of the MSS. of Dr. Ducarel has produced the following additional Anecdotes.

In a letter to Dr. Ducarel, June 26, 1756, he [Browne Willis] mentions "the death of his only son in a fourth fit of the gout inwardly, which he brought on himself very early. He [Willis' son Thomas] was ill 12 weeks, and would not believe himself in danger. He [Browne Willis] vastly lamented his [son's] leaving his family minors [Thomas had three children by two wives], especially the heir of it, who has been bred up to sports, &c." By his [son's] death, Browne Willis's manor-house reverted to him [Browne Willis] again; and he wished for a good tenant for it.

In another letter to the Doctor, Nov. 13, 1756, he says, "I am 100*l*. out of pocket by what I have printed; except my Octavo of Parliaments, which brought me 15*l*. profit, though I gave it all away, and above 20*l*. more, to build Buckingham tower steeple; and now, as I hoped for subscription to this book (the History of the Town and Hundred of Buckingham) am like to have half the impression on my hands. Sold only 69 copies, of which to gentlemen of Buckinghamshire only 28."

In a letter dated Dec. 20, 1756, he says, "Rheumatisms and gout in his right hand made him get the minister and his daughter to write his letters;" and adds "I have worked for nothing; nay, except in one book, I have been out of pocket, and at great expence in what I printed."

In March 1757 "he was 74 years of age, full of aches and pains in his neck, rheumatism, gout, and gravel, and both his heels flew up on his coming out of the church."

He heard, in 1757, "that his cousin Robert Browne, esq. of Frampton, Dorset, had left him 100*l*."

He amused himself in 1759 by making inquiries after Bells. He had return of Bells in the county of Lincoln, from Dr. Reynolds, archdeacon of Lincoln, of near 600 parishes in that great county. He wanted the same from Archdeacon Denne for the county of Kent. May 8, 1759, he "grew so weak and infirm, that he could not apply to antiquities and study, or draw up accounts as formerly. He had not strength to reach down and turn over books. He entered the Bells in the *Parochiale Anglicanum*."

[Editor's note: Willis inquires after bells in a letter in the Osborn Collection, dated 27 December 1759 and written from Whaddon. It is directed to "Dear Doctor": probably Ducarel, since in it he says, "I am ever glad to hear of AB[p] Whitgift's Health & M[rs] Talbot's & begg my Duty ever to His Grace, & respects to the Lady." Ducarel's duties as Keeper of the Library at Lambeth would have put him in a position to convey a message to Abp. Secker, to whom Willis gave the name of *Whitgift*. In this same letter, Willis requests information on "any accounts of antiquity." He also says, with reference to his health, that "I am unfit for business, & have gone no where out of late nor been at church & scarce wrote an Answer to any letter." He adds that "I am little able to get out of my parlour & sleep but poorly a nights & doze away in the day."

A year earlier, Willis had written the following letter (Br. Mus. Add. Mss. 42,560. f. 57) to Thomas Warton, directed "To the Revd Mr Wharton / Fellow of / Trinity College."

>Whaddon Hall near Fenny Stratford
>January 13 1758
>
>Sir
>
>As you wrote me a letter ab^t 2 or 3 years agoe to enquire whether I could help you to any materials ab^t Dr Bathurst; as I remember I told you that I had no account of Him; & indeed I could not recollect that I had met with any. But this day looking over some of my old papers, I met with the enclosed wch I had bound up in some miscellaneous collections, & so begg your acceptance of it. The obligations I stand indebted to your college in; will for ever command all that is in the power of Sir
>
>Your devoted humble Servant
>Browne Willis]

The Delegates of the Press sent him Lord Clarendon's "Life," 1759, by which he thought they could not raise so much as by the "History."

He kept his eyes by two issues in his neck 40 years.

In his last letter, dated Jan 9, 1760, he "desires Dr. Ducarel and Archbishop *Whitgift's* (Secker's) prayers."

[Nichols' note: [The following Letter was addressed to Dr. Ducarel by Mr. Cole, April 23, 1760:] "Dear Sir, I have an opportunity, by the return of Mr. Cartwright to London, of transmitting these papers to you, which I beg may be returned to me as soon as you have done with them; as they belong, not to me, but to Mr. Willis, who was so kind as to lay by a basket of papers for me when he was looking over his grandfather's Letters, &c. among which I found only these adapted to your present enquiry. I heard Mr. Gibberd say you wanted to see one of Mr. Willis's printed queries relating to his designed History of Buckinghamshire: this is the only one to be met with, and therefore, when you have made what use you think proper of it, beg you would give it to Mr. Cartwright, who will convey it to me again. I met with a second printed paper of queries, but whose it is I know not, which I have sent with the rest. The diploma will please you, and the note of his collection for Stony Stratford fire will be a specimen of his industry and success in his applications of that sort. I have sent you the account of the expences for Bletchley church; and could send papers without end of that sort relating to Fenny Stratford chapel, but imagine them useless to you. I am now quite at large and at leisure, and no school-boy from Eton at his breaking up enjoys the holydays more exquisitely than myself after so tiresome a task as I have gone through. I sent the MSS. I had to Oxford yesterday together with the rest, and hope they are all safely arrived to their place of repose, where probably they will meet with no great interruption after the first curiosity of people is a little satisfied: therefore, if you have any particular queries in regard to the design you are about, please to communicate them and I will resolve them in the best manner I am able. I suppose Mr. Gibberd has been with you, as he was to set out for town on Monday. W.C."

[In a subsequent letter, addressed also to Dr. Ducarel, Dec. 22, 1781, Mr. Cole says,] "A friend of mine (Mr. Tyson) having etched last month a print of your old friend and my patron, Mr. Browne Willis, from an original picture by Mr. Dahl, I would not omit sending one to my old friend and schoolfellow Dr. Ducarel, from whom I have not heard these many years. You was so kind, many years ago, to give me a private print of Archbishop Hutton: I beg now to return the obligation. You will probably object, that it is not like Mr. Willis: agreed, and God forbid it should! But no doubt it was like him in his best days, in queen Anne's time, when Dahl drew him: and no one, that reveres the memory of Mr. Willis, would wish to have a caricature of him, such as he made of himself, when you and I were acquainted with him. W.C."[—Mr. Tyson's original etching is here annexed.]

Dr. Willis had five sons and five daughters [whose names, dates, heirs, etc., are repeated by Nichols in a note because, he says, they were "rather incorrectly given in vol. VI. p. 194" (actually 194-195)].

In his will, dated Dec. 15, 1741, after directing the funeral charges not to exceed 20*l.* he states, that by his eldest son's marriage-settlement, 1735, he got an augmentation of 1000*l.* for the younger children; of this his eldest daughters Gertrude and Catharine were to have 300*l.* each, and his youngest, Mary and Alice, 200*l.* each, and no part of the 1000*l.* was to go to any of his sons. 5000*l.* to younger children was given by his own marriage-settlement, with power to repay himself expences of apprenticing, or otherwise preferring or advancing his sons Henry and Elliot, of whom the former having cost him above 60*l.* a year for above then years past, 20*l. per annum* to be deducted out of the principal and interest of his portion, to be paid by 10*l.* for five years, after his decease, to Gertrude and Catharine, it having been so concluded and adjudged by Richard Fleming, esq. that what has been advanced to him above 30*l. per annum* since he became of age, ought to be so deducted and distributed; and my son Elliot to pay in like manner to Mary and Alice 30*l.* all the sisters' fortunes having been diminished by the brothers. His wife having desired that Mary and Alice should each have 150*l.* out of the 400*l.* put out to interest for her, he confirms it; and what shall remain after such distribution to go to Henry and Elliot. Coins of five guineas value to Bishop Benson, hon. Dr. Thomas Symonds, and Daniel Willis, esq.; rings to sister Jane Sheppard, brother John, W[illis,] Thomas Lingen, Robert Browne, Robert Gwillym, Richard Elliot, the bishops of Gloucester, Lincoln, and St. David's, Thomas Cartwright, Judge Willes, James West, Drs. Mead and Richard Frewen, Mr. Benjamin Pomfret, Richard Eyre, John Barton, and Thomas Cooke; and to each Alderman of Buckingham a copy of his Notitia Parliamentaria; to the poor of Bletchley and Whaddon, exclusive of Nash, 5*l.* each parish, to be paid at the next anniversary of his death on his grave, after divine service; to each servant who had lived with him seven years, half a year's wages.

"Item, I give and bequeath to the Chancellor, masters, and scholars, of the University of Oxford all my silver, copper, brass, and pewter coins, to be kept together in the School gallery, in like manner as those I have already given are placed by my direction; and my will is, that the said University shall have my gold coins, in case they shall in two years after my decease think proper to purchase them, after the rate of 4*l*. for every ounce thereof, which I desire may be preserved in one series, and kept together in one distinct cabinet, they having been adjudged by the greatest Virtuosos to be the *entirest* and most of a *complete series* of any collection of English coins whatsoever; for which reason it is that I give them, that a true value may be set upon them somewhere, as the best and most grateful return I am capable of making that learned body for their many generous favours conferred on me, and mine and Dr. *Thomas* Symonds's eminently learned grandfather, the celebrated physician Dr. Thomas Willis,[7] whom they in a singular manner honoured by choosing one of their Professors. And whereas the chief amusement of my life has been in the study of national Antiquities, and particularly those of Buckinghamshire, and the History of Parliamentary Boroughs, I give all my *Collections* relating thereto, and all my MSS. whatsoever, to the said chancellor, masters, and scholars of the said University of Oxford, to be placed in the School gallery next to those of my friend Bishop [of St. Asaph, Thomas] Tanner's, hoping that they may be consulted, and deemed worthy of publication by some member of that learned body."

Executor benefited by his building Whaddon-hall on jointure ground, agreeable to his father's will, together with paying off considerable sums, exceeding all together 7000*l*.; desired to see to further endowing St. Martin's donative curacy in Fenny Stratford by future purchase, to make it 40*l. per annum,* exclusive of town subscriptions, and to have all fees and offerings, as agreed with the archdeacon of Buckingham's official and the bishops of Lincoln and Gloucester, for a resident unmarried graduate of either University, and native of South Britain, and not rector of Bletchley; the executor in seven years to fit up the house he purchased; and if he neglect, the rector of Bletchley to do this, by getting subscriptions, and getting 6*l*. in, out of the tithes of Fenny Stratford; the minister of Bletchley to appoint future curates; Thomas Symonds, John Hulme, esq. and Mr. Benjamin Pomfret, trustees of Whaddon-hall, purchased by him by sale of a capital house and lands of the same value in St. Mary Blandford, to sell for payment of debts and children's portions. His four daughters to have the use of the house and goods till the sale, and to account for furniture. All the rest and residue, real and personal, to his eldest son Thomas and his heirs.

---

7. In a note, Nichols gives the tombstone inscription, from a stone placed by Browne Willis, to the memory of Thomas Willis and his wife Rachell, "in the chancel of North Hinksey church, Berks."

Codicil, 1758, 21 Feb. revokes the additions to marriage-settlement portion of 200*l*. to his daughter Alice Eyre, and instead of it 300*l*.; the 1000*l*. given to be divided, her brothers Henry and Elliot being dead; and of the remaining 700*l*. 400*l*. to Gertrude and 300*l*. to Catherine; the fortune of his daughter Hervey to be made 300*l*. by moiety of South-sea stock sold for Eyre, his claim and interest in the fortune of Elliot to go to the children of Hervey, provided the heir and executor of his son Thomas does the same with his share, else to go to the daughters of Hervey, with all such monies as he gave to the widow and son of Dr. Henry Willis. After the death of the relict of his son Thomas, power to charge Whaddon with 20*l*. *per annum*, to go to Dr. Eyre and Robert-Lingen Burton, of Radbrook, co. Gloucester, esq. Clause of future settlement of St. Martin revoked, provided his heir confirms the settlement, the minister's house, and obliges him to reside.

His son Thomas dying in 1756, he appoints executor *his* son Thomas, gentleman-commoner at New College, with all rest and residue; he to pay an annuity of 20*l*. to his cousin Thomas, only child of Dr. Henry Willis. All coins of five guineas, and rings, and appointment of Benjamin Pomfret trustee, revoked. All writings and papers in his custody to be locked up, and sealed by his son-in-law Mr. Richard Eyre, and Mr. Thomas Cooke (each 5*l*. for their trouble), till the hon. Thomas Symonds, of Pengelly, co. Hereford, peruse them, and destroy at his discretion. His daughters Gertrude and Catharine to pay back 100*l*. to Hervey's children.

"And whereas in my said will and testament, dated Dec. 15, 1741, I have given my coins and MS. books to the University of Oxford, the former of which have been received, and placed in a cabinet in the School gallery (which I desire may remain there and be annually visited on the festival of St. Frideswide), I do hereby direct and appoint that the latter, *viz.* my MSS. should be given into the hands of my son-in-law Richard Eyre, B.D. John Gibberd, and Mr. Humphrey Owen, B.D. Librarian, to be placed and disposed of according to my said will; and that my executors therein named permit the said Mr. Eyre, Mr. Gibberd, and Mr. Owen, to take and receive the same for that purpose within three months after my decease.["]

[Nichols' note:] [From his codicil to the said will (here said to bear date Dec. 15, 1741), dated Feb. 25, 1748:] "Next I give the library of Trinity College in Oxford, Rymer's Foedera, in seven volumes; and to the Rev. Mr. Wise, B.D. the liberty of choosing a book out of my study. And whereas my sons have declared, shewn, and testified their dislike and aversion to the study which hath been my chief delight and amusement, I give all my printed books, and also all my pictures, to my eldest grandson Thomas Willis; and do order a catalogue and inventory to be taken of the same, and that the same shall continue in my house at Whaddon-hall, as they do now, until he shall have attained the age of twenty-two years. I will and devise that my son-in-law Richard Eyre shall have the use of my said books and my said house at Whaddon at his free will and pleasure, if he continues so long vicar of Whaddon."

[This ends the addition to the life of Browne Willis from Vol. VIII of *Lit.*

Anec. The material that follows comes from a life of Sneyd Davies in *Illustr.*, I, 682-685.]

[There is a very humourous collection of Letters in the second volume of "The Repository,[8] published in 1777. The title is, "ORIGINES DIVISIANAE, or the ANTIQUITIES OF THE DEVIZES, in familiar Letters to a Friend, in 1750 and 1751, by DR. DAVIES; first printed in 1754."
The Letters are nine.
I was informed, upon authority which I cannot resist, that SNEYD DAVIES, unquestionably was the writer of them.
As they occupy several pages, and contain ridicule upon my *respected friends* the *Antiquaries,* I am loth to copy more than one passage, which appears to me in a very different style from his other works,—an admirable specimen of his comic powers. It is in the Fourth Letter.]

"Though I am sensible the list (of the *Wardens*) is very imperfect, I have not leisure to make it complete by passing *six months* in the Tower.
"If you would have it exact, you may go and consult *Browne Willis,* a man of singular character—a genuine Antiquary, in learning, manners, habit, and person—so extraordinary, that I think it worth a digression to give you an account of him, to acquaint you with his family, and point out his residence by such marks that you will know it the moment you see it.
"The fortune of his family was acquired by the celebrated *Thomas Willis,* M.D. out of Cavaliers who were sick of the war. It was acquired by *single fees,* before the *Funds* were created, and *Change Alley* turned into a *Court of Requests.*
"He was a man of uncommon penetration, and saw farther into the *head* than his contemporaries. He wrote many ingenious Romances, in a *nervous* and pleasing style.
"He was known to have dealt much with familiar spirits called *animal.* Having command over them, he could make, for the entertainment of his acquaintance, a million of them dance a jigg on the pineal gland of a fine lady, or on the point of a needle. He would send them on errands, God knows where, and remand them back, as quick as thought. These obsequious beings always perched upon his elbow when he wrote prescriptions, after which they instantly whipped into the palm of his right hand. He could place them spread over all that was exterior in fribbles, or confine them to the finger of a celebrated fiddler—the hand of a cheat—the foot of a dancing-master—the toe of a soldier—the posteriors of a bully—or the heart of a lover, and make them jump through little crevices into the hollow pericranium of a Methodist.
"The Doctor gave the money thus acquired for his grandson's purchase of this antique place, which indeed is a little crowded with *natural plantations,* the owner having made a vow to live *in a wood.*
"The house is invested with tall and large trees, which look formidable in decay, yielding an occasional habitation to a colony of rooks, who legally

---

8. This work, printed by the Bowyer-Nichols press, is thus described in *Lit. Anec.,* III, 249: "The Repository, a Select Collection of Fugitive Pieces of Wit and Humour, in Prose and Verse, by the most eminent Writers," 2 vols. small 8vo; selected by Isaac Reed, esq.; by whom two more Volumes were published in 1783.

have enjoyed them by authentic prescription from the days of *Richard the First*.

"The *vallum* that encloses the garden, is a little out of repair, but is never to be rebuilt by his heirs. The penalty is a curse of pulling an old wall upon their heads.

"The *moat* that surrounds the house has from all time enjoyed a melancholy and slumbering stillness, unruffled by winds, and stranger to a dimple; but has been for several years changing its nature, and thickening into earth.

"His unmolested gate loves its threshold; a little wicket lets you into a little court, lined and overshadowed with yews, which present a very solemn gloom. You need not strike your hand upon the door; you may with ease creep through it; or the walls that are pervious can give you ample room for admittance.

"The furniture of the inside is green, but resembles the *verde antique*. The parlour is wainscoated with oak, indigenous, and more than coeval with its tenement. The panels are little squares, intermixed with fluted *pallustrade,* which, by way of capital, support the faces of men, but which bear no resemblance to human nature. The chambers are hung with silks and velvets, in a kind of *Mosaic,* in the manner of patchwork. His father must have purchased them out of the *Arundelian* wardrobe; for the son, by his indefatigable erudition, can prove them to be genuine remnants of *Queen Elizabeth's* hoop-petticoat.

"A variety of ornaments appear in furniture which Time has impaired. You see an assortment of statues that fell at the Reformation from their crosses, and have looked as if they had been scared ever since.||

"There is many a *Saxon* bust, of man, or beast, but which is not well determined; numberless fragments of painted glass, scraps of inscriptions, and shreds of deeds.

"In his library, adorned with fretwork of pendent spiders'-webs, you will find a large collection of *Coins,* down from *Abraham* to the *Borough halfpenny.*

"He *had,* before he gave them to the University of *Oxford,* the most ample collection of Townsmen's Halfpence; ten of which are nearly equal in their *intrinsic* value to one of the farthings issued by *Wood,* but in the *extrinsic* are infinitely superior.

"Amongst his MSS. written all of them in his own hand with incredible assiduity, you will see a laborious Dictionary of Lords, Abbots, Parliamentmen, Gentlemen, Clergymen, and Parish clerks, ever since the *Saxon* Invasion; and in what may be called his *family pictures* you have the most copious registers of marriages, births, and burials, that is to be found in the world.

"The territory around him has been remarkable for considerable actions heretofore; but is now disfigured with pits, dug, not for marle, gravel, or earthly use, but in search of *Roman* spears, and *Saxon* stirrups.

"He shews a botanical curiosity, unparalleled in *England, Europe,* or the Universe. It is a willow basket, propagated from the identical *wicker basket* of *Druidism* recorded by *Julius Caesar;* though some carry it no higher than to the *bucking basket,* well known in the facetious reign of *Henry the Fourth.*"

|| This appears to me very like the manner of *Horace Walpole* in his lively and amusing Letters. NICHOLS.

Samuel Pegge the Elder

[Nichols' memoir of Samuel Pegge the Elder in *Lit. Anec.*, VI, 224-259, is introduced with a parenthetical acknowledgment, *"Taken principally from Memoirs compiled by his Son."* The son was Samuel Pegge the Younger, author of *Anecdotes of the English Language* (1803) and of *Curialia* (1782-1806), whose style has a quality of pomposity contrasting with Nichols' more plain and direct statement.

The memoir of the elder Pegge, in its first form, appeared in the *Gentleman's Magazine* for June and subsequent months of 1796, reprinted partially (the June and August sections) in *A Selection of Curious Articles from the Gentleman's Magazine*, ed. John Walker (London, 4 vols., 1814), IV, 245-257. This place of first publication is fitting because Pegge contributed a great many articles over the years to the *Gentleman's Magazine*, often using the pseudonym *Paul Gemsege,* formed, says Nichols, "by an ingenious transposition of the letters of his name" (*Lit. Anec.*, V, 53, n.).

In reprinting the memoir in *Literary Anecdotes*, Nichols used essentially the same materials but with additions to the text and to the notes; for instance, after the name of the Rev. Seth Ellis, Nichols added in the latest version: "a man of reprobate character, and a disgrace to his profession." This one example should be sufficient to explain why the text here has been taken from *Literary Anecdotes*. Some other additions introduced by Nichols will be pointed out in the notes.

The letters and other manuscripts of Pegge are scattered in a number of depositories. The British Museum has ten of his manuscripts; the Osborn Collection has five of his letters, including one to Richard Gough and two to Nichols. Another letter from Pegge to Nichols is in the Nichols collection at Columbia. The Folger Library and Harvard University each possesses one of Pegge's autograph letters.

John Nichols edited, printed, and was otherwise concerned in the publication of a number of works of the two Samuel Pegges. Information on this subject will be found in the list of works appended to the life Nichols wrote of himself, which is a part of this volume. A short life of the elder Pegge, written by Warwick William Wroth, is in the DNB; *Literary Anecdotes* is listed as the primary source, but there is no mention of the *Gentleman's Magazine*.]

THE REV. SAMUEL PEGGE, LL.D. and F.S.A. was the representative of one of four branches of the family of that name in Derbyshire, derived from a common ancestor, all which existed together till within a few years. The eldest became extinct by the death of Mr. William Pegge, of Yeldersley, near Ashborne, 1768; and another by that of the Rev. Nathaniel Pegge, M.A. vicar of Packington, in Leicestershire, 1782.

The Doctor's immediate predecessors, as may appear from the Heralds-office, were of Osmaston, near *Ashborne,* where they resided, in lineal succession, for four generations, antecedently to his father and himself, and where they left a patrimonial inheritance, of which the Doctor died possessed.*

Of the other existing branch, Mr. Edward Pegge having (1662) married Gertrude, sole daughter and heir of William Strelley, esq. of Beauchief, in the Northern part of Derbyshire, seated himself there, and was appointed high sheriff of the county in 1667; as was his grandson, Strelley Pegge, esq. 1739; and his great-grandson, the present Peter Pegge, esq. 1788.

It was by Katharine Pegge, a daughter of Thomas Pegge, esq. of Yeldersley, that King Charles II. (who saw her abroad during his exile) had a son born (1647), whom he called Charles *Fitz-Charles,* to whom he granted the royal arms, with a baton sinister, Vairé, and whom (1675) his Majesty created Earl of *Plymouth,* Viscount *Totness,* and Baron *Dartmouth.*† He was bred to the sea, and, having been educated abroad, most probably in Spain, was known by the name of Don Carlos.‡ The Earl married the Lady Bridget Osborne, third daughter of Thomas Earl of Danby, lord high treasurer (at Wimbledon, in Surrey), 1678,§ and died of a flux at the siege of Tangier, 1680, without issue. The body was brought to England, and interred in Westminster Abbey.|| The Countess re-married Dr. Philip Bisse, Bishop of Hereford, by whom she had no issue, and who, surviving her, erected a handsome tablet to her memory in his cathedral. Katharine Pegge, the Earl's mother, married Sir Edward Greene, bart. of Samford in Essex, and died without issue by him.#

But to return to the Rev. Dr. Pegge, the outline *only* of whose life we propose to give. His father (Christopher) was, as we have observed, of Osmaston, though he never resided there, even after he became possessed of it; for, being a younger brother, it was thought proper to put him to business; and he served his time with a considerable woolen-draper at Derby, which line he followed till the death of his elder brother (Humphry, who

* In Church-street, at Ashborne, is an alms-house, originally founded by Christopher Pegge, esq. The name occurs also on the table of benefactors in Ashborne church. NICHOLS.
† Docquet book in the Crown-office. NICHOLS.
‡ See [Francis] Sandford, [*A Genealogical History of the Kings of Portugal,*] p. 647, edit. 1707. [James] Granger [in *A Biographical History of England*] erroneously calls him Carlo; and also, by mistake, gives him the name of *Fitz-roy.* NICHOLS.
§ See Mr. [Daniel] Lyson's Environs of London, vol. I. p. 537. NICHOLS.
|| [John] Dart's History of Westminster Abbey, vol. II. p. 55. NICHOLS.
There is a half-length portrait of the Earl, in a robe de chambre, laced cravat, and flowing hair (with a ship in the back ground of the picture), by Sir Peter Lely, now in the family: and also two of his mother, Lady Greene; one a half-length, with her infant son standing by her side; the other, a three-quarters; both either by Sir Peter Lely, or by one of his pupils. NICHOLS.

died without issue 1711) at Chesterfield in Derbyshire, when he commenced lead-merchant, then a lucrative branch of traffick there; and, having been for several years a member of the corporation, died in his third mayoralty, 1723.

He had married Gertrude Stephenson (a daughter of Francis Stephenson, of Unston, near Chesterfield, gent.) whose mother was Gertrude Pegge, a daughter of the before-mentioned Edward Pegge, esq. of Beauchief; by which marriage these two branches of the family, which had long been diverging from each other, became re-united, both by blood and name, in the person of Dr. Pegge, their only surviving child.

He was born Nov. 5, 1704, N.S. at Chesterfield, where he had his school education; and was admitted a pensioner of St. John's college, Cambridge, May 30, 1722, under the tuition of the Rev. Dr. William Edmundson; was matriculated July 7; and, in the following November, was elected a scholar of the house upon Lupton's foundation.

In the same year with his father (1723) died the heir of his maternal grandfather (Stephenson), a minor; by whose death a moiety of the real estate at Unston (before mentioned) became the property of our young collegian, who was then pursuing his academical studies with intention of taking orders.

Having, however, no immediate prospect of preferment, he looked up to a fellowship of the college, after he had taken the degree of A.B. in January 1725, N.S.; and became a candidate upon a vacancy which happened favourably in that very year; for it was a lay-fellowship upon the Beresford foundation, and appropriated to the founder's kin, or at least confined to a native of Derbyshire.

The competitors were, Mr. Michael Burton (afterwards Dr. Burton), and another, whose name we do not find; but the contest lay between Mr. Burton and Mr. Pegge. Mr. Burton had the stronger claim, being indubitably related to the founder; but, upon examination, was declared to be so very deficient in literature, that his superior right, as founder's kin, was set aside, on account of the insufficiency of his learning, and Mr. Pegge was admitted, and sworn fellow March 21, 1726, O.S.

In consequence of this disappointment, Mr. Burton was obliged to take new ground, to enable him to procure an establishment in the world; and therefore artfully applied to the College for a testimonial, that he might receive orders, and undertake some cure in the vicinity of Cambridge. Being ordained, he turned the circumstance into a manoeuvre, and took an unexpected advantage of it, by appealing to the visitor (the Bishop of Ely, Dr. Thomas Greene), representing, that, as the College had, by the testimonial, thought him qualified for ordination, it could not, in justice, deem him unworthy of becoming a fellow of the Society upon such forcible claims as founder's kin, and also as a native of Derbyshire.

These were irresistible pleas on the part of Mr. Burton; and the Visitor found himself reluctantly obliged to eject Mr. Pegge, when Mr. Burton took possession of the fellowship, which he held many years.*

Thus this business closed; but the Visitor did Mr. Pegge the favour to recommend him, in so particular a manner, to the master and seniors of the College, that he was thenceforward considered as an honorary member of the body of fellows (*tanquam socius*), kept his seat at their table and in the chapel, being placed in the situation of a fellow-commoner.

In consequence, then, of this testimony of the Bishop of Ely's approbation, Mr. Pegge was chosen a Platt-fellow on the first vacancy, A.D. 1729. He was therefore, in fact, *twice* a fellow of St. John's.

[[Nichols' note:] The *Platt-fellowships* at St. John's are similar to what are called *Bye-fellowships* in some other Colleges at Cambridge, and are not on the foundation. The original number was *six*, with a stipend of 20*l.* per annum each, besides rooms, and commons at the fellows' table. They were founded by William Platt, esq. (son of Sir Hugh Platt, knt.) an opulent citizen of London, out of an estate then of the annual value of 140*l.* Being a rent-charge, the fellowships cannot be enlarged in point of revenue, though the number has been increased to *eight*, by savings from the surplus. There is a good portrait of Mr. Platt in the master's lodge at St. John's, with the date of 1626, aet. 47. He died 1637. More of him may be seen in Mr. Lyson's Environs of London, vol. III. pp. 59, 66, 70, 71, 110, 376.]

There is good reason to believe that, in the interval between his removal from his first fellowship, and his acceding to the second, he meditated the publication of Xenophon's "*Cyropaedia*" and "*Anabasis*," from a collation of them with a Duport MS. in the library at Eton, to convince the world that the master and seniors of St. John's college did not judge unworthily in giving him so decided a preference to Mr. Burton in their election. It appears that he had made very large collections for such a work; but we suspect that it was thrown aside by being anticipated by Mr. Hutchinson's edition, which was formed from more valuable manuscripts.

While resident in College (and in the year 1730) Mr. Pegge was elected a member of the Zodiac Club, a literary Society, which consisted of twelve members, denominated from the twelve signs. This little institution was founded, and articles, in the nature of statutes, were agreed upon Dec. 10, 1725. Afterwards (1728) this Society thought proper to enlarge their body, when six select additional members were chosen, and denominated from six of the planets, though it still went collectively under the name of the Zodiac Club.† In this latter class Mr. Pegge was the original Mars, and

* Dr. Burton was president (*i.e.* vice-master) of the College when Mr. Pegge's son was admitted of it, 1751; but soon afterwards took the living of Staplehurst, in Kent. NICHOLS.
† Of this little academical literary Society the late Samuel Pegge, esq. possessed a particular History in MS. NICHOLS.

continued a member of the Club as long as he resided in the University. His secession was in April 1732, and his seat accordingly declared vacant.

In the same year, 1730, Mr. Pegge appears in a more public literary body, viz. among the members of the Gentleman's Society at Spalding, in Lincolnshire, to which he contributed some papers which will be noticed below.

[[Nichols' note:] In 1734, he sent them a critical letter on the name and town of Wye. In 1733, his Life of Archbishop Kempe was in forwardness for press, and he solicited assistance for it from MSS. 1739, an Account of a Religious House in Canterbury, not noticed before, his conjectures on which were approved by Mr. Thorpe. An Account of the Endowment of the Vicarage of Westfield in Sussex, by Richard second Bishop of Chichester, 1249, in the hands of Sir Peter Webster, bart. Account of the Amphitheatre in the Garden of the Nuns of Fidelite at Angers: the arena 150 feet diameter, outer wall 20 feet thick, the caveae 14 feet long and wide, with layers of Roman brick and stone 3 or 4 feet asunder.]

Having taken the degree of A.M. in July 1729, Mr. Pegge was ordained deacon in December in the same year; and, in the February following, received priest's orders; both of which were conferred by Dr. William Baker, bishop of Norwich.

It was natural that he should now look to employment in his profession, and, agreeably to his wishes, he was soon retained as curate to the Rev. Dr. John Lynch (afterwards [1733][1] dean of Canterbury), at Sundrich in Kent, on which charge he entered at Lady-day 1730; and in his principal, as will appear, soon afterwards, very unexpectedly, found a patron.

The Doctor gave Mr. Pegge the choice of three cures under him; viz. of Sundrich, of a London living, or the chaplainship of St. Cross, of which the Doctor was the master. Mr. Pegge preferred Sundrich, which he held till Dr. Lynch exchanged that rectory for Bishopsbourne, and then removed thither at Midsummer 1731.

Within a few months after this period, Dr. Lynch, who had married a daughter of Archbishop Wake, obtained for Mr. Pegge, unsolicited, the vicarage of Godmersham (cum Challock) into which he was inducted Dec. 6, 1731.

We have said *unsolicited,* because, at the moment when the living was conferred, Mr. Pegge had more reason to expect a *reproof* from his principal than a *reward* for so short a service of these cures. The case was, that Mr. Pegge had, in the course of the preceding summer (unknown to Dr. Lynch) taken a little tour, for a few months, to Leyden, with a fellow collegian (John Stubbing, M.B. then a medical pupil under Boerhaave), leaving his curacy to the charge of some of the neighbouring clergy. On his return,

---

1. Square brackets here supplied by Nichols.

therefore, he was not a little surprized to obtain actual preferment through Dr. Lynch, without the most distant engagement on the score of the Doctor's interest with the Archbishop, or the smallest suggestion from Mr. Pegge.

Being now in possession of a living, and independent property, Mr. Pegge married (April 13, 1732) Miss Anne Clarke, the only daughter of Benjamin, and sister of John, Clarke, esqrs. of Stanley, near Wakefield, in the county of York, by whom he had one son, the late Samuel Pegge, esq. who, after his mother's death, became eventually heir to his uncle, and one daughter, Anna-Katharina (now living) the wife of the late Rev. John Bourne, M.A. of Spital, near Chesterfield, rector of Sutton cum Duckmanton, and vicar of South Winfield, both in Derbyshire. From the son, by Martha, a daughter of Dr. Henry Bourne, an eminent physician in Derbyshire, descended Charlotte-Anne, who died unmarried, March 17, 1793,‡ and Christopher Pegge, M.D.F.R.S. and fellow of the College of Physicians, reader of anatomy, on Dr. Lee's foundation, at Christ Church, Oxford: Mrs. Bourne's issue being two daughters, Elizabeth, who married Robert Jennings, esq. and Jane, who married Benjamin Thompson, esq.

While Mr. Pegge was resident in Kent, where he continued 20 years, he made himself acceptable to every body, by his general knowledge, his agreeable conversation, and his vivacity; for he was received into the familiar acquaintance of the best gentlemen's families in East Kent, several of whom he preserved in his correspondence after he quitted the county, till the whole of those of his own standing gave way to fate before him.

Having an early propensity to the study of antiquity among his general researches, and being allowedly an excellent classical scholar, he here laid the foundation of what in time became a considerable collection of books, and his little cabinet of coins grew in proportion; by which two assemblages (so scarce among country gentlemen in general) he was qualified to pursue these collateral studies, without neglecting his parochial duties, to which he was always assiduously attentive.

The few pieces which Mr. Pegge printed while he lived in Kent will be mentioned hereafter, when we shall enumerate such of his writings as are most material. These (exclusively of Mr. Urban's obligations to him, in the Gentleman's Magazine) have appeared principally, and most conspicuously, in the *Archaeologia,* which may be termed the Transactions of the Society of Antiquaries. In that valuable collection will be found more than 50 memoirs, written and communicated by him, many of which are of considerable length, being by much the greatest number hitherto contributed by any individual member of that respectable Society.

In returning to the order of time, we find that, in July 1746, Mr. Pegge had the great misfortune to lose his wife; whose monumental inscription, at Godmersham, bears ample testimony of her worth:

‡ See Gent. Mag. vol. LXIII. p. 285. NICHOLS.

MDCCXLVI.
Anna Clarke, uxor Samuelis Pegge vicarii hujus parochiae;
mulier, si qua alia, sine dolo, vitam aeternam et beatam
fidenter hic sperat; nec erit frustra.

This event entirely changed Mr. Pegge's destinations; for he now zealously meditated on some mode of removing himself, without disadvantage, into his native county. To effect this, one of two points was to be carried; either to obtain some piece of preferment, tenable in its nature with his Kentish vicarage; or to exchange the latter for an equivalent; in which last he eventually succeeded beyond his immediate expectations.[2]

We are now come to a new epoch in the Doctor's life; but there is an interval of a few years to be accounted for, before he found an opportunity of effectually removing himself into Derbyshire.

His wife being dead, his children young and at school, and himself reduced to a life of solitude, so ungenial to his temper (though no man was better qualified to improve his leisure), he found relief by the kind offer of his valuable friend, the late Sir Edward Dering, bart.

At this moment Sir Edward chose to place his son (the present baronet) under the care of a private tutor at home, to qualify him more competently for the University. Sir Edward's personal knowledge of Mr. Pegge, added to the family situation of the latter, mutually induced the former to offer, and the latter to accept, the proposal of removing from Godmersham to Surrenden (Sir Edward's mansion-house) to superintend Mr. Dering's education for a short time; in which capacity he continued about a year and an half, till Mr. Dering was admitted of St. John's college, Cambridge, in March, 1751.

Sir Edward had no opportunity, by any patronage of his own, permanently to gratify Mr. Pegge, and to preserve him in the circle of their common friends. On the other hand, finding Mr. Pegge's propensity to a removal so very strong, Sir Edward reluctantly pursued every possible measure to effect it.

The first vacant living in Derbyshire which offered itself was the perpetual curacy of *Brampton,* near Chesterfield; a situation peculiarly eligible in many respects. It became vacant A.D. 1747; and, if it could have been obtained, would have placed Mr. Pegge in the centre of his early acquaintance in that county; and, being tenable with his Kentish living, would not have totally estranged him from his friends in the South of England. The patronage of Brampton is in the Dean of Lincoln, which dignity was then filled by the Rev. Dr. Thomas Cheyney, to whom, Mr. Pegge being a stranger, the application was necessarily to be made in a circuitous manner, and he was obliged to employ more than a double mediation before his name could be mentioned to the Dean.

2. This ends the material contained in the *Gent. Mag.* for June 1796.

The mode he proposed was through the influence of William, the third Duke of Devonshire, to whom Mr. Pegge was personally known as a Derbyshire man (though he had so long resided in Kent), having always paid his respects to his Grace on the public days at Chatsworth, as often as opportunity served, when on a visit in Derbyshire. Mr. Pegge did not, however, think himself sufficiently in the Duke's favour to make a direct address for his Grace's recommendation to the Dean of Lincoln, though the object so fully met his wishes in moderation, and in every other point. He had, therefore, recourse to a friend, the Right Rev. Dr. Fletcher, bishop of Dromore, then in England; who, in conjunction with the late Godfrey Watkinson, of Brampton Moor, esq. (the principal resident gentleman in the parish of Brampton), solicited, and obtained, his Grace's interest with the Dean of Lincoln; who, in consequence, nominated Mr. Pegge to the living.

One point now seemed to be gained towards his re-transplantation into his native soil, after he had resisted considerable offers had he continued in Kent; and thus did he think himself virtually in possession of a living in Derbyshire, which in its nature was tenable with Godmersham in Kent. Henceforward, then, he no doubt felt a satisfaction that he should soon be enabled to live in Derbyshire, and occasionally visit his friends in Kent, instead of residing in that county, and visiting his friends in Derbyshire.

But, after all this assiduity and anxiety (as if *admission* and *ejection* had pursued him a second time), the result of Mr. Pegge's expectations was far from answering his then present wishes; for, when he thought himself secure by the Dean's nomination, and that nothing was wanting but the Bishop's licence, the Dean's *right of patronage* was controverted by the parishioners of Brampton, who brought forward a nominee of their own.

The ground of this claim, on the part of the parish, was owing to an ill-judged indulgence of some former Deans of Lincoln, who had occasionally permitted the parishioners to send an incumbent directly to the *bishop* for his licence, without the intermediate nomination of the *dean* in due form.

These measures were principally fomented by the son of the last incumbent, the Rev. Seth Ellis,[3] a man of a reprobate character, and a disgrace to his profession, who wanted the living, and was patronized by the parish. He had a desperate game to play; for he had not the least chance of obtaining any preferment, as no individual patron, who was even superficially acquainted with his *moral* character alone, could with decency advance him in the church. To complete the detail of the fate of this man, whose interest the deluded part of the mal-contents of the parish so warmly espoused, he was soon after suspended by the Bishop from officiating at Brampton.

[[Nichols' note:] The Bishop's inhibition took place soon after the deci-

---

3. As pointed out in the headnote, "a man of reprobate character, and a disgrace to his profession" was added after publication of the account in the *Gentleman's Magazine*, as was the rest of the paragraph beginning with "He had a desperate game to play."

sion of the cause at Derby, and was not revoked till late in the year 1758, which was principally effected by Mr. Pegge's intercession with his Lordship, stating Mr. Ellis's distressed circumstances, and his having made a proper submission, with a promise of future good behaviour. This revocation is contained in a letter (now before us) addressed to Mr. Pegge, under the Bishop's own hand, dated Oct. 30, 1758.]

Whatever inducements the parish might have to support Mr. Ellis so strenuously we do not say, though they manifestly did not arise from any pique to one Dean more than to another; and we are decidedly clear that they were not founded in any aversion to Mr. Pegge as an individual; for his character was in all points too well established, and too well known (even to the leading opponents to the Dean), to admit of the least personal dislike in any respect. So great, nevertheless, was the acrimony with which the parishioners pursued their visionary pretensions to the patronage, that, not content with the decision of the jury (which was highly respectable) in favour of the Dean, when the right of patronage was tried in 1748, they had the audacity[4] to carry the cause to an assize at Derby, where, on the fullest and most incontestible evidence, a verdict was given in favour of the Dean, to the confusion and indelible disgrace of those parishioners who espoused so bad a cause, supported by the most undaunted effrontery, and we may add—villainy.

The evidence produced by the parish went to prove, from an entry made nearly half a century before in the accounts kept by the church-wardens, that the *parishioners,* and not the *deans of Lincoln,* had thitherto, on a vacancy, nominated a successor to the Bishop of the diocese for his licence, without the intervention of any other person or party. The parish accounts were accordingly brought into court at Derby, wherein there appeared not only a palpable erasement, but such an one as was detected by a living and credible witness; for a Mr. *Mower* swore that, on a vacancy in the year 1704, an application was made by the parish to the *dean of Lincoln* in favour of the Rev. Mr. Littlewood.§

In corroboration of Mr. Mower's testimony an article in the parish accounts and expenditures of that year was adverted to, and which, when Mr. Mower saw it, ran thus:

"Paid William Wilcoxson, for going *to Lincoln to the Dean,* concerning Mr. Littlewood, five shillings."

The parishioners had before alleged, in proof of their title, that THEY had *elected* Mr. Littlewood, and, to uphold this asseveration, had clumsily altered the parish account-book, and inserted the words "to *Lichfield* to the BISHOP," in the place of the words "to *Lincoln* to the DEAN."

§ We believe this witness to have been *George Mower, esq.* of Wood-seats, in this county, who served the office of sheriff, 1734. NICHOLS.
4. The phrase "had the audacity" does not appear in the *Gentleman's Magazine* account, nor does the ending of the paragraph following "in favour of the Dean."

Thus their own evidence was turned against the parishioners; and not a moment's doubt remained but that the patronage rested with the DEAN of Lincoln.

We have related this affair without a strict adherence to chronological order as to facts, or to collateral circumstances, for the sake of preserving the narrative entire, as far as it regards the contest between the *Dean of Lincoln* and the *Parish of Brampton;* for we believe that this transaction (uninteresting as it may be to the publick in general) is one of very few instances on record which has an exact parallel.

The intermediate points of the contest in which Mr. Pegge was more peculiarly concerned, and which did not prominently appear to the world, were interruptions and unpleasant impediments which arose in the course of this tedious process. He had been nominated to the perpetual curacy of Brampton by Dr. *Cheyney,* dean of Lincoln; was at the sole expence of the suit respecting the right of patronage, whereby the verdict was given in favour of the Dean; and he was actually licensed by the Bishop of Lichfield. In consequence of this decision and the Bishop's licence, Mr. Pegge, not suspecting that the contest could go any farther, attended to qualify at Brampton, on Sunday, Aug. 28, 1748, in the usual manner; but was repelled *by violence* from entering the church.

In this state matters rested regarding the patronage of Brampton, when Dr. Cheyney was unexpectedly transferred from the deanry of *Lincoln* to the deanry of *Winchester,* which (we may observe by the way) he solicited on motives similar to those which actuated Mr. Pegge at the very moment; for Dr. Cheyney, being a native of Winchester, procured an exchange of his deanry of Lincoln with the Rev. Dr. William George, provost of Queen's college, Cambridge, for whom the deanry of Winchester was intended by the minister on the part of the Crown.

Thus Mr. Pegge's interests and applications were to begin *de novo* with the patron of Brampton; for, his nomination by Dr. Cheyney, in the then state of things, was of no validity. He fell however into liberal hands; for his activity in the proceedings which had hitherto taken place respecting the living in question, had rendered fresh advocates unnecessary, as it had secured the unasked favour of Dr. George, who not long afterwards voluntarily gave him the rectory of *Whittington,* near Chesterfield, in Derbyshire; into which he was inducted Nov. 11, 1751, and where he resided for upwards of 44 years without interruption.

[[Nichols' note:] Dr. (William) George's letter to Mr. Pegge on the occasion has been preserved, and is conceived in the most manly and generous terms. On account of the distance, Mr. Pegge then residing in Kent, the Dean was so obliging as to concert matters with Bishop (Frederick) Cornwallis, who then sat at Lichfield, that the living might *lapse* without injury to Mr. Pegge, who therefore took it, in fact, from his Lordship by *collation*.]

Though Mr. Pegge had relinquished all farther pretensions to the living of *Brampton* before the cause came to a decision at Derby, yet he gave every possible assistance at the trial, by the communication of various documents, as well as by his personal evidence at the assize, to support the claim of the new nominee, the Rev. John Bowman, in whose favour the verdict was given, and who afterwards enjoyed the benefice.

Here then we take leave of this troublesome affair, so nefarious and unwarrantable on the part of the parishioners of *Brampton;* and from which PATRONS of every description may draw their own inferences.

Mr. Pegge's ecclesiastical prospect in Derbyshire began soon to brighten; and he ere long obtained the more eligible living of *Whittington.* Add to this that, in the course of the dispute concerning the patronage of Brampton, he became known to the Hon. and Right Rev. Frederick (Cornwallis) Bishop of Lichfield and Coventry; who ever afterwards favoured him not only with his personal regard, but with his patronage,[5] which extended even beyond the grave, as will be mentioned hereafter, in the order of time.

We must now revert to Mr. Pegge's old friend Sir Edward Dering, who, at the moment when Mr. Pegge decidedly took the living of *Whittington,* in Derbyshire, began to negotiate with his Grace of Canterbury (Dr. Herring) the patron of *Godmersham,* for an exchange of that living for something tenable with Whittington.

The Archbishop's answer to this application was highly honourable to Mr. Pegge: "Why," said his Grace, "will Mr. Pegge leave my diocese? If he will continue in Kent, I promise you, Sir Edward, that I will give him preferment to his satisfaction."‡

No allurements, however, could prevail; and Mr. Pegge, at all events, accepted the rectory of *Whittington,* leaving every other pursuit of the kind to contingent circumstances. An exchange was, nevertheless, very soon afterwards effected, by the interest of Sir Edward with the *Duke of Devonshire,* who consented that Mr. Pegge should take his Grace's rectory of *Brinhill** in Lancashire, then luckily void, the Archbishop at the same time engaging to present the *Duke's* Clerk to *Godmersham.* Mr. Pegge was accordingly inducted into the rectory of *Brindle,* Nov. 23, 1751, in less than a fortnight after his induction at *Whittington.*†

In addition to this favour from the family of *Cavendish,* Sir Edward Dering obtained for Mr. Pegge, almost at the same moment, a *scarf* from the

---

‡ Mr. Pegge became known, at least by name, to Dr. [Thomas] Herring, when Archbishop of York, by an occasional sermon (which will be adverted to among Mr. Pegge's writings) on the publication whereof his Grace sent him a letter in handsome terms. When the Archbishop was translated to Canterbury, Mr. Pegge was, most probably, personally known to him as the diocesan. NICHOLS.

* More usually called *Brindle.* NICHOLS.

† The person who actually succeeded to the vicarage of Godmersham was the Rev. *Aden Ley,* who died there, 1766. NICHOLS.

5. The remainder of this paragraph was added to the account in the *Gentleman's Magazine.*

Marquis of Hartington (afterwards the fourth Duke of Devonshire), then called up to the House of Peers, in June 1751, by the title of Baron *Cavendish,* of *Hardwick.* Mr. Pegge's appointment is dated Nov. 18, 1751; and thus, after all his solicitude, he found himself possessed of two livings and a dignity, honourably and indulgently conferred, as well as most desirably connected, in the same year and in the same month; though this latter circumstance may be attributed to the voluntary lapse of Whittington.

[[Nichols' note:] Soon after the present Duke of Devonshire came of age, 1769, finding that he had many friends of his own to oblige, it was suggested to the senior chaplains that a resignation would be deemed a compliment by his Grace. Mr. Pegge, therefore (among some others), relinquished his chaplainship, though he continued to wear the *scarf.*]

After Mr. Pegge had held the rectory of *Brinhill* for a few years, an opportunity offered, by another obliging acquiesence of the *Duke of Devonshire,* to exchange it for the living of *Heath* (alias *Lown*), in his *Grace's* Patronage, which lies within seven miles of Whittington; a very commodious measure, as it brought Mr. Pegge's parochial preferments within a smaller distance of each other. He was accordingly inducted into the vicarage of *Heath,* Oct. 22, 1758, which he held till his death.[6]

This was the last favour of the kind which Mr. Pegge *individually* received from the DUKES OF DEVONSHIRE; but the Compiler of this little Memoir regarding his late father, flatters himself that it can give no offence to that noble family if he takes the opportunity of testifying a sense of his own *personal* obligations to the late DUKE OF DEVONSHIRE, when his Grace was *Lord Chamberlain* of his MAJESTY's *Household.*

As to Mr. Pegge's other preferments, they shall only be briefly mentioned in chronological order; but with due regard to his obligations. In the year 1765 he was presented to the perpetual curacy of *Wingerworth,* about six miles from Whittington, by the Honourable and Rev. James *Yorke,* then *Dean of Lincoln,* afterwards *Bishop of Ely,* to whom he was but little known but by name and character. This appendage was rendered the more acceptable to Mr. Pegge, because the seat of his very respectable friend Sir Henry Hunloke, bart. is in the parish, from whom, and all the family, Mr. Pegge ever received great civilities. We have already observed, that Mr. Pegge became known, insensibly as it were, to the Honourable and Right Rev. Frederick (*Cornwallis*), Bishop of Lichfield, during the contest respecting the living of *Brampton;* from whom he afterwards received more than one favour, and by whom another greater instance of regard was intended, as will be mentioned hereafter.

---

6. This ends the material contained in the *Gent. Mag.* for August 1796.

Mr. Pegge was first collated by his Lordship to the prebend of *Bobenhull* in the church of *Lichfield,* 1757; and was afterwards voluntarily advanced by him to that of *Whittington,* 1763, which he possessed at his death.

[[Nichols' note:] It is rather a singular co-incidence, that Mr. Pegge should have been at the same time *rector* of *Whittington* in *Derbyshire* and *prebendary* of *Whittington* in *Staffordshire,* both in one diocese, under different patronages, and totally independent of each other. These two *Whittingtons* are likewise nearly equidistant from places of the name of *Chesterfield.*]

In addition to the stall at Lichfield, Mr. Pegge enjoyed the prebend of *Louth,* in the cathedral of *Lincoln,* to which he had been collated (1772) by his old acquaintance, and fellow-collegian, the late Right Rev. John *Green,* bishop of that see.

[[Nichols' note:] The prebend of *Louth* carries with it the *patronage* of the vicarage of the *parish* of *Louth,* to which Mr. Pegge presented more than once. On the first vacancy, having no clerk of his own, he offered the nomination to his benefactor Bishop *Green;* at the last, he gave the living, uninfluenced, to the present incumbent, the Rev. *Wolley Jolland,* son of the Recorder of Louth.]

This seems to be the proper place to subjoin, that, towards the close of his life, Mr. Pegge declined a situation for which, in more early days, he had the greatest predilection, and had taken every active and modest measure to obtain, *viz.* a *residentiaryship* in the church of *Lichfield.*

Mr. Pegge's wishes tended to this point on laudable, and almost natural motives, as soon as his interest with the Bishop began to gain strength; for, it would have been a very pleasant interchange, at that period of life, to have passed a portion of the year at *Lichfield.* This expectation, however, could not be brought forward till he was too far advanced in age to endure with tolerable convenience a removal from time to time; and therefore, when the offer was realized, he declined the acceptance.

The case was literally this. While Mr. Pegge's elevation in the church of *Lichfield* rested solely upon Bishop (*Frederick*) Cornwallis, it was secure, had a vacancy happened: but his patron was translated to *Canterbury* 1768, and Mr. Pegge had henceforward little more than personal knowledge of any of his Grace's successors at *Lichfield,* till the Hon. and Right Rev. *James* Cornwallis (the Archbishop's nephew) was consecrated bishop of that see, 1781.

On this occasion, to restore the balance in favour of Mr. Pegge, the Archbishop had the kindness to make an *option* of the *residentiaryship* at *Lichfield,* then possessed by the Rev. Thomas *Seward.* It was, nevertheless, several years before even the tender of this preferment could take place; as his *Grace* of *Canterbury* died 1783, while Mr. *Seward* was living.

Options being personal property, Mr. Pegge's interest, on the demise of the *Archbishop,* fell into the hands of the Hon. Mrs. *Cornwallis,* his relict and executrix, who fulfilled his *Grace's* original intention in the most friendly manner, on the death of Mr. *Seward,* 1790.

The little occasional transactions which primarily brought Mr. Pegge within the notice of Bishop *(Frederick)* Cornwallis at Eccleshall-castle led his Lordship to indulge him with a greater share of personal esteem than has often fallen to the lot of a private clergyman so remotely placed from his diocesan. Mr. Pegge had attended his Lordship two or three times on affairs of business, as one of the parochial clergy, after which the Bishop did him the honour to invite him to make an annual visit at Eccleshall-castle as an *acquaintance.* The compliance with this overture was not only very flattering, but highly gratifying, to Mr. Pegge, who consequently waited upon his Lordship for a fortnight in the autumn, during several years, till the Bishop was translated to the metropolitical see of *Canterbury,* 1768. After this, however, his Grace did not forget his humble friend, the *rector of Whittington,* as will be seen; and sometimes corresponded with him on indifferent matters.

About the same time that Mr. Pegge paid these visits at Eccleshall-castle, he adopted an expedient to change the scene, likewise, by a journey to London (between Easter and Whitsuntide); where, for a few years, he was entertained by his old friend and fellow-collegian the Rev. Dr. *John Taylor,* F.S.A. Chancellor of Lincoln, &c. (the learned editor of Demosthenes and Lysias), then one of the Residentiaries of St. Paul's.

After Dr. Taylor's death (1766), the Bishop of Lincoln, Dr. *John Green,* another old college-acquaintance, became Mr. Pegge's London-host for a few years, till *Archbishop Cornwallis* began to reside at Lambeth. This event superseded the visits to Bishop *Green,* as Mr. Pegge soon afterwards received a very friendly invitation from his *Grace;* to whom, from that time, he annually paid his respects at Lambeth-palace, for a month in the spring, till the *Archbishop's* decease, which took place about Easter, 1783.

All these were delectable visits to a man of Mr. Pegge's turn of mind, whose conversation was adapted to every company, and who enjoyed *the world* with greater relish from not living in it every day. The society with which he intermixed, in such excursions, changed his ideas, and relieved him from the *taedium* of a life of much reading and retirement; as, in the course of these journeys, he often had opportunities of meeting old *Friends,* and of making new *literary acquaintance.*

On some of these occasions he passed for a week into *Kent,* among such of his old associates as were then living, till the death of his much-honoured friend, and former parishioner, the elder *Thomas Knight,* esq. of Godmersham, 1781.‡ We ought on no account to omit the mention of some *extra-visits* which Mr. Pegge occasionally made to Bishop *Green,* at *Buckden,* to which we are indebted for the life of that excellent prelate *Robert Grosseteste,* Bishop of *Lincoln;*—a work upon which we shall only observe here, that it is Dr. Pegge's *chef d'oeuvre,* and merits from the world much obligation. To these interviews with Bishop *Green,* we may also attribute those ample collections, which Dr. Pegge left among his MSS. towards a history of the *Bishops* of *Lincoln,* and of that *Cathedral* in general, &c. &c.

With the decease of Archbishop Cornwallis (1783) Mr. Pegge's excursions to London terminated. His old familiar friends, and principal acquaintance there, were gathered to their fathers; and he felt that the lot of a long life had fallen upon him, having survived not only the *first,* but the *second* class of his numerous distant connexions.

While on one of these visits at Lambeth, the late *Gustavus Brander,*[7] esq. who entertained an uncommon partiality for Mr. Pegge, persuaded him, very much against his inclination, to sit for a drawing, from which an octavo *print* of him might be engraved by Basire. The work went on so slowly that the plate was not finished till 1785, when Mr. Pegge's current age was 81. Being a *private print,* it was at first only intended for, and distributed among, the particular friends of Mr. Brander and Mr. Pegge. This print, however, *now* carries with it something of a publication; for a considerable number of the impressions were dispersed after Mr. *Brander's* death, when his library, &c. were sold by auction; and the print is often found prefixed to copies of "The Forme of Cury," a work which will hereafter be specified among Mr. Pegge's literary labours.

[[Nichols' note:] This print has the following inscription:]

SAMUEL PEGGE, A.M. S.A.S.
A.D. MDCCLXXXV. Aet. 81.
Impensis, et ex Voto, Gustavi Brander, Arm.
Sibi et Amicis.

[We cannot in any degree subscribe to the resemblance, though the print is well engraved. There is, however, a three-quarters portrait in oil (much valued by the family) painted in 1788, by Mr. Elias Needham, a young provincial artist, and a native of Derbyshire, which does the painter great credit, being a likeness uncommonly striking. Dr. Pegge being an old gentleman well known, with a countenance of much character, the portrait was taken at the request of Mr. Needham; who, after exhibiting it to his patrons and friends, made a present of it to Mr. Pegge. Those who knew Dr.

---

‡ The very just character of Mr. *Knight* given in the Gentleman's Magazine, vol. LI. p. 147, was drawn by Mr. *Pegge,* who had been intimate with him very nearly half a century. NICHOLS.

7. Nichols has a life of Brander immediately following that of Pegge in *Lit. Anec.,* VI, 260-261.

Pegge, and have had an opportunity of comparing the portrait with the print, will agree with us, that no two pictures of the same person, taken nearly at the same point of life, and so unlike each other, can both be true resemblances.]

The remainder of Mr. Pegge's life after the year 1783 was, in a great measure, reduced to a state of quietude; but not without an extensive correspondence with the world in the line of antiquarian researches: for he afterwards contributed largely to the *Archaeologia,* and the *Bibliotheca Topographica Britannica,* &c. &c, as may appear to those who will take the trouble to compare the dates of his writings, which will hereafter be enumerated, with the time of which we are speaking.

The only periodical variation in life, which attended Mr. Pegge after the Archbishop's death, consisted of summer visits at Eccleshall-castle to the present Bishop (*James*) Cornwallis, who (if we may be allowed the word) *adopted* Mr. Pegge as his guest so long as he was able to undertake such journeys.

We have already seen an instance of his Lordship's kindness in the case of the intended *residentiaryship;* and have, moreover, good reasons to believe that, had the late *Archdeacon* of *Derby* (Dr. Henry Egerton) died in an earlier stage of Mr. Pegge's life, he would have succeeded to that dignity.

This part of the memoir ought not to be dismissed without observing, to the honour of Mr. Pegge, that, as it was not in his power to make any individual return (in his life-time) to his patrons, the two Bishops of *Lichfield* of the name of *Cornwallis,* for their extended civilities, he directed, by testamentary instructions, that *one hundred volumes* out of his collection of books should be given to the library of the Cathedral of *Lichfield.*§

During Mr. Pegge's involuntary retreat from his former associations with the more remote parts of the kingdom, he was actively awake to such objects in which he was implicated nearer home.

Early in the year 1788 material repairs and considerable alterations became necessary to the Cathedral of *Lichfield.* A subscription was accordingly begun by the members of the church, supported by many lay-gentlemen of the neighbourhood, when Mr. Pegge, as a prebendary, not only contributed handsomely, but projected, and drew up, a circular letter, addressed to the Rev. Charles Hope, M.A. the minister of All Saint (the principal) church in Derby, recommending the promotion of this public design. The letter being inserted in several provincial newspapers, was so well seconded by Mr. Hope, that it had a due effect upon the clergy and laity of the diocese in general; for which Mr. Pegge received a written acknowledgment of thanks from the present Bishop of *Lichfield,* dated May 29, 1788.

§ He specified, in writing, about fourscore of these volumes, which are chiefly what may be called library-books; the rest were added by his Son; of whom some account shall be given at the end of this memoir, [*Lit. Anec.,* VI], p. 259. NICHOLS.

This year (1788), memorable as a centenary in the annals of England, was honourable to the little parish of *Whittington,* which accidentally bore a subordinate *local* part in the History of the *Revolution:* for it was to an inconsiderable public-house *there* (still called the *Revolution-house*) that the Earl of Devonshire, the Earl of Danby, the Lord Delamere, and the Hon. John D'Arcy, were driven for shelter, by a sudden shower of rain, from the adjoining common (*Whittington-Moor*) where they had met by appointment, disguised as farmers, to concert measures, unobservedly, for promoting the succession of King William III. after the abdication of King James II.||

The celebration of this jubilee, on Nov. 5, 1788, is related at large in the Gentleman's Magazine of that month; on which day Mr. Pegge preached a sermon, apposite to the occasion, which was printed at the request of the gentlemen of the committee who conducted the ceremonial,‡ which proceeded from his church to Chesterfield in grand procession.

In the year 1791 (July 8) Mr. Pegge was created LL.D. by the University of OXFORD, at the commemoration. It may be thought a little extraordinary that he should accept an advanced academical degree so late in life, as he wanted no such aggrandizement in the learned world, or among his usual associates, and had *voluntarily* closed all his expectations of ecclesiastical elevation. We are confident that he was not ambitious of the compliment; for, when it was first proposed to him, he put a *negative* upon it. It must be remembered that this honour was not conferred on an unknown man (*novus homo*); but on a *Master of Arts of* CAMBRIDGE, of name and character, and of acknowledged literary merit.* Had Mr. Pegge been desirous of the title of *Doctor* in earlier life, there can be no doubt but that he might have obtained the superior degree of D.D. from Abp. Cornwallis, upon the bare suggestion, during his familiar and domestic conversations with his Grace at Lambeth-palace.

Dr. Pegge's manners were those of a gentleman of a liberal education, who had seen much of the world, and had formed them upon the best models within his observation. Having in his early years lived in free intercourse with many of the principal and best-bred gentry in various parts of Kent, he ever afterwards preserved the same attentions by associating with respectable company, and (as we have seen) by forming honourable attachments.

In his avocations from reading and retirement, few men could relax with

---

|| In this year he printed a Narrative of what passed at the Revolution-house at Whittington in the year 1688, with a view and plan of the house by Major Rooke (reprinted in Gent. Mag. vol. LIX. p. 124.) NICHOLS.

‡ This solemnity took place on *Wednesday;* and, the church being crowded with strangers, the sermon was repeated to the parochial congregation on the following *Sunday.* Mr. Pegge was then very old, and the 5th of November N.S. was his birthday, when he entered into the 85th year of his age. NICHOLS.

* Mr. Pegge, at the time, was on a visit to his grandson, the present Sir Christopher Pegge, M.D. then lately elected reader of anatomy at Christ Church, Oxford, on Dr. Lee's foundation. NICHOLS.

more ease and cheerfulness, or better understood the *desipere in loco;*—could enter occasionally into temperate convivial mirth with a superior grace, or more interest and enliven every company by general conversation.

As he did not mix in business of a public nature, his better qualities appeared most conspicuously in private circles; for he possessed an equanimity which obtained the esteem of his friends, and an affability which procured the respect of his dependents.

His habits of life were such as became his profession and station. In his clerical functions he was exemplarily correct, not entrusting his parochial duties at *Whittington* (where he constantly resided) to another (except to the neighbouring clergy during the excursions before mentioned) till the failure of his eye-sight rendered it indispensably necessary; and even *that* did not happen till within a few years of his death.

As a preacher, his discourses from the pulpit were of the didactic and exhortatory kind, appealing to the understandings rather than to the passions of his auditory, by expounding the Holy Scriptures in a plain, intelligible, and unaffected manner. His voice was naturally weak, and suited only to a small church, so that when he occasionally appeared before a large congregation (as on visitations &c.), he was heard to a disadvantage. He left in his closet considerably more than 230 sermons composed by himself, and in his own hand-writing, besides a few (not exceeding 26) which he had transcribed (in substance only, as appears by collation) from the printed works of eminent Divines. These liberties, however, were not taken in his early days from motives of idleness, or other attachments, but later in life, to favour the fatigue of composition; all which obligations he acknowledged at the end of each such sermon.

Though Dr. Pegge's life was sedentary, from his turn to studious retirement, his love of antiquities, and of literary acquirements in general; yet these applications, which he pursued with great ardour and perseverance, did not injure his health. Vigour of mind, in proportion to his bodily strength, continued unimpaired through a very extended course of life, and nearly till he had reached *"ultima linea rerum:"* for he never had any chronical disease; but gradually and gently sunk into the grave under the weight of years, after a fortnights [sic] illness, Feb. 14, 1796, in the 92d year of his age.

[[Nichols' note:] He was buried, according to his own desire, in the chancel at *Whittington*, where a mural tablet of black marble (a voluntary tribute of filial respect) has been placed, over the East window, with the following short inscription:]

At the North End of the Altar Table, within the Rails,
lie the Remains of
SAMUEL PEGGE, LL.D.
who was inducted to this Rectory Nov. 11, 1751,

and died Feb. 14, 1796;
in the 92d year of his Age.

Having closed the scene, it must be confessed, on the one hand, that the biographical history of an individual, however learned, or engaging to private friends, who had passed the major part of his days in secluded retreats from what is called *the world,* can afford but little entertainment to the generality of readers. On the other hand, nevertheless, let it be allowed that every man of acknowledged literary merit, had he made no other impression, cannot but have left many to regret his death.

Though Dr. Pegge had exceeded even his "*fourscore* years and ten," and had outlived all his more early friends and acquaintance; he had the address to make new ones, who *now* survive, and who, it is humbly hoped, will not be sorry to see a modest remembrance of him preserved by this little memoir.

Though Dr. Pegge had an early propensity to the pursuit of *Antiquarian* knowledge he never indulged himself materially in it, so long as more essential and *professional* occupations had a claim upon him; for he had a due sense of the *nature* and *importance* of his *clerical* function. It appears, that he had read the Greek and Latin *Fathers* diligently at his outset in life. He had also re-perused the *Classicks* attentively before he applied much to the *monkish* historians, or engaged in *Antiquarian* researches; well knowing that a thorough knowledge of the learning of the *Antients,* conveyed by *classical* authors, was the best foundation for any literary structure which had not the *Christian religion* for its *corner-stone.*

During the early part of his incumbency at Godmersham, in Kent, his reading was principally such as became a *Divine,* or which tended to the acquisition of *general knowledge,* of which he possessed a greater share than most men we ever knew. When he obtained allowable leisure to follow *unprofessional* pursuits, he *attached* himself more closely to the study of *Antiquities,* and was elected a fellow of the SOCIETY OF ANTIQUARIES, Feb. 14, 1751, N.S. in which year the *charter of incorporation* was granted (in November), wherein his name stands enrolled among those of many very respectable and eminently learned men.†

Though we will be candid enough to allow that Dr. Pegge's *style* in general was not sufficiently terse and compact to be called elegant; yet he made ample amends by the matter, and by the accuracy with which he treated every copious subject, wherein all points were matured by close examination and sound judgment.[8]

Frivolous as many detached *morsels,* scattered up and down in the GENTLEMAN'S MAGAZINE, may appear to some readers, they may be called the ruminations of a busy mind; which shews an universality of reading, a love

---

† The only member of the Society at the time of its incorporation, who survived Dr. Pegge, was *Samuel Reynardson,* esq. NICHOLS.

8. In a long note, Nichols here gives titles and dates of publication of a large group of early miscellaneous works, sermons, and so on.

of investigation, and a fund of knowledge, more than would have displayed itself in any greater work, where the subject requires but *one* bias, and *one* peculiar attention.‡

It is but justice to say, that few men were so liberal in the diffusion of the knowledge which he had acquired, or more ready to communicate it, either *vivâ voce,* or by the loan of his MSS, as many of his living friends can testify.

In his publications he was also equally *disinterested* as in his private communications; for he never, as far as can be recollected, received any *pecuniary* advantage from any pieces that he printed, committing them all to the press, with the sole reserve of a few copies to distribute among his particular friends.

In the following catalogue we must be allowed to deviate from chronological order, for the sake of preserving Dr. Pegge's *contributions* to various *periodical* and *contingent* Publications, distinct from his independent works; to all which, however, we shall give (as far as possible) their respective dates.

The greatest honour, which a literary man can obtain, is the *eulogies* of those who possessed equal or more learning than himself. *"Laudatus à laudatis viris"* may peculiarly and deservedly be said of Dr. Pegge, as might be exemplified from the frequent mention made of him by the most respectable contemporary writers of the *Archaeological* line; but modesty forbids our enumerating them.

The following articles were added by Mr. Gough.

"While vicar of Godmersham, Mr. Pegge collected a good deal relative to the College at Wye, in its neighbourhood, which he thought of publishing, and engraved the seal, before engraved in Lewis's Seals. He had 'Extracts from the Rental of the Royal Manor of Wye, made about 1430, in the hands of Daniel Earl of Winchelsea;' and 'Copy of a Survey and Rental of the College, in the possession of Sir Windham Knatchbull, 1739.'

"Dr. Pegge's early application to literature appears from a collation of Xenophon's Cyropaedia and Anabasis with a Duport MS. in the library of Eton college (1924 Cat. MSS. Angl.), and with a view to publication, had not Hutchinson superseded it from more valuable manuscripts.

"He possessed a MS Lexicon Xenophonticum by himself, as well as a Greek Lexicon in MS.; and had also 'An English Historical Dictionary,' in 6 volumes, folio; a French and Italian, a Latin, a British and Saxon one, in one volume each; all corrected by his notes; a 'Glossarium Generale;' and two volumes of Collections in English History.

"During his residence in Kent, he formed a 'Monasticon Cantianum,' in two folio MS volumes; a MS Dictionary for Kent; an alphabetical List of Kentish Authors and Worthies; Kentish Collections; Places in Kent; and

---

‡ An accurate list of these detached publications may be seen in the Gentleman's Magazine for December 1796. . . . NICHOLS. (There follows in this note a long list of works written by Pegge for the Society of Antiquaries.)

many large MS additions to the account of that county in the 'Magna Britannia.' "

SAMUEL PEGGE, esq. the Doctor's only surviving son, was born 1731.§ He was a barrister of the Middle Temple, one of the grooms of his Majesty's privy-chamber, and one of the esquires of the King's household; F.A.S. 1796. He married, 1. Martha, daughter of the Rev. Dr. Henry Bourne, of Chesterfield (where he died, in his 89th year, 1775), and sister to the Rev. John Bourne, who married Mr. Pegge's sister. By this lady, who was born in 1732, and died in 1767, he had one son, Christopher Pegge, M.D.F.R.S.; knighted in 1799, and Regius Professor of physic; and a daughter, Charlotte-Anne, who died unmarried, March 17, 1793.

Mr. Pegge married, secondly, Goodeth Belt, aunt to Robert Belt, esq. of Bossal, co. York.

To Mr. Pegge we are indebted for the foregoing Memoir of his learned Father; and for several occasional communications to the Gentleman's Magazine. He was the author also of "Curialia; or an historical Account of some Branches of the Royal Household," Part I. 1782; Part II. 1784; Part III. 1791; and assisted Mr. Nichols in publishing his father's posthumous "History of Beauchief Abbey."||

He was buried on the West side of Kensington church-yard; where the following epitaph is placed on an upright stone:

SAMUEL PEGGE, Esq.
died May the 22d, 1800, aged 67 years.
MARTHA, wife of SAMUEL PEGGE, Esq.
died June 28, 1767, aged 35 years.
CHARLOTTE-ANNE, the only daughter
of SAMUEL and MARTHA PEGGE,
died March 17, 1793, aged 31 years.
Mrs. CHRISTIANA PEGGE died July 1, 1790.

He had been several years engaged in preparing the remaining Numbers of his "Curialia" for the press; the materials for which, and also his "Anecdotes of the English Language," he bequeathed to Mr. Nichols; who presented to the publick the "Anecdotes of the English Language" in 1803, 8vo; and the "Curialia," Parts IV. and V. in 1806.‡

§ Another son, Christopher, died, an infant, in 1736. NICHOLS.
|| See [*Lit. Anec.*, VI,] p. 257. NICHOLS.
‡ I have the outlines of Three succeeding Numbers, the appearance of which the fatality attending the publication of the Fourth and Fifth will probably for ever prevent. NICHOLS. (In a note in *Lit. Anec.*, VIII, 119, Nichols wrote concerning *Curialia:* "The intended publication of Three more Numbers was put aside by the fatal accident which has occasioned the former Parts [particularly Parts IV. and V.] to be ranked among the scarcest ornaments of an Antiquarian Library." The *fatality* referred to was probably the fire of 8 February 1808 that destroyed Nichols' "printing-office and ware-houses, with the whole of their valuable contents.")

Joseph Warton and Thomas Warton the Younger

[Nichols' memoir of the Wartons, in *Lit. Anec.*, VI, 168-185, is a basic source of materials for the lives of the two brothers, containing original materials not provided by his more ambitious contemporary biographers. In his account of the Wartons, Nichols drew upon personal resources: a long acquaintance and possession of many letters to and from his subjects. Interest in antiquities, along with an interest in literature in general and in poetry in particular, inevitably brought about an acquaintance between the brothers and the leading printer and publisher, not only of antiquarian books, but of works of such literary importance as Johnson's *Lives of the Poets*.

As he usually did, Nichols published most of the materials found in his accounts in *Literary Anecdotes* in earlier versions in the *Gentleman's Magazine*. One advantage of this practice was that the materials could be put before the public quickly, while general interest in the subject was at its peak; secondarily, the readers of the magazine could send in corrections and additions to the editor, who could incorporate them when the materials went into a book.

A considerable amount of attention has been given to the three Wartons in the twentieth century. Thomas Warton the Elder was the subject of a work by David Horace Bishop, *The Father of the Wartons* (1917); and he figures, of course, in Eric Partridge's *The Three Wartons* (1927). Joseph Warton was one of the subjects considered in the Warton Lecture on English Poetry, No. 6, by Edmund Gosse, *Two Pioneers of Romanticism: Joseph and Thomas Warton* (1915); and he was the center of attention in a work by Edith J. Morley, *Joseph Warton: A Comparison of his Essay on the Genius and Writings of Pope with his edition of Pope's Works* (1924). Thomas Warton the Younger has received the most attention of the three. In the British Academy Warton Lecture, No. 1, William P. Ker wrote about him in a work entitled *Thomas Warton* (1911). Clarissa Rinaker wrote a work intended to be his definitive biography, *Thomas Warton; A Biographical and Critical Study* (University of Illinois, 1916). David Nichol Smith produced a work entitled *Warton's History of English Poetry* (1929); and Vol. 3 of the *Percy Letters* series is the *Correspondence of Thomas Percy and Thomas Warton* (1944). Publication No. 39 of the Augustan Reprint Society is *A History of English Poetry: an Unpublished Continuation*, ed. with an introduction by Rodney M. Blaine (Los Angeles, 1953).

Future work on the Wartons will certainly have to begin with the important collection of letters to Thomas Warton the Younger in the British Museum. These letters, which scholars have scarcely begun to make use of, are Additional Mss. 42,560 (containing 236 folios) and 42,561 (containing 239 folios). "The present material," says the *Catalogue of Additions to the Manuscripts in the British Museum, 1931-1935* (1967), "was apparently not known to Clarissa Rinaker when writing her *Thomas Warton*." Relatively few other scholars since have made use of the letters, whose copyright subsists indefinitely with the publishing firm of John Murray, London.

In addition to the valuable holdings of the British Museum, many other sources exist, of course, for manuscript materials regarding the Wartons. The Osborn Collection at Yale possesses twelve letters and two other manuscripts of Joseph Warton and four letters of his brother Thomas. The Folger Library has three of Joseph Warton's letters, two of his brother's, and a number of others in which the Wartons are mentioned, including one from Hannah More to Mrs. Garrick, 31 May 1790, mentioning Thomas Warton's death (W. b. 487). The Bodleian Library has at least a dozen letters written by the Warton brothers in its MS. Montagu d. 2 collection, including the one from Joseph Warton to Nichols dated 18 April 1784, put by Nichols in *Literary Anecdotes* and reproduced in the account that follows. In another collection in the Bodleian, MS. Autogr. d. 4, is a letter from Thomas Warton to John Prince, 17 August 1773. Harvard University Library possesses thirty-one letters written by Thomas Warton, twenty-nine of which are to Thomas Percy, and five letters to him, four of which are from Percy, in addition to miscellaneous papers; Harvard also has one letter by and one to Joseph Warton.

Sidney Lee is the author of lives of both the Warton brothers in the DNB. Nichols' account in *Literary Anecdotes* is listed as a source at the end of both lives. A portrait of Thomas Warton the Younger is in *Illustr.*, IV, 738, opposite more of his letters.]

THE Lives of these learned and benevolent Brothers (whom with honest pride I call my Friends) have so lately been given to the publick by Mr. Mant and Mr. Wooll;[1] and still more recently, and not less ably, by Mr. Alexander Chalmers, in the Biographical Prefaces to his valuable Collection of the English Poets, 1810; that I shall content myself by a mere epitome of dates.

Their father, the Rev. Thomas Warton, B.D. descended from an antient and honourable family at Beverley in Yorkshire, was fellow of Magdalen College, Oxford, Poetry Professor there, and vicar of Basingstoke; where he died in 1746; and where his tomb is thus inscribed by his sons:

D. O. M.
THOMAE WARTON, S.T.B.
hujus parochiae vicario,
viro erudito,
probo, pio;

---

1. A memoir of Thomas Warton the Younger, written by Richard Mant, was prefixed to the collected edition of Warton's poems of 1802; a memoir of Joseph Warton, written by John Wooll, was published in the first volume of a selection from his works and correspondence in 1806.

> qui vixit annos LVI.
> ob. MDCCXLVI.
> filii moerentes
> F.

JOSEPH, the eldest son, was born at Dunsford in Surrey, at the house of his maternal grandfather, the Rev. Joseph Richardson, in 1722; and, except being a small time at New College school, was principally instructed by his father, till at the age of 14 he was admitted on the foundation at Winchester, under Dr. [George] Sandby, the present venerable Chancellor of Norwich; and at this noble seminary he commenced a poetical correspondence with Mr. Urban.

In September 1740, being superannuated at Winchester, he was entered at Oriel College, Oxon; where he sedulously cultivated his poetical talents; and, taking the degree of B.A. in 1744, was ordained to his father's curacy at Basingstoke; which, in February 1746, he exchanged for Chelsea; whence, to complete his recovery from the small-pox, he went to Chobham; and, after accepting for a few months the duty of Chawton and Droxford, returned to the curacy of Basingstoke.

In 1746 he published a small volume of "Odes;" and in 1747-8 was presented by the Duke of Bolton to the rectory of Winslade; soon after which, he happily united himself in marriage to Miss Daman.

[Editor's note: A number of letters in the Warton collection in the British Museum are from the period of the writing and publication of the odes; I shall introduce a few here by way of illustration. The first (Add. Mss. 42,560. ff. 3-4), from Joseph Warton to his brother Thomas, is not dated but was obviously written sometime shortly before the reply (Add. Mss. 42,560. f. 5), dated 19 April (1745). The third letter (Add. Mss. 42,560. ff. 9-10) is again from Joseph to Thomas Warton and is dated 18 March (1746).]

> Dear Tom.
>
> John is setting out so suddenly that I have scarce time to say a word to you. I desire you will take particular care of every single paper that comes from Hartwells, & put 'em all by themselves in some separate drawer or box. I should be obliged to you too if at a leisure hour you would take a catalogue of my books. I hope you have got every thing from Hartwells at your room at this time.
>
> I desire you will finish the two poems you mention to me & send them hither. The Odes you speak of I suppose by this you know are Akinsides, & some of 'em are extremely insipid & flat. Collins sent them to me with Tancred & Sigismunda:[2] in which there are some moving

---

2. This story from *Gil Blas*, IV, iv, was made into a play by James Thomson and published in 1745. *Tancred and Sigismunda* was produced with Garrick as Tancred in 1752.

strokes. Yesterday I read the Story in the second Vol. of Gil Blas where it is inimitably related.

I should be very glad if you could send one or two of my paper books of manuscripts by John Holder: as they are light enough for him to carry. I met with very little pleasure in Surrey, where they all Love Money more than ever. We are very dismal now my Mother is in London. . . .

You know I had entirely laid aside the Temple of Pity: but I have now begun to write an Ode to Pity: which I will make as correct as I can. . . . Which of Akinsides Odes are most approved; or are any of 'em approved? The thoughts to me are generally trite & common. You see by his Advertisement that he thinks to set up for the first correct English lyric poet. . . . Adieu dear Tom.—I am to preach here twice next Sunday & have no Sermon.

Your most affec. Bro.
Jos. Warton

Dear Jo,   Oxon Ap 19 [1745].

To answer your first point, I shall take particular care of all your things from Hartwell's, & I assure the Papers shall never be seen by any one; as to the Books I took a Catalogue of them the day after I gott them into my own room.

I wish I had finished the two poems I mentioned to send them by Holder.—As to Akenside's Odes I have to agree with you that they have a vast deal of ye frigid. Tancred & Sigismunda has some good strokes here & there but I think in the whole it is a very bad Tragedy.

I am glad you have laid aside the Temple of Pity, for that of writing an ode to it, in which you may not only mention her temple with all its' attendants, but likewise bring in several of the unfortunate characters. . . .

[Editor's note: Before the following letter appears here, part may have appeared in the *Correspondence of Edward Young*, edited by Henry Pettit and scheduled for publication by Oxford University Press.]

Dear Tom

I am very sorry to hear that Geering has no more humanity than to turn a Dun. I am more & more every day convinced that Hutcheson's "Moral Sense"[3] is Utopian & Imaginary and to this purpose must tell you what Dr YOUNG said to me, (with whom I breakfasted the other

---

3. See Francis Hutcheson, *An Essay on the Nature and Conduct of the Passions and Affections, with Illustrations on the Moral Sense*, 1728.

morning)—"Proper D[istrust of] All Mankind is one of the most prudential Maxims." I spent two or three [hours] very agreeably & in Conversation he is a very . . . [hole in paper] & sensible & entertaining man. I have [rene]wed my Acquaintance with Mr Spense, who is the most charming fellow in the World; he read to me two of his Dialogues in M.S. He is pleas'd to be very fond of my *"Ode to Solitude";* I shewed all of them to him, & he strongly advised me not to publish this Season. I gave him & Dr Young subscription papers. Dodsley has vex'd me extremely not to send the proposals to Fletcher as he was ordered a week ago. I was surprised to find he had not done it. But you will receive some on Thursday or Friday night; that is, they are sent to Fletcher from whom you will take whatever you want. I hope you were able to get a little money by them to stop [Geering's] Mouth. Whatever subscriptions are got in Oxford I think may be applied to that purpose. I hope you will be able to raise enough, if not let me know. Payne is too worldly-minded to be compassionate. What you say about Misfortunes is just. And I think you & I, tho we have lived so little a while in the World, have felt our proper share of them. Let us bear up against them as well as We can. My situation here is far from eligible: it will do this Summer, but I shall not be able to hold it the Winter.—I am writing a new "Ode to FANCY": in which I think I have succeeded; it will be very long. I desire [your] opinion of this Image which pleases me much, as it does that Aristarchey[4] HOLLOWAY, who by the way is an excellent tho severe Critic: speaking of a most wild, uncultivated Country—

> "Where Nature seems to sit alone
> Majestic on a rocky throne."

You shall see the whole—I have altered several expressions in the Odes, that upon stricter review were faulty.

My Mother desires you would write to her. Poor old Mrs May was buried at Basingstoke last Friday.

I am obliged to leave off here, & am

your most affection. Bro.
J Warton

Chelsea
    March 18 [1746].

In 1748, in conjunction with his brother, he published by subscription, and inscribed to Lord Craven, an octavo volume of his Father's Poems; and in 1751 accompanied the Duke of Bolton to Paris.

---

4. The OED labels the word *Aristarchy* as "obs. rare" and defines it as "A body of severe critics."

[[Nichols' note:] In this volume (which was published partly with a view to do honour to his father's memory, but principally for the laudable purpose of paying the few debts he left behind him), the "Ode on the Death of the Author by a Lady" was by his daughter, Jane Warton, who died at Wickham, Nov. 3, 1809, at the advanced age of 87.]

In 1753 he was an assistant in "The Adventurer;" and published his poetical version of the Eclogues and Georgics of Virgil, which was begun in 1748-9.

[Editor's note: The following letter (British Museum Add. Mss. 42,560. ff. 24-25) from Joseph to Thomas Warton is from this period.]

Dearest Tom

You must give me joy! for all Virgil is finished off except the dedication, & I yesterday returned to Quiet in the Country. I longed to have a Line from you in London, but I believe must reserve the thousand things I have to say till I see you here, which I hope will be soon.

I have seen Johnson so very often that we have contracted close friendship & are quite intimate. Dodsley behaved throughout with the utmost civility & kindness. The last night he made a grand Supper & invited all my acquaintance, Vansittart among the rest—who was glad to see Johnson. Twice to [Robert] Bedingfield. I left the play houses in combustion raised by Hill; but was Wednesday with little Garrick who despised it. [Bonnell] Thornton called & seemed piqued I should say to Johnson that He wrote the *Adventurers*. I told him I heard it at a coffeehouse openly from 20 people which is true. He's cursedly nettled & with Justice at Hill, who deserves caning. I have brought down the 4 Vols—*stitch'd* in *blue!* to look over for errata & I wish you could go over them with me—and therefore I should be very glad if you could take a ride to Winslade as soon as possible. Can't you be absent a little at present? & come again at Xmas. Let me know. Mr May brings this— you can't think how kind he has been in preaching so often for me Here.

A folio w^d not contain all I have to communicate, could therefore wish you'd come over—if only for a few days—if you cant stay long— & if you come next Week, I can shew you the Dedication which *is critical*, & I brought it down to revise tho finished quite in Town—so come!

I am most affectionately yours

J Warton.

Nov. 17 [1752]. Friday eve—
    Winslade.
Mother & all are well.

[The cover has written on it "To Mʳ Warton / Trinity College / Oxon." In Joseph Warton's hand also are two notes on the cover: "Pray come this week" and "P.S. The Roads are now very good."]

In 1754 he was presented, by the Jervoise family, to the rectory of Turnworth; and in 1755 was elected second master of Winchester school.

The first volume of his "Essay on the Writings and Genius of Pope" was published anonymously in 1756; and in the same year, Sir George Lyttelton having obtained a peerage, Mr. Warton was honoured by the noble Baron with a chaplain's scarf.

In May 1766 he was advanced to the head mastership of Winchester school; and, visiting Oxford, proceeded to the degree of B. and D.D.

[Editor's note: The following excerpt is from a manuscript in the British Museum Warton collection (Add. Mss. 42,560. f. 144).]

Dearest Tom   Win[chester]. May. 8. [17]66.

You may now give me joy of being Head master of Winchester College, which crowns all my Views & all my Wishes in Life. All was done & conferred in the most handsome & polite manner—no improper & impertinent questions or tests asked or proposed. After all was over, the Warden told us of the proposed stipend, which we said we should *consider* of so important a thing, & give in an answer. Thus you see we got *elected* without being *pinned* down to take the Salary—a great Point gained. My Speech has been immensely liked, & I went thro it to my Wish. I added &c &c. . . .

Adieu dearest Tom

I am most affectˡʸ
Jᵒˢ Warton

In 1772, he lost an affectionate wife, by whom he had six children; but, in the following year, was induced again to enter into the marriage state, with Miss Nicholas, daughter of Robert Nicholas, esq.; and, in the intervals of attendance on the school, passed such leisure as he could obtain amongst his intimates in London. It was at this period I had the satisfaction of becoming personally acquainted with Dr. Warton; and experienced from him abundant proofs of that inclination to forward the literary labours of others, for which he was peculiarly famed. I had, then recently, published four volumes of a small Collection of "Miscellaneous Poems;" in the selecting of which I had the assistance of many first-rate literary characters; and in four subsequent volumes was particularly indebted to Bishops Lowth and Percy, Dr. Warton, and Mr. Kynaston.

[Editor's note: Nichols is referring here to his *A Select Collection of Poems: with Notes, Biographical and Historical*. The first four volumes were issued in 1780 and the second four, in 1782. That Nichols made use of the suggestions made by Joseph Warton (in the letters that follow) is evident from an inspection of the second four-volume series of the *Select Collection*. Thirty poems of John Whaley are included in Vol. 6 (pp. 143-241); three poems by Walter Harte and a note on his life are in Vol. 7 (pp. 302-308); a series of sea-eclogues by John Diaper and a note on his life appear in Vol. 5 (pp. 209-255); seven poems by Samuel Cobb(e) and a note on his life are in Vol. 7 (pp. 238-286); and four poems of George Sandys, including "To the King," "To the Queen," and "Deo Optimo Maximo," and a note on Sandys' life are in Vol. 8 (pp. 238-246).]

[[Nichols note:] I hope to stand excused in exhibiting some proofs of Dr. Warton's kind attention.]5

SIR,   *College, Winchester, April* 25, 1780.

When I was last in town, I proposed to myself the pleasure of calling on you, to thank you for the care you had taken in printing some books for the use of this school; and likewise to have asked you if you had remaining in your hands any copies of that excellent edition of the *Two Iphigenia's* by Markland; for our bookseller has orders to procure some, as I shall be glad to use it at the upper end of the school. Suffer me to return you my thanks for the great pleasure you have given me in the perusal of your *Four Volumes of Poems,* and of the very entertaining Notes and Anecdotes that accompany them. I am glad to find that you intend giving more of that sort to the publick. We have a good many old Miscellaneous Poems in our College Library; and, if I thought your plan was not completed, might perhaps point out some to you. I believe there are some things in the Miscellanies of *Husband,* of *Lewis,* of *Harte,* and of *Diaper, Whalley,* and *Cobbe* (author of a very fine Ode in Dodsley's Miscellanies),6 that might deserve to be inserted. Why should you not take some of *Sandys's* Psalms, as a pattern of his excellent versification? His introductory verses to the King and Queen; and a concluding copy, intituled, *"Deo Opt. &c."* containing an account of his Life and Travels, are really excellent. I hint these things; not as imagining you want either *matter* or *information;* but rather to express the pleasure I have received from your publication. Will you please to tell Mr. Reed* I have found Fenton's letter, which I promised to shew him.7 I am, Sir,
              Your very obedient and humble servant,   JOS. WARTON.

---

* The late Isaac Reed, esq. of Staple Inn. NICHOLS.

5. This sentence and the following three letters from Joseph Warton to Nichols are in a note in *Literary Anecdotes*.

6. Nichols' *Select Collection* was intended as a supplement to the collections of Dodsley and Pearch. It was supposed to include no poem that had appeared in Dodsley, in Pearch, or in the sixty volumes of the *English Poets*. See the "Advertisement" to the *Select Collection*, I, viii.

7. Elijah Fenton and William Broome were Pope's collaborators in the translation of Homer.

[Editor's note: The next letter is interesting in that very few of the suggestions made by Warton were followed by Nichols. The obvious implication is that Nichols was not accepting suggestions blindly but was exercising an active editorship. None of Sandys' translations of psalms is included, nor is Solomon's Song. The verses "to Sandys from the great Lord Falkland," however, are in Vol. 8 (pp. 247-258). Walter Harte's "To Mr. Pope" is included (VII, 306-308), but the "*Essay* on Painting" is omitted for lack of space (p. 304n). The poem "To Mr. Pope" is described by Nichols in his note on Harte in Warton's own words: "much laboured, and went through Mr. Pope's hands" (p. 302n). The rest of Warton's suggestions were not used.]

SIR, *Winton, May 7,* 1780.
I am heartily glad to find that any hints I could give you about your very entertaining Work have been acceptable to you; and, in that confidence, shall add one or two more. I did not know that the Dryades of *Diaper* was in the Poetical Calendar. There is a thin volume of *Cobb's* Poems, from whence I have a notion something might be selected. His Ode in Dodsley is most excellent. *Sandys*, besides his Psalms, translated also, and most elegantly, Solomon's Song. All which might be inserted; as well as a Copy of Verses to Sandys from the great Lord Falkland, and Sandys's Epistle before his Translation of Ovid. From *Walter Harte's* Poems, the *Essay* on Painting, and his Epistle to Pope, and his *Essay* on *Reason,* a very fine poem, which was much laboured, and went through Mr. Pope's hands; and which I wonder has not lately been reprinted. Have you Lord *Paget's* Essay on Human Life; and an Epistle of *his* to Mr. Pope? I have the very copy he gave *Pope,* which I will send you by the carrier, if you wish to see it. I think Mr. *Merrick's* Tryphiodorus, the *Destruction of Troy,* might be inserted. It is admirably well done, very good versification indeed, and better than the original; and would, as it has never been re-printed without his large notes, be, I should think, acceptable. Do you know *Jones's* Translation of *Oppian's Halieutics?* This, perhaps, might be taken in whole or in part. I forgot to say that something might be also selected from *The Amaranth* of *Walter Harte;* the *Vision of Death* particularly. Why not give a *specimen* of *Chapman's* Homer, which is much talked of, and little known? As I see you have given some of *Creech's* Translations (who, by the way, is a most nervous and vigorous translator), why not insert some of his *Theocritus,* many parts of which are admirable? Look at the *Hylas,* the *Anacreontic* on the Death of Adonis, the Young Hercules, &c. &c. And, though *Francis* seems to have demolished Creech's Horace, yet give me leave to say that some parts of Creech's Horace are good, and I wish you would insert some of his Odes. As you have taken some Songs out of *Dryden's* Plays, why should you not also take those Songs that *Ben Jonson* has inserted in his Plays, some of which are most elegant and harmonious? "*Still to be neat, &c.*" in the *Silent Woman,* &c; and some excellent lyric pieces, from what he calls his *Underwood,* To *Charis* 10 pieces, and *An Ode,* and Epistle to Selden. I must now *earnestly* entreat you, *for many strong reasons, not* to select any thing out of the collection you mention of my Father's, 1748. And I am sure you will oblige me by believing that I do not ask this without reason. [See p. 169.][8]

---

8. Square brackets are Nichols'; the reference is, of course, to *Literary Anecdotes.*

I have a poem called *Henry and Minerva,* by J.B. esq. printed for Roberts, 1729. I know not the author; but there is much fancy and taste, on the introduction of *Literature* after the Dark Ages, &c. And another poem, "*A Prospect of Poetry,* to Lord Orrery, by *J. Dalacourt.* Dublin. 1734." Would you see them? I am, Sir,
   Your very obedient and faithful servant,   Jos. WARTON.

SIR,   *Winton, June* 3, 1782.
I am very certain that your candour will induce you to excuse the trouble I give you of a letter, when it is to rectify a great mistake with respect to myself in your very last Magazine, p. 233. The *whole note,* inserted in my Virgil, on which some animadversions are made, is Dr. [Richard] *Hurd's,* and is by me quoted *as such* in the Virgil, as the Critic might have seen, if he had turned to my volumes, as he ought to have done. And I have nothing to do with his objections relating to *ardentes,* or *accingor,* or *Tithonus,* &c. &c. I will therefore beg the favour of you to say, in any little note or remark, in any part of your *next* Magazine, that the whole passage *animadverted upon* is Dr. Hurd's, and not mine. And be so kind as to put it, *not as coming from me,* but as a remark of your own.†—I cannot but be highly pleased with the clear and candid review of my second volume on Pope. If you *happen* to know the author, I will beg you to make my compliments to him, and to return him my thanks.—Your Magazine is justly in the greatest credit here; and, under your guidance, is become one of the most useful and entertaining Miscellanies I know. I am, dear Sir, with much regard,
   Your obedient humble servant,   Jos. WARTON.

In 1782 his friend Bp. Lowth gave him a prebend in St. Paul's, and the rectory of Thorley, Herts; which, after some arrangements, he exchanged for Wickham, Hants. And in this year he published the second volume of his "Essay on Pope."

In 1784 he began to print a small volume of some curiosity, not completed till 1787; which, though little noticed at the time, is now become exceedingly rare. I make no apology, therefore, for transcribing his short Advertisement.

"The Public has paid, of late, so much attention to our *old Poets,* that it has been imagined a perusal of some of our *old Critics* also may be found equally agreeable. Two pieces of criticism, accordingly, are here selected, of no common merit; and, indeed, the two earliest in our language, that deserve much attention; but which are not sufficiently known and read, by the situation in which they happen to stand; the one at the end of so tedious and unnatural a Romance as the *Arcadia;* and the other at the end of *Ben Jonson's* Works; which, being very voluminous, and not all of equal value, fall not into many hands.

"The characters of the two authors are too well known to require to be here displayed. Suffice it to say, that there are few rules and few excellencies of Poetry, especially epic and dramatic, but that Sir *Philip Sydney,* who had diligently read the best Latin and Italian commentaries on *Aristotle's*

---

† This was accordingly done, in vol. LII [June 1782]. p. 290. NICHOLS. (The letter to the editor criticising Hurd's note, May 1782, is signed *H.* The answer correcting the mistaken attribution is signed *Bob Short.*)

Poetics, has here pointed out and illustrated with true taste and judgment; and that the observations of *Ben Jonson* have all that closeness and precision of style, weight of sentiment, and accuracy of classical learning, for which he is so justly celebrated. For the few antiquated expressions, in both pieces, no apology can be required."

[Editor's note: Nichols inserted the three following letters in a note to the paragraph preceding the last, where he introduces them with this statement: "Which, previous to its being begun, he thus characterizes."]

DEAR SIR, *Winton, April* 18, 1784.
I have a little printing scheme to mention to you, and imagine you will not dislike to join with me in the *profit* and *loss*. We all know what a taste is diffused for reading our old *Poets*. I think some of our old *Critics* might be made as popular and pleasing. I therefore propose to you to print, in a very neat volume in twelves, these two pieces, both of which are excellent in their way: "A Defense of Poetry by Sir Philip Sydney;" and, "Observations on Eloquence and Poetry, from the *Discoveries* of Ben Jonson." Neither of these pieces are read frequently, because one is at the end of the *Arcadia*, into which few people look; and the other at the end of Jonson's works, consisting, you know, of many volumes.—I would wish it were soon done, if you approve it. I should be glad to see the proofs, and to have it perfectly correct. And I will find you the copy to print from. Believe me, dear Sir, very sincerely,
Yours, JOS. WARTON.

DEAR SIR, *Winton, April* 27, 1784.
I here send you the copy to print our Work from, with such directions to your Compositor as I could recollect. I think he cannot well mistake in *omitting* the parts of *Jonson's Discoveries* that are marked out; and I would beg he would be attentive to the *pointing*, which I have gone through as carefully as I could. It will make a larger volume than I thought, especially as I wish to add some Notes. Neither of these pieces are sufficiently known and read by being in their present situations; and they will shew the state of criticism and taste at so early a period of our Literature. I am, dear Sir,
Your obedient and very faithful humble servant, J. WARTON.

DEAR SIR, *Winton, Dec* 12, 1786.
At length I here send you what I think necessary to prefix to our little publication, as also the title-page, just as I wish it to be *printed*. Indeed I am afraid it could be of no use to have published for the many last dead months. I shall be in town about January 6 or 7, and wish all were then ready for publication—or sooner, if you, who understand these matters better than I can do, think it necessary. My friend and old acquaintance Mr. Dodsley declining shop-business, I wish to have the name of Mr. [John] *Walter* at Charing Cross, as one of our *publishers,* joined with whatever other person you approve. I am, dear Sir,
Your obedient and faithful servant, J. WARTON.

In 1788, he obtained a prebend at Winchester; and the rectory of Easton, which in the same year he was permitted to exchange for that of Upham.

He resigned the mastership of Winchester school in July 1795; and retired to his rectory at Wickham; where, in 1797, he completed his edition of "Pope's Works" in nine octavo volumes.

[Nichols note:] [On this occasion he thus mentions some books which I had lent him, enriched by some valuable MS notes by Mr. Bowyer.]

DEAR SIR, *Wickham, by Fareham, Hants, Sept.* 13, 1797.
I hope you will not think me forgetful of your kindness in lending me Mr. Bowyer's *ten* volumes of Pope, and *six* of *Curll's* Letters. If you wish it, I will return them to you by the carrier immediately, or bring them when I come to town.

I have a little inclination to know, and perhaps you may be able to inform me, who is the writer of a peevish, feeble, and therefore contemptible criticism, on the edition of Pope, published in the last *******Review. The good man seems to be principally angry at my inserting the observations formerly made in my *Essay* on Pope, and which it would have been absurd, and improper, and impossible, and contrary to the very design of undertaking the Edition, not to have done; and if they had been omitted, then I should have been called on for such an unexpected omission. I am too callous a veteran to regard such sort of objections.—Is our friend Mr. [John] Wilkes returned to town? and is he well? I was very unfortunately prevented from visiting him.‡ I beg my best remembrances to him, and to tell him that I have safe his six volumes of Pope. Believe me, dear Sir, very sincerely and faithfully yours, JOS. WARTON.

He afterwards undertook an edition of Dryden; of which, in 1799, he had completed two volumes, with notes; which are now in the possession of his son, the Rev. John Warton; who has undertaken to give them to the world. At this time he was afflicted by an incurable disorder in his kidneys, which terminated his useful and honourable life, Feb. 23, 1800, in his 78th year. He left a widow, who died in 1806; a son, and three daughters; the youngest by his second wife. He was buried in the same grave with his first wife, on the North side of Winchester cathedral; and the grateful Wiccamites have evinced their respect for his memory by placing an elegant monument, designed by Mr. Flaxman, against a pillar next to the entrance of the choir, with the following very handsome inscription:

H. S. E.
JOSEPHUS WARTON, S.T.P.
hujus Ecclesiae
Praebendarius;
Scholae Wintoniensis
per annos ferè triginta
Informator:
Poeta fervidus, facilis, et politus:
Criticus eruditus, perspicax, elegans:
Obiit XXIII° Feb. MDCCC,
aetat. LXXVIII.
Hoc qualecunque

---

‡ At Sandown Cottage, his *villakin* in the Isle of Wight. NICHOLS.

> Praeceptori optimo,
> desideratissimo,
> Wiccamici sui
> P. C.

THOMAS WARTON, the younger brother of Dr. Joseph, was born at Basingstoke in 1728; and in very early life evinced a fondness for reading, and a taste for poetry. [Nichols' note:] [This appears by a translation from Martial, in his ninth year, authenticated by a letter to his sister, dated "from the School, Nov. 7, 1737."] After passing some time under his father's tuition, and at Basingstoke school, he was, in March 1743, admitted a commoner of Trinity college, Oxford, in his sixteenth year.

In 1745 he published five "Pastoral Eclogues;" and became a correspondent in Dodsley's Museum, to which his brother was also a contributor.

In 1747 and 1748 he had the office of "poet laureate" conferred upon him, according to an antient practice, in the common room of Trinity college. [Nichols' note:] ["The duty of his office was, to celebrate the lady chosen by the same authority as the Lady Patroness; and Warton performed his task, on an appointed day, crowned with a wreath of laurel. The verses, which Mr. Mant says are still to be seen in the common room, are written in an elegant and flowing style, but have not been thought worthy of preservation." *Chalmers, Poets,* vol. XVIII. p. 76.]

His next publication, "The Pleasures of Melancholy," was followed by "The Triumphs of Isis, 1749."[9]

He was a contributor to "The Student" in 1750 [Nichols' note:] [In which Mr. Warton's "Progress of Discontent," which had been written in 1746, deserves especial notice.]; and in that year took his master's degree. In 1751 he succeeded to a fellowship; and published his excellent satire called "Newmarket;" an "Ode to Music;" and "Verses on the Death of Frederick Prince of Wales;" and was, in 1753, the editor of "The Union," printed at Edinburgh.

The Bodleian and Savilian Statutes were drawn up by him in 1754; in which year he published his "Observations on the Faerie Queen of Spenser;" enlarged in 1762 to two volumes.

In 1757 he was elected Poetry Professor; which, as is the usual custom, he held for ten years; and his lectures were elegant and original.

In 1758 he published "Inscriptionum Romanarum Metricarum Delectus," a collection of the best Roman epigrams and inscriptions, with a few modern epigrams, one by Dr. Jortin, and five by himself, on the model of the antique; and between 1758 and 1760 he wrote three numbers in "The Idler." [Nichols' note: Numbers 33, 93, and 96.]

---

9. In the British Museum Warton collection (Add. Mss. 42,560. f. 17) is a letter from Joseph to Thomas Warton on the subject of the *Triumph of Isis,* a political defense of Oxford in opposition to Cambridge. Joseph Warton gives some detailed critical advice to his brother about the poem and tells him, "I w^d have you lie snugg at the first publication."

He published, in 1760, without his name, "A Description of the City, College, and Cathedral of Winchester," 12mo; and, in the same year, "A Companion to the Guide, and a Guide to the Companion, being a complete Supplement to all the Accounts of Oxford hitherto published."

About the same time he wrote, for the Biographia Britannica, a "Life of Sir Thomas Pope" (which he republished in 1772, and again in 1780).

In 1761 he published the "Life and Literary Remains of Dr. Bathurst;" and in that and the next year contributed to the Oxford Verses on the Royal Marriage, and on the Birth of the Prince of Wales; and "The Complaint of Cherwell, an Ode."

His next publication was "The Oxford Sausage," 1764; of which a second edition appeared in 1777, and a third in 1806.[10]

In 1766 he superintended, at the Oxford press, an edition of *"Cephalus'* Anthology;" and announced his edition of Theocritus, which appeared in 1770.

In 1767 he took the degree of B.D. and was elected F.A.S.; and in that year was instituted to the rectory of Cuddington, otherwise Kiddington, in Oxfordshire.

The first volume of his most important work, "The History of English Poetry," appeared in 1774; a second in 1778; and the third in 1781; and, finally, a fragment, but a valuable one, of a fourth. [He had long been engaged in preparing the fourth volume; of which a few sheets only were printed at the time of his death.][11]

[Editor's note: Two letters to Thomas Warton are reproduced below from manuscripts in the British Museum. Dating from the time of the production of the work referred to in the paragraph above, they are from George Steevens and William Warburton (Add. Mss. 42,561. ff. 35 and 10 respectively).]

Dear Sir.   Hampstead Heath. Augt 6th 1774

I had the favour of yours this evening, and immediately prepare to send you the Bibliotheque Bleue. If you will inform me in what particular part of the notes on Shakespeare I have mentioned Wynkyn de Worde's Edition of the Gesta Romanorum I will furnish you with the exact title of it, provided the book is in my possession; and, if it is not, will enquire after it that I may procure the intelligence you desire. You are welcome to keep the Bibliotheque as long as you please. I have a very ancient copy of the Gesta, bound up with Guido of Columpna, and some other pieces, but have lent the volume, or otherwise would have forwarded it to Winton. I perceive you and I

---

10. Concerning the accuracy of these dates see n. 14 to the life of Browne Willis.
11. This sentence appears as a note in Nichols.

have differed concerning the dates of the several publications of this work.

I have enclosed to you the unfinished proof of a plate which I have had engraved from a window in Staffordshire. It contains all the characters of the ancient Morris-dance; viz. Maid Marian, Friar Tuck, the Hobby-horse, Tom Piper, the Fool &c. I design it for the future illustration of many passages in Shakespeare, Ben Jonson & B. and Fletcher. Perhaps you may know more about the matter than I have been able to collect.

I shall be happy if I can prove myself a worthy pioneer in your service:—but I must beg you will not mention the purpose for which my plate is meant, lest the sale of our present edition of Shakespeare should be injured by too early a proclamation that a more ample and correct one is in hand.

I seal my letter &c with a confidence that they will be transmitted to you in a package which Mr Collins of this place (the commentator who writ so subtly on the potatoe) is to pack up for his sister. If that resource should fail me, my servant shall carry the parcel to town on Monday Morning early enough for it to go by the Winchester Fly.

I am Dear Sir
Your most faithful and obliged
humble Servt
G Steevens

I think I know *the person eminent in the republic of letters* who advised you to exclude from your Hist. of Poetry any mention of the English Drama; and am not less acquainted with his reasons for so doing; but I hope his counsels will have no more weight with you than they ought to have:—I hate monopolists in literature.

Dear Sir   Gloucester Octr 9th 1771

Your Favour of the 6th from Winchester has afforded me great pleasure, as it is a mark of your Chanceller's real regard & esteem for you; in which yet, he does himselfe more honour, than he confers on you.—There was a little hardship in their usage of you ab^t the professorship: but that even adds to the merit of this Obligation; for men are, in general, more backward to repair a hardship than to confer an unsought Favour.

I was in hopes of hearing some thing of the progress of your great Work; which will not only be a lasting Honour to you, but to your country likewise. For while letters remain amongst us, this fine performance (as I more than predict it will be) will be one of the lasting honours of our Island.—Make my best compliments to your worthy Brother and believe me to be, my dear Sir, your very

Affectionate & Faithfull Friend & humble Servt
W. Gloucester.

In 1776 he was called upon, as an intelligent umpire, to decide a friendly dispute between some eminent Antiquaries; which will be best illustrated by the correct narrative transcribed below.

[Editor's note: In a long note Nichols quotes correspondence and other materials relating to the establishment of the identity of a body discovered "on new-paving the choir at Winchester."]

Mr. Warton published a Collection of his Poems in 1777; a second edition in 1778; a third in 1779; and a fourth in 1789.

For some time he had been making collections for a Parochial History of Oxfordshire; of which, in 1781, he printed a few copies of the "History of Kiddington," as a specimen, to be given to his friends; and of which, in 1782, a second edition was printed for sale.

[On this subject he thus wrote to Mr. Nichols.[12]]

SIR, *Winton, Sept.* 22, 1782.
I address you as a Publisher in the Antiquarian branch. I have made very considerable additions to a small tract, of which I printed a few copies for the use of friends last winter. It is a *Specimen of a History of Oxfordshire,* containing one parish, with which I am connected. I mean to re-print it for sale, with a new preface. If you have no objections, I wish to have you concerned with me in the publication—on this plan:—You and I to share profit and loss equally; you to pay the expences of paper, printing, &c. immediately; and those to be accounted for in the final balance between us. I am sensible there is a great impropriety in my not engaging you as a *printer also* in this business; but, on account of the badness of my copy, and for other reasons, it is absolutely necessary for me to print the piece at Oxford, where I mean to employ Mr. [Daniel] Prince, both for printing and paper. It will make about 80 pages, in quarto. Our number 250. If you please, I will choose a decent and reasonable paper; on a long-bodied English, with long-primer notes—to be ready for publication in or before next January. After your own, the names of any booksellers you choose shall follow in the title-page. I will overlook the press business with great care. If this proposal should be perfectly agreeable, a speedy answer, directed to me at the Rev. Dr. Warton's, Winchester, will oblige, Sir, your most obedient humble servant,
T. WARTON.

SIR, *Winton, Sept.* 29, 1782.
Dr. Warton is greatly obliged to you for Pope's letter about Fenton's death.§ As you have no objection, we will print my *specimen* as an *inde-*

---

12. This sentence, the four letters from Thomas Warton, and the paragraph following the letters are a note in *Literary Anecdotes.*

§ The letter to Mr. Broome, in Dr. Johnson's Life of Fenton. NICHOLS. (Nichols contributed information to Johnson's lives of both Elijah Fenton and William Broome, Pope's two assistants in his translation of Homer. See my "Some New Sources of Johnson's *Lives,*" PMLA, LXV [December 1950], 1094-1099. The letter was sent to Nichols by George Steevens, *pendent* Pamphlet, according to the plan I first proposed. As to profit, I know full well the limited sale of publications of this kind; and shall think we are sufficient gainers if we pay the expences. I who, being an old author, am a piece of a printer, will conduct every thing in a frugal yet decent way. I am, Sir, &c. T. WARTON.

DEAR SIR, *Trinity College, Oxon, Dec.* 9, 1782.
The *Specimen* is almost finished at press. I wish you would let me know what names (of publishers) you would have inserted in the title-page, after your own. Messrs. Fletchers are my booksellers here, but I will put any other Oxford name you like.
Your most obedient humble servant, T. WARTON.

DEAR SIR, *Trinity College, Oxon, Dec.* 17, 1782.
You will in a day or two receive 150 of the *Specimen*. The rest we have kept back, from Oxford. The price, for *selling*, 3s. I will take care of advertising in the Oxford paper. You will take care of London advertising. I expect the pleasure of seeing your *Hinckley* to day; and am, dear Sir, &c.
T. WARTON.

[It is needless to add, that the proposal was readily accepted on the terms prescribed; or that the book was accordingly printed, much to the credit of the Author, but without any profit.]

Topography had long formed one of his favourite studies; and the acuteness with which he had investigated the progress of antient Architecture gave him undoubtedly high claims to the honour of being an eminent Antiquary; but his Poetical History had a much stronger claim to his attention.

[[Nichols' note:] The "History of Kiddington" is certainly an excellent specimen of parochial history; and, if I were asked which was the best of this species, I should name *three* works, in the following gradation: 1, Sir John Cullum's "History of Hawsted;" 2, Mr. Gough's elaborate "History of Pleshy;" and, 3, Mr. Warton's "History of Kiddington."—The Authors being all dead, I shall not here be suspected of flattery. Next to those, if I were to name living persons, I should select the Histories of "Stoke-Newington" and of "Shoreditch."]

[Editor's note: Apparently the cost of the joint publication venture of Warton and Nichols fell mostly upon Nichols. In a letter from Daniel Prince to Nichols, *Lit. Anec.*, III, 694-695, dated 5 July 1780, the following appears: "*Entre nous* (for perhaps Mr. Warton will not like to have it made known) I am printing a History of *Kiddington* in this County, where *T.W.* is Minister, intended as a Specimen of Parochial History and Antiquities."

---

who asked Nichols to give it to Johnson, advising him at the same time "to set it up before you part with it" *Lit. Anec.*, VIII, 388-389. This letter appeared as part of the life of Fenton for the first time in the edition of 1783 and in Nichols' collection of *Corrections and Additions to the Lives*, 1783, intended to be distributed free by Nichols to purchasers of the 1781 edition of the *Lives*.)

In a note to the above Nichols adds: "This was a very small impression, not for sale; and of which a second edition was printed, under Mr. Warton's inspection, at my expence, in 1783." Three additional letters from Warton to Nichols are in *Lit. Anec.*, VI, 640-641. In one of these, dated 5 October 1782, Warton writes: "*Our quarto pamphlet* will be at press at Oxford next month. I am much obliged to you for the great entertainment you have given me in the Life of Bowyer." The "Life of Bowyer" referred to is, of course, the *Biographical and Literary Anecdotes of William Bowyer* of 1782.]

In 1782 he took an active part in the *Chattertonian* controversy; and was decidedly of opinion that the poems were a fabrication. In the same year he became a member of the famous *Literary Club*, which could boast the names of a Johnson, a Burke, a Reynolds, and many other literary Luminaries. In the same year he published his verses on Sir Joshua Reynolds's Painted Window in New College Chapel; and was presented by his College to the donative of Hill Farrand in Somersetshire.

He was compelled, in self-defence, to vindicate his "History of English Poetry" from the scurrilous Observations of [Joseph] Ritson; which he did, very ably, under the signature of *Verax*, in Gent. Mag. vol. LII. p. 527; as did a friend of his, under the signature of A. S. in the same volume, p. 574. —In the succeeding volumes of the Magazine are several other letters on the subject, some of them from Mr. Ritson, others from Dr. Warton, Rev. John Bowle,[13] &c.; and an original letter to Mr. Warton from the Poet Gray is given in vol. LIII. p. 100.

He was chosen Camden Professor in 1785; and delivered an inaugural lecture, ingenious, and full of promise;[14] but "suffered the *rostrum* to grow cold while it was in his possession."

The office of Poet Laureat was accepted by him this year, as it was offered at the express desire of his Majesty; and he filled it with credit to himself and to the place.

His last publication was an edition of the "Juvenile Poems of Milton," with notes; which he had purposed to extend to a second volume, by the "Paradise Regained" and "Sampson Agonistes;" for both which he left notes.

His death was somewhat sudden. Till his 62d year he enjoyed vigour and uninterrupted health. Being seized with the gout, he went to Bath; whence he returned, recovered in his own opinion; but it was evident to his friends that his constitution had received a fatal shock. On Thursday May 20, 1790, he passed the evening in the common room, and was for some time more cheerful than usual. Between 10 and 11 o'clock he was suddenly seized with a paralytic stroke, and expired next day about two o'clock.

---

13. Nichols here has a long biographical note on Bowle.
14. Nichols here includes two letters from Warton to Gough on the subject of a Saxon font.

On the 27th his remains were interred, with the highest academical honours, in the ante-chapel of Trinity college; where his tomb is thus inscribed:

> THOMAS WARTON, S.T.B. & S.A.S.
> hujus Collegii Socius,
> Ecclesiae de Cuddington
> in com. Oxon, Rector,
> Poetices interum Praelector,
> Historices Praelector Camden.
> Poeta Laureatus.
> Obiit 21 die Maii,
> anno Domini 1790, aetat. 63.

In this brief account of the WARTONS, I have purposely abstained from enlarging on the merit of their writings; as I am unwilling to deprive the reader of the pleasure of perusing the criticisms of Mr. Chalmers, which are so judiciously condensed that partial extracts would be unpardonable.||

|| See also Mr. [Richard] Mant's edition of the Works of Thomas Warton, in two volumes, 8vo, Oxford, 1802, with the Author's Portrait. NICHOLS.

John Nichols

[Nichols' memoir of himself is in *Lit. Anec.*, VI, 627-637. John Bowyer Nichols, son of John Nichols, wrote a continuation of the memoir and placed it in *Illustr.*, VIII, 566-569, in a section of "Additions and Corrections to Vol. VI" of *Literary Anecdotes*. John Nichols' list of his own works (misnumbered fifty-seven because of having two entries numbered twenty-four), is continued by John Bowyer Nichols, who follows his father's numbering and brings the total number of items listed to seventy-one.

The list of John Nichols' works is reprinted at the end of Alexander Chalmers' memoir of him in the *Gent. Mag.*, XCVI (December 1826), 489-504; but it is reprinted with some differences in numbering, caused first by Nichols' numeration error and second by Chalmers' incorporation of three items from Nichols' list with earlier items because they were merely new editions or parts of an edition. The incorporated items were:

52. An enlarged Edition of "The Epistolary Correspondence of Sir R. Steele," in two vols. 8vo. 1809

55. The Seventh and concluding portion of the ["] History of the County of Leicester."

56. A Fourth Edition, enlarged and corrected of Mr. Bowyer's "Conjectures on the New Testament," 1812, 4to.

The new items added in *Illustrations* and in Chalmers' memoir are works completed by Nichols between the issuing of the first six volumes of *Anecdotes* in 1812 and his death in 1826. As far as any major works are concerned, these lists are complete. John Bowyer Nichols notes, in addition, works in the preparation of which he was assisted by his father.

The text of Chalmers' memoir of John Nichols is reprinted at the beginning of the eighth volume of *Illustrations,* immediately followed by "Visit to an Octogenarian," which was written by Thomas Frognall Dibdin, author of *Bibliomania*.

Innumerable references to himself and his relations with literary men are given by Nichols throughout his works. Further information concerning biographical work done on John Nichols is given in the introduction to this volume.

Some letters to or from John Nichols are in almost every important collection of eighteenth-century manuscripts. The Bodleian, for instance, has letters to him from Cole, Pegge, Joseph Warton, and others, as well as a number of important letters from Nichols to Malone (in MS Malone 39). The British Museum, among other items, possesses the letters of Johnson to Nichols, 1778-1784 (Add. Mss. 5159). Harvard University Library has four letters written by Nichols and twelve to him. The Folger Shakespeare

Library also holds a few Nichols letters, and the Osborn Collection, quite a few, including a letter from George Crabbe to Nichols, 19 October 1797, about a natural history of a county to be written by Crabbe.

By far the most important cache of Nichols materials as yet unassimilated by scholars is the great collection of papers in the Special Manuscript Collection of Columbia University Library. This collection was acquired from the "Typographic Library and Museum of the American Type Founders Company" and contains 1,064 items. Most of these papers, though by no means all, are private family letters. For this reason, most of those who have known about this collection have regarded it as of secondary importance. For a scholar studying Nichols, however, it is indispensable for two reasons: first, because the Nichols business was a family business, and, second, because Nichols as a private man is revealed in this collection in glimpses that he did not allow to appear in the public view of himself in his works. As one evidence of the importance of the first reason, I merely point to the letter from David Henry (reproduced later in his life in this volume) in which he turns over the complete management and editorship of the *Gentleman's Magazine* to John Nichols; in the dozens of letters from John Nichols to his son John Bowyer Nichols, whom he usually addresses as "Dear Bowyer," there are innumerable references to the conduct of the family business. As evidences of the second reason, I shall transcribe a few of the letters from the Columbia collection in the life of Nichols that follows this headnote. In this new view of him, we shall find a John Nichols who has essentially the same character in private as in public. To say that the view is *new* is simply to assert that here are some heretofore unseen manifestations of the character of John Nichols in relation to his family and closest friend. In all the unused material in the Columbia collection lies the possibility of a new and more nearly comprehensive biography of John Nichols.]

JOHN NICHOLS, son of Edward and Anne Nichols, was born at Islington, Feb. 2, 1744-5; and received his education in that village, at the academy of Mr. John Shield.[1]

His original designation was to the Royal Navy; which was rendered abortive by a Relation's death.

[[Nichols' note:] See before, in this volume, p. 451. [The reference is to a note on Daines Barrington, which is reproduced following this interpolation.] The worthy Judge has already been mentioned, as the friend and patron of Mr. Bowyer; and I cannot pass by this fair opportunity of expressing my own obligations both to him and to his brother the Bishop

---

1. Nichols has here a long biographical note on John Shield.

(Shute Barrington). To the Admiral (Samuel Barrington) I was also indebted, for his friendship to Mr. Thomas Wilmot, who shared with him in the perils and the laurels of War, which he did not long survive: had his life been spared, the Writer of this Note (instead of having been employed as a Pioneer of Literature) would probably have been engaged, under the banners of the gallant Admiral, in the Naval service of his country.—Mr. Wilmot (my maternal uncle) was a Lieutenant of the Bellona, under Captain Barrington, when, in August 1747, he captured the Duke of Chartres East Indiaman.]

In 1757, before he was quite 13, he was placed under the care of Mr. Bowyer; who, in a short time received him into his confidence, and intrusted to him the management of his Printing-office.

In 1765, he was sent to Cambridge, to treat with the University for a lease of their exclusive privilege of Printing.

[[Nichols' note:] See vol. II. p. 458. [The material referred to in Nichols' note is introduced following this interpolation.] In consequence of overtures from a few respectable friends at Cambridge, Mr. Bowyer had some inclination, towards the latter end of 1765, to have undertaken the management of the University Press, by purchasing a lease of their exclusive privileges, by which for several years they had cleared a considerable sum. To accomplish this, he took a journey to Cambridge; and afterwards sent the Compiler of these Anecdotes[2] to negotiate with the Vice-Chancellor. The treaty was fruitless; but he did not much regret the disappointment. [In a note to the foregoing, Nichols gives his impressions of his journey to Cambridge.] At the distance of 45 years [hence written by Nichols in 1810] I have great satisfaction in recollecting this pleasant journey. The world was then all fair before me; and I was looking forward to my future settlement in life. I had never before been above 20 miles from London; and my heart expanded when I mounted on the outside of the coach to undertake so long a journey as to Cambridge. Like other young Travellers, I wrote an account of my tour; which I still carefully preserve as *first impressions*. The Colleges, the Libraries, the Public Walks, and the fertile Gardens, were a source of inexpressible delight; and, though drenched with rain on my lofty seat in returning, I enjoyed my few holidays to the last moment.]

But that learned Body having determined to keep the property in their

---

2. Nichols introduces here several letters that passed between him and Bowyer on the subject of the University Press. At the end of a letter to Bowyer, Nichols says: "I shall not offend by compliments; but shall only assure you, that in whatever state of life I am thrown, I shall be the better man for your good example; and shall ever retain the liveliest sensation of gratitude for the more than paternal kindnesses I have ever met with at your hands."

own hands, he in the following year (having previously become a Freeman of London, and a Liveryman of the Company of Stationers) entered into partnership with his Master; with whom in 1767 he removed from White Friers into Red Lion Passage, Fleet Street. This union continued till the death of Mr. Bowyer in 1777.

[Editor's note: Although Nichols has covered the period of his life from 1765 to 1777 in one sentence, there are, fortunately, surviving letters that supply glimpses of his apprenticeship and eventual partnership. Three of these letters, which I shall introduce here, are to his friend William Tooke, described by Nichols in a note in *Lit. Anec.*, II, 552-553 as "the companion of my boyish days, and the steady friend through a pilgrimage of sixty years." Tooke was present at Nichols' funeral (*Illustr.*, VIII, xxv). It was Tooke who, after having been introduced to Johnson by Nichols, told Johnson that the *Rambler* had been translated into Russian (see Hill-Powell, *Boswell*, IV, 276-277 and 277 n. 1; see also Johnson's letter No. 931 and the notes to it).

The letter that follows, written in August 1765, is from the Columbia University Nichols collection. One sheet and some of the margins are illegible or barely legible; but since, in the same collection, there exists a copy of extracts from this letter in the hand of John Bowyer Nichols, it can be mostly reconstructed. I have, however, placed brackets around words or parts of words not actually distinguishable in Nichols' own writing.]

[August 1765]
White Fryars, Monday afternoon

At length, my Friend, the ardently-expected Packet is received, which assures me of your safe Arrival at Shirburn [in Oxfordshire].—Poor P.! what distress did she feel on Friday Evening when I had no pleasing Tale to relate to her; no soft endearing word from the idol of her affections, to alleviate her misery!—But judge how this was heightened when the next day elapsed also without any tidings!—"Some accident has happened;" "they are overturned;" "they are robbed and murdered;" were the exclamations of the affected fair.—To say the truth, I began myself to fear you had met with some Delay on the Road.— I consoled her as much as possible; fulfilled the injunction you laid on me, in respect to Mˣˢ CASH; and promised to call on your Father, to enquire if he had heard from you.—This, *en passant,* I did; but no news stirring.—I was not from Islington all day yesterday; I did not, therefore, get your epistle till this morning; and have not been able to reach Butcher Row since.—For this reason, I shall not send to you till To-morrow night, that I may be [more] explicit about P.—Now for other Business.

I was much pleased to find your *Tibia* so fortunately escaped the concussion of Mr *Surplice's corpulent occiput.*—As no accident happened, the adventure must have been laughable.—Had you no Females to participate your m[ost] fortunate Jaunt?—(Your vindicating the *sacred gospels* and the *propriety* of the English Language is a circumstance no less serviceable to your *credit,* than agreeable to your *inclinations.*)—I am rejoiced to find you [have] met with company *qualified* to relish your conversation.

A morning walk, with sentimental reflexions!—Yes, my friend; you are much a Philosopher to take such a ramble *unimproved.*—Though *alone,* in the most engaging company, Nature and grateful Sensations! —Certainly these self-examinations, these *retirings within ourselves,* are some of the most amiable Moments we experience in this *vale of tears!*—But tell me (you are asked [by] one in whom you may repose an unbounded confidence) did no tender ideas obtrud[e] on your most serious meditations? no thoughts of P. impede for a mome[nt] the exertion of the silent yet sonorous adoration of gratitude?—I shall ma[ke] no scruple of confessing to you that ideas of past pleasures have frequently rushed into [my] mind in the midst of the most religious sentiments; and have chained my soul [by] a momentary delusion, even whilst "I knelt at the throne of my God;" (if I may be permitted to use the Language of Mr Kelly).—But these wandering[s] I conceive to be the portion of mortality.—Aid me then, my worthiest friend, to soar with you beyond this enfeebled state of misery; and enable me, by your prudent counsels, to meet with pleasure the *dies irae* which awaits us. But in our search for spiritual blessings, it were in the highest degree culpable, to *neglect* our *temporal.* Let us descend, therefore, from the starry regions, and assume an humbler theme.

You seem to hint—Ah! Tooke, are you smitten? (Nay don't blush. I may, perhaps, set you the example.—I have at last met with a girl [Note in hand of *JBN*: Miss Anne Cradock, whom Mr Nichols married at St Giles in the Fields, June 22, 1766] who answers ALL my expectations; whose unaffected goodness and amiable temper, joined to the sprightliest imagination, render her in my eyes the summit of perfection—who, if Fortune should so far smile on your friend, would amply recompence him for every former disappointment! Heaven knows what may happen. I begin to be very serious! No frolics to the *Garden* now, nor breaking Pier Glasses nor battering enfeebled watchmen!) But whither have I got? How this Self operates!—Oh! I was asking if you was *smitten.*—Has the capricious son of Cytherea transfixed the bearded shaft? Are you determined to take the Lovers Leap?—If so, may every conjugal felicity attend you! May the Nymph prove propitious to your wishes; and deserving of your esteem. *Esteem?* did I say? your *Love;* your *unalienable affections.*—What in the name of matrimony is your brother doing all this Time?—When are his nuptials to be solemnized? Are you to fix the time before you leave Shirburn? If not, you may chance to be married before him.—But then poor *P.* and *Em.* The former I tremble for;—the latter will be compelled to quit the embraces of a mother. Heart-breaking thought! Excuse me, my dear friend, if I affect you too closely. Whilst I write, the tear of sympathy hangs heavy in my eye!—a tear [that] is ready to start at the apprehensions of what your sensibility must exper[ience] at so melancholy a parting; However, since your union is barred, let [mar]riage wean you from the too-fond remembrance! Find some worthy wom[an] whom you think can make you happy; and I am confident, she will ha[ve] no reason to repent of matrimony!

"I may be happy"! "May be not!" Alas, my Friend, I have learned that Happiness is not of *mortal* growth!—Content however shall supply the vacant throne—and animate the most languid hour.—But consider my *uncertainties*—Entirely a dependant!—Should my views in life succeed—should business turn out to my expectations—should the *beauteous girl* I adore return the tender regard I entertain for her—then may I set Fortune at defiance, and smile at the frowns of the world.—But, should this golden dream vanish, this airy delusion disperse, how horible the thought!

Think how ill I should brook the situation of a Journeyman Printer, the most despicable drudge in the un[iverse]—[Note in hand of JBN: In 1807, 51 years afterwards, Mr Nichols left 500£ four per cent annuities to be disposed of by the Company of Stationers to *three Journeyman Printers*—one to have 10£. & two others 5£. a year each] No hopes of promotion! In youth, a slave to this position for a moderate subsistence; in age, the scoff of the profligate and the pity of [the] benevolent! From this situation, my Friend, we may heartily pray; "Good Lord deliver us!" [Note in hand of *JBN*: His Correspondent Mr Tooke was also at this time a Printer.]

I have just got a Proof brought me. Shall add no more, therefore, at present. . . .

Islington and Love are at this moment *uppermost* [in my thoughts], but not so predominantly high as to make me insensible to the ties of your Friendship, which will ever afford me the highest satisfaction. . . .

Tuesday afternoon, ½ past 3.

Just returned from bestowing a Benediction on Em.—P. in good spirits (I had revived her last night with the news);—but all impatience for your return. . . . you to write instantaneously on receiving this; and to delay not her happiness in seeing you longer than *Saturday.*—She is in good health; transmits you a fresh assurance of her love,—and the duty of E.—Let me beg a Line from you, to satisfy the Fair-one, and myself.—How goes on the Copy of Othmiel? Have not y[ou] conceived a volume of it?—If you have, our idle Presses will have reason to hold Shirburn in grateful remembrance.—M^r B[owyer]. asked me this morning when you was to return.—Have you ventured again to mount the cart for a fishing-bout? or has more material business engaged you? If so, strike while the iron is hot; and secure the bargain.—I should be pleased to see you bring your Lady to town [for] a preparatory *visit* of *formality*.—How it would surprize xxxx and xxxx and xxxx!—no matter!—If it appears *suitable,* let the world scowl, friends chide, or enemies laugh;—pursue the combat; and win the maid and we[d] her.— You will pardon my levity; and believe me when I assure you, that, however ludicrously my sentiments are expressed, there is not a person on earth who more seriously would rejoice at your felicity, or participate your griefs if necessary, than, Sir

Yours most sincerely
J Nichols

Be so kind as to present my respects to Mr Toovey.

[Editor's note: The letter that follows is also from Nichols to Tooke and from the Columbia University Library's Nichols collection, sent shortly after the preceding letter.]

[August 1765]
Friday Afternoon, Past 3.

Yes, my dear Friend, you do me Justice in ascribing my not answering your last (this should be *penult*), to the *only* cause which *could* have restrained my Pen.—The Hazard of a Letter falling into *improper* hands, in case it missed you, alone with-held it;—for, though *names* would have been mute, yet *circumstances* (for such must have been the *main purport* of the whole), might be alarming!—But I know you have long ere now overlooked the *Fault,* if any, of this Omission.

It is not quite an hour since the Post convinced me of your Health, of which I began to have some apprehensions. Since then, I have strolled across the Temple, and have administered some trifling Consolation to my lovely Charge.—But (Dî boni!) how grievous pass her moments! —Worn out by excess of Sorrow, she has communicated the Contagion of Grief to *Imm.,* who, sleeping, raves and cries, as if sensible of the Anguish which wrings her Mother.—In short, if you stay much longer, you will never more see *either of them* alive.—In her serious Intervals, the double Pangs of *Mother* and *Daughter* rend her to Distraction.— The affections of a Child paint to her the Horrors she has raised in a maternal Bosom; but these thoughts are soon absorbed in the Excess of Love for you. "I have disobliged every Friend; and still would do it, to preserve the Esteem of Mr Tooke!"—You may easily guess, my good Friend, the Pain I feel at Distress so pungent; a Pain not lessened by the recollection of my worthiest Friend's being so deep a Sharer in it!—Pardon me if the Picture I draw affects me to too great a degree to proceed with it.—I will therefore snatch a few minutes for a topic of a different nature.

I have called three Times at your house without meeting your Father 'till last Night.—On enquiring if they had heard from you, I found him, as I thought, *displeased,* at not having had more than *one* Letter from you.—But this I only hint, *nec tali Patri displiceas.*

Caution!

Need I ask Remission for my M^r B[owyer]. has been for some time very solicitous about your Return.—I wished for you here.—Schemes of Chariots and Forty Thousands have been in agitation; work for your Brother!—But, I fear, they are vanished in fumes.—However, they are subsided at least.—When I see you, more may be said.—Mr B. urging me to acquaint him with the Cause of your long absence, and enquiring whom you was with, I so far satisfied him as to the latter part of his Queries, as to tell him something of your Connexion (or at least your Brother's) with the Daughter of Mrs T.—The former Part he accounted for himself—in a strange manner, you will say.—Tomorrow being the Day appointed for Journeymen Typographers to eat Goose and drink the Liquor of the Immortals, he imagines a *point of Honour* kept you *away;* as being above accepting so *trifling* an Entertainment.—In this I did not contradict him; as that might have produced some Interrogatories I could not so well have answered. —*Suidas sleepeth!* Hasten to rouze him!³

I will not close this till I have seen P. To-morrow Morning; if possible, not before I have seen your Letter to your Father, but this I fear, I shall not compass; as I have an appointment this Evening with *all that Earth contains of lovely!* and To-morrow will be rather a disagreeably-busy kind of a day! all Confusion! You are best absent; unless I had you with me to enjoy a private walk.—Oh! how I destest a Crowd!—How different from my Taste is a noisy Revel.—But I am M^r O, and must perform the Honours of the Table.—McIntosh has just brought me a *Revise,* and I must break off abruptly.

Saturd. Morning, almost 7.

Just arrived from Islington.—Have Four Proofs now lying before me—Criticism! Natural History! Novels! & Mathematicks!—By your leave, dear P. I must seal my Letter before I see you.—But this shall not prevent my calling on you this Morning.—I have not been at Albemarle Street; but will pass that way to-day.—Connor and Hutchin-

---

3. *Emendations in Suidam* by Jonathan Toup was printed at the Bowyer-Nichols press. In a note in *Lit. Anec.,* II, 339, Nichols wrote: "In 1760 Mr. Toup published the first Part of his *Emendations in Suidam,* and in 1764 the second Part of the same work (on both which the Author of these Anecdotes was the Compositor)." According to *Lit. Anec.,* III, 37, the third part of Toup's work on Suidas went through the press in 1766.

son are *considerable* men this Day—*Stewards* of the Feast!—I almost envy their *Honour!* Apropos to Feasting and Honour, I have a printed Letter in my Window which was sent to request Mr Tooke's Company at the last Venison-eating in Stationers-Alley. Am not I unreasonable in writing so far without enquiring after the *demoiselle de Fortune?*— Let it suffice, however to assure you that if any Counsels can assist you, they never shall be wanting.—It depends, meantime, on yourself to form a tolerable Judgment of the Rectitude of the measure in agitation; I mean, as to Similarity of Sentiment in the Charmer; and those delicate Feelings, those rapturous Inspirers of Felicity, which *dead Life* (if I may so express myself) never can produce.—But to whom am I talking?—Need I use this Language of Caution to a man so little likely to be seduced by *empty* Charms, so susceptible of the Beauties of the Mind?—To speak more plain:—If the Lady be one you know you can be happy with, strike the Bargain, and hasten its Conclusion.—But, poor P.—what will become of her?—I tremble to reflect on her Condition!—How *can* you part?—How will you be able to conceal the Connexion of past Times?— Extricate yourself from this Labyrinth, and Marriage is your surest Card.—I am called. Farewell!—If you stay two days in the Country after receiving this, I insist on hearing from you, for the sake of our Friends in B[utcher]. Row. Once more Farewell; and believe me

                                            Unchangeably Yours,
                                                J Nichols.

[Editor's note: Nichols entered into a partnership with William Bowyer at the beginning of the year 1766 (*Lit. Anec.*, III, 1). The following manly and determined letter (also from Columbia) from Nichols to his former master was, therefore, written when the partnership was only a few months old. In it, Nichols announced his intention to marry Anne Cradock; he carried out his intention and married her twelve days after this letter was written, 22 June 1766.]

Sir,   Tuesday Morn^g June 10 [17]66.

Receiving a Letter with my Name signed to it will doubtless occasion Astonishment.—But let me beg your Indulgence for a Perusal.—If the Freedom offends, destroy it; but let it first be *read*.—The Subject concerns *me* NEARLY; and, of course, cannot be wholly *uninteresting* to YOU.—I *would* speak; but the Delicacy of my Situation deprives me of the Power of speaking to you as I ought.

It is in vain any longer to wear the Mask.—The Distraction I have already experienced, in endeavouring to conceal my Sentiments, convinces me it is impossible.—You may, perhaps, think but little of the merit of a Discovery in such a Case; yet there is at least some Honesty in revealing what *might* (if longer kept in Silence) tend to *your* Detriment.—In short, Sir, you cannot but have observed, of late, a strange Absence of Mind in a Person you once (not without Reason) thought *alert*.—You *must* have *seen* a Remissness in my Behaviour; an eager Desire of *retreating from Business* at every Leisure minute.— I acknowledge all.—However, neither Business nor *your Interest* has been on that account neglected.—To deal openly with you, I *love*, love with *my Eyes open,* and *must* MARRY.—In the first Rise of my Passion, I acquainted you with the most material of the Measures I had taken.—You disapproved.—I *strove* to comply—but found my Esteem too justly fixed to be removed by *any* Argument.—This Warmth of Expression may perhaps be deemed *partial*, but let me beg you, Sir, to consider to how great a Degree of Affection two Minds not wholly devoid of Sensibility may attract each other.—Pity me; but spare your Blame!

The Name of the Lady is *Cradock*. She is the only Daughter of *a Taylor,* in *Little Wyld Street, Linc. Inn-Fields,* A Man of Character, and of improved Understanding. If you would deign to interfere in the Promotion of *my Happiness,* you may, by calling on him as you come from Dinner *this afternoon,* be satisfied of every Particular relating to her Connexions and Expectations.—I will not pretend to trust myself with acquainting you *at second hand,* as Fondness may incline me to exaggerate.—

Marriage I am determined on:—How far it may coincide with the Engagement I am under to you, you will best judge when you have talked with Mr C. who, I make no Doubt, will *give* (or, if you prefer it, *procure*) much better Security for Performance of Articles with you, than I can even hope for from any of my own Friends. And even *that* is a Point that contributes to my Unhappiness at present.—You have no Trust but my Honour, which (tho' I would hope it should be far safer than any Bond) no Man can answer for.—The Domestic Oeconomy of your Family need not undergo the least Change. Her Father's House is, and shall be, HER *Home*.

You may believe me, Sir, when I assure you, I am too Sensible of the Favours I have received from you, to be capable of making an ill use of them; and if, in Consequence of my having laid open to you my Soul, you should entertain the least Fear of *your* being injured, I will readily recede from every advantage you have given me: will resign to you your House and Business, in as great Perfection as possibly I can; will settle all Accounts immediately; and will quit you, on your giving me a single Week's Notice; or, if you desire it, will carry on the Work (*as your Servant,*) for *one, three* or *six* Months; or till you can provide a proper Person.—But all this is far foreign to my Desire; and is only in case you should totally disapprove my Conduct.

Do not be alarmed with any Apprehensions of my Parents having *drawn me* into a bad Match.—They are unacquainted with any Particulars; and even disapprove of general Circumstances, because I have not informed them of the *minutiae*.—My Uncle too, Mr *Mitchell*, whom you perhaps think my *most reputable* Friend, as indeed he is, knows nothing at all either of the Person or the Matter.—Nor does any one of my Acquaintance or Relations; as I never chose to risque my Peace of Mind to the Secrecy of any *Confident*.

I am sensible, you detest Disputes.—We will therefore *have none*. —And *I here give it you under my hand, that whatever your Humanity shall suggest to you in the present Case, I will never say you have dealt ungenerously with me, but shall ever acknowledge myself greatly indetted to you for the Intentions you had to serve me*.—If you think I am doing *improperly*, dissolve the Partnership; and I will enter into any Engagement you shall require that the Time we have been together shall not in the least prejudice you.—This may be now done to your own Satisfaction; as our Connexion is scarcely known.—But if (as I would hope) Mr C. and You should come to an Agreement, you may assure yourself of an unwearied attention to our mutual Interest being on every occasion testified, by, Sir

Your much-obliged Servt

J Nichols

P.S. I am sensible I ought to apologize for the abruptness of this address to you.—But I have gone too far to think of retreating.— Whatever you may think of my Schemes, do not upbraid me with Levity or Ingratitude.—I am too full to speak to you; but will answer in Writing any Question you may propose.—But I would rather you would apply to Mr C. who can give you the most ample Information.— Let your Resolution be what it will, let me request Dispatch.—If you are offended at my Presumption in asking your Protection, it is not too late for you to gain Redress for *yourself*. As to *me*, I can at the most but remain *unhappy*.—This much I will however say, that if you discover the least Fallacy, I will entirely decline every *Pursuit*.—If you should see Mr C. shew him as much of this Letter as you think necessary.

[Editor's note: With reference to the preceding letter, Jeremiah Markland wrote to Bowyer on 30 June 1766 as follows: "I wish you had not reason to be less pleased with *John's* Letter of the 10th of this month than I am. There seems to me to be a great deal of ingenuity and natural eloquence in it. . . . You must consider, that he is at present under a distemper which is to be cured by matrimony, as an ague is by the bark. This cannot be avoided, because it is part of the constitution of his mortality; but if it be suffered to run on, without taking the recipe, perhaps it may fly into the head, and end in madness, or some other permanent disorder." *Lit. Anec.,* IV, 335-336.

The concluding material from this early period of Nichols' life is a large extract from one letter and a small extract from another letter from Nichols to William Tooke. The extracts, which I believe to be in the hand of John Bowyer Nichols, are in the Osborn Collection.]

Dec. 10. 1774

Amongst other troubles I have been much alarmed for Mr Bowyer. You who know my every connection in Life will not be surprized that I should feel more for that worthy man than even for a Father. Alas, what a real Father. With a Heart truly grateful for the Lot of Life into which I am fallen, I am indebted to Mr Bowyer for more than my existence for the very means of obtaining a Living not to add for a prospect of a better establishment in the world than my most sanguine hopes would have aspired to. A great part of mankind might think me interested in my praise of Mr Bowyer but you know both *him* and *me* too well to join them! and I assure you his Life in even a lucrative view is of infinitely more advantage to me than his Death can possibly be. Last Sunday three weeks he was affected with a terrible complaint indeed, something of a Palsy. It attacked none of his Limbs but his Speech was almost taken from him for some hours. When the first shock was over he continued for two days in a situation infinitely more shocking than Death; that great, that learned, that good Man could not make himself understood by any one about him, not even by me who am so used to him. He was not in a state of Idiotcy for he himself understood distinctly whatever was said to him, but when he attempted to speak, any word of a quite different meaning came out very articulately. He attempted to write but equaly faltered there; though he made every Letter exactly right he could not connect two Words; I cannot give a specimen but it was something like this "I, *you, can, can, can, I can, you, you, can, that can, that.*" These are not his Words, but whatever he wrote was full as unconnected and as untelligible. D^r [William] Heberden very kindly and very diligently attended him and in the course of a Week Mr Bowyer in great measure got the better of his disorder, though it has left behind a bodily weakness which at 73 cannot be of any service to him. You know his turn to Literature, he always, *whilst he is alive* must be pursuing some Plan or other. Since his last Illness he has turned his thoughts to the Art of Printing, and we have been all this week, I mean he and I as an Amanuensis immersed in [Michael] Maittaire, [Conyers] Middleton, [Samuel] Palmer and [Gerald] Meerman, we have plenty of materials. I wish you were here to compile and to correct them as Mr Bowyer, I fear, will not have strength to go through with it or I sufficient leisure to attend to it. It will be an excellent subject for you and me when you take up your abode in this foggy Country. I say foggy for it is so at present, and I believe colder than Cronstadt.

In another letter:

> I have had a multiplicity of Employments. I have written a Book, I have planted a Tree, and have in some sense built a House, that is to say I have added a Main Room to the House I already possess. The Book I speak of must answer for itself [;] you will see it is an hasty production, and will be rather astonished it is so well as it is, than be inclined to find fault with it. Such as it is, however, let me persuade you to set to work upon it at your leisure, and we may be able perhaps at some future time to make an useful Publication between us. The subject is the Origin of Printing.

[Editor's note: *The Origin of Printing* (in two essays by Conyers Middleton and Gerald Meerman), ed. by Bowyer and Nichols, was published in 1774 and republished in 1776; a supplement was added in 1781 (see Item 3 of the works of Nichols at the end of this life).

William Tooke, in 1771, married Elizabeth, "daughter of Thomas Eyton, Esq. of Llangynhaval in the county of Denbigh." In the same year he took orders and received an appointment as "Minister of the English Church at Cronstadt, an Island in the Gulph of Finland, subject to Russia, and serving as the great Sea-port to that part of the Empire." Later he "was appointed Chaplain to the Factory at St. Petersburg." In 1782 he was elected a Fellow of the Royal Society, and in 1792 he was enabled to return to England by means of an inheritance from a relative who died that year. (See Nichols' biographical note on Tooke, *Lit. Anec.*, IX, 168-180; see also ibid, p. 159; VI, 627; and III, 249, the latter of which deals with Nichols' publication of a work by Tooke.)

The text of Nichols' autobiography is resumed after this lengthy interpolation.]

In August 1778, he became associated with his Friend Mr. David Henry in the management of the Gentleman's Magazine; and since that time not a single month has elapsed, in which he has not written several articles in that Miscellany; some of them with his name, or his initials; and others (as is essential to a periodical work) anonymously. [Nichols' note]: [Under the signatures, very frequently, either of *Alphonso; Eugenio; M. Green; A London Antiquary; J.N. &c. &c. &c.*] But he can truly say, that he never wrote a single line, either in the Magazine or elsewhere, that he would not at the time have avowed had it been necessary, or that he now wishes to recall.

In 1781 he was elected an honorary member of the Society of Antiquaries at Edinburgh; and in 1785 received the same distinction from the Society of Antiquaries at Perth.

In December 1784, he was elected into the Common Council, for the Ward of Farringdon Without; whence, in 1786, on a violent collision of parties, he was ousted. In the Summer of 1787 he was unanimously re-elected; and received from Mr. Alderman Wilkes the unsolicited appointment of one of the Deputies of the Ward.

At the end of 1797, on the death of Mr. Wilkes, he withdrew from his seat in the Common Council; but in the following year, on the pressing solicitation of some of his friends, again accepted of it.

In 1804, he attained the summit of his ambition—in being elected Master of the Stationers' Company.

On the 8th of January 1807, by an accidental fall, he fractured one of his thighs; and, on the 8th of February 1808, experienced a far greater calamity, in the destruction of his printing-office and warehouses, with the whole of their valuable contents.

Under these accumulated misfortunes, sufficient to have overwhelmed a much stronger mind, he was supported by the consolatory balm of friendship, and the offers of unlimited pecuniary assistance—till, cheared by unequivocal marks of public and private approbation (not to mention motives of a higher and far superior nature)* he had the resolution to apply with redoubled diligence to literary and typographical labours.

In December 1811, having completed the "History of Leicestershire," and made a considerable progress in the Volumes in which this article appears, he bad a final adieu to civic honours;—intending also to withdraw from a business in which he has been for 54 years assiduously engaged; and hoping (*Deo volente*) to pass the evening of life in the calm enjoyment of domestic tranquility.

[Editor's note: Nichols mentions the resignation of his honors in a letter to his daughter, Martha Sadelbia. The letter is from the Columbia University Nichols collection.]

My dear Martha,   Decr 6 [,1811]

I thank you heartily for all your kind Attention to our beloved, *gentle Anne;* of which I am sure she will always retain a grateful Remembrance, as well as of her excellent Sister Sarah's. Give my Love to her; and say that I hope to see her before it is long.

I inclose you Ten Pounds; and beg that you will give my Kind Love to her, and desire that she will allow you to buy some Coals, to replace the large Quantity that must have been lately unavoidably consumed; and I hope she will buy anything else that she may have

---

* "I thank God, I had the hope of a Christian; and that supported me." *Bishop Hough to Lady Knightley, Feb. 2, 1731-2.* NICHOLS.

occasion for, and let me pay for it—I will send her Christmas Dividend very soon. Let me know when you want more Money yourself.

At Christmas there will be Three Guineas due to Molly Argyll at the Bank; but as she may be in need of it, and it will make no Difference to me, I send it her beforehand.

You will be surprized to hear that I have given up Two high Honours—the *Common Council,* and the *Alderman's Club.*

I dined yesterday with the Canonbury Club at Mr Brown's, and had a pleasant day.

The last sheet of *Leicestershire* is this Day going to Press.

I remain, my dear Martha and Anne,

Your affectionate Father
J Nichols

[Editor's note: John Bowyer Nichols inserted in *Illustr.,* VIII, 566-567, an addition to the life of his father at the point just preceding the above interpolated letter. The entire addition consists of the introductory statement and the letter to Charles Price, after which the text of Nichols' life of himself is resumed.]

Mr. Nichols thus resigned his *civic* honours, in a letter addressed "To the Right Worshipful Sir Charles Price, Bart. M.P. Alderman of the Ward of Farringdon Without:

DEAR SIR, *St. Thomas's Day,* 1811

I am arrived at a time of life when domestic comfort is more essential than even public honours, and have therefore declined becoming a candidate for a seat in the Common Council. I can reflect with satisfaction that I have long discharged the various duties of an important trust, faithfully, diligently, and conscientiously. Unbiassed by the prejudices of party, and enjoying a political opinion which I have never concealed, my vote has always been consonant to the feelings of an independent man, and such as I have not had occasion to be ashamed of. I beg leave, Sir, on retiring, to return my most cordial thanks to yourself as presiding officer, to my late worthy colleagues, and to our constituents in general, for the unequivocal marks of friendly attention which I have experienced during a residence among them of more than half a century, for forty-six years of which time I have been an inhabitant householder, and a freeman and liveryman of London. With a hearty wish of perpetual prosperity to that great and opulent city, of which the Ward of Farringdon Without forms so proud and prominent a part; and that you, Sir, may long enjoy the honour of continuing one of its representatives in parliament; I subscribe myself, Sir,

Your greatly obliged and very faithful servant, J. NICHOLS.

He was married, in 1766, to Anne daughter of Mr. William Cradock, of Leicester, and again, in 1778, to Martha daughter of Mr. William Green, of

Hinckley. By the first wife (who died in 1776) he has two daughters living, 1812; by the second (who died in 1788) one son and four daughters.

[Editor's note: More complete information concerning Nichols' family can be found in *Illustr.*, VIII, xxiv; *History of Leicester*, III, 1149, and IV, 709, and in the various places in the *Gentleman's Magazine* where the obituaries and other facts regarding members of his family are given. Additional details, of course, can be found in the family papers. Following is a summary of the pertinent information regarding the children of each of his two wives:

A. By Anne Cradock (baptized 9 August 1737; m. John Nichols 22 June 1766; d. 18 February 1776);
   1. Anne (b. 3 August 1768; m. John Pridden [1758-1825] 4 September 1787; d. 12 November 1815);
   2. Sarah (b. 14 May 1771; d. unmarried 13 January 1843);
   3. William Bowyer (b. 1 April 1775; d. 6 April 1776);
B. By Martha Green (b. 25 January 1756; m. John Nichols 11 June 1778; d. 29 February 1788);
   1. John Bowyer (b. 15 July 1779; m. Eliza Baker [1784-1846] 6 June 1805; d. 19 October 1863);
   2. Thomas Cleiveland (b. 31 May 1781; d. 2 April 1782);
   3. Martha Sadelbia (b. 10 November 1782; d. unmarried 19 April 1816);
   4. Mary (b. 30 January 1784; m. John Morgan [1784-1832] 1814; d. 1 August 1850);
   5. Isabella (b. 26 May 1785; living in 1862);
   6. Charles Howard (b. 6 September 1786; d. 13 November 1786);
   7. Anne Susannah (b. 15 February 1788; d. 17 March 1853).

At this point, a few more items will be introduced to illustrate Nichols' relations with his family. That which follows is, first, a verse proposal of marriage to Sarah, and, second, a letter accompanying the verse, sent by Nichols to Sarah. They are from the Columbia Nichols collection, the guardians of which also kindly supplied me with some of the dates in the above summary.]

To Miss Nicholls

A Youth there is, who loves you True,
He's one among those very few;
Who're candid, open, generous,
Sincere, discreet, and virtuous.
He's young, not handsome; short not tall,
Just Nineteen years, and that is all.
A dark, a grave complexion,
And fond of contemplation;
His Temper is precarious,
His Manners gentle, various,

His Hopes are both great and many
His fears but few,—indeed scarce any.
A Tradesman,—his Business such
Does not require a Wife's help much.
Not poor, nor very affluent,
But cash, he needs not any lent.

He wishes much to have a Wife,
Who's free from trouble in this Life;
Of manners gentle, and not rude,
Polite, well bred, but not a prude;
Some Wit, and Conversation
Without any Malversation—
Good sense, that's fluent, true and such,
But Modesty, not over much.
Falsehood with Truth, he will not mix
Yet wishes much on *You* to fix—

Now, if you think, you cou'd him like,
Pray let him know before 'tis night;—
A Letter directed to A. B. C.
In which I hope you will agree,
And sent to Nott's* in Butcher Row
Near Temple Barr—the House is Low.
He gladly will unfold and read
And send an Answer with all speed—
      Veritas—

*Notts Coffe House and Tavern in Butchers Row n^r Temple Barr.

Throw the *inclosed,* my dear Child, into the Fire; and banish from your Thoughts forever the Idea you may have too fondly indulged. If any forgiveness on my Part were necessary, you have it *a Thousandfold*. Much as I respect the Abilities of the Person you speak of, there is *that* about him which rendered him wholly *unworthy of you*—a total Neglect of Religious Duties.—Thank Heaven for your Escape; and may the Almighty restore you speedily to Strength of Body and Serenity of Mind!—Your *Worth*, in every Sense of the Word, and your *Fortune*, entitle you to *as good*, or even a *far superior* Match.—No earthly Consideration can prevent my remaining, whilst I enjoy my Senses,
      Your truly affectionate Father
Dec. 29   J. Nichols
Burn these Lines.

[Editor's note: The following letter, also from the Columbia collection, is from Nichols to his daughter Martha Sadelbia and was sent from Hinckley, Leicestershire.]

My dear Martha, Tuesday, March 12 [1799].

I give you Joy of the important Business you are this Day to transact at *St. Paul's*. It is a memorable Æra, my good Child, in your Life; and I doubt not but you will ever entertain a due Sense of that Divine Goodness, which has hitherto preserved and protected you to an Age in which you are fully competent to judge properly of the Blessings you enjoy in the free Exercise of a pure Religion, and in the Comfort of a domestic Happiness amongst affectionate Relatives. But, as Devotion does not consist in Gloom, I will leave off Preaching for the present; and shall hope very shortly to lead you to the Altar, that you may partake of the Blessed Sacrament.

Now then for innocent Amusements.—I expect that your Brother has received Lady Mayor's Card. If so, he will take you and M[rs] Gutch—and any one other Friend, if he thinks proper. Perhaps sister [Anne Nichols] Pridden may like to go, if she should not come to Dunstable.—M[r] Gutch . . . and your Parcel just received.—I have not Time to answer all your kind Letters—but will send a Parcel Tomorrow—I find I need not have been anxious about the *Rout* but the Ticket may yet come.

M[r] [Joseph] Cradock was from home—but we dine at Gumley Tomorrow *in our way back*—and sleep there at Night—Hope to reach Dunstable *in good Time* Thurs *Evening*—but should any thing detain us on the Road, P[ridden] may expect us there to *Breakfast* early on Friday Morning.

We are all well—Farewell—All on the best Terms possible with Uncle John and *every body*.

Yours affectionately

Love *from all* JN
to all.

[Editor's note: The concluding letter of this interpolated digression also comes from the Columbia University Nichols collection and is from Nichols to Mrs. John Reep of Ridgeway, Devonshire. In the letter, Nichols recommends his wife's brother, John Green, as a suitor to Mrs. Reep's daughter. According to the pedigree of the Green family in the *History of Leicester*, IV, 709, John Green and Anne Reep were married and produced six children.]

Madam, Sept. 17. 1783.

To my very great Astonishment I have this *Moment* received a Letter from my Brother-in-law M[r] John Green, who is unspeakably distressed by a Letter he has just received from Ridgeway.

Of his Pretensions to *your Daughter* I know nothing. But *this* I know, and *affirm*, that in 1778 I married his Sister, and have never since had Reason to be sorry for the connexion with her Family. Their Father

[William Green] has for many Years carried on with Reputation the Business of a Plumber and Glazier and has at the same Time carried on that of Worsted-making. The Family were for many Years possessed of a considerable Estate at Somerby in Leicestershire.—Old Mr Green, so far from being in Necessity, is at this Moment fitting up a House to retire from Business—and has already given his Son *John* what has settled him in an exceeding good Business. His Brother *Charles* is quite in a distinct Trade in London. Nor is there any partnership between them. The Connexion there was between his Father and him in the Worstedmaking and Hosiery is now at an End and is entirely his own.—As to his Dependence on his Uncle, I can only say that his Uncle is a very worthy Man, has a good deal of Property, and no Family. Mr John Green (nor any of his Family) has never had any thing from him; but they are on very friendly Terms.

I ought to apologize for this Intrusion; but it is in Justification of my Friend. You know nothing of me; but I flatter myself there is not a Printer or Bookseller in the Kingdom, who is not able to tell you something not to the Discredit of

      Madam,
        Your very obed^t Servant
         J Nichols
        Printer, Red Lion
       Passage Fleet Street

My best Respects attend
your Daughter; from whom
or from yourself I should
be happy to receive a
few Lines.

[Editor's note: This concludes the interpolated matter regarding Nichols' family. The text of the autobiography continues.]

He never affected to possess any superior share of erudition, or to be profoundly versed in the learned languages; content, if in plain and intelligible terms, either in conversation or in writing, he could contribute his quota of information or entertainment.

[Nichols' note, following this introductory comment, is actually given to the first item in his list of works, but is placed here in order to avoid interrupting the list:].

[Among other youthful votaries of the Muses, Mr. Nichols very early aspired to distinction; and employed some leisure hours in writing verses, which generally found their way into the Newspapers and Magazines of the time, to most of which (and to the Gentleman's and Ladies Diaries) he was an occasional contributor from 1761 to 1766, when the term of his apprenticeship expired. At an early part of that period he furnished Mr. [Hugh] Kelly with a few numbers of "The Babler:" and his old friend Mr. [George] Redmayne, then Printer of the Westminster Journal, with a series of Letters from "The Cobler of Alsatia." He assisted Mr. Bowyer in the publication of "Verses on the Coronation of King George the Second, 1761:" and translated many of the Latin epigrams. In 1765, he contributed several poems to a miscellaneous collection, published by Dr. [William] Perfect of Town-Malling, under the title of "The Laurel Wreath," 2 vols. 12mo.; and in 1778 gave, in the Public Advertiser, a few numbers of "Modern Characters," selected from the Works of Dean Swift.

Some notes, communicated by him to the re-publication of Mr. Dodsley's Collection of Old Plays in 1780, are acknowledged by Mr. Reed in the preface to that work.

In 1789 his old friend the Rev. Samuel Pegge inscribed to him his "Annales Eliae de Trickenham, 4to;" and in 1802, Mr. Hutton of Birmingham, in a dedicatory epistle, addressed to him a pleasant "History of the Roman Wall," 8vo.]

The Publications of which he has been either the Author or the Editor are numerous.

1. "Islington, a Poem, 1763," 4to.

2. "The Buds of Parnassus, 1763," 4to; republished in 1764, with some additional Poems.

3. "The Origin of Printing, 1774," 8vo; the joint production of Mr. Bowyer and himself; reprinted in 1776; and a Supplement added in 1781.

4. "Three Supplemental Volumes to the Works of Dean Swift, with Notes, 1775, 1776, 1779," 8vo.

5. "Index to the Miscellaneous Works of Lord Lyttelton, 1775," 8vo.

6. "Index to Lord Chesterfield's Letters to his Son, 1776," 8vo.

7. "The Original Works, in Prose and Verse, of William King, LL.D. with Historical Notes, 1776," 3 vols. small 8vo.

8. "Brief Memoirs of Mr. Bowyer, 1778," 8vo; distributed, as a tribute of respect, amongst a few select friends.

9. "History of the Royal Abbey of Bec, near Rouen, 1779," small 8vo.†

10. "Some Account of the Alien Priories, and of such Lands as they are known to have possessed in England and Wales, 1779," 2 vols. small 8vo.‡

11. "Six Old Plays," on which Shakspeare grounded a like number of his; selected by Mr. Steevens, and revised by Mr. Nichols, 1779, 2 vols. small 8vo.

---

† From a MS. communicated by Dr. [Andrew Coltée] Ducarel. NICHOLS.

‡ These volumes, originally compiled from the MSS. of John Warburton, esq. were revised through the press by Dr. Ducarel and Mr. Gough: many valuable notes were added by both, and a Glossary by Mr. Gough. NICHOLS.

12. Mr. Rowe-Mores having left at his death a small unpublished impression of "A Dissertation upon English Typographical Founders and Founderies;" all the copies of this very curious pamphlet were purchased at his sale by Mr. Nichols; and given to the publick in 1779, with the addition of a short explanatory "Appendix."

13. "A Collection of Royal and Noble Wills; 1780," 4to.§

14. "A Select Collection of Miscellaneous Poems, with Historical and Biographical Notes; 1780;" 4 vols. small 8vo; to which four other volumes, and a general Poetical Index by Mr. Macbean, were added in 1782.

15. In 1780, on the suggestion, and with the assistance, of his firm friend Mr. Gough, and with him concurring in a wish to save from the chandler and the cheesemonger any valuable articles of British Topography, MS or printed, he began to publish the BIBLIOTHECA TOPOGRAPHICA BRITANNICA; which was completed (in LII Numbers) 1790.

16. "Biographical Anecdotes of William Hogarth, 1781," 8vo;|| re-published in 1782,‡ again in 1785;* and a fourth edition, in two very handsome quarto volumes, with CLX genuine Plates, 1810; each edition being considerably enlarged.

17. "Biographical Memoirs of William Ged, including a particular Account of his Progress in the Art of Block-printing, 1781," 8vo.

18. A Third Edition (much enlarged) of Mr. Bowyer's "Conjectures and Observations on the New Testament, 1782," 4to.†

19. "Biographical and Literary Anecdotes of William Bowyer, Printer, F. S. A. and of many of his learned Friends, 1782," 4to.

20. "The History and Antiquities of Hinckley, in Leicestershire, 1782," 4to.; of which a second edition, in folio, extracted from the "History of Leicestershire," was printed in 1812.

21. Mr. Bowyer's "Apology for some of Mr. Hooke's Observations concerning the Roman Senate, with an Index to the Observations, 1782," 4to.

22. "Novum Testamentum Graecum, ad fidem Graecorum solùm Codi-

---

§ In which he was again assisted by Dr. Ducarel; and also by Mr. Gough, who contributed the Preface and the Glossary. NICHOLS.

|| "Since the First Edition of this work (*the Anecdotes of Painting*) a much ampler account of HOGARTH and his Works has been given by Mr. Nichols; which is not only more accurate, but much more satisfactory than mine; omitting nothing that a Collector would wish to know; either with regard to the history of the Painter himself, or to the circumstances, different editions, and variations of his Prints. I have completed my list of Hogarth's Works from that source of information." *Lord Orford's* [Horace Walpole's] *Works, 4to. vol. III. p.* 453. NICHOLS.

‡ A translation into German of the *second edition* was published at Leipsic, by Mr. A. Crayen, in 1783. NICHOLS.

* In this work he was indebted for nearly every critique on the Plates of Hogarth, to the late George Steevens, esq. who wrote the Prefaces to the second and third editions; and by whom large additions for a fourth were made, in a copy purchased at his sale, by the late George Baker, esq. of St. Paul's Church-yard; who politely allowed them to be copied for the last edition. NICHOLS.

† A translation into German of the second edition of this Work also was published at Leipsic, by Professor Schultz, in 1774. NICHOLS.

cum MSS. expressum; adstipulante Joanne Jacobo Wetstenio: juxta Sectiones Jo. Alberti Bengelii divisum; et novâ Interpunctione saepiùs illustratum. Editio Secunda, Londini, curâ, typis, & sumptibus Johannis Nichols, 1783."

23. In 1783, he collected "The principal Additions and Corrections in the Third Edition of Dr. Johnson's Lives of the Poets, to complete the Second Edition" (of 1781).

24. "Bishop Atterbury's Epistolary Correspondence, with Notes," vols. I. and II. 1783; vol. III. 1784; vol. IV. 1787.—A new Edition of this Work, corrected and much enlarged, was published in 1799, with Memoirs of the Bishop; and a Fifth Volume, entirely new.

24. In conjunction with the Rev. Dr. Ralph Heathcote,‡ he revised the second edition of the "Biographical Dictionary," 12 vols. 8vo, 1784; and added several hundred new lives.

25. "A Collection of Miscellaneous Tracts, by Mr. Bowyer, and some of his learned Friends, 1785," 4to.

26. "The History and Antiquities of Lambeth Parish, 1786."§

27. "The Tatler, 1786," *cum Notis Variorum*, 6 vols. small 8vo.||

28. "The Works, in Verse and Prose, of Leonard Welsted, Esq. with Notes and Memoirs of the Author, 1787," 8vo.

29. "The History and Antiquities of Aston Flamvile and Burbach, in Leicestershire, 1787," 4to.

30. "Sir Richard Steele's Epistolary Correspondence, with Biographical and Historical Notes, 1788," 2 vols. small 8vo.

31. "The Progresses and Royal Processions of Queen Elizabeth, 1788." 2 vols. 4to.—Of this Collection a Third Volume was published in 1804.

32. "The History and Antiquities of Canonbury, with some Account of the Parish of Islington, 1788," 4to.[4]

33. "The Lover and Reader, by Sir Richard Steele, illustrated with Notes, 1789," 8vo.

34. "The Town Talk, Fish Pool, Plebeian, Old Whig, Spinsters, &c. by Sir Richard Steele; illustrated with Notes, 1790," 8vo.

35. "Collections towards the History and Antiquities of the Town and County of Leicester, 1790," 2 vols. 4to.#

---

‡ Of whom see memoirs in vol. III. [of *Lit. Anec.*] p. 531. NICHOLS.

§ Compiled principally from papers communicated by Dr. Ducarel, in return for assistance which had been given him by Mr. Nichols in the Histories of the Two Archiepiscopal Palaces of Lambeth and Croyden. NICHOLS.

|| The principal merit of this edition is due to the Rev. Dr. John Calder, who was furnished with the notes of the late learned and venerable Prelate, Bishop Percy. Mr. Nichols wrote the preface, and contributed several notes. NICHOLS.

Very few copies were printed, principally with a view of soliciting communications towards a regular history of that County. NICHOLS.

4. John Bowyer Nichols, in a correction in *Illustr.*, VIII, 567, says "History of Canonbury and *Islington*." The remainder of J. B. Nichols' note to this entry, tribute to John Nichols' history of Islington, will be introduced into the text later.

36. "An Edition of Shakspeare, 1790," in seven volumes, 12 mo; accurately printed from the Text of Mr. Malone;[5] with a Selection of the more important Notes.

37. "The Theatre and Anti-theatre, &c. of Sir Richard Steele, illustrated with Notes, 1791," 8vo.

38. "Miscellaneous Antiquities, in continuation of the Bibliotheca Topographica Britannica," Six Numbers, 4to. 1792-1798.

39. "The History and Antiquities of the Town and County of Leicester;" Parts I. and II. 1795. Folio.—A Third Part was published in 1798; a Fourth in 1800; a Fifth in 1804; a Sixth in 1807. (reprinted in 1810); and the Seventh in 1811.

40. "Illustrations of the Manners and Expences of Antient Times in England, 1797," 4to.

41. Bishop [White] Kennett[']s Funeral Sermon, with Memoirs of the Cavendish Family, 1797," 8vo.*

42. "Chronological List of the Society of Antiquaries of London, 1798," 4to. compiled in conjunction with Mr. Gough.†

43. "An Edition of Shakspeare, 1799," in eight volumes, 12 mo; accurately printed from the Text of Mr. Steevens: with a Selection of the Notes.

44. Having recovered the MS. of the Reverend Kennett Gibson's "Comment upon Part of the Fifth[6] Journey of Antonius through Britain" (which in 1769 Mr. Gibson proposed to publish by subscription, but which upon his death was supposed to have been lost); Mr. Gough and Mr. Nichols jointly published it in 1800, with the Parochial History of Castor and its Dependencies; and an Account of Marham, and several other places in its neighbourhood.

45. In 1800, he completed "The Antiquaries Museum," which had been begun in 1791 by his friend Jacob Schnebbelie.‡

46. In 1801, he published Dr. Pegge's "Historical Account of Beauchief Abbey, in the County of Derby."§

---

* Printed from a corrected copy of the former edition, purchased from the Rev. Henry Freeman. See [*Lit. Anec.*, VI,] p. 323. NICHOLS. (On the page referred to, Nichols says that Richard Gough "superintended the second edition of Dr. White Kennett's famous Sermon, preached at the funeral of William Duke of Devonshire, 1707; to which he added several Notes, and an Appendix." A long note to this, signed "R. G.," describes the copy from which the sermon was printed.)

† To which Mr. Gough intended to have added biographical memoirs of the several members;

"—— *quique sui memores alios fecere merendo.*["] NICHOLS.

‡ Who dying in 1792, before the third number was completed, the Work was continued, for the benefit of his family, to XIII numbers (the last of which contains memoirs of the Author) by Mr. Gough and Mr. Nichols. NICHOLS.

§ The MS. of this Work had been entrusted to him for that purpose by his venerable and much respected friend, Dr. Pegge. NICHOLS.

5. Nichols here introduces a long biographical note on Edmond Malone.

6. The text in *Lit. Anec.*, VI, 636, erroneously reads "Fourth Journey," though the entry that discusses the work in greater detail, in IX, 237, reads "Fifth Journey."

47. In the same year, he published a new and complete Edition of the "Works of Dean Swift," in XIX vols. 8vo; which in 1803 were reprinted in XXIV volumes, 18mo; and again in XIX volumes, 8vo, in 1808.

48. In 1803, in conformity to the last will of Samuel Pegge, esq. (son of the learned Antiquary already named), he ushered into the world, "Anecdotes of the English Language, &c." 8vo.

49. "Journal of a very young Lady's Tour from Canonbury to Aldborough, through Chelmsford, Sudbury, Ipswich; and back, through Harwich, Colchester, &c. Sept. 14-21, 1804; written hastily on the Road, as occurrences arose;" not intended for publication; but a very few copies only printed, to save the trouble of transcribing.

50. In 1806, he published, from the MSS. of his Friend Mr. Samuel Pegge, "The Fourth and Fifth Parts of Curialia: or, An Historical Account of some Branches of the Royal Household, &c." 4to.

51. In 1809 he printed from the Originals, and illustrated with Literary and Historical Anecdotes, "Letters on various subjects, to and from Archbishop [William] Nicolson," 2 vols. 8vo.

52. An enlarged Edition of "The Epistolary Correspondence of Sir R. Steele," in two vols. 8vo. 1809.

53. In the same year he edited another posthumous Work of Dr. Pegge's, under the title of "*Anonymiana*: or, Ten Centuries of Observations on various Authors and Subjects," 8vo.

54. A new edition of Fuller's History of the Worthies of England, with brief Notes, 1811. 2 vols. 4to.

55. The Seventh and concluding Portion of the HISTORY OF THE COUNTY OF LEICESTER.

56. A Fourth Edition, enlarged and corrected of Mr. Bowyer's "Conjectures on the New Testament," 1812, 4to.

57. "Literary Anecdotes of the Eighteenth Century, 1812," 6 vols. 8vo.

[Editor's note: This ends the account from *Lit. Anec.*, VI, 627-637. John Bowyer Nichols continues the list in *Illustr.*, VIII, 567-569, in "Additions and Corrections to Vol. VI" of *Literary Anecdotes*, where the list begins thus: "P. 637. Add to the works published by John Nichols."]

58. "Literary Illustrations of the Eighteenth Century, being a Sequel to the Literary Anecdotes." 4 vols. 1815-1822.

59. A new edition of his friend Sir John Cullum's "History of Hawsted." 4to. 1813.

60. A third edition of the Rev. Thomas Warton's "History of Kiddington, Oxfordshire;" revised through the press by Sir H. Ellis, F.R.S., Sec. S.A.

61. In 1817, Mr. Nichols published a Third Volume of "The Works of

Wm. Hogarth, with Biographical Anecdotes;" with 50 additional plates, 4to. The first two volumes, published in 1810, are mentioned in [*Lit. Anec.*] Vol. VI. p. 632.

62. Mr. N[icholas] Hardinge's "Latin, Greek, and English Poems." 8vo. 1818.

63. "Miscellaneous Works of George Hardinge, Esq." 3 vols. 8vo. 1819.

64. In 1818 he prefixed to the Third Volume of the "General Index to the Gentleman's Magazine" a Prefatory Introduction, descriptive of the rise and progress of the Magazine, with Anecdotes of its Projector and his early associates.

65. "Taylor and Long's Music Speeches at Cambridge," 1819, 8vo; in conjunction with Dr. [Samuel] Parr.

66. "Four Sermons, by Dr. Taylor, and Bishops Lowth and Hayter," 8vo; in conjunction with the same learned Divine.

67. Explanation of the Subjects of Hogarth's Plates, for the complete and new edition of them, as engraved by Hogarth and retouched by Heath, folio. 1822.

68. "Progresses of Queen Elizabeth." New edition, 3 vols. 4to. 1823.

69. "Progresses of James the First." 4 vols. 4to; were nearly completed by Mr. Nichols, and published after his death.

In this work Mr. Nichols was very materially assisted by his grandson J. Gough Nichols, then a very young man.

70. A portion of the fifth volume of "Literary Illustrations" was printed before Mr. Nichols's death.

71. "Birthday Odes and Domestic Poems, by the late John Nichols, F.S.A." 1827. (Privately printed after Mr. Nichols's death.)

The following works, edited by J. Bowyer Nichols, and printed during the lifetime of his father, had the benefit of his kind revision through the press:—

1. The Second Edition of Hutchins's History of Dorsetshire, Vols. III. and IV. This work was undertaken at the cost and risk of Major-Gen. John Bellasis, who prevailed on Richard Gough, esq. (who, with other friends, had edited in 1774 the first edition of that work) to become the editor of the new edition. Mr. Gough, with his usual ardour, proceeded with the work, assisted by several antiquaries in Dorsetshire, and, in 1796, published the first volume, which, in 1804, was followed by the second volume. But in 1808 three events occurred within a short time of each other that put a stop to the progress of the work. The first was the commencement of the serious illness of Mr. Gough, which only terminated with his death. The second was the complete destruction by fire of all the unsold copies of Vols. I. and II., and of all the part of the third volume that was edited by Mr. Gough and not published; and the third was the lamented death of Major-Gen. Bellasis, who was to supply the funds to complete the work. He died Feb. 18, 1808, just ten days after the work was destroyed by fire.

About 112 copies had been called for by purchasers; and, in 1811, Mr.

Nichols issued proposals to print that number of copies of the third and fourth volumes to perfect the sets of the work already in the hands of the purchasers. This labour was undertaken, at a cost not nearly remunerative, from motives thus expressed by Mr. Nichols: "An ardent desire to do honour to the memory of Mr. Hutchins; to the filial piety of his son-in-law Major-Gen. Bellasis; and to the unremitted exertions of my excellent friend Mr. Gough in his improvement; also to do justice to those who had already purchased the former volumes, that the world might not be deprived of so important a link in British Topography."

This eventually was carried out by J. B. Nichols, who became editor of the work after Mr. Gough's death, and published the third volume in 1813, the fourth volume in 1815, and an Appendix, containing additions and corrections, and general indexes, in the same year. The surviving editor has the satisfaction to know that it is one of the best and scarcest works on topography; it is also one of the highest in price whenever a copy occurs for sale.

2. The Life and Errors of John Dunton, Citizen of London, with the Lives and Characters of more than 1,000 contemporary Divines, and other persons of literary eminence; to which are added, Dunton's Conversation in Ireland; Selections from his other genuine Works. By J. B. Nichols. Prepared from copious memoirs of the author, with his portrait.

3. A brief Account of the Guildhall of the City of London. By J. B. Nichols, 1819.

4. The Athenian Oracle abridged; containing the most valuable Questions and Answers in the original Works on History, Philosophy, Divinity, Law, and Marriage, 8vo. 1820. Originally published by John Dunton. This work is commended by the Rev. T. D. Fosbroke in Gent. Mag. 1820, ii. 241.

5. Account of the Royal Hospital and Collegiate Church of St. Katharine, near the Tower of London, 4to. 1824.

[Editor's note: A note given earlier by J. B. Nichols to item 32, Nichols' history of Canonbury and Islington, was reserved for the end of Nichols' account of his own life and the additions of J. B. Nichols in order that the list of works might not be unnecessarily interrupted. The material below comes from *Illustr.*, VIII, 567.]

The following grateful acknowledgment from Mr. J. Norris Brewer, on his own behalf, and that of Mr. J. Britton and E. W. Brayley, appeared in 1816, in Mr. Brewer's account of the parish of *Islington*:

"We cannot quit Islington without observing, that this parish also claims as a native John Nichols, Esq. F.S.A. In the Literary Anecdotes of the Eighteenth Century, this judicious historian and antiquary has narrated the principal events in the early part of his private life; and in the general detail of that interesting work, his public character stands illustrated; for with the most conspicuous literary men of his era he has been closely connected. Still we must be allowed to remark, that the author of the History of Leicestershire cannot fail to be regarded as the Dugdale of the present age.

"Perhaps, to no individual of any period are topography and the study of antiquities more highly indebted than to this native of the suburban village under notice; and, while alluding to the stores of information which Mr. Nichols has collected, and takes pleasure in dispensing around, we beg permission, in the name of the principal editors concerned in this present publication, to return thanks for the loan of many scarce and valuable books, and for undeviating politeness and attention when such intelligence was requested as could only satisfactorily be expected from himself. Mr. Nichols has for many years occupied a residence in his native village."

[Editor's note: This concludes the account of Nichols as written by himself and his son. Interesting as the memoirs written by Chalmers and Dibdin may be, and even though they are in Volume VIII of *Illustrations,* I shall not reproduce them here because I am trying to include, insofar as it is possible, the writings of John Nichols himself.

One of the great remaining problems concerning Nichols is finding what has become of some of the letters which he printed and which have since disappeared. Here is the history of some of the disappearances.

The bulk of manuscript letters once owned by John Nichols turned up for auction after the death, in 1873, of John Gough Nichols, grandson of John Nichols. The first and more important sale was held by Sotheby's in December 1874, and a second one, in April 1879. For the dates of the sales see the index to the *List of Catalogues of English Book Sales 1676-1900 now in the British Museum* (London, 1915). Lot 975 of the 1874 sale, the correspondence of Richard Gough, was bought by the Bodleian Library at Sotheby's on 29 April 1947, at which sale it was lot 295. It came from the library of the eminent collector, E. P. Shirley. Lot 975 was described in the catalogue of 1874 as "arranged in 11 vols." But by the time the set was purchased by the Bodleian, five volumes had disappeared. As yet nothing is known of the missing volumes, whether they have been destroyed or are still hidden somewhere.

It is not too fantastic to imagine that they may yet be found, if one may speculate in accordance with what has happened to other letters printed by Nichols and long thought missing. Every year some of the lost letters make an appearance in the Bodleian or British Museum. Perhaps some of Nichols's carefully bound volumes of correspondence were broken up and sold individually as autographs. If so, the missing pieces may yet be recovered, but it is most unlikely that the whole collection will ever be reassembled.

In the meantime, Nichols remains the sole authority for many important letters. There is, for instance, letter number LV from *The Correspondence of Thomas Percy and Richard Farmer,* ed. Cleanth Brooks (Louisiana State

University Press, 1946). This letter implies both antecedent and subsequent letters, and it is known today only by the text in *Illustrations*. (See the *Percy-Farmer Correspondence,* p. xiii.)

A third sale of manuscripts from the library of John Gough Nichols was held by Sotheby's on 18 November 1929: see *Catalogue of valuable autograph Letters and Manuscripts, printed Books, &c. from the Collection of the late John Gough Nichols. . . . (sold by order of his grandson, J. C. M. Nichols, Esq.).* Bodleian shelfmark 2591 d. 1. (-33). At this sale "the MS. of Goldsmith's 'Haunch of Venison' brought £4,800, and another MS. of the same author £2,700" (see *Times Literary Supplement* [9 December 1939], p. 724).

The important Upcott collection, sold at auction in 1846, contained letters printed in *Illustrations*. But they are letters of little importance and were probably thrown out after being printed.

The Folger Shakespeare Library possesses a great amount of correspondence with and contributions to the *Gentleman's Magazine,* dating from 1762 to 1888, along with bound volumes of the magazine annotated by the editors and containing many manuscripts of accepted materials: altogether about 4,500 items. Letters are to Nichols, his son, and his grandson as they successively became editors.

As noted in the introduction to this volume, Nichols, as well as owning a remarkable collection of manuscript letters, possessed an exceptionally fine collection of newspapers. A part of this latter collection came into the Bodleian Library: "In 1865 the Library acquired for the sum of £200 a remarkable collection of London newspapers from 1692 [mistake for 1672] to 1737 which had been formed by John Nichols, the printer and antiquary. They were originally contained in 96 thick volumes, cased in boards and arranged in one chronological series, but for their better preservation and consultation they have recently been rebound in a permanent form in 305 volumes": see *A Catalogue of English Newspapers and Periodicals in the Bodleian Library 1622-1800,* ed. R. T. Milford and D. M. Sutherland (Oxford, 1936), p. 5. The portion of Nichols' collection of newspapers now in the Bodleian is particularly rich in material relating to the 1688 revolution and the early years of George I. For the year 1688, Nichols' collection in the Bodleian is probably the most complete in existence.]

Part II. Booksellers and Printers

John Dunton

[Nichols' memoir of John Dunton is in *Lit. Anec.,* V, 59-83. Scattered throughout *Anecdotes* and *Illustrations,* however, are numerous quotations from Dunton's *Life and Errors,* mostly brief character sketches made by Dunton and used by Nichols to illustrate the lives of the various subjects about whom they were written. Nichols was early attracted to the writings of the erratic Dunton; he quoted him extensively throughout his own works; and late in life Nichols assisted his son, John Bowyer Nichols, in editing (1818) an edition of the *Life and Errors.* Part of the attraction was certainly the result of the fact that Dunton was in the bookselling trade. Nichols included the lives of a great many booksellers among his biographies.

Fairly extensive accounts of Dunton are in Knight, *Shadows of the Old Booksellers,* pp. 21-42, and in Roberts, *Earlier History of English Bookselling,* pp. 281-313, though neither account contains much of significance not in Nichols. Briefer accounts occur in other books dealing with the bookselling trade in the eighteenth century.

A life of John Dunton by Leslie Stephen is in the DNB, at the end of which the only sources listed are: "Dunton's Life and Errors (1705), reprinted in 1818 with life by J. B. Nichols, also in Lit. Anecd. v. 59-83."

C. H. Timperley has a life of Dunton (as he has of most of the people in the book trade included in this volume) in his *Dictionary of Printers and Printing* (1839). But since he frequently copies Nichols verbatim, I shall pay little further attention to him.]

This eccentric Bookseller was born May 14, 1659,[1] at Graffham in Huntingdonshire, where his father, John Dunton, fellow of Trinity college, Cambridge, was then rector. His mother Lydia Dunton, was daughter of Mr. Daniel Carter, of Chesham; and died March 3, 1660. On the loss of his wife, Mr. Dunton went to Ireland, where he continued some years; and the son was placed, at a very early age, at the school of Mr. William Readings, at Dungrove, near Chesham.

In 1669 his father returned into England, obtained the rectory of Aston Clinton, where he married a second wife, and removed the son from school to his own immediate tuition, intending him for the Church. The acquire-

---

1. In a section called "Additions to the Fifth Volume," in *Lit. Anec.,* IX, 592, Nichols has a correction to p. 59, the one on which the life of Dunton begins: "John Dunton was born Dec. 5, 1681; and died in 1735." In his life of Dunton in the DNB, Leslie Stephen gives his birth date as 4 May 1659 and his death year as 1733. I cannot account for the peculiar dating given by Nichols in his "correction."

ment of Latin he found easy; but the difficulty of Greek overcame all his resolutions. He made some little progress in logic, metaphysics, and morality; but at the age of fourteen was found too volatile for the Church; to the no small mortification of his father, who was himself the third John Dunton, in a lineal descent, that had been a minister. When nearly fifteen, to suit the peculiarity of his genius, he was apprenticed to Mr. Thomas Parkhurst, a respectable bookseller.* In 1676 he lost his father; and, when his apprenticeship was nearly expired, made himself conspicuous in the great political dispute between the Tories and the Whigs. He, being a prime mover on the part of the Whig apprentices, and selected for their Treasurer, the Tories, to the number of 5000, presented an address to the King against the petitioning for parliaments. The dissenting party made their remonstrances to the former address, in another they presented to Sir Patience Ward, then lord mayor of London, who promised he would acquaint the King with their address; and then bid them return home, and mind the business of their respective masters.

By his own statement, his conduct during the seven years was not very regular; and at the expiration of the term 100 apprentices were invited to celebrate *the funeral*.[2] He now entered on business as a bookseller on his own account; but, to avoid too large a rent, took only half a shop, a warehouse, and a fashionable chamber. "Printing," he says, "was the uppermost in my thoughts; and hackney authors began to ply me with specimens, as earnestly, and with as much passion and concern, as the watermen do passengers with oars and scullers. I had some acquaintance with this generation in my apprenticeship, and had never any warm affection for them; in regard I always thought their great concern lay more in how much a sheet, than in any generous respect they bore to the commonwealth of learning; and indeed the learning itself of these gentlemen lies very often in as little room as their honesty; though they all pretend to have studied you six or seven years in the Bodleian Library, to have turned over the Fathers, and to have read and digested the whole compass both of humane and ecclesiastic history: when, alas! they have never been able to understand a single page of Saint Cyprian, and cannot tell you whether the Fathers lived before or after Christ. And as for their honesty, it is very remarkable, they will either persuade you to go upon another man's copy, to steal his thought, or to abridge his book, which should have got him bread for his life-time.

---

* John Dunton says, his master, Mr. Thomas Parkhurst, was "a religious and a just man;" and adds, "My honoured Master is the most eminent Presbyterian Bookseller in the Three Kingdoms, and (now) chosen Master of the Company of Stationers; he has printed more practical books than any other that can be named in London. He has met with very strange success, for I have known him sell off a whole impression before the book has been almost heard of in London. He is scrupulously honest in all his dealings, a good master, and very kind to all his relations; and, which is an argument of something in him above the common rate of mankind, he is a great admirer, and constant hearer of the Rev. John How." NICHOLS. (In "Additions and Corrections," *Lit. Anec.*, V, 696: addition to p. 59.)

2. The funeral, of course, for the death of his apprenticeship.

When you have engaged them upon some project or other, they will write you off three or four sheets perhaps, take up three or four pounds upon an urgent occasion, and you shall never hear of them more."—"The first copy I would venture to print, was written by the Reverend Mr. [Thomas] Doolittle, and intituled 'The Sufferings of Christ.'[3] This book fully answered my end; for, exchanging it through the whole trade, it furnished my shop with all sorts of books saleable at that time; and it also brought me acquainted with those ingenious gentlemen, Mr. Waters, Mr. Shewel, Mr. Clark, Mr. Benson, Mr. Wells, and Mr. Sanders, who were then students under the care of Mr. Doolittle. There was a copy of Greek verses prefixed to this book, which occasioned a poetical duel between the two private Academies of Islington and Stepney; Mr. [Samuel] Wesley, then pupil under Mr. Veale, endeavouring to ridicule the Poem; with whom, and Mr. Kingston, his fellow student, I contracted a very intimate friendship. Mr. Wesley was much celebrated for his vein at poetry; though those that allow of no second rate in that art have endeavoured to lessen his reputation—The second adventure I made in printing, was a copy written by Mr. Jay, rector of Chinner, intituled, 'Daniel in the Den; or, the Lord President's Imprisonment, and miraculous Deliverance.'[4] It was dedicated to the Lord Shaftsbury, and published upon the occasion of his being acquitted by an ignoramus jury. This piece was well furnished with wit, and being published at the critical time, sold well.

> Books have their time of life as well as we;
> They live by chance, but die by destiny.
> Our fate is less severe, in this alone,
> That books no resurrection have, we hope for one.

"This extraordinary success in my first attempts, gave me an ungovernable itch to be always intriguing that way. The next thing I printed was a Sermon preached by the Rev. Mr. John Shower, at the funeral of Madam Anne Barnardiston.[5] The growing reputation of the author made the Sermon move very well. There have been three editions of it, two of my own printing, and a third by my worthy friend Mr. John Lawrence. When I was thus fixed in the trade, I resolved to make public a Collection of Funeral Discourses preached by my reverend father, Mr. John Dunton, intituled, 'The House of Weeping.'[6] The success was well enough; but my chief design was to perpetuate my father's name, for whose memory I have always entertained a very great and just veneration."

---

3. See Donald Wing, *Short-title Catalogue, 1641-1700*, 3 vols. (Columbia University Press, 1945, 1948, 1951), I, 462, Entry D1885: "The Lords last sufferings shewed in the Lords-Supper. *For John Dunton*, 1682. 12o."
4. See Wing, II, 268, Entry J497: "J[ay], S[tephen]. Daniel in the den. *By J. A. for John Dunton*, 1682. 4o."
5. See Wing, III, 255, Entry S3690: "Shower, John. A sermon preacht upon the death of Mrs Anne Barnardiston. *By J. A. for Benjamin Alsop, and John Dunton*, 1682. 4o."
6. See Wing, I, 479, Entry 2627: "The house of weeping. *For John Dunton*, 1682. 12o."

Dunton's reputation grew with his circumstances; and, Aug. 3, 1682, he married Elizabeth, one of the daughters of Dr. [Samuel] Annesl[e]y,[7] who at that time was a celebrated preacher among the Dissenters. He now opened a shop at the Black Raven in Princes-street; where he carried on business very prosperously, till the universal damp upon trade which was occasioned by the defeat of the Duke of Monmouth in the West; when, having 500l. owing him in New England, he determined, after much deliberation, to make a trip thither; and, after a long and tedious voyage of four months, and the loss of a venture of 500l. in another ship, which was cast-away, he arrived safe at Boston in March 1685-6; and opened a warehouse for the sale of the books which he had taken thither. Carrying with him powerful recommendations, and his books being of a class adapted to the Puritans, the success was equal to his wishes. His rivals in trade were but few; Mr. Usher, Mr. Philips, Mynheer Brunning, and Duncan Campbell, an industrious Scotchman, being then the only booksellers in Boston; and Mr. Green the principal if not the only printer. He had taken with him a steady apprentice, Samuel Palmer, to whom he entrusted the whole charge of his business; which left him at leisure to make many pleasant excursions into the country.

He visited Harvard college particularly, and the town of Salem; where he opened another warehouse for his books. He also visited Wenham, an inland town; where he was most kindly received by Mr. Geery, the then minister of that place; whose character he thus delineates: "It were endless to enter on a detail of each faculty of learning Mr. Geery is master of, and therefore take his character in shorthand. The Philosopher is acute, ingenious, and subtle; the Divine curious, orthodox, and profound; the Man of a majestic air, without austerity or sourness; his aspect is masterly and great, yet not imperious or haughty. The Christian is devout, without moroseness, or starts of holy frenzy and enthusiasm; the Preacher is primitive, without the accessional colours of whining or cant; and methodical without intricacy or affectation; and, which crowns his character, he is a man of a public spirit, zealous for the conversion of the Indians, and of great hospitality to strangers. He gave us a noble dinner, and entertained us with such pleasant fruits as, I must own, Old England is a stranger to."—In a ramble to Ipswich he had an opportunity of seeing much of the customs of the Indians.

In the autumn he returned to London; and, being received by his wife and her father with all the marks of kindness and respect, expected nothing but a golden life of it for the future, though all his satisfactions were soon withered; for, being deeply entangled for a sister-in-law,[8] he was not suf-

7. The elder Samuel Wesley, father of John Wesley, married Susannah, another daughter of Samuel Annesley. Nichols has memoirs of the Wesleys in *Lit. Anec.*, V, 212-247. Samuel Wesley wrote much verse published by Dunton; in his memoir of Samuel Wesley, Nichols quotes a character sketch of him written by Dunton and a letter in which Wesley addresses Dunton as "Dear Brother."
8. Before undertaking his trip to America, Dunton had become security for the debt

fered to step over the threshold in ten months. Wearied with this confinement, he determined to take a trip to Holland, Flanders, Germany, &c.; and stayed four months at Amsterdam; whence he travelled to Cleves, Rhineberg, Dusseldorp, Cologne, Mentz, &c.; and, returning through Rotterdam to London, Nov. 15, 1688, found his wife in health, and all her affairs in peace. On the day the Prince of Orange came to London, he again opened shop, at the Black Raven, opposite the Poultry Compter, where he traded ten years, with variety of successes and disappointments. The following books, among many others, may serve to give a taste of what he was engaged in: "Heads of Agreement, assented to by the United Ministers."[9]— "The Morning Exercises, published by the London Ministers."[10]—"Malebranche's Search after Truth, which was made English by Mr. Sault."[11]— "Mr. Coke's Detection of the Court and State of England."[12]—"The Works of the Lord Delamere, published by Consent of the Earl of Warrington."[13] —"Dr. Burthogg's Essay on Reason, and the Nature of Spirits; dedicated to Mr. Locke."[14]—"The Tigurine Liturgy; published by the Approbation of Six learned Prelates."[15]—"Bishop Barlow's Remains; published from his Lordship's original Papers, by Sir Peter Pet, Knight."[16]—"The Life of the Reverend Mr. Thomas Brand."[17]—"The Life and Death of the Reverend Mr. John Elliot, who first preached the Gospel to the Indians in America."[18] —"The Bloody Assizes, which contain the Trials and Dying Speeches of those that died in the West."[19]—"Sermons on the whole Parable of Dives and Lazarus, by Joseph Stephens, Lecturer of Cripplegate and Lothbury

---

of a brother and sister-in-law. The debt amounted to £1,200; his trip to Holland, etc., was for the purpose of evading creditors.

9. *"By R. R. for Tho. Cockerill and John Dunton, 1691. 4o."* See Wing, II, 171, Entry H1282A.

10. Probably the work listed in Wing, I, 61, as Entry A3225: "[Annesley, Samuel.] Casuistical morning-exercises. The fourth volume. *By James Astwood for John Dunton, 1690. 4o.*"

11. See Wing, II, 395, Entry M315: "Malebranche's search after truth ... Vol. I. *For J. Dunton, and S. Manship, 1694. 8o.*"

12. See Wing, I, 351, Entry C4973: "Coke, Roger. A detection of the court and state of England, *Printed, 1694. 2 v. 8o.*"

13. See Wing, I, 436, Entry D873: "Delamere, Henry Booth, *earl of.* The works of. *For John Lawrence, and John Dunton, 1694. 8o.*"

14. See Wing, I, 224, Entry B6150: "Burthogge, Richard. An essay upon reason. *For John Dunton, 1694. 8o.*"

15. See Wing, II, 365, Entry L2589: "Liturgia Tigurina: or, the book of common prayers. *For D. Newman, R. Baldwin, J. Dunton, 1693. 8o.*"

16. See Wing, I, 111, Entry B832: "Barlow, Thomas, *bp.* The genuine remains. *For John Dunton, 1693. 8o.*" In 1690 Dunton had published, by William Barlow of Chalgrove, Oxford, "A treatise of fornication." See Wing, I, 112, Entry B848.

17. See Wing, I, 61, Entry A3230: "[Annesley, Samuel.] The life and funeral sermon of the Reverend Mr. Thomas Brand. *For John Dunton, 1692. 4o.*"

18. This work is not listed by Wing under John Eliot, the missionary to the Indians, nor is it listed under him in the *British Museum Catalogue.*

19. See Wing, I, 135, Entry B1905: "[Bent, James.] The bloody assizes. *For J. Dunton, and sold by R. Janeway, 1689. 4o.*"

Churches."[20]—"The Tragedies of Sin, by Mr. Jay, Rector of Chinner."[21]—"Mr. Williams's Gospel Truth."[22]—"Machenzye's Narrative of the Siege of Derry."[23]—"Mr. Boyse's Answer to Bishop King."[24]—"Mr. Shower's Mourners Companion."[25]—"Mr. Roger's Practical Discourses."[26]—"Poems, written by Madam Singer, the Pindarick Lady."[27]—"Mr. Baxter's Life."[28]—"The History of the Edict at Nantes, translated by several Hands."[29]—"It was a wonderful pleasure," he says, "to Queen Mary to see this History made English, and was the only book to which she ever granted her Royal Licence."

Of 600 books which he had printed, he had only to repent, he adds, of *seven*: "The second Spira,"[30] "The Post-boy robbed of his Mail,"[31] "The

---

20. See Wing, III, 298, Entry S5499: "Steevens, Joseph. The whole parable of Dives. *For John Dunton*, 1697. 8o." The entry preceding this, S5498, by the same author, was also published by Dunton: "A narrative of the extraordinary penitence of Rob. Maynard. *For John Dunton*, 1696. 4o."

21. See Wing, II, 268, Entry J498: "J[ay], S[tephen]. . . . The tragedies of sin. By *J. Astwood, for John Dunton*, 1689. 8o."

22. See Wing, III, 490, Entry W2649: "Williams, Daniel. Gospel-truth stated. *For John Dunton*, 1692. 12o." Possibly another work by the same author and published by Dunton may have been intended; it is in the same column as the preceding, Entry W2646: "A defence of gospel-truth. *For John Dunton*, 1693. 4o." Three other works by the same author and published by Dunton at this same period also appear in the same column of Wing, Entries W2648, W2653, and W2657: "The excellency of a publick spirit," 1697, 8o, "Man made righteous," 1694, 12o, and "The vanity of childhood," 1691, 8o.

23. In Wing, II, 393, Entry M216, this work is not assigned to Dunton: "Mackenzie, John. A narrative of the siege of London-derry. *For the author, and are to be sold by Richard Baldwin*, 1690. 4o."

24. The author of this work was Joseph Boyse, father of the Samuel Boyse whose life is in this volume. Joseph Boyse carried on a controversy with William King, the Archbishop of Dublin, concerning the sanction given the office of bishop by the New Testament. Boyse, as a Dissenter, denied the sanction. See Wing, I, 178, Entry B4072: "[Boyse, Joseph.] Remarks on a late discourse. *For J. Lawrence, and J. Dunton*, 1694. 8o." The work to which it was an answer is (Wing, II, 298, Entry K520): "King, William, abp. An admonition to the dissenting inhabitants of . . . Derry. *Dublin, by Andrew Crook*, 1694. 4o."

25. See Wing, III, 255, Entry S3673: "Shower, John. The mourners companion. By *J. A. for J. Dunton*, 1692. 8o."

26. See Wing, III, 150, Entry R1852: "Rogers, Timothy, M. A. Practical discourses on sickness & recovery. *For Thomas Parkhurst, Jonathan Robinson, and John Dunton*, 1691. 8o." Dunton is listed as the sole publisher of another work by Rogers, in the same column of Wing, Entry R1850: "Fall not out by the way," 1692, 8o; and he and J. Robinson are listed as joint publishers of a third work by Rogers, same column of Wing, Entry R1849: "Early religion," 1683, 4o.

27. See Wing, III, 155, Entry R2062: "[Rowe, Mrs. Elizabeth Singer.] Poems on several occasions. *For John Dunston* [sic], 1696. 8o." According to the CBEL, the pseudonym used here was *Philomela*.

28. See Wing, I, 123, Entry B1370: "[Baxter, Richard.] Reliquiae Baxterianae. *For T. Parkhurst, J. Robinson, J. Lawrence and J. Dunton*, 1696. fol." Dunton also published the second edition of Baxter's "Poetical fragments" in 1689, 12o (Wing, I, 122, Entry B1350).

29. See Wing, I, 135, Entry B1898: "[Benoit, Elie.] The history of the famous edict of Nantes. *For John Dunton*, 1694. 2 v. 4o."

30. See Wing, III, 182, Entry S733: "[Sault, Richard.] The second spira. *For John Dunton*, 1693. 12o." According to Wing, Dunton also published a fourth edition of this work the same year. He also published by J. Sault "A conference betwixt a modern atheist," 1693, 12o (Wing, ibid, Entry S732).

31. See Wing, II, 107, Entry G735A: "Gildon, Charles. The post-boy rob'd of his mail. *For John Dunton*, 1692. 12o."

Voyage round the World,"[32] "The New Quevedo,"[33] "The Pastor's Legacy,"[34] "Heavenly Pastime,"[35] "The Hue and Cry after Conscience."[36] These he heartily wished he had never seen, and advised all who had them to burn them. After confessing his errors in printing, he says, "As to bookselling and traffick, I dare stand the test, with the same allowance that every man under the same circumstance with me would wish to have, for the whole trading part of my life. Nay, I challenge all the Booksellers in London to prove I ever over-reached them or deceived them in any one instance. And when you come to that part of my life that relates to the *Auctions I made in Dublin,* you will find that in all the notes I made for Dublin, that I put the same price to every man. And would any Bookseller be at the pains to compare all my notes together (though I exchanged with all the trade), for every penny he finds charged more to himself than to other men, he shall have ten pounds reward, and a thousand thanks into the bargain, for rectifying a mistake I never designed."—In 1692, having been "put in possession of a considerable estate upon the decease of my cousin Carter, the Master and Assistants of the Company of Stationers began to think me sufficient to wear a Livery, and honoured me with the cloathing. My Livery-fine upon that occasion was twenty pounds, which I paid; and the year following, Mr. Harris (my old friend and partner), and about fifty more of the Livery-men, entered into a Friendly Society, and obliged ourselves to pay twenty shillings a man yearly to the Renter-warden, in regard that honour was usually once a year attended with a costly entertainment to the whole Company.

"The first year I wore the Livery, Sir William Ashhurst being then Lord Mayor, I was invited by our Master and Wardens to dine with his Lordship. We went in a body from the Poultry church to Grocers-hall; where the entertainment was very generous, and a noble spoon he sent to our wives. To speak the truth, I do not think Sir William Ashhurst ever acted a little or a mean thing in his whole life. The world now smiled on me. I sailed with wind and tide; and had humble servants enough among the Booksellers, Stationers, Printers, and Binders; but especially my own relations, on every side, were all upon the very height of love and tenderness, and I was caressed almost out of my five senses.—And now, making a considerable figure in the Company of Stationers, the Right Hon. the Earl of

---

32. See Wing, III, 431, Entry V742: "A voyage round the world. *For Richard Newcome,* 1691. 8o." According to the *Brit. Mus. Cat.* "*The author's name appears in the anagram* '*Hid unto none*' *on sig.* b4 *verso.*"

33. I have not been able to identify the work of Francisco Gomez de Quevedo y Villegas referred to here.

34. This work is identified in the *Brit. Mus. Cat.* thus: "DUNTON (John) *Rector of Aston Clinton.* Dunton's Remains: or, the Dying Pastor's Last Legacy to his friends and parishioners, *etc.* pp. 387. *J. Dunton: London,* 1684. 8o." See Wing, I, 479, Entry D2633. The author of this work was, of course, the father of John Dunton the publisher.

35. See Wing, I, 479, Entry D2625: "Dunton, John. Heavenly pastime. *For John Dunton,* 1685. 12o." A second edn. (Entry 2626) appeared the same year.

36. See Wing, I, 479, Entry D2628: "Dunton, John. An hue and cry after conscience. *For John Dunton,* 1685. 12o."

Warrington did me the honour to send me a letter (the original of which I have still by me) in behalf of Mr. Humphreys, desiring all the interest I could make, to procure him the Clerk's place to the Company of Stationers. Upon my reading the Earl's letter, I did all that lay in my power to get Mr. Humphreys chosen Clerk, though by the majority of voices it was carried against him. However, the many civilities I received from the Company of Stationers, for the fifteen years I traded amongst them, do oblige me, out of mere gratitude, to draw the character of the most eminent of that profession in the three kingdoms." Here Mr. Dunton proceeds to characterize the principal Booksellers, Printers, Stationers, Bookbinders, &c. who were his contemporaries (as in a former part of the volume he had the several Authors with whom he had been connected in trade); several of whom have already been mentioned in the present work, and others shall be noticed in future pages.

In delineating the characters of others, Mr. Dunton has not forgot to describe his own *Projects*; "for I have been sufficiently convinced," he says, "that unless a man can either think or perform something out of the old beaten road, he will find nothing but what his forefathers have found before him. A Bookseller, if he is a man of any capacity and observation, can tell best what to go upon, and what has the best prospect of success. I remember Mr. Andrews, a learned and ingenious Scotsman of this age, has offered me several translations, and told me they would certainly sell; the substance of the book was so and so, and could not miss. He added, I had printed more than any other, and yet none had printed less. This was sharp enough, I confess; however, it is a difficult matter to attack a man in his own science. I have, it is true, been very plentifully loaded with the imputation of *Maggots,* &c. And what is the reason? Why, because I have usually started something that was new; whilst others, like footpads, ply only about the high-roads, and either abridge another man's book, or one way or other contrived the very life and soul out of the copy, which perhaps was the only subsistence of the first Proprietor. I once printed a book, I remember, under the title of *Maggots*;† but it was written by a Dignitary of the Church of England. However, I am willing to submit myself, and to stand or fall by the impartial judgment of the Reader. My *first Project* was the 'Athenian Gazette.'[37] As the Athenian Society had their first meeting

---

† "*Maggots*; or, Poems on several Subjects never before handled. 1685." 8vo; with the portrait of the Author (*Samuel Wesley*); a maggot on his forehead. See more particulars relating to this publication (which is anonymous) in Granger, vol. IV. 8vo. p. 329. NICHOLS. (The 8vo edition of James Granger's *Biographical History of England* was the second, 1775.)

37. The *Athenian Gazette; or, Casuistical Mercury,* continued as the *Athenian Mercury* from No. 2, was written by Dunton with the assistance of Richard Sault, John Norris, and Samuel Wesley the Elder (V. 1-19, March 17, 1690/91—Feb. 8, 1696, thirty nos. in a volume; V. 20, May 14—June 14, 1697, ten nos.) See R. S. Crane and F. B. Kaye, *A Census of British Newspapers and Periodicals, 1620-1800* (University of North Carolina Press, 1927), p. 16, Entry 32. A bibliography at the beginning of Crane, pp. 3-6, will lead the reader to other works on the subject of early English periodicals, as will also the bibliogra-

in my brain—so it has been kept ever since religiously secret: but I will now oblige the Reader with a true discovery of the *Question-project,* and of the several persons that engaged in it.

"I had received a very flaming injury, which was so loaded with aggravations, that I could scarce get over it; my thoughts were constantly working upon it, and made me strangely uneasy: sometimes I thought to make application to some Divine, but how to conceal myself and the ungrateful wretch, was the difficulty. Whilst this perplexity remained upon me, I was one day walking over St. George's-fields, and Mr. [George] Larkin and Mr. Harris[38] were along with me, and on a sudden I made a stop, and said, 'Well, Sirs,' I have a thought I'll not exchange for fifty guineas!' They smiled, and were very urgent with me to discover it; but they could not get it from me. The first rude hint of it, was no more than a confused idea of concealing the Querist, and answering his question. However, so soon as I came home, I managed it to some better purpose, brought it into form, and hammered out a title for it, which happened to be extremely lucky, and those who are well acquainted with the Grecian History may discover some peculiar beauties in it.—However, the honest Reader that knows nothing of criticism may see the reason why this Project was intituled the 'Athenian Gazette,' if he only turns to Acts xvii. 21. When I had thus formed the design, I found that some assistance was absolutely necessary to carry it on, in regard the Project took in the whole compass of Learning, and the nature of it required dispatch. I had then some acquaintance with the ingenious Mr. Richard Sault; who turned Malebranche into English for me, and was admirably well skilled in the mathematicks; and over a glass of wine I unbosomed myself to him, and he very freely offered to become concerned. So soon as the design was well advertised, Mr. Sault and myself, without any more assistance, settled to it with great diligence (and Numbers 1. 2. were entirely of Mr. Sault's composure and mine). The Project being surprizing and un-thought-of, we were immediately overloaded with letters; and sometimes I have found several hundreds for me at Mr. Smith's coffee-house in Stocks-market, where we usually met to consult matters.

"The 'Athenian Gazette' made now such a noise in the world, and was so universally received, that we were obliged to look out after more members; and Mr. Sault, I remember, one evening came to me in great transport, and told me he had been in company with a gentleman, who was the greatest prodigy of learning he had ever met with; upon inquiry, we found it was the ingenious Dr. [John] Norris,‡ who very generously offered his

---

phies in the CBEL (1940) at the beginnings of sections dealing with magazines and reviews, II, 668-670, and the newspaper, II, 688-691.

38. Partner with Dunton in some publishing ventures; see *Lit. Anec.,* I, 60.

‡ "He search'd Malebranche; and now the Rabbi knows,
   The secret springs whence truth and error flows.
   Directed by his leading light we pass,

assistance *gratis*, but refused to become a stated member of Athens. He was wonderfully useful in supplying hints; for, being universally read, and his memory very strong, there was nothing could be asked, but he could very easily say something to the purpose upon it.

"In a little time after, to oblige *Authority,* we altered the title of 'Athenian Gazette,' into 'Athenian Mercury.' The undertaking growing every week upon our hands, the impatience of our Querists, and the curiosity of their questions, which required a great deal of accuracy and care, did oblige us to adopt a third member of Athens; and the reverend Samuel Wesley[39] being just come to town, all new from the University, and my acquaintance with him being very intimate, I easily prevailed with him to embark himself upon the same bottom, and in the same cause. With this new addition we found ourselves to be masters of the whole design, and thereupon we neither lessened nor increased our number.

"The success of Athens growing so very considerable, Mr. [Thomas] Brown and Mr. [W.] Pate began to ape our design in a paper they entituled the 'Lacedemonian Mercury,'[40] which immediately interfered with us under a title, which, it is true, was pretty and pertinent enough. Upon this, I was resolved one way or other to blow them up, in regard, it was both ungenerous and unjust to interlope upon a man, where he has the sole right and property; for the children of the brain are as much ours, as those we beget in lawful wedlock. I first of all advertized, that all the questions answered in the 'Lacedemonian Mercury' should be answered over again in our 'Athenian Mercury,' with amendments, with the life of Tom Brown, the chief antagonist. This news startled them pretty much. At that time I was altogether unacquainted with Mr. Brown. However, one evening he comes to me, with all the civility imaginable, and desires to take a glass with me. I sent for my Athenian brethren, and we went to the Three Cranes, where we discoursed the matter with him at large: but, Mr. Sault being a gentleman of courage, and a little inclined to passion, was going to draw upon Mr. Brown, for an uncivil reflection; upon which Mr. Brown cried *peccavi,* and promised very faithfully that he would never meddle any more with the 'Lacedemonian Mercury;' and though they had not dropt it, yet the flaming wickedness, and the blasphemy that was in it, would have ruined the design.

> Through Nature's rooms, and tread in ev'ry maze;
> A throng of virtues in his soul repose,
> Which, single, would as many Saints compose;
> Or if all graces you would see in one,
> View his *humility* for there 'tis found.
> He is distinguish'd by his low retreat
> To Bemerton, far from a Bishop's seat:
> Yet dignified, for Learning makes him great."

(*This is* Dunton's *Character of Mr.* Norris.) NICHOLS.

39. The father of John Wesley and brother-in-law of Dunton. See n. 4.
40. The *London Mercury* was continued as the *Lacedemonian Mercury* with the 9th number, 7 March 1692. See Crane, p. 146, Entry 1524, and CBEL, II, 658.

Browne Willis, Esq.

Reverend Samuel Pegge, LL.D., F.S.A.

Reverend Thomas Warton, B.D., F.S.A.

James Basire

"A little after this was published, 'The New Athenian Comedy,'[41] containing, 'The Politicks, OEconomicks, Tacticks, Crypticks, Apocalypticks, Stypticks, Scepticks, Pneumaticks, Theologicks, Poeticks, Mathematicks, Sophisticks, Pragmaticks, Dogmaticks, of our most Learned Society.' This Play was a poor performance, writ, however, on purpose to expose us; but failed so far in the design of it, that it promoted ours. There was nothing of wit through the whole of it, and the reader may take notice that Mr. S——'s§ genius was quite run out towards the conclusion of the third act, and could not carry it an inch farther.

"The Earl of —— was once pleased to frown upon the 'Athenian Mercury,' and forced us into silence; but, when men are pleased to make personal application (for the offence was only taken at a question that was sent us, of a father that had two daughters), it is a sign there is a sore place, else they would never wince for the matter; however Captain M—al procured us liberty to proceed, and had twenty-five guineas for that service. I have waded through these, and many other difficulties with this design; and nothing could discourage me, when my cause was so great and good.

"The 'Athenian Mercury' began at length to be so well approved, that Mr. [Charles] *Gildon* thought it worth his while to write 'A History of the Athenian Society;' to which were prefixed several poems written by the chief Wits of the age (*viz.*[42] Mr. [Peter] Motteux, Mr. Foe,[43] Mr. [William] Richardson, &c. and in particular, Mr. [Nahum] *Tate* (now Poet Laureat), was pleased to honour us with a Poem directed to the Athenian Society. Mr. *Swift*,|| a country gentleman, sent an Ode to the Athenian Society; which, being an ingenious poem, was prefixed to the Fifth Supplement of the 'Athenian Mercury.' Many other persons did also rhime in the praise of our Questions. Our Athenian Project did not only obtain among the populace, but was well received by the politer sort of mankind. That great and learned Nobleman, the late Marquis of Halifax, was once pleased to tell me, that he constantly perused our Mercuries, and had received great satisfaction from very many of our Answers. The late Sir William Temple,[44] a man of clear judgment, and wonderful penetration, was pleased to honour me with frequent letters and questions, very curious and uncommon; in particular, that about the *Talismans* was his. The Honourable Sir Thomas Pope Blount, when he resided in town, has very frequently sent for me to his chamber, and given me particular thanks for my Athenian Project; and the last visit I made him, he told me the Athenian Society was certainly the

---

§ Mr. S—— is Mr. Elkanah Settle. JOHN BOWYER NICHOLS. (*Illustr.*, VIII, 540.)

|| Afterwards the celebrated Dean; see his Works, vol. XVI. p. 23. NICHOLS. (The reference would be to the London booksellers' trade edition, the 16th volume of which was edited by Deane Swift and published in 1765.)

41. See Wing, III, 232, Entry S2701 (1693, 4o). See also Joseph Wyeth, *The Athenian Society Unvail'd* (1692, fol.), Wing, III, 514, Entry W3760.
42. The parenthesis before *viz.* is left without a mate.
43. Daniel Defoe was born without the *De*.
44. Swift's patron.

most useful and informing design that had even been set on foot in England. Sir William Hedges was pleased to tell me, he was so well pleased with the 'Athenian Mercuries,' that he would send several complete sets into the Indies, to his friends; and that he thought the publick, and himself in particular, so much obliged to me, that I should be always welcome to his house, and that he would serve me to his utmost with reference to my trade. I could mention many more honours that were done me, by Sir Peter Pett, and several others, whose learning and judgment the world has little reason to question.

"Our 'Athenian Mercuries' were continued till they swelled, at least, to twenty volumes folio; and then we took up, to give ourselves a little ease, and refreshment; for the labours and the travels of the mind are as expensive, and wear the spirits off as fast, as those of the body. However our Society was never formally dissolved.

"The old Athenian volumes, a while ago, growing quite out of print, a choice collection of the most valuable questions and answers, in three volumes, have lately been re-printed, and made publick, under the title of 'Athenian Oracle;'[45] two of which I dedicated to the most illustrious and magnanimous Prince, James Duke of Ormond (Chancellor of the Universities of Oxford and Dublin), and Lord Lieutenant of Ireland. These two volumes I presented to his Grace with my own hand; and if any thing could make me vain of the Athenian Project, it would be the generous reception his Grace gave to each of the volumes. I have no need here to shew the reason of this dedication; for his Grace's fame is improved already to an undoubted immortality. His courage, conduct, and success in war, have raised him as far above the reach of flattery, as above all parallel. He has waded through blood and battles, and has freely ventured his life and fortunes in the great cause of liberty and religion; and now, at last, we cannot but applaud the judicious choice of our gracious Queen, in making him the Guardian of a Kingdom which owes so much to his Family, and where his presence is as acceptable, as it is necessary; and therefore, as the Duke of Ormond is Patron of Learning, as well as of Arms, the Athenian Society thought they had a natural right to his protection; and they found it in so ample a manner, that his Grace not only honoured each volume with his own perusal, but was pleased afterwards to mention to some Lords the great satisfaction he took in the Athenian Oracles that had been presented to him. And may his Grace live long, the great encouragement of Arms and Arts! The copy of these three volumes I sold to Mr. Bell in Cornhill, and is all (as appears by our articles) that he has any right to; and much good may his success do him! For it is thought he will get above a thousand pounds by it.

"A *second Project* of mine, which was set on foot by the Old Athenians,

---

45. Vols. I and II were issued in 1703 by Dunton and Vol. III, in 1704. A second edn. of Vols. I and II came out in 1704, and of Vol. III, in 1706. See CBEL, II, 186-187.

and lately published by the New, is intituled, 'The Athenian Spy; or the Secret Letters of Platonic Courtship, between the Athenian Society, and the most ingenious Ladies in the Three Kingdoms; with the form of solemnizing Platonic Matrimony, invented by the Athenian Society.'[46]

"A *third Project* of mine, for the promotion of Learning, was a monthly Journal of Books printed in London, and beyond Sea; which was chiefly extracted out of 'The Universal Bibliotheque,' and 'Journal des Sçavans;'[47] and it first appeared under the title of 'A Supplement to the Athenian Mercury,' but was afterwards called, 'The Complete Library.'[48] This design was carried on about ten months, when Monsieur Lecrose[49] interfered with me in a Monthly Journal, intituled 'The Works of the Learned;' upon which I dropped my own design, and joined with Lecrose's Bookseller, in publishing 'The Works of the Learned.' But Lecrose dying, it was discontinued; though the same design, under the same title, is yet on foot, and managed by several hands, one of which is the ingenious Mr. [George] Ridpath.

"IV. *Another Project* (which I writ myself, and published a year ago) was intituled 'The Post Angel: or Universal Entertainment.'[50]

"My *fifth Project* has been preparing for the press for these ten years, and is intituled, 'The New Practice of Piety. Writ in imitation of Dr. [Thomas] Brown[e]'s *Religio Medici*: or, a System of uncommon Thoughts, extracted from the Experience of Forty Years.'[51]

"My *sixth Project* was 'The Challenge, sent by a young Lady to Sir Thomas ———, intituled *The Female War*; wherein the present Dresses and Humours of the Fair Sex, are vigorously attacked by Men of Quality, and as bravely defended by several Ladies.'[52]

"VII. My next *Project* was intituled, 'The Post-Boy robbed of his Mail; or, The Pacquet broke open, containing Five Hundred Letters that were taken from several Posts, discovering the Secrets of Men and Women of all Ranks and Qualities.'[53] The Club of Gentlemen supposed to have been

---

46. Published by Dunton in 1709, 12o. See entry for this under the *Athenian Society* (LONDON. III. "Miscellaneous Institutions, Societies, and other Bodies,") *Brit. Mus. Cat.*

47. For a discussion of these French journals in connection with the development of English periodicals, see Walter Graham, *English Literary Periodicals* (New York, 1930), pp. 22-32. Graham also gives considerable attention to Dunton, pp. 32-48.

48. *The Compleat Library: Or, News for the Ingenious* began in May 1692 and ran till June 1694. See CBEL, II, 675.

49. Jean Cornand de la Crose, a Huguenot, began *The Works of the Learned* in 1691, and it ran to April 1692. La Crose's *The History of Learning* had been begun July 1691 and was transformed into *The Works of the Learned*. Ridpath's continuation was called *The History of the Works of the Learned* (January 1699–March 1712). See CBEL, II, 675, and Graham, pp. 38-42.

50. This dialogue paper appeared between January 1701 and June 1702. See CBEL, II, 659.

51. Issued by Dunton in 1704, 8o; see *Brit. Mus. Cat.*

52. See Wing, I, 272, Entry C1796: "The challenge sent by a young lady. *Printed and sold by E. Whitlock,* 1697. 12o." The fullest description in the *Brit. Mus. Cat.* is under the pseudonym *Philaret*.

53. See n. 27; see the title of this book also in the *Brit. Mus. Cat.* under the entry

concerned in this frolick make remarks upon the Letters as they break them up. This Project obtained so well, that both volumes are now out of print.

"My *eighth Project* was a design to expose vice, intituled, 'The Night Walker; or, Evening Rambles in search after lewd Women; with the various Conferences held with them.'[54] This Project was so well received, that I purposed to continue it monthly."

[[Nichols' note:] Dunton's greatest Project was intended for the extirpating of lewdness from London; a scheme highly creditable to the schemer, had it been practicable. Armed with a constable's staff, and accompanied by a clerical companion, he sallied forth in the evening, and followed the wretched prostitutes home, or to a tavern, where every effort was used to win the erring fair to the paths of virtue; but these, he observes, were "perilous adventures," as the Cyprians exerted every art to lead him astray, in the height of his spiritual exhortations.]

"IX. My last *Project* (amongst many that I shall leave unmentioned) was intituled 'The Merciful Assizes; or, a Panegyrick on the late Lord [George] Jeffreys' hanging so many in the West.'[55] You must know, Reader, in the book intituled 'The Bloody Assizes'[56] (of which I sold above six thousand) the Lord Jeffreys is made a very cruel man: but in this new Project I (wholly) change the scene, and turn the Bloody Assizes into Merciful Assizes. But let none be surprized that I make Jeffreys the subject of a panegyrick; for there is a witty Author has defended the bloody Nero; and of late, a learned gentleman has published an Apology for the Failures of Dr. Walker;[57] and with the same design that these gentlemen writ, do I venture to praise that *nonsuchman,* George Lord Jeffreys. This panegyrick was so well accepted,

---

G., C. (for Charles Gildon). Vol. I was published in 1692, 12o. The next volume is called the "second edition," containing many additions, 1705, 8o.

54. See Crane, p. 78, Entry 628, where this is dated 1696-97.

55. See the *Brit. Mus. Cat.*: "2 pt. 1701. 8o."

56. See n. 15. Dunton had also published earlier, Wing, I, 135, Entry B1906, by James Bent, "An impartial history of the life and death of George Lord Jeffreys. *For John Dunton,* 1689. 4o."

57. In 1758 the Bowyer press printed "Mr. George Walker's 'Narrative of the Siege of Londonderry,' republished by Dr. [John] Brown, who did all he could to reform and revive us, 'as a useful Lesson to the Present Times, with a prefatory Address to the Publick,' 8vo." In a note to the above entry, Nichols gives the following information about Walker: "Rector of Donaghmoore, in the county of Tirone. The work was originally published in 1689; and occasioned a considerable controversy. Mr. Walker acquired such a military taste by this gallant atchievement, that he sacrificed his life at the battle of the Boyne. It was thought, had he lived, he would have been presented to the see of Derry, vacant by the death of Dr. Hopkins, three days before. *Gough's British Topography,* vol. II. p. 808." *Lit. Anec.,* II, 311. (Regarding another book published by Bowyer in 1758, Nichols writes, *Lit. Anec.,* II, 303: "*This was one of the first Works on which I was employed as a Compositor.*")

that my friend Mr. George Larkin[58] was pleased to explain the Project by an ingenious Poem.

"Thus have I given a brief account of the Projects I formerly engaged in; and whether they give me the title of *Maggot,* or Promotor of Learning and Virtue, is left to the candour and judgment of the honest Reader."

After this ample account of himself and of his various Projects, little remains to be added, but the title-pages of several[59] of Dunton's publications.

1. *"The Dublin Scuffle*: being a Challenge sent by John Dunton, Citizen of London, to Patrick Campbel, Bookseller in Dublin; together with the small Skirmishes of Bills and Advertisements. To which is added, the *Billet Doux,* sent him by a Citizen's Wife in Dublin, tempting him to Lewdness: with his Answers to her. Also some Account of his Conversation in Ireland, intermixt with particular Characters of the most eminent Persons he conversed with in that Kingdom; but more especially in the City of Dublin. In several Letters to the Spectators of this Scuffle. With a Poem on the whole Encounter. '*I wear my Pen as others do their Sword.*' OLDHAM. London, printed for the Author; and are to be sold by A. Baldwin, near the Oxford-Arms in Warwick-Lane, and by the Booksellers in Dublin; 1699."[60]

This volume is inscribed "To the Honourable Colonel Butler, a Member of the House of Commons in Ireland;" as a compliment due to the generous encouragement that gentleman had been pleased to give to his *Auction of Books* at Dublin in the year 1698, and the extraordinary and unmerited kindnesses he had received. The *Scuffle* relates to disputes in trade with Patrick Campbel, a Dublin Bookseller, who was jealous of Dunton's success; which are amusing, though not very generally interesting. But the "Account of his Conversation in Ireland" contains a pleasing description of several parts of that Island, not generally known to an English reader, and well worth perusing.[61]

2. His next regular publication was, "The Life and Errors of John Dunton, late Citizen of London; written by himself in Solitude. With an Idea of a new Life; wherein is shewn how he'd think, speak, and act, might he live over his days again: intermixed with the new Discoveries the Author has made in his Travels abroad, and in his private Conversation at home. Together with the Lives and Characters of a Thousand Persons now living in London, &c. Digested into Seven Stages, with their respective Ideas.

---

58. Larkin published a newspaper called *The Old Post-Master* (June–July 1696); see CBEL, II, 706.

59. This word reads *three* in the text in *Lit. Anec.,* V, 74, but is corrected to *several* by John Bowyer Nichols in *Illustr.,* VIII, 540. Nichols actually lists *ten* publications, misnumbered *eleven.*

60. See Wing, I, 479, Entry D2622.

61. Long after writing this account of Dunton, John Nichols assisted his son John Bowyer Nichols in the editing and republication of several of Dunton's works, including the conversation in Ireland (see headnote).

> 'He that has all his own mistakes confess'd,
> Stands next to him that never has transgress'd;
> And will be censur'd for a fool by none,
> But they who see no errors of their own.'
>   FOE's Satyr upon himself, p. 6.

London: printed for S. Malthus, 1705." This genuine and simple narrative of his own history is a very curious performance, and abounds in literary history of an interesting nature.

[[Nichols' note: At the end of this volume was advertized, as preparing for the press, "A Ramble through Six Kingdoms, by John Dunton, late Citizen of London. Wherein he relates, 1. His Juvenile Travels. 2. The History of his Sea Voyages. 3. His Conversation in Foreign Parts. With Characters of Men and Women, and almost every Thing he saw or conversed with. The like Discoveries (in such a Method) never made by any Traveller before. Illustrated with Forty Cuts, representing the most pleasant Passages in the whole Adventure. With Recommendatory Poems, written by the chief Wits in both Universities."][62]

3. "The Case of John Dunton with respect to Madam Jane Nicholas of St. Alban's, his Mother-in-law, 1700," 4to.

[[Nichols' note in "Additions to the Fifth Volume," *Lit. Anec.*, IX, 592:] "Madam Jane Nicholas" was a considerable benefactrix to the Town of St. Alban's by her will dated 14 October and proved 18 December 1708. Her bequests were to take effect within a year after the decease of her daughter Sarah Dunton without issue, who is recorded to have been buried in the Abbey Church 21 March 1720. Among other things she bequeathed to the Minister of the Parish 5*l. per annum* for ever for preaching an annual Sermon, which I have heard, I believe, more than once. She desired to be buried in the Abbey Church; and directed that the annuities she had left might be expressly engraven on her tomb-stone, that the memory thereof might not be lost, but preserved for future ages. It was a wise provision; but, like many other testamentary directions, never attended to, for there appears not the smallest vestige of any of the family through the whole church. J[AMES]. BROWN (of St. Alban's).]

4. "A Cat may look on a Queen: or a Satyr on Her present Majesty."[63]

---

62. If this work and the one following were actually published, I have not been able to identify them.
63. This work is listed under Dunton in the *Brit. Mus. Cat.* (1708, 8o), where it is

5. "Plain French: or a Satyr upon the Tackers. To which is added the Character of a True Patriot: written to caution and direct English Freeholders in the Choice of a New Parliament; and particularly the Electors in Bucks. By John Dunton, a Freeholder in the same County. The Fourth Edition, corrected and enlarged."[64]

6. "The New Athenian Oracle; under Three General Heads, *viz.* The Divine, Philosophic, and Secret Oracle. The whole resolving such nice and curious Questions as were never answered in the Old Athenian Oracle. vol. I. with a General Table.—The Second Volume of The New Athenian Oracle will be published when a thousand of the first Volume is sold off; and then this New Oracle will be continued in Volumes, at 3*s.* each, till the Question Project is completed in Six Volumes; all which will not exceed the bulk (or price) of the Three Volumes of the old Athenian Oracles. This Notice is given, that so the ingenious Querists may continue to send what nice and curious Questions they have still by them. But take notice, that no Questions will be answered, or received, but what are sent to the Athenian (or Smith's) Coffee-house in Stock's-market, and postage paid."[65]

7. "The Athenian Catechism: containing, The Atheist's Catechism, Numb. 1. A Continuation of the Atheist's Catechism, Numb. 2. The Player's Catechism, Numb. 3. The High Flyer's Catechism, Numb. 4. The bigotted Dissenter's Catechism, Numb. 5. The Atheist at Confession: or, the Atheist's penitential Catechism, Numb. 6. A Continuation of the Atheist's penitential Catechism, Numb. 7. The occasional Conformists's Catechism, Numb. 8. The occasional Nonconformist's Catechism, Numb. 9. A Continuation of the occasional Nonconformist's Catechism, Numb. 10. The Lady's Catechism for Paint and Patches, Numb. 11. A Catechism for our late Pamphleteers, Numb. 12. A Catechism for Coffee-houses, Numb. 13. A Continuation of the Coffee-house Catechism, Numb. 14. The Catechism for Coffee-houses continued, Numb. 15. The finishing Catechism for the Coffeehouses, Numb. 16. The Political Catechism, for the Improvement of Newsmongers, Numb. 17. A Continuation of the Political Catechism, Numb. 18, 19, 20.—These several Catechisms are a Continuation of the Athenian Catechism. To which is added, The Gentleman's Courant, or, News for the Ingenious. These 20 Numbers complete the first Volume of the Athenian Catechism; and are sold at 18*d.* A second Volume of this Catechetical Project will be published, if due encouragement be given.—By the New Athenian Society."[66]

---

called the "second edition." A work with the title *A Cat may look upon a King*, by Sir Anthony Weldon, was published in 1652; see Wing, III, 461, Entry W1271.

64. I have not been able to identify this.

65. See n. 44 for information concerning the various volumes and editions of this work. See also the *Brit. Mus. Cat.* entries under the *Athenian Society* (LONDON. III. "Miscellaneous Institutions, Societies, and other Bodies.") See also item No. 4 of the additions to the works of John Nichols as supplied by John Bowyer Nichols (in the life of John Nichols).

66. I have not been able to identify this.

8. "Dunton's Whipping-post: or, a Satire upon every body. To which is added, A Panegyrick on the most deserving Gentlemen and Ladies in the Three Kingdoms; &c. &c. Vol. I. To which is added, The Living Elegy: or, Dunton's Letter to his few Creditors. With the Character of a Summer Friend. Also, the secret History of the Weekly Writers, in a distinct Challenge to each of them. Printed, and are to be sold by B. Bragg, at the Black Raven in Paternoster-row. 1706."[67]

9. "The Bull-baiting: or, Sacheverell[68] dressed up in Fireworks. Lately brought over from Bear-garden in Southwark; and exposed, for the Diversion of the Citizens of London, at Six-pence-a-piece. By John Dunton, Author of the Answer to Dr. [White] Kennett, intituled *"The Hazard of a Death-bed Repentance."*[69] Being Remarks on a scandalous Sermon bellowed out at St. Paul's on the fifth of November last, before the Right Honourable the Lord Mayor, and Court of Aldermen, by Dr. Sacheverell. Printed for the Author, and are to be sold by John Morphew, near Stationers-hall; and take notice whatever of these Books are published, not having Mr. Morphew's name to them (or that are sold at a lower price than 6*d*.) are a wrong to the Author, and a cheat to the Buyers; all such stolen and imperfect Books not containing the fourth part of Mr. Dunton's original Copies. 1709."

11. [Sic] The latest of his publications that I have seen is intituled, "*Athenianism*; or, the new Projects of Mr. John Dunton, Author of the Essay intituled, '*The Hazard of a Death-bed Repentance*;['] being *six hundred* distinct Treatises (in Prose and Verse) written with his own Hand; and is an entire Collection of all his Writings, both in Manuscript and such as were formerly printed.

[[Nichols' note to the above:] Dunton is honoured with an incidental notice in the Dunciad, II. 144;[70] on which Warburton remarks, that "he was an auction [broken] bookseller, and an abusive scribler. He wrote Neck or Nothing,[71] a violent satire on some Ministers of State; [The danger

---

67. See entry for this work under Dunton in the *Brit. Mus. Cat.*; see also CBEL, II, 187.
68. Henry Sacheverell, a high-church Tory, on 5 November 1709 preached a sermon in extremely violent language on "the perils of false brethren in church and state" on a text from 2 Corinthians xi. 26. He declared that the church was in danger from toleration, occasional conformity, and schism; and he characterized the Whig ministers as false friends. For publishing his sermon without authorization, Sacheverell was impeached by the Commons and found guilty by the Lords on 20 March 1710. He was forbidden to preach for three years. See entry for *The Bull-baiting* under Dunton in the *Brit. Mus. Cat.*.
69. See entry for this work (1708, 8o) under Dunton in the *Brit. Mus. Cat.*.
70. Nichols' reference is to the four-book *Dunciad* of 1742, since the reference to Dunton occurs in line 144 of the second book in that edition; it occurs in line 136 of the second book of the variorum *Dunciad* of 1729. The couplet in both versions reads:
        A shaggy Tap'stry, worthy to be spread
        On Codrus' old, or Dunton's modern bed;
see *The Poems of Alexander Pope*, vol. V, *The Dunciad*, ed. James Sutherland, 2nd edn. (London, 1952), pp. 117, 302.
71. See entry for this work (1713, 12o) under Dunton in the *Brit. Mus. Cat.*.

of a death-bed repentance,] a libel on the Duke of Devonshire and the Bishop of Peterborough, &c."

"I am informed," says Swift in the *Tale of a Tub,* "that worthy Citizen and Bookseller Mr. John Dunton has made a faithful and painful Collection, which he shortly designs to publish in *twelve volumes in folio, illustrated with copper-plates*; a work useful and curious, and altogether worthy of such a hand."[72]

In his "Public Spirit of the Whigs," Swift says, "Among the present Writers on that side I can recollect but three of any great distinction, which are the Flying Post, Mr. Dunton, and the author of the Crisis [Steele]. The first of these seems to have been much sunk in reputation, since the sudden retreat of the only true genuine original author, Mr. [George] Ridpath, who is celebrated by the Dutch Gazetteer as one of the best pens in England. Mr. Dunton hath been longer and more conversant in books than any of the three, as well as more voluminous in his productions: however, having employed his studies in so great a variety of other subjects, he hath, I think, but lately turned his genius to politicks. His famous tract, intituled *Neck or Nothing,* must be allowed to be the shrewdest piece, and written with the most spirit, of any which hath appeared from that side since the change of the Ministry: it is indeed a most cutting satire upon the Lord Treasurer and Lord Bolingbroke; and I wonder none of our friends ever undertook to answer it. I confess, I was at first of the same opinion with several good judges, who from the style and manner suppose it to have issued from the sharp pen of the Earl of Nottingham; and I am still apt to think it might receive his Lordship's last hand."[73]

Dunton was certainly a most voluminous writer, as he seems to have had his pen always ready, and never to have been at a loss for a subject to exercise it upon. Though he generally put his name to what he wrote, it would be a difficult task to get together a complete collection of his various publications. As containing notices of many persons and things not to be found elsewhere, they certainly have their use; and his accounts are often entertaining.]]

[Editor's note: Nichols added the following note as comment on the *"six hundred* Treatises," after which his text resumes.]

[This dipper into a *thousand* books formed *ten thousand* projects, six hundred of which he appears to have thought he had completely methodized. His mind seemed to be like some tables, where the victuals have been

---

72. See *A Tale of a Tub,* ed. Herbert Davis (Oxford, 1957), p. 35.
73. See *Political Tracts: 1713-1719,* ed. Herbert Davis and Irvin Ehrenpreis (Oxford, 1953), pp. 31-32.

ill-sorted, and worse dressed.] To which is added, *Dunton's Farewell to Printing,* in some serious Thoughts on those Words of Solomon, 'Of making many Books there is no End; and much Study is a Weariness of the Flesh.' With the Author's Effigies, to distinguish the original and true Copies from such as are false and imperfect. Take care also of being cheated by Wooden Cuts: the right is that which is drawn and 'graved by those two celebrated Artists, *Knight* and *Vander Gucht.* To this Work is prefixed an Heroick Poem upon Dunton's Projects, written by the Athenian Society; with an Alphabetical Table of the several Projects, Questions, Novelties, Poems, and Characters inserted in this Volume. Printed by Tho. Darrack; and sold by John Morphew. 1710."[74]

In the Preface to this volume, which breathes all the pride of self-consequence, he informs his readers, that he does not write to flatter, or for hire.

As a specimen of the better parts of this performance, take the characters of three eminent Divines, of whom some memoirs have been given already.

[Editor's Note: Dunton's verse characterizations of George Stanhope, Benjamin Hoadly, and Robert Moss, quoted at length by Nichols, are omitted. Two of Nichols' notes to the last sentence of text above are quoted following this interpolation, along with an addition to the first note.]

[[First note:] Other subjects are, 1. "The Funeral of Mankind, a paradox proving we are all dead and buried." 2. "The Spiritual Hedge-hog; or, a new and surprising Thought." 3. "The Double Life, or a new way to redeem Time, by living over to-morrow before it comes." 4. "Dunton preaching to himself; or every man his own Parson." 5. His "Creed, or the Religion of a Bookseller," in imitation of Browne's Religio Medici, has some humour and merit. This he dedicated to the Stationers Company.]

[[Addition to first note by John Bowyer Nichols, *Illustr.,* VIII, 540:] The subjects here noticed were five out of thirty-five projects which Dunton promised to give in his second volume of *Athenianism,* which probably was never published.]

[[Second note:] As a satirist, he appears to most advantage in his Poems, intituled, "The Beggar mounted;" "The Dissenting Doctors;" "Parnassus hoa! or Frolics in verse;" "Dunton's Shadow, or the character of a Summer Friend." Throughout the whole of his writings, however, he is exceedingly prolix and tedious, and sometimes obscure. His "Case is altered, or Dunton's Re-marriage to his own Wife,"[75] has some singular notions, but very little merit in the composition.]

This volume [*Athenianism,* the last item under discussion before the

---

74. Vol. I of *Athenianism* was published in 2 pts., 1710, 8o, and no other volumes were published. See *Brit. Mus. Cat.*.
75. See entry for this work (1701, 12o) under Dunton in the *Brit. Mus. Cat.*.

interpolations], on the whole, is a strange mixture of sense and folly; containing some good articles in prose and verse, a few of a licentious turn, and some deeply tinctured with insanity; a misfortune under which Dunton appears to have long laboured.

12. Dunton published, after this, "An Appeal to Her Majesty, with a List of his Political Pamphlets;" of which a copy is in the British Museum.[76]

I find no farther particulars of him till Oct. 17, 1723, when he advertised the volume noticed below; which I have never seen. He survived till 1733; and died at the age of 74.

[[Nichols' note to the above:] *"Upon this Moment depends Eternity:* or, Mr. John Dunton's serious Thoughts upon the present and future State, in a Fit of Sickness that was judged mortal; in which many new Opinions are started and proved; in particular this, That the sincere practice of known Duties, or dying daily to this Life and World, would of itself resolve the most ignorant Person in all the abstruse Points of the Christian Religion—being a new Directory for holy living and dying; composed of the Author's own Experience in Religion, Politicks, and Morals, from his Childhood to his Sixty-third Year (but more especially during his dangerous Disease in Ireland in the Year Ninety-eight, when his Life was despaired of); and completed in Twenty Essays upon such nice and curious points in Divinity as were never handled before. To which is added, the Sick Man's Passing-Bell, to remind all Men of that Death and Eternity to which they are hastening. Containing, 1. God be merciful to me a Sinner; or, Dunton at Confession; in which he discovers the secret Sins of his whole Life; with his Resolution in what penitent Manner (by the help of God) he'll spend the short Time he has yet to live. 2. Dunton's Legacy to his native Country; or, a dying Farewell to the most remarkable Persons and Things both in Church and State; with his last Prayer (or those very Petitions to Almighty God) with which he hopes to expire. 3. A living Man following his own Corpse to the Grave: or, Dunton represented as dead and buried, in an Essay upon his own Funeral. To which is added (for the Oddness and Singularity of it) a Copy of his last Will and Testament. His living Elegy, wrote with his own Hand; and the Epitaph designed for his Tombstone in the new Burying-place. Together with, 4. The real Period of Dunton's Life; or, a Philosophical Essay upon the Nature of that Grand Climacteric Year Sixty-three, in which (as few Persons outlive that fatal Time) he expects to be actually buried with the best of Wives Mrs. Elizabeth Annesley *alias* Dunton; with their Reasons for sleeping together in the same Grave till the general Resurrection; as contained in two Letters that passed between Mr. Dunton and his Wife a few Days before she died. The whole Directory and Passing-Bell submitted to the impartial Censure of the Right Reverend

---

76. Probably the work to which Nichols refers is under Dunton in the *Brit. Mus. Cat.* as "An appeal to his majesties most gracious promise of never forgetting those that have distinguished themselves in his service; or the humble Petition of John Dunton. . . . *etc.* (With a list of his political pamphlets, against the Pretender.) (London, 1730?) 4o."

Father in God William Lord Bishop of Ely. By Mr. John Dunton, a Member of the Athenian Society, and Author of the Essay intituled, 'The Hazard of a Death-bed Repentance.'

> We are all seiz'd with the Athenian Itch,
> News, and New Things do the World bewitch.
>
> Dr. WILDE.[77]

Printed for S. Popping in Paternoster-row, price 1s. 6d."]

[Editor's note: In his life of Dunton in the DNB, Leslie Stephen wrote, "Dunton also advertised in 1723 a volume, the enormous title of which begins 'Upon this moment depends Eternity;' it never appeared." A "first part," however, is entered in the British Museum Catalogue, with the shelf-mark G. 14056. The entry ends, "No more published."

Following this interpolation is a note on Dunton, written by John Whiston and quoted by John Nichols in *Lit. Anec.*, I, 506. John, a bookseller, was a younger son of William Whiston, of whom Nichols has a memoir in ibid., 494-506.]

[*John Dunton,* an eminent Printer and Author among the Dissenters, and a great Projector, and ruined himself thereby. He wrote a book which he called his "Life and Errors;" very candidly confessing them. He gives an account of his dealing in trade; and intersperses the characters of the most eminent Booksellers from 1670 to 1700. It is an entertaining work. Those whom he speaks in particular very well of are, [Richard] Chiswell, [James] Knapton, [R.] Knaplock, [Daniel] Browne senior, [Richard] Grafton, &c.]

[Editor's note: The following is from "Additions and Corrections" to p. 59, *Lit. Anec.*, V, 696.]

[To the numerous Works of John Dunton, may be added, 1. "The Preaching Weathercock,"[78] written against Wm. Richardson, once a Dissenting Teacher, 8vo.—2. "Mordecai's Memorial; or, There's nothing done for him; a just Representation of unrewarded Services,["][79] 1716, 8vo.—3. "Kainopholos," a curious rhapsody; noticeable (Mr. D'Israeli informs me) for its extreme rarity, and for two elegant pieces of poetry, which, if John's own, entitle him to a higher degree of praise than he has been usually thought

---

77. In *Illustr.*, VIII, 540, John Bowyer Nichols has the correction: "for 'WILD,' r. 'WILDE.'" The index to *Lit. Anec.* identifies him as Dr. Robert Wilde, author of "Iter Boreale."
78. 1712; see *Brit. Mus. Cat.* under Dunton.
79. I have not been able to identify this.

to merit. It is obscurely noticed in his "Life and Opinions;" but the Anagram of the Author's name prefixed to a copy of verses declares him. It has a frontispiece, which is a large folding cut, with 24 circles, exhibiting the Author's adventures.]

[Editor's note: In "Additions to the Fifth Volume," *Lit. Anec.*, IX, 631, is a note by Nichols to the above.]

[I have been favoured, by Mr. D'Israeli, with the following particulars of the scarce Tract noticed in this page [V, 696]:
"The publication of John Dunton, you will recollect, though transmitted by me, is not mine; it was the communication of a well-known literary Friend, who trusted to his memory.—I have at length examined the Work; and, had it not been already mentioned, it would deserve no further notice. It turns out to be one of those seven books, out of six hundred, which Dunton repents of publishing. It is intituled, 'A Voyage round the World; or, a Pocket Library, divided into several Volumes; the first of which contains the rare Adventures of *Don Kainophilus,* from his Cradle to his 15th Year, 1691.'[80] To the Work are prefixed Panegyrical Verses, 'by the Wits of both Universities,' who, however, offer no evidence of their residence or their quality; and may be suspected to be Wits of the University of Grubstreet. One of these wretched panegyricks tells us that 'the Author's name, when anagrammatised, is *hid unto none,*' by which *John Dunton*E would, and would not, conceal himself. These volumes were published in our Scribbler's thirtieth year, on his return from America; and are, in fact, a first essay towards that more mature 'Life and Errors' which he gave the World in 1705. He seems to have projected a series of what he calls 'The Cock-rambles of all my Four and Twenty Volumes;' but his readers, probably, deserted him at the third. *Kainophilus,* as he calls himself, 'signifies *a Lover of News,* not any thing of *Kain,* as if I were a-kin to him.' It is a low rhapsody; but it bears a peculiar feature, a certain whimsical style, which he affects to call his own, set off with frequent dashes, and occasionally a banter on false erudition. These cannot be shewn without extracts; and your volumes must not admit of such trifles. I would not add an idle accusation to the already injured genius of STERNE; but I am inclined to think he might have caught up his project of writing Tristram's life, in 'twenty-four Cock-rambling' volumes; have seized on the whim of Dunton's style; have condescended even to copy out his breaks and dashes. But Sterne could not have borrowed wit or genius from so low a scribbler.

"The elegant pieces of poetry were certainly never composed by Dunton, whose mind had no elegance, and whose rhimes are doggrel. On a rapid

---

80. See Wing, III, 431, Entry V742; see also *Brit. Mus. Cat.* under Dunton.

inspection, I have detected him transcribing from Francis Osborn and Cowley, without acknowledgment; and several excellent passages, which may be discovered amidst this incoherent mass, could not have been written by one who never attained the slightest arts of composition. He affects, however, to consider himself as 'a great Original' in what he calls 'this hop-stride-and-jump round the World;' and says, 'So great a glory do I esteem it to be the *Author* of these *Works,* that I cannot, without great injury to myself and justice, endure that every one should own them, who have nothing to do with them; like the fellow at Rome who pretended to Virgil's Verses. But I need take no other way to refute these *plagiaries* than *Virgil* himself did, requiring the tally to his *Vos non Vobis*. Let any man write on at the rate this is already written, and I will grant he is the Author of this book, that before, and all the rest to the end of the Chapter. No; there is such a sort of a *Whim in the Style,* something so like myself, so incomprehensible (not because 'tis nonsense), that whoever throws but half an eye on that and me together, will swear 'twas spit out of the mouth of Kainophilus. This by the bye.'["] I. D'I. *July,* 1812.]

Bernard Lintot

[The most important part of the life that follows is taken from *Lit. Anec.,* Vol. VIII (1814). In Vols. I and II (1812) Nichols has a good deal of information regarding Lintot, for the most part desultory and in conformity with the popular opinion, in particular with the opinion handed down by Johnson in his life of Pope. It is evident that Nichols' opinion of Lintot underwent a change between 1812 and 1814. In the earlier volumes he joined to some extent in the jesting at Lintot, but later he took a stand in defense of a maligned character.[1] A life of Bernard Lintot, signed Peter Cunningham, and an article on the "Family of Lintot," signed Mark Antony Lower, are in the *Sussex Archaeological Collections* (London, 1856), VIII, 276. The material concerning Bernard Lintot and his immediate family in Lower's article is derived almost wholly from Nichols, though there is no acknowledgement of indebtedness. The life of Lintot in the DNB by George A. Aitken relies heavily upon Nichols and lists him as a source. The new information which Nichols sought and found regarding Lintot between 1812 and 1814 probably was acquired, at least partially, as a result of the letter to the *Gentleman's Magazine* with which the life below begins. Nichols' insertion of such letters by himself in his magazine was his habitual way of soliciting help.

The British Museum has a letter from Lintot to a Mr. Parker on his disappointment at not being chosen King's Bookseller, 15 October 1714 (Stowe Mss. 750. f. 72); and Harvard University Library holds two of his publisher's agreements. Brief accounts of Lintot occur in a number of works concerning the bookselling trade in the eighteenth century: e.g., in Henry Curwen, *A History of Booksellers* (London, 1873), pp. 33-38; William Roberts, *The Earlier History of English Bookselling* (London, 1889), pp. 188-214; Edward Marston, *Sketches of Some Booksellers of the Time of Dr. Johnson* (London, 1902), pp. 56-71; Charles Knight, *Shadows of the Old Booksellers* (New York, 1927), pp. 94-99; and J. A. Cochrane, *Dr. Johnson's Printer* (Harvard University Press, 1964), p. 39. These accounts are largely derived from Nichols and his sources.]

MR. URBAN   MARCH 10 [1813]

BERNARD LINTOT, the celebrated Bookseller, immortalized by Pope and Swift, after having many years been the Rival of Jacob Tonson, retired, about the year 1730, to the enjoyment of an easy fortune, very honourably acquired, to Horsham in Sussex. In November 1735 he

---

1. A. S. Collins, in *Authorship in the Days of Johnson* (London, 1926), pp. 41-42, chose to interpret charitableness of this type in Nichols as "that typical bias which we have to discount in his judgments" and as "that bias favourable to the trade," though I believe he does not produce evidence to indicate that Nichols' facts are incorrect.

was appointed High Sheriff of that County, but died on the 3d of February following, before he had actually entered on the duties of the office; to which his son, Henry Lintott, esq. was appointed in his room, February 5, 1735-6.[2] Henry died in the year 1758; his widow in 1763; and their only daughter, Catharine, was married in 1768, with a fortune of £45,000, to Captain Henry Fletcher, afterwards Sir Henry Fletcher, bart.

Any further particulars of either of the Lintotts, or their Epitaphs, either at Horsham or elsewhere, would be a favour conferred on.

BIOGRAPHICUS.[3]

Of these very respectable Booksellers [Bernard and Henry Lintot], Father and Son, the little that is known being principally through the dense and partial medium of "The Dunciad," I feel a peculiar pleasure, as a Brother of the Craft, in endeavouring to vindicate their memories.

"BARNABY BERNARD LINTOTT,* son of John Lintott, late of Horsham in Sussex, yeoman," [born 1 December 1675] was bound apprentice, at Stationers' Hall to Thomas Lingard, Dec. 4, 1690; turned over to John Harding 169..; and made free, March 18, 1699.† He soon after commenced business, as a Bookseller, at the sign of the Cross Keys, between the Temple Gates, where he was patronized by many of the most eminent Writers of a period which has been styled the Augustan age of English Literature.

The earliest Work published by him that at present occurs to recollection is a volume intituled *Examen Miscellaneum.* . . . He published some of Dryden's Poems singly; and several, afterwards, for Lady Chudleigh, Pope, Gay, Farquhar, Dr. King, Fenton, and Parnell. . . .

In 1708 he was called on by the Company of Stationers, to take upon him their livery.

In 1709 he published, but without a date, "Oxford and Cambridge Miscellany Poems: chiefly written by Mr. Fenton, Mr. Prior, Mr. Charles Hopkins, Mr. Philips, Mr. Gardiner, Sir John Denham, Lord Halifax, Dr. Sprat, Dr. Yalden, . . . and Mr. Warmstry." Of this volume Mr. Fenton was avowedly the Editor, as appears by his Dedication. . . .

In 1712 he published a similar volume, under the title of "Miscellaneous Poems and Translations by several Hands;

---

* This was the name under which he was bound apprentice; but he soon dropped *Barnaby;* and after some years, wrote Lint*o*t with a single *t* at the end. NICHOLS.

† He was Renter-warden in 1715; elected into the Court of Assistants 1722-3; and served the office of Under Warden in 1729, and again in 1730; but died before the Upper Wardenship came to his turn. NICHOLS.

2. This, of course, would be 1736 by the new style of dating introduced at the time of calendar reform in 1752. When double years are given hereafter for a date falling between 1 January and 25 March, the later year should be taken as the correct one under our present calendar.

3. *Gent. Mag.,* 83:200 (March 1813). "Sylvanus Urban" was the title adopted by the first editor of the magazine, and it was continued by each successive editor.

"Multa Poetarum veniet manus, auxilio quae Sit mihi." HOR.

The Volume contains two copies of verses addressed to Bernard Lintot, on the publication of the Miscellanies; one of them, as it afterwards appeared, and as indeed the *last line* would prove, by Swift, who afterwards enlarged them:[4] the other by a nameless but not inelegant Bard, perhaps Dr. William King of the Commons.[5]

In 1712-13 Mr. Lintot's name occurs among the generous Benefactors to Mr. Bowyer after his loss by fire. (See Vol. I. p. 61)[6]

In 1714 he reprinted his "Miscellanies;" and thus displayed the names of the several Writers. "Miscellaneous Poems and Translations by several Hands; particularly, 'The First Book of Statius his Thebais translated:' 'The Fable of Vertumnus and Pomona, from the Fourteenth Book of Ovid's Metamorphoses;' 'To a young Lady, with the Works of Voiture;' 'On Silence;' 'To the Author of a Poem intituled *Successio*;' 'The Rape of the Lock, an Heroi-comic Poem;' 'An Ode for Musick on St. Cecilia's Day;' 'Windsor Forest, to the Right Hon. George Lord Lansdown;' 'An Essay on Criticism.'—'BY MR. POPE.'—The Second Edition. London; printed for Bernard Lintot between the Two Temple Gates in Fleet Street; and William Lewis, in Russel Street, Covent Garden, 1714."

I have given the full title of this volume for various reasons. It shews the estimation in which the name of POPE was held even at that early period. The name of that great Poet, it may be objected, is placed in the Title-page *ad captandum*, as if he were the actual Editor of the Work, an idea which he afterwards affected to discountenance.[7] It is plain, however, that he must

---

4. These lines, "*Verses designed to be prefixed before* BERNARD LINTOT's *New Miscellany*, 1712," are reprinted fully by Nichols in *Lit. Anec.* from his earlier editions of Swift, of whose works Nichols brought out the first fairly complete edition. Sir Walter Scott, who borrowed much text and many notes from Nichols, likewise included the verses to Lintot in his edition of Swift's works. I cannot find these verses, however, in *The Poems of Jonathan Swift*, ed. Harold Williams (Oxford, 1958); they are not among the genuine works nor are they listed with the "Poems Attributed to Swift." The last six lines of the poem are:

> But Lintot is at vast expence,
> And pays prodigious dear for—sense.
> Their [other publishers'] books are useful but to few,
> A scholar or a wit or two;
> Lintot's for general use are fit;
> For some folks read, but all folks****.

5. This poem ends, "So long shall live thy Praise in Books of Fame, / And *Tonson* yield to *Lintot's* lofty Name."

6. William Bowyer, the Younger, had been Nichols' employer and, later, partner.

7. Nichols' opinion that Pope actually edited the *Miscellanies* was earlier voiced by Addison; see *The Works of Alexander Pope*, ed. W. Elwin and W. J. Courthope (London, 1871-1889), I, 11, n. 1. Pope, writing to Christopher Pitt, had made an ambiguous statement on the subject in a letter dated 23 July 1726. Regarding this, Norman Ault, in his *New Light on Pope* (London, 1949), p. 38, says: "This disclaimer of Pope's, for whatever reason made, has generally been taken at its face value to mean that his connection with 'Lintot's Miscellany' was as temporary and slight as it seems to suggest. But on examination it is seen actually to deny irrelevant things like reviewing, recommending, and some proof-correction; and the word 'publisher' having several meanings, even at that date, a

have consented to the publication of the several Poems above enumerated; a circumstance which the name of Mr. William Lewis (Pope's early Friend) tends also to confirm. Nor had Pope any reason to be ashamed of the company in which he was introduced—Dryden—Bate—Swift—Gay—Broome—Southcote—Edmund Smith—Fenton—Betterton, &c. &c.

In the same year, 1714, Mr. Lintot entered into a very liberal agreement with Mr. Pope, for his Translation of Homer's Iliad; the printing of which was soon after begun by Mr. Bowyer, and diligently attended to by all parties.—Mr. Gay, in a Letter to Congreve, April 7, 1715, facetiously says, "Mr. Pope's Homer is retarded by the great rains that have fallen of late, which causes the sheets to be long a-drying. This gives Mr. Lintot great uneasiness; who is now endeavouring to engage the Curate of the Parish to pray for fair Weather, that his work may go on." The progress of the publication, and the loss sustained by Lintot, has been fully detailed in the First Volume of these "Anecdotes," pp. 77, 78, 109.[8]

It has been there observed [i.e., in the pages referred to at the end of the preceding paragraph], from Dr. Johnson,[9] "that the subscribers were 575; and the copies for which subscriptions were given were 654." To this I am enabled to add, from original documents, that the bargain with the subscribers (of printing no more copies in quarto than were actually engaged for) was so strictly complied with, that the number printed in that size was only 660. By the manner in which the Folio Edition of this Work is mentioned by Dr. Johnson, it might be supposed to have been a fraudulent transaction on the part of Mr. Lintot.[10] But the slightest inspection of the Advertisement copied in vol. I. p. 110. will shew that the Folios were printed on paper of two sizes, with the full concurrence of the Translator, and with the sanction of a Royal Patent; the smaller at 12s. a volume, the Royal paper at a Guinea. The number which was printed of the first volume was 250 large and 1750 small—but of the subsequent Volume, the number on small paper was only 1000.

---

repudiation of that office in its connotation of bookseller might, if carefully left undefined, seem to cover any or all of the others—editor, author, owner of copyright, or what not. Such a quibble might serve Pope's immediate purpose with a comparative stranger like Pitt; but it can avail little in face of the foregoing evidence, all of which testifies that Pope spoke no more and no less than the truth in his letter to his friend Broome when, referring to the collection known as 'Lintot's Miscellany', he called it simply 'my Miscellany.'" In addition to proving that Pope actually edited each successive edition of *Lintot's Miscellany*, Ault in another work, *Pope's Own Miscellany* (London, 1935), p. li, shows how Pope edited and inserted anonymous pieces of his own in another miscellany published by Lintot, the extremely rare *Poems on Several Occasions* of 1717. As this publication proved a failure, Pope transferred pieces from it to the successful *Lintot's Miscellany*.

8. The loss suffered by Lintot was caused by the importation from Holland of a pirated duodecimo edition.

9. In *Lit. Anec.*, I, 77-78, Nichols reproduces a part of Johnson's life of Pope concerning the relations of Pope and Lintot.

10. Johnson had said that Lintot had perpetrated "a fraud of trade" by impressing the same pages as used for the quarto on folio pages and selling these for half the price of the quartos (which were to be printed for subscribers only). Later, Johnson says, the buyers of the folios cut the excess paper off to make the folios look just like the quartos.

In 1715–16 we find Mr. Lintot pursuing his profession on the frozen River Thames:

"In this place *Bowyer* plies; there's *Lintot's* stand."[11]

Mr. Lintot afterwards published "Poems on several Occasions, by his Grace the Duke of Buckingham, Mr. Wycherly, Lady Winchelsea, Sir Samuel Garth, N. Rowe, esq. Mrs. Singer, Bevil Higgins, esq. and other eminent Hands, 1717;" without any Introduction or Preface; but dedicated by "Mr. Fenton," to "the Earl of Orrery."

Bernard Lintot‡ was appointed, with Jacob Tonson and William Taylor, by the Hon. Spencer Compton, then Speaker of the House of Commons, to be one of the Printers of the Votes; and so continued till 1727. . . .

There does not appear to have been any altercation between the Bookseller and the Author during the whole period of the publication of the *Iliad* or *Odyssey,* which continued till 1725; but, from whatever cause it may have arisen, the friendship between Mr. Pope and his Publisher appears to have terminated with the conclusion of Homer.

In an *undated* Letter, addressed by Mr. Pope to the Earl of Burlington about that period, his description of his old friend *Bernard Lintot* is given with the most exquisite humour.[12] "I know of nothing in our language," says Dr. Warton, "that equals it, except, perhaps Mr. Colman's description, in a *Terrae Filius,* of an expedition of a Bookseller and his Wife to Oxford."[13]

Perhaps Mr. Pope conceived that Lintot had risen *above his proper level;* for it appears that early in 1726, having, by successful exertions in business, acquired a decent competence, and made some additions to his paternal inheritance in Sussex, he was desirous of tracing the origin of his family; and for that purpose consulted Humphrey Wanley, who had then the custody of the Earl of Oxford's Heraldic MSS. and in whose Diary is the following memorandum: "Young Mr. Lintot the Bookseller came enquiring

---

‡ *Joshua Lintot* had a similar appointment jointly with Jacob Tonson, Timothy Goodwin, and John Roberts, from 1708 till 1710, whilst Sir Richard Onslow was Speaker. NICHOLS.

11. Nichols wrote in *Lit. Anec.,* I, 118: "In the severe frost of January and February 1715-16, the river Thames was one solid block of ice; and shops of almost every description were erected on its surface. Amongst these, printers and booksellers were also found pursuing their profession."

12. At the end of the memoir of Lintot, Nichols added some corrections and additions (*Lit. Anec.,* VIII, 304) which begin with this statement: "I shall take this opportunity of adding some Notes on the *undated* Letter from Mr. Pope to the Earl of Burlington, p. 170; which must have been written between September 1715, when Lord Lansdown was committed to the Tower, and February 1716-17, when he was released." The letter, which Nichols quoted in full as a note to the text, is in *The Correspondence of Alexander Pope,* ed. George Sherburn (Oxford, 1956), I, 371-375, where it is conjecturally dated November 1716.

13. *Terrae Filius* of George Colman, the Elder, was issued from Oxford in four numbers, 5-8 July 1763.

after *Arms,* as belonging to his father, mother, and other relations, who now, it seems, want to turn *gentlefolks*. I could find none of their names."§

Mr. Pope, in a letter to Mr. [Christopher] Pitt, on the subject of his Translation of Vida, July 23, 1726, says,

. . . . But as to my being the publisher, or any way concerned in reviewing or recommending of "Lintot's Miscellany," it is what I never did in my life, though he (like the rest of his tribe) makes a very free use of my name. He has often reprinted my things, and so scurvily, that, finding he was doing so again, *I corrected the sheets as far as they went, of my own only;* and, being told by him that had two or three copies of yours (which you also had formerly sent me, as he said, through his hands,) I obliged him to write for your consent before he made use of them. This was all: your second book he has just now delivered to me, the inscription of which to myself I will take care he shall leave out; and either return the rest of your verses to him, or not, as you shall like best. . . .||

Mr. Pope had at this period undoubtedly conceived a very ill impression of his *quondam* Bookseller; and in 1727 vented his indignation without mercy in the "Dunciad." His principal *delinquency,* however, seems to have been, that he was a stout man, clumsily made, not a very considerable Scholar, and that he filled his shop with *rubric posts*. Against his benevolence and general moral character there is not even an insinuation. In the First Book, he is thus ungraciously introduced,[14]

> Hence Miscellanies spring, the weekly boast[15]
> Of Curll's choice press,[16] and Lintot's rubric post.

§ Arms were granted, 1723, to *Tho. Lintot,* of Wadhurst. NICHOLS. (From additions at end of memoir of Lintot, VIII, 304. Many entries from Wanley's Harleian Journal are published by Nichols in *Lit. Anec.,* I, 86-94.)

|| Mr. Christopher Pitt, Mr. Broome, Mr. Fenton, Mr. Walter Harte, and Mr. Somervile, *condescended* (as Mr. Pope had done before them) to receive liberal payments for their several contributions to Lintot's "Miscellanies." See pp. 294. 296. 301 [of *Lit. Anec.,* Vol. VIII, where Nichols has reproduced many pages from Lintot's account books.] NICHOLS. (From additions at end of memoir of Lintot, VIII, 304. This letter, of which part is given here, is in Sherburn, *Correspondence of Pope,* II, 382-383. The text here, including the italics, is from Nichols. See above, n. 9, for Ault's statement regarding Pope's deliberately misleading ambiguity in this letter.

14. Even so ardent an admirer of Pope as Edith Sitwell has nothing but good to say of Lintot for his part in the publication of the *Iliad*. She wrote, in her *Alexander Pope* (New York, 1930), pp. 129-130: "It is pleasant to think that Lintot, the publisher (who was usually referred to in Pope's letters, as 'that fool,' as though there were no other fool), behaved with real courage and generosity in this enterprise." The quarrel between Pope and Lintot arose, in reality, out of the publication of the *Odyssey,* and for two reasons. In the first place, Lintot objected to supplying free copies to Broome's as well as to Pope's subscribers. The agreement called for copies to be given only to Pope's subscribers, but Pope encouraged William Broome to collect subscriptions and told him that he could have the money for himself. This was Pope's way of paying for part of Broome's services to himself out of Lintot's pocket. The second phase of the quarrel was over the large share of the translation done by Broome and Elijah Fenton (twelve of the twenty-four books) and the consequent loss in the commercial value of the whole *Odyssey*. See Johnson's lives of Broome and Fenton and Elwin-Courthope, *Works of Pope,* VIII, 94-95nn.

15. Nichols' reading of this line is that of the later *Dunciad;* earlier versions read: "Hence springs each weekly Muse, the living boast," etc.

16. For a discussion of the significance of Edmund Curll as a biographer see "Early

On which the learned Annotator[17] remarks, that "The former was fined by the Court of King's Bench for publishing obscene Books; the latter *usually adorned his shop with titles in red letters.*["]

In the Race described in the Second Book of the Dunciad, in honour of the Goddess of Dulness, Lintot and Curll are entered as Rival Candidates:

> But lofty Lintot in the circle rose:
> "This prize is mine; who 'tempt it are my foes;
> With me began this genius, and shall end."
> He spoke: and who with Lintot shall contend?
> Fear held them mute. Alone, untaught to fear,
> Stood dauntless Curll; "Behold that Rival here!
> The race by vigour, not by vaunts, is won;
> So take the hindmost, Hell!" (he said,) and run.
> Swift as a Bard the Bailiff leaves behind,
> He left huge Lintot, and out-strip'd the wind.
> As when a dab-chick waddles thro' the copse
> On feet and wings, and flies, and wades, and hops;
> So lab'ring on, with shoulders, hands, and head,
> Wide as a Windmill all his figure spread,
> With arms expanded Bernard rows his state,
> And *left-legg'd Jacob* seems to emulate.[18]

The remaining part of the description (in which Curll, after escaping from a *dirty* accident, outstripped his competitor) I forbear to copy—sanctioned by the authority of Dr. Warton, who pronounces it to be "as nauseous as it is stupid, though Warburton defends it by a note if possible more nauseous."[19]

Bernard Lintot appears to have soon after relinquished his business to his son Henry; and to have retired to Horsham in Sussex; for which county he was nominated High Sheriff in November 1735; an honour which he did not live to enjoy; as his death happened Feb. 3, 1735-6, at the age of 61. In the Newspapers of the day he was styled "Bernard Lintot, esq. of the Middle Temple, late an eminent Bookseller in Fleet-street."[20]

Henry Lintot, his only son, was born about August 1709; was admitted to the freedom of the Company of Stationers, by patrimony, Sept. 1, 1730;

---

lives of the Poets" in Walter Raleigh, *Six Essays on Johnson* (Oxford, 1927), pp. 116-117. Nichols did not know, of course, of the very involved use Pope had made of Curll in the publication of his letters. For a discussion of the early phases of the quarrel between Pope and Curll see *The Prose Works of Alexander Pope*, ed. Norman Ault (Oxford, 1936), I, xciv ff. Nichols misreads "choice" for "chaste" in this line of the couplet.

17. The "learned Annotator" of this note was Pope himself, though Nichols may have supposed it written by William Warburton.

18. "Left-legg'd Jacob" is Jacob Tonson, the publisher whom Dryden described as having two left legs. Again, Nichols' text for the lines quoted here is that of the later *Dunciad* with some punctuation variations of his own.

19. The note defending the passage in the *Dunciad* was written not by Warburton but by Pope himself, and the objection that both passage and note were "nauseous" was made by W. L. Bowles.

20. See, e.g., an entry for 3 February under "A List of Deaths for February, 1736," in the *Gent. Mag.*, 6:111 (misnumbered 55; February 1736).

obtained the Livery the same day;‡ and from that time their business was carried on in the joint names of Bernard and Henry; but the Father passed the principal part of his time in Sussex.—Two days after the death of Bernard, Henry was appointed High Sheriff for that county, where his residence was at Southwater, in the Rape of Bramber, about two miles from Horsham.—He married, first, Elizabeth, daughter of Sir John Aubrey, Bart. of Llantrythed in Glamorganshire, (whose mother was Margaret, daughter of Sir John Lowther, Bart.); by whom he had an only daughter and heiress, Catharine, who was married, Oct. 20, 1768, (with a fortune of 45,000*l.*) to Captain Henry Fletcher, at that time a Director of the East India Company. —Mr. Linton married, secondly, Philadelphia ――, by whom he had no issue. He died in 1758; and his widow Jan. 31, 1763.[21]

Many Months after the article on the LINTOTS (pp. 161-176) was printed off, the unwearied researches of Mr. D'Israeli brought to light a small Memorandum-book of those enterprizing Booksellers, intituled, "Copies when purchased;" and, from this document, his "Quarrels of Authors" are illustrated by some very interesting particulars respecting Mr. Pope and other Writers.[22] But the plan of his publication not admitting of *minutiae* which may be pardonable in these desultory pages; I am tempted (by the permission of Mr. [James] Nunn, the present Owner of the MS.) to enter

---

‡ He obtained the patent of Law Printer about 1748; and in 1754 was elected into the Court of Assistants of his Company. (The following addition to this note occurs in VIII, 304.) Miss Catharine Lintot, after her Father's death, was Joint Patentee, with Mr. Samuel Richardson, in the office of "Law Printer to his Majesty."—They were succeeded by the late Henry Woodfall and William Strahan, esqrs. NICHOLS.

21. This ends the main account of the life of Lintot in *Lit. Anec.*, VIII, 161-176. That which follows is a later addition to the same volume, pp. 293-304.

22. Isaac D'Israeli's *Quarrels of Authors* was issued in 1814, the same year in which Nichols published Vol. VIII of *Lit. Anec.* D'Israeli's work is reviewed in the *Gent. Mag.* for April 1814, and Nichols' in the issue for June. Each acknowledged the help of the other. D'Israeli wrote in his preface: "Of my old and respected friend Mr. JOHN NICHOLS, who has devoted a life to Literature, and who aided the researches of Johnson, it is no common gratification for me to add, that he has even as zealously, aided mine." Nichols listed D'Israeli among the contributors to Vol. VIII of *Lit. Anec.* in his "Advertisement" to the volume. There is specific evidence that Nichols and D'Israeli assisted each other in delving into the relationship between Pope and Lintot. D'Israeli, for example, uses some of Nichols' own phrasing from Vol. VIII, and D'Israeli's book was published several months before Nichols', indicating that D'Israeli had access either to Nichols' manuscript or to certain printed pages before they were published. Regarding *Lintot's Miscellany*, D'Israeli wrote: "Mr. NICHOLS has obliged me by supplying the title—'Miscellaneous Poems and Translations, by several Hands, 1712.'—The second Edition appeared in 1714; and in the title-page are enumerated the Poems mentioned in this account; and Pope's name affixed, as if he were the actual Editor;—an idea (adds Mr. Nichols) which he affected to discountenance. It is probable that POPE was the Editor. We see, by this account, that he was paid for his contributions." "An idea which he afterwards affected to discountenance" is Nichols' own wording. Nichols was printer of D'Israeli's *Quarrels of Authors* of 1814. This example of mutual assistance is included here because it illustrates the kind of relationship that existed between Nichols and nearly all other anecdotists and antiquarians of his day. This relationship of Nichols with others illustrates, in turn, the great interchange among writers typical of the whole eighteenth-century antiquarian movement.

more particularly into its Contents; and the rather, as a considerable number of the Books enumerated were produced from Mr. Bowyer's press.

The period which, from conjecture, I had assigned for Lintot's commencing business is literally accurate; the earliest Copies which he purchased appearing to be three different Works of Toland, in 1701–2. In July he purchased "Love and Business; in a Collection of occasional Verse and Epistolary Prose, not hitherto published," and "A Discourse on Comedy, in reference to the English Stage. In Fourteen Letters. By George Farquhar." In November he bought a share in Cibber's "Last Shift;" employed Mr. Gildon as Editor of the "Examen Miscellaneum;" and from that period, till the time of his quitting business, he was a very considerable Purchaser, as the following List of his Copies (some of which were *Old Works* bought from his Brethren of the Trade) may testify. For the sake of readier reference, I place them in alphabetical order.

[Over 11 pages of the account book are reproduced at this point by Nichols. After his printing of this material, the original account book itself disappeared, leaving Nichols the only authority for many of these entries, since only a few were used by D'Israeli. Fifty-three of Nichols' 206 entries are given below by way of illustration.]

BETTERTON.

			£	s.	d.
1712,	April 7.	The Miller's Tale, with some Characters from Chaucer	5	7	6

BROOME.

1726-7,	Feb. 22.	Miscellany Poems	35	0	0

Mr. CIBBER

1701,	Nov. 8.	A Third of Love's Last Shift	3	4	6
1705,	Nov. 14.	Perolla and Izadora	36	11	0
1707,	Oct. 27.	Double Gallant	16	2	6
——	Nov. 22.	Lady's last Stake	32	5	0
——	Feb. 26.	Venus and Adonis	5	7	6
1708,	Oct. 9.	Comical Lover	10	15	0
1712,	Mar. 16.	Cinna's Conspiracy	13	0	0
1718,	Oct. 1.	The Nonjuror	105	0	0

Mr. DENNIS

1703,	Feb. 24.	Paid Mr. George Strahan, Bookseller, for Half Share of "Liberty Asserted"	7	3	0
1708,	Nov. 10.	Appius and Virginia	21	10	0
1711,	April 25.	Essay on Public Spirit	2	12	6
——	Jan. 6.	Remarks on Pope's Essay	2	12	6

Mr. Farquhar.

			£	s.	d.
1701,	July 3.	Letters and Poems	3	4	6
1702,	Dec. 22.	Twin Rivals	15	0	0
1705,	Feb. 12.	Recruiting Officer	16	2	6
1706,	Jan. 27.	Beaux Stratagem	30	0	0

Mr. Fenton.

1716,	Oct. 14.	Paid Mr. Fenton for his Miscellanies	21	10	0
——	——	Paid more for the said Miscellanies	13	4	3

Mr. Gay.

1713,	May 12.	Wife of Bath	25	0	0
1714,	Nov. 11.	Letter to a Lady	5	7	6
1715,	Feb. 14.	The What d'ye call it	16	2	6
——	Dec. 22.	Trivia	43	0	0
——	——	Epistle to the Earl of Burlington	10	15	0
1717,	May 4.	Battle of the Frogs	16	2	6
——	Jan. 8.	Three Hours after Marriage	43	2	6
		Revival of the Wife of Bath	75	0	0
		[The Mohocks, a Farce, 2*l*. 10*s*.—Sold the Mohocks to him again.]	£234	10	0

Mr. Gildon.

1701,	Nov. 15.	For Examen Miscellaneum	5	7	6

Harte.

1726,	Nov. 18.	Mr. Harte's Miscellaneous Poems	30	0	0

Mr. Pope.*

1712,	Feb. 19.	Statius, First Book	16	2	6
		Vertumnus and Pomona			
1712,	Mar. 21.	First Edition of the Rape	7	0	0
1712,	9 April.	To a Lady presenting Voiture Upon Silence	3	16	6
		To the Author[23] of a Poem called *Successio*†			

---

* These purchases from Mr. Pope sufficiently vindicate Lintot from the coarse sarcasm of Warburton in Vol. II, p. 165 (of *Lit. Anec.*) Nichols. (This refers to a letter from Warburton to William Bowyer: "You will oblige me with telling me that beast Lintot's steps. I would do him all reason while he acts with decency and justice, and shall never print any part of his property with my Notes and Commentary without his leave; but if he acts like a rogue, I have but one word with him, the Chancery and Mr. Murray.")

† "These anonymous lines," Mr. D'Israeli judiciously observes, "appear to be a literary satire by Pope, written when he had scarcely attained his fourteenth year. . . ." See in the "Quarrels of Authors," vol. I. p. 302, Pope's Satire on Settle. . . . [Settle's poem "The Succession" was] Written in June 1702, when the Act of Settlement was passed in consequence of the Duke of Gloucester's death. Nichols.

23. Elkanah Settle was the author of this poem.

			£	s.	d.
1712-13,	Feb. 23.	Windsor Forest	32	5	0
1713,	July 23.	Ode on St. Cecilia's Day	15	0	0
1714,	Feb. 20.	Additions to the Rape	15	0	0
——	Mar. 23.	Homer, vol. I	215	0	0
		650 Books on Royal Paper	176	0	0
1715,	Feb. 1.	Temple of Fame	32	5	0
1715,	April 3.	Key to the Lock	10	15	0
1716,	9 Feb.	Homer, vol. II	215	0	0
1716,	May 7.	650 Royal Paper	150	0	0
——	July 17.	Essay on Criticism	15	0	0
1717,	Aug. 9.	Homer, vol. III	215	0	0
1718,	Jan. 6.	650 Royal Paper	150	0	0
——	Mar. 3.	Homer, vol. IV	210	0	0
		650 Royal Paper	150	0	0
——	Oct. 17.	Homer, vol. V	210	0	0
1719,	April 6.	650 Royal Paper	150	0	0
1720,	Feb. 26.	Homer, vol. VI	210	0	0
1720,	May 7.	650 Royal Paper	150	0	0
1721,	Dec. 13.	Parnell's Poems	15	0	0
		Paid Mr. Pope for the Subscription-money due on the Second Volume of his Homer; and on his Fifth Volume, at the Agreement for the said Fifth Volume.—(I had Mr. Pope's Assignment for the Royal Paper that were then left of his Homer)	840	0	0
		Copy-money for the Odyssey, Volumes I. II. III.; and 750 of each Volume printed on Royal Paper, 4to.	615	6	0
		Copy-money for the Odysey [sic], Volumes IV. V.; and 750 of each Volume, Royal	425	18	7½
			£4244	8	7½

N. Rowe, Esq.

1713,	Dec. 12.	Jane Shore	50	15	0
1715,	Apr. 27.	Jane Grey	75	5	0

Settle.

1711,	Sept. 8.	The City Ramble	3	10	0

Sir Richard Steele.

1703–4,	June 11.	Lying Lovers	21	10	0

David Henry

[Nichols' memoir of David Henry is from *Lit. Anec.*, III, 423-426; and this was taken, with only small changes: rearrangements and minor additions, from Nichols' obituary of Henry in the *Gentleman's Magazine*, reprinted as an obituary of June 1792 in *A Selection of Curious Articles from the Gentleman's Magazine,* ed. John Walker (London, 4 vols., 1814), IV, 390-392.

David Henry was the second editor of the *Gentleman's Magazine*, succeeding his brother-in-law, Edward Cave, the founder. Appropriately, Henry wrote Cave's epitaph (*Lit. Anec.*, V, 58). Nichols became associated with Henry in the management of the magazine in 1778 and took over the editorship completely in 1791, shortly before Henry's death in 1792.

Henry was instrumental in the preservation and publication of a number of Johnson's letters to Edward Cave. "Of these eleven letters," wrote Nichols in a note, *Lit. Anec.*, V, 18, "nine of the originals are in the possession of Miss Cave, great-niece of Edward. The other two were given by Mr. Henry to Thomas Astle, esq. and by him communicated to Mr. Boswell." In the text above this note, Nichols wrote that these letters, which he reproduced in full in *Literary Anecdotes,* were "first through my intervention communicated to the publick."

A few of Henry's letters to Nichols are in the great collection of Nichols materials in the Special Collections of Columbia University Library, and two of these will be inserted into Nichols' memoir (including the very important and, I think, hitherto unknown one in which he turned the editorship of the *Gentleman's Magazine* over to Nichols.

There is no life of Henry in the DNB.]

DAVID HENRY, ESQ. was born in the neighbourhood of Aberdeen, Dec. 26, 1710; "of a family," to use his own expressive words in a letter which Death prevented his finishing, "more respected for their good sense and superior education than for their riches; as at every neighbouring meeting of the gentlemen they were amongst the foremost. . . . I left both country and friends," he adds, "before the age of 14; and may be truly said never to have seen either since, if by *friends* are meant assistants."

[[Nichols' addition (*Lit. Anec.*, III, 759):] Mr. Henry was born at a place called Fovron, about 16 miles from Aberdeen. As his father lived in a genteel style, and was at great pains to instruct his children, young Henry was put to the college of Aberdeen, but left it, and went to London, in his 14th year, much to his father's regret, being a favourite son, and it was the old man's wish that he should be a clergyman. Several of his relations, desirous also to try their fortune, went to America, where they acquired considerable property; and in Virginia, where several of them are settled, their name is held in reverence.—Patrick Henry, esq. son of John Henry (a first cousin of our printer) was the first governor of Virginia after the late memorable revolution, and next in fame there to Washington.]

Mr. Henry was literally the artificer of his own fortune. His inclinations having fixed him in the profession of a Printer, and a concurrence of circumstances placing him within the notice of Mr. Edward Cave, an universal encourager of merit, he favoured our young Printer with his protection; and in 1736 Mr. Henry became related to his patron, by marrying his sister, Miss Mary Cave. About this period he lived in habits of intimacy with the celebrated Dr. [Benjamin] Franklin and the late Mr. [William] Strahan, who, like himself, were both at that time Journeymen Printers. Soon after his marriage, Mr. Henry commenced business at Reading, where he established a provincial newspaper, for the use of that town, and of Winchester, where he had likewise a printing-office. In 1754 we first find his name used in the Gentleman's Magazine as a partner at St. John's Gate, where he continued to reside for many years with great reputation; and he possessed the freehold property of the Gate and its appurtenances at the time of his death, which happened at Lewisham, June 5, 1792, in his 82d year; after having for more than half a century taken an active part in the management of the Magazine; in which the most painful portion of the labour is the frequent occasions that occur of lamenting the loss of those whom we more particularly esteem. In this class our late very worthy Associate might with great sincerity be ranked.

[Editor's note: Two letters concerning the management of the *Gentleman's Magazine,* sent by Henry to Nichols (and preserved in the Nichols collection of manuscripts at Columbia University), follow, after which the text of Nichols is resumed.]

    Dear Sir
    I think on the most serious Consideration that 750 of the Gen Index will be fully sufficient to answer all Demand.
    I thank you for your offer of printing the whole at your own Risque, but I should be unworthy of such Generosity, were I to accept it. Live or die I or those who succeed me shall share in the Loss, Gain there can be none but the Credit of acting honourably by our Customers.
    I think the printing may be contracted—but of this at Leisure. Hope M^{rs} N's Cold wears off favourably, and am Sir
                                               Yours friendly
June 26th [17]87   DH

Dr Sir [1791]

Finding myself unfit for the Business of the Magazine and sensible how much I trespass on your Time and Patience in supplying my Defects, I beg leave to commit the whole and entire managem{t} of it with the Salary anexd into your Hands, in sure and certain hope of seeing it flourish in greater Perfection from the Improvem{t} it will receive from an abler Compiler.

My Infirmities are such and so many that I dare not trust myself alone in London, till it shall please the Giver of all good Things to restore me to better Health. When that time comes, if ever it should come, I shall not fail to embrace the Opportunity to pay you my most grateful Acknowledgm{t}, and in the mean time to do my best to supply the Press till the Hurry of yr Business shall be so far abated as to allow you full time to make Choice of an Assistant, if you should think such a one necessary. Then, when things are settled to your Mind, and you should have half a Day to spare it will gratify me much to see You and Family at Lewisham to eat a Bit of South-down Mutton with the Family of

Sir   your most assured Friend   D. Henry.

His literary labours would reflect much credit on his memory if an accurate list of them could be obtained; but his modest merit ever disclaimed the just praise which talents and industry like his deserved. The only printed volume, that we recollect, which bears his name, was an admirable compilation (whilst he lived at Reading) under the patronage of Dr. [Theophilus] Bolton, Dean of Carlisle, intituled, "Twenty Discourses on the most important Subjects, carefully abridged from the Works of the late Archbishop [John] Tillotson, and adapted to the meanest Capacities, with a View to their being dispersed by those who are charitably inclined;" of which a second edition was published in 1763, a fourth in 1779. "The motive," says Mr. Henry, "that I had to abridge these most valuable compositions was, that I might spread them, that I might make them the more easily purchased, and thereby the more generally read. Few of my readers are likely to acknowledge the pains I have taken. Praise, indeed, of any kind, is not to be expected from a work of this nature. The most it has to hope is, that it may escape censure. If I have furnished any occasion for a just one, I have this to say in my excuse, that no care was wanting in me to avoid it."

Those useful and popular publications which describe the curiosities in Westminster Abbey, St. Paul's Church, and the Tower of London, were originally compiled by Mr. Henry; and had been improved by him through many successive impressions.*

* Mr. *John Newbery,* many years a respectable Bookseller in St. Paul's Church-yard,

One of the principal amusements of his life was the study of Agriculture, which he understood from practice as well as theory. During his residence at Reading, the management of his newspaper occasioned him many long journeys, in all which he treasured up great stores of useful information; and, on his quitting St. John's Gate, he occupied a considerable farm at Beckenham in Kent. The result of these observations he gave to the publick, in 1772, under the title of "The complete English Farmer; or, a Practical System of Husbandry; in which is comprised a general View of the whole Art of Husbandry;" but from this he withheld his name, as he did also from "An Historical Account of all the Voyages round the World, performed by English Navigators," 1774, in four volumes, 8vo, of which the first and second were compiled by Mr. Henry; the third and fourth by another hand; to which, in 1775, Mr. Henry added a fifth, containing Capt. Cooke's Voyage in the Resolution; and in 1786 a sixth, containing the last Voyage of Capt. Cook; introduced by an admirable summary of all the Voyages undertaken for *discovery only,* in both the Southern and Northern Hemispheres, and in the Pacific and Atlantic Oceans. Of the more immediate productions of his pen in the Magazine, the enumeration would be endless; but I may be allowed to suggest, that in every line he wrote is demonstrated a rectitude of heart, and a soundness of understanding, particularly in the general politicks of every quarter of the globe, that will not easily be surpassed; and that his death, though at a ripe old age, was truly lamented by all who had the happiness of his acquaintance. By himself it was foreseen with a confidence which the *mens conscia recti* alone could inspire. With a look of inexpressible benevolence, not many hours before his departure, he squeezed the hand which now records his loss, declaring his entire resignation to the divine pleasure. "My death-warrant," he said, "is signed; and I have no dread of dissolution. Why should we fear?" Then, calmly reclining back his head, he placidly repeated, "I will lie down, and die."

His remains, attended by a small party of select friends (amongst whom was one who now records his history), were placed, on the 13th, in the vicar's vault under the church of Lewisham.

Mr. Henry, after having been almost nine years a widower, and having also lost one only daughter, married secondly, in 1762, Mrs. Hephzibah

---

is characterized by the late Sir John Hawkins as "a man of good understanding, and of great probity."—"He suggested (as Mr. Chalmers observes, in his Preface to The Idler) the plan of many useful compilations for the young, or those who had more curiosity than leisure to read; and generally employed men of considerable talents in such undertakings." Many now living may perhaps remember the pleasure they derived from Mr. Newberry's little books, for "masters and misses," of some of which he was the reputed author. Among the best of these may be reckoned the brief Histories of the Tower of London, of St. Paul's Cathedral, and of Westminster Abbey, all compiled by David Henry, esq. and of which several large editions were rapidly sold; and "The World Displayed," to which Dr. Johnson wrote an historical introduction. . . . NICHOLS. (*Lit. Anec.,* III, 731-732.)

Newell;† who survived him till Feb. 2, 1808; when she closed a long life, passed in acts of beneficence, at the age of 82. She died at Charlton in Kent, and was buried at Lewisham.

Richard Henry, Esq. an only son by the second marriage, entered early in life into the military service of the East India Company; and died unmarried, Dec. 27, 1807, having at that time acquired the rank of Major.

His only sister, Hephzibah, is the wife of Mr. F. Hommey, Master of the well-known Military Institution at Charlton.

---

† The first husband of this lady (whose maiden name was Appletree) was the well known and respectable master of the old Jerusalem Tavern in Clerkenwell, by whom she had one daughter, still living, the wife of Mr. John Bonnycastle, a name well known in the Republick of Letters as the Author of many valuable scientific publications, and Principal Mathematical Master of the Royal Academy at Woolwich. NICHOLS.

(In "Additions to the Third Volume," *Lit. Anec.*, VIII, 446-447, there is the following additional information:)

Mrs. Henry (formerly Mrs. Newell) had two children when she married Mr. Henry, a son and a daughter. The former, who was lame both in person and conduct, died a young man; the daughter married, as you truly say, Mr. Bonnycastle.

Thomas Davies

[Thomas Davies had the unique privilege of introducing James Boswell to Samuel Johnson on 16 May 1763. The event occurred in the "back-parlour" of Davies' book shop in Russell Street, Covent Garden; and is as much responsible as anything Davies did during his lifetime for the preservation of his memory.

Nichols' life of Davies comes primarily from *Lit. Anec.*, VI, 421-443, though, as should be expected, there are numerous references to him elsewhere in the writings of Nichols. Nichols was personally acquainted with Davies (they were fellow members of a booksellers' club) and he preserved some of Davies' correspondence. Nichols' memoir of Davies is the source of most of the material in such lives of Davies as appear in books about the eighteenth-century book trade: for example, Edward Marston's *Sketches of Some Booksellers of the time of Dr. Samuel Johnson* (London, 1902), pp. 28-44; Charles Knight's *Shadows of the Old Booksellers* (New York, 1927), pp. 227-229; or the brief sketch in Plomer, Bushnell, and Dix's *Dictionary of the Printers and Booksellers who were at work in England Scotland and Ireland from 1726 to 1775* (Oxford University Press, 1932), pp. 71-72. Leslie Stephen's life of Davies in the DNB also relies heavily upon Nichols, who is listed first among the sources.

Quite a large number of manuscripts of Davies' letters are divided among various collections. The Osborn Collection at Yale contains three of Davies' letters: one to James Granger, one to James Robertson, and one to Robert Dodsley in which he offers to sell him shares in the new edition of Beaumont and Fletcher (c. 1780). Yale's Beinecke Library has an autograph letter from Davies to an unidentified recipient, 19 August 1775, bound with Boswell's *Life of Johnson* (London, 1874), IV, after p. 400 (shelfmark Im, J637, +W791gh). A number of Davies items are in the Bodleian and in the British Museum: for example, there are "Notes and Corrections for a new contemplated edition of the History of English Poetry," sent from Davies to Thomas Warton (Add. Mss. 42,561. ff. 236-237); there is also a letter from Davies to Willis, 23 November 1736 (Add. Mss. 5829. f. 47b). The Folger Shakespeare Library has a letter from Davies to Garrick (W.b. 473) and a facsimile of another and several other letters of Davies to various people. In the Harvard University Library are four Davies letters and two other items. Columbia University's Special Collections holds a letter from Davies to W. J. C. Miller.]

Mr. THOMAS DAVIES, a man of uncommon strength of mind, who prided himself on being through life a companion for his superiors, was born in or about the year 1712. In 1728 and 1729 he was at the University of Edinburgh, completing his education; and became, as Dr. Johnson used to say of him, "learned enough for a Clergyman."[1]

Mr. Davies imbibed very early a taste for theatrical pursuits; and in 1736 his name occurs among the Dramatis Personae of Lillo's celebrated tragedy of "Fatal Curiosity," at the Theatre in the Haymarket; where he was the original performer of young Wilmot; under the management of Henry Fielding.

In a short time he commenced Bookseller, in Duke's-court, opposite the church of St. Martin in the Fields; and afterwards in Round-court, near the Strand; but met with misfortunes in trade, which induced him to return to the stage; and on the 24th of January 1746, "Venice Preserved" was acted for his benefit at Covent-Garden Theatre; when, as the play-bill says, the part of Pierre was *attempted* by him. Not succeeding, probably, to his hopes on a London stage, he became an itinerant, and performed at York; where he married Miss Yarrow, daughter of an actor there, whose beauty was not more remarkable than her private character was ever unsullied and irreproachable. He also performed at Edinburgh (where he appears to have been the Manager of the Theatre) the characters of Romeo, Richard III. and Ranger.

[[Nichols' note:] During the period of Mr. Davies's performance at Edinburgh, his superiority seems to have given umbrage to some of his brethren, as appears by the following undated hand-bill:

To the Publick.
"Habeo, quae possunt Fabium delassare loquacem,
Sed pauca nunc sufficient."

Whereas Mr. Davies, in the *Caledonian Mercury* of the 26th of last month, *insinuated,* that his playing the principal characters in Tragedy proceeded from *sad necessity:* In order that the Publick should not be so grossly imposed on, it is hoped they will take the following facts, all of which can be justly attested, into consideration; and then judge, whether his playing some principal characters proceeded from his *ambition* or *necessity.* . . .

'Tis surprizing to think, that a man who publicly confesses he is not a Performer, should before every Character he plays say, that such a part is to be performed by Mr. Davies;* neither can he, nor will he, suffer any man's name to be printed in the Bills within a size or two of his, lest it should take off from the merit of his *attempt.*

THEATRICUS.

*My kind and very intelligent friend Mr. F. G. Waldron, to whom I am

---

1. Johnson said, "Sir, Davies has learning enough to give credit to a clergyman." See Hill-Powell, *Boswell,* IV, 13.

indebted for this curious morsel of theatrical history, observes, that this was "a customary mode formerly of aggrandizing an actor."

NICHOLS.]

He then went to Dublin; and, with his wife, performed several characters there.

In 1753 he came, with his wife, to Drury-lane Theatre; and, on Mr. Havard being taken ill, appeared first in the character of Stukely, in Moore's tragedy of "The Gamester." Here Mr. and Mrs. Davies remained several years, in good estimation with the Town, and played many characters, if not with excellence, at least with propriety and decency.

In his "Dramatic Miscellanies" he thus modestly speaks of his own performance on a particular occasion: "When sickness deprived the stage of this valuable man (Mr. Edward Berry), Mr. Garrick called the Writer of this Miscellany to represent the character of Gloster (in the tragedy of 'King Lear'); the candour of the audience gave him much more encouragement than he expected."

In the same entertaining Work he thus speaks of his wife: "Mrs. Davies, during Mrs. Cibber's illness, was invited to supply her place. But she did not pretend to imitate that which was not to be attained by imitation, the action, voice, and manner of Mrs. Cibber. Mrs. Davies's figure, look, and deportment, were esteemed to be so correspondent with the idea of this amiable character (Cordelia in King Lear), that she was dismissed with no inconsiderable degree of approbation."

Churchill's indiscriminate satire, in the "Rosciad"[2] endeavoured to fix some degree of ridicule on Mr. Davies's performance; but the pen of a Satirist is not entitled to implicit credit. It, however, had the ill effect, Dr. Johnson said, of driving this respectable performer from the stage.[3]

[[Nichols' note:] The following correspondence, which appeared in the public Newspapers in September 1761, between Mr. *T. Davis* and Mr. Churchill, the former deprecating an apprehended satirical attack from

---

2. With him came mighty Davies.—On my life,
   That Davies hath a very pretty wife!
   Statesman all over!—In plots famous grown!—
   He mouths a sentence, as curs mouth a bone.
                 (*Rosciad*, 11. 319-322)

3. "After he [Tom Davies] went away, Johnson blamed his folly in quitting the stage, by which he and his wife got five hundred pounds a year. I said, I believed it was owing to Churchill's attack upon him,
      'He mouths a sentence, as curs mouth a bone.'
JOHNSON. 'I believe so too, Sir. But what a man is he, who is to be driven from the stage by a line? Another line would have driven him from his shop.'" Hill-Powell, *Boswell*, III, 223.

the latter, was not from our worthy bookseller, but from a Comedian of inferior talents. . . .[4]]

In 1762, a few years before he finally quitted the Theatre, he resumed his former occupation of a Bookseller, in Russel-street, Covent Garden.

[Editor's note: Davies' resumption of bookselling was most likely his real reason for leaving the stage, though both Churchill and Garrick were blamed for his departure. Davies wrote as follows to Garrick in a letter dated 10 August 1763. The full letter, of which this is a part, is in *The Private Correspondence of David Garrick*, ed. James Boaden (London, 1831-1832), 2 vols., I, 162-163; a facsimile in Davies' handwriting of the part reproduced here is bound with Boswell's *Life of Johnson* (London, 1874), IV, in Yale's Beinecke Library (Im, J637, +W791gh) and placed above a picture of Davies' shop. The same facsimile is also in Folger's PN, 2598, G3, D3, 1781, Cage.

Sir
    Mr Johnson can remember that I declared to him above 12 Months since that I sho^d not have quitted the Theatre when I did, if your warmth of temper had not provoked me to it. At ye same time I own I told my friends that my motive for so doing was ye being unable to attend my shop & ye business of ye Stage together—
                                                            Thomas Davies[5]

For nearly a year before Churchill's attack in the *Rosciad,* which came out in March 1761, Davies had been advertising heavily in the *Public Advertiser* (e.g., 7 May, 23 May, and 5 June 1760) and elsewhere. The probability is that he had decided to become a bookseller before anything had been said or written against him by either Churchill or Garrick, that he had already given up the stage except for an occasional appearance, but that after the unkind words he gave up even occasional acting.]

In 1772 he collected and republished, in three volumes, the beautiful Pastoral Poems, &c. of William Browne;* who flourished in the reign of

---

* It is a great blemish in Davies's edition of "The Works of William Browne," that, owing to some oversight, or from their having been re-printed from an imperfect copy, the contents of three pages, 78, 79, and 80, and a couplet in page 81, of edition 1625, are wanting. They should follow page 99, in vol. I. of Davies's edition, 1772. *F.W.* (initials not identified by Nichols). NICHOLS.

4. The text of the correspondence given by Nichols is omitted because, as he informs us, the writer was not Davies.

5. See Garrick's reply to this letter in *The Letters of David Garrick,* ed. David M.

James I. and who was complimented with commendatory Verses by three of the best Pastoral Poets this nation has produced: Drayton, Jonson, and the unjustly contemned Wither.

He also re-published "The Poems of Sir John Davies; consisting of his Poem on the Immortality of the Soul; the Hymn of Astrea; and Orchestra, a Poem on Dancing: All published from a corrected Copy formerly in the Possession of W. Thompson, of Queen's College, Oxon. 1773," 12mo.

In the same year he was the editor of "Miscellaneous and Fugitive Pieces (by the Author of The Rambler), 1773," in two volumes, 8vo; to which was afterwards added a third Volume. In these volumes, Dr. Johnson is the prominent feature; but we meet in them likewise with the names of Garrick, Colman, Cradock, Goldsmith, Francklin, Lloyd, and others. Dr. Johnson was for a short time displeased at the publication; and his behaviour on that occasion is thus described by Mrs. Piozzi: "When Davies printed the Fugitive Pieces without his (Dr. Johnson's) knowledge or consent,[6] 'How,' said I, 'would Pope have raved, had he been served so!' 'We should never,' replied he, 'have heard the last on't, to be sure; but then Pope was a narrow man. I will, however,' added he, 'storm and bluster myself a little this time:'—so went up to London in all the wrath he could muster up. At his return, I asked how the affair ended. 'Why,' said he, 'I was a fierce fellow, and pretended to be very angry; and Thomas was a good-natured fellow, and pretended to be very sorry: so *there* the matter ended. I believe the dog loves me dearly. Mr. Thrale,' turning to my husband, 'What shall you and I do for Tom Davies? We will do something for him, to be sure.' "[7]

In 1774 he published "The Works of Dr. John Eachard, late Master of Catharine Hall, Cambridge. Consisting of the Grounds and Occasions of the Contempt of the Clergy; his Dialogues on the Writings of Mr. Hobbes; and other Tracts. A new Edition; with a Second Dialogue on the Writings of Mr. Hobbes, not printed in any former Edition; and some Account of the Life and Writings of the Author," 3 vols. 12 mo.[8]

"The Works of Mr. George Lillo; with some Account of his Life, 1775," 2 vols. 12 mo.

[[Nichols' note:] The lovers of the Drama are obliged to Mr. Thomas Davies, not only for an edition of the Works of the moral, the feeling, the

---

Little and George M. Kahrl (Harvard University Press, 1963), 3 vols., I, 382-383 (letter 313); see also letters 312, 314.

6. Nichols, in a note at this point, quotes from Boswell concerning Davies' publication of the *Fugitive Pieces*, citing "*Boswell's Life of Johnson, vol.* II. *p.* 273." See Hill-Powell, *Boswell*, II, 270-271.

7. The 4th edn. of Piozzi's *Anecdotes of the late Samuel Johnson* (1786) is reproduced in Hill, *Johnsonian Miscellanies* (Oxford, 1897), I, 141-350. See p. 184 for the episode quoted by Nichols. Essentially the same material is in *Thraliana*, ed. K. C. Balderston (Oxford, 1951), I, 164.

8. Nichols here gives a long biographical note on John Eachard.

natural, and the sensible George Lillo, but for a more critical and more perfect account of the life of that esteemed and popular Bard, than had before been given by any of our biographical compilers.—The world, as Dr. Davies remarks in his Dedication to Mr. Garrick, "is indebted to this Writer for the invention of a new species of Dramatic Poetry, which may properly be termed the inferior or lesser Tragedy."—We cannot better sum up the merits of this Writer as a Moralist, than in the Editor's words: "A love of truth, innocence and virtue, a firm resignation to the will of Providence, and a detestation of vice and falsehood, are constantly insisted upon, and strongly inculcated in all the compositions of honest Lillo."

Monthly Review, vol. LII. p. 54.]

[Editor's note: In 1775 also Davies wrote the following letter to an unidentified correspondent. The letter is from Yale University Library, where it is bound with Boswell's *Life of Johnson* (London, 1874), IV, after p. 400, shelfmark Im, J637, +W791gh:]

Dear Sir,   London 19 August 1775

Pardon me for saying that it does not become so open and generous a mind as you bear to be suspicious.

Pigeon assured me that he sent ye sheets you demanded, but could not get at them so soon as he could have wished. I stipulated that you should have 20 setts of your book in 8vo, so pray demand them. I am sure they will not be withheld. I am sorry you still retain some hard thoughts of Cadell, believe me he does not deserve them. I did not come to Town till last night or should have answer'd yours sooner. Mrs Davies & I have made a short tour in hopes to establish our health. We think our selves much better for ye journey.

If any difficulty arises about your share of books, pray let me know your complaint & I will certainly do all in my power to convince you how much I would consult your ease & pleasure.

                                        I am Dear Sir
                                        Your ever obliged
                                        & most obedient
                                        humble Servant
                                        Thomas Davies

In 1777, he was the Author of "The Characters of George the First, Queen Caroline, Sir Robert Walpole, Lord Hardwicke, Mr. Fox, and Mr. Pitt, reviewed. With Royal and Noble Anecdotes, and a Sketch of Lord Chesterfield's Characters," 12mo.

[[Nichols' note:] There are several entertaining *anecdotes* and *remarks* in this little pamphlet; and the ingenious Author appears to have written with great candour, and freedom from prejudice.
Monthly Review, vol. LIV. *p.* 436.]

"Some Memoirs of Henderson, 1778."
In 1779 he published "Some Account of the Life and Writings of Massinger; prefixed to a new and improved Edition of his Works," in 4 volumes, 8vo.

[[Nichols' note:] From the name subscribed to a short inscription of this Life to Dr. Samuel Johnson, "as a small but sincere tribute to his liberal and extensive learning, his great and uncommon genius, and his universal and active benevolence," we learn that the writer is Mr. Thomas Davies, who, as we remember, for his very generous treatment of the late Mr. [James] Granger, Dr. [John] Campbell said, was "not a bookseller, but a gentleman dealing in books." To this uncommon character we are glad to find that he has now added that of Author.
Gent. Mag., vol. XLIX. *p.* 88.]

A series of very curious Letters from Mr. Davies was inserted, by Mr. Malcolm, in "Letters between the Rev. James Granger, M.A. Rector of Shiplake, and many of the most eminent Men of his Time, 1805;" many of them highly characteristic both of Mr. Granger and Mr. Davies.

Not meeting with that success which his attention and abilities merited, Mr. Davies, in 1778, was under the disagreeable necessity of submitting to become a bankrupt; when, such was the regard entertained for him by his friends, that they readily consented to his re-establishment; and none, as he said himself, were more active to serve him, than those who had suffered most by his misfortunes. But all their efforts might possibly have been fruitless, if his great and good friend Dr. Johnson[9] had not exerted all his interest in his behalf. He called upon all over whom he had any influence to assist Tom Davies; and prevailed on Mr. Sheridan, patentee of Drury-lane Theatre, to let him have a benefit; which he granted on the most liberal terms. This event took place May 27, 1778; when Mr. Davies made his last appearance on the stage, in the character of Fainall, in Congreve's comedy of "The Way of the World," and acquitted himself to the satisfaction of his friends and the publick.

---

9. Nichols, in a note at this point, quotes from the *Life of Johnson*. See Hill-Powell, *Boswell,* I, 390-391.

In 1780, by a well-timed publication, "The Life of Mr. Garrick,"[10] in two volumes, which passed through four editions, he not only acquired considerable fame, but realized money.

[[Nichols' note:] It happened that, nearly at the time of its first publication, being then engaged in the former edition of these Anecdotes,[11] I had occasion to give some particulars of Mr. Garrick; and, studiously wishing to avoid all interference with what might in any degree be thought anticipating the novelty of Mr. Davies's volumes, I forbore to make extracts from them, confining myself principally to what had appeared in the "Biographia Dramatica" from the pen of Mr. Steevens;[12] a circumstance which gave offence to the nice feelings of a somewhat too susceptible mind, as I afterwards found by the following complaint:]

DEAR SIR, *Russel-street, Wednesday, April* 14 (1784).
I return your "Bibliotheca Topographica," with thanks; and beg you to lend me your "Anecdotes of Bowyer."[13]—You will please to recollect that the "Memoirs of Garrick" were published in 1780, and the "Anecdotes of Bowyer" in 1782.—By referring to the Index, you will find the article *Garrick*—you will there read how *T.F.* strains with all his nerves to prove, contrary to all evidence, that Mr. Garrick was an avaricious man. That he was a great oeconomist, no man denies; nor can any man be charitable or generous without that virtue.—In my next edition of Garrick I shall perhaps take notice of this malevolent remark.—You will also find that *T.F.* quotes the "Life of Garrick," merely to misrepresent a sentence, by an over-strained and ill-natured comment. I confess I was disappointed, not to find in your valuable Work, which I esteem an excellent monument of gratitude to a kind Master, a favourable mention of a Book you have always professed to approve.

I yesterday told you truly, that my "Miscellanies" were published with a view to secure a tolerable income to the partner of my life. And I am convinced that an unfavourable or cold account of them in a Magazine so well established as the Gentleman's would greatly hurt my present Book. And, farther give me leave to say, it would prevent my making any addition to the present volumes, should my health and spirits permit me to go on and complete my original intention.

To a Gentleman of your humanity I need say no more. I am, dear Sir,
Your most obedient servant, THO. DAVIES.
P.S. There are so many blots and interlineations in my letter, that, if I had time, I would write it over again. Pray excuse me.

He also published, "Dramatic Miscellanies, consisting of Critical Observations on several Plays of Shakspeare; with a Review of his principal

10. Nichols here again quotes from Boswell's *Life of Johnson* and from a review in the *Gentleman's Magazine*.
11. Nichols habitually refers to the *Biographical and Literary Anecdotes of William Bowyer* of 1782 as the "first edition" of *Literary Anecdotes*.
12. See n. 7 to the life of Steevens.
13. See n. 11, above.

Characters, and those of various eminent Writers, as represented by Mr. Garrick, and other celebrated Comedians. With Anecdotes of Dramatic Poets, Actors, &c. 1785." 3 vols. 8vo. A second edition appeared a few days only before his death.

[[Nichols' note:] On the "Dramatic Miscellanies" the Reviewer in the Gentleman's Magazine thus candidly delivered his opinion:

"The Life of Garrick we have already taken occasion to commend. Our theatrical Nestor, unimpaired by years, and animated by his subject, proceeds, in the present Work, to delineate the portraits of his theatrical compeers, and to comment on the productions of 'Nature's darling child.' In relating the Historiettes of the Theatre Mr. Davies excels; and his characters of the performers in general are amusing and impartial."

That this praise, however, was not deemed sufficient, appears by the following remonstrance:

SIR, *Russell-street, Sunday, May* 2, (1784).
I have read the Critique on my "Miscellanies" in the Gentleman's Magazine. I cannot be proud of the high rank in which I am there placed amongst authors. An old woman, who tells her stories fluently, with a pipe in her mouth, sitting by a winter's fire, may deserve as ample a panegyrick as the writer has bestowed on me. My pudding, I find, is not made all of plumbs—the Critick cries out for more Anecdotes. That is to say, he would not have me trouble myself about remarkable Observations upon Shakspeare, for of that species of writing, he ingeniously hints, I am not capable; by telling the Publick that *there is enough of them.*
Seriously I am concerned to see a man with an excellent heart, under the influence of one who is as well known for his treacherous and invidious conduct as the abuse of his ingenuity and abilities.
My remarks on authors have been approved by judges as well qualified to decide upon them as Mr. *T.F.* How could you suffer this man to shed his venom in some notes which he has been permitted to insert in your valuable "Anecdotes of Bowyer?" In the article *Garrick,* you neglected an opportunity to do that justice to my Life of the English Roscius, which I expected from one who loudly, and I hoped sincerely, commended it. But the Devil at your elbow prevented your kind intention. Honest Mr. [Isaac] Reed, under the same influence I believe, was hindered from doing me that justice his heart prompted him to; for though, in two or three places of his "Biographia Dramatica," he mentioned my "Life of Garrick," it was in so cold a manner, that my Book could receive no advantage from his notice. The cold distillation of Nightshade, composed by the poisoning Chemist, infected his Work in more places than I shall pretend to enumerate.
I am not discouraged by the sale of my "Miscellanies" to proceed in my remarks on Shakspeare.
I have hitherto treated *T.F.* more gently and politely than his behaviour to me has deserved. Be assured, in future, that I will not spare him. I dread neither his rancour, nor his power of writing.
When I have the pleasure to see you next, I will entertain you with two or three pretty stories of this worthy gentleman. I am, Sir, &c.
THO. DAVIES.

Wishing, if possible, to conciliate the irritability of an offended Author, the Reviewer was requested to revise his former article, which he did in these words: "On an attentive re-perusal of these volumes, we must again declare, that we are abundantly more pleased with the anecdotes they contain, than with the criticism, however excellent. Without the least derogation to the 'Antient Learning,' or 'Historical Information,' for which Mr. Davies has been (we do not say too highly) extolled, we still assert that his history of the heroes of the stage, including 'the manner in which great actors delivered particular passages,' is by far the most valuable portion of this entertaining book."

The whole of these uncomfortabe sensations in the mind of my very worthy, but in this instance somewhat too captious friend, arose from a supposition, which he had erroneously formed, that Mr. George Steevens was both the Reviewer in the Magazine, and the Writer of the Notes signed *T.F.;* when, in fact, he was neither the one nor the other. Nor had I myself at that time any power over the *Review*. The Writer of it (who made no secret of his name, and really wished to befriend Mr. Davies) was the Rev. John Duncombe.

The initials *T.F.* designated *Dr. Taylor's Friend,* now known to be the late Rev. George Ashby; whose short Notes on the Life of Garrick were written (as were nearly all the other Notes which he communicated) in the margin of the proof-sheets whilst they were preparing for the press.

With myself, personally, Mr. Davies continued on his usual friendly terms.

SIR, *Russel-street, Monday, Nov.* 15, 1784.
I return thanks for the "Anecdotes of Bowyer," a book replete with agreeable biography and literary amusement.
I have in my last edition of Garrick's Life answered, and I hope with temper, the acrimonious and malevolent remarks of *T.F.* upon the bounty of Mr. Garrick.   THO. DAVIES.]]

Mr. Davies was also the writer of essays without number, in prose and verse, in the St. James's Chronicle, and some other of the public newspapers.

The Compiler of the present Volumes knew Mr. Davies well; and for several years passed many convivial hours in his company at a social meeting; where his lively sallies of pleasantry were certain to entertain his friends by harmless merriment.

[[Nichols' note:] In this Society Mr. Davies originally started the idea of writing the Life of Mr. Garrick; and, encouraged by their approbation, he frequently produced, at their dinners, a small portion of his intended work, which he would read to them with much complacency, and not a little to their general information.

This pleasant Association originated in occasional evening meetings of a few Booksellers, at the Devil Tavern, Temple Bar. That house, however, having been converted into private dwellings, a regular club was held, once a week, at the Grecian Coffee-house; where I recollect with no small satisfaction many happy hours that passed in rational and improving conversation.

After a trial of three of four years, the evening club was changed to a monthly dinner at *The Shakspeare;* and truly proud was *honest Campbell,* in producing his prime bottles to a Literary Society, whom he justly considered as conferring celebrity on his house, and to whom he constantly devoted the *Apollo* Room.

This Club has been already mentioned in Vol. V. p. 324 (actually 325) . . .]

[Editor's note: The reference to *Literary Anecdotes* in the last sentence above provides the following:

[Though very far removed from the character of a *bon vivant,* he (James Robson) was a member of a monthly dining-club at the Shakspeare tavern; a society which the writer of this article can scarcely mention without emotions of the tenderest concern, as it brings to mind the many rational hours of relaxation it has afforded him, when congenial spirits, warmed not heated with the genuine juice of the grape, have unreservedly poured out their whole souls in Attic wit and repartee. But of this friendly band, after an association of about 35 years, Mr. Robson was nearly the last survivor! The late Mr. Alderman (Thomas) Cadell, with Messrs. James Dodsley, Lockyer Davies, Thomas Longman, Peter Elmsly, honest Tom Payne of the Mews-gate, and Thomas Evans of the Strand, were members of this society; from which originated the germ of many a valuable publication. Under their auspices, Mr. Thomas Davies (who was himself a pleasant member of the club) produced his "Dramatic Miscellanies," and his "Life of Garrick;" and here first were suggested the ideas which led to the publication of Dr. Johnson's invaluable "Lives of the most eminent English Poets."[14] The last time, however, that [Mr. Davies] visited them he wore the appearance of a spectre; and, sensible of his approaching end, took a solemn valediction. Poor Ghost! how it would comfort thee to know, that, at a subsequent meeting of thy sincere friends, the impression of thy last appearance was not eradicated; and that every breast heaved a sympathetic sigh, lamenting the loss of so excellent an associate!

He died May 5, 1785, aged about 73; for, in the Postscript to the second edition of his "Dramatic Miscellanies," published 1785, he mentions a circumstance which occurred, he says, when he was in his 73d year. He

---

14. Nichols was printer of the *Works of the English Poets* (1779-1781) and of the first and succeeding editions of Johnson's prefaces, collected from the *Works* and given the title *Lives of the Poets.*

was buried, by his own desire, in the vault of St. Paul Covent Garden; and the following lines were written on the occasion:

> Here lies the Author, Actor, Thomas Davies;
> Living, he shone a very *rara avis*.
> The scenes he play'd Life's audience must commend,
> He honour'd Garrick—Johnson was his friend.

Mrs. Davies, his widow, died Feb. 9, 1801.

[Nichols' addition to the foregoing (from *Lit. Anec.*, IX, 665) is reproduced below.]

Mr. T. Davies published a new Edition of Bolingbroke's Letters on the Spirit of Patriotism, &c. with a Dedication to Mr. Burke, dated Nov. 17, 1774, and a Preface by the Publisher, 1775. He also published Manilius with *Bentley's Notes*.

In his "Dramatic Miscellanies" he observes, that "he had part of his education at an University; and was through life a companion of his superiors.—About the year 1742," he adds, "I was smit with the desire of turning Author, and publishing a silly pamphlet (Qu. was this 'The Blackest Beast, a Poem, 1742?'); and, though a Bookseller myself, chose to have it come out at the famous Jacob Robinson's shop in Ludgate-street. [Ralph] Griffith[s] was brought up under this man, who was first a dealer in spectacles, afterwards a considerable Publisher; and then a learned Critick, for he printed a periodical Criticism on 'the Works of the Learned;' from which work, I suspect, R.G. [Ralph Griffiths] borrowed his hint of 'A Review.' Robinson was intelligent, and I conversed with him; but, being nearer of age to Griffith[s], I preferred his company and conversation to that of the old man. Many years after this, we were partners, with several others, men of superior abilities, in an Evening Paper; and for 16 or 17 years successively we dined together at least eight or ten times in a year."

In a Postscript, after complimenting the Writers in several of the Reviews and Magazines, for their "candid and generous panegyricks," he subjoins a strong Philippick against his old friend Dr. Griffith[s]; and, in an Appendix, anathematizes George Steevens for having withheld the Notes on Shakspeare with which Mr. Davies had furnished him, on the pretence "that the distribution of the Notes in the Edition of 1773 was lodged with Dr. Farmer; whose answer to a letter on that subject is here subjoined":]

Sir, March 2, 1785.
An accidental avocation has deprived me of the opportunity of giving you an answer by an earlier post. Give me leave to assure you, that though I have read your *printed* Notes on Shakspeare with pleasure, if not always

with conviction, and shall be glad to read more; yet I never saw, or asked to see, or was offered to be *shewn,* any manuscript Note of yours in my life. I hope this fully answers your question; and that you will believe me, Sir, your most obedient servant,

R. FARMER.

James Dodsley

[Nichols' brief biographical sketch of James Dodsley appears in *Lit. Anec.*, VI, 437-439, as a note (along with similar sketches of several other booksellers) on Thomas Davies and the club of booksellers to which he, Dodsley, Nichols, and others belonged.

A number of biographical sketches have been written of James Dodsley's more famous brother Robert, including one by Alexander Chalmers.

References and brief memoirs occur in a number of books about booksellers and the bookselling trade of the eighteenth century. There is, for example, a short account in Edward Marston, *Sketches of Some Booksellers of the Time of Dr. Samuel Johnson* (London, 1902), pp. 85-86, and a reference in Charles Knight, *Shadows of the Old Booksellers* (New York, 1927), p. 172. The highest tribute paid him occurs in J. A. Cochrane, *Dr. Johnson's Printer: The Life of William Strahan,* where the author writes, p. 33: "Perhaps the first publisher in the modern idiom was James Dodsley, who succeeded to his famous brother Robert's publishing and bookselling business in Pall Mall; it is recorded that he was the first man to sell only his own publications in his shop."

Quite a few of James Dodsley's letters and printing agreements exist in a number of repositories. His letter to Garrick of 26 January 1763, for example, is in the Folger Shakespeare Library. His agreement with Goldsmith for the publication of a proposed chronological history of the lives of eminent persons of Great Britain and Ireland, dated 31 March 1763, is in the British Museum (Add.Mss. 19022). The Beinecke Library and the Osborn Collection at Yale hold several letters from him and to him from Richard Graves, George Keate, Samuel Jackson Pratt, etc. (along with several publication agreements). The Harvard University libraries have seven letters to him.

There is no life of James Dodsley in the DNB.]

Mr. *James Dodsley* was the brother, the partner, and successor in business, of the late ingenious Mr. Robert Dodsley, of whom see [*Lit. Anec.,*] vol. II. pp. 374-376.

James Dodsley was very early in life invited by his brother Robert (who was 22 years older than himself) to assist him in business. Their father kept the free-school at Mansfield, Nottinghamshire; and, being very much respected, had also many other scholars of neighbouring farmers and gentlemen. He was a little deformed man; married a young woman of 17, at the age of 75, and had a child by this union at 78. Besides Robert and James, he had many other children. One son (named Avery) lived with the late

Sir George Savile, bart. and died in his service. Another, Isaac, lived as gardener with Mr. [Ralph] Allen, at Prior-park, and afterwards with Lord Weymouth, at Long Leate. Isaac was 52 years in these families, and may justly be named the father of the beautiful plantations at Prior-park and at Long Leate. He retired from the latter situation at 78, and died in his 81st year.

Mr. James Dodsley became an active and useful partner to his brother; in conjunction with whom he published many works of the first celebrity; "A Collection of Poems," "The Preceptor," "The Annual Register," &c. &c.

Robert quitted business in 1759; but James perservered in acquiring wealth by the most honourable literary connexions. In 1782 he suggested to the Rockingham Administration the plan of the tax on receipts; which, though troublesome to the trader, has been productive of considerable revenue to the state. A few years after (1788) he was nominated as a proper person to be sheriff of London and Middlesex; in excuse for which, he cheerfully paid the customary fine. It is worthy noticing, as a literary anecdote, that he sold no less than 18,000 copies of Mr. Burke's famous "Reflections on the French Revolution;" with considerable advantage both to himself and to the Author, to whom he made a very handsome compliment for the profits.

His property (which was estimated to be about 70,000l.) he gave principally to nephews and nieces, and their descendants; to some of them 800l. 3 per cents each, and to others 4 or 500l. each, in specific sums, or in higher funds: to each of his executors 1000l. These were Mr. Thomas Tawney, of Brooke's-place, Lambeth, who married a daughter of his brother Isaac; Mr. John Walter, of Charing Cross (with whom he had been in habits of friendship, Mr. Walter having served his apprenticeship with his brother Robert); and Mr. George Nicol, his Majesty's bookseller, in Pall Mall. To his attorney, Mr. Webster, 1000l.; to Mr. John Freeborn, who had been for several years his assistant in business, 4000l.; to his maid-servant 500l.; to his coachman 500l. and also his carriage and horses; to the poor of St. James's, Westminster, 200l. 3 per cents; and to the Company of Stationers, nearly 400l.

By a habit of secluding himself from the world, Mr. James Dodsley (who certainly possessed a liberal heart and a strong understanding) had acquired many peculiarities. He at one time announced an intention of quitting trade; but, in less than a fortnight, repenting the resolution, again advertised that he should continue in business, and re-solicited the favour of his friends. For some years past, however, he kept no public shop, but continued to be a large wholesale dealer in books, of his own copy-right. Of these a part, to the amount of several thousand pounds, was burnt by an accidental fire in a warehouse which he had not prevailed on himself to insure; but the loss of which he was philosopher enough to bear without the least apparent emotion; and, in the presence of the writer of this article, who dined with him before the fire was well extinguished, sold, to a gentleman in company, the chance of the fragments of waste-paper that might be saved, for a single hundred pounds. This agreement was not fulfilled, but the whole remainder was afterwards sold for 80 guineas. He kept a carriage many years; but studiously wished that his friends should not know it; nor did he ever use it on the Eastern side of Temple Bar. He purchased some years since an estate, with a small house on it, between Chiselhurst and Bromley; on the house he expended an incredible sum, more than would have re-built one of twice the size, which afterwards he rarely visited, and at length lett, with the estate, on a long lease, at a very low rent.

Though he often expressed his apprehension that the Law (if he should die intestate) would not dispose of his property as he could wish, he never could persuade himself to make a will till he was turned of 70; after which time he made four; the last of them Jan. 4, 1797, not long before his decease. He left every legacy clear of the tax, and appointed six residuary-legatees.

He was buried in St. James's church, Westminster; and in the chancel an open book of marble is inscribed,

> Sacred to the memory of JAMES DODSLEY,
> many years an eminent bookseller in Pall Mall.
> He died Feb. 19, 1797, aged 74.
> His body lies buried in this church.
> He was a man of a retired and contemplative turn of mind,
> though engaged in a very extensive line of public business.
> He was upright and liberal in all his dealings;
> a friend to the afflicted in general,
> and to the poor of this parish in particular.

[Editor's note: The following is from "Additions to the Sixth Volume," *Lit.* Anec., IX, 666.]

[I shall give one kind Billet from Mr. Dodsley:]

Sept. 23, 1795.

Mr. Dodsley presents his best compliments to Mr. Nichols, and has received Two Volumes of his History of Leicestershire, together with his very polite Note; which he is unable to answer in terms so elegant and flattering. He can only return his thanks, with a request, that, *though a Bookseller, he may pay for them as a Gentleman.*

[The following two letters were written in connection with Nichols' printing and Dodsley's publishing of *A Treatise on the Study of Antiquities* (1782) by Thomas Pownall. They appear in *Lit. Anec.,* VIII, 111. Omitted is a letter from Pownall to Nichols inquiring concerning the sale of another work, "With," say Nichols, "an anxiety not uncommon."]

Mr. Dodsley, *June* 30, 1782.

The person who corrects the press is so perfect a scholar, and so accurate in his attentions, that I not only think myself obliged to him, but shall take it as a particular favour, if, where he sees any *inaccuracy in the orthography* or *stopping,* or any intricacy in the *diction* of the sentences, he will be so good as to put, at least, his mark against such; or even correct them.

T. Pownall.

Mr. Nichols, *June* 30, 1782.

Your business, in the department of Printer and Corrector, is conducted by men perfect masters of their business; and well done. We shall, I see, perfectly understand one another. I return both the proofs; that which was *under correction,* and that which has been printed off *corrected.*

T. Pownall.

[Editor's note: This characterization of the accuracy of Nichols as a printer is in keeping with Edward Gibbon's addressing him in a letter as "to the last, or one of the last, of the learned Printers in Europe, a most respectable order of men." See *Lit. Anec.,* VIII, 557.]

Thomas Longman

[The Thomas Longman of whom Nichols has the following short note in *Lit. Anec.*, VI, 439, was another member of the booksellers' club which claimed Thomas Davies, Nichols, and others as members. The Thomas Longman of this note was a nephew of Thomas Longman (1699-1755), founder of the publishing house of Longman, and the father of Thomas Norton Longman, who carried on the business after the death of his father and became important as a publisher of the Romantic poets.

The most important study of the Longman family is that of Harold Cox and John E. Chandler, *The House of Longman, 1724-1924* (London, 1925). There are, of course, shorter accounts and references in nearly all books dealing with the history of publishing in England. A brief entry occurs, for instance, in H. R. Plomer, G. H. Bushnell, and E. R. McC. Dix, *A Dictionary of the Printers and Booksellers who were at work in England, Scotland, and Ireland from 1726 to 1775* (Oxford, 1932). A somewhat longer entry appears in Charles Knight, *Shadows of the Old Booksellers* (New York, 1927), pp. 233-234; and a fairly lengthy account is in Henry Curwen, *A History of Booksellers, the Old and the New* (London, 1873), pp. 79-109.

The Longman firm in the eighteenth century did an extensive business, and it is to be expected that many letters and business agreements survive. A few of these are mentioned by way of illustration. The Bodleian Library has two letters from Thomas Longman, one each to Joanna Baillie and H. Ellis; the Osborn Collection at Yale has a letter to Longman from John Calder and an agreement drawn up by him between himself and Longman and Strahan. The Harvard University Libraries possess two letters written by Longman, three letters to him, and four agreements and petitions.

Lives of the Longmans, including that of Nichols' subject (who was born in 1730), by Francis Espinasse are in the DNB, where of course are other biographical references.]

Mr. *Thomas Longman,* many years a considerable bookseller in Paternoster Row, was a man of the most exemplary character both in his profession and in private life, and as universally esteemed for his benevolence as for his integrity. He died at Hampstead, Feb. 5, 1797, aged 66; and was succeeded by a son of both his names; who, with a considerable portion of the well-earned wealth, inherits the good qualities of his father; and has carried on the business of a wholesale bookseller to an extent far beyond what was ever known in the Annals of *The Row.* Another son, George (M. P. for Maidstone), is of equal consequence as a wholesale stationer.

[Editor's note: Longman, as one of the proprietors of Chambers' *Cyclopaedia*, was involved in a scheme to have a new edition published, to be edited by John Calder. The history of this project is given by Nichols in a memoir of Calder, *Illustr.*, IV, 799-848. Below are a few excerpts from this history, particularly as Longman is involved. A great deal of interspersed correspondence is omitted, including some letters from Johnson, who became involved as an arbiter in the dispute.]

[One of the most important events of Dr. Calder's Literary Life was a contract which he made, in 1773, to prepare for the press a new Edition of Chambers's "Cyclopaedia." This project unfortunately terminated to the dissatisfaction of all parties, and was the cause of some unhappy years to Dr. Calder; and as the circumstance may possibly find a niche in a future Volume either of the "Quarrels" or the "Calamities of Authors," [works by Nichols' friend Isaac D'Israeli] some further account of it shall here be given. . . .

By a regular contract between Dr. Calder and the Proprietors of the Work, Oct. 29, 1773, it was stipulated that the Doctor should complete the new Edition of Chambers's Dictionary, begun by the late Dr. [Owen] Ruffhead, in the best manner he was able, and as soon as conveniently might be, according to his own written Proposal. . . .

Dr. Calder now began heartily to work on the new "Cyclopaedia," and, as was his usual custom, soon overstocked himself with materials; having secured the voluntary assistance of many persons eminent in various departments of science. . . .

In the beginning of 1776 the Work was so far advanced, that specimens of it was printed; and the first sheet, by general consent, was submitted to Dr. Johnson, who made many judicious remarks on it, which I possess in his own hand-writing. . . .

Mr. Longman, whose amenity of manners is pleasingly recollected by all who knew him, endeavoured in vain to mediate between Dr. Calder and the Proprietors. The breach was made; and after much epistolary altercation, the contract was wholly dissolved, and the Cyclopaedia placed in the hands of Dr. Abraham Rees, under whose superintendence it has since increased to 39 large quarto volumes, which has added much to his literary reputation, and not a little to the emolument of the Proprietors.]

Thomas Payne

[Nichols' brief memoir of Thomas Payne is taken primarily from *Lit. Anec.*, VI, 439-440, although there are references to him elsewhere in this same work, including a list of books published by him (III, 655-660). There are also a number of references to Payne in *Illustrations*.

Payne was another member of the booksellers' club referred to at greater length in the life of Thomas Davies. Comparatively little work has been done on his life, though short accounts occur, for the most part derived from Nichols, in such books as Charles Knight, *Shadows of the Old Booksellers* (New York, 1927), p. 233, and Plomer, Bushnell, and Dix, *A Dictionary of the Printers and Booksellers who were at work in England, Scotland, and Ireland from 1726 to 1775* (Oxford, 1930), p. 195. His letters have found their way into a number of libraries, including some in America. The Beinecke Library at Yale, for example, has a letter from Payne to Frances (Burney) d'Arblay, 24 April 1820. The Harvard University Libraries and the Osborn Collection each hold one of Payne's letters. The Bodleian Library at Oxford holds a letter to Payne from C. N. Cole.

A life of Thomas Payne (as well as one of his son of the same name) by William Prideaux Courtney is in the DNB. It relies heavily upon Nichols, as will be observed by a comparison of two sentences.

Nichols	Courtney
This little shop, in the shape of an L, was the first that obtained the name of a Literary Coffeehouse in London, from the knot of Literati that resorted to it. . . .	. . . and constructed the shop in the shape of the letter L. The convenience of the situation made it the favourite place of resort for the literati of the day, and it became known as the Literary Coffeehouse. . . .
This he continued to do till 1790; when he resigned the business to his eldest son, who had for more than twenty years been his partner. . . .	Payne continued in business with increasing success until 1790, when he retired in favour of his son. . . , who had been his partner for more than twenty years. . . .]

Mr. *Thomas Payne,* for more than 40 years a bookseller of the highest reputation at the Mews-gate, was a native of Brackley in Northamptonshire; and began his career in "Round-court in the Strand, opposite York buildings;" where, after being some years an assistant to his elder brother, Olive Payne (with whom the idea and practice of printing Catalogues is said to have originated), he commenced bookseller on his own account, and issued "A Catalogue of curious Books in Divinity, History, Classicks, Medicine, Voyages, Natural History, &c. Greek, Latin, French, Italian, and Spanish, in excellent condition, and mostly gilt and lettered," dated Feb. 29, 1740, being almost the first of the Catalogists, except Daniel Brown, at the Black Swan without Temple Bar, and the short-lived Meers and Noorthouck. From this situation he removed to the Mews-gate, in 1750, when he married Elizabeth Taylor, and succeeded her brother in the shop and house, which he built, whence he issued an almost annual succession of Catalogues, beginning 1755; and, in the years 1760 and 1761, two Catalogues during the year; a list of which may be seen in Gent. Mag. vol. LXIV. p. 901. This he continued to do till 1790; when he resigned the business to his eldest son, who had for more than twenty years been his partner, and who opened a new literary channel, by a correspondence with Paris, whence he brought, in 1793, the library of the celebrated Chancellor, Lamoignon. This little shop, in the shape of an L, was the first that obtained the name of a Literary Coffeehouse in London, from the knot of Literati that resorted to it; and, since the display of new books on the counter has been adopted from the Oxford and Cambridge booksellers, other London shops have their followers. If a reasonable price, and a reasonable credit for his goods, be the criterion of integrity, Mr. Payne supported the character of an *honest* man to the last; and, without the modern flash of wealth, which, ostentatiously exposed in a fine shop, has involved so many traders of all descriptions in difficulties and ruin, he acquired that fortune which enabled him to bring up two sons and two daughters with credit, and to assist some relations who wanted his aid. Warm in his friendships as in his politicks, a convivial, cheerful companion, and unalterable in the cut and colour of his coat, he uniformly pursued one great object, *fair dealing,* and will survive in the list of booksellers the most eminent for being adventurous and scientific, by the name of *honest* Tom Payne. The Author of "The Pursuits of Literature,"[1] who is an excellent appreciator of character, calls him "that *Trypho emeritus,* Mr. Thomas Payne, one of the honestest men living, to whom, as a bookseller, Learning is under considerable obligations."

He died Feb. 2,[2] 1799, in his 82d year; and was buried, on the 9th, at Finchley, near the remains of his wife and brother.

The present *Thomas Payne* of Pall Mall was the eldest, and is now the only surviving son; and inherits every good quality of his Father.

1. T. J. Mathias; see 11. 190-194 and note.
2. Originally Nichols wrote his death date as 8 February, which he corrected in *Lit. Anec.,* IX, 666.

[The following is from an addition to the above in "Additions to the Sixth Volume," *Lit. Anec.*, IX, 666.]

[Epitaph in memory of Mr. Thomas Payne, who died, at the age of 82, Feb. 2 (not the 9th [8th in original]), 1799:

> Around this Tomb, ye Friends of Learning, bend!
> It holds your faithful, though your humble Friend:
> Here lies the Literary Merchant, PAYNE,
> The countless Volumes that he sold contain
> No name by liberal Commerce more carest
> For virtues that become her Votary's breast;
> Of cheerful probity, and kindly plain,
> He felt no wish for disingenuous gain;
> In manners frank, in manly spirit high,
> Alert good-nature sparkled in his eye;
> Not learn'd, he yet had Learning's power to please,
> Her social sweetness, her domestic ease:
> A Son, whom his example guides and cheers,
> Thus guards the hallow'd dust his heart reveres;
> Love bade him thus a due Memorial raise,
> And friendly Justice penn'd this genuine praise.]

[Among those who frequented the shop of Payne were two whose lives appear in this volume: George Steevens and Richard Gough. References to Payne in the correspondence of Steevens may be found in *Illustr.*, V, 428, 435.]

Peter Elmsly

[Nichols' memoir of Peter Elmsly (or Elmsley) occurs along with other members of Thomas Davies' club of booksellers in *Lit. Anec.*, VI, 440-441. References to him occur also in other places in this same work and in *Illustrations*.

Elmsly appears as a personal friend of the Nichols family in a note in the Nichols Collection at Columbia University: "For John, Martha & Mary Nichols, from the Garden of their affectionate Friends Peter & Isabella Elmsly. Aug. 2. 1791." An attached note in the hand of John Bowyer Nichols reads: "Kept in grateful Memory of a kind Friend & his Wife—Mr Peter Elmsly, of Sloane Street, then in the Country; sent with Fruit from their Garden at that Time—the Fruit sent to me & my Sisters. J. B. Nichols. 1850."

References to Elmsly occur in the usual histories and dictionaries of eighteenth-century publishers (see particularly Knight and Plomer, Bushnell, and Dix). Such references, however, tend to be brief and derivative. Manuscripts relating to Elmsly are held in a number of repositories. The British Museum, for instance, possesses copies of correspondence of Elmsly and Jonathan Toup (of whom Nichols has a memoir in *Lit. Anec.*, II, 339-346). The Osborn Collection at Yale contains a letter, dated 20 June 1807, from Elmsly to Charles Burney, Jr. The Bodleian Library has two of Elmsly's letters, one of which is to Thomas Cadell; and the Harvard University Libraries have one of Elmsly's receipts and two letters to him.

A life of Elmsly by Henry Richard Tedder in the DNB is remarkable for the similarity of its language to that used in Nichols' account, although this statement is made not by way of disparagement but merely to point up the importance of Nichols as a source for the life of almost any contemporary. It may, nevertheless, be of interest to compare two passages.

Nichols	Tedder
To the tolerable education which is in the power of almost every North Briton without much difficulty to attain, he had gradually superadded. . . a fund of general knowledge. . . . Nor was he less critically nice in the French language than his own. . . .	To the usual Scottish schooling Elmsly added a large fund of information acquired by his own exertions in after life. He knew French well. . . .
His remains were brought to Sloane-street; whence, on the 10th, they were removed, in solemn funeral procession, and deposited in the family vault at Marybone. . . .	His remains were conveyed to his house in Sloane Street, London, and were buried at Marylebone 10 May. . . .]

Mr. *Peter Elmsly,* who succeeded *Paul Vaillant,* esq. at his well-known shop in the Strand, in the department principally of an Importer of Foreign Books, was respected by every human being who knew him. To the tolerable education which it is in the power of almost every North Briton without much difficulty to attain, he had gradually superadded, as he advanced in life and prosperity, such a fund of general knowledge, and so uncommonly accurate a discrimination of language, that, had he chosen to have stood forward as a Writer, he would have secured a permanent niche in the Temple of Fame. For the truth of this assertion I can boldly appeal to all who have been favoured with his epistolary correspondence. Nor was he less critically nice in the French language than in his own.

Mr. Elmsly died at Brighthelmstone, in the 67th year of his age, May 3, 1802.

For a short time before his death he had wholly quitted business, with a competent fortune, most handsomely acquired by consummate ability and the strictest integrity. The respect which he experienced from the late Duke of Grafton, the Hon. Topham Beauclerk, Mr. Stuart Mackenzie, Mr. Gibbon, Mr. Cracherode,[1] Mr. Wilkes, &c. &c. is well recollected; and among the many living characters of eminence by whom he was beloved and regarded were his more immediate friends and patrons Earl Spencer, Earl Stanhope, Sir Joseph Banks, Dean Rennell, Mr. Dutens,[2] &c. &c.

His remains were brought to Sloane-street; whence, on the 10th, they were removed, in solemn funeral procession, and deposited in the family vault at Marybone, attended by a large party of friends, sincere mourners on the melancholy occasion; as, for strength of mind, soundness of judgment, and unaffected friendship, he left not many equals.

He left a widow, to whom he had long been an affectionate husband, and who had the consolation to reflect that she had for many years soothed the pillow of anguish by unwearied assiduity.

[The following appears as a biographical note on Paul Vaillant, whose successor in business was Peter Elmsly. The text is from *Lit. Anec.,* III, 310, n.]

[At the time of the revocation of the Edict of Nantes he [Paul Vaillant] escaped with his life from the bloody *Dragonade* of the Hugonots by that merciless tyrant Louis XIV.; and, 1686, settled as a Foreign Bookseller in the Strand, opposite Southampton-street; where himself, his sons Paul and

---

1. Nichols has a biographical note on Clayton Mordaunt Cracherode in *Lit. Anec.,* IX, 666-667.
2. Lewis Dutens translated into French the second volume of *Marlborough Gems;* see *Lit. Anec.,* IV, 669.

Isaac, his grandson the late Mr. Vaillant, and Mr. Elmsly, successively carried on the same trade, in the same house, till nearly the end of the eighteenth century—when Mr. Elmsly resigned the business to his shopman Mr. David Bremner: whose anxiety for acquiring wealth rendered him wholly careless of indulging himself in the ordinary comforts of life, and hurried him prematurely to the grave. He was succeeded by Mess. James Payne and J. Mackinlay; the former of whom was the youngest son of the late well-known and much-respected Mr. Thomas Payne, of the Mews-gate; the latter shopman to Mr. Elmsly. Both these are also lately dead; Mr. Payne having unfortunately fallen a victim to a long and cruel confinement as a prisoner in France, and the latter having unfortunately perished in a momentary absence of reason.]

[The following material comes from *Lit. Anec.*, VIII, 557-560, and deals with Elmsly's relations with both Nichols and Edward Gibbon. Elmsly is called by Nichols the "confidential Friend" of him and Gibbon.
Some of the material which follows is from letters and some is Nichols' filling in of connections between letters. The first letter is to Nichols.]

SIR, *Lausanne, February* 24, 1792.
At this distance from England you will not be surprised that this morning only, by a mere accident, the *Gentleman's Magazine* for August 1788 should have reached my knowledge. In it I have found, pp. 698-700, a very curious and civil account of the Gibbon Family, more particularly of the branch from which I descend, with several circumstances of which I was myself ignorant, and several concerning which I should be desirous of obtaining some further information. . . .
I address myself to you, as to the last, or one of the last, of the learned Printers in Europe, a most respectable order of men; in the fair confidence that you will assist the gratification of my curiosity. Perhaps, if it be not a secret, you may be able to disclose the name of the Author of this article, which is subscribed N.S.; and through your channel I might correspond directly with a gentleman to whom I am already obliged. . . .
It is not improbable that I may do myself the pleasure of calling upon you in London before the close of the year. I shall be happy to form an acquaintance with a person from whose writings I have derived both amusement and information.
I am, your obedient humble servant, E. GIBBON.*

[To Mr. Gibbon's inquiry in the preceding Letter, I immediately answered, "that I did not know with any certainty the Gentleman from whom the information was received; but that I fortunately possessed some

---

* This Letter was first printed in the Magazine, vol. LXIV. p. 5, a few days only after the death of Mr. Gibbon; which happened Jan. 16, 1794, in his 57th year.—See, in that volume, pp. 174. 178. 199. 322. some articles respecting Mr. Gibbon's Life and Writings, which the elegant Memoirs by Lord Sheffield have since superseded. NICHOLS.

Genealogical documents relating to Mr. Gibbon's Family" (which had been presented to me by John Beardsworth, esq.† of Lincoln's Inn).—Those original MSS. (with my Letter) were soon after dispatched to Mr. Gibbon, through the medium of his and my confidential Friend Mr. Peter Elmsly; in whose multiplicity of business, the parcel was unfortunately mislaid, as will appear by the subsequent Correspondence.

In the conclusion of a Letter to Lord Sheffield, May 30, 1792, Mr. Gibbon says, "Call upon Mr. John Nichols, Bookseller and Printer, at Cicero's Head, Red Lion Passage, Fleet-street; and ask him whether he did not, about the beginning of March, receive a very polite Letter from Mr. Gibbon of Lausanne? to which, either as a man of business, or a civil gentleman, he should have returned an answer...."

This produced a proper explanation; and accordingly, in a subsequent Letter to Lord Sheffield, Oct. 27, 1793, Mr. Gibbon says, "I am much indebted to Mr. Nichols for his Genealogical communication; which I am impatient to receive, but I do not understand why so civil a gentleman could not favour me in six months with an answer by the post. Since he entrusts me with these valuable papers, you have not, I presume, informed him of my negligence and awkwardness in regard to Manuscripts."

I had actually written a second time, though unluckily *not by the post;* for again my Letter was delayed at Mr. Elmsly's; and Mr. Gibbon, on its finally reaching him, says,]

SIR, *Lausanne, Jan. 16, 1793.*
It gives me serious concern to find that I have been the innocent occasion of injuring a very respectable man, in the very act in which he intended a kindness to me.

Last February, on the credit of your general character, I addressed you by letter on the subject of an article, in the Gentleman's Magazine, relative to my Family. I am now assured that my expectation was fulfilled; and that my curiosity would have been gratified by the communication of several interesting papers, which you procured for my use, and deposited in Mr. Elmsly's hands: and I can only lament that you did not at the same time favour me with a line by the post, to inform me of the success of my application. During the whole Spring and Summer I remained in a state of ignorance; nor was it till late in the Autumn, and after several fruitless enquiries, that I was informed at once of your deposit, and of Mr. Elmsly's inexcusable neglect. I then wrote to him, requesting, first, that the parcel might be sent to Lausanne; and afterwards, on cooler thoughts, that it might be returned to you, to await my approaching arrival in England. You may guess at my surprize and concern, when he informed me, by a letter which I received last post, "that it was lost, mislaid, taken away perhaps by some workmen repairing his house," &c. By this state of the case, you will acknowledge how perfectly I am guiltless of this unfortunate accident. You are on the spot: you have but too good a right to interrogate Mr. Elmsly closely and sharply. Perhaps an advertisement, with an handsome reward,

---

† To whom they came, with the original seat of the Family, *The Hole,* in the parish of Rolvenden, Kent. . . . The MSS. accompanied the title-deeds. NICHOLS.

might detect these papers, which are of little value except to ourselves. I should willingly take any trouble, or support any expence, to repair the mischief which has been the consequence of my application, and your kindness.

I beg the favour of an immediate answer; and you will perhaps give me some account of these papers, which I hope will not turn out to be the bill of lading of a shipwreck.

E. GIBBON.

[Mr. Elmsly having assured Mr. Gibbon of the real causes of delay, the following explanation [by Gibbon to Nichols] took place.]

SIR, *Lausanne, April 4, 1793.*
Mr. Gibbon might perhaps have expected the favour of an answer to his first or second letter; but he is himself so indifferent a correspondent, and he feels himself so much indebted to Mr. Nichols's good offices, that he will not complain of this apparent neglect. It gave him great pleasure to learn by Elmsly's last letter, that the Family Papers are found, and most probably returned into Mr. Nichols's hands. It was Mr. Gibbon's intention to have left them there till his arrival in England; but his journey there this Summer appears so uncertain, that he is tempted to make use of a very favourable opportunity. Mr. Françillon, a Swiss Clergyman, established in London, and his particular friend, is setting out on a visit of three or four months to his family at Lausanne. He will call on Mr. Nichols; and, should the papers be entrusted to his care, their conveyance will be safe and speedy. According to the time that may be allowed, Mr. Gibbon will either return them by the same messenger, or bring them to England himself.

[The MSS. were once more forwarded, perused, and punctually returned, and are still in my possession.

On Mr. Gibbon's return to England, he very condescendingly paid me several short visits; and, in one of those interviews, dictated the following lines, which were printed in the Gentleman's Magazine, for July 1793, vol. LXIII. p. 536.

"If the Gentleman who signs N.S. (vol. LVIII. p. 698, vol. LIX. p. 584), on the Gibbon Family, will communicate his address, it will be a particular favour."—To which, with his concurrence, I added, "Mr. Gibbon is returned to England; and a new work from the pen of that celebrated Writer is expected next Winter."

Within a few days after, he sent the two following notes:

"Mr. Gibbon will be much obliged to Mr. Nichols for Philpot and Lambarde. The shortness of his stay in town will oblige him to carry them to Lord Sheffield's in Sussex; but they shall be carefully used, and speedily returned."

"If the invitation in this Month's Magazine has revealed the Author of the article relative to the Gibbon Family, Mr. Gibbon will be much obliged to Mr. Nichols for a line inclosed to Lord Sheffield, Sheffield Place, Uckfield, Sussex."

The consequence of the inquiry was, an epistolary intercourse between

Mr. Gibbon and Mr. Brydges (now Sir Egerton Brydges, K.J. and M.P.) the original communicator of the Anecdotes of the Gibbon Family in Gent. Mag. vol. LVIII. p. 699; and in vol. LXII. p. 523; and whose signature is annexed to some corrections in the "Memoirs of Mr. Gibbon," vol. LXVI. p. 272.[3]

The substance of the above narrative having been stated in the Magazine for 1796, vol. LXVI. p. 459, my books were returned, new bound; and I was honoured by the following Letter:]

Sir, *Sheffield Place, Jan. 10, 1797.*
Having observed in one of your late Magazines that you had lent Philpot and Lambarde to Mr. Gibbon in the year 1793, I intended to call on you as soon as I shall go to London (which has been prevented for some time by the severe indisposition of Lady Sheffield) to mention that I had kept those two books, supposing they had been purchased by Mr. Gibbon. They have been *new dressed*, which I hope will make some amends for their stay at this place. I am, Sir,
Your most obedient humble servant, Sheffield.

[Editor's note: It appears that there was some difficulty over another box of manuscripts left with Elmsly (though this box does not seem to have been lost). The following is from a letter from Henry Meen to Thomas Percy.]

My Lord, Bread Street Hill, April 8, 1801.
... The day I received your box, I opened it as desired, and acquainted Mr. Bremner [Elmsly's former shopman and his successor in business], bookseller, that at my house was a parcel containing two folio volumes of MSS. directed for Mr. Foulis, printer; that it was your Lordship's desire that he would take particular care of this parcel till orders were given for the disposal of it. The parcel is still at their house, under the protection of Mr. Elmsly; for Mr. Bremner, who has been long ill, is since dead. It is somewhat strange that Mr. Foulis should not once in all this time have either written or sent after this parcel.... H. Meen.[4]

3. The edition of Lord Sheffield, 2 vols., 1796.
4. *Illustr.*, VII, 52-53.

Thomas Cadell

[Thomas Cadell was another member of the club of booksellers (to which Nichols, Davies, and others belonged) which met at the Shakespeare Tavern. Nichols' memoir of Cadell is taken from *Lit. Anec.*, VI, 441-443, where it appears as a note, along with the lives of other members of the booksellers' club. This memoir, as could be expected, appeared previously in the *Gent. Mag.*, 71:1173-1222 (December 1802). Numerous references to Cadell occur in *Literary Anecdotes* and *Illustrations*. Of special interest are those relating to his son of the same name, in partnership with William Davies, and their connection with Thomas Percy in the publication of some of his works (see *Illustr.*, VII, 30, 126-127, 132, 139, 152-153, 190-191; VIII, 320).

Short accounts of Cadell occur in the books dealing with the book trade of the eighteenth century. He is in the dictionary, for example, compiled by Plomer, Bushnell, and Dix. He appears briefly also in Knight (pp. 201-203) and in Marston (p. 96) as well as in Cochrane (pp. 32-33; 138-141). A more extensive and important study is *The Publishing Firm of Cadell and Davies. Select Correspondence and Accounts, 1793-1836. Edited with an Introduction and Notes by Theodore Besterman* (Oxford University Press, 1938).

Many manuscripts relating to Cadell survive. In the Osborn Collection housed at Yale are twenty-four items, including a letter from James Currie to Cadell concerning the danger of unauthorized publication of the manuscripts of Robert Burns (9 February 1798). Yale's Beinecke Library holds about 550 letters to the firm of Cadell and Davies from various authors, along with approximately 100 miscellaneous manuscripts and 125 replies from Cadell and Davies. Harvard University possesses twenty-nine letters by Cadell, sixteen to him, and two receipts. The British Museum has letters from Cadell and Davies to Samuel Ireland, dated circa 1796 (Add. Mss. 30348. ff. 246, 247). The Folger Library has a letter from Joseph Warton to Cadell and Davies concerning the agreement for an edition of Dryden (ART vol. a12). Among the Folger's other writers of letters to Cadell and Davies are Hannah More and Arthur Murphy (W.b. 476; W.a. 167). The Folger also possesses a letter from Sir John Hawkins to Cadell (ART vol. a12); one from Samuel Johnson to him (W.b. 473); and one from Henry McKenzie to him (PN, 2598, G3F3, Copy 4, Ex-ill). In the William Cowper Collection at Princeton is a letter from William Hayley to Cadell and Davies, 15 December 1812. The Bodleian Library holds several letters to Cadell and a collection of letters to the firm of Cadell and Davies.

A brief memoir of Cadell by Sidney Lee, listing at the end no sources other than those provided by Nichols, is in the DNB.]

Mr. *Thomas Cadell,* a striking instance of the effects of a strong understanding when united to unremitting industry, was born in Wine-street,

Bristol; and served an apprenticeship to that eminent bookseller *Andrew Millar,* the steady patron of Thomson, Fielding, and many other eminent authors; who, by remunerating literary talent with a liberality proportionate to its merit, distinguished himself as much, as the patron of men of letters of that day, as Mr. Alderman *Boydell* did afterwards of the Arts. Mr. Cadell in 1767 succeeded to the business; and, at an early period of life, was at the head of his profession. Introduced by Mr. Millar to writers of the first rank in literature, who had found in him their best Maecenas —to Johnson, Hume, Warburton, Hurd, &c. &c.—he pursued the very same commendable track; and, acting upon the liberal principle of his predecessor in respect to authors, enlarged upon it in an extent, which, at the same time that it did honour to his spirit, was well suited to the more enlightened period in which he carried on business. In conjunction with the late William Strahan, esq. M.P. for Wotton Basset, and, after his death, with his son Andrew Strahan, esq. now member for *Catherlogh,* munificent remunerations have been held out to writers of the most eminent talents; and it is owing to the spirit and generosity of these gentlemen, that the world has within these fifty years been enriched by the masterly labours of Robertson, Blackstone, Gibbon, Burn, Henry, and numberless other of the ablest writers of the age.*

In 1793 Mr. Cadell retired from trade, in the full possession of his health and faculties, and with an ample fortune, the sole and satisfactory fruits of unremitted diligence, spirit, and integrity; leaving the business which he had established as the first in Great Britain, and perhaps in Europe, to Thomas, his only son, conjointly with Mr. Davies, who, following the Alderman's example, have preserved the high reputation acquired from the liberality, honour, and integrity of their predecessors.[1] Accustomed, however, from early days, to business, and conscious that an idle life was a disgrace to a man of clear intellects, sound judgment, and an active mind, he, with a laudable ambition, sought, and most honourably obtained, a seat in the Magistracy of the City of London; being unanimously elected, March 30, 1798, to succeed his friend Mr. Gill, as Alderman of Walbrook ward. At Midsummer 1800, a period when party spirit ran high, he was elected by a very honourable majority on a poll, with his friend Mr. Alderman Perring, to the shrievalty of London and Middlesex; an office, which, it may be said without disparagement to any other gentleman, was never more honourably or more splendidly discharged. To a conscientious attendance on the severer duties of that important station (for he was never absent a single Sunday from the Chapel of one of the Prisons) he owed the foundation of that asthmatic complaint, which so fatally terminated at a

---

* Mr. Cadell often spoke of *B* as a very successful letter to him; and instanced Blackstone, Blair, Buchan, Burn. NICHOLS ("Additions to the Sixth Volume," *Lit. Anec.,* IX, 667).

1. See notes on Thomas Cadell the Younger and William Davies, his partner, reproduced at the conclusion of this life.

period when the Citizens of London, who justly revered him as an independent, humane, and intelligent Magistrate, anticipated the speedy approach of his attainment to the highest civic honours. He had dined out on Sunday, and returned in the evening to his own house, apparently in as good health as usual. In the morning, a little before one, he rang his bell, and told the servant that he thought he was dying. A person was immediately dispatched for medical assistance; but, before it arrived, the worthy Alderman had expired. He had been for some months subject to severe fits of coughing; by the effects of one of which fits, it is supposed, his death was occasioned.

[Editor's note: The following five sentences, which run to the end of this paragraph, are from an addition in *Illustr.*, VIII, 552.]

[Alderman Cadell died Dec. 27, 1802. The death of Thomas Cadell, jun., his only son, took place Nov. 26, 1837. Mr. Cadell's daughter married Dr. Charles Lucas Eldridge, rector of Shipdham, Norfolk, and chaplain in ordinary to his Majesty. He died Jan. 4, 1826; and his widow died Sept. 20, 1829. His second son, Lieut. Henry Thomas Eldridge, Royal Engineers, died at Worcester, Nov. 6, 1828.]

To the Asylum, where he had long been a valuable Treasurer, the Foundling Hospital, and various other public charities, of which he was an active governor, and where his presence gave animation to their proceedings, while his purse liberally aided their funds, his loss was great:—to a very extensive circle of friends (and there are several, as well as the writer of this article, who had unbent their inmost souls with him for more than 40 years) it was incalculable.

He was eminently characterized by the rectitude of his judgment, the goodness of his heart, the benevolence of his disposition, and the urbanity of his manners; and, whether considered in his magisterial character, or in the more retired walks of social or domestic life, few men could be named, so well deserving of private veneration or public esteem.

One of the latest public acts of his life was the presenting to the Company of Stationers, of which he had been thirty-seven years a liveryman, a handsome painted window for the embellishment of their Hall.[2]

2. In *Lit. Anec.*, III, 580-581, Nichols describes the window as part of a larger description of Stationers' Hall: "At the North end is a large arched window, entirely filled with painted glass, the border and fan of which are very vivid and splendid. Seven compartments are filled with the arms of London, the Royal arms, the Company's arms, their crest, the arms of Thomas Cadell, esq. and two emblematic figures designed by [Robert] Smirke. At the bottom is the following inscription: 'This window (except the arms and crest of the Company, which for their excellence and antiquity it has been thought adviseable to preserve) was the gift of Thomas Cadell, esq. Alderman, and Sheriff of London, 1801.'"

In an addition to the above, in IX, 549 (with a plate of the window facing this page), Nichols has a note on the creator of the window: "Mr. Francis Eginton, of Handsworth,

By an affectionate wife, who died in January 1786, he had one son and one daughter; both of whom he lived to see united in marriage, to his entire satisfaction; and who now have the comfort to reflect, that their father fulfilled the various duties allotted to him with the honour of a man and the integrity of a Christian.

He died, at his house in Bloomsbury-place, in his 60th year.

In a Sermon preached by Mr. Hutchins (then Chaplain to the Lord Mayor) on the 9th of January following, a handsome compliment is paid to Mr. Alderman Cadell, for "gentleness of manners, benevolence of disposition, purity of morals, tenderness to the unfortunate, and an unaffected deportment, in the various offices of citizen, magistrate, parent, and friend."

The Alderman's great success in life is one of the many proofs that this Metropolis has for years afforded, that application and industry, when unforeseen misfortune and severe ill health do not intervene, seldom fail to meet with their due reward; and, more especially, where those necessary qualifications for business are accompanied with a spirit of enterprize unalloyed by rashness or want of caution. Mr. Andrew Millar, the predecessor of Alderman Cadell, was in possession of very humble means when he commenced business, and lived some years facing St. Clement's church. He died rich, and very deservedly, as he was a liberal patron of authors. Previous to his time, Lintott and the Tonsons were at the head of the bookselling trade.

[Editor's note: The following brief but significant reference to Cadell comes from a group of anecdotes collected by Nichols about "the latest periods of the life" of Johnson, *Lit. Anec.*, II, 552.]

[He [Johnson] was earnestly invited, by his warm friend the late Mr. Alderman Cadell, to publish a volume of *Devotional Exercises;* but this (though he listened to the proposal with much complacency, and a large sum of money was offered for it by Mr. Cadell), he declined, from motives of the sincerest modesty.]

[Editor's note: The following note on Robin Lawless, an assistant of Andrew Millar, occurs as a note to the life of the latter; but since it is related more to Cadell than to Millar, I have chosen to place it here. It comes from *Lit. Anec.*, III, 387-388n.]

---

near Birmingham, justly celebrated for his ingenious discovery of painting and staining of glass, far surpassing that of the Antients, in which his numerous works (of which a good specimen may be seen in the annexed Window in Stationers' Hall, presented to that Company by the late Alderman Cadell) will long continue monuments of his unrivaled abilities, died March 25, 1805."

[This diligent and honest servant [Robin Lawless], who for considerably more than half a century, had been so well known to, and much distinguished by, the notice and regard of many of the most eminent literary characters of his time, as one of the principal assistants to Mr. Andrew Millar, afterwards to Mr. Alderman Cadell, and finally, to Messrs. Cadell and Davies, the present conductors of that extensive business, died at his apartments in Dean Street, Soho, June 21, 1806, at the advanced age of 82. He was a native of Dublin, and related, not very distantly, to the respectable and recently ennobled family of the same name, as well as to the Barnewalls and Aylmers. . . . In his character were united the soundest integrity of mind with a simplicity of manners rarely equalled. His reading had been extensive; his judgment was remarkably correct; his memory uncommonly strong; and the anecdotes with which it was stored often afforded gratification to his friends, who delighted to draw him into conversation. Humble as was his walk in life, few men had stronger claims to affectionate regard. A purer spirit never inhabited the human bosom. One remarkable instance of his singleness of heart we can add on the most indisputable authority. Not very long before Mr. Cadell obtained the scarlet gown, on taking stock at the end of the year, honest Robin very seriously applied to his master, to ask a favour of him. Mr. Cadell, of course, expected that it was somewhat that might be beneficial to the applicant. But great indeed was his surprize to find that the purport of the request was, that his annual salary might be lowered, as the year's accompt was not so good as the preceding one; and Lawless really feared that his master could not afford to pay him such very high wages. On retiring from business, the benevolent master had a picture of the faithful servant painted by Sir William Beechey, which he always shewed to his friends as one of the principal ornaments of his drawing-room.]

[Editor's note: The following two obituaries, Thomas Cadell the Younger and his partner William Davies, are taken from a group of obituaries of "Printers and Booksellers," given as an addition to *Literary Anecdotes* and found in *Illustr.*, VIII, 463-527. Davies' obituary is from pp. 492-493; Cadell's is from p. 510.]

[Nov. 26 [1836]. In Charlotte-street, Fitzroy-square, aged 63, Thomas *Cadell,* Esq. bookseller and publisher in the Strand. He was the only son of Mr. Alderman Cadell, and carried on the business from his father's retirement in 1793 to 1820, in partnership with Mr. Wm. Davies; and afterwards in his own name alone. There for 43 years he followed his father's example, and sustained the reputation the house had acquired for liberality, honour, and integrity. See Lit. Anecd. VI. pp. 441-443, and p. 493 of this volume. In 1802 he married a daughter of Robert Smith, Esq. solicitor, of

Basinghall-street, and sister of Messrs. J. and H. Smith, authors of "Rejected Addresses," and other works. Mr. Cadell had a numerous family; but after his death none of his sons continued in the trade, and the old concern was broken up. Mr. Cadell was one of the Court of Assistants of the Company of Stationers. Mrs. Cadell, his widow, died May 11, 1848.

1820, April 28. William *Davies,* Esq. of the respectable firm of Messrs. Cadell and Davies, booksellers, in the Strand. On the retirement of Mr. Alderman Cadell in 1793, he selected Mr. Davies as the partner of his son, Mr. Thomas Cadell, junr. and the business was most ably conducted by Mr. Davies for upwards of 30 years. Those who knew him best never witnessed in him anything but the most liberal conduct as a friend, and a straightforward man of business, in which he was assiduous and attentive, always giving most valuable advice, and acting with the utmost fairness and liberality in the position in which his good conduct had placed him. His connection with authors, artists, and persons of splendid acquirements, added to his superior abilities, might have given him that appearance of conscious superiority which to strangers might appear to be hauteur. Mr. Davies was many years one of the Stockkeepers of the Company of Stationers. The family of Mr. Davies was, at his death, not left so well provided for as might have been hoped, from his large concerns in business for so long a period. His widow, Mrs. Jesse Davies, died at Bushy, Herts, Oct. 14, 1854, aged 76.]

[Editor's note: In *Illustr.,* VIII, 460, John Bowyer Nichols states that in the Court Room of Stationers' Hall is "A Portrait of Thomas Cadell, Esq., by Sir Wm. Beechy, R.A."]

Andrew Millar

[Nichols' life of Andrew Millar comes from a section entitled "Booksellers and Printers" in *Lit. Anec.*, III, 386-389. Numerous references to him appear other places in Nichols' works since Millar published a number of books printed at the press of Bowyer and Nichols: e. g., Warburton's *Divine Legation* (*Lit. Anec.*, II, 387-388). Millar was thoroughly involved, also, with many other men about whom Nichols wrote. The *Free and Candid Disquisitions* of John Jones, for instance, was published by Millar (*Lit. Anec.*, I, 586).

Nichols credits Millar and Jacob Tonson with being the best patrons of literature of their time. Johnson is reported to have said that Millar had no great taste in literature himself, but that he was surrounded by capable assistants who helped him choose and reward well the best writers; thus he became the publisher of works written by Thomson, Fielding, and others. He was also chiefly responsible for seeing Johnson's *Dictionary* though the press. Of him, Johnson said that "he has raised the price of literature" (Hill-Powell, *Boswell*, I, 288).

Millar (and of course many others included in this volume) is found in C. H. Timperley's *Dictionary of Printers and Printing*. Millar is also in most of the other works dealing with the book trade in the eighteenth century. Henry Curwen has a page about him in *A History of Booksellers* (London, 1873); and similar space is given to him by Knight and by Cochrane. Knight is quoted as a source in the entry concerning Millar in the *Dictionary of Booksellers and Printers* compiled by Plomer, Bushnell, and Dix. Marston's material on Millar is almost entirely attributed to Nichols. The most important recent study of Millar is Austin Dobson's *Fielding and Andrew Millar* (London, 1916; reprinted from *The Library* for July 1916).

The British Museum has a letter from Millar to Sir Hans Sloane, n.d. (Add. Mss. 4059. f. 353) and several to the Society for the Encouragement of Learning, 1736-1739 (Add.Mss. 6190. ff. 9, 10, 17, 62). The Bodleian has letters from several authors, including Edward Young, to Millar; and the Osborn Collection contains two Millar letters. Additional letters, no doubt, exist in other depositories.

There is a brief life of Millar, with Nichols listed at the end as the first source, written by Gordon Goodwin in the DNB.]

ANDREW MILLAR, Esq. [born 1707] was literally the artificer of his own fortune. By consummate industry, and a happy train of successive patronage and connexion, he became one of the most eminent Booksellers of the eighteenth century. He had little pretensions to Learning; but had a thorough knowledge of mankind; and a nice discrimination in selecting his literary counsellors;[1] amongst whom it may be sufficient to mention the late eminent Schoolmaster and Critick, Dr. William Rose,* of Chiswick; and the late William Strahan, Esq. the early friend and associate of Mr. Millar in private life, and his partner in many capital adventures in business.

Mr. Millar had three children; but they all died in their infancy. He was *not extravagant;* but contented himself with an occasional regale of humble port at an opposite Tavern; so that his wealth accumulated rapidly. He was fortunate also in his assistants in trade. One of these was the present worthy veteran Mr. Thomas Becket, who afterwards colonized into another part of the Strand, in partnership with Mr. P. De Hondt; and thence transplanted himself, first to the corner of the Adelphi, and afterwards to Pall Mall, where he has long been stationary, and, it is hoped, will remain so whilst he can enjoy the comforts of life.

Mr. Millar's next assistant was *Robin Lawless,*[2] a name familiar to every Bibliomaniac and every Bookseller who recollects the latter half of the eighteenth century.

In 1758 Mr. Millar met with an apprentice congenial to his most ardent wishes; who, combining industry with intellect, relieved him in a great measure from the toil of superintending an immense concern; whom in 1765 he readily admitted as his partner: and in 1767 relinquished to him the whole business. I need not add, that this was the late worthy and successful Bookseller Mr. Alderman Cadell.

Mr. Millar now retired to a villa at Kew Green. He died in the following year [1768]; and was buried in the cemetery at Chelsea,† near the King's private road; where in 1751 Mr. Millar had erected an obelisk** over a vault appropriated to his family, where three infant children were deposited; and afterwards his own remains, and those of his widow, who had been re-married to Sir Archibald Grant, Bart. of Monymusk, Aberdeenshire. She died, at her house in Pall Mall, Oct. 25, 1788; and left many charitable

---

* A gentleman well known in the republick of letters, and highly esteemed for his public spirit, his friendly disposition, his amiable and chearful temper, and his universal benevolence. He published an edition of Sallust, and was largely concerned in the Monthly Review. He left one son, Samuel Rose, Esq, barrister at law, a young man of considerable talents, and universally beloved for his truly mild and unobtrusive manners; who was the friend and correspondent of Cowper the Poet; and in 1804 was the Editor of Goldsmith's Works, 4 vols. 8vo. . . . NICHOLS.

† This Cemetery, about a quarter of a mile from the Church, was given to that parish by Sir Hans Sloane. NICHOLS.

1. Here Nichols quotes from Boswell's *Life of Johnson* the anecdote concerning Millar's goading of Johnson for copy for the *Dictionary:* "When the messenger who carried the last sheet to Millar returned, Johnson asked him, 'Well, what did he say?'—'Sir, (answered the messenger) he said, thank GOD I have done with him.' 'I am glad (replied Johnson, with a smile,) that he thanks GOD for any thing.' " Nichols includes Boswell's notational refutation of Hawkins, who said that the above was written in notes instead of being merely spoken. See Hill-Powell, *Boswell,* I, 287.

2. Nichols' note here on Robin Lawless is reproduced in the life of Thomas Cadell, to which it seemed more closely related.

benefactions; among others, the whole residue of her estate (supposed to be at least 15,000*l*.) to be disposed of at the discretion of her three executors, the Rev. Dr. Trotter, Mr. Grant, and Mr. Cadell.

[**On which are the several following inscriptions:]

    1. Mindful of Death and of Life;
ANDREW MILLAR
of the Strand, London, Bookseller,
erected this
near the Dormitory
intended
for himself and his beloved wife
JANE MILLAR
when it shall please Divine Providence
to call them hence,
as a place of like repose
for other near relations,
and in memory of
the sacred pledges of their mutual love,
MDCCLI

    2. ROBERT MILLAR, aged one year, died in 1736,
interred not far from hence.
ELIZABETH MILLAR, of the same age, died in 1740,
Buried in the Church-yard of St. Clements Danes.
Innocent in their short lives,
and therefore happy in their Deaths.
Though lost to their human,
they live to their Eternal Parent.

    3. Sacred to the Remembrance of
ANDREW MILLAR
the fleeting Joy, the lasting Grief
of those who dedicate this Monument.
Having shewn such goodness in this frail life
as attracted the love of all,
he was taken to a better
at Scarborough July 30, 1750,
aged five years and six months,
interred here August 28 following.

    4. Here lie the remains of ANDREW MILLAR, Esq.
who departed this Life, June the 8th, 1768,
aged 61 years.

    5. Dame JANE GRANT,
widow of Sir ARCHIBALD GRANT, Bart.
who died Oct. 25, 1788, aged 81 years.
Her remains are deposited here,
near those of her first husband,
ANDREW MILLAR, Esq.

    6. Here lie the remains of Mrs. MARGARET JOHNSTON;
who departed this life July the 30, 1757.

[Editor's note: The following is taken from a life of George Robinson in *Lit. Anec.*, III, 448.]

[During the better half of the past century, Jacob Tonson and Andrew Millar were the best Patrons of Literature; a fact rendered unquestionable, by the valuable works produced under their fostering and genial hands. Their successors, Mr. Alderman Cadell, the late Mr. Strahan, and his surviving son, exceeded their predecessors in the spirit of enterprise, which led them, at great expence, to publish the works of the many celebrated Writers that have ornamented the age in which we live. Mr. Robinson, standing alone and unconnected, boldly rivalled these, the most powerful of his competitors; and, by his liberality to Authors, his encouragement to engravers, and other artists of the press, has considerably added to the stores of science and taste.]

William Strahan

[The sketch of the life of William Strahan by John Nichols comes primarily from *Lit. Anec.*, III, 390-397, although there are, additionally, numerous references to him elsewhere in Nichols' writings. Nichols had a personal acquaintance with Strahan, both being members of Johnson's Essex Head Club (though Strahan left shortly after its founding); see *Lit. Anec.*, II, 553, and Hill-Powell, *Boswell*, IV, 436-439.

With the sons of William Strahan, Nichols had many associations also. George Strahan, editor of Johnson's "Prayers and Meditations" (1785), is listed as a contributor to *Literary Anecdotes* (see Advertisement, IX, v); and information in the same volume is attributed to his brother Andrew: "Lord Mansfield, we are here informed on the unquestionable authority of Mr. Andrew Strahan, was of opinion, that 'Mr. [John] Wilkes was the pleasantest companion, the politest gentleman, and the best scholar he ever knew'" (p. 479n). Nichols and Andrew Strahan are linked elsewhere, also; in a letter from Richard Gough to John Cullum, dated 13 June 1780, Gough asserts that Nichols and Strahan suffered from the Gordon Riots: "Poor Nichols being personally threatened, as well as the King's Printer [Andrew Strahan], all business stopped there last week. The distress of his family affected me more than all the shocking scenes I saw in London last Thursday, or that my servant related to me on his return from the scene of action that morning" (*Lit. Anec.*, VIII, 678).

Strahan's association with Johnson has led to his having received more scholarly attention than any of the other printers or booksellers included in this volume. The work in which he is most recently studied is by J. A. Cochrane, *Dr. Johnson's Printer: the Life of William Strahan* (Harvard University Press, 1964). At earlier dates he appeared briefly in the *Dictionary of Booksellers and Printers* of Plomer, Bushnell, and Dix and in Knight's *Shadows of the Old Booksellers*. G. B. Hill edited the Letters of *David Hume to William Strahan* (Oxford, 1888).

For a guide to other sources of information about Strahan, the scholar should turn to Cochrane, who also gives the locations of many important Strahan manuscripts, including his ledgers in the British Museum (see Cochrane, pp. 7-8). Harvard University Libraries hold three letters to Strahan, and the Folger Library has one of Johnson's letters to him. The Osborn Collection and the Beinecke Library at Yale have letters to and from William and Andrew Strahan, including some from Benjamin Franklin to William Strahan. The Columbia University Library has two letters to David Hall from Strahan; and the Bodleian Library holds several letters to him.

William Strahan has a life in the DNB written by Thomas Secombe; Nichols is listed first among the sources at the end.]

This distinguished Printer was born in Scotland in April 1715; and was apprenticed there to the profession which he pursued through life. He came early to London, where his capacity, diligence, and probity, raised him to great eminence. The good humour and obliging disposition, which he owed to nature, he cultivated with care, and confirmed by habit. His sympathetic heart beat time to the joy or sorrow of his friends. His advice was always ready to direct youth, and his purse open to relieve indigence. Living in times not the purest in the English annals, he escaped unsullied through the artifices of trade, and the corruption of politicks. In him a strong and natural sagacity, improved by an extensive knowledge of the world, served only to render respectable his unaffected simplicity of manners, and to make his truly Christian philanthropy more discerning and more useful. The uninterrupted health and happiness which accompanied him half a century in this capital, proves honesty to be the best policy, temperance the greatest luxury, and the essential duties of life its most agreeable amusement. In his elevated fortune none of his former acquaintance ever accused him of neglect. He attained prosperity without envy, enjoyed wealth without pride, and dispensed bounty without ostentation. His ample property he bestowed with the utmost good sense and propriety. After providing munificently for his widow and his children, his principal study seems to have been to mitigate the affliction of those who were more immediately dependant on his bounty; and to not a few who were under this description, who would otherwise have severely felt the drying up of so rich a fountain of benevolence, he gave liberal annuities for their lives; and, after the example of his old friend and neighbour Mr. Bowyer, bequeathed 1000*l.* to the Company of Stationers for charitable purposes.[1] He had been Master of the Company in 1774.

Mr. Strahan married, early in life, a sister of Mr. James Elphinston,[2] a schoolmaster of considerable reputation. He died July 9, 1785; and Mrs. Strahan on the 9th of August following.

They lived to see two daughters respectably married; who are now both dead, leaving several children.

Of Mr. Strahan's three sons:

1. William, the eldest carried on the profession of a printer for some years on Snow Hill; but died, in his father's life-time, April 19, 1781.

2. George, of University College, Oxford, M.A. 1771; and B. and D.D. 1807; is now a Prebendary of Rochester, Rector of Cranham in Essex, and Vicar of St. Mary's Islington. This worthy Divine was honoured in his

---

1. Andrew Strahan added another £1,000 to the bequest made by his father; to that, in February 1815, he added £1,225. "At the same time Mr. Strahan presented to the Company [of Stationers] a Portrait of his Father, an excellent likeness, copied by Sir William Beachy from an Original by Sir Joshua Reynolds." See *Lit. Anec.,* IX, 705-706.

2. Nichols has a biographical sketch of James Elphinston in *Lit. Anec.,* III, 30-37n. Strahan left his brother-in-law a bequest, ibid., p. 34n.

youth by the peculiar regard of Dr. Johnson (of whose "Prayers and Meditations" he was in 1785 the Editor.)[3]

3. Andrew, (M.P. for Newport in the Isle of Wight 1797; for Wareham 1802; and now for Catherlogh) is one of the Joint Patentees as Printer to his Majesty; has also the patent of Law Printer; and for many years has been at the head of his profession.[4]

[Editor's note: The following material appears as a note to Nichols' life of William Strahan.]

[The following character of him is copied from "The Lounger," a periodical paper, published at Edinburgh, Aug. 20, 1785. . . .]

"Mr. Strahan was born at Edinburgh in the year 1715. His father, who had a small appointment in the Customs, gave his son the education which every lad of decent rank then received in a country where the avenues to Learning were easy, and open to men of the most moderate circumstances. After having passed through the tuition of a grammar-school, he was put apprentice to a Printer; and, when a very young man, removed to a wider sphere in that line of business, and went to follow his trade in London. Sober, diligent, and attentive, while his emoluments were for some time very scanty, he contrived to live rather within than beyond his income; and though he married early, and without such a provision as prudence might have looked for in the establishment of a family, he continued to thrive, and to better his circumstances. This he would often mention as an encouragement to early matrimony; and used to say, that he never had a child born, that Providence did not send some increase of income to provide for the increase of his household. With sufficient vigour of mind, he had that happy flow of animal spirits, which is not easily discouraged by unpromising appearances. By him who can look with firmness upon difficulties, their conquest is already half achieved; but the man on whose heart and spirits they lie heavy, will scarcely be able to bear up against their pressure. The forecast of timid, or the disgust of too delicate minds, are very unfortunate attendants for men of business; who, to be successful, must often push improbabilities, and bear with mortifications.

"His abilities in his profession, accompanied with perfect integrity and unabating diligence, enabled him, after the first difficulties were overcome, to get on with rapid success. And he was one of the most flourishing men in the trade, when, in the year 1770, he purchased a share of the patent for King's Printer of Mr. Eyre, with whom he maintained the most cordial intimacy during all the rest of his life. Besides the emoluments arising from this appointment, as well as from a very extensive private business, he now drew largely from a field which required some degree of speculative sagacity to cultivate; I mean, that great literary property which he acquired by

---

3. A sketch of George Strahan by Nichols is in *Illustr.*, VI, 149-151n.
4. A sketch of Andrew Strahan by Nichols is in *Illustr.*, VIII, 505-506.

purchasing the copy-rights of some of the most celebrated Authors of the time. In this his liberality kept equal pace with his prudence, and in some cases went perhaps rather beyond it. Never had such rewards been given to the labours of literary men, as now were received from him and his associates in those purchases of copy-rights from Authors.

"Having now attained the first great object of business, wealth, Mr. Strahan looked with a very allowable ambition on the stations of political rank and eminence. Politicks had long occupied his active mind, which he had for many years pursued as his favourite amusement, by corresponding on that subject with some of the first characters of the age. Mr. Strahan's queries to Dr. Franklin in the year 1769, respecting the discontents of the Americans, published in the London Chronicle of 28th July, 1778, shew the just conception he entertained of the important consequences of that dispute, and his anxiety as a good subject to investigate, at that early period, the proper means by which their grievances might be removed, and a permanent harmony restored between the two countries. In the year 1775 he was elected a member of parliament for the borough of Malmsbury, in Wiltshire, with a very illustrious colleague, the Hon. C. J. Fox; and in the succeeding parliament for Wotton Bassett, in the same county. In this station, applying himself with that industry which was natural to him, he attended the House with a scrupulous punctuality, and was a useful member. His talents for business acquired the consideration to which they were entitled, and were not unnoticed by the Minister.

"In his political connections he was constant to the friends to whom he had been first attached. He was a steady supporter of that party who were turned out of administration in spring 1784, and lost his seat in the House of Commons by the dissolution of parliament with which that change was followed; a situation which he did not shew any desire to resume on the return of the new parliament.

"One motive for his not wishing a seat in the next parliament, was a feeling of some decline in his health, which had rather suffered from the long sittings and late hours with which the political warfare in the last had been attended. Though without any fixed disease, his strength was visibly declining; and though his spirits survived his strength, yet the vigour and activity of his mind were also considerably impaired. Both continued gradually to decline till his death, which happened on Saturday, the 9th of July 1785, in the 71st year of his age.

"Endued with much natural sagacity, and an attentive observation of life, he owed his rise to that station of opulence and respect which he attained, rather to his own talents and exertion, than to any accidental occurrence of favourable or fortunate circumstances. His mind, though not deeply tinctured with learning, was not uninformed by letters. From a habit of attention to style, he had acquired a considerable portion of critical acuteness in the discernment of its beauties and defects. In one branch of writing himself excelled, I mean the epistolary, in which he not only shewed the precision and clearness of business, but possessed a neatness, as well as fluency of expression, which I have known few letter-writers to surpass. Letter-writing was one of his favourite amusements; and among his correspondents were men of such eminence and talents as well repaid his endeavours to entertain them. One of these, as we have before mentioned, was the justly-celebrated Dr. Franklin, originally a Printer like Mr. Strahan, whose friendship and correspondence he continued to enjoy, notwithstanding the difference of their sentiments in political matters, which often afforded pleasantry, but never mixed any thing acrimonious in their letters. One of the latest he received from his illustrious and venerable friend, contained a humourous allegory of the state of politicks in Britain, drawn from the profession of Printing, of which, though the Doctor had quitted the exercise, he had not forgotten the terms.

"There are stations of acquired greatness, which make men proud to recall the lowness of that from which they rose. The native eminence of Franklin's mind was above concealing the humbleness of his origin. Those only who possess no intrinsic elevation are afraid to sully the honours to which accident has reared them, by the recollection of that obscurity whence they spring.

"Of this recollection Mr. Strahan was rather proud than ashamed; and I have heard those who were disposed to censure him, blame it as a kind of ostentation in which he was weak enough to indulge. But methinks ''tis to consider too curiously, to consider it so.' There is a kind of reputation which we may laudably desire, and justly enjoy; and he who is sincere enough to forego the pride of ancestry and of birth, may, without much imputation of vanity, assume the merit of his own elevation.

"In that elevation he neither triumphed over the inferiority of those he had left below him, nor forgot the equality in which they had formerly stood. Of their inferiority he did not even remind them, by the ostentation of grandeur, or the parade of wealth. In his house there was none of that saucy train, none of that state or finery, with which the illiberal delight to confound and to dazzle those who may have formerly seen them in less enviable circumstances. No man was more mindful of, or more solicitous to oblige the acquaintance or companions of his early days. The advice which his experience, or the assistance which his purse could afford, he was ready to communicate; and at his table in London every Scotsman found an easy introduction, and every old acquaintance a cordial welcome. This was not merely a virtue of hospitality, or a duty of benevolence with him; he felt it warmly as a sentiment: and that paper in 'The Mirror,' of which I mentioned him as the author (the letter from London in the 94th number), was, I am persuaded, a genuine picture of his feelings on the recollection of those scenes in which his youth had been spent, and of those companions with which it had been associated.

"Such of them as still survive him will read the above short account of his life with interest and with pleasure. For others it may not be altogether devoid of entertainment or of use. If among the middling and busy ranks of mankind it can afford an encouragement to the industry of those who are beginning to climb into life, or furnish a lesson of moderation to those who have attained its height; if to the first it may recommend honest industry and sober diligence; if to the latter it may suggest the ties of antient fellowship, and early connection, which the pride of wealth or of station loses as much dignity as it foregoes satisfaction by refusing to acknowledge; if it shall cheer one hour of despondency or discontent to the young; if it shall save one frown of disdain or of refusal to the unfortunate; the higher and more refined class of my readers will forgive the familiarity of the example, and consider, that it is not from the biography of Heroes or of Statesmen that instances can be drawn to prompt the conduct of the bulk of mankind, or to excite the useful, though less splendid, virtues of private and domestic life."

[The material below appears as a note to the text of Nichols' life of William Strahan.]

[The following "Sketch of a Character, attempted on the loss of a much respected Friend," came from the heart of one who both loved and revered him.]

> If industry and knowledge of mankind,
> Could prove that Fortune is not always blind;
> If wealth acquir'd could prompt a generous heart,
> To feel new joys its blessings to impart;
> Lament with me such worth should be withdrawn,
> And all who knew his worth must weep for STRAHAN!
> In business, which became his pleasure, keen:
> Tho' not enough the tradesman to be *mean*;
> Social and frank, a zealous friendly guide,
> With sage advice, and ready purse beside,
> And far above the littleness of pride:
> Pride that, exacting homage, meets, in place
> Of true respect, contempt beneath grimace.
> A breast thus warm could not with coolness bear
> Those base returns the good must sometimes share;
> Sincere himself, his feelings stood excus'd,
> Never by one man to be twice abus'd:
> For natures alter not; the leopard's skin
> Is stain'd without, as hearts are stain'd within.
> Numbers, whose private sorrows he reliev'd,
> Have felt a loss, alas! but ill conceiv'd;
> He's gone! and those who miss him, never will
> Find equal excellence his place to fill.
> Thy darts, O Death, that fly so thick around,
> In such a victim many others wound.
>   *Bernard's Inn.*   J. NOORTHOUCK.

[Editor's note: The ensuing quotation from the will of William Strahan and Nichols' concluding comment on it appear as a note in Nichols' life of William Strahan.]

"I give and bequeath unto my Executors hereinafter named, the sum of One Thousand Pounds, of lawful money of Great Britain, to be paid unto them by and out of such part of my personal Estate, of which I have a disposing power, upon trust, that they my said Executors, and the survivor of them, and the Executors or Administrators of such survivor, do and shall pay and assign the said sum of One Thousand Pounds unto the Master, Wardens, and Court of Assistants of the Company of Stationers of London, to whom I give and bequeath the same sum of One Thousand Pounds, upon trust, That they the said Master, Wardens, and Court of Assistants of the said Stationers Company, and their successors, the Master, Wardens, and Court of Assistants of the said Stationers Company of London, for the time being, do and shall, from time to time, lay out, and invest the said sum of One Thousand Pounds, in the purchase of Government Security or Securities, or place and continue the same sum at Interest on such other security or securities, and in the name or names of such person or persons as they, or the major number of them, shall from time to time think fit, and as touching one Moiety or Half-part of the annual Interest, Dividends and Proceeds that shall from time to time arise, or be made by or from the said sum of One Thousand Pounds, my mind and will is, and I do hereby order and direct, that such one Moiety or Half-part of the same annual Interest, Dividends and Proceeds, from time to time arising from the said Sum of One Thousand Pounds, shall yearly, and every year for ever, in the week after Christmas-day annually, be paid, distributed, and divided, in equal shares or proportions, 'to such Five poor Journeymen Printers, natives of that part of Great Britain, called England or Wales, and who shall be Freemen of the said Company of Stationers,' as the Master, Wardens, and Court of Assistants for the time being of the said Company of Stationers, or the major number of them, shall annually elect and choose as proper persons to partake of the said charitable donation; and as touching the remaining Moiety or Half-part of the annual Interest, Dividends and Proceeds that shall from time to time arise, or be made by or from the said sum of One Thousand Pounds, my mind and will is, and I do hereby order and direct, that such last mentioned Moiety or Half-part of the same annual Interest, Dividends and Proceeds, from time to time arising from the said sum of One Thousand Pounds, shall yearly, and every year for ever, in the week after Christmas-day annually, be paid, distributed, and divided, in equal shares or proportions, 'to such Five poor Journeymen Printers, natives of that part of Great Britain, called Scotland, without regard to their being freemen or being non-freemen' of the said Company of Stationers, as the Master, Wardens, and Court of Assistants, for the time being, of the said Company of Stationers, or the major number of them, shall annually elect and choose, as proper persons to partake of the said charitable donation; and upon, to, or for no other trust, intent, or purpose whatsoever"—

[The Sum of 1000*l.* was laid out in the purchase of Three *per Cent.* Annuities, 1726, and from the Yearly Dividend ten persons receive each 4*l.*[5]

Mr. Strahan, among many other generous legacies, gave also 100*l.* to the poor of the parish of St. Bride's, in which he had many years resided.]

5. These pensions of £4 were raised to £8 by a later bequest of Andrew Strahan; see n. 1.

Joseph Johnson

[The following account of the life of Joseph Johnson, written by John Aikin for the *Gent. Mag.* (December 1809), was reprinted by Nichols in *Lit. Anec.*, III, 461-464, where it is attributed to *J. Aikin*. Certain other materials from other places in the writings of Nichols follow Aikin's memoir.

It is typical of Nichols to be meticulous about attributing borrowed material to its proper source. In working closely with him over a period of twenty years, I have yet to find an example of his using another man's work without acknowledgment. Though Nichols did not write this life, he is responsible for its publication twice, and possibly even for its being written; he also made interesting additions to it. More important, Johnson's life helps round out the cycle of lives of men in the book trade in this volume.

Joseph Johnson was a publisher of works by Anna Letitia Aikin (Mrs. Barbauld), Joseph Priestley, William Cowper, Erasmus Darwin, Mary Wollstonecraft, and Maria Edgeworth. His biographers, in addition to John Aikin, are Timperley and Henry Richard Tedder, whose brief life in the DNB is greatly indebted to Aikin in fact and phraseology. Plomer, Bushnell, and Dix have a fair-sized entry for Johnson in their *Dictionary of Booksellers and Printers*, p. 141. Knight gives even more space to him in his *Shadows of the Old Booksellers*, pp. 244-248.

A person undertaking further study of Joseph Johnson would do well to begin with the manuscripts in the collections of Princeton University Library, which has not only original letters from Cowper to Johnson and Johnson to Cowper but also extracts and copies of much more of their correspondence in the Hannay Collection of William Cowper. Yale's Beinecke Library possesses an autograph letter of Johnson to William Wordsworth, 14 September 1798; and the Folger Shakespeare Library has a letter from Anna Letitia Aikin to Johnson, Y.c.82(1), dated 29 April ca. 1780.]

Mr. JOSEPH JOHNSON, a respectable Bookseller in St. Paul's Church-yard, was born at Liverpool in November 1738, of parents who were Dissenters of the Baptist persuasion. He was sent to London at the age of fourteen; and after some time was apprenticed with Mr. George Keith of Gracechurch-street. He began business for himself in a shop on Fish-street-hill, a situation he chose as being in the track of the Medical Students resorting to the Hospitals in the Borough, and which probably was the foundation of his connexions with many eminent members of that profession. From that place he removed to Paternoster-row, where he lived some years in partnership first with Mr. Davenport, and then with Mr. John Payne. His house and stock were entirely destroyed by fire in 1770; after which misfortune he removed to the shop in St. Paul's Church-yard, in which he thenceforth carried on business without a partner to the time of his death, Dec. 20, 1809; an event greatly regretted by his numerous friends; and had been for some years past considered as the Father of the Trade.

The character of Mr. Johnson, established by his integrity, good sense, and honourable principles of dealing, soon raised him to eminence as a Publisher; and many of the most distinguished names in Science and Literature during the last half century appear in works which he ushered to the world. Of a temper the reverse of sanguine, with a manner somewhat cold and indifferent, and with a decided aversion to all arts of puffing and parade, the confidence and attachment he inspired were entirely the result of his solid judgment, his unaffected sincerity, and the friendly benevolence with which he entered into the interests of all who were connected with him. Although he was not remarkable for the encouragement he held out to Authors—the consequence of his being neither sanguine nor pushing; yet it was his invariable rule, when the success of a work surpassed his expectations, to make the Writer a partaker in the emolument, though he lay under no other obligation to do so than his own notions of justice and generosity. The kindness of his heart was equally conspicuous in all the relations of life. His house and purse were always open to the calls of friendship, kindred, or misfortune; and perhaps few men of his means and condition have done more substantial services to persons whose merits and necessities recommended them to his notice.

It is well known that Mr. Johnson's literary connexions have lain in great part amung the free Enquirers both on religious and political topics. He was himself, on conviction, a friend to such large and liberal discussion as is not inconsistent with the peace and welfare of Society, and the preservation of due decorum towards things really respectable. But these were limits within which, both by temper and principle, he wished to see such discussion confined; for turbulence and sedition were utterly abhorrent from his nature. When, therefore, for the unconscious offence of selling a few copies of a pamphlet of which he was not the publisher, and which was a reply to one of which he had sold a much larger number, the opportunity was taken of involving him in a prosecution that brought upon him the infliction of fine and imprisonment, it was by many considered as the ungenerous indulgence of a long-hoarded spleen against him on account of publications not liable to legal censure, though displeasing to Authority.[1] It is gratifying, however, to relate, that during the height of party animosity, so little was he regarded personally as a party-man, that he continued to number among his intimate friends, several worthy persons of opposite

---

1. The pamphlet was by Gilbert Wakefield; Johnson was sentenced to nine months' imprisonment and fined £50 in 1797.

sentiments and connexions, who, with himself, were capable of considering a man's performance of the duties of life apart from his speculative opinions.

Although the majority of his publications were of the theological and political class, yet the number of those in science and elegant literature was by no means inconsiderable. Besides all the scientific writings of Dr. Priestley, he published many important works in Medicine and Anatomy; and others in different branches of knowledge. Two Poets of great modern celebrity were by him first introduced to the publick—[William] Cowper and [Erasmus] Darwin. The former of these, with the diffidence, and perhaps the despondency, of his character, had actually, by means of a friend, made over to him his two volumes of Poems on no other condition than that of securing him from expence; but when the Publick, which neglected the first volume, had discovered the rich mine opened in "The Task," and assigned the Author his merited place among the first-rate English Poets, Mr. Johnson would not avail himself of his advantage, but displayed a liberality which has been warmly acknowledged by that admirable though unfortunate person.

It is proper to mention that his true regard for the interests of Literature rendered him an enemy to that typographical luxury which, joined to the necessary increase of expence in printing, has so much enhanced the price of new books as to be a material obstacle to the indulgence of a laudable and reasonable curiosity by the reading Publick. On this principle he usually consulted cheapness rather than appearance in his own publications; and if Authors were sometimes mortified by this preference, the purpose of extensive circulation was better served.

Mr. Johnson was of a weak and delicate frame of body, and was much afflicted with asthmatic complaints, which visibly gained ground upon him as he advanced in years. The immediate cause of his dissolution was a pleuritic attack, under which he quietly sunk after three days of patient suffering. His remains were deposited in the church-yard of Fulham, in which parish he had a country house. He was never married.

J. AIKIN.

[Editor's note: Johnson's part in the foundation of the *Analytical Review* is described in the following paragraph from Nichols' life of Thomas Christie (*Lit. Anec.*, IX, 388).]

[Never neglecting his [Christie's] medical pursuits, and to all appearances having nothing else in view; his mind constantly ran on topics of classical, theological, and philosophical Literature. He had carefully perused the best of the Foreign Literary Journals, and could refer with ease to their contents;

and he loved the society in which subjects of literary history and criticism were discussed. More than one of his intimate friends, some of them much senior in years, and not wholly inattentive to such pursuits, had often occasion to be surprized at the extent of his acquirements. It was this accumulation of knowledge which suggested to Mr. Christie the first outline of a Review of Books upon the *analytical* plan; and finding in the late Mr. Johnson of St. Paul's Church-yard, a corresponding spirit of liberality and enterprise, the "Analytical Review" was begun in May 1788; and the Preface, it is believed, was from Mr. Christie's pen.]

[Editor's note: Another reference is made to Johnson in Nichols' life of Thomas Christie, who was, wrote Nichols, "At this period. . . frequently a welcome visitor at my house; and an entertaining Correspondent, both as a private friend, and a contributor to the labours of Sylvanus Urban" (*Lit. Anec.*, IX, 368). The reference to Johnson is in a letter from Christie to Nichols, written from Edinburgh and dated 20 August 1786 (ibid., pp. 372-373).]

How does Mr. Bonnycastle do? . . . I hope he is not now, or at least will not be long in that state, in which it is said, that *it is not good for man to be—alone* I mean. The day before I left London, I dined at Mr. Johnson's; and who should come in, about tea-time, but a certain lady, whom I was glad to have seen, and whom I am disposed to think very highly of. If I have any skill in physiognomy, I should pronounce her possessed of a great share of good sense, and of good temper. Am I right?*

[*He was in this instance perfectly correct, both in his ideas of Physiognomy; and in the good opinion he formed of Miss Bridget Newell, the daughter-in-law of my old and much esteemed Friend David Henry, esq. [Nichols' predecessor as editor of the *Gentleman's Magazine*, whose life is in this volume]—She soon after became the wife of Mr. [John] Bonnycastle [whose publisher was Joseph Johnson]. NICHOLS.]

[Editor's note: The following is Nichols' addition to Aikin's life. It appears in *Lit. Anec.*, VIII, 447.]

[A handsome monument in the North-east corner of Fulham church-yard is thus inscribed:]

<blockquote>
Here lie the remains of
Joseph Johnson, late of St. Paul's, London,
who departed this life on the 20th day of
December, 1809, aged 72 years.
</blockquote>

A Man equally distinguished by Probity, Industry, and Disinterestedness in his intercourse with the Publick, and every domestic and social virtue in private life; beneficent without ostentation, ever ready to produce merit, and to relieve distress; unassuming in prosperity, not appalled by misfortune; inexorable to his own, indulgent to the wants of others; resigned and cheerful under the torture of a malady which he saw gradually destroy his life.

Part III. Illustrators and Designers

Isaac Basire and the Three James Basires

[Nichols' lives of the Basires cover four generations of engravers. Isaac Basire was the founder of the dynasty, and his son James was the most important member of it. It is of this first James that Nichols has the longest life. James Basire, son of Isaac, had a son named James, and he in turn had a son named James; the latter two are treated only briefly by Nichols, as is the founder Isaac.

The first James Basire had the distinction of having the young William Blake apprenticed to him for seven years as his pupil and assistant. Many references to him will be found in Gilchrist's biography of Blake.

A passing mention of one or another of the Basires finds its way into many of the books dealing with the history of engraving. The first James, for instance, is referred to by Malcolm C. Salaman in *The Old Engravers of England* (London, 1907); and all three of the Jameses are introduced by Arthur M. Hind in *A Short History of Engraving and Etching* (London, 1911). The first James, again, makes an appearance in Jean Adhémar, *La Gravure originale au XVIIIe siècle* (Paris, 1963). Manuscripts and letters of the Basires do not seem to have survived in great abundance, but some are now located in a number of repositories. The Osborn Collection contains several bills from the second James Basire to Nichols for work done; it also contains three letters from the third James Basire, including one to John Bowyer Nichols in which the death of John Nichols is mentioned. The British Museum has a letter from the second James to Richard Gough, dated 7 January 1789; and Harvard University Libraries hold one James Basire letter.

A portrait of the first James by his son is prefixed to Vol. IX (sometimes Vol. VIII) of *Literary Anecdotes*. The lives that follow this headnote are from this same work (III, 717-718). A memoir of the Basires by Frederick Wedmore, citing Nichols as a source, is in the DNB.]

Mr. *Isaac Basire*, Engraver and Printer, born 1704, lived near St. John's Gate, Clerkenwell. He engraved the Frontispiece to an improved edition of Bailey's Dictionary, 1755, &c. &c. and died in 1768. He was a fine chubby-faced man, as appears by an excellent portrait of him, a drawing by his son.

Mr. *James Basire*, son of Isaac, born Oct. 6, 1730, was bred from infancy to his Father's profession, which he practiced with great reputation for 60 years. He studied under the direction of Mr. Richard Dalton; was with him at Rome; made several drawings from the pictures of Raphael, &c, at the time that Mr. Stuart, Mr. Brand Hollis, and Sir Joshua Reynolds, were there. He was appointed Engraver to the Society of Antiquaries about

1760; and to the Royal Society about 1770. As a specimen of his numerous works it may be sufficient to refer to the beautiful Plates of the "Vetusta Monumenta," published by the Society of Antiquaries; and to Mr. Gough's truly valuable "Sepulchral Monuments." With the Author of that splendid Work he was most deservedly a Favourite. When Mr. Gough had formed the plan, and hesitated on actually committing it to the press, he says, "Mr. Basire's specimens of drawing and engraving gave me so much satisfaction, that it was impossible to resist the impulse of carrying such a design into execution." The Royal Portraits and other beautiful Plates, in the "Sepulchral Monuments," fully justify the idea which the Author had entertained of his Engraver's talents; and are handsomely acknowledged by Mr. Gough. The Plate of *Le Champ de Drap d'Or* was finished about 1774; a Plate so large, that paper was obliged to be made on purpose, which to this time is called *Antiquarian Paper*. Besides the numerous Plates which he engraved for the Societies, he was engaged in a great number of public and private works, which bear witness to the fidelity of his *burin*. He engraved the Portraits of Fielding and Dr. Morell, 1762; Earl Camden, in 1766, after Sir Joshua Reynolds; Pylades and Orestes, 1770, from a picture by West; Portraits of the Rev. John Watson and Sir George Warren's family; Dean Swift, and Dr. Parnell, 1774; Sir James Burrow, 1780, Mr. Bowyer, 1782; Portraits of Dr. Munro, Mr. Gray, Mr. Thompson, Lady Stanhope, Sir George Saville, Bp. Hoadly, Rev. Dr. Pegge, Mr. Price, Algernon Sydney, Andrew Marvell, William Camden, William Brereton, 1790; Captain Cooke's Portrait, and other Plates, for his First and Second Voyages; a great number of Plates for Stuart's Athens (which are well drawn.) In another branch of his Art, the Maps for General Roy's "Roman Antiquities in Britain" are particularly excellent.

He married, first, Anne Beaupuy; and, secondly Isabella Turner. He died Sept. 6, 1802, in his 73d year, and was buried in the vault under Pentonville chapel.[1]

The ingenuity and integrity of this able Artist are inherited by a second *James*, his eldest son by the second wife, who was born Nov. 12, 1769; and of whose Works it may be enough to mention the "Cathedrals," published by the Society of Antiquaries, from the exquisite drawings of Mr. John Carter.[2] He married, May 1, 1795, Mary Cox, by whom he has several children; of whom the eldest, a third *James Basire*, born Feb. 20, 1796, has already given several proofs of superior excellence in the arts of Drawing and Engraving.

1. The portrait of the first James Basire by his son is referred to in the Advertisement to Vol. IX of *Lit. Anec.* (p. vi): "To Mr. JAMES BASIRE (whose modest worth, even in his boyish days, secured my hearty esteem) I am indebted for a Portrait of his Father; whose animated features I felicitate myself in thus having first been the medium of introducing to the Publick."

2. As engraver to the Society of Antiquaries, the second James Basire made three trips across Dorsetshire in the company of Nichols and Gough; see *Lit. Anec.*, VI, 283n (reproduced in this volume as n. 24 to the life of Gough).

John Baskerville

[Nichols' life of Baskerville comes, primarily, from *Lit. Anec.*, III, 450-461. According to Nichols' typical (and sometimes maddening) practice, a good deal of the material is in notes. On two pages, only two lines of text float across the top, while all the rest of the page is dark with the small print of notes. For the sake of easier reading, I have brought a good deal of the notational material into the consecutive place in the text where it belongs but have indicated its original location.

Baskerville has had a good deal of attention in the twentieth century, beginning with a *Handlist* of books printed by him or with his types (Cambridge University Press, 1904). This was followed by a work by Ralph Straus and R. K. Dent, *John Baskerville: A Memoir* (London, 1907). A work on the ancestry of Baskerville appeared next: *John Baskerville*, written by Thomas Cave (London, 1923). In 1927 (London) came *The Baskerville Types, a Critique*, published as Vol. 26, No. 221, of *The Monotype Recorder*, with the cover title "The Roman & Italic of John Baskerville. A Critical Work." Hans H. Bockwitz produced two works on Baskerville; the first was *Baskerville in Letters* (1935) and the second, *John Baskerville, Buchdrucker, im Urteil Deutscher Zeitgenossen* [in the judgment of German contemporaries] (1937). Also in 1937, William Bennett of Birmingham published his work, *John Baskerville, the Birmingham Printer. His Press Relations and Friends.*

In the 1940's, four more books on Baskerville were published, two of them in 1944; they were Benjamin Walker, *The Resting Places of the Remains of John Baskerville, the Thrice-buried Printer*, and Josiah H. Benton, *John Baskerville, Type-founder and Printer* (New York, 11th Chap Book of the Typophile series). In 1945 appeared, by Paul A. Bennett, *John Baskerville's Types in America* (Boston, Society of Printers); and in 1949, by John Dreyfus, *The Survival of Baskerville's Punches*.

Two additional books, these published in the 1950's, complete this list of works about Baskerville in this century; they are Henry H. Evans, *John Baskerville: The Gracious Infidel* (Peregrine Press, 1953), and Philip Gaskell, *John Baskerville: A Bibliography* (Cambridge University Press, 1959).

A life of Baskerville by Henry Richard Tedder is in the DNB. Tedder uses Nichols as a source and gives many additional references. Almost every history or dictionary of typography and printing has in it some brief account of Baskerville.

Letters and other manuscripts of Baskerville are in the holdings of a number of libraries. One letter from the Beinecke Rare Book and Manuscript Library at Yale and two from the Special Manuscript Collection of the Columbia University Library (all three probably addressed to Robert Dodsley) will be introduced in the life by way of illustration.]

This celebrated Printer was born at Wolverley, in the county of Worcester, in 1706, heir to a paternal estate of 60*l. per annum,* which fifty years after, while in his own possession, had increased to 90*l.*; and this estate, with an exemplary filial piety and generosity, he allowed to his parents till their deaths, which happened at an advanced age.

He was trained to no occupation, but in 1726 became a writing-master at Birmingham.

In 1737, he taught at a school in the Bull-ring, and is said to have written an excellent hand.

As painting suited his talents, he entered into the lucrative branch of japanning, and resided at Nº 22, in Moor-street; and in 1745 he took a building lease of eight acres and two furlongs, North-west of the town, to which he gave the name of *Easy Hill,* converted it into a little Eden, and built a house in the centre: but the town, daily increasing in magnitude and population, soon surrounded it with buildings.—Here he continued the business of a japanner for life: his carriage, each panel of which was a distinct picture, might be considered the pattern-card of his trade, and was drawn by a beautiful pair of cream-coloured horses.

[[Nichols notes:] Mr. [Samuel] Derrick, in a letter written to the Earl of Corke, July 15, 1760, containing a description of Birmingham, says, "I need not remind your Lordship, that Baskerville, one of the best Printers in the world, was born in this town, and resides near it. His house stands at about half a mile's distance, on an eminence that commands a fine prospect. I paid him a visit, and was received with great politeness, though an entire stranger. His apartments are elegant; his staircase is particularly curious; and the room in which he dines, and calls a smoking room, is very handsome. The grate and furniture belonging to it are, I think, of bright wrought iron, and cost him a round sum.

"He has just completed an elegant Octavo Common Prayer Book; has a scheme for publishing a grand Folio edition of the Bible; and will soon finish a beautiful collection of Fables by the ingenious Mr. [Robert] Dodsley. He manufactures his own paper, types, and ink; and they are remarkably good. This ingenious Artist carries on a great trade in the japan way, in which he shewed me several useful articles, such as candlesticks, stands, salvers, waiters, bread-baskets, tea-boards, &c. elegantly designed and highly finished. Baskerville is a great cherisher of genius, which, wherever he finds it, he loses no opportunity of cultivating. One of his workmen has manifested fine talents for fruit-painting, in several pieces which he shewed me."

Dr. [Andrew] Kippis, who has copied this Letter, adds "his own testimony concerning Mr. Baskerville's politeness to strangers, and the chearful hospitality with which he treated those who were introduced to him. He was well known," says the Doctor, "to many ingenious men, and was particularly intimate with the late Mr. Robert Dodsley and Mr. Shenstone."]

His inclination for letters induced him, in 1750, to turn his thoughts towards the press. He spent many years in the uncertain pursuit; sunk 600*l*. before he could produce one letter to please himself, and some thousands before the shallow stream of profit began to flow.

[Editor's note: Three letters from Baskerville to a recipient identified, in another hand than Baskerville's, only as Dodsley (probably Robert Dodsley) will be introduced here, two of them written in 1752 and one in 1756. The two written in 1752 are in the Special Manuscript Collection of the Columbia University Library and the one written in 1756 is in the Beinecke Rare Book and Manuscript Library of Yale University. After these three interpolated letters, the text of Nichols' life is resumed.]

Dear Sr Birmingham 2^d Oct. 1752

To remove in some Measure y^r Impatience, I have sent you an Impression of 14 punches of the two lines Great Primer, which have been begun & finish'd in 9 Days only, & contain all the Roman Letters necessary in the Titles & half Titles. I can't forbear saying they pleased me, as I can make nothing more Correct, nor shall you see any thing of mine much less so. You'll observe they strike the Eye much more sensibly than the smaller Characters tho Equally perfect, till the press shows them to more Advantage. The press is creeping slowly towards perfection. I flatter my self with being able to print nearly as good a Colour & smooth a stroke as the inclos'd. I should esteem it a favour if you'd send me the Initial Letters of all the Cantos, lest they should not be included in the said 14, & three or four pages of any part of the poem, from whence to form a Bill for the Casting a suitable Number of each Letter. The R. wants a few light Touches & the Y. half an hour's Correction.

This Day we have resolutely set about 13 of the same siz'd Italick Capitals, which will not be at all inferior to the Roman, & I doubt not to compleat them in a fortnight. You need therefore be in no pain about our being ready by the time appointed. Our best Respects to Mrs Dodsley & our friend Mr Beckett concludes me
                    Y^r most obed Servt John Baskerville

[Verso] Pray put it in no One's power to let Mr Caslon see them.

Dear Sr Birmingham 19 Oct. 1752

As I propos'd in my last I have sent you Impressions from a Candle of 20, two Lines Great Primer Italick, which were begun & finish'd in 10 Days only. We are now about Figures which are in a good forwardness, & changing a few of those Letters we concluded finish'd. My next Care will be to strike the punches into Copper & justify them with all the

Care & Skill I am Master of. You may depend on my being ready by y^r time (Christmas) but if more time could be allow'd I should make use of it all in Correcting & justifying. As so much depends on appearing perfect on first starting, I have with great pains justified the plate for the platten & stone on which it falls, so that they are as perfect planes as it will ever be in my power to procure; for instance, if you Rest one End of ye Plate on the Stone, & let the other fall the height of an Inch, It falls soft as if you dropt it on feathers or several folds of Silk, & when you raise it, you manifestly feel it suck (if you'll excuse so unphilosophical a Term). Wet the two, & either would support the other with (I believe) 500 W^t added to it, if held perpendicularly. To as perfect a plane will I endeavour to bring the faces of the Types, if I have time. Nor do I despair of better Ink & printing (the Character must speak for itself) than has hitherto been seen.

I must beg Leave to remark on the Plate sent me, that I fear the performer is capable of doing nothing. Much better, as he's greatly deficient in Design Drawing & Execution with the Needle, the composition of the Ornament if it will bear that Name is mean, or if you will, means Nothing. To Speak in my own Way the D. is as bad a one as can well be made. If you are determin'd to have the Initials 'grav'd, I would refer you to Pine's Horace, where the Execution is neat, tho' the Proportion is bad. The Letter is Suppos'd rais'd, consequently the side next the light is express'd by a very faint Line, its Opposite very strong, like the light & Shadow in a picture. If you'll accept my Judgm^t & Skill it is at y^r Service. Give me the Initials & Size, or if you please I'll give the Size to 5 or 6 Lines great primer, & the Letters as correct as I can draw them in black Lead, the Ornament as you & the 'Graver can agree. Thus Dear S^r you see I readily accept the Terms you are so kind to offer me of treating you freely as my Friend. Pray consider the above inter nos only & give me a Line as soon as you have Leisure. As you are in the Land of Franks, half a Doz. would do me a particular pleasure, as a good many things not worth a Groat might be communicated by

Y^r most obed & hble Servt
J Baskerville

Hast had almost made me forget complem^{ts} of the Family &c.

Dear Sir,   Birm^m 20 Dec. 1756

I have for some past hoped a line from you in relation to the paper Scheme. Whether you have sent, or chose to send any of the thin post to Mr Culver, as that is the only Article I lay any stress upon in his hands; pray do not send it, if you are more inclined to keep it. He shall stay till I can furnish him, which probably may be six Weeks or two Months. I have more than six Ream of that sort, which If I chose to do it, I could sell tomorrow in Birm^m at 24/. & if inserting his name makes the least difference in y^r Scheme of Advertising, I shall like it quite as well left out. I have sent Samples of the ornamented paper & thin post gilt to several neighbouring towns & have receiv'd Orders freely from them. I told you in my last the Prices, but that need not be a Rule to you, perhaps some of y^r Customers would like them less if sold too low, all I fear'd was laying an Embargo on them. I propose reducing the Price of the octavo from 21 to 18 as it will be more suitable to the Quarto. Pray therefore make me D^r for that difference in all y^r Stock of that Sort. Pray give me y^r opinion if it would be wrong to make a present of a quire of each sort, & the thin gilt, to the Princes of Wales, as a Sample of English Manufactory: to be had at Mr Dodsley's; the Present mine.

I copied with great Pleasure from our Birm. Paper a fine Complem^t made you which I shall learn by heart, & of which I give you Joy. I shall have Virgil out of the Press by the latter end of Jan^y & hope to produce the Volume as smooth as the best Paper I have sent you. Pray will it not be proper to advertize how near it is finishing, & beg the Gentlemen who intend favouring me with their Names to send them by that time?

When this is done, I can print nothing at home but another Classick, (a Specimen of which will be given with it) which I cannot forbear thinking a grievous hardship, after the infinite pains & great expence I have been at. I have almost a mind to print a Pocket Classick in one size larger than the old Elzivers as the Difference will on Comparison be obvious to every Scholer nor should I be very sollicitous whether it paid me or not.

You have not fulfill'd y^r promise in sending me the Printer's Scheme. I am with due Respect to Mr James Dodsley & comp^ts of the ensuing Season

D^r S^r

Y^r obed^t Servt

J Baskerville

His first attempt was a quarto edition of Virgil, in 1756, price one guinea, now worth several.[1] This he reprinted in octavo 1758; and in that year was employed by the University of Oxford on an entirely new-faced Greek type.

The University of Oxford have lately contracted with Mr. Baskerville of Birmingham, for a complete Alphabet of Greek types, of the Great Primer size; and it is not doubted but that ingenious artist will excel in that character, as he has already done in the Roman and Italic, in his elegant edition of Virgil, which has gained the applause and admiration of most of the literati of Europe, as well as procured him the esteem and patronage of

---

1. See an addition of Nichols concerning the date of the quarto Virgil in *Lit. Anec.*, VIII, 447.

such of his own countrymen as distinguish themselves by paying a due regard to merit.
St. James's Chronicle, Sept. 5, 1758[2]

Soon after this he printed many other works, with more satisfaction to the literary world than emolument to himself; and obtained leave, from the University of Cambridge, to print a Bible in Royal Folio, and two Editions of the Common Prayer in three sizes; for the permission of doing which, he paid a great premium to that University.

The next in order of his works was "Dr. [Thomas] Newton's Edition of Milton's Poetical Works, 1759," 2 vols. 8vo.

In May 1760 he circulated Proposals for printing a Folio Bible; and in that year he printed "The Book of Common Prayer, 1760," in octavo.

"Dodsley's Select Fables of AEsop, 1761," 8vo.

"Juvenal and Persius, 1761," 8vo.

"Congreve's Works, 1761," 3 vols. 8vo.

"The Book of Common Prayer, 1762," in long lines.

Another very neat edition, in 12mo, 1762.

"Horace, edited by J. Livie, A.M. 1762," 8vo.

"Addison's Works, 1763," 4 vols. 4to.

Dr. [David] Jennings's "Introduction to the Knowledge of Medals, 1763," 8vo.

"The Holy Bible, for the use of Churches, 1763," a beautiful Royal Folio.

He also printed editions of Terence, Catullus, Lucretius, Sallust, and Florus, in Royal Quarto.

These publications rank the name of Baskerville with those persons who have the most contributed, at least in modern times, to the beauty and improvement of the art of Printing. Indeed, it is needless to say to what perfection he brought this excellent art. The paper, the type, and the whole execution of the works performed by him, are the best testimonies of his merit.

After the publication of the Folio Bible;* Mr. Baskerville appears to have been weary of the profession of a Printer; or at least he declined to carry it on, except through the medium of a confidential agent.†

[The following letter and Nichols' introduction of it appear as a note in *Literary Anecdotes*, to the word *Printer* in the above paragraph. See *Illustr.*, VIII, 458.]

* The subscribers were desired to send for those volumes to Mr. Baskerville's Printing Office, at Mr. Paterson's, at Essex-house, in Essex-street, in the Strand. NICHOLS.

† "Robert Martin has agreed with Mr. Baskerville for the use of his whole Printing Apparatus, with whom he has wrought as a journeyman for ten years past. He therefore offers his service to print at Birmingham for Gentlemen or Booksellers, on the most moderate terms, who may depend on all possible care and elegance in the execution. Samples, if necessary, may be seen, on sending a line to John Baskerville or Robert Martin." *June* 8, 176.. NICHOLS.

2. The quotation from the *St. James Chronicle* appears as a note in Nichols.

[The following is a copy of a Letter from Mr. Baskerville.]

To the Hon'ble Horace Walpole, Esq. Member of Parliament, in Arlington-street, London, this.

SIR, *Easy Hill, Birmingham,* 2d. *Nov.* 1762.

As the Patron and Encourager of Arts, and particularly that of Printing, I have taken the liberty of sending you a specimen of mine, begun ten years ago at the age of forty-seven; and prosecuted ever since, with the utmost care and attention; on the strongest presumption, that if I could fairly excel in this divine art, it would make my affairs easy, or at least give me Bread. But, alas! in both I was mistaken. The Booksellers do not chuse to encourage me, though I have offered them as low terms as I could possibly live by; nor dare I attempt an old Copy till a Law-suit relating to that affair is determined.

The University of Cambridge have given me a Grant to print their 8vo and 12mo Common Prayer Books; but under such shackles as greatly hurt me. I pay them for the former twenty, and for the latter twelve pounds ten shillings the thousand; and to the Stationers' Company thirty-two pounds for their permission to print one edition of the Psalms in Metre to the small Prayer-book; add to this, the great expence of double and treble carriage; and the inconvenience of a Printing-house an hundred miles off. All this summer I have had nothing to print at home. My Folio Bible is pretty far advanced at Cambridge, which will cost me 2000*l.* all hired at 5 *per Cent*. If this does not sell, I shall be obliged to sacrifice a small patrimony, which brings me in 74*l.* a year, to this business of Printing, which I am heartily tired of, and repent I ever attempted. It is surely a particular hardship, that I should not get bread in my own country (and it is too late to go abroad) after having acquired the reputation of excelling in the most useful art known to mankind; while every one who excels as a Player, Fiddler, Dancer, &c. not only lives in affluence, but has it in their power to save a fortune.

I have sent a few specimens (same as the inclosed) to the Courts of Russia and Denmark, and shall endeavour to do the same to most of the Courts in Europe; in hopes of finding in some one of them, a purchaser of the whole scheme, on the condition of my never attempting another type. I was saying this to a particular friend, who reproached me with not giving my own country the preference, as it would (he was pleased to say) be a national reproach to lose it: I told him, nothing but the greatest necessity would put me upon it; and even then I should resign it with the utmost reluctance. He observed, the Parliament had given a handsome premium for a great Medicine; and, he doubted not, if my affair was properly brought before the House of Commons, but some regard would be paid to it. I replied, I durst not presume to petition the House, unless encouraged by some of the Members, who might do me the honour to promote it; of which I saw not the least hopes. Thus, Sir, I have taken the liberty of laying before you my affairs, without the least aggravation; and humbly hope your patronage: To whom can I apply for protection, but the Great, who alone have it in their power to serve me? I rely on your candour as a Lover of the Arts, and to excuse this presumption in your most obedient and most humble Servant,

JOHN BASKERVILLE.

P.S. The folding of the Specimens will be taken out, by laying them a short time between damped papers.—N.B. The Ink, Presses, Chases, Moulds for casting, and all the apparatus for Printing, were made in my own Shops.

[How greatly must we regret the projected sale of his estate, for payment of a debt incurred for borrowed capital to print his Bible, when we witness the price which it now produces, whenever offered for sale; more particularly when we reflect, that, though entitled to this estate from his birth, Baskerville appropriated the produce of it, during the lives of his parents, to their comfort and support.[3]]

In 1764, he had the honour of presenting to his Majesty, and to the Princess Dowager of Wales, his then newly printed Octavo Common Prayer book; which was most graciously received.

In 1765, he applied to his friend the eminent and excellent Dr. [Benjamin] Franklin, then at Paris, and who had before in vain endeavoured to assist him in London[4] to sound the Literati respecting the purchase of his types; but received for answer, "That the French, reduced by the war of 1756, were so far from being able to pursue schemes of taste, that they were unable to repair their public buildings, and suffered the scaffolding to rot before them."

After this, we hear little or nothing of Mr. Baskerville as a Printer.

He died, without issue, Jan. 8, 1775; but it is painful to observe that, in the last solemn act of his life, he unblushingly avowed his total disbelief of Christianity.

[Editor's note: Baskerville's will, following this interpolation, appears as a note in *Literary Anecdotes*.]

---

3. This paragraph concludes the interpolated note, of which the letter and its introduction were a part.

4. [Editor's note: The following letter to Baskerville appears as a note in *Literary Anecdotes*.]

DEAR SIR,   *Craven-street, London,* 1764.

Let me give you a pleasant instance of the prejudice some have entertained against your Work. Soon after I returned, discoursing with a Gentleman concerning the Artists of Birmingham, he said "you would be a means of blinding all the readers in the nation, for the strokes of your letters, being too thin and narrow, hurt the eye, and he could never read a line of them without pain:" "I thought," said I, "you were going to complain of the gloss on the paper, some object to." "No, no," says he, "I have heard that mentioned; but it is not that; it is in the form and cut of the letters themselves; they have not that natural and easy proportion between the height and thickness of the stroke, which makes the common Printing so much the more comfortable to the eye."

You see this gentleman was a connoisseur. In vain I endeavoured to support your character against the charge; he knew what he felt, and could see the reason of it; and several other gentlemen among his friends had made the same observation, &c.

Yesterday he called to visit me, when, mischievously bent to try his judgment, I stept into my closet, tore off the top of Mr. Caslon's specimen, and produced it to him as yours brought with me from Birmingham, saying, "I had been examining it since he spoke to me, and could not for my life perceive the disproportion he mentioned, desiring him to point it out to me." He readily undertook it, and went over the several founts, shewing me every where what he thought instances of that disproportion; and declared, "that he could not then read the specimen without feeling very strongly the pain he had mentioned to me." I spared him that time the confusion of being told, that these were the types he had been reading all his life with so much ease to his eyes; the types his adored Newton is printed with, on which he has pored not a little; nay, the very types his own book is printed with, for he is himself an Author, and yet never discovered this painful disproportion in them, till he thought they were yours.

I am, &c.   B. FRANKLIN.

Memorandum, That I, John Baskerville, of Birmingham, in the county of Warwick, on the 6th day of January, 1773, do make this my last will and testament, as follows: First, I give, bequeath, and devise unto my executors hereafter named, the sum of 2000*l*. in trust, to discharge a settlement made before my marriage to my wife Sarah. I also give to my executors the lease of my house and land, held under the late John Ruston, in trust, for the sole use and benefit of the said Sarah my wife, during the term of her natural life, and after her decease to the uses mentioned below. And my further will is, that the sum of 2000*l*. shall be raised and paid to my wife out of my book debts, stock in trade, and household furniture, plate and china. (N.B. The use of my furniture, plate, and china, I have already given by deed to my wife for the term of her natural life, but this will makes it entirely her own.) I appoint and desire my executors to take an inventory and appraisement of all my effects whatsoever, within six weeks after my decrease. I also give to my executors hereafter named, the sum of 100*l*. in trust, to the sole use and benefit of my nephew John Townsend, to whom I also give my gold watch as a keepsake. I further give to my executors, in like trust, the sum of 100*l*. for the sole use and benefit of my niece Rebecca, the wife of Thomas Westley, as an acknowledgement of relationship.

I have heretofore given by will, to each of the last-named relations, a more considerable sum: but as I have observed with pleasure that Providence has blessed their endeavours with success, in acquiring a greater fortune than they ever will expend the income of; and as they have no child or chick to inherit what they leave behind them, I have stayed my hand, and have thereby reserved a power to assist any branch of my family that may stand in need of it. I have the greatest respect and esteem for each of the above parties.

I also give to my executors, in like trust, the sum of 150*l*. for the use of my nephew Richard Townsend, butcher. I further give to my executors the sum of 300*l*. to be disposed of as follows: To Joseph, Thomas, and Jacob, sons of Thomas Marston by his wife Sarah, my niece, 100*l*. each, as they shall severally attain the age of twenty-one years. But should any of them die before they come of age, then such 100*l*. shall be divided, share and share alike, among the survivors.

I also give to Isaac, the son of Thomas Marston, the sum of 10*l*. for pocket-money; and my reason is, his being patronized by his worthy uncle Mr. Thomas Westley, who, if he behaves well, will put him in a way to acquire an easy fortune. But I must not forget my little Favourite—I therefore give to my executors, in trust, the sum of 500*l*. for the sole use and benefit of Sarah, the daughter of Ferdinand and Sarah De Mierre (my wife's daughter), to be paid her when she attains the age of twenty-one years: but should she happen to die before that age, my pleasure is, that my wife shall have the disposal of the said 500*l*. at her pleasure, signified in her last will. I also give to my executors the further sum of 1400*l*. in trust, to the following uses, viz. to Rebecca Westley, John Townsend, Richard Townsend, and to the four sons of Thomas Marston, by his wife Sarah my niece, the sum of 200*l*. each, to become due and payable (only) on the day of my wife's future marriage, which, if she chuses, I wish her happy equal to her merit; but if she continues a widow the last-mentioned legacies are entirely void. I further give to my executors, in trust, all my goods and chattels, household furniture, plate, and china, not disposed of as above, to the following uses: first, for the payment of my several legacies and debts (if any), and all the residue and remainder (except the sale of my lease as below) to the sole use and benefit of my wife Sarah. I further give to my executors, in trust, the reversion of the lease of my house and land, held under my good friend the late Jonathan Ruston, together with fixtures in the house (particularly the fire place, including the grate, fender, &c. together with three leaden figures) all plantations of trees and shrubs of every kind, including my grotto, and whatever contributes to beautify the place:—That the whole shall be sold by public auction, after being properly advertized in some of the London and neighbouring Country Papers. The money arising from such sale I give to the following uses; (viz.) first, 500*l*. to the Committee for the time being of the Protestant Dissenting Charity School at Birmingham, in trust, towards erecting a commodious building for the use of the said charity; 700*l*. more arising from the said sale I give and bequeath as follows: 400*l*. to be shared equally among the sons of Thomas Marston, by his wife Sarah; to Jonathan, John, and Richard Townsend, my nephews, 100*l*. each; to Rebecca Westley, my niece, 100*l*. and my will is, that this and the above-mentioned sum of 100*l*. shall be entirely at her own disposal, and not subject to the controul or intermeddling of her husband, and yet her receipt alone shall be a sufficient discharge to my executors; 800*l*. more arising from the said sale I give to the three sons of the late Jonathan Ruston, in even and equal shares, viz. John, Daniel, and Josiah Ruston. What further sum of money may arise from the sale of the above lease I give to the sole disposal of my wife Sarah, by her last will. As I doubt not the children of my late worthy friend will endeavour to traduce my memory, as they have already done my character, in having my lease on too easy terms, I therefore think proper to declare, that at the time I took the aforesaid lease I paid the full value of it, and have laid out little less than 6,000*l*. upon the premises. But as the increase of the town has since enhanced its value I have made an acknowledgement as above, which I always proposed to the sons of my most valuable friend, and which would have been much more considerable if they had refrained from injuriously abusing me. I had even given, by will, the reversion of my lease to Martha ———, upon the death of my wife's eldest son, and my intended successor; but her unprovoked petulant malice and spleen, and abusive treatment of me without cause, convinced me of the rancour of her heart, and determined me as above. My farther will and pleasure is, and I do hereby declare, that the devise of my goods and chattels, as above, is upon this express condition, that my wife, in concert with my executors, do cause my body to be buried in a conical building in my own premises, heretofore used as a Mill, which I have lately raised higher and painted, and in a vault which I have prepared for it.

This, doubtless, to many, will appear a whim; perhaps it is so, but it is a whim for many years resolved upon, as I have a hearty contempt of all Superstition. (*What follows is by far too indecent for repetition* [NICHOLS].) * * * * * * * * * * *
* * * * * * * * * * * * * *

* I expect some shrewd remarks will be made on this my declaration by the ignorant and bigoted, who cannot distinguish between Religion and Superstition, and are taught to believe that Morality (by which I understand all the duties a man owes to God and his fellow creatures) is not sufficient to entitle him to divine favour without professing to believe * * (*Here again we must leave a blank* [NICHOLS].) * * * * *
* * * * * * * * * * * * * *

This morality alone I profess to have been my religion and the rule of my actions, to which I appeal how far my profession and practice has been consistent. Lastly, I do hereby appoint my worthy friends, Mr. Edward Palmer, and Josiah Ruston, my wife's brother, joint executors of this my will, in most perfect confidence (as I know the integrity of their hearts) that they will jointly and cordially execute this my most important trust committed to them with integrity and candour; to each of which I leave six guineas to buy a ring, which I hope they will consider as a keepsake. In Witness, &c. SARAH STUART, JOSEPH BRIDGWATER, JOHN WEBSTER.

Agreeably to the singularity of his opinions, he was buried in a tomb of masonry, in the shape of a cone, under a windmill in his garden, belonging to a handsome house which he had built at the upper end of the town of Birmingham. On the top of the windmill, after it fell into disuse, he had erected an urn, for which he had prepared the following inscription:

> Stranger,
> beneath this cone, in *unconsecrated* ground,
> a friend to the liberties of mankind directed his
> body to be inurn'd.
> May the example contribute to emancipate thy mind
> from the idle fears of *Superstition,*
> and the wicked arts of Priesthood.

The principal part of his fortune, amounting to about 12,000*l.* he left to his widow; who sold the stock, and retired to the house which her husband had built.

That building was destroyed in the riots of 1791; but his remains continued undisturbed.

She had before been the widow of a person who having been guilty of some fraudulent practices in regard to a relation's will, was obliged to quit the kingdom, having first made over his property to a person at Birmingham, who after his return refused to resign it. His son, reduced to drive waggons for his livelihood, by the assistance and support of Mr. Baskerville (to whom his mother retired, and who afterwards married her) recovered his estate, and made a handsome provision for his two sisters.
Gough's British Topography, 1780, vol. II. *p.* 306.[5]

In regard to his private character, he was much of a humourist, idle in the extreme; but his invention was of the true Birmingham model, active. He could well design, but procured others to execute: wherever he found merit, he caressed it: he was remarkably polite to the stranger, fond of shew: a figure rather of the smaller size, and delighted to adorn that figure with gold lace. Although constructed with the light timbers of a frigate, his movement was stately as a ship of the line.

During the twenty-five last years of his life, though then in his decline, he retained the singular traces of a handsome man. If he exhibited a peevish temper, we may consider that good-nature and intense thinking are not

---

5. The quotation from Gough appears as a note in *Lit. Anec.*

always found together. Taste accompanied him through the different walks of agriculture, architecture, and the fine arts. Whatever passed through his fingers, bore the lively marks of John Baskerville.

In April 1775, Mrs. Baskerville wholly declined the Printing business; but continued that of a Letter Founder till February 1777.

Mrs. Baskerville, being to decline business as a Printer, purposes disposing of the whole of her apparatus in that branch, comprehending, amongst other articles, all of them perfect in their kind, a large and full assortment of the most beautiful types, with the completest printing presses, hitherto known in England. She begs leave to inform the Publick, at the same time, that she continues the business of Letter-founding, in all its parts, with the same care and accuracy that was formerly observed by Mr. Baskerville. Those gentlemen who are inclined to encourage so pleasing an improvement may, by favouring her with their commands, be now supplied with Baskerville's elegant types at no higher expence than the prices already established in the trade. *April 6, 1775.*[6]

The late Mr. Baskerville having taken some pains to establish and perfect a Letter-foundry for the more readily casting of Printing-types for sale, and as the undertaking was finished but a little before his death, it is now become necessary for his widow, Mrs. Baskerville, to inform all Printers, that she continues the same business, and has now ready for sale, a large stock of types, of most sizes, cast with all possible care, and dressed with the utmost accuracy. She hopes the acknowledged partiality of the world, in regard to the peculiar beauty of Mr. Baskerville's types, in the works he has published, will render it quite unnecessary here to say any thing to recommend them—only that she is determined to attend to the undertaking with all care and diligence; and to the end that so useful an improvement may become as extensive as possible, and notwithstanding the extraordinary hardness and durability of these types above all others, she will conform to sell them at the same prices with other Letter-founders. *Feb. 25, 1777.*[7]

Many efforts were used after his death, to dispose of the types; but, no purchaser could be found in the whole commonwealth of letters. The Universities rejected the offer.

The London Booksellers preferred the sterling types of Caslon and his apprentice Jackson. The valuable property lay a dead weight, till purchased by a literary society at Paris, in 1779, for 3700*l*.

It is an old remark, that no country abounds with genius so much as this Island; and it is a remark nearly as old, that genius is no where so little rewarded: how else came Dryden, Goldsmith, and Chatterton, to want bread? Is merit like a flower of the field, too common to attract notice? or is the use of money beneath the care of exalted talents?

Invention seldom pays the inventor. If you ask what fortune Baskerville

---

6. This quotation, source unidentified, appears as a note in *Lit. Anec.*
7. This quotation, like the preceding, is a note in *Lit. Anec.* The paper in which Mrs. Baskerville's notice appeared is not identified.

ought to have been rewarded with? The most which can be comprised in five figures. If you farther ask what he possessed? the least; but none of it squeezed from the press. What will the shade of this great man think, if capable of thinking, that he has spent a fortune of opulence, and a life of genius, in carrying to perfection the greatest of all human inventions, and that his productions, slighted by his country, were hawked over Europe in quest of a bidder?

We must admire, if we do not imitate, the taste and oeconomy of the French nation, who, brought by the British arms in 1762 to the verge of ruin, rising above distress, were able, in seventeen years, to purchase Baskerville's elegant types, refused by his own country, and to expend an hundred thousand pounds in poisoning the principles of mankind by printing the works of Voltaire.

Mrs. Baskerville died in March 1788.

[Editor's note: The following two quotations, numbered by me (1) and (2) appear in *Lit. Anec.* as notes to the penultimate paragraph with no further attribution than that given here.]

(1) The English language and learning are so cultivated in France, and so eagerly learned, that the best Authors of Great Britain are now re-printing in this Metropolis: Shakspeare, Addison, Pope, Johnson, Hume, and Robertson, are to be published here very soon. Baskerville's types, which were bought it seems for a trifle, to the eternal disgrace of Englishmen, are to be made use of for the purpose of propagating the English language in this country. *Letter from Paris, Aug. 8, 1780.*

(2) A complete edition of the Works of Voltaire, printed by subscription, with the types of Baskerville. This work, the most extensive and magnificent that ever was printed, is now in the press at Fort Khel, near Strasburgh, a free place, subject to no restraint or imprimatur, and will be published towards the close of the present year. It will never be on sale. Subscribers only can have copies. Each set is to be numbered, and a particular number appropriated to each subscriber at the time of subscribing. As the sets to be worked off are limited to a fixed and small number, considering the demand of all Europe, those who wish to be possessed of so valuable a work must be early in their applications, lest they be shut out by the subscriptions being previously filled. Voltaire's Manuscripts and Port Folios, besides his Works already published, cost twelve thousand guineas. This and the other expences attending the publication will lay the Editors under an advance of 100,000*l.* sterling. The Publick may from thence form a judgement of the extraordinary care that will be taken to make this edition a lasting monument of typographical elegance and grandeur. Subscriptions are taken in at the following Banking-houses, London, Sir Robert Herries and Co.; Edinburgh, Sir William Forbes, J. Hunter and Co.; Dublin, Messrs. Blacke and Murray. Proposals and particulars may be had, and subscriptions taken in, at Mr. Elmsly's, bookseller, in the Strand; Mr. Woodmason's, Leadenhall-street; Mr. Farquharson's, agent to the undertaking, and at John Henderson's, esq. Milk-street, Cheapside. *June* 4, 1782.

[Editor's note: This completes the memoir proper of Baskerville as found in Vol. III of *Literary Anecdotes*. The material immediately following is an addition to the above, taken from *Illustr.*, VIII, 458.]

[The following Letter from Mr. Allen Everitt of Birmingham to Mr. D. Parkes of Shrewsbury, describes the state of the body of Mr. Baskerville.]

DEAR SIR, *Aug.* 15, 1829.
 ... The body was exhibited at Mr. Marston's, a plumber and glazier of Birmingham. It was in a good state of preservation, considering the time it had been interred. All the teeth were perfect with the exception of one. I have since heard that the teeth are taken away. A few years ago the premises and property were let to a Mr. Gibson, who on cutting of a branch canal into the land discovered the lead coffin, when it was opened, and the body found in a very fresh state. Since that time, shameful to relate, the coffin and contents have been in the warehouse of Mr. Gibson. They are now in the warehouse of Mr. Marston, for the purpose of having a new lid to the lead coffin; and it is said to be the intention of Mr. Ryland of Edgbaston, who I believe is a distant relation of his wife, to have him interred.

[The body was finally buried in a field adjoining Cradely Chapel, the property of a branch of the Baskerville family.]

[Editor's note: A number of interesting references to Baskerville occur elsewhere in Nichols' writings, and a few of these will be introduced here. The following reference is from a letter written by Samuel Paterson[8] to John Nichols, dated 23 August 1779; it is from *Lit. Anec.*, VIII, 483.]

I could give you also a note on *Baskerville,* to demonstrate that he knew very little of the excellences of Typography, beyond the common productions which are to be found every day in Pater-noster Row; and therefore, in a comparative view, might readily conclude he had outstript them all.

[Editor's note: The following is from a letter written by William Warburton, *Lit. Anec.*, V, 653n.]

Dec. 27, 1761, I think the Booksellers have an intention of employing Baskerville to print Pope in 4to; so they sent me the last Octavo to look over. I have added the inclosed to the long note in the beginning of the "Rape of the Lock," in answer to an impertinence of Joseph Warton. When you have perused it you will send it back. *Letter to Mr.* [Richard] *Hurd, Dec.* 27, 1761.

[Editor's note: The concluding reference to Baskerville is from a letter written by John Bedford to Richard Richardson from Durham and dated 29 October 1758, taken from *Illustr.*, I, 813.]

---

8. Nichols has a memoir of Paterson, a bookseller, in *Lit. Anec.*, III, 733-737.

By Baskerville's Specimen of his types, you will perceive how much the elegance of them is owing to his paper, which he makes himself, as well as the types and his ink also: and I was informed, whenever they come to be used by common pressmen, and with common materials, they will lose of their beauty considerably. Hence, perhaps, this Specimen may become very curious (when he is no more, and the types cannot be set off in the same perfection), and a great piece of *vertû*.

William Caslon

(With Accompanying Brief Memoirs of THOMAS COTTRELL, JOSEPH JACKSON, and VINCENT FIGGINS)

[Nichols' memoir of William Caslon, along with the brief sketches of the lives of Cottrell, Jackson, and Figgins, appears as a note in *Lit. Anec.*, II, 355-361. A few additions and corrections from other places are identified as they are introduced.

Nichols made use, in his memoir, of materials provided by Edward Rowe-Mores in *A Dissertation upon English Typographical Founders and Founderies*, which was issued by Nichols with an appendix of his own in 1779. Nichols' work on Caslon illustrates his long and abiding interest in everything connected with the printing trade. A cause of additional interest here is the fact that Nichols and his Bowyer predecessors had been patrons of Caslon, Jackson, and Figgins.

The reputation of Caslon as a type designer is secure; and therefore mention of him will be found in any history of type design or printing. An entry regarding him, heavily indebted to Nichols, is in Plomer, Bushnell, and Dix, *Dictionary of Booksellers and Printers*. This work also contains an entry for Thomas Cottrell, though it identifies the Jackson who was dismissed from the employ of William Caslon the Younger as a *Thomas* Jackson. J. A. Cochrane, in his *Dr. Johnson's Printer*, calls William Caslon, without reservation, "the greatest of English type-founders" (p. 15); and he reports that Benjamin Franklin, after visiting a number of type-founders on a tour of England and Scotland, eventually purchased Caslon's types for the *Gazette* in Philadelphia (p. 105). A letter dated June 1788 from Franklin to William Caslon is in the Special Manuscript Collection of Columbia University.

An account of William Caslon the Elder and William Caslon the Younger by John Westby-Gibson is in the DNB. Nichols is heavily relied upon as a source, as indicated in the following comparison, intended (as are those comparisons made elsewhere) not to denigrate the later biographers but to reveal the importance of Nichols to all biographers who have followed him.

Nichols	Westby-Gibson
In the year 1720 (the year in which his eldest son was born) the Society for Promoting Christian Knowledge. . . deemed it expedient to print, for the use of Eastern Churches, the New Testament and Psalter in the Arabic language, . . . and Mr. Caslon was pitched upon to cut the fount which in his specimens is distinguished by the name of *English Arabic*. Mr. Caslon, after	. . . in 1720 his first child, named William, was born. In the same year he was chosen by the Society for Promoting Christian Knowledge to cut the fount of 'English Arabic' for the New Testament and Psalter required for the christians of the East. He afterwards

he had finished his Arabic fount, cut the letters of his own name in Pica Roman, and placed the name at the bottom of a specimen of the Arabic; and Mr. Palmer (the reputed author of Psalmanazar's "History of Printing") seeing this name, advised Mr. Caslon to cut the whole fount of Pica. Mr. Caslon did so; and as the performance exceeded the letter of the other founders of the time. . . .	cut in 'pica roman' the letters of his own name and printed them at foot of his Arabic specimens. By the advice of Samuel Palmer (reputed author of that 'History of Printing' really written by George Psalmanazar) he then cut the whole fount of pica roman and italic, and this he did in very superior style.]

Mr. William Caslon, born in that part of the town of Hales Owen which is situated in Shropshire,[1] in 1692, and who is justly styled by Mr. Rowe-Mores "the Coryphaeus of Letter-founders," was not trained to that business; "which is a handy-work, so concealed among the artificers of it," that Mr. [Joseph] Moxon, in his indefatigable researches on that subject, "could not discover that any one had taught it any other; but every one that had used it learnt it of his own genuine inclination." Dissertation upon English Typographical Founders and Founderies, p. 17.

He served a regular apprenticeship to an engraver of ornaments on gun-barrels; and was taken from that instrument to an employment of a very different tendency, *the propagation of the Christian faith*. In the year 1720 (the year in which his eldest son was born) the Society for promoting Christian knowledge, in consequence of a representation made by Mr. Salomon Negri, a native of Damascus in Syria, well skilled in the Oriental languages, who had been professor of Arabic in places of note for a great part of his life, deemed it expedient to print, for the use of the Eastern Churches, the New Testament and Psalter in the Arabic language, for the benefit of the poor Christians in Palestine, Syria, Mesopotamia, Arabia, and Egypt; the constitution of which countries allowed of no printing; and Mr. Caslon was pitched upon to cut the fount which in his specimens is distinguished by the name of *English Arabic*. Mr. Caslon, after he had finished his Arabic fount, cut the letters of his own name in Pica Roman, and placed the name at the bottom of a specimen of the Arabic; and Mr. [Samuel] Palmer (the reputed author of [George] Psalmanazar's "History of Printing") seeing this name, advised Mr. Caslon to cut the whole fount of Pica. Mr. Caslon did so; and as the performance exceeded the letter of the other founders of the time, Mr. Palmer, whose circumstances required credit with those who, by this advice, were now obstructed, repented of having given

---

1. A correction in *Lit. Anec.*, II, 720, reads: "Mr. Caslon was born at Cradley, a large hamlet of Hales-Owen (the whole town and borough of which are in Shropshire), about two miles distant from it, and situated in Worcestershire, near Stourbridge."

the advice, and discouraged Mr. Caslon from any farther progress; a circumstance which was verified by the celebrated Dr. [Benjamin] Franklin, who was at that time a journeyman under Mr. [John] Watts, the first printer that employed Mr. Caslon. Mr. Caslon, disgusted, applied to Mr. Bowyer;[2] under whose inspection he cut, in 1722, the beautiful fount of English which was used in printing Selden's Works, 1726; and the Coptic types which were used for Dr. [David] Wilkins's edition of the Pentateuch (which letter, having accidentally escaped the conflagration of 1808, I still possess); Mr. Caslon was encouraged to proceed farther both by Mr. Bowyer and his brother-in-law Mr. Bettenham;[3] and had the candour to acknowledge Mr. Bowyer as his master, and that he had taught him an art, in which, by diligence and unwearied application, he arrived to that perfection, as not only to remove the necessity of importing types from Holland; but in the beauty and elegance of those made by him so far surpassed the best productions of foreign artificers, that his types have not unfrequently been exported to the Continent; and it may still with great justice and confidence be asserted, that a more beautiful specimen than his is not to be found in any part of the world. It appears by the Dissertation of Mr. Mores, p. 86,[4] that Mr. Caslon had a brother named Samuel, who was his mould-maker, and afterwards lived with Mr. George Anderton, of Birmingham, in the same capacity. Mr. Caslon's first foundery was in a small house in Helmet Row in Old Street; he afterwards removed into Ironmonger Row; and about the year 1735 into Chiswell-street, where the foundery was carried on at first by himself, and afterwards in conjunction with William, his eldest son; whose name first appeared in the specimen of 1742. In or about the year 1750, Mr. Caslon was put into the commission of the peace for the county of Middlesex; and retired from the active part of business to a house opposite the Nag's Head, in the Hackney road; whence he removed to another house, in Water Gruel Row; and afterwards to Bethnal Green; where he died, Jan. 23, 1766; at the age of 74; and was buried in the church-yard of St. Luke, Middlesex; in which parish all his different founderies were situated. A monument, erected to his memory, is thus briefly inscribed:

> W. CASLON, esq. ob, 23 Jan, 1766, aet. 74.
> Also, W. CASLON, esq. (son of the above)
> ob. 17 Aug. 1778, aet. 58 years.

2. William Bowyer the Elder (1663-1737), father of the younger William Bowyer (1699-1777), with whom Nichols was associated as apprentice, partner, and successor.

3. James Bettenham was married to "Mrs. Bowyer's daughter (by a former husband)," *Lit. Anec.*, I, 65n. Nichols has introduced a confusion here between the two William Bowyers (see n. 2). Bettenham would have been the "brother-in-law" of the younger Bowyer, but he would have been the "son-in-law" of the elder Bowyer. After 1722, the two were in business together; and after that date, wrote Nichols, "I shall in general speak of them as one person," *Lit. Anec.*, I, 230.

4. "Mr. [Edward] Rowe-Mores having left at his death a small unpublished impression of 'A Dissertation upon English Typographical Founders and Founderies;' all the copies of this very curious pamphlet were purchased at his sale by Mr. Nichols; and given to the publick in 1779, with the addition of a short explanatory 'Appendix,'" *Lit. Anec.*, VI, 631.

One particular in his character is thus excellently described by Sir John Hawkins (History of Music, vol. V. p. 127). "Mr. Caslon, meeting with encouragement suitable to his deserts, settled in Ironmonger row, in Old-street; and, being a great lover of music, had frequent concerts at his house, which were resorted to by many eminent masters; to these he used to invite his friends, and those of his old acquaintance, the companions of his youth. He afterwards removed to a large house in Chiswell-street, and had an organ in his concert-room; after that he had stated monthly concerts; which, for the convenience of his friends, and that they might walk home in safety when the performance was over, were on that Thursday of the month which was nearest the full moon; from which circumstance his guests were wont humorously to call themselves Lunatics. In the intervals of the performance the guests refreshed themselves at a sideboard, which was amply furnished; and when it was over, sitting down to a bottle of wine, and a decanter of excellent ale, of Mr. Caslon's own brewing, they concluded the evening's entertainment with a song or two of Purcell's, sung to the harpsichord, or a few catches; and about twelve retired." There is a good mezzotinto print of him by J. Faber, from a painting by F. Kyte, inscribed Gulielmus Caslon. His second son, Thomas, was for many years a bookseller of eminence in Stationers' court; where he died, March 29, 1783.

Of the modern state of this undoubtedly most capital foundery in the world, the particulars are given by Mr. Mores, with some attempts at pleasantry. His ridicule, however, before the publication of his book, had lost its sting by the death of the *second* of the Caslons, who, as an artist, had certainly great merit, though not equal to his father. He died in 1778; leaving a widow, whom, in the history of this celebrated foundery, it would be improper to pass unnoticed. She was the only child of Dr. [John] Cartledge; and her mother marrying again imprudently, she was put to school by an uncle, who took care to provide for her. Her merit and abilities in conducting a capital business during the life of her husband, and afterwards till her son was capable of managing it, can only be known to those who had dealings with that manufactory. In quickness of understanding, and activity of execution, she has left few equals among her sex. On the death of her husband, and their eldest son's establishing himself in the magnificent building now occupied by Messrs. Lackington and Co. in Moorfields (the Temple of the Muses), she conducted the foundery herself, and continued to do so till disabled by an attack of the palsy; which she survived but a few months, dying Oct. 23, 1795, aged about 70. After the death of the mother, there were still two very large founderies carried on; one of them by a third *William Caslon*,* who, having quitted Moorfields, had become the purchaser of the *Jackson* foundery in Dorset-street; since given up to his son, a fourth *William Caslon*, a young man of considerable abilities, to whom I cannot recommend a better model than

---

* Mr. William Caslon died in Sept. 1883. See Gent. Mag. 1850, ii. p. 96, note. JOHN BOWYER NICHOLS. (*Illustr.*, VIII, 448)

his great grand-father, who was universally esteemed as a first-rate artist, a tender master, and an honest, friendly, and benevolent man.

The original foundery in Chiswell-street was purchased by Mr. Charles Catherwood, a distant relation, who died June 7, 1809, aet. 45; and is still carried on by Mr. Henry Caslon[5] (another great-grandson of the first William) under the firm of Caslon and Catherwood.

[Editor's note: The following long paragraph, enclosed in brackets, appears in *Lit. Anec.*, II, 720-721, as an addition to the above. After this paragraph, Nichols' text resumes.]

[Mr. Caslon's first residence was in Vine-street in the Minories, where one considerable branch of his employment was to make tools for the bookbinders and for the chasing of silver plate. Whilst he was engaged in this employment, the elder Mr. Bowyer accidentally saw in the shop of Mr. Daniel Browne, bookseller, near Temple-Bar, the lettering of a book uncommonly neat; and inquiring who the artist was by whom the letters were made, Mr. Caslon was introduced to his acquaintance, and was taken by him to Mr. James's foundery in Bartholomew Close. Caslon had never before that time seen any part of the business; and being asked by his friend if he thought he could undertake to cut types, he requested a single day to consider the matter, and then replied he had no doubt but he could. From this answer Mr. Bowyer lent him 200*l*. Mr. Bettenham lent the same sum, and Mr. Watts 100*l*.; and by that assistance our ingenious artist applied himself assiduously to his new pursuit, and was eminently successful. The three printers abovementioned were of course his constant customers. It appears by Ged's "Narrative of his Scheme for Block-printing," that so early as 1730 "he had eclipsed his competitors in the art of letter-founding; but found more difficulty than he apprehended in an attempt to make plates for block-printing." In the Universal Magazine for June 1750, is a good view of Mr. Caslon's work-shop in Chiswell-street, with portraits of six of his workmen.†—Mr. Caslon was three times married. The name of his second wife was Longman; of the third, Waters; and with each of these two ladies he had a good fortune. The abilities of his son William appeared to great advantage in a specimen of types of the learned languages in 1748.—His younger son, Mr. Thomas Caslon, was Master of the Stationers' Company in 1782; and died March 29, 1783.]

† The figure marked 3. is the portrait of Jackson; and 4. Cottrell. NICHOLS.
5. The following two obituary notices are from *Illustr.*, VIII, 474 and 521: "[1808] March . . . At Bristol Hotwells, Mrs. Henry *Caslon*, letter-founder, who, with her able assistant Mr. Drury, renewed the credit of the Caslon letter foundry. See an article on the Caslon family, where this lady is noticed, under May 28, 1850 [of the *Gentleman's Magazine*]."
"1850, May 28. Aged 64, Mr. Henry *Caslon*, letter-founder."

It is but common justice to mention in this place the names of Cottrell and Jackson, as Letter-founders who were trained up under the auspices, and pursued with commendable industry the steps, of their excellent instructor. Mr. Mores says, "Mr. Thomas Cottrell is in order *à primo proximus*. He was in the late Mr. Caslon's house, an apprentice to *dressing*, but not to *cutting*. This part he learned, as Mr. Moxon terms it, 'of his own genuine inclination.' He began in the year 1757, with a fount of English Roman;" [and afterwards cut a fount of Norman, intended (but not used) for Domesdaybook].[6] "He lives in Nevil's-court, in Fetter-lane; obliging, good-natured, and friendly; rejecting nothing because it is out of the common way, and is expeditious in his performances."

Mr. Cottrell died in 1785, I am sorry to add, not in affluent circumstances, though to his profession of a Letter-founder were superadded that of a Doctor for the Tooth-ache, which he cured by burning the ear; and had also the honour of serving in the Troop of his Majesty's Life-guards.

"Mr. Joseph Jackson[7] was in Mr. Caslon's house too, an apprentice to the whole art, into which he launched out for himself upon the same principle as did Mr. Cottrell; for, actuated by the same motives, they both flew off together. Mr. Jackson lives in Salisbury-court, in Fleet-street; he is obliging, and communicative, and his specimen will, *adjuvante Numine*, have place amongst the literate specimens of English letter-cutters."

Of Mr. Jackson Mr. Mores would have said more, if he had lived to witness the progress of his diligent exertions. He too, after cutting a variety of types for the Rolls of Parliament (a work which will ever reflect honour on the good taste and munificence of the present Reign), employed his talents on Domesday, and in a manner more successful than his fellow-labourer. I have much gratification in stating, that the two beautiful volumes of that valuable record were finished at the press in 1783, on a plan which I had the honour of projecting, and Mr. Jackson the skill to execute, under the title of "Domesday Book; sive Liber Censualium Willielmi Regis Angliae, inter Archivis Regiis in Domo Capitulari Westmonasterii asservatus. Jubente Rege Augustissimo Georgio Tertio prelo mandatus. Londini, Typis J. Nichols, 1783."

To Mr. Jackson's Occidentals may also be added a beautiful Pica Greek, which he cut under the express direction of Mr. Bowyer, who used to say, "the types in common use were *no more Greek than they were English.*" And (under the direction of Joshua Steele, esq. the ingenious author of "Prosodia Rationalis, an Essay towards establishing the Melody and Measure of Speech,") Mr. Jackson augmented the number of *musical types*, by such as represent the emphasis and cadence of prose. *See Mores' Dissertation on Typographic Founders*, pp. 82, 83. 97.

Mr. Jackson,‡ born in Old-street, Sept. 4, 1733, was the first child baptised

---

6. The square brackets here are provided by Nichols.
7. A portrait of Joseph Jackson is in *Lit. Anec.* facing p. 358.

‡ In the Gentleman's Magazine for 1792, p. 166, is an Elegy on Mr. Joseph Jackson, letter-founder, and on his types used in Hume's History of England. . . . JOHN BOWYER

in St. Luke's church; and received his education at a school in that neighbourhood, the gift of a Mr. Fuller; whence he was apprenticed to Mr. Caslon. Being exceedingly tractable in the common branches of the business, he had a great desire to learn the method of cutting the punches, which is in general kept profoundly secret; his master and master's father locking themselves in whenever they were at that branch of the business. This difficulty he surmounted by boring a hole through the wainscot, and observing them at different times, so as to form some idea of the mode in which the whole was performed; and applied himself at every opportunity to the finishing of a punch. When he had completed one to his own mind, he presented it to his master, expecting to be rewarded for his ingenuity; but the premium he received was a hard blow, with a threat that he should be sent to Bridewell if he again made a similar attempt. This circumstance being taken in dudgeon, his mother bought him what tools were necessary, and he improved himself at her house whenever he had an opportunity. He continued to work for his master, after he came out of his time, till a quarrel arose in the foundery about the price of work; and a memorial, which terminated in favour of the workmen, being sent to the elder Caslon (who was then in the commission of the peace, and had retired to Bethnal-green) young Jackson and Mr. Cottrell were discharged, as the supposed ringleaders. Compelled thus to seek employment, they united their slender stock in a partnership, and went on prosperously till, Jackson's mother dying, he entered, in 1759, on board the Minerva frigate, as armourer; and in May 1761 was removed, with Captain Alexander Hood, into the same situation in the Aurora; and proved somewhat successful, having about 40*l.* prize-money to receive at the Peace of 1763. During the time he was at sea, he was visited by a severe fit of sickness, in which he vowed, if he recovered, to lead in future a very penitent life; which promise he punctually fulfilled. On his return to London, he worked for some time under Mr. Cottrell; till, determining to adventure into business for himself, he was encouraged to do so by two Life-guardsmen, his fellow-workmen, who engaged to allow him a small pittance for subsistence, and to supply money for carrying on the trade, for two years. Taking a small house in Cock-lane, he soon satisfied his partners that the business would be productive before the time promised. When he had pursued his labours about six months, Mr. Bowyer accidentally calling to inspect some of his punches (for he had no specimen), approved them so much, that he promised to employ him; adding, "My father was the means of old Mr. Caslon riding in his coach: how do you know but I may be the means of your doing the same?" A short time after this, he put out a small specimen of one fount; which his young master carrying to Bethnal-green with an air of contempt, the good old Justice treated it otherwise; and desired his son "to take it home, and preserve it; and whenever he went to

---

NICHOLS. (*Illustr.*, VIII, 448. A life of Joseph Jackson, using Nichols almost exclusively as a source, by Henry Richard Tedder is in the DNB).

cutting again, to look well at it." It is but justice to the third William Caslon to add, that he always acknowledged the abilities of Jackson; and though rivals in an art which requires the greatest exertions of ingenuity, they lived in habits of reciprocal friendship. Business increasing rapidly, Mr. Jackson removed to Dorset-street, for a more capacious workshop; and about 1771 was applied to by the late Duke of Norfolk to make a mould to cast a hollow square. Telling the Duke that he thought this was practicable; his Grace observed, that he had applied to all the skilful mechanicks in London, Mr. Caslon not excepted, who declared it impossible. He soon convinced the Duke of his abilities; and in the course of three months producing what his Grace had been years in search of, was ever after held in great estimation by the Duke, who considered him as the first mechanick in the kingdom.

In 1762 he married Eliz. Tassel, originally a whinster in Spital-fields, a very worthy woman, and an excellent wife, who greatly contributed, by her care and industry, to his getting forward, on his first entering into business. She died Dec. 3, 1783, at the age of 49; and, in about six months after, he married Mary Pasham (the widow of a printer in Black Friars), who died Sept. 14, 1791, at the age of 52. Surviving the second of his wives but a few months; he died of a scarlet-fever, at his foundery, in Dorset-street, Salisbury-square, Jan. 14, 1792; and his remains were on the 23d deposited, in the same grave with them both, in the front ground of the Spa-Fields Chapel, a neat oration being delivered on the occasion by the Rev. Mr. Towers; who preached also a funeral sermon on the 29th, at his meeting-house in Barbican, of which Mr. Jackson was one of the Deacons. By the death of this ingenious artist, and truly worthy man, the poor lost a most excellent benefactor, his own immediate connexions a steady friend, and the literary world a valuable coadjutor to their labours. To particularize the articles of his foundery which were more peculiarly superior, when all were excellent, would be unnecessary. Let it suffice to mention, as matters of difficulty and curiosity, the fac-simile types which he formed for Domesday Book, and for the Alexandrian New Testament; and, as a pattern of the most perfect symmetry, the types which printed the splendid edition of the Bible published by Mr. Macklin. Mr. Jackson had acquired some considerable property, the bulk of which, having left no child, he directed to be equally divided between fourteen nephews and nieces.

On his only apprentice, Mr. Vincent Figgins, the mantle of his predecessor has fallen. With an ample portion of his kind instructor's reputation he inherits a considerable share of his talents and his industry; and has distinguished himself by the many beautiful specimens he has produced, and particularly of Oriental types. And here I hope I shall not be accused of being ostentatiously vain, if I close this note with a P.S. which is subjoined at the particular request of the only person it could possibly offend. "I am greatly obliged to you for the very flattering mention of my name; but you have not done yourself the justice to record your own kindness to me: that, on Mr. Jackson's death, finding I had not the means to purchase the

Foundery, you encouraged me to make a beginning. You gave me large orders, and assisted me with the means of executing them; and, during a long and difficult struggle in pecuniary matters for fifteen years, you, my dear sir, never refused me your assistance: without which I must have given it up. Do mention this—that, as the first Mr. Bowyer was the means of establishing Mr. Caslon—his son, Mr. Jackson—it may be known, that Vincent Figgins owes his prosperity to Mr. Bowyer's successor."[8]

[Editor's note: The following excerpt is from a letter written by John Lewis to Joseph Ames, dated 10 December 1740; see *Illustr.*, IV, 173-174.]

I thank you for sending Mr. Caslon's Picture; I think I once saw him at Mr. Mount's. The Picture is well done. Cannot you get for me his Specimen, &c?

[Editor's note: The following excerpt is from a letter written by Charles Lyttelton (later Bishop of Carlisle) to Joseph Ames. It is dated 25 April 1744 and is in full in *Illustr.*, IV, 231.]

Some unforseen business prevents Dr. Pococke and myself dining with Caslon to-morrow. [Nichols' note to the foregoing mention of *Caslon:*] This first of that name distinguished in the Annals of Letter-founding, was a most worthy and amiable man; and at his hospitable board were frequently assembled large parties of literary men, particularly the amateurs of musick.

8. Nichols purchased large quantities of type from both Jackson and Figgins. The accounts, showing amounts and kinds of type, are in the Bodleian, MS. Eng. misc. c. 142. See Albert H. Smith, "John Nichols, Printer and Publisher," *The Library*, Fifth Series, 18:181 (3 September 1963).

Part IV. Curate, Scholar, Grub, Poet

John Jones

[As will appear in this brief memoir of Jones, taken from *Lit. Anec.*, I, 637-639, he left at his death, a bundle of papers to be delivered to Nichols. Soon afterwards, Nichols (using the pseudonym *Eugenio*) began to send extracts from Jones's papers to the *Gentleman's Magazine*. Eugenio's first letter on the subject of Jones is dated 13 February 1783 (53:101-103). Accompanying the letter is Jones's note on Gilbert West, which, as mentioned in the introduction to this volume, is now part of Johnson's life of West. Other letters from Eugenio followed, along with additional excerpts from the writings of Jones. A good deal of interest seems to have been aroused by these publications, if one may judge by the number of letters to the editor on the subject of Jones's comments after the publication of each letter. Later still, most of the material contributed by Jones and published in the *Gentleman's Magazine* was reprinted by Nichols in *Literary Anecdotes*, where every excerpt is marked by an acknowledgment of the source, the usual designation being "Mr. Jones of Welwyn, MS." or merely the initials "J.J." In addition to the materials drawn from the *Gentleman's Magazine*, Nichols, of course, also used in *Literary Anecdotes* a great many of Jones's letters and short character sketches that had not been used previously anywhere else. Those papers of Jones not given to Nichols were deposited by Thomas Dawson, a dissenting minister, in the library of Dr. Daniel Williams.

A life of Jones by William Connor Sydney, relying heavily upon Nichols as a source, is in the DNB.]

Mr. JOHN JONES was born in the year 1700; and was a native, it is believed, of Carmarthen. He was admitted of Worcester College, Oxford; where he took the degree of B.A. about 1721. He quitted the University in or before 1726; and his earliest pastoral cure was in the Diocese of Lincoln, but in what part of it does not appear.

In 1741 he was resident at Abbots Ripton in Huntingdonshire, and soon after was presented to the vicarage of Alconbury. In 1749 he was the Editor of the "Free and Candid Disquisitions;" and, in 1750 and 1751, of "An Appeal to Common Reason and Candour," &c. in two parts.

In 1751 he resigned Alconbury for the rectory of Boulne-Hurst, in Bedfordshire. In 1759 he accepted the curacy of Welwyn from Dr. Young;[1] and continued there till 1765, when the Doctor died, and Mr. Jones was appointed one of his executors. He afterwards returned to Boulne-Hurst; and probably obtained no other preferment.

1. Edward Young, author of *Night Thoughts*.

He was, in 1765, the Author of "Catholic Faith and Practice," &c. and of "A Letter to a Friend in the Country."

The time of his death I have not been able to discover, though some pains have been taken in search for it. In answer to a query on that subject, I was favoured with the following particulars; "Having passed some months at Welwyn in the Summer of 1764, my father's family were well acquainted with Mr. Jones; and the acquaintance with that very worthy man continued to the last period of his life. He was a plain, honest, and most sincere Christian—well-read—of singular and simple manners. He was Curate some years to Dr. Young, and resided in a small house at Welwyn—a single man, of a very retired disposition, visiting few people, but attending to all the poor in the parish of Welwyn. He usually spent two hours every evening with Dr. Young in useful conversation, and in reading to relieve Mrs. Hallows (the good Doctor's housekeeper), whose eyes were much impaired by constant reading. Mr. Jones told us many very good anecdotes of Dr. Young; and had collected a great variety of interesting and curious accounts of eminent and pious persons, some of which he published in your useful Miscellany, which he was very partial to, and left orders to his executors to insert the rest occasionally, after his death. On the death of good Dr. Young, Mr. Jones left Welwyn, and went to reside at his living in Huntingdonshire,* at or very near Little Gedding, where that extraordinary man Mr. [Nicholas] Ferrar lived. Some extracts from the original copy of the Life of Mr. Ferrar Mr. Jones had in his possession, and we compared it with the printed one, and found it perfectly correct; he likewise shewed us some of the books bound by Mr. Ferrar's nieces, with their hand-writing in them. The correspondence between my father and Mr. Jones continued to the end of Mr. Jones's life, who fell from his horse in going to his parish in Huntingdonshire, and never spoke more.† The letters that passed between my father and Mr. Jones were full of pious and useful information; the account given in them of good Dr. Young's death is truly affecting. These letters are probably now in the hands of some of my family; and if I ever get them again in my possession, I may be able to give you farther particulars of Mr. Jones; happy in the opportunity of bearing testimony to a worthy character, whose memory I shall ever revere."

That Mr. Jones was ready to communicate information to others, is evident from the preceding Letters to Dr. Birch.[2]

After Mr. Jones's death, many (if not all) of his MSS. passed into the hands of the Rev. Thomas Dawson, M.D. a Dissenting Minister of Hackney; and early in 1783 a large bundle of Biographical Fragments were presented to

---

* Boulne Hurst is in Bedfordshire; but nearly adjoining to the county of Huntingdon. NICHOLS.

† It is strange that this circumstance should not have led to the exact date of his death. NICHOLS.

2. The memoir of Jones is preceded by 52 pages of his correspondence with Thomas Birch, frequently summarized by Nichols rather than given in full.

me (conformably, it should seem, to Mr. Jones's intentions) by an unknown hand.³ They were folded in a paper, indorsed, by Mr. Jones, "Various little Anecdotes, Memorials, and other the like Notices,—perhaps none of them of so much significance; yet not to be destroyed in too much haste." Many of these have at various times been inserted in the Gentleman's Magazine;‡ several others are interspersed in the present Volumes; and an unpublished specimen or two shall here be given.⁴

[Editor's note: The following paragraph appears in Nichols as a note to the next-to-last paragraph, above.]

[The amiable Mr. [William] Gilpin, also, in the Preface to his "Life of Cranmer," 1784, p. iv. says, "In gratitude I must acknowledge particular obligation to the late Mr. Jones of Welwyn; the learned friend, and (I believe) the executor, of the celebrated Author of the Night-thoughts. But I never was personally acquainted with him. This gentleman had once entertained the design of writing the life of Archbishop Cranmer, and with this intention had made considerable collections: but laying his design aside, he was so obliging as to put his papers, near twenty years ago, into my hands. We had both, I found, drawn from the same authorities; only I had the mortification to observe, that he had been much the more industrious compiler. He had also, through the means of several of his learned friends at Cambridge, particularly the late Mr. [Thomas] Baker [of St. John's], gained access to many sources of information, less obvious to common enquirers.—Our plans too rather differed. His was chiefly to explain the opinions of the Archbishop: mine attempts rather to illustrate his character. Notwithstanding, however, this difference, Mr. Jones's papers were of considerable use to me. I have now deposited them, agreeably to his last will, in the library of Dr. [Daniel] Williams, in Red-cross-street, London."]

[Editor's note: The following material is taken from a note in *Lit. Anec.*, III, 15-16, to Francis Blackburne, Archdeacon of Cleveland, who was for a time and by some taken to be the compiler of the *Free and Candid Disquisitions*.]

‡ See particularly his Anecdotes of Gilbert West, Bp. Burnet, Bp. Atterbury, Apb. Herring, Dr. Doddridge, Mr. James Harvey, and Dr. Samuel Clarke, vol. LIII. pp. 101, 227. NICHOLS.
3. In *Lit. Anec.*, VIII, 380, Nichols says he received the manuscripts from Thomas Dawson: "Wishing to obtain better information than I possessed respecting Dr. *Benjamin Dawson*, one of the Writers on the subject of 'The Confessional,' and Dr. *Thomas Dawson*, from whom I received the MSS. of the Rev. John Jones; I solicited assistance in the Gentleman's Magazine for October 1811, p. 357."
4. The lives given here in a note by Nichols are of John Norris and a Dr. Ingram.

[In 1749 appeared, for the first time, "Free and Candid Disquisitions relating to the Church of England;" containing many sensible observations on the defects and improprieties in the liturgical forms of faith and worship of the Established Church, and proposals of amendments and alterations of such passages as were liable to reasonable objections. This work was a compilation of authorities taken from the writings of some eminent Divines of the Church of England, tending to shew the necessity, or at least the expedience, of revising our public Liturgy, and of extracts of Letters sent, or supposed to be sent, to the compiler, from his correspondents in different parts of the kingdom, approving of his design, and signifying their disposition to promote and encourage it, as there should be occasion.

The compiler, the Rev. Mr. John Jones, vicar of Alconbury near Huntingdon, was a man of very singular character, pious and regular in his deportment, diligent in his clerical functions, and indefatigable in his studies, which were chiefly employed in promoting this scheme of reformation, conceived and digested long before his "Disquisitions" were made public, but withal affecting a mysterious secresy even in trifles, and excessively cautious of giving offence to the higher powers.

With Mr. Blackburne this gentleman, on the recommendation of Dr. Edmund Law, afterwards Bishop of Carlisle, held a correspondence; and to him Mr. Jones sent the greatest part of his Work in manuscript, which was returned to him without so much as the correction of a single slip of the writer's pen; nor was there a single line or word in the "Free and candid Disquisitions" written or suggested by Mr. Blackburne, notwithstanding many confident reports to the contrary.

The truth is, Mr. Blackburne, whatever desire he might have to forward the work of ecclesiastical reformation (which was as earnest at least as Mr. Jones's) could not possibly conform his style to the milky phraseology of the "Disquisitions;" nor could he be content to have his sentiments mollified by the gentle qualifications of Mr. Jones's lenient pen. He was rather (perhaps too much) inclined to look upon those who had in their hands the means and the power of reforming the errors, defects, and abuses, in the government, forms of worship, faith and discipline, of the Established Church, as guilty of a criminal negligence, from which they should have been roused by sharp and spirited expostulation. He thought it became Disquisitors, with a cause in hand of such high importance to the influence of vital Christianity, rather to have boldly faced the utmost resentment of the class of men to which they addressed their work, than, by meanly truckling to their arrogance, to derive upon themselves their ridicule and contempt, which all the world saw was the case of these gentle suggesters, and all the return they had for the civility of their application. . . .]

[Editor's note: In *Illustr.*, III, 438-450, several letters from John Jones to Philip Doddridge have the following note accompanying their introduction.]

Of this well-meaning and industrious Divine [Jones] many interesting particulars may be seen in the "Literary Anecdotes," vol. I. p. 637, to which the Rev. Thomas Stedman enables me to add an Extract from Dr. Doddridge's papers; which affords a pleasing idea of Mr. Jones, and of a small circle of his acquaintance, and does honour to the Doctor's catholic and friendly disposition.

Reflections on a Visit received from Mr. Jones, Nov. 9, 1736:
This day I enjoyed a great deal of the company of my pious and worthy friend, Mr. Jones, of Ripton-Abbots; a Clergyman, for whom I have the tenderest respect. He shewed me several papers especially relating to Lady ——, which I read with pleasure, and with confusion, when I observed her shining and eminent piety, which I think as conspicuous as most I have ever seen; her daily and nightly devotions, watching over her family as a guardian angel while they sleep; referring, as it were, all her other passions into the love of God and her husband; passing through the world as a stranger in it, always tending homewards. What also I heard of Sir John Thorold, Mr. R ——, Mr. B ——, and many others of the Established Church, relating to their real goodness and zeal for the glory of God, and the salvation of their own souls, put me to the greatest shame, when I compared it with my unprofitable life; particularly what I saw of some hints, which Mr. Jones had drawn up, for self-examination, which contained so much elevated and spiritual devotion, and betokened a mind so thoroughly devoted to the glory of God, and good of mankind, that I thought I had never seen any thing of the kind that equalled it.

[Editor's note: In a series of letters from William Warburton to Philip Doddridge (*Illustr.*, II, 811-837), Jones is discussed in two. In the first letter, dated 25 June 1741 (p. 828), Warburton quotes his friend Lyndford Caryl, Master of Jesus College, Cambridge (of whom Nichols has a brief note in *Lit. Anec.*, V, 159). The quotation from Caryl concerning Jones follows.]

Mr. Jones, the Huntingdonshire Clergyman, came hither with the Doctor [Doddridge]. By two or three things which dropped from him I find he suspects you slight his acquaintance; and truly, if it were my case, I should continue so to do; for, betwixt friends, I take him to be a mere solemn coxcomb, &c.

[Editor's note: Warburton is speaking himself in the second excerpt, from a letter (pp. 828-829) dated 5 August 1741.]

As I came down from London I dined at Bugden with the Bishop of Lincoln, where I accidentally met with Mr. Jones. He has a very good look, and I believe is a good man; but is too trifling where he proposes to be most serious; for I had his company some miles on the road.
Dr. [John] Newcome, Master of St. John's, was much taken with you; but blamed Mr. Jones for not telling him that it was Dr. Doddridge of

Northampton, because he believes he said some things too freely of the Dissenters.[5]

[Editor's note: Nichols prints a series of five letters from Jones to Zachary Grey in *Lit. Anec.*, VIII, 289-292, and in a note says: "These Letters illustrate the early History of Mr. Jones; of whom see vol. I. p. 687." A note written by Nichols to the second letter reads: "By this and some of the subsequent passages, it should seem that Mr. Jones was a principal assistant to Mr. [John] Wilford the Bookseller, in his publication of 'Memorials of Eminent Persons,' which originally appeared in Monthly Numbers."
In a letter dated 12 July 1814, John Calder wrote to Nichols (*Illustr.*, IV, 848) concerning Jones' manuscripts. An excerpt from the letter follows.]

Very many of Mr. Jones of Welwyn's MS papers were safe in Dr. Williams's Library when I had the care of it. They were all sealed up carefully, and under the stipulation when deposited of not being inspected for *twenty* years, long since expired. The reason commonly alledged for this restriction, was that they related to many in the Established Church who were writers in the "Candid Disquisitions," and desirous of alterations and reforms in it, who were still alive and adherents to it, whose desire and temporal interest it was, that nothing of such inconsistency should be publicly known till after their deaths. Whether this was precisely as I have stated it to have been the case, I cannot inform you, having never inspected any of these MSS. since the time of their concealment expired, and they have been unsealed and open to examination. I wish to know whether you have ever seen them, or inserted in your "Literary Anecdotes" any thing from them. It is more than thirty years that they have been open to public and general inspection.

[Editor's note: Nichols has a brief life of Thomas Dawson, from whom he received his share of Jones's mss., in *Illustr.*, VI, 858-860. On p. 859 is the following note.]

[Dr. Dawson was on terms of the strictest friendship with the Rev. John Jones, the learned author of "Free and Candid Disquisitions;" many, if not all of whose MSS. passed into his hands after Mr. Jones's death, and were by him ultimately deposited in the Dissenters' Library in Redcross-street.]

[Editor's note: As a sample of the kind of biographical notes left by Jones in his mss. and used by Nichols throughout *Literary Anecdotes* and *Illustrations*, I have chosen the following passage dealing with two literary men, Edward Young and Samuel Richardson. The excerpt comes from the "Additions and Corrections" at the end of *Lit. Anec.*, IV, 726-727, and is an addition to Nichols' life of Richardson, pp. 578-598.]

---

5. Philip Doddridge had exerted some effort to effect a reconciliation of Churchmen and Dissenters. See *Lit. Anec.*, III, 748-749; V, 544-545n.

[Mr. Jones of Welwyn, in his MS. says, "Dr. Young tells me, that he has been long and intimately acquainted with Mr. Richardson; and has always had the highest esteem for him, on account of the many excellences, natural and moral, which he discerned in him. As the Doctor has had much free conversation with him, he is acquainted with many particulars relating to him, which are known to none, or to but very few, besides himself.

"Mr. Richardson having not had the advantage of a complete education (as the situation and circumstances of his father§ would not allow him to bestow it)|| Dr. Young, to whom he was recounting the various difficulties he had passed through, asking him, 'How he came to be an author?' he answered, 'when I was about 12 years of age, I drew up a short character of a certain gentlewoman in the parish, who was reputed a great Saint, but I looked upon her to be a great hypocrite. The character, it seems, was so exactly drawn, that, when it came to be privately handed about amongst some select friends, every one could discern the features, and appropriate the picture to the true original, though no name was affixed to it. This little success at first setting out did, you will naturally suppose, tempt me at different times to employ my pen yet further in some trivial amusements or other for my own diversion, till at length, though many years after, I sat down to write in good earnest, going upon subjects that took my fancy most, and following the bent of my natural inclination, &c.'

"Dr. Young made this pertinent and just observation, that this man, with the advantages only or chiefly of mere nature, improved by a very moderate progress in education, struck out at once, and of his own accord, into a new province of writing, and succeeded therein to admiration. Nay, what is more remarkable, and seldom seen in any other writers, he both began and finished the plan on which he set out, leaving no room for any one after him to make it more complete, or even to come near him: and it is certain that not one of the various writers that soon after, and ever since, attempted to imitate him, have any way equalled him, or even come within a thousand paces of him. That kind of Romance was and is peculiarly his own, and seems like to continue so. 'I consider him,' said Dr. Young, 'as a truly great natural genius; as great and super-eminent in *his* way, as were Shakspeare and Milton in theirs.[']

"Mr. Shotbolt tells me, that when Mr. Richardson came down to Welwyn, with the late Speaker Onslow, and other friends, to visit Dr. Young, he took up his quarters with Mr. Shotbolt, there being not room enough at the Doctor's; and that, getting up early, about five of the clock, he wrote two of the best letters in Sir Charles Grandison in one or two mornings before breakfast. Mr. Onslow had a high esteem for him; and not only might, but actually would have promoted him to some honourable and profitable station at Court; but the good man neither desired nor would accept of

---

§ A farmer in Derbyshire. NICHOLS.
|| He was educated at Christ's Hospital. NICHOLS.

such posts, &c. being much better pleased with his own private way of living.‡

"Mr. Richardson, besides his being a great genius, was a truly good man in all respects; in his family, in commerce, in conversation, and in every instance of conduct. Pious, virtuous, exemplary, benevolent, friendly, generous, and humane to an uncommon degree; glad of every opportunity of doing good offices to his fellow-creatures in distress, and relieving many without their knowledge. His chief delight was doing good. Highly revered and beloved by his domesticks, because of his happy temper and discreet conduct. Great tenderness towards his wife and children, and great condescension towards his servants. He was always very sedulous in business, and almost always employed in it; and dispatched a great deal by the prudence of his management, &c.

"*Mem.* The tender touches of his compositor Mr. Tewley,[6] in his letter to Dr. Young, soon after the death of his good master."]

[Editor's note: This account of Jones will be concluded with a few excerpts from his correspondence with Thomas Birch, the 52 pages of which precede Nichols' memoir of Jones in *Lit. Anec.*, I, 585-637. The passages are chosen to throw light upon himself and upon Edward Young, his patron. They are introduced by Nichols as follows:

"AMONG the Letters to Dr. Birch* in the British Museum, vol. XII. (Ayscough's Catalogue, No. 4311.) are several from the Rev. John Jones, from 1741 till 1765, with various papers concerning the 'Free and Candid Disquisitions,' and on literary subjects in general; which having never been published, a selection from them shall here be given.

"In the earliest of them, dated from *Abbots Ripton, in Huntingdonshire, June* 24, 1741, Mr. Jones tenders Mr. Birch his assistance in the publication of the Thurloe State Papers."]

Jan. 4, 1749-50. I have at last accepted of the benefice offered me;† and purpose to leave this (which has been so troublesome to me) when the Spring is more advanced, and the roads better for a removal. I am indeed loath enough to part with so many people, who so heartily express their concern on the prospect of my leaving them. But I love ease and honesty so much, that the few litigious spirits I have found here,‡ have fixed my resolution to give them up, and to go to a smaller parish, being a rectory; though I intend, without any the least engagements, to resign that also, if I live, after some years are elapsed.

---

‡ His business being profitable, and his fortune easy. NICHOLS.

* Mus. Brit. Bibl. Birch, 4311. Plut. III. H. NICHOLS.

† Boulne-Hurst, a rectory rated at 9*l.* in the King's books. Fleetwood Churchill, clerk, was patron in 1772. NICHOLS.

‡ Alconbury is a vicarage of small value, in a populous village, in the gift of the Dean and Chapter of Westminister. NICHOLS.

6. In his last will, Richardson bequeathed rings to his overseer, William Tewley, and to Edward Young; see *Lit. Anec.*, IV, 596. Tewley, according to Nichols, "was remarkably deaf" (p. 597), which was the reason for Richardson's giving directions in writing.

Boulne-Hurst, in Bedfordshire, 20*th of June,* 1750. . . . in my present situation I have very little leisure to read any thing, being not yet fully settled in my new little parish, but hoping to be so by degrees. I like this obscure retreat, and am glad to find myself released from a large and troublesome vicarage, though I had been at great charge and pains to make every thing as convenient as possible, and to rectify many disorders which I found there at my first coming. My successors and the parish will, I hope, reap the benefit. I am busying myself about repairs and improvements here also. If at any time you should come into this neighbourhood, I should extremely rejoice to pay my respects to you at Boulne-Hurst. It lies about four or five miles North of Bedford.

May 1, 1754. My kind and much-esteemed Dr. Birch will, I know, be concerned when he finds that I have lately received a shock, which brought my life into imminent danger, and hath had a very considerable effect upon my state of health ever since: though I am now, I thank God, much better than I have been; and hope to receive still more benefit from pursuing the directions which have been given me by my physician, who has a true desire to do me service. If God spare my life and health till after Whitsuntide, I design to turn my face towards the Sea-coast, and to try the effect of bathing, and drinking the sea-water, hoping it will prove salutary.

The shock I mentioned, you will rightly imagine, reminds me, as it ought to do, of mortality. I have for some years been considering, at different intervals, how to dispose of my manuscript-papers, which, such as they are, upon a variety of subjects, make up pretty nigh a press full: but have not yet determined. I have indeed requested a particular friend, not far from me, to take care of them; and given him directions what to do, in case of my being removed out of this world before I shall have fixed my last resolution. Farther than this I have not as yet gone; and what conclusion I may come to hereafter, I know not. I remember, I mentioned this matter transiently once to you, Sir; and I am desirous to consult you again upon the topick. I should be glad they might come into your hands in time, after proper revisal, if you can make free to tell me how you intend to dispose of your own. I cannot imagine you would have them go into the hands of booksellers, any more than I would have mine. I will tell you freely what I think, and could wish to have done, as far as I have yet considered about the matter. If they should come into your hands, I should be glad that they might accompany your papers, on supposition that you design yours for a friend, or friends, who will take proper care of them; as supposing, for instance, any of the Lord Chancellor's [Philip Yorke, first Earl of Hardwicke] family: or else (if circumstances should render it expedient) that they should be disposed of by way of sale, according to reasonable valuation, to such friend or friends, by your direction and management; the sum received for them going to my heir-at-law, or appointed executor, as I shall either make, or should happen not to make, a will. In case of such a sale, I know I can depend upon your kindness and prudence, supposing you survive me; and perhaps I may desire another friend to join in the trust.

When you shall have considered about what I have said, I shall be glad to be favoured with your answer; and hope to have it soon, if your business will permit. I do not, after all, imagine my papers to be of any considerable worth: but, as I would not willingly have them all destroyed, and as I may not live to look them over as I desire to do, I judge it prudent to make some sort of provision about them in time, to prevent their falling into hands into which I could not wish them to fall. This is my main view in applying to you as I now do.

Everton, Nov. 17, 1755. . . . The time draws near when I am reminded of the considerations on which I took upon me the charge of Boulne-Hurst, which I have no thoughts of retaining any longer than till I am advertised (which I have not been as yet) by the Patron concerning his design to succeed me. This I have all along resolved, though they never asked me in the least to give them any promise; nor did I at all, till after I was in full possession; and then, in gratitude, I spoke my mind freely: which was kindly taken. . . .

Excuse this trouble. I am at Everton, near St. Neot's, Huntingdonshire, for this winter. . . .

March 20, 1756. The crisis about which I dropped some intimations to you more than once in town, and more lately in a letter of November last, seems now to be gradually approaching. I do not mention some assurances voluntarily given me by the Patron soon after my entrance, which tempted me to run myself into great expences upon the place, when I never intended any: of those assurances I am now reminding the gentleman by letter in a gentle and respectful manner; waiting the issue, and only wishing to be re-imbursed those expences: but as for resigning, I fully purpose it, if farther requested of me, with all the expedition I fairly can. Indeed, the place never answered my expences, any one year.

Now if my worthy friend Dr. Birch can put me in a way of acquiring any thing suitable for me, and what I can in honour and with integrity accept, I readily assure myself that he will be very free to do it, and will neither forget nor neglect me in such a difficult situation. If nothing of the ecclesiastical kind can be attained, on such terms as I mention, I should judge it agreeable to reason, in a case of real difficulty, to accept of some secular provision. If a pension, or the like, cannot well be hoped for; a place, not disagreeable, even in some Hospital, might be of service. Confinement, or close air, would not suit me, as I have often experienced. If I could be of use as a Catechist in such an airy place as the Foundling Hospital, I should like it much. And the Charter-house, I think, is not ill situated for openness. But then I know not the terms of admission there, nor what maintenance is assigned for the pensioners. Nor can I tell where Guy's Hospital is situated, or for what sort of persons, or what allowance they have. There may be many other things, in different parts of the kingdom, that might suit one in my case; but I can have little or no intelligence about them; nor know either where they are to be met with, or how to be come at.

Have you any account to give of the disposal of the Preaching-lectures (instituted, I suppose, by his present Majesty's Father) for the mountainous parts of Lancashire, in the summer months? I am told, the salary is pretty good. Such exercise of riding would be agreeable and useful to me: and I should take great pleasure in instilling principles of Religion and Loyalty into the minds of poor ignorant people. . . .

I suppose no Bishop would readily approve, or perhaps admit, a remonstrance at the time of subscription. But if ever I should be inclined to accede to the terms of admission, I would surely enter my protest in writing, and leave it there upon record; let the consequence be what it might. But I had rather be free, than involved in such restraints.

I purpose to return to Boulne-Hurst about a week before Easter. . . .

Boulne-Hurst, June 25, 1756. . . . No encouraging prospect hath as yet opened. Since my coming home, I have found my reasons for resigning confirmed. . . .

I know you will not be surprized, when I tell you, that some clerical men have lately been very busy, in criticizing upon my poor affair: for they have, by some means or other, got a notion of it, though, I see plainly, a very imperfect one. . . . I bear with patience, saying very little; knowing it would be to little purpose, with such men, to make any remonstrance. I cannot but think it very unbecoming their profession, either to invent or spread falsehoods; which they have not failed to do. . . . Even friends, and men of understanding, have been tampered with. My intention is, to be quiet, and to let truth find out its way in time. Attempts of this kind may possibly incommode me a little, in respect of future livelihood; but cannot, I hope, always do it.

P.S. When I am dead, you will not deny any friendly direction or assistance you can conveniently give, in favour of those who shall execute any trust for me, and apply to you. . . .

[Editor's note: In 1759 Jones received the curacy of Welwyn from Edward Young. His first letter to Birch from Welwyn is dated 13 June 1759. He remained at Welwyn until the death of Young in 1765. The few remaining excerpts from Jones's letters to Birch are concerned primarily with Young.]

2 *April* [1765.] Dr. Young very ill; attended by two physicians.—Having mentioned this young gentleman (Dr. Young's son [Frederick]), I would acquaint you next, that he came hither this morning, having been sent for, as I am told, by the direction of Mrs. Hallows.§ Indeed, she intimated to me as much herself. And if this be so, I must say, that it is one of the most prudent acts she ever did, or could have done in such a case as this; as it may prove a means of preventing much confusion after the death of the Doctor. I have had some little discourse with the son; he seems much affected, and I believe really is so. He earnestly wishes his father might be pleased to ask after him: for you must know he has not yet done this, nor is, in my opinion, like to do it. And it has been said farther, that, upon a late application made to him on the behalf of his son, he desired that no more might be said to him about it. How true this may be, I cannot as yet be certain: all I shall say, is, it seems not improbable. Mrs. Hallows has fitted up a suitable apartment in the house for Mr. Young; where I suppose he will continue till some farther event.

I heartily wish the antient man's heart may prove tender towards his son; though, knowing him so well, I can scarce hope to hear such desireable news. He took to his bed yesterday about eleven in the forenoon, and hath not been up since.|| I called soon after my coming home, but did not see him: he was then in a doze. I imagine his further stay upon earth can be of no long duration. When that is over, I must, it seems, again emigrate. . . .

April 13, [1765.] I have now the pleasure to acquaint you, that the late Dr. Young, though he had for many years kept his son at a distance from him, yet has now at last left him all his possessions, after the payment of

§ Dr. Young's housekeeper. NICHOLS.
|| He had performed no duty for the last three or four years of his life; but he retained his intellects to the last. . . . NICHOLS.

certain legacies; so that the young gentleman (who bears a fair character, and behaves well, as far as I can hear or see) will, I hope, soon enjoy and make a prudent use of a very handsome fortune. The father, on his death-bed, and since my return from London, was applied to in the tenderest manner, by one of his physicians, and by another person, to admit the son into his presence, to make submission, intreat forgiveness, and obtain his blessing. As to an interview with his son, he intimated that he chose to decline it, as his spirits were then low, and his nerves weak. With regard to the next particular, he said, *I heartily forgive him;* and, upon mention of the last, he gently lifted up his hand, and, letting it gently fall, pronounced these words; *God bless him!* After about a fortnight's illness, and enduring excessive pains, he expired, a little before eleven of the clock, in[7] the night of Good-Friday last, the 15th instant; and was decently buried yesterday, about six in the afternoon, in the chancel of this church, close by the remains of his lady, under the communion-table; the Clergy who are the trustees for his charity-school, and one or two more, attending the funeral; the last office at interment being performed by me. I know it will give you pleasure to be farther informed, that he was pleased to make respectful mention of me in his will; expressing his satisfaction in my care of his parish, bequeathing to me a handsome legacy, and appointing me to be one of his Executors, next after his sister's son. . . .

7. In "Additions and Corrections to Vol. I," *Illustr.*, VIII, 444, is this correction: "for 'on,' r. 'in.'"

Thomas Tyrwhitt

[The greater part of Nichols' memoir of Thomas Tyrwhitt is contained in a biographical note in *Lit. Anec.*, III, 147-151. Several later additions to this will be included, however, along with letters concerning Tyrwhitt's death, taken from *Illustrations*. The source of each will be pointed out as it is introduced.

Tyrwhitt is remembered chiefly in connection with Chatterton and Chaucer. With regard to the former, he gave to the world the first edition of the Rowley poems (1777), purported by Chatterton to have been written by a fifteenth-century monk. That Tyrwhitt believed them to be genuine until "after his volume was actually completed at the press" is asserted by Nichols in this life of Tyrwhitt in a note to a contrary assertion of Steevens that Tyrwhitt had become convinced that Chatterton's manuscripts were not genuinely ancient before the volume was finished but decided, despite his conviction, to complete it. Nichols' version is supported by his evidence that after the Rowley volume was completed at the press, Tyrwhitt "canceled *several sheets* which had been printed to demonstrate that the Poems were genuine." The controversy as to whether the Rowley poems were taken from genuine medieval manuscripts continued for many months. Tyrwhitt, Steevens, Thomas Warton the Younger, and others wrote against the authenticity of the medievalism. Jeremiah Milles, dean of Exeter and president of the Society of Antiquaries, published an edition of the Rowley poems in 1782 and wrote an elaborate defense of their authenticity. The whole thing is seen in a much different light by the modern reader, who interprets Chatterton's transparent mask of the medieval monk as a youthful invention behind which lay much real poetic ability. Johnson, Warton, Walpole, and Malone all expressed admiration for Chatterton's talents, which had little chance to be developed. He died by suicide in 1770, three months before his eighteenth birthday.

Tyrwhitt's contribution to Chaucer scholarship is of inestimable value. He is credited by W. P. Ker with being "the restorer of Chaucer" (in Chapter X of CHEL, X, 241, 1952): "No other piece of medieval scholarship in England can be compared with Tyrwhitt's in importance. . . . The art of the grammarian has seldom been better justified and there are few things in English philology more notable than Tyrwhitt's edition of Chaucer." Tyrwhitt restored the proper reading of Chaucer's line, "mainly by getting the value of the *e* mute, partly by attending to the change of accent." Dr. Charles Burney (*Lit. Anec.*, IV, 660) lists Tyrwhitt as one of the seven greatest critics of the century, along with Richard Bentley and Richard Porson.

Through his interest in the medieval, Tyrwhitt became associated with other antiquarians, particularly Steevens, Farmer, and Reed (see *Lit. Anec.*, II, 670).

In view of the importance of Tyrwhitt as an English scholar, it seems that no great foresight is needed to predict that inevitably he will be the subject of thorough study. He was generous with help to other scholars; and therefore many of his letters survive in libraries and collections. The locations of a few of these letters will be detailed here, and two others relating to him, one from his brother Robert to Thomas Warton and one from his nephew Thomas to George Steevens, will be interpolated at the end of Nichols' life. The British Museum, which possesses the letter from Robert Tyrwhitt just referred to, also holds a letter dated 1758 from Thomas Tyrwhitt to the Bishop of Durham (Add. Mss. 32,881. f. 436), written while Tyrwhitt held a post at the War Office. The Bodleian Library has a number of Tyrwhitt's letters, as has the Osborn Collection; and Harvard University owns two annotated manuscripts. The letter from Tyrwhitt's nephew to Steevens is in the Steevens collection at the Folger Shakespeare Library.

A life of Tyrwhitt by William Prideaux Courtney in the DNB lists Nichols as a source.]

Thomas Tyrwhitt, esq. F.R.S. and F.A.S. (whose critical abilities distinguished him as a scholar, and his unlimited benevolence as the friend of humanity) was born in 1730; came from Eton to Queen's college, Oxford, 1747; took the degree of B.A. in 1750; was elected fellow of Merton in 1755; took the degree of M.A. in 1756; and remained Fellow of that College seven years; *i. e.* till 1762; when he was made Clerk of the House of Commons, in the room of the late Jeremiah Dyson, esq. and resigned his Fellowship. He had been previously Deputy Secretary at War, which he also at the same time relinquished. In 1768, preferring to that "post of honour" a "private station" devoted to learned ease, he resigned it to John Hatsell, esq. (whose abilities and long service in that important department require no encomium.) From that time he occupied himself chiefly in critical and other literary studies, to which the greater part of his former life had been devoted. Mr. Tyrwhitt is one of the Pleiades celebrated by Dr. [Charles] Burney, as noticed under the article of Mr. Markland, in [*Lit. Anec.,*] vol. IV. p. 660. Besides a knowledge of almost every European tongue, he was deeply conversant in the learning of Greece and Rome, of which latter acquisition some valuable tracts are distinguished proofs. He was thoroughly read in the old English writers; and, as his knowledge was directed by a manly judgment, his critical efforts have eminently contributed to restore the genuine text of Shakspeare. The admirers of Chaucer are also greatly indebted to him, for elucidating the obscurities, and illustrating the humour, of that antient Bard. His loss as a Curator of the British Museum (to which office he was elected in 1784, which his friend Mr. [Clayton Mordaunt] Cracherode, on the deaths of Mr. [Daniel] Wray and Mr. [Matthew] Duane, and in the duties of which he was indefatigably diligent) was greatly regretted.

The publications of Mr. Tyrwhitt were, 1. "An Epistle to Florio (Mr. Ellis of Christ Church), at Oxford, London, 1749," 4to. 2. "Translations in Verse. Mr. Pope's Messiah, Mr. Phillips's Splendid Shilling, in Latin; the Eighth Isthmian of Pindar in English," 1752, 4to. 3. "Observations and Conjectures on some Passages of Shakspeare, 1766," 8vo. (Many other judicious remarks on our great Dramatic Bard were afterwards communicated by him to his friend Mr. Steevens for the Edition of 1778, and others to Mr. Reed for the Edition of 1785.) 4. "Proceedings and Debates in the House of Commons in 1620 and 1621; from the original MS. in the Library of Queen's College, Oxford: with an Appendix. Printed at the Clarendon Press, 1766," in 2 vols. 8vo. 5. "The Manner of holding Parliaments in England: by Henry Elsynge, Cler. Par. Corrected and enlarged from the Author's original MS. Lond. 1768," small 8vo. With a view to raise a spirit of research into classical antient MSS. unnoticed, his first critical publication in Literature was, 6. "Fragmenta Duo Plutarchi, 1773," 8vo. from a Harleian MS. 5612, not, he observes, of any great merit, but to induce further enquiries after such (see p. 156) [of *Lit. Anec.*, Vol. III]. 7. "The Canterbury Tales of Chaucer, 1773," in 4 vols. crown 8vo; to which, in 1778, he added a fifth volume, with a Glossary. Of this performance it is not too much to say, that it is the best edited English Classick that ever has appeared. 8. "Dissertatio de Babrio, Fabularum AEsopearum Scriptore. Inseruntur Fabulae quaedam Esopeae nunquam antehac editae, Cod. MS. Bodl. Accedunt Babrii Fragmenta, 1776;" shewing that the Collection of Fables which pass under the name of AEsop, are inserted many from another antient Writer, of the name of Babrius, whose Fragments in Verse are preserved in Suidas's Lexicon, and many of whose Fables, translated into prose, are here printed from a Bodleian MS. This is a small pamphlet, but sufficient to establish the celebrity of his critical acumen on the broadest basis. He published also, 9. some "Notes on Euripides," of which I do not recollect the exact title or the date. 10. "Poems, supposed to have been written at Bristol, by Thomas Rowley and others, in the 15th century; the greatest part now first published from the most authentic copies, with an engraved specimen of one of the MSS. To which are added, a Preface, an introductory Account of the several Poems, and a Glossary, 1777," 8vo. This was twice re-published in 1778, "with an Appendix, containing some Observations upon their Language, tending to prove that they were written, not by any antient Author, but entirely by Chatterton." This affair became the foundation of a vehement controversy. Mr. Malone and the Rev. T. Warton entered the lists professedly on the side of Mr. Tyrwhitt; and were supported by the sterling wit of the "Archaeological Epistle," addressed, with the most poignant brilliancy of satire, to Dean Milles, who, with Mr. Bryant and some other writers, defended the originality of the Poems. The business, however, was completely settled, by, 11. "A Vindication of the Appendix to the Poems called Rowley's, in Reply to the Answer of the Dean of Exeter, Jacob Bryant, esq. and a Third Anonymous Writer, with some further Observations upon those Poems, and an Examination of the Evidence which has been produced in support of their Authenticity. By Thomas Tyrwhitt, 1782," 8vo. The active spirit of our learned Commentator had produced, meantime, a very accurate and judicious Edition of, 12. "ΠΕΡΙΑΙΘΩΝ, de Lapidibus, Poema Orpheo à quibusdam adscriptum, Graecè et Latinè, ex editione Jo. Matthaei Gesneri. Recensuit, notasque adjecit, Thomas Tyrwhitt. Simul prodit Auctarium Dissertationis de Babrio, 1781," 8vo. The Poem on Stones, ascribed to Orpheus, is by this enlightened Critic referred to the age of Constantius. The Supplement to Babrius consists of additional Notes. Of, 13. his "Conjecturae in Strabonem," printed only for private use, 1783, see Gent. Mag. vol. LIII. p. 103. His amiable disposition also prompted him to superintend the publication of, 14. "Two Dissertations, I. On the Grecian Mythology. II. An Examination of Sir Isaac Newton's Objection to the Chronology of the Olympiads. By the late Samuel Musgrave, M.D. 1782." For this Work a very liberal subscription was raised, entirely by the exertions of Mr. Tyrwhitt. The last public literary labour which passed through his hands was, 15. A newly-discovered Oration of Isaeus, against Menecles, which he revised in 1785, and enriched with some valuable remarks (at the request of Lord Sandys, one of the few Noblemen who have condescended to unite to the talents of a Statesman the taste and abilities of a polite Scholar). These few specimens are from the Medicean Library, and are sufficient to shew Mr. Tyrwhitt's powers, and to make us regret that his modesty declined the proposal made to him of directing the publication of the second volume of Inscriptions collected by Mr. Chishull, and first laid open to the publick by the sale of Dr. Askew's MSS. How he succeeded in the illustration of such subjects will best appear by that most happy explanation of the Greek Inscription on the Corbridge altar, which had baffled the skill of all preceding Criticks, and will be a lasting proof how critical acumen transcends elaborate conjecture. (See Archaeologia, vol. III. p. 324, compared with vol. II. pp. 92, 98.) Nor must his Observations on some other Greek Inscriptions in Archaeologia, vol. III. p. 230, be forgotten. His "Conjecturae in Strabonem," were published by Charles Hailes, in 1788.

He left to the British Museum all such of his printed books as were not before in the rich Library of that admirable repository.

"Mr. Tyrwhitt's intimate acquaintance with the antient English Poets (a Correspondent observes) enabled him to detect the pretensions of an Impostor, whose principal merit, if there be merit in forgery, was, that he conducted his deception so well, that less enlightened criticks could not penetrate the disguise. The first edition of the Poems ascribed to Rowley was superintended by Mr. Tyrwhitt, who left the question of their authenticity to the impartial publick, only intimating his opinion, that the external evidence on both sides was so defective as to deserve but little attention. In an Appendix to the *third* edition of these Poems, he shewed that the internal evidence, founded on the language, was sufficient to prove that they were not written in the fifteenth century, but that they were written entirely by Chatterton. When the late Dean of Exeter, Mr. Bryant, and an Anonymous Writer, had ranged the field of controversy, Mr. Tyrwhitt published, 1782, 8vo, a "Vindication of his Appendix." To this last Pamphlet he put his name; and it clearly proved that all these Poems were written by Chatterton. With this, we presume, the controversy is brought to a fair conclusion. It can never be enough lamented, that Mr. Tyrwhitt did not continue the publication of the Writings of Chaucer, and compile the Glossary for the whole of them, which he so much regrets the want of."

The following account of Mr. Tyrwhitt is from an anonymous hand: "Mr. Tyrwhitt was naturally of a calm and contemplative disposition: He manifested the strongest propensities to Literature at an age when other boys are employing every moment they can steal from books, in pursuit of pleasure. From the University he carried with him an uncommon fund of various knowledge, to which he afterwards added, by the most unwearied application. Even while he sustained a public character, his vacant hours were appropriated to the closest study of the dead and living languages. The profundity and acuteness of his remarks on Euripides, Babrius, Chaucer, Shakspeare, and Pseudo-Rowley, &c. bear sufficient witness to the diligence of his researches and the force of his understanding. His mode of criticism is allowed to have been at once rigorous and candid. As he never availed himself of petty stratagems in support of doubtful positions, he was vigilant to strip his antagonists of all such specious advantages. Yet controversy produced no unbecoming change in the habitual gentleness and elegance of his manners. His spirit of enquiry was exempt from captiousness, and his censures were as void of rudeness, as his erudition was free from pedantry.

"Of his virtues a record no less honourable might be made. *Ab uno disce omnes*. To the widow of the late Dr. [Samuel] Musgrave he is said to have given up a bond for several hundred pounds, which her husband had borrowed of him. At the same time he undertook the patronage and correction of one of his posthumous Works; which produced, by subscription, an ample sum for the benefit of his children. No political sentiments could be at greater variance than those of the Doctor and Mr. Tyrwhitt; yet the latter was an unshaken friend to the former throughout all his misfortunes. True generosity is uninfluenced by party considerations, which operate only upon narrow minds. What Mr. Tyrwhitt was, may indeed more exactly be inferred from the characters of those with whom he lived in intimacy— a set of gentlemen as conspicuous for their amiable qualities as for their rank in life and their literary acquisitions.

"I had almost added, that, by exhibiting a list of the adversaries and associates of any private man, his genuine merits might be ascertained. But, in the present instance, such an experiment, if attempted, would be incomplete; for he who, like Mr. Tyrwhitt, had no enemies, must be content to lose the benefit of contrast, and be estimated only by the value and number of his friends.

"Of the Royal Society Mr. Tyrwhitt was many years a Fellow; and, to his honour be it remembered, that one of the Trusteeships of the British Museum, an office not unfrequently courted by the great and the vain, was conferred on him without the slightest private interest or solicitation.

"His constitution had never been of the athletic kind, and therefore easily gave way to a joint attack from two violent disorders, which hurried him with uncommon speed to his grave.

"Can it be necessary to subjoin, that he died lamented by all who knew the worth of his friendship, or enjoyed the honour of his acquaintance?" Τὸγάζ, γέζας ἐστὶ θανόντων.

He died in Welbeck-street, Cavendish-square, Aug. 15, 1786, in his 56th year.

[Editor's note: In 1776 the Bowyer-Nichols press issued " 'Dissertatio de Babrio, Fabularum AEsopicarum Scriptore. Inseruntur Fabulae quaedam AEsopeae nunquam antehac editae, ex Cod. MS. Bodl. Accedunt Babrii Fragmenta.' By Mr. Tyrwhitt, 8vo." Following is a note to the above entry from Lit. Anec., III, 234.]

[See some Memoirs of this illustrious Scholar in p. 147; to which may be added, that he was the son of the Rev. Dr. Robert Tyrwhitt, a gentleman of considerable eminence in the Church; who was of Magdalen College, Cambridge, B.A. 1718; M.A. 1722; D.D. Com. Reg. 1728; rector of St. James's Westminster 1729, which he resigned in 1732, on being appointed a canon residentiary of St. Paul's. He held also the prebend of Kentish Town in that Cathedral; and was archdeacon of London. He obtained a canonry of Windsor in 1740; died June 15, 1742; and was buried in St. George's chapel at Windsor. By his mother's side he was grandson to Bp. [Edmund] Gibson. At the age of six he was sent to school at Kensington, and thence removed to Eton, in 1741. He was appointed, in 1756, Under Secretary at War to Lord Barrington.]

[Editor's note: The following addition to Nichols' life of Tyrwhitt appears in the "Additions to the Third Volume" in Lit. Anec., IX, 527-531.]

[Pp. 147, 234. The name of Mr. Tyrwhitt is so justly dear to every Scholar, that I make no scruple of enlarging his article, by a Letter from Dr. [John] Loveday; who says to Mr. Urban, "I have reason to think that every thing relating to Mr. Tyrwhitt will be well received by you and all your Readers, either as good men, or as literary men; but I do not intend to take up any more of your Miscellany than will suffice to supply what was omitted in your account of that gentleman; so that, if you or any of his friends think it worth while to interweave and arrange both accounts, there will be a pretty correct history of that benevolent and learned man. Mr. Tyrwhitt's father was the Rev. Dr. Robert Tyrwhitt, of a very antient (Baronet's) family in Lincolnshire (whose elder Brother had also a very considerable estate there; but who, on his travels, preferring the Roman Catholic Religion, settled in France, and died there; but left the shipwreck of his fortune to his Nephew): and I have heard that at the death of the last Sir John Tyrwhitt, the late Mr. Tyrwhitt might have claimed the title; but, as Sir John gave all the estates to the female line (now possessed by Mr. Drake Tyrwhitt, who took that name by Sir John's Will), Mr. Tyrwhitt never thought proper to stir in it. Dr. Tyrwhitt might be called in those times a Pluralist; for he was Residentiary of St. Paul's, Canon of Windsor, and Archdeacon of London, and at one time Rector of St. James's also, which he resigned, though he had interest enough to have kept them all, by his connexions with the Walpole family, as well as his father-in-law. Mr. Tyrwhitt's mother was the eldest daughter of that excellent Prelate Dr. Gibson, Bishop of London, whose virtues of liberality and hospitality Dr. Tyrwhitt so well followed, that, dying at the age of 44 years, he left a numerous family, very moderately provided for. Mr. Tyrwhitt was the eldest son. The second (Edmund, of Katharine Hall, Cambridge, B.A. 1753, M.A. 1756) was many years Chaplain to Bp. Sherlock, from whom he got some preferment in Essex or Hertfordshire. The third (Robert, Fellow of Jesus College, Cambridge, B.A. 1757, M.A. 1760) had the offer of being Chaplain to Bishop Thomas of Winchester, which he declined; and growing more and more dissatisfied with the Articles and Establishment of the Church, after fighting for many years the battles of Reformation in vain, he resigned all his present and future prospects, and at last his Fellowship. The fourth is an Officer in the Army or Navy, and lives (1787) retired in the country with a large family; he married a woman with some fortune and connexions, whose eldest son has lately changed his name for a large estate in Shropshire. Three other children are dead.

"Mr. Thomas Tyrwhitt was educated at Eton, which place foretold what he would be (for he never was a boy); and these prophecies were fully confirmed by Queen's and Merton Colleges in Oxford. He studied the Law at the Temple, and was called to the Bar: but his health was visibly unequal to the fatigues of the profession; therefore, in December 1756, he accepted the post of Deputy Secretary at War, under his noble friend and patron Lord Barrington, with whom and his family he preserved (and valued highly) the most intimate friendship to the last hour of his life. In August 1762 he left the War-office, and was appointed Clerk of the House of Commons; and if the too constant fatigues and late hours of that office had not proved too much for his constitution, there is no saying how high he might have soared; his friends used to think then that the highest offices of the State were within his abilities, if not within his reach. After getting through one long Parliament, he retired in 1768 to his beloved books, and the remainder of his life was devoted entirely to literary pursuits; how well he employed himself, and how well he succeeded, your Miscellany has very correctly recorded. You say truly, that no difference in politicks (nor indeed difference in any thing) could interrupt his benevolence, as Mrs. Musgrave and others have experienced for many years. His love of learning carried him to the encouragement, and partly to the support, of young men of promising abilities and application. His love of his family and friends, and his care of his dependents, made them all sharing in his fortune. "Ex unô disce omnes." I have heard that in one year of his life he gave away 2000*l*.; but he had no luxuries, no follies, no vices to maintain. Such was this excellent man; and to him belonged this uncommon eulogium, 'he had no enemy.' He left the most valuable and scarce books of his Library, to the amount of a great many hundreds, to the Museum; a generous and suitable return for the unsolicited and unexpected honour conferred on him by the Trustees."

P. 147. The following Letter, by Mr. Steevens, as it is connected with the name of Tyrwhitt, will, I think, be deemed interesting.]

Mr. Urban, March 24, 1788.

My Father (says Tristram Shandy) *had such a skirmishing, cutting kind of way with him in his disputations, thrusting and ripping, and giving every one a stroke to remember him by in his turn; that, if there were twenty people in company, in less than half an hour he was sure to have every one of them against him.* Somewhat, perhaps, of this characteristick is discernible in the Correspondence of the late Dr. Samuel Johnson.

In two of his Letters, published by Mrs. Piozzi, are the following strictures; and on each of these I shall trouble you with a few remarks, extracted from an explanatory Note I have just received from a Friend, who thinks (like Falstaff) that such *sneaps should not be undergone without reply.*

Vol. I. p. 326. *Steevens seems connected with Tyrwhitt in publishing Chatterton's Poems; he came very anxiously to know the result of our enquiries; and, though he says he always thought them forged, is not well pleased to find us so fully convinced.*

That eagerness in Mr. Steevens, which Dr. Johnson construed into anxiety, was merely the effect of haste. When he called in Bolt-court, he had little time to spare; and, being kept waiting till the Doctor could be prevailed on to leave his bed, might reasonably be allowed to urge the questions he came to propose with some degree of earnestness and impatience. Mr. Steevens was that morning to set out for the country, where he expected to meet Mr. Tyrwhitt, who, having heard of Dr. Johnson's peremptory decision in the business of Rowley, very naturally wished to be acquainted with the particular circumstances on which that decision was founded. To obtain such intelligence for Mr. Tyrwhitt, was the sole object of Mr. Steevens's early visit and precipitate enquiries.

That Mr. Steevens always thought the Poems forged, is certain. That he was not pleased to find Dr. Johnson so fully convinced, is by no means a fact. It might rather be observed, that Dr. Johnson himself was piqued at finding Messrs. Tyrwhitt and Steevens resolved to make their own eyes and understandings their judges in the Chattertonian Controversy, instead of expressing complete acquiescence in his decrees. On his determinations, however, he wished them to repose; strove to laugh Mr. Steevens out of his intended journey to Bristol; and finally dropped this stroke of satire on him, because he persisted in his design to accompany Mr. Tyrwhitt, and look at manuscripts, of which the Doctor himself could be no competent examiner, for want of eye-sight keen enough to trace the weak vestiges of almost evanescent ink. On the score of knowledge in antient hand-writing, his qualifications for the same task were equally disputable. Had Mr. Steevens, however, been the *first* to declare against the genuineness of these verses, was it not possible that his friend the Doctor, to whom the cause of the Savage or the Citizen (see Mrs. Piozzi's Collection, vol. I. p. 115) was indifferent, for the sake of mere contradiction, might have stood forth the Champion of the Counterfeit Rowley?

But this sarcasm on Mr. Steevens is of little moment. What follows is of importance, because it may, perhaps, be considered as some oblique reflection on the literary integrity of Mr. Tyrwhitt; which, to those who enjoyed the happiness of his personal acquaintance, can want no justification.

Vol. I. p. 337. *Catcot has been convinced by Barret, and has written his recantation to Tyrwhitt, who still persists in his Edition of the Poems, and perhaps is not much pleased to find himself mistaken.*

As Mr. Tyrwhitt (unfortunately for the Publick as well as his particular Friends) can no longer vindicate himself, that office must devolve on one who honours his memory, and, knowing all his gradations of belief as to the authenticity or illegitimacy of the pieces in question, thinks he ought not to suffer the most remote insinuation to his disadvantage (and especially from the pen of a Writer so eminent as Dr. Johnson) to pass without proper notice.

Before Mr. Tyrwhitt published his Chaucer, the productions of the fictitious Rowley were only known to him through the medium of partial transcripts, and extracts of very doubtful authority. When he was first favoured with these specimens, he was sufficiently willing to have supposed them genuine; but soon discovered reason enough for wavering in his opinions concerning their value, if considered in the light of antient compositions. Till he visited Bristol, however, he had not seen the smallest fragment of their boasted archetypes. His judgment, therefore, might be allowed to fluctuate till the means of complete decision were in his reach. No sooner had he examined the many-coloured "Rolles" (those *simiae vetustatis*), than his sentiments became immutably fixed. Nevertheless, he resolved to proceed in printing the Poems, which had been already purchased (as curiosities of dubious character) by his recommendation.

[[Nichols' note: Mr. Tyrwhitt changed his opinion after his volume was actually completed at the press; and canceled *several sheets* which had been printed to demonstrate that the Poems were genuine. J. N.]]

Still he forbore to obtrude on the Publick a single hint of his own concerning their spuriousness or originality; though he reserved to himself a right of delivering his undisguised opinions of them on some future occasion. Of this privilege he availed himself in an Appendix about a year afterwards; and, had Dr. Johnson been acquainted with the gentleman whose conduct he undertook to censure, he would never have urged against him, either as a weakness or as a fault, that he *persisted in his Edition of the Poems, and was not much pleased to find himself mistaken.* Mr. Tyrwhitt was wholly uninterested in the result of the publication. He was equally content whether he was employed to enlist a Poetical Recruit, or to detect an Impostor who strove to disguise himself in the uniform of one of the oldest regiments of Parnassus. Mere truth was the object of his researches; and, in the present instance, he discovered it by his own sagacity, his judgment being alike uninfluenced by the recantations of Catcot, the disquisitions of Barret, and the decretals of Johnson. And yet, had the Doctor's representation of this matter been strictly just, could it have been amiss if the Visitant of Fanny the phantom had been disposed to manifest a little more indulgence to a quondam sceptick in the cause of the Pseudo-Rowley?

[Editor's note: This ends Steevens' letter and the addition to Tyrwhitt's life from Vol. IX of *Literary Anecdotes*. Johnson's death (13 December 1784) had occurred three years before Steevens' letter was written. Since Steevens himself had died in 1800, all of the people involved were dead when Nichols placed the letter in *Literary Anecdotes*.

The three letters which follow are taken from *Illustr.*, VIII, 220-223. The Thomas Tyrwhitt writing the second letter and receiving the third is the nephew of the editor of Chaucer.]

[THOMAS TYRWHITT, Esq. to Bishop Percy.]

MY DEAR LORD, *Welbeck Street, Feb. 1, 1783.*
I send with this the Appendix, as you desired. The pretended Letter to Mr. Walpole is a mere catch-penny, without either wit or argument. It is supposed to be addressed to him by one of his fellow-conspirators against the fame of poor Rowley. I just ran over it, but my conscience would not permit me to be instrumental in promoting the sale of it. There has been a more decent pamphlet published lately on the same side by Mr. [Thomas J.] Mathias. He calls it a State of the Evidence on *both* sides. But he allows himself at the end to be a *well-wisher* to Rowley, and therefore you will easily suppose that his State is not quite impartial. However, I do not see that he has said anything which should occasion a renewal of the controversy. I really begin to hope that it is ended; especially if what the papers tell us be true, that Dr. [R.] Glynne is married. Of literary news there is a great dearth. I think I understood from Mr. Malone, the other day, that he had some Supplement in hand to his two volumes of Shakespear. I suppose, too, we shall have Mr. [Edward] Capell at last this spring, though I have not heard any certain intelligence about him. I am, my dear Lord, your very faithful and obedient T. TYRWHITT.

[THOMAS TYRWHITT, Esq. [nephew of the above] to Bishop Percy.]

MY LORD, *Welbeck Street, Aug. 18, 1786.*
I am exceedingly concerned that it falls to my lot to apprise your Lordship of the loss of so intimate a friend as the one who lately inhabited this house. He died on Tuesday last, after a short though severe illness. It has been beyond my exertions to write to all his numerous acquaintances in the course of two days' time, which, together with my present situation, I hope will prevent your Lordship from the supposition that I have been guilty of any intentional neglect in not having given the melancholy information

at an earlier period. I am, with the greatest respect, your Lordship's most faithful, humble servant, THOMAS TYRWHITT.

P.S. I am well aware that it becomes me to enter into further particulars to your Lordship, as I may say the most intimate friend of my departed uncle, but at present I am greatly pressed for time; the first opportunity I shall take the liberty of transmitting them to your Lordship.

[Bishop PERCY to THOMAS TYRWHITT, Esq. [Nephew]]

SIR, *Dromore House, Aug.* 31, 1786.

I received with most sincere grief the account of the death of my very ingenious, learned, and ever honoured friend Mr. Tyrwhitt, which you were pleased to impart to me. I beg you will accept both my best acknowledgments for the early communication of an event to me so interesting, and my unfeigned condolence on so great a loss. He was an honour to his age and country, not more for his extensive erudition, his fine genius and deep and solid judgment, than for his candour, elegance, and probity of his manners, his unassuming modesty and simplicity of character, and distinguished virtues.[1] His memory will be dear to his friends and to all that knew him for the short time they have to survive; but will be transmitted to posterity for unceasing duration among the first scholars and greatest critics to whom the world has been indebted for the improvement of learning.

You give me hope of being favoured at some future hour with further particulars concerning the last illness of my dear departed friend, &c. I am too sensible of the present urgent demands on you for all your time and attention to require so great a sacrifice at present; but if at your future leisure you should be inclined to gratify and indulge me with any detail of whatever kind relating to a man I so much loved and honoured, it will lay me under the deepest obligation. I hope you and all his family will allow me to mingle my tears with theirs on this afflicting occasion, and will believe me to be, Sir, your most obliged and very faithful servant.

T. DROMORE.

P. S. If at this distance I can be of any use in respect to any information, &c. concerning his books or papers, I beg my best services may be commanded.

If his library should be disposed of, I should be exceedingly obliged if I may be allowed to purchase two or three little Spanish books of historical songs, particularly one intituled "El Cancionero de Anvers," in a very small volume.

[Editor's note: Thomas Tyrwhitt's nephew of the same name also wrote to George Steevens on the day after his uncle's death. The letter, in the Folger Library Steevens Collection (C.b.10.f. 172), is reproduced here.]

Dear Sir,

I think it an office incumbent upon me however disagreeable, to acquaint you, as a dear friend of my late uncle, of the melancholy event of his death, which took place yesterday afternoon.

---

1. A note to the text signed "J.M." reads: "Mr. Tyrwhitt well deserved this praise. His scholarship and his critical talents were of the first order; but it is to be lamented that he employed too much of his time on authors of inferior value."

His illness was very severe thoʰ short, & in that short period he was fairly worn to a listless state; could do no one single thing, or even order it. Dʳ Gisborne paid him I understand that attention which became one who professed so sincere a regard for him. You will, I know, excuse me for troubling you with this line, & permit me to say that I am, your most obedient,

Humble Servant,
Thomas Tyrwhitt.

Welbeck Street.
Aug. 16. 1786.

[Editor's note: The concluding interpolation is a letter from Thomas Tyrwhitt's brother Robert, then a fellow of Jesus College, Cambridge, to Thomas Warton. The letter is in the British Museum Warton Collection (Add. Ms. 42,561. f. 192).]

Revᵈ Sir,

The inclosed papers were sent to my Brother not long before his death, on the Idea of his being employed in preparing some account of the Life & Writings of Spenser: and are now transmitted to you through Mʳ Dodsley by desire of the Writer of them; in hopes, as he expresses himself, that if you should take up Spenser again they may afford some little light.

I am Sir your humble Servᵗ
Robᵗ Tyrwhitt

Jesus College,
Cambridge.
7 Decʳ 1786.

Samuel Boyse

[This account is taken from Nichols, *A Select Collection of Poems: with Notes, Biographical and Historical,* 8 vols. (London, 1780-1782), II, 161-163; VI, 328-348; VIII, 288-290. The first four volumes of the *Select Collection* were issued in 1780; and the account of Boyse given in Vol. II relies heavily upon information given in *The Lives of the Poets of Great Britain and Ireland to the Time of Dean Swift,* 5 vols. (London, 1753), V, 160-176. Mr. Cibber is called the author of this work on the title page, by which, said Nichols (*Lit. Anec.,* V, 308), "a double literary fraud was here intended. Theophilus Cibber, who was then in the King's Bench, had ten guineas for the use of his name, which was put ambiguously Mr. *Cibber,* in order that it might pass for his father Colley's. The real publisher was Mr. Robert Shiels, an amanuensis of Dr. Johnson. . . ." A life of Boyse was also in the *Annual Register* for 1764, pp. 54-58, derived entirely from Shiels, mostly verbatim.

After the publication of his initial account of Boyse, Nichols received a great deal of fresh information. Some of it came directly from Samuel Johnson, who had known Boyse well, and the rest came from correspondents, among them Francis Stewart, another of Johnson's amanuenses. Perhaps the most important part of the new information consisted of fragments of letters from Francis Stewart and from Boyse himself. The new materials tend to make Boyse more human than he is in Shiels' account in *Cibber's Lives,* where he appears almost grotesque: a defect in the portrayal of Boyse which is also in his latest biography, that by Norman Moore in the DNB. Moore did not mention Nichols as a source, nor did he make use of the unique materials offered by Nichols.

A more recent account with the title "The Paradox of Samuel Boyse" by Edward A. Bloom appeared in *Notes and Queries* (April 1954), p. 163. An article of mine, "Portrait of a Grub: Samuel Boyse," was in *Studies in English Literature,* 7:415-425 (Summer 1967). References to works in which Boyse is mentioned are in n. 2 to Chapter XIII of James L. Clifford, *Young Sam Johnson* (New York, 1955), p. 349.]

Son of Joseph Boyse, a Dissenting minister of great eminence in Dublin (who was one of the 16 children of Mr. Matthew Boyse of Leeds) well known by his controversial writings against Abp. King.—Samuel was born in 1708, and received his education at Dublin; at 18, he was sent to the university of Glasgow; and, marrying before he was 20, returned to Dublin with his wife, where the conduct of neither was commendable. The husband, who had no graces of person and fewer still of conversation, passed his time in abject trifling; the wife, in intrigue: and their extravagance reduced his father to indigence. In 1731 young Boyse resided at Edinburgh, where he published a volume of poems, addressed to the countess of Egleton,[1] the patroness of all men of wit. Here also Mr. Boyse particularly distinguished himself by an elegy, called "The Tears of the Muses," on the death of the viscountess Stormont; which introduced him to the noble viscount; and also to the dutchess of Gordon, who had engaged for him an office in the customs, which he lost by an unpardonable remissness. The dutchess sent him to London with recommendations to Mr. Pope and the lord chancellor King. He went to Twickenham; but, the poet not being at home, he never repeated the visit; by the peer he was most graciously received. From this period he wrote many poems; but those, though excellent in their kind (and sufficient, it is said, to have filled at least six volumes) were lost to the world, by being introduced with no advantage. He had so strong a propensity to groveling, that his acquaintance were generally of such a cast as could be of no service to him; and those in higher life he addressed by letters, not having sufficient confidence or politeness to converse familiarly with them; a freedom to which he was intitled by the power of his genius. His genius was not confined to poetry only; but he had a taste for painting, music, and heraldry, with the latter of which he was well acquainted. Many of his poems are in the Gent. Mag.[2] signed Y. and Alceus. In 1743 he published his "Albion's Triumph," an ode on the battle of Dettingen; and in or about 1745 wrote an admirable poem called "The Deity," which Mr. Pope declared, on its publication, contained many lines of which he should not be ashamed. It was also commended by the late Henry Fielding, who gave a quotation from it, (See Tom Jones, B. vii. C. 1.) and at the same time very justly styled it *a noble one*.[3] This unfortunate man,[4] by addicting himself to

---

1. On their tour to the Hebrides, Johnson and Boswell visited Lady Eglintoune, or Eglinton, then in her eighty-fifth year. Of her, Boswell said, "She had been the admiration of the gay circles of life, and the patroness of poets." See Hill-Powell, *Boswell*, V, 374. Johnson's relationship with Boyse, as reported to Boswell by Nichols, is given in ibid., IV, 407, n. 4.

2. Nichols purchased a share of the *Gentleman's Magazine* in 1778, assisted David Henry in the management of it until 1792, and was sole editor from 1792 until 1826, the year of Nichols' death.

3. In the introductory chapter of Book VII of *Tom Jones,* Fielding, after quoting the lines from *Macbeth* about the poor player strutting and fretting his hour upon the stage, continues: "For which hackneyed quotation I will make the reader amends by a very noble one, which few, I believe, have read. It is taken from a poem called the Deity, published about nine years ago, and long since buried in oblivion; a proof that good books, no more than good men, do always survive the bad." At this point Fielding quotes 12 lines from Boyse's poem, among which are these:

> See the vast Theatre of Time display'd,
> While o'er the scene succeeding heroes tread!
>
> * * *
>
> Then at Thy nod the phantoms pass away;
> No traces left of all the busy scene,
> But that remembrance says—*The things have been!*

4. In transferring the matter that occurs between here and the end of the paragraph to

low vices, among which were gluttony and extravagance, rendered himself so contemptible and wretched, that he frequently was without the least subsistence for days together. After squandering away in a dirty manner any money which he acquired, he has been known to pawn all his apparel; [[This circumstance has been since confirmed to me by Dr. Johnson, who knew him well; and who once collected a sum of money to redeem his cloaths, which in two days after were pawned again.[5] "This," said the Doctor, "was when my acquaintances were few, and most of them as poor as myself. The money was collected by shillings."[6]]] and in that state was frequently confined to his bed, sitting up with his arms through holes in a blanket, writing verses in order to procure the means of existence. It seems hardly credible, but it is certainly true, that he was more than once in that deplorable situation, and to the end of his life never derived any advantage from the experience of his past sufferings. A late collector of poems (Mr. Giles) says, he was informed by Mr. Sandby the bookseller,[7] that this unhappy man at last was found dead in his bed, with a pen in his hand, and in the act of writing, in the same manner as above described. He died in Shoe-lane, in May, 1749, and was buried at the expense of the parish.[8]

I can assert from the same respectable authority [Dr. Johnson][9] that Mr. Boyse translated *well* from the French; but if any one employed him, by the time one sheet of the work was done, he *pawned* the original. If the employer redeemed it, a second sheet would be completed, and the book again be pawned; and this perpetually. He had very little learning; but wrote verse with great facility, as fast as most men write prose. He was constantly employed by Mr. Cave, who paid him by the hundred lines, which after a while his employer wanted to make what is called the *long* hundred. The circumstance related by Mr. Giles about his death, Dr. Johnson assures me, is not true; it being supposed that, in a fit of intoxication, he was run over by a coach; at least, he was brought home in such a condition as to make this probable, but too far gone to give the least account of the accident.

From another worthy friend I have received the following supplementary narrative: "Your account of Mr. Boyse must have been furnished by one who was acquainted with him. I knew him well from the year 1732 to the time of his death; have often relieved his necessities, and frequently cor-

---

Lit. Anec., IX, 777, Nichols introduces it with this authenticating statement: "The following particulars of the unfortunate Mr. Samuel Boyse, I had from his [Johnson's] own mouth."

5. This note was added in the *Select Collection*, VIII, 288, under "Additional Remarks on the Second Volume," p. 163.

6. This sentence and the one preceding it were added by Nichols when he transferred this material to *Lit. Anec.*, IX, 777. See above, n. 4.

7. The bookseller was William Sandby; in 1771 Joseph Giles edited a volume of *Miscellaneous Poems on Various Subjects and Occasions*.

8. The material up to this point, with the exceptions noted, is from the *Select Collection*, II, 161-163.

9. The material that follows is from ibid., VIII, 288-290.

responded with him. I have preserved, I believe, at least, 30 of his letters; and have, in manuscript, some of his poems that were never published. I never saw any thing in his wife's conduct that deserved censure. He published a second volume of poems in the year 1738. He was a man of learning; when in company with those by whom he was not awed, an entertaining companion; but so irregular and so inconsistent in his conduct, that it appeared as if he had been actuated by two different souls on different occasions. The account of his death by Mr. Sandby, I believe, is fictitious. I send you inclosed a letter from a Mr. Stewart,[10] the son of a bookseller at Edinburgh, who had been long intimately acquainted with Mr. Boyse, giving me an account of his death."

Poor Mr. Boyse was one evening last winter attacked in Westminster by two or three soldiers, who not only robbed him, but used him so barbarously, that he never recovered the bruises he received, which might very probably induce the consumption of which he died. About nine months before his death he married a cutler's widow, a native of Dublin, with whom he had no money; but she proved a very careful nurse to him during his lingering indisposition. She told me, that Mr. Boyse never imagined he was dying, as he always was talking of his recovery; but perhaps his design in this might be to comfort her, for one incident makes me think otherwise. About four or five weeks before he breathed his last, his wife went out in the morning, and was surprised to see a great deal of burnt papers upon the hearth, which he told her were old bills and accompts; but I suppose were his manuscripts, which he had resolved to destroy, for nothing of that kind could be found after his death. Though from this circumstance it may be inferred that he was apprehensive of death; yet I must own, that he never intimated it to me, nor did he seem in the least desirous of any spiritual advice. For some months before his end, he had left off drinking all fermented liquors, except now and then a glass of wine to support his spirits, and that he took very moderately. After his death, I endeavoured all I could to get him decently buried, by soliciting those Dissenters who were the friends of him and his father, but to no purpose; for only Dr. Grosvenor, in Hoxton Square, a Dissenting teacher, offered to join towards it. He had quite tired out those friends in his life-time; and the general answer that I received was, "That such a contribution was of no service to him, for it was a matter of no importance how or where he was buried." As I found nothing could be done, our last resource was an application to the parish; nor was it without some difficulty, occasioned by the malice of his landlady, that we at last got him interred on the Sunday after he died. Three more of Mr. Johnson's amanuenses, and myself, attended the corpse to the grave. Such was the miserable end of poor Sam, who was obliged to be buried in the same charitable manner with his first wife; a burial, of which he had often mentioned his abhorrence.

Yours most sincerely, FRA. STEWART.[11]

10. Francis Stewart, the son of George Stewart of Edinburgh, was another of Johnson's amanuenses. In a letter to Boswell, Johnson refers to Francis Stewart as "an ingenious and worthy man." See Hill-Powell, *Boswell*, III, 421.

11. The remaining part of the life of Boyse comes from the *Select Collection*, VI, 328-348.

I will now add an extract from an original letter which in July 1741 he [Boyse] sent to a friend, with some citations from his poem called "Deity."

I have no great reason to brag of the success of the poem, though "The Champion" early recommended it. Divine poetry is not the taste of the age, but I hope it shall be the support of mine. It is the only subject I now take pleasure in. I have all last summer been employed by Mr. Cave[12] in French translation, a province highly agreeable to me, and the most profitable business stirring. I have been since last September almost constantly with Dr. Douglas in the slavish work of index-making, alias word-catching: and am only now interrupted by his "Osteology," which takes up his whole attention, and will soon be published; the plates, which are the noblest of the kind I ever saw, being taken from the life. I have the prospect of having a new translation from the French in a few days; but Booksellers are so undistinguishing, and Authors, or rather Scriblers, so plenty, that Learning, unless supported, bids fair to starve between them. I hope the best, as I begin to be a little known, and would endeavour, as far as I could, to support a good character in the literary way.

All I am sorry for, is, that the taste runs strong against every thing that is just and sensible—unless it is consecrated by the infallibility of a Pope, whose *ipse dixit* is as much revered as that of his Holiness at Rome.

[Editor's note: Two letters, from among others in the British Museum, will be introduced following this note. They illustrate directly Boyse's life and his work on the *Gentleman's Magazine* during three months of 1742. The letters are dated 20 and 21 July (Stowe Mss. 748. ff. 180, 181). Both are directed to "Mr Cave at St John's Gate," the editor and founder of the *Gentleman's Magazine*.]

Sir

Mr Voltaire's ode on the Q[ueen]. [of] Hungary seems to me rather an affected Compliment to Card[inal]. Fleury, for this Reason instead of translating it, I have thought proper to address an ode to Mr Voltaire on this occasion always keeping the original in view which I think it would do well to print opposite to it in a different Character, if you judge mine worth the Inserting. I shall this day sett about Mr Van Harens ode on the British Nation, which I think highly worth your Inserting this month as it does us Honour to receive the Compliments of such a Genius. His Incomparable Poem on Peace shall be my Care to finish as well and as soon as possible. I want a Copy of the last mag. a Gentleman having got mine. I am with Sincere Respect

Sir

Y.^{rs}

S. Boyse.

---

12. Edward Cave, the founder of the *Gentleman's Magazine*, was also one of Johnson's early employers in London.

July 20. 1742

I send you the other Stowe, & expect y^r further directions on that Subject.

PS. I intreat the favour you would send me 2^s 6 or 3^s by the Bearer which shall be fully accounted [for at] the end of the Week.

[Notation in another hand] Sent 3^s

[Editor's note: The extent of Boyse's contributions to the *Gentleman's Magazine* becomes clear only as the references in the above letter are traced to the issues for June, July, and August of 1742. In those three issues, three works referred to by Boyse in his letter, by themselves, amount to 592 lines of verse; and July alone has 318 of these, aside from whatever else he may have been doing that was not alluded to in his letter.

The "Stowe" mentioned by Boyse at the end of his letter, after his signature, turns out to be a poem of 478 lines with the title "The Triumphs of Nature. A Poem. On the magnificent Gardens at Stowe in Buckinghamshire, the Seat of the Rt. Hon. Ld. Cobham." It appeared in three installments in the *Gent. Mag.*, 12: 324, 380-382, 435-436 (June, July, August 1742). Boyse's translation of Van Haren's (spelled *Van Haaren* elsewhere) "Ode in praise of the British Nation," 36 lines, appeared in July, pp. 383-384, as did his "Ode addressed to M. Voltaire occasioned by his Ode in praise of the Queen of Hungary," 78 lines, p. 383. The latter poem is introduced by a letter signed *Y*, which Nichols identifies as one of Boyse's signatures:

SIR,

I was greatly disappointed on reading M. Voltaire's ode, published last month at the Hague in praise of the Queen of Hungary; for I expected it would have answered the title by giving us some idea of the glorious character of that august princess—instead of which I found only a wild panegyrick on his own nation and some well turn'd compliments to Cardinal Fleury. If therefore you think the following stanzas to that gentleman on this occasion worth inserting, I may perhaps next month trouble you with a poem that will do more justice to her Hungarian majesty.

Your constant reader and correspondent,
London, July 26, 1742.   Y

The poem that would "do more justice to her Hungarian majesty" did not appear the next month, but in December the first installment of "Ode to the Queen of Hungary: From the Dutch of M. Van Haaren" was on p. 656 (misnumbered 634). In May, p. 270, had appeared "Extracts of Mr. Van Haren's Love of Peace. A Poem." At the end is this note: "If this extract from M. Van Haaren meets with encouragement, we may perhaps publish the whole poem translated by the same hand."

Boyse's second letter to Cave, written the day following that on which the preceding one was written, follows this note. It begins with a Latin inscription, which I have omitted. After this letter, the text of Nichols' life of Boyse is resumed.]

S^r

I wrote you yesterday an account of my unhappy Case. I am every moment threatned to be turnd out here because, I have not money to pay for my bed two Nights past, which is usually paid beforehand and I am loth to go into the Compter [prison for debtors] till I can see if my affair can possibly be made up. I hope therefore you will have the Humanity to send me half a Guinea for Support, till I finish your papers in my hands. The ode on the British Nation I hope to have done to-day & want a Copy proof of that part of Stowe you design for the present magazine, that it may be improved as far as possible from y^r assistance. Y^r papers are but ill transcribed. I agree with you as to St Augustine's Cave. I humbly intreat y^r answer, having not tasted any thing since Tuesday Evening I came in here, & my Coat will be taken off my Back, for the charge of the Bed. To that I must go into Prison naked, which is too shocking for me to think of. I am with Sincere Regard

S^r

Y^r unfortunate
humble Servt
S. B.

Crown Coffee House, Grocers Alley, Poultry
   July 21. 1742
[The following is noted below the preceding:]

July 21. 1742

Receivd from Mr Cave the Sum of half a Guinea by me in Confinement.
S. Boyse

[The following in Boyse's hand is written sideways to the left of the address:]
I send Mr Van Haren's ode on Brittain.

To the same gentleman [unidentified by Stewart], in June 1747, he [Boyse] affectingly laments the loss of his first wife Emilia, and describes his situation as "not wholly uncomfortable." He was then at Reading, and employed by Mr. Henry[13] in compiling "An Historical Review of the Transactions of Europe."

---

13. David Henry was Edward Cave's brother-in-law and preceded Nichols as editor of the *Gentleman's Magazine*. David Henry was a first cousin of John Henry, the father of Patrick Henry of Virginia. See *Lit. Anec.*, III, 759.

My salary is wretchedly small (half a guinea a week) both for writing the history and correcting the press; but, I bless God, I enjoy a greater degree of health than I have known for many years, and a serene melancholy, which I prefer to the most poignant sensations of pleasure I ever knew.

All I sigh for, is a settlement with some degree of independence, for my last stage of life, that I may have the comfort of my poor dear girl to be near me, and close my eyes. I should be glad to know if you have seen my *History*; from which you must not expect great things, as I have been overpersuaded to put my name to a composure, for which we ought to have had at least more time and better materials, and from which I have neither profit nor reputation to expect. I am now beginning "The History of the Rebellion," a very difficult and invidious task. All the accounts I have yet seen are either defective, confused, or heavy. I think myself, from my long residence in Scotland, not unqualified for the attempt, but I apprehend it is premature; and, by waiting a year or two, better materials would offer. Some account, I think, will probably be published abroad, and give us light into many things we are now at a loss to account for. I am about a translation (at my leisure hours) of an invaluable French work, intituled, "L' Histoire Universelle," by the late M. Bossuet, Bishop of Meaux, and preceptor to the Dauphin, eldest son of Lewis XIV. I propose only to give his Dissertations on the Ancient Empires, viz. the Egyptian, Assyrian, Grecian, and Roman, which he has described with surprising conciseness, and with equal judgement and beauty. I design to inscribe it to the Right Honourable Mr. Lyttelton, one of the Lords of the Treasury, one of the most amiable men I have ever known, and to whose uncommon goodness if you knew my obligations, you would esteem him as much as he deserves.

[Boyse was a man of no party: whatever were his private sentiments, his public political creed was influenced by his necessities. In regard to his person, he was of a middle size, of a thin habit, slovenly in his dress, which was increased by his necessities, very near-sighted, and his hearing imperfect; these circumstances, added to his natural diffidence, and his not having been accustomed to appear in good company but as necessitous, and a mendicant, gave him an awkward sheepish air, which by no means prejudiced strangers in his favour. His liberal translation of Voltaire's three epistles on Happiness, Freedom of Will, and Envy, are well executed. They were published, without his name, in the year 1738; but I am a good witness they were written by him; for, when finished, as his cloaths were then deposited at the pawnbroker's, I treated with the late Mr. Dodsley for the manuscript, of whom I could only obtain a poor two guineas. The sheets were sent to me from the press for correction.[14]]

[The following material appears in the *Select Collection* as notes to some

---

14. This paragraph is a note signed *C, Select Collection*, VI, 348. The *C* who wrote it may have been Dr. William Cuming, a physician, whose father was an Edinburgh merchant. William Cuming lived in Edinburgh until 1735, when he left to spend nine months in Paris. An "Ode, to Mr. William Cuming, on his going to France, August 31, 1735," is in the *Select Collection* as is also a poem dedicated to Alexander Cuming, an older brother of William. A note describing the loss at sea of Alexander is signed *C*, and immediately after, Nichols refers to "my worthy friend Dr. William Cuming of Dorchester."

of Boyse's poems. The first note is to a poem called "Horace and Lydia, B. III. O. IX. Imitated."]

[Written on a slight temporary jarring between Boyse and his wife, whom he thought too much attached to Miss Atcheson, her sister, a woman, to say no worse of her, of an equivocal character.[15]]

[A line in the "Horace and Lydia" referred to above reads: "And Peter's folk never are out of your head." The following note is to "Peter's folk."]

[By *Peter's folk* is meant the hospitable and agreeable family of a Mr. Stewart, a merchant in Edinburgh; who had two amiable daughters, to whom Mr. Boyse addressed some poems printed in his second volume; and in the Gentleman's Magazine for 1741, p. 380, there is one to Hilaria on the death of her elder sister Clarissa; of which Boyse thus speaks in a letter already quoted:]

I am sorry any part of your letter should be cruel or disagreeable to me— Yet such, greatly such, was the news of Clarissa's death. It affected Mrs. Boyse so, that, on reading it, she and the letter dropped together!

Never was greater sweetness inshrined in the tomb. My next will convey you my sentiments on so dear, so affecting a subject; and, as I address them to my admired Hilaria, I hope you will convey them to that once happy, but justly disconsolate, family. They will, I hope, be such as gratitude dictates, and her virtues deserve.

[It was in this family that the friendly communicator of these anecdotes became acquainted with Mr. Boyse about the latter end of the year 1732.[16]]

[The following is a note to Boyse's poem "Epistle to Henry Brooke, Esq."]

["In 1738," says the gentleman to whom I am obliged for this poem,[17] "Mr. Boyse did me a real favour by introducing me to the acquaintance of the amiable and ingenious Mr. Brooke, the author of 'Gustavus Vasa.' I visited Mr. Brooke almost every day while he was composing that tragedy; I perused it, scene by scene, as it was written. On that account perhaps, and the esteem which I bear to the author, I may be biassed in its favour;

---

15. This note is also signed *C*.
16. This note is signed *N* for Nichols. The fragment of Boyse's letter quoted here belongs, apparently, with one of those quoted in part earlier. The "friendly communicator" referred to may be Dr. Cuming.
17. The "gentleman" referred to may, again, be Dr. Cuming. As nearly as I can tell, Cuming, Boyse, and Brooke, author of *The Fool of Quality*, were all in London in 1738.

but I do not think that a tragedy of equal merit has appeared since that time. I have now by me the four first acts of it in manuscript, given me by the author, before the fifth was finished. During our acquaintance, poor Boyse, by his irregularities, somehow gave offence to Mr. Brooke, who for a time declined his visits. Boyse, sensible of his fault, (for no man's repentance was more poignant for the time, but, alas! it was brief and fleeting) addressed to Mr. Brooke this penitentiary epistle, which, with a solemn promise of amendment, restored him to favour."]

John Hughes

[This short account from the *Select Collection*, IV, 301-302, is more a note to Johnson's life of Hughes than an original memoir. Since Johnson had given details of Hughes's life and publications, Nichols no doubt felt that it would have been superfluous to repeat them; he confined himself instead to some comments which seem rather bold when one reviews the fact that in giving assistance to Johnson, Nichols was usually happy to be seen merely as a willing helper of the great luminary.]

[From Johnson's life of Hughes:] The character of his genius I shall transcribe from the correspondence of Swift and Pope.

"A month ago," says Swift, "was sent me over by a friend of mine the works of John Hughes, Esquire. They are in prose and verse.[1] I never heard of the man in my life, yet I find your name as a subscriber (too). He is too grave a poet for me; and I think among the *mediocrists* in prose as well as verse."

To this Pope returns: "To answer your question as to Mr. Hughes; what he wanted in genius, he made up as an honest man; but he was of the class you think him."

In Spence's collections Pope is made to speak of him with still less respect as having no claim to poetical reputation but from his tragedy.[2]]

---

1. An edition of Hughes' *Poems on Several Occasions, with some Select Essays in Prose*, ed. W. Duncombe, had been published in 2 vols. in 1735. Swift's letter to Pope was written on 3 September of that year and Pope's reply was written in November. See Johnson's *Lives*, ed. G. B. Hill (Oxford, 1905), II, 164, n. 6. William Duncombe, editor of Hughes's poems, had won a thousand pounds in the lottery of 1725 in partnership with Elizabeth Hughes, John's sister. Duncombe and Elizabeth were married that same year. An account of John Hughes was prefixed by Duncombe to the 1735 edition of Hughes's poems. See *Lit. Anec.*, VIII, 266, 268.

2. This paragraph was introduced by Johnson after the first edition. See Hill, *Lives*, II, 165, n.1. In *Spence's Anecdotes*, ed. S. W. Singer (London, 1820), Pope is reported by Joseph Spence to have said, "Hughes was a good humble-spirited man, a great admirer of Mr. Addison, and but a poor writer, except his play, that is very well." In a note to this, Singer wrote, in an obvious reference to Nichols' note from the *Select Collection:* "It has been said that Pope, in this case acted with duplicity, because he praises the Siege of Damascus in a letter to Hughes, written the very day he died; and in a subsequent letter to his brother, praises both the work and the author.—Dr. Johnson gives his sanction to this character of Hughes, and has also been censured for doing so.—We have here a proof that Pope's opinion of Hughes's talents, was not a mere echo of that of Swift, and we see that he excepts his play from the censure. But this is not the only instance of Pope's insincerity in his epistolary commerce with mankind, all his correspondents are made easy by flattery, laid on without conscience or remorse." The preceding comment by Singer (pp. 302-303n) is not reproduced along with the anecdote concerning Hughes in the new edition of James M. Osborn, *Joseph Spence: Observations, Anecdotes, and Characters of Books and Men* (Oxford, 1966), I, 211-212, Entry 496.

This Poet's Life has employed the pleasing pen of Dr. Johnson, who has given the character of his genius from Pope; but I am sorry to say that our English Homer appears to have acted in this case with duplicity. In a letter to Mr. Hughes, just before his death, he [Pope] thus expresses himself: "Would to God you might live as long as, I am sure, the reputation of your Tragedy must!" Letters from Eminent Persons, Lett. 290.[3] In one to his [Hughes's] brother, just after his [Hughes's] death, with other elogiums, "I am glad of an occasion to give you, under my hand, this testimony both how excellent I think this work to be, and how excellent I thought the author." Ibid. I. 197. And, which is still more to the purpose, this last "testimony of his real regard (as he styles it) for Mr. Hughes," being given after his death, the editor of his Works was allowed by Mr. Pope to publish, as "a greater instance of the sincerity with which it was given." Ibid. I. 205. These are his words. And now which is most deserving of credit, a testimony thus solemnly given to the world, or the echo, as it were, of his peevish friend, whom he was afraid to contradict, in a letter which he little thought would have been preserved and printed; and which, with his others to Swift, he wanted to recall? At every tribunal, a witness who contradicts himself is disbelieved; if such an opinion is not allowed to establish, much less should it be admitted to traduce a character: and, on the whole, the passage which Dr. Johnson has thus quoted can, with the considerate, only degrade and condemn the author of it, though "what HE wanted as an *honest* man, he made up as a genius." I transcribe this passage from a writer in "The Gentleman's Magazine, 1779," p. 457, who appears to be well informed.—Dr. Johnson having observed that, "though Mr. Hughes's advances in literature are in the Biographia very ostentatiously displayed, the name of his master is somewhat ungratefully concealed;" the Reviewer in "The Gentleman's Magazine, 1779," p. 549, exculpates Dr. Campbell by observing, "that it does not appear, or is likely, that he knew it; and all that can be known is, that Hughes was a fellow-student in logic and philosophy with Dr. Watts and Mr. Say, perhaps under Mr. Thomas Rowe."—It must be owned, however, that concealing a master's name is a venial fault. If it is always to be mentioned, how often must the masters of Eton and Westminster be named, though perhaps they have contributed little! A lad may leave school before he comes under them; or even if he does, all the five or six previous ushers ought to have their proportionate share of praise. . . .

3. *Letters by Several Eminent Persons Deceased, including the Correspondence of John Hughes. . . and several of his friends* [Pope, Addison, etc.]: *with Notes* (London, 1772), 2 vols.

Index

Abingdon, Thomas, 108
Adams, ——, 102
Addison, Joseph, xv, 296, 303
Addison, Mr., a pseudonym, xvii
Adhémar, Jean, 289
Aesop, 296, 333, 334
Aikin, Anna Letitia, 282
Aikin, John, 282
Aitken, George A., xviii, 221
Akenside, Mark, xx, 151
Allan, George, 82, 91
Allen, Ralph, 251
Allenson, ——, 37
Almon, John, xvii, 45
Alphonso, pen name of Nichols, 179
Ame, ——, 73
American Revolution, 23
Ames, Joseph, 314
Ana, collection of, xv-xviii
Analytical Review, 284-285
Anamaboe, Prince of, 66
Anderton, George, 308
Andrewes, Gerrard, 18
Andrews, ——, 204
Anecdotes, collection of, xv-xviii
Annesley, Mrs. Elizabeth, 217
Annesley, Samuel, 200
Antiquarian: defined, xv; Nichols as, xviii; Cole as, 75-76
Antiquarians, Society of, xx; Farmer elected to, 19; and Hardyknute, 55; Cole elected to, 74; Gough elected to, 86, 98; history of, 90; and Willis, 111, 113; Pegge's writings for, 132, 145-146; Basire engraver to, 289-290; Apthorp, Charles, 64, 65
Apthorp, Stephen, 64, 67, 74
Archaeologia, 132, 142, 332
Argyll, Molly, 181
Armsteed, ——, 71
Ash, John, 28
Ashby, George, 102, 104, 112, 115, 246
Ashhurst, Sir William, 203
Askew, Anthony, 20, 21, 46, 332
Astle, Thomas, 232
Atcheson, Miss, 349
"Athenae Cantabrigienses," 63, 71, 72, 75, 78-79
"Athenae Oxonienses," 73
Athenian Gazette, 204-206
Athenian Mercury, 206-208
Athenian Oracle, 208
Atterbury, Francis, xxiv, 62; *Epistolary Correspondence* published by Nichols, xxviii, 89, 188
Atterbury, Mrs., xxiv
Aubrey, Elizabeth, 228
Aubrey, John, xvi
Ayloffe, Thomas, 101

Babbes, Elizabeth, 65
Babrius, 332, 333, 334
Baillie, Joanna, 254
Baker, David Erskine, 7
Baker, Sam, 46, 92
Baker, Thomas, 69, 73, 115, 319
Baker, William, 131
Baldwin, A., 211
Baldwin, Henry, 21, 53
Bale, John, 56, 57
Ballard, George, 119
Banks, Sir Joseph, 42, 56, 60, 260
Barbarossa, portrait of Steevens as, 46
Barbauld, Mrs. *See* Aikin, Anna Letitia
Barlow, Thomas, 201
Barnardiston, John, 24, 85
Barnewitz, ——, 84
Barret, ——, 337, 338
Barrett, Dr. John, xxxi
Barrington, Daines, 91, 168
Barrington, Samuel, 169
Barrington, Shute, 168-169
Barrington, Lord, 334
Barton, John, 122
Basire, Isaac, 289
Basire, James, 55, 90, 98-99, 141; Nichols on, 282, 289-290
Basire, James (son of the above), 290; (grandson of the above), 290
Baskerville, John: Nichols on, 291-303; letters to R. Dodsley by, 293-295; edition of Virgil by, 295; Greek type designed by, 295-296; works printed by, 296, 304; letter to Walpole from, 297; will of, 299-301; posthumous sale of printing business of, 302; disinterment of body of, 304; perfection of type by, 305
Baskerville, Mrs. John, 302-303
Baskerville, Mrs. Sarah, 300-303
Bate, Dudley, 224
Bates, William, xviii
Bathurst, Richard, 121
Baxter, Richard, 202
Beardsworth, John, 262
Beauclerk, Topham, 39, 260

Beaupuy, Anne, 290
Beaver, ———, 52
Becket, Thomas, 272
Beckett, ———, 293
Bedford, Duchess of, 90
Bedford, John, 304
Bedingfield, Robert, 153
Beechey, Sir William, 269, 270
Beecroft, John, 21
Bell, ———, 208
Bellasis, Major-Gen. John, 88, 191
Beloe, William, xvi, 11
Belt, Goodeth, 147
Belt, Robert, 147
Benet, Sir Simon, 104-105
Bennet, William, 23, 71, 91
Bennett, Paul, 291
Bennett, William, 291
Benoit, Elie, 202n
Benskin, Miss, 38
Benson, Martin, 101, 103, 113, 116, 122
Benson, ———, 199
Bent, James, 201n
Bentham, James, 67
Bentley, Richard, 329
Berry, Edward, 239
Besterman, Theodore, 265
Bettenham, James, 308, 310
Betterton, Thomas, 224, 229
Bible, the: printed by Baskerville, 292, 296, 297; types designed by Jackson for, 313
Bibliotheca Farmeriana, 36
Bibliotheca Topographica Britannica, xvii, xxvii, 142, 187, 189
Bickerstaffe, William, 27
Bickham, James, 18, 19, 37
Bicknell, John, 60
Bindley, James, 15, 25n; life of Reed by, 3, 4
Biographical and Literary Anecdotes of William Bowyer, xxvi
Biographical Anecdotes of William Hogarth, xxvi-xxvii
Birch, Thomas, 318; letters from J. Jones to, 324-328
Bishop, David Horace, 148
Bisse, Philip, 128
Blackburne, Francis, 319-320
Blackstone, Sir William, 266
Blaine, Rodney M., 148
Blake, William, 289
Blanchard, Rae, xxviii
Bliss, Philip, 73
Bloom, Edward A., 341
Blount, Sir Thomas Pope, 207
Boaden, James, 240
Bockwitz, Hans H., 291
Bodleian Library: collection of newspapers in, xxi, 194; Cole papers in, 63; Gough's library to, 82, 87, 91, 96; gifts of Willis to, 104, 109; purchase of Nichols letters by, 193-194
Bohun, Humfrey de, 83
Bolingbroke, Lord, 248
Bolton, Duke of, 150, 152
Bolton, Theophilus, 234
Bonnycastle, John, 285
Bossuet, Bishop Jaques Bénigne, translated by Boyse, 348
Boston, Mass., Dunton a bookseller in, 200
Boswell, James, xvi, xviii, 35, 232; and Nichols, xix, xxv, xxxii; *Life of Johnson* by, 35, 44n, 232; on Steevens, 44n; introduced to Johnson, 237
Bourne, Henry, 147
Bourne, John, 132
Bourne, Martha, 132, 147
Bowle, John, 165
Bowman, John, 137
Bowyer, Thomas, 4-5
Bowyer, William the elder, 308; patron of Caslon, 310, 314; and Jackson, 311, 312
Bowyer, William, xviii, xx, xxvi, 69, 83, 95, 174, 186, 223, 271, 276; publisher of Swift, xxviii; on Pope, 159; Nichols' relationship to, 169-170, 175-176, 178; Pope's *Iliad* printed by, 224; portrait of, 290
Boydell, ———, 266
Boyse, Joseph, 202, 341
Boyse, Matthew, 341
Boyse, Samuel, xix, xxvii; Nichols on, 341-350; death of, 343-344; letters to Cave from, 345; translations by, 345-347
Bragg, B., 214
Braithwaite, Daniel, 15, 16
Brampton, dispute over curacy of, 134-137
Brand, Thomas, 201
Brander, Gustavus, 141
Bray, William, 91
Brayley, E. W., 192
Bremner, David, 261, 264
Brereton, William, 290
Brewer, J. Norris, 192
Bridgwater, Joseph, 301
British Topography, 85, 87; Gough's contributions to, 90n, 97, 98, 301
Britton, J., 192
Brooke, Henry, 349
Brooke, J. C., 91
Brooks, Cleanth, 17, 193
Broome, William, xxvii, 35, 155n. 163n, 224, 226n; published by Lintot, 229
Brown, Daniel, 257
Brown, James, 212
Brown, Thomas, 206
Brown, ———, 102

Browne, Alice, 100
Browne, Daniel, senior, 218, 310
Browne, Robert (father-in-law of Browne Willis), 100
Browne, Robert (cousin of Browne Willis), 120, 122
Browne, Thomas, 206, 209, 216
Browne, William, 240-241
Brunning, ——, 200
Bryant, Jacob, 54, 71, 331, 333
Bryce, John C., xvii
Brydges, Sir Egerton, 264
Brydges, John, 103
Buckinghamshire, history of, 120, 121
Burke, Edmund, 165, 248, 251
Burn, Richard, 266
Burney, Charles, 28, 329, 330
Burney, Charles, Jr., 259
Burns, Robert, 265
Burrow, Sir James, 290
Burthogge, Richard, 201
Burton, Michael, 129-130
Burton, ——, 88
Busby, Richard, xxxii
Bush, S., 112
Bushnell, G. H., 254, 256, 259, 265, 271, 275, 282, 306
Butts, ——, 65
Byerley, Thomas, xvii

Cadell, Thomas, the elder (Mr. Alderman Cadell), 53, 242, 247, 259, 272, 273, 274; Nichols on, 265-269
Cadell, Thomas, the younger, 266, 269-270
Calder, John, xxviii, 254, 255, 322
Cambridge University: Farmer's connection with, 23-27, 33-34, 37-38; Dennis expelled from, 36
Camden, Earl, 290
Camden, William, 290
Camden, ——, 98
Camden's Britannia, 85, 87, 97, 98
Campbel, Patrick, 211
Campbell, Duncan, 200
Campbell, John, 243
Campbell, ——, 91
Campbell, ——, 352
Candale, Pyramus de, 46
Canterbury Tales, edited by Tyrwhitt, 331
Capell, Edward, 51, 338
Carte, Samuel, 22
Carter, Daniel, 197
Carter, John, 91, 290
Cartledge, John, 309
Cartwright, Thomas, 71, 115, 121, 122
Caryl, Lyndford, 321
Caslon and Catherwood, 310
Caslon, Henry, 310
Caslon, Samuel, 308
Caslon, Thomas, 309, 310

Caslon, William, 293, 298n, 302; Nichols on, 306-311; Jackson discharged by, 312
Caslon, William (son of the above), 308, 310; (grandson of the above), 309, 313; (great-grandson of the above), 309
Caslon, Mrs. William, 309
Catcott, George, 54, 337, 338
Catherwood, Charles, 310
Catullus, xx, 296
Cave, Edward, xxi, 232; relation of Henry to, 233; employer of Boyse, 343, 345
Cave, Mary, 233
Cave, Thomas, 291
Chaderton, Laurence, 17
Chalmers, Alexander, xviii, 250; life of Reed by, 5; on Nichols' article on Reed, 6n; on Steevens, 41; on Cole, 63, 73-78; on the Wartons, 149, 160, 166; on Nichols, 167, 193
Chambers, Ephraim, *Cyclopaedia* of, 255
Chandler, John E., 254
Chapman, George, 156
Charlemont, Lord, xxvii, xxix-xxx, 12n
Charles I, 25, 46
Charles II, 128
Charles Fitz-Charles, 128
Charlett, ——, 119
Chatterton, Thomas, 302; and the Rowley controversy, 54, 72, 165, 329, 331; Tyrwhitt on, 322-33; Steevens on, 336. See also Rowley poems
Chaucer, Geoffrey, xv, 229; work of Tyrwhitt on, 329, 330, 333
Chedder, ——, 45
Chesterfield, Lord, 186, 242
Cheyney, Thomas, 133-136
Chishull, Edmund, 332
Chiswell, Richard, 218
Christie, Thomas, 284-285
Chudleigh, Lady, 222
Churchill, Charles, 239-240
Churton, Ralph, 91
Cibber, Colley, 229, 341
Cibber, Theophilus, 341
Cibber, Mrs., 239
Clair, Colin, xx
Clarendon, Lord, 121
Clarendon Press, 331
Clark, ——, 46
Clark, ——, 199
Clarke, Anne, 132, 133
Clarke, Benjamin, 132
Clarke, John, 132
Clarke, Samuel, 77
Clarke, William, xxv
Clifford, James L., 341
Cobbe, Samuel, 155, 156
Cochrane, J. A., 221, 250, 265, 271, 275, 306
Coine, collection by Willis, 103-104, 123
Coke, Roger, 201

Cole, Charles, 104
Cole, C. N., 256
Cole, William, 5, 17, 91, 167; at Stirbitch Fair, 11; manuscripts from, 13-14; as source of Nichols data, 18n; and Woolsey manuscript, 24-25; on Farmer, 27; and Steevens, 42, 53n; sources of life of, 63-64; Nichols on, 65-73; Chalmers on, 73-78; D'Israeli on, 78-81; and Walpole, 89; and Willis, 100, 102, 106, 112, 116, 119, 121; on publication of Willis, 109-111
Cole, William (father of the above), 64, 65
Collins, William, 151, 162
Colman, George, the elder, 27, 38, 225, 241
Common Prayer, Book of, printed by Baskerville, 292, 296, 297, 298
Compton, Spencer, 225
Congreve, William, 224, 243; printed by Baskerville, 296
Cook, Captain James, 74, 290
Cooke, Thomas, 122, 124
Cooper, Thompson, 17, 63; on Gough, 82
Corke, Earl of, 292
Cornwallis, Frederick, 137, 138, 139-140, 141, 143
Cornwallis, James, 139, 142
Cott, John, 85
Cotton, Sir John, 11
Cottrell, Thomas, 306, 311, 312
Courayer, Father, 66
Courtney, William Prideaux, 100, 256, 330
Cowley, Abraham, 220
Cowper, William, 282, 284
Cox, Harold, 254
Cox, Mary, 290
Crabbe, George, xx, 168
Cracherode, Clayton Mordaunt, 260, 330
Cradock, Anne, 171, 176, 181; children of, 182
Cradock, Joseph, 20, 184, 241
Cranmer, Thomas, 319
Craven, Lord, 152
Creech, ——, 156
Critical Review, 54
Crose, Jean Cornand de la, 209
Croxall, Samuel, 9
Cullum, Sir John, 91, 164, 190, 275
Cuming, William, 348n
Cunningham, Peter, 221
Curialia, 147, 190
Curll, Edmund, xvi, 9, 89, 159, 226; *Dunciad* on, 227
Currie, James, 265
Curwen, Henry, 221, 254, 271

Dahl, Michael, 116, 122
Dalton, Richard, 289
Daman, Miss, 151
D'Arblay, Frances Burney, 256

Darrell, ——, 117-118
Darwin, Erasmus, 282, 284
Davenport, ——, 283
Davies, Sir John, 241
Davies, Lockyer, 247
Davies, Sneyd, 125-126
Davies, Thomas, 44, 54; Nichols on, 237-249; acting career of, 238-240; publications of, 240-243, 248; bankruptcy of, 243; life of Garrick by, 244-246; literary club of, 247, 250, 254, 256, 259, 265
Davies, William, 265, 269, 270
Dawson, Thomas, 317, 318, 322
Debrett, ——, 54
Defoe, Daniel, 207, 212
DeHondt, P., 272
Delamere, Henry Booth, 201
De Mierre, Ferdinand, 299
De Mierre, Sarah, 299
Denham, Sir John, 222
Denne, ——, 120
Dennis, John, 36, 299
Dent, R. K., 291
Derbyshire, history of, 191-192
Dering, Sir Edward, 133, 137
Derrick, Samuel, 292
Devonshire, Duke of, 96, 134, 137-138
Diaper, John, 155, 156
Dibdin, Thomas Frognall, xv, 38; *Bibliomania*, 36n; on Steevens, 41, 61-62; on Gough, 92-93; on Nichols, 167, 193
Dictionary of National Biography, xxv
Dillingham, ——, 17
Disney, Matthew, 101
D'Israeli, Issac, xvii, 44n; on Cole, 73, 78-79; on Dunton, 218, 219-220; on Pope and Lintot, 228; *Quarrels of Authors*, 228n, 255
Dix, E. R. McC., 254, 256, 259, 265, 271, 275, 282, 306
Dobson, Austin, xviii, 271
Doddridge, Philip, 320-321; letters from Warburton to, 321-322
Dodsley, Avery, 250
Dodsley, Isaac, 251
Dodsley, James, 22, 247; Nichols on, 250-253
Dodsley, Robert, 4, 7, 8, 9, 52, 59, 152, 153, 237, 291, 340; as collector of poems, 155, 158, 160, 186; association of with James, 250, 251; and Baskerville, 292, 296
Domesday Book, xxxii, 311, 313
Doolittle, Thomas, 199
Dormer, Sir Clement, 46
Dorsetshire, history of, 88, 191
Dowden, Edward, 5, 12n
Drayton, Michael, 241
Dreyfus, John, 291
Droit d'Aubaine, 66, 75
Dryden, John, xv, xvi, xxxi, 53, 156, 265,

302; Malone as editor of, xxx; J. Warton as editor of, 159; published by Lintot, 222, 224
Duane, Matthew, 330
Ducarel, Andrew Coltée, 63, 67, 88n, 186n; on Willis, 100, 105, 111-113; letter from Willis to, 120-121; letter from Cole to, 121-122
du Deffand, Mme., 72
Dugdale, William: *Monasticon*, xv; history of Warwickshire by, 88
Dunciad, 214, 222; on Lintot and Curll, 226-227
Duncombe, John, 44n, 86
Dunstone, G. E., xix
Dunton, John, senior, books by, 199, 203, 211-212
Dunton, John, xvi, xviii; life of, edited by J. B. Nichols, 192; J. Nichols' life of, 197-218; works printed by, 199, 201-203; trip to U.S. by, 200; trip to Holland by, 201; *Athenian Gazette*, 204-207; *Athenian Oracle*, 208; projects of, 208-211; list of other publications, 211-214, 216-218; Swift on, 218; D'Israeli on, 218, 219-220
Dunton, Lydia, 197
Dunton, Sarah, 212
Dutens, Lewis, 260
Dyer, George, 17
Dyer, Samuel, 84
Dyson, Jeremiah, 330

Eachard, John, 241
Edgeworth, Maria, 282
Edmundson, William, 129
Edward VI, 56, 57
Edwards, ——, 90
Egerton, Henry, 142
Eginton, Francis, 267n
Eglintoune, Countess, 342
Eldridge, Charles Lucas, 267
Eldridge, Lieut. Henry Thomas, 267
Eliot, John, 201
Elizabeth I, 52
Elizabeth, Queen, *Progresses* of, xxvii, 95, 191
Elliott, Catharine, 102
Elliot, Daniel, 102
Elliot, Richard, 122
Ellis, Henry, 91, 190, 254
Ellis, Seth, 127, 134-135
Ellis, ——, xxiv
Ellis, ——, 331
Elmsley, Peter, 53-54, 247, 303; Nichols on, 259-264
Elphinstone, James, 276
Elsynge, Henry, 331
Ely, history of, 67
Espinasse, Francis, 254

Essex, James, 91
Essex Head Club, 28n, 44n, 275
Etoniensis, *Pseudonym* on Steevens, 57-61
Eugenio, pen name of Nichols, xxiii, 179, 317
Eumélean Club, 28
Euripides, 331, 333
European Magazine, 24, 36, 41; on Reed, 3; Reed as contributor to, 10; on Steevens, 41
Evans, Henry H., 291
Evans, Thomas, 247
Everitt, Allen, 304
Eyre, Richard, 122, 124, 277
Eyton, Thomas, 179

Faber, John, 309
Facius, 70
Falconer, Thomas, 91
Falkland, Lord, 156
Farmer, John, 18
Farmer, Capt. Joseph, 30, 32
Farmer, Richard, xxiv, 5, 6, 43, 53, 91, 248-249, 329; and the Stirbitch Fair, 11-14; and Reed, 14; Nichols on, 18-28; *History of Leicester*, 19-22; various posts of, 23-26; refusal of bishopric by, 26-27; letters on health of, 29-31; epitaph of, 31; library of, 36-37; Martyn on, 36-37; Johnson's visit to, 39-40; and Steevens, 42, 57; on Rowley controversy, 54; and Cole, 63, 68, 71, 73, 77-78; letters to Percy from, 193-194
Farmer, Thomas, 30, 32
Farmer, Tom (son of the above), 30
Farquhar, George, 222, 229, 230
Farquharson, ——, 303
Farringdon Without, xx, 181
Fastolf, Sir John, 95
Faulder, Robert, 54
Fenn, Sir John, 91
Fenton, Elijah, 155, 163, 222, 224, 225, 226n, 230
Ferrar, Nicholas, 318
Fielding, Henry, 238, 266, 271; portrait of, 290; on Boyse, 342
Figgins, Vincent, 306, 313-314
Fisher, Edward, 85
Flaxman, John, 45, 47, 159
Fleming, John Willis, 107
Fleming, Richard, 122
Fletcher, Bishop, 134
Fletcher, Sir Henry, 222, 228
Fletcher, John, 162
Fletcher, ——, 152
Fleury, Abbé, 84
Florus, 296
Foe. *See* Defoe
Folger Shakespeare Library, Reed collection in, 5-6

Forster, Benjamin, 85
Foulis, ———, 264
Fox, Charles James, 26, 242, 278
France, purchase of Baskerville type by, 302-303
Françillon, ———, 263
Francis, ———, 106
Franklin, Benjamin, xxii, 233, 275; and Wm. Strahan, 278-279; correspondence with Baskerville, 298, 298n; purchase of Caslon types by, 306, 308
Freeborn, John, 251
Freestone, Abraham, 101
Frewen, Richard, 122
Fry, Thomas, 72
Fuller, Thomas, xvi, 54; *Worthies* published by Nichols, xxviii, xxxii, 190
Fuller, ———, 312
Fuseli, Henry, 42

Gale, Samuel, 107
Gardiner, James, 222
Garrick, David, 42, 51, 153, 250; and Tom Davies, 237, 239, 240, 241, 242; "Life of," 244
Garrick, Mrs., 149
Garth, Sir Samuel, 225
Gaskell, Philip, 291
Gay, John, 222, 224, 230
Ged, James, 310
Ged, William, 187, 310
Geering, ———, 151, 152
Gemsege, Paul. *See* Pegge, Samuel
General Biographical Dictionary, The, xxvii-xxviii
General Evening Post, 54
Gentleman's Magazine, xi, xxi-xxii, 41; Nichols as editor of, xxi-xxv, 168, 179, 191, 233-234; Steevens' contributions to, 45, 54; life of Pegge in, 127; on the Wartons, 148; J. Warton on, 157; on Lintot, 221-222; Henry as editor of, 232; founded by Cave, 233; Jones' papers in, 317; Boyse's poems in, 342, 346
George I, 194, 242
George II, 186
George III, 25-26, 87
George, William, 136
Gibberd, John, 105, 121, 124
Gibbon, Edward, xx, 253, 260, 266; Elmsly as friend of, 261; correspondence of with Nichols, 261-263
Gibson, Edmund, 334, 335
Gibson, Kennett, 189
Gibson, ———, 98
Gibson, ———, 304
Gifford, Edward, 107
Gifford, Walter, 107
Gilchrist, Alexander, 289
Gildon, Charles, 202, 207, 229, 230

Giles, Josiah, 343
Gillray, James, 55
Gilpin, William, 319
Gleig, George, 17, 25, 32-33
Glynn, Robert, 54, 338
Goldsmith, Oliver, 194, 241, 250, 302
Gomez, de Quevedo y Villegas, Francisco, 203
Gooch, Bishop, 66
Goodwin, Gordon, 271
Gordon Riots, 275
Gosling, Francis, 108
Gosling, R., 102-103, 108
Gosse, Edmund, 148
Gough, Elizabeth, 83
Gough, Henry, 83-84
Gough, Sir Henry, 85
Gough, John, 85
Gough, Richard, xxvii, 5, 43, 187, 258, 275, 289; at the Stirbitch Fair, 11, 13; and Reed, 15; letter from Farmer to, 24; and Steevens, 55-56; and Cole, 63, 67, 69, 71, 81, 109; attack by Cole on, 79-80; Nichols on, 82-97; as antiquarian, 97-99, 164; and S. Pegge, 127, 146-147; and history of Dorsetshire, 191-192; auction of letters of, 193; Basire as engraver for, 290; on Baskerville, 301
Gough, Mrs. Richard, 97
Gough, Sir Richard, 83
Grace, William, 71
Grafton, Richard, 218
Granger, James, 63, 70, 237, 243
Grant, Sir Archibald, 272, 273
Graves, Richard, 250
Gray, George J., 63
Gray, Thomas, 17, 35, 63, 71, 165; on the Woolsey ms., 25; portrait of, 290
Green, Berkeley, 65
Green, John, 67, 139, 140-141, 184
Green, M., pen name of Nichols, xxiv, 179
Green, Margaret, 65
Green, Martha, 181-182; children of, 182
Green, Thomas, 16
Green, William, 181, 185
Green, ———, 200
Greene, Sir Edward, 128
Greene, Thomas, 24, 129
Grey, Zachary, 63, 73, 322
Griffiths, George, 85
Griffiths, Ralph, 248
Grose, ———, 67
Grose, Capt., 88
Grosseteste, Robert, 141
Guido of Columpna, 161
Gutch, John, 91
Gwillym, Robert, 122

Hailes, Charles, 332
Haistwell, Edward, 79, 85

Halifax, Lord, 222
Hall, Anne, 93
Hall, David, 275
Hall, Thomas, 93
Hallows, Mrs., 318, 327
Hamilton, Archibald, 53
Harcourt, George Simon Earl, 96
Harding, John, 222
Harding, Sylvester, 46
Hardinge, George, 191
Hardinge, Nicholas, 191
Hardwicke, Lord, 242
Hardyknute stone, 55-56
Harper, ——, 91
Harris, ——, 203, 205
Hart, E. L., xix, xxiv, xxxii, 341
Harte, Walter, 155, 156, 230
Harvard College, 200
Harwood, ——, 30
Hatsell, John, 330
Hatton, Miss, 27, 38
Hatton, Sir Thomas, 19, 27
Havard, ——, 239
Hawkesworth, John, xxviii-xxx
Hawkins, Sir John, 44n, 54, 67, 84n, 265, 309
Hawkins, John Sidney, 36
Hayley, William, 6, 15, 265; epitaph for George Steevens by, 45, 51
Hearne, Thomas, 119
Heathcote, Ralph, 188
Heberden, William, 178
Hedges, Sir William, 208
Henderson, John, 303
Henderson, Patrick, 5
Henderson, William, 5
Henebert, ——, 65
Henry VI, 90
Henry, David, xxi, 168, 179, 266, 285; Nichols on, 232-236; and *Gentleman's Magazine*, 233-234; on agriculture, 236; and Boyse, 347
Henry, Hephzibah, 236
Henry, Patrick, 233
Henry, Richard, 236
Herbert, of Cherbury, Edward Lord, 25
Herbert, William, 73
Herries, Sir Robert, and Co., 303
Herring, Thomas, 102, 137
Hervey, Charlotte, 107
Hervey, Edward, 107
Higgins, Bevil, 225
Hill, Aaron, 153
Hill, G. B., 275
Hinckley, History of, 69, 76, 164, 187
Hind, Arthur M., 289
History of English Poetry, The, 161, 165
History of Leicester, xxvii
Hoadly, Benjamin, 68, 77, 216, 290
Hobbes, Thomas, 241

Hodgson, ——, 6
Hogarth, William, 13, 59; Nichols on, xxvi-xxvii, 46, 76, 187, 191; Steevens on, 46-47, 59; later pictures ascribed to, 55; Cole on, 68, 76
Holbein, Hans, 56
Holder, John, 151
Holdom, Joe, 72
Hollis, Brand, 289
Holloway, ——, 152
Homer, 156; translated by Pope, 224, 226n
Hommey, F., 236
Hood, Captain Alexander, 312
Hooke, ——, 187
Hope, Charles, 142
Hopkins, Charles, 222
Horace, 156, 223; printed by Baskerville, 296
Hoskins, ——, 6
House of Commons, Nichols as printer of votes of, xx
Howard, John, 86
Howel, ——, 88
Hubbard, Henry, 18, 23, 30, 37
Hughes, John, 351-352
Hulme, John, 123
Hume, David, 266, 275, 303
Humphreys, ——, 204
Hunloke, Sir Henry, 138
Hurd, Richard, 24, 157, 266, 304
Husbands, John, 155
Hutcheson, Francis, 151
Hutchins, John, 88, 191, 192
Hutchins, ——, 268
Hutchinson, ——, 130
Hutton, James, 122, 186
Hynde, Morgan, 83

Iles, ——, 104
Illustrations of the Literary History of the 18th Century, xi, xxvi; on Steevens, 42
Ireland, Samuel, 52, 55, 265
Isaeus, 332
Islington, 192

Jackson, Joseph, 302, 306, 311-313
James I, 52, 241
James I, *Progresses* of, xxvii, 191
James II, 143
Jay, Stephen, 199, 202
Jebb, John, 19, 23
Jeffreys, Lord George, 210
Jenkins, John G., 100
Jenkinson, ——, 80
Jennings, David, 296
Jennings, Robert, 132
Jenny, Henry, xxxi
Jervoise, ——, 154
Johnson, Joseph: Aikin on, 282-284; Nichols on, 285-286

Johnson, Samuel, xvi, xviii, 7, 15, 28, 51, 84, 165, 170, 265; relation of Nichols to, xix, xxiv, xxvii, xxxii, 167, 188; Nichols as printer of, xx; Cave as employer of, xxi; letters of, xxv; contributions of Reed to, 10; and Farmer, 36; visit to Cambridge by, 39-40; edition of Shakespeare by, 43, 52, 58; and Steevens, 53; and the Wartons, 153; *Lives of the Poets*, 148, 163n, 188, 247; on Lintot, 221, 224; and Davies, 237, 238, 240, 241, 243; on Chambers, 255; and Cadell, 266, 268; on Millar, 271; Essex Head Club, 28, 275; Strahan as printer of, 275; printed in France, 303; on Chatterton, 329, 336-338; on Boyse, 341, 343; and Hughes, 351
Johnston, Margaret, 273
Jones, Claude E., 4, 12n, 47, 48
Jones, John, xxiv, 156, 271; Nichols on, 317-324; letters to Birch from, 324-328
Jones, Sir William, 9
Jonson, Ben, 156, 157, 158, 162, 241
Jortin, John, 19
Journal to Stella, xxviii-xxx
Juvenal, 296

Kainophilus, 219, 220
Kearsley, George, 9, 10, 53
Keate, George, 7, 250
Keene, Bishop, 67, 75, 85
Keith, George, 282
Kelly, Hugh, 186
Kemble, J. P., 15
Kempe, Archbishop, 131
Kennett, White, 96, 189, 214
Ker, William P., 148, 329
Kerrich, Thomas, 70
Kidlington, History of, xv, 163-165, 190
King, Archbishop, 341
King, William, 222, 223; *Works* of, published by Nichols, xxvi, 10, 186
King, ———, 36
Kingston, ———, 199
Kinnoul, Thomas Earl of, 74
Kippis, Andrew, xxv, 36, 95, 292
Kirby, ———, 12
Knaplock, R., 218
Knapton, James, 218
Knatchbull, Sir Windham, 146
Knibb, Hannah, 18
Knight, Charles, 197, 221, 237, 250, 254, 256, 259, 265, 271, 275, 282
Knight, Thomas, 140-141
Knightley, Miss, 107
Kuist, James M., xix
Kynaston, John, 115-116, 154
Kyte, F., 309

Lacedemonian Mercury, 206

Lackington and Co., 309
Lamoignon, ———, 257
Larkin, George, 205, 211
Laud, Archbishop, 71
Law, Edmund, 320
Lawless, Robin, 268, 272
Lawrence, John, 199
Ledwick, Edward, 91
Lee, Sidney, 5, 42, 43, 149
Leicester, History of, xxvii; undertaken by Farmer, 17, 19-22, 32; transferred to Nichols, xxiv, 22, 167, 180, 181, 188; Gough's contributions to, 90
Leigh and Sotheby, 96
Leland, Thomas, 21
Lewis, John, 314
Lewis, William, 223, 224
Lewis, D., 155
Lichfield, 139, 142
Lillo, George, 238, 241-242
Lingard, Thomas, 222
Lingen, Thomas, 122
Lintot, Barnaby Bernard, 268; Nichols on, 221-227; publisher of Pope's Homer, 224-225; Popes quarrel with, 225-227; list of purchases by, 230-31
Lintot, Catherine, 222
Lintot, Henry, 222; Nichols on, 227-228
Literary Anecdotes of the 18th Century, xi, xx, xxvi, 82n; on Steevens, 42; on the Wartons, 148
Literary Club, 28, 44n, 165
Littlewood, ———, 135
Lloyd, Charles, 241
Long, William, 15, 47, 49
Long, ———, 191
Longman, George, 254
Longman, Miss, 310
Longman, Thomas, 53, 247; Nichols on, 254-255
Longman, Thomas Norton, 254
Lord, William, 218
Lort, Michael, 38n, 53n, 91; correspondence of with Cole, 63, 71, 73
Lounger, The, sketch of Strahan in, 277-279
Loveday, John, 334-336
Lower, Mark Antony, 221
Lowndes, Richard, 112
Lowndes, William, 106
Lowth, Robert, 154, 157
Lowther, Sir John, 228
Lucretius, 296
Lum, Aubrey Joseph, 16
Lum, Robert, 16
Lynch, John, 131
Lysons, Daniel, 41, 45
Lysons, Samuel, 60
Lysons, ———, 130
Lyttelton, Charles, 314

Lyttelton, Sir George, xx, 154, 186

Macbean, ——, 187
Machenzye, John, 202
Mackenzie, Stuart, 260
Mackinlay, J., 261
Macklin, Charles, 313
Maittaire, Michael, 178
Malcolm, J. P., 70
Malcolm, ——, 243
Malebranche, Nicolas de, 201, 205
Malone, Edmond, xvi, xxvii, 5, 12n, 15, 51; as editor of Swift, xxx, xxxi-xxxii; and Farmer, 17; and Steevens, 42; letters from Nichols to, 167; on Chatterton, 329, 331; on Shakespeare, 338
Malthus, S., 212
Manning, ——, 91
Mant, Richard, 149, 160, 166
Mapletoft, Matthew, 74
Markham, Gervase, 40
Markland, Jeremiah, 155, 177, 330
Marston, Edward, 221, 237, 250, 265, 271
Marston, Isaac, 299
Marston, Jacob, 299
Marston, Joseph, 299
Marston, Sarah, 299, 300
Marston, Thomas, 299, 300
Martin, Robert, 296n
Martin, Thomas, 88
Martyn, Thomas, on Farmer, 37-39
Marvell, Andrew, 290
Mason, William, 89
Massinger, Philip, 243
Masters, Robert, 80
Mathias, Thomas J., 40n, 257n, 338
Mawson, ——, 85
May, ——, 153
McKenzie, Henry, 265
Mead, ——, 122
Meen, Henry, 3, 16, 264; on Farmer, 29; on Steevens, 57
Meerman, Gerald, 178, 179
Meers and Noorthouck, 257
Merrick, James, 156
Mewburn, Francis, 4
Middleton, Conyers, 178, 179
Middleton, Thomas, 7
Milford, R. T., 194
Millar, Andrew, 266, 268, 269
Millar, Jane, 272, 273
Miller, W. J. C., 237
Milles, Dean Jeremiah, 45, 54, 86, 91; on the Rowley poems, 329, 331
Milner, John, 82
Milton, John, 15, 165; printed by Baskerville, 296
Mitchell, ——, 177
Mole, Anne, 65
Montague, Lady Mary Wortley, 7

Montfaucon, Bernard de, 98
Montfort, Lord, 72, 74, 75
Monthly Mirror, 41
Moore, Daniel, 94
Moore, Edward, 239
Moore, Norman, 341
Morant, ——, 108
More, Hannah, 149, 265
Morell, Thomas, 290
Morley, Edith J., 148
Morphew, John, 214, 216
Moss, Robert, 216
Mostyn, ——, 102
Motteux, Peter, 207
Mount, ——, 314
Mountstuart, Lord, 76
Mower, George, 135
Moxon, Joseph, 307, 311
Mudge and Dutton, watch-makers, 53
Munro, [or Monro] Alexander, 290
Murphy, Arthur, 44n, 54, 265
Murray, John, xvi, 149
Murray, ——, 13
Musgrave, Samuel, 332, 333
Musgrave, Mrs., 336
Myers, Christopher, 46

Nantes, Edict of, 202, 260
Nash, Treadway, 88
Nasmith, ——, 80
Needham, Elias, 141
Negri, Salomon, 307
Nelson, Robert, 101
Nettleshipp, ——, 47, 50, 51
New Athenian Comedy, 207
New Testament, 313
Newberry, Francis, 15
Newbery, John, 234n
Newcome, John, 112, 321
Newell, Bridget, 285
Newell, Hephzibah, 235-236
Newton, Isaac, 332
Newton, Thomas, 296
Nicholas, Jane, 212
Nicholas, Robert, 154
Nichols, Anne, 82, 180-181, 184
Nichols, John, xv; as antiquarian, xviii; books about, xviii-xx; as printer, xx-xxxi; editor of *Gentleman's Magazine*, xxi-xxv; compiler of obituaries, xxii, xxiv; borrowing from, xxv; as author, xxv-xxviii; on Hogarth, xxvi-xxvii, 46, 52, 76, 187, 191; as editor, xxviii; work on Swift, xxviii-xxxii; as friend of Reed, 6, 15, 16; at Stirbitch Fair, xi, 12; letters from J. Warton to, 155-159; memoir on himself, 167-170, 179-180, 181, 185-193; letters to Tooke from, 170-175, 178; letter on proposed marriage of, 175-177; continuation of memoir by his son, 181;

children of, 182; letters to his children from, 182-184; list of works of, 186-191; disappearance of letters owned by, 193-194; collection of newspapers by, 194; and Gibbon, 253, 261-263; in booksellers' club, 254, 265; friend of Elmsly, 259, 261; and Christie, 285; and Caslon, 306; and Figgins, 314-315; on Rowley controversy, 329, 337
Nichols, John Bowyer, xviii, xxvi, 42, 97, 182, 259, 289; continuation of father's memoir by, 167, 190-191; letters of his father to, 168; works edited by, 191-192, 197; notes on Dunton by, 216, 218n
Nichols, John Gough, xviii, 82, 191, 193, 194
Nichols, Martha Sadelbia, 180-181
Nichols, Mary, 182
Nichols, Sarah, letter to, 182-183
Nichols, Thomas Cleiveland, 182
Nichols, William Bowyer, 182
Nicol, George, 15, 16, 251
Nicolson, William, 190
Noble, Mark, xvi
Noorthouck, J., 280
Norfolk, Duke of, 313
Norris, John, 205-206
North, Lord, 25
Nunn, James, 228

Oakes, Abraham, 74
Obituaries, in the *Gentleman's Magazine*, xxii-xxiii, xxiv-xxv
O'Keefe, John, 59
Oldham, ——, 211
Oldys, William, 52
Onslow, Arthur, 323
Ord, Craven, 91
Origin of Printing, The, 179
Ormond, James Duke of, 208
Orrery, Earl of, 157, 225
Osborn, Francis, 220
Osborn, James M., xvi
Osborne, Lady Bridget, 128
Osborne, S. J., xix
Osborne, ——, 108
Ovid, 223
Owen, Humphrey, 124
Oxford University, Gough's papers left to, 96-97
Oxford Sausage, the, 161; poem on Willis in, 117-118

Paget, Lord, 156
Palmer, Edward, 300
Palmer, Samuel, 178, 200, 307
Park, John James, 41
Parker, Archbishop, 97
Parker, ——, 221
Parkes, D., 304

Parkhurst, Thomas, 198
Parnell, Thomas, 222, 290
Parr, Samuel, 31, 35, 39, 191
Partridge, Eric, 148
Pasham, Mary, 313
Pate, W., 206
Paterson, Samuel, 92, 296n, 304
Payne, James, 261
Payne, John, 283
Payne, Oliver, 257
Payne, Thomas, 54, 87, 98, 247; Nichols on, 256-258
Payne, ——, 152
Pearch, George, 7, 155n
Pegge, Anna-Katharina, 132
Pegge, Charlotte-Anne, 132, 147
Pegge, Christopher (father of Samuel Pegge), 128-129; (grandson of Samuel Pegge), 132, 143n, 147
Pegge, Edward, 128, 129
Pegge, Gertrude, 129
Pegge, Humphrey, 128-129
Pegge, Katharine, 128
Pegge, Nathaniel, 128
Pegge, Peter, 128
Pegge, Samuel, the elder, xvii, 4, 55, 91, 167; memoir of, by his son, 127-146; Gough on, 146-147; works of published by Nichols, 186, 189, 190; portrait of, 290
Pegge, Samuel, the younger, xvii, 91, 190; memoir of father by, 127-146; note on, 147
Pegge, Strelley, 128
Pegge, William, 127
Pemberton, ——, 76
Pennant, Thomas, 104, 111
Pennington, Isaac, 12
Percy, Reuben. *See* Byerley, Thomas
Percy, Sholto. *See* Robertson, Joseph Clinton
Percy, Thomas, xv, 3, 16, 29, 57, 154, 264; notes on *Tatler* by, xxviii; letters of, 17, 193; letters to Farmer to, 29, 30-31; letters from Steevens to, 42; letters from T. Warton to, 149; and Cadell, 265; letters from Tyrwhitt to, 338-339
Perfect, William, 186
Perot, Francis, 71
Perrot, John, 71
Perrott and Hodgson, attorneys, 6
Pett, Sir Peter, 201, 208
Pettit, Henry, 151
Philips, Ambrose, 35, 222
Philips, ——, 200
Phillips, ——, 331
Philpot, ——, 88
Pickering, Roger, 84
Pindar, 331
Pindar, Peter. *See* Wolcot, John

Piozzi, Hester Lynch Thrale, 241, 336
Pitt, Christopher, 226
Pitt, William, 26-27, 38, 242
Platt, Hugh, 130
Platt, William, 130
Pleshy, history of, 91, 164
Plomer, H. R., 254, 256, 259, 265, 271, 275, 282, 306
Plumptre, Charles, 68
Plutarch, 331
Pococke, ——, 314
Pomfret, Benjamin, 122, 123, 124
Pope, Alexander, xv, 51, 53, 156, 214, 304, 345; *Life of,* xvi; J. Warton on, 154, 157, 159, 163; and Lintot, 221, 223-227, 230-231; translation of Homer by, 224-225; D'Israeli on, 228n; printed in France, 303; and Boyse, 342; and Hughes, 351
Pope, Sir Thomas, 161
Popping, S., 218
Porson, Richard, 329
Portland, Duchess of, 90
Powell, L. F., 39
Pownall, Thomas, 252-253
Pratt, Samuel Jackson, 250
Price, Sir Charles, 181
Price, John, 91, 290
Pridden, John, 82, 184
Priestley, Joseph, 282, 284
Prince, Daniel, 82, 163, 164
Prince, John, 149
Prior, Matthew, 222
Psalmanazar, George, 307
Pseudonyms of John Nichols, xxiii, xxiv
Purchas, ——, 52

Raleigh, Walter, xvi
Rapin, ——, 52
Raspe, E. E., xxxii
Rawlinson, ——, 98, 108
Readings, William, 197
Redmayne, George, 186
Reed, Isaac, 28, 155, 186, 245, 329; Nichols on, 5-16; publications of, 7-11; at Stirbitch Fair, 11-14; friends of, 14-15; on Farmer, 17, 33-35, 36, 38; correspondence with Steevens, 42, 47, 49-51, 52, 53, 57, 59; edition of Shakespeare by, 43, 331
Reep, Mrs. John, 184
Rees, Abraham, 255
Rennell, Thomas, 260
Reynolds, Sir Joshua, 28, 165, 289
Reynolds, Richard, 103
Reynolds, ——, 120
Richard II, 91
Richardson, Joseph, 150
Richardson, Richard, 304
Richardson, Samuel, 61; Jones' note on, 323

Richardson, William, 18, 23, 37, 70, 98, 207, 218
Riddell, Robert, 91
Ridpath, George, 209, 215
Rinaker, Clarissa, 148
Ritson, Joseph, 42, 165
Roberts, Sydney C., 17, 197
Roberts, William, 221
Robertson, James, 237
Robertson, Joseph Clinton, xvii
Robertson, William, 266, 303
Robinson, George, 274
Robinson, Jacob, 88, 248
Robson, James, 54, 247
Rogers, Timothy, 202
Romney, George, 15, 28
Rose, William, 272
Rowe, Nicholas, 51, 225, 231
Rowe, Thomas, 352
Rowe-Mores, Edward, 187; on the Caslons, 306, 308; on Cottrell, 311
Rowley poems, the, xv; Steevens on, 45, 54; Cole on, 72; and Tyrwhitt, 329, 331, 332-333. *See also* Chatterton, Thomas
Roy, Gen. William, 290
Ruding, Rogers, 91
Ruffhead, Owen, xvi, 255
Ruggles, George, 36n
Ruston, Daniel, 300
Ruston, John, 299
Ruston, Jonathan, 300
Ruston, Josiah, 300
Ryland, ——, 304

Sacheverell, Henry, 214
St. James's Chronicle, 45, 54, 296
Salaman, Malcolm C., 289
Salem, Mass., 200
Sallust, 296
Sandby, George, 150
Sandby, William, 343, 344
Sandwich, Lady, 66
Sandys, George, 155, 156
Sandys, Lord, 332
Sault, Richard, 201, 202, 205
Saville, Sir George, 290
Sawbridge, Wanley, 19, 37
Sayer, James, 15
Schick, G. B., xix
Schnebbelie, Jacob, 55, 189
Schuckburgh, E. S., 17
Scott, Sir Walter, xxxi
Secker, Abp. Thomas, 114, 120, 121
Secker, Mrs., 114
Secombe, Thomas, 275
Selby, Thomas James, 106, 107
Selden, ——, 308
Select Collection of Poems, xxiii, xxvii, 154-155, 187

Sepulchral Monuments, 89, 90, 97, 98-99; Basire as engraver for, 290
Settle, Elkanah, 207, 230n, 231
Seward, Thomas, 140
Seward, William, xvii, 24, 28, 60; on Farmer, 17
Shakespeare, William, 244; edition published by Nichols, xxvii, 189; edited by Reed, 7-8; Farmer on, 17, 20, 32, 34, 35, 37, 39; edited by Steevens, 43-44, 52, 53, 58, 61, 161-162; published in France, 303; work of Tyrwhitt on, 330, 331, 333
Shakespeare tavern, literary club at, 247, 250, 254, 256, 259, 265
Sharp, Richard, 15
Sharpe, Gregory, 86
Shaw, Stebbing, 82
Sheffield, John Earl of, 262-264
Shelley, Sir Richard, 84
Shenstone, William, 292
Sheppard, Germanicus, 101
Sheppard, Jane, 122
Sheppard, Thomas, 101
Sheridan, Richard Brinsley, 243
Sheridan, Thomas, xx; editor of Swift, xxx
Sherlock, Bishop Thomas, 66, 70, 74, 335
Sherwen, John, 94
Shewel, ———, 199
Shield, John, 168
Shiels, Robert, 341
Shirley, Sir Anthony, 68
Shirley, E. P., 193
Shotbolt, ———, 323
Shower, John, 199, 202
Siddons, Mrs. Sarah, 13
Simon, ———, 88
Singer, Mrs. Elizabeth, 202n, 225
Singer, Samuel Weller, xvi, 351n
Sir Charles Grandison, 323
Sitwell, Edith, 226n
Sliford, William, 103
Sloane, Sir Hans, 271, 272n
Smallwood, Sarah, 71
Smith, Albert H., xix
Smith, David Nichol, 148
Smith, Edmund, 224
Smith, Edward Orlebar, 107
Smith, Robert, 269
Smorles, Francis, 5
Sotheby's, 193, 194
Southcote, ———, 224
Specimen of a History of Oxfordshire, 163-164
Spence, Joseph, xviii; collection of anecdotes by, xvi; and Hughes, 351n
Spencer, George John, 2nd Earl, 47, 52, 57
Spense, ———, 152
Spenser, Edmund, 15, 160, 340
Sprat, Bishop Thomas, 222

Stanhope, George, 216
Stanhope, Lady, 290
Stationers' Company, xx; painted window presented to, 267; bequest from Strahan to, 276, 280
Staveley, Thomas, 19, 22
Staveley, William. *See* Staveley, Thomas
Stedman, Thomas, 321
Steele, Joshua, 311
Steele, Sir Richard, 215; Nichols as publisher of, xxiv, 167, 188, 189; letters of, edited by Nichols, xxviii, 190; published by Lintot, 231
Steevens, Mrs. Anna, 42-43
Steevens, Elizabeth, 6; letters of, 47-48, 50-51; death of, 57n
Steevens, George, xxvii, xxxii, 5, 7, 16, 187n, 258; correspondence of with Reed, 5-6; at the Stirbitch Fair, 11-14; letters from and about Farmer, 17, 28, 30-31, 38n; general correspondence of, 42; editor of Shakespeare, 43-44, 52, 61, 189; satire of, 44, 54; library of, 46-47, 52; on the Rowley controversy, 54, 329, 336-338; and the Hardyknute forgery, 55-56; Etoniensis on, 57-61; Dibdin on, 61-62; and Cole, 71, 81, 110, 111; letter to Warton from, 161-162; and reviews of Davies, 244, 246, 248; and Tyrwhitt, 330, 331, 339-340
Steevens, William S., 42
Stephen, Leslie, 197, 218, 237
Stephens, Joseph, 201
Stephenson, Francis, 129
Stephenson, Gertrude, 129
Sterne, Laurence, 219
Stewart, Clarissa, 349
Stewart, Francis, 341; letter on Boyse by, 344
Stewart, Hilaria, 349
Stirbitch (Sturbridge) Fair, xi-xii, 5, 11-14
Stockdale, John, 52, 54, 88
Stormont, viscountess, 342
Strahan, Andrew, 266, 275, 277
Strahan, George, 229, 275, 276
Strahan, William, the Elder, 233, 254, 266, 272, 274; Nichols on, 275-277, 280-281; sketch of in *Lounger*, 277-279
Strahan, William (son of the above), 276
Straus, Ralph, 291
Strelley, Gertrude, 128
Strelley, William, 128
Strype, John, 108
Stuart, James, 289, 290
Stuart, Sarah, 301
Stubbing, John, 131
Stukeley, William, 85
Suidas, 331
Surrey, history of, 91
Sutherland, D. M., 194

Swift, Deane, 290; as editor of J. Swift, xxviii-xxx, 207n
Swift, Jonathan: Nichols as publisher of, xxiv, xxviii-xxxii, 10, 186, 190; on Dunton, 215; and Lintot, 221, 223, 224; on Boyse, 251
Sydney, Algernon, 290
Sydney, Sir Philip, 157-158
Sydney, William Connor, 317
Sylvanus Urban, pen name of Editor of Gent. Mag., xxi, xxiii
Symonds, Thomas, 122, 123, 124

Talbot, Catharine, 113-115
Tancred and Sigismunda, 150-151
Tanner, John, 108
Tanner, Bishop Thomas, 108, 123
Tanquerary, ———, 72
Tassel, Elizabeth, 313
Tate, Nahum, 207
Tatler, the, edition of printed by Nichols, xxviii
Tatton, William, 25
Tawney, Thomas, 251
Taylor, Elizabeth, 257
Taylor, Harry, 68
Taylor, John, 102, 115, 140
Taylor, William, 225
Taylor, ———, 191
Tedder, Henry Richard, 259, 282, 291
Temple, Sir Richard, 102, 104
Temple, Sir William, 207
Terence, 296
Terrick, ———, 20
Territ, ———, 66
Territt, ———, 74
Tewley, William, 324
Theobald, Lewis, 51
Thespian Dictionary, 41
Thetford, history of, 88
Thomas, Bishop, 335
Thomas of Woodstock, 91
Thomas, ———, 88
Thompson, Benjamin, 132
Thompson, William, 241, 290
Thomson, James, 266, 271
Thoresby, Ralph, 52
Thornton, Bonnell, 153
Thorold, Sir John, 321
Thoroton, ———, 88
Thorpe, ———, 131
Thrale, Henry, 15, 241
Thrale, Hester Lynch, xvii-xviii, 241; *See also* Piozzi
Throsby, ———, 88
Thurlowe, Lord Chancellor, 27
Tillotson, John, 234
Timperley, C. H., 197, 281, 282
Todd, H. J., 15
Toft, Mary, 52

Toland, John, 229
Tonson, Jacob, 221, 223n, 225, 268, 271, 274
Tooke, William, letters from Nichols to, 170-175, 178-179
Toovey, ———, 173
Topography, Gough's work in, 98
Toup, Jonathan, 174, 259
Townsend, John, 299, 300
Townsend, Jonathan, 300
Townsend, Richard, 299, 300
Travel, H., 72
Travel, William, 71
Trotter, ———, 273
Tuer, Catharine, 65, 70
Tuer, Theophilus, 64, 65, 70
Tunstall, ———, 25
Turner, Baptist Noel, 39-40
Turner, Isabella, 290
Tyrwhitt, Drake, 335
Tyrwhitt, Edmund, 335
Tyrwhitt, Sir John, 335
Tyrwhitt, Robert (father of Thomas), 334, 335; (brother of Thomas), 330, 340
Tyrwhitt, Thomas, 14, 53, 329-340; Nichols on, 330-340; publications of, 331-332; on the Rowley poems, 332-333; note by Loveday on, 334-336; letter by Steevens on, 336-338; letter to Percy from, 338
Tyrwhitt, Thomas (nephew of the above), 330, 338-340
Tyson, Michael, 79, 85, 116, 122

Unicreasable Club, 15, 28
Upcott collection, 194
Usher, ———, 200

Vaillant, Isaac, 261
Vaillant, Paul, Nichols on, 260-261
Vaillant, Paul (father of the above), 260; (grandfather of the above), 260
Van Haren (Van Haaren), 345, 346
Vansittart, ———, 153
Veale, ———, 199
Venn, J. A., 17, 43
Verax, *Pseudonym* of Thomas Warton, 165
Vertue, ———, 88
Virgil, 153, 157; printed by Baskerville, 295
Voltaire, Arouet de, 303; translated by Boyse, 345, 346, 348

Wake, Archbishop, 131
Wakefield, Gilbert, 283n
Waldron, F. G., 52, 238
Walker, Benjamin, 291
Walker, George, 210
Walker, John C., 91, 127, 210
Walpole, Horace, xv, xxxii, 338; compiler of anecdotes, xvi-xvii; on Hogarth, xxvi-xxvii; correspondence with Cole, 63, 66,

71, 72, 75, 76, 77, 78, 79, 81; note to Gough from, 89; letter from Baskerville to, 297
Walpole, Sir Robert, 84, 242
Walter, John, 158, 251
Wanley, Humphrey, 71, 103, 225-226
Warburton, William, xvi, 51, 58, 214, 227, 266; letter to J. Warton from, 162; published by Millar, 271; letter to Hurd from, 304; on John Jones, 321
Waring, ——, 19
Warmstry, Thomas, 222
Warren, Sir George, 290
Warrington, Earl of, 203-204
Warton, Jane, 153
Warton, John, 159
Warton, Joseph, xix, xxxii, 163, 227, 265, 304; Nichols on, 148-160; correspondence with T. Warton, 150-154; letters to Nichols from, 155-159, 167
Warton, Thomas, the elder, 148, 149-150; poems by, 152-153, 156
Warton, Thomas, the younger, xv, xiii, 6, 21; correspondence with Steevens, 42, 54, 161-162; correspondence with Gough, 82; "Oxford Sausage" by, 117; letter from Willis to, 121; correspondence with J. Warton, 150-154; Nichols on, 160-166; letter from Warburton to, 162; letters to Nichols from, 163-164; on the Rowley poems, 329, 331; and Tyrwhitt, 330, 340
Waters, ——, 199
Waters, Miss, 310
Watkinson, Godfrey, 134
Watson, John, 290
Watts, John, 308, 310
Waugh, James, 84
Webster, John, 301
Webster, Sir Peter, 131
Webster, ——, 251
Wedmore, Frederick, 289
Weldon, Sir Anthony, 212n
Wells, Edward, 101
Wells, ——, 199
Welsted, Leonard, *Works of* published by Nichols, xxviii
Wenham, Mass., 200
Wesley, Samuel, 199, 200n, 204n, 206
West, Benjamin, 290
West, Gilbert, xxiv
West, James, 122
Westby-Gibson, John, 306
Western, Thomas, 68
Westley, Rebecca, 299
Westley, Thomas, 299
Westminster Magazine, 10
Westmoreland, Earl of, 26
Weymouth, Lord, 251
Whaley, John, 155

Whiston, John, 218
Whiston, William, 218
White, Ben, 13, 52, 53
Whittingham, ——, 88
Whittington, 136, 137, 139, 143, 144
Wiclif, John, 57
Wilcocks, Bishop, 65
Wilcox, ——, 12, 13
Wilcoxson, Williams, 135
Wilde, Robert, 218
Wilford, John, 322
Wilkes, John, xx, 159, 260, 275
Wilkes (Mr. Alderman), 180
Wilkins, David, 308
Willes, Judge, 122
William III, 143
Williams, Daniel, 202, 317, 319, 322
Williams, Harold, xxviii, xxx
Willis, Alice (Mrs. Richard Eyre), 122, 124
Willis, Browne, 63, 66, 69, 73, 74, 237; Nichols on, 100-124; coin collection of, 103-104, 123, 124, 126; writings of, 107-109; publication of, 109-111; Ducarel on, 111-113; Miss Talbot on, 113-115; Kynaston on, 115-116; portrait of, 116, 122; Cole on, 116, 119, 121-122; satirical poem on, 117-118; work on bells by, 120; will of, 122-124; Sneyd Davies on, 125-126
Willis, Catharine, 102-103, 122, 124
Willis, Daniel, 122
Willis, Elliot, 122, 124
Willis, Gertrude, 122, 124
Willis, Henry, 102, 122, 124
Willis, Hervey, 124
Willis, Jane, 101
Willis, John, 102, 122
Willis, Katharine, 119
Willis, Mary, 122
Willis, Mrs., 71
Willis, Rachel, 119
Willis, Thomas (father of Browne Willis), 107, 125; (son of Browne Willis), 120, 124; (grandson of Browne Willis), 102, 124
Willis, Dr. Thomas (uncle of Browne Willis), 74, 100, 104, 123, 125
Wilmot, Thomas, 169
Winchelsea, Daniel Earl of, 146
Winchelsea, Lady, 225
Winchester, history of, xv
Winchester College, J. Warton headmaster of, 154, 159
Windham, William, 28, 47, 52, 57
Wingfield, ——, 25
Wise, Francis, 107, 124
Wither, George, 241
Wolcot, John, xxii-xxiii, 53n
Wollstonecraft, Mary, 282

Wood, Anthony à, xvi, 73, 76, 77, 78-79
Wood, Will, 71
Woodmason, ——, 303
Wooll, John, 149
Woolsey, Cardinal Thomas, 24-25
Worcestershire, Collections for a History of, 88
Wordsworth, William, 282
Wotton, William, 102
Wray, Daniel, 330
Wroth, Warwick William, 127
Wycherley, William, 225
Wynkyn de Worde, 161

Xenophon, 130, 146

Yalden, Thomas, 222
Yarrow, Miss, 238
Yorke, James, 138
Young, Frederick, 327
  Reed as editor of, 8; John Jones' relation to, 317-318; note on Richardson and, 323; death of, 327-328
Young, Edward, xxiv, 3, 7, 151-152, 271;

Zoffanii, Johan, 46
Zodiac Club, 130-131